LEMON-AID

USED CAR

GUIDE 1996

LEMON-AID

USED CAR

GUIDE 1996

Phil Edmonston

Published in 1995 by
Stoddart Publishing Co. Limited
34 Lesmill Road
Toronto, Canada
M3B 2T6

Canadian Cataloguing in Publication Data

The National Library of Canada has catalogued this publication as follows:

Edmonston, Louis-Philippe, 1944-
    Lemon-aid used car guide

1982-
Continues in part: Edmonston, Louis-Philippe,
1944-   . Lemon-aid, ISSN 0383-7084.
ISSN 0714-587X
ISBN 0-7737-5750-3 (1996)

1. Used cars - Purchasing - Periodicals.
I. Edmonston, Louis-Philippe, 1944-   . Lemon-aid.
II. Title.

TL162.E3397   629.2'222'05   C82-031620-2

Cover design: Leslie Styles
Typesetting and text design: Studio Apostrophe, Montreal
Editorial services: Don Loney/Word Guild

Printed and bound in Canada

CONTENTS

Part One:
DEALS ON WHEELS
1

Part Two:
FIGHTING BACK FOR PRINCIPLE AND PROFIT
41

Part Three:
USED VEHICLE RATINGS
84

SMALL CARS
91

v

COMPACT CARS
154

MID-SIZE CARS
233

LARGE CARS/WAGONS
265

LUXURY CARS
299

SPORTS CARS
369

MINIVANS
428

Appendix I:
LEMON-PROOFING BEFORE YOU BUY
471

Appendix II:
SURVEY AND BULLETIN SEARCH
476

Part One

DEALS ON WHEELS

NEW YORK—His [Iacocca's] taste in cars runs to wire wheel covers, vinyl roofs and heavy chrome trim. When he dictated design in the late 1980s, those features dominated Chrysler's cars, making them a veritable generation gap on wheels. Some models (notably the Imperial and Fifth Avenue) were so embarrassing that company executives wouldn't even show pictures of them at analysts' meetings…. An Iacocca Restoration probably would scare so many (good) people out of the company that the term "Chrysler Bailout" would acquire a new meaning.

> Paul Ingrassia, co-author of
> Comeback: The Fall and Rise of the
> American Automobile Industry
> (Simon & Schuster),
> from an address given on April 19, 1995

This is a great year to buy a used vehicle with a minimum of risk. Most cars and multipurpose vehicles (minivans, vans, 4X4s and pickups) are far more reliable than they were a few years ago. Plus, if you do get a vehicle with some problems, chances are the manufacturer's five-to-seven-year warranty will fix it for free. The ultimate irony is now that Chrysler has dropped its seven-year new car warranty on its 1995 models, your '93 Chrysler will be under warranty until the year 2000—exceeding the warranty of '95 models by two years.

Vehicles manufactured between 1990 and 1994 have gotten progressively safer, too, as airbags, traction control, ABS brakes, and side impact crash protection have been installed as standard equipment in a broader range of inexpensive, entry-level models.

If you're looking to save paying tax, consider buying privately. You will save at least $70 per $1000 paid (more if the provincial tax is applied to the federal tax) because the 7 percent federal Goods and Services Tax only applies to dealers' sales—private sales are exempt. Additionally, many 1991 models cost thousands of dollars less than previous model years because the 13.5 percent manufacturer's tax was replaced by the GST. This reduced cost is carried through some models' used prices.

1

An airbag-equipped '91 Dodge Caravan sold for $15,200 new. Present cost is about $9000 and the vehicle is still under warranty.

Why Buy Used?

In Canada, the average cost of a new car is $20,416, up a little more than 8 percent over the cost of a new 1993 model ($18,893), according to the Canadian Automobile Dealers Association. Interestingly, while dealers continue to claim they make only marginal profits from new car sales, the CADA reports the average profit margin on new vehicle sales is $1,490— a 13.1 percent increase over a 1993 model—giving Canadian dealers a 53 percent increase in pre-tax profits for 1994. The CADA reports that new vehicle sales make up 60 percent of a dealer's profits, used cars represent 20 percent, and service, parts and financing charges make up the remaining 20 percent.

Owning and operating the average new car (for example, a Chevrolet Cavalier RS with automatic transmission) costs $7403 annually—a 5.3 percent increase over a year ago. This works out to 30.8 cents per kilometer versus 29.3 cents last year. Depreciation alone ($3,287) represents 44 percent of the car's total cost.

Again this year, the costs of operating a car in Quebec are the highest and in Alberta are the lowest.

Three million vehicles are sold each year in Canada, with a 50-50 split between new and used. Unfortunately for many new car purchasers, the status of owning a new car fades away just about the time that the neighbors buy theirs and the new car warranty protection promised by the manufacturer has turned into a flip-the-coin contest. Despite advances made in terms of technology, buying a new car is still no absolute guarantee of trouble-free driving. So, the new car purchaser may ultimately find out that he or she has still gotten stuck with somebody else's troubles—the auto manufacturer's!

Smart buyers can avoid problems like these by purchasing a used vehicle with a good reliability and crashworthiness record, sticking to the prices listed in this *Guide*, making sure some of the original warranty is still available, and insisting upon an independent mechanical inspection before parting with their money. In a nutshell, they know that in buying a car, one is simply buying transportation—not a "statement."

There are several other important advantages in buying used, and in particular from a private party.

1. Less initial cash outlay; slower vehicle depreciation; better and cheaper parts availability.

In buying a car, one is simply buying transportation. The amount of the initial cash outlay is very important, because it may reduce your spending requirements in other areas such as investments where your money may generate a return, or paying down a mortgage. Because the purchase of many used cars only requires half the cash or credit of a new car, it is easy to see that the used car purchaser need not invest as much income in a depreciating investment, and may be fortunate enough not to require a loan.

If someone were to ask you to invest in stocks or bonds that were guaranteed to be worth about half their initial purchase value after two years, you would probably tell him to get lost. But this is exactly the trap you are falling into when buying the average new car that normally depreciates 30 percent in the first year and 10 percent in the second. The following illustration shows how new cars are infinitely more expensive than a good used car.

TABLE 1

New Car Cost	
Purchase Price	$20,000
Provincial Tax (e.g, Ont. - 8%)	$ 1,600
Federal GST (7%)	$ 1,400
Total Price	$23,000

Now, the motorist buying a new car is certain that the warranty and status far outweigh any inconvenience. He happily forks over $23,000 and takes possession of his new automobile.

For the used car buyer, the situation is altogether different. That same vehicle can be purchased two years later, in good condition, with much of the manufacturer's warranty remaining, for about half its original cost. The following illustration shows what happens.

TABLE 2

Used Car Cost	
Purchase Price (2 years old, 40,000 km)	$12,000
Provincial Tax (8%)	$ 960
No GST (if sold privately)	—
Total Price	$12,960

In this example, the used car buyer saves $1400 in federal taxes, $640 in provincial taxes, and gets a good car for almost half its original price.

Generally, a new car is expected to run at least 200,000 km (125,000 miles) to 240,000 km (150,000 miles) in its lifetime. The United States Department of Transportation has concluded that the average vehicle requires major repairs after five years of use. Once these repairs are done, it can then be run relatively trouble free for another five years. Furthermore, three years after a model has been sold, the replacement parts market starts to fill up due to cars being declared a total loss by insurance companies, or because of the increased competition from parts wholesalers and independent parts manufacturers. So, after a few years have passed, replacement parts are unquestionably easier to come by through bargaining with local garages or through a careful search of auto wreckers' yards. A reconditioned or used part costs one-third to one-half less than one bought new.

2. Cheaper insurance rates.
The difference in costs between insuring a new car and a used car may not seem much at first, but by carefully negotiating the deductible, the smart shopper can reduce insurance premiums by hundreds of dollars. For example, as a car gets older, the amount of deductible should be increased to a maximum of $500 per collision. As the amount of deductible is increased, the annual premiums for collision coverage decrease.

By agreeing to a $500 deductible, the motorist agrees to repair the vehicle for all damages under the $500 figure. Generally, by purchasing used parts (remember, you bought a used car) from a local auto wrecker and having the work done by small, specialized garages, the total amount of your repair losses can be controlled. What may have been an estimated repair cost of $500 may even be reduced to less than half that amount with sharp repair bargaining.

3. The right to a mechanical examination.
A used car buyer can have a vehicle checked out by an independent mechanic for $75 to $100 before concluding the deal. This examination before purchase protects against hidden defects. It's also a tremendous bargaining tool, because it allows the customer to evaluate the cost of

any needed repairs and then bargain down the purchase price.

If you can't get permission to have the vehicle inspected elsewhere, walk away from the deal, no matter how tempting the selling price. The seller is obviously trying to put something over on you. Ignore the usual excuses that the car is not insured, the licence plates have expired or the vehicle has a dead battery.

4. You can be better informed about a used car before its purchase.

Smart customers will want to get answers to the following questions before paying a penny for any used vehicle: What did it first sell for and what is its present value? How much of the original warranty is left? How many times has the car been recalled for safety-related defects? Are parts easily available? Does the vehicle have a history of costly performance-related defects that can be corrected under a secret warranty, a safety recall campaign or with an upgraded part? (See *Service Tips* in Part Three.)

5. Freedom from the "new car warranty blues."

Used car purchasers are also protected from manufacturing defects and deceptive practices under provincial and federal legislation. There is no expressed warranty made by the manufacturer that can restrict the hapless consumer's right to damages. In fact, the courts have ruled that the manufacturer of a product is liable for the damages caused by that product, even if the person injured is not the original purchaser. As for exaggerated statements or "puffery," as many advertisers call the practice, the federal Competition Act and provincial consumer protection laws take a dim view of anyone using the technique to sell products (especially cars) to unsuspecting consumers.

So, the typical used car buyer is protected by a multitude of federal and provincial laws that go far beyond whatever protection may be offered by the standard new car guarantee. Furthermore, the used car purchaser doesn't have to conform to any arbitrary rules or service guidelines to get this protection.

6. Litigation is quicker, easier and less costly.

Let's say you do get stuck with a lemon. Most provincial small claims courts have a jurisdiction limit between $3000 and $5000. Because many used cars are purchased for less than this amount, any dispute between buyer and seller can be settled within a few months, without lawyers or excessive court costs.

Choosing the Right Time to Buy

Few used cars are sold in the winter months of December through March. Car salespeople see few customers, and used cars generally show their worst in a vehicle they aren't used to, from defective heating and defrosting systems, poor suspensions, etc. It is precisely for these reasons that the smart used car buyer should shop during these months for real bargains.

One danger in buying in winter is that body defects can be concealed by snow or dirt. Nevertheless, an inspection by an independent garage should disclose any serious corrosion or accident damage to the sheet metal or the vehicle's chassis.

Choosing the Right Seller

New car dealers

Buying from a dealer is the most expensive way to buy a used vehicle. Used cars bought from dealers usually sell for 20 percent to 30 percent more than they would if purchased from a private seller. Dealers get their used cars as trade-ins, from auto auctions and rental car companies, and off the street. They then have to recondition them, add a warranty and pay advertising and sales commissions. Twenty years ago, according to the Federation of Automobile Dealer Associations of Canada (now called the Canadian Automobile Dealers Association), 86 percent of used cars were sold by new car dealers. Today, that number is less than 25 percent, due mainly to the GST driving buyers into the arms of private sellers.

Dealers do offer important advantages. They're insured against selling stolen vehicles or cars with finance owing or other liens. Financing is available, cars are sometimes permitted to be examined by an independent garage, and there is a much wider choice of models. Repair facilities are also available for warranty work. Finally, dealers have "deeper pockets" than private sellers, so there's a better chance of getting paid should a court judgment be won against the firm.

A good dealer provides honest and reliable service. A dealer's honesty and reliability can be verified in a variety of ways. A call to the local consumer protection agency or the clerk of the regional small claims court usually will turn up some leads. It is also a good idea to talk with motorists driving vehicles identified by that dealer's nameplate on the trunk lid. If they have been treated fairly by the dealer, they will be glad to recommend him. You can also ascertain the quality of the dealer's cars and servicing by renting a car from the dealer for a weekend or by having your own vehicle serviced there.

Used car dealers

Used car dealers sell their vehicles for almost as much as new car dealers. They, too, offer easy credit, advertise low prices and stock a variety of models with varying warranties. On the other hand, they usually are marginal operations that can't invest much money in reconditioning their vehicles, and they don't usually have repair facilities to honor what warranties they do give.

Certain used car dealers use their customers' desire to get a good used car for practically nothing to their own advantage. The search for the perfect used car for a couple of hundred dollars holds an endless fascination for some buyers; but as with most other goods, you get what you pay for, and that "bargain" may bring you nothing but headaches.

Be sure to find out whether a used car dealer is licensed by the provincial government, how long the company has been in business, and where the dealer purchases his cars.

Private parties
Private sellers are your best source for a cheap and reliable used vehicle because you have lots more vehicles to choose from and you're bargaining with a vendor who isn't trying to profit from your inexperience. This translates into a golden opportunity to negotiate a fair price, which is not common in many dealer transactions.

Apart from newspaper classified ads, you can track down good private deals and get a good idea about prices through:

- word of mouth
- grocery store bulletin boards
- coming across cars for sale while you drive about town or take a walk
- specialty publications (e.g., *Auto Trader* or *Buy and Sell Bargain Hunter*)
- The *Canadian Red Book* (2908 South Sheridan Way, Oakville, Ont. L6J 7M1).

Car brokers are a risky alternative because they are unregulated and can pocket much more than their commission or disappear with their customers' money.

The best method of determining the price range for a particular model is reading the publications listed above prior to the actual purchase. This will give you a reasonably good idea of how low you can drive the price asked by the seller. Remember, nobody expects to get his or her asking price—be it a dealer or private party. A 10 percent reduction from the advertised price is common.

In assessing sales tax, the selling price may be arbitrarily fixed by government officials. For example, each year Ontario regulations require that over 800,000 used car buyers provide a signed bill of sale, accept the *Canadian Red Book* value, or have their vehicle independently appraised. There are some common sense exceptions. For example, buyers of vehicles that have a *Red Book* estimated wholesale value less than $1000 can pay the retail sales tax on the purchase price they declare without an appraisal. Furthermore, vehicles that are worth more than $1000 (according to the *Red Book*), but are damaged or run down, can be appraised before the buyer pays the sales tax, and the tax will be calculated upon either the selling price or the appraised price, whichever is higher. Where there is a dispute, an independent appraiser may be used.

Traditional sales tax exemptions remain. For example, transactions and gifts between family members will have the sales tax rebated. Sales involving status Indians and diplomats, vehicles registered from out-of-province, and bequests for estate settlements are not subject to Ontario sales tax.

Private sellers in Ontario need to buy a Vehicle Transfer Package

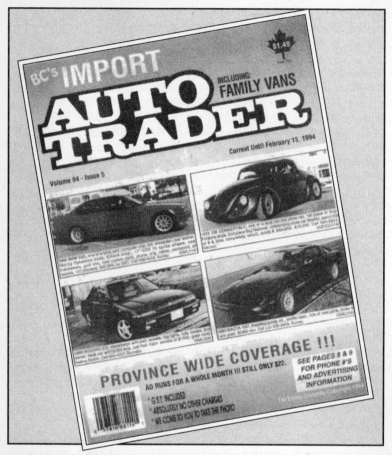

Auto Trader bargains are quickly snapped up.

(about $20) from the Ministry of Consumer and Commercial Relations. This kit contains lien information, details as to what is covered in a safety inspection, sales tax information, forms for an affidavit and bill of sale. These measures have been taken to drive "curbsiders" (professional sellers posing as private individuals) from the used car business and to stop buyers from paying less sales tax than they should.

As a buyer, you should get a written sales agreement, even if it is handwritten, that includes a clause stating there are no outstanding traffic violations or liens against the vehicle. Whether or not the car will be purchased "as is" or certified under provincial regulation doesn't make a great deal of difference. A vehicle sold as safety "certified" can still be dangerous to drive or turn into a lemon (see Part Two). The certification process can be sabotaged by incompetent mechanics, poorly calibrated instruments, or a minimal number of components checked. Certified is not the same as having a warranty to protect you from the engine blowing or the transmission falling out. Certified means only that the vehicle has met minimum safety standards on the day tested. Make sure the vehicle is lien-free and hasn't been written off from an accident. In fact, Canada has become a haven for rebuilt U.S. wrecks. U.S. sellers of salvage vehicles are preying upon Canada's lack of title-branding laws to ship accident-damaged vehicles to unsuspecting Canadians. This problem has increased greatly due to the large number of states enacting title-branding laws.

In most provinces, you can conduct a lien and registration search yourself. If a lien does exist, you should contact the creditor(s) listed to find out whether any debts have been paid. If a debt is outstanding, you should arrange with the vendor to pay his creditor directly and pay him or her any balance. If the debt is larger than the purchase price of the car, it is up to you to decide whether or not you wish to complete the deal. If the seller agrees to clear the title personally, make sure that you receive a written relinquishment of title from the creditor before paying any money to the vendor. Make sure the title doesn't show an "R" for "restored."

Even if all documents are in order, ask the seller to show you the vehicle's original sales contract and a few repair bills to ascertain how well the car was maintained. The bills will show you if the odometer was turned back and will also indicate which repairs are still guaranteed. If none of these can be found—**run, don't walk**—away. If the contract shows the car was financed, verify that the loan was paid. If you are still not sure that the vehicle is free of liens, ask your bank or credit union manager to make a check for you. If no clear answer is forthcoming, look for another car.

Government and commercial auctions

You swim with piranha at these auctions—the place where the mythical $50 Jeep is sold. Government auctions are fun to watch but are risky ventures because you can't determine the condition of the vehicles put up for bid. Commercial auctions are another risky place to buy a used car or truck. They are frequented by professional dealers who pick up cheap, worn-out cars unloaded by new car dealers who are afraid to sell them to their own customers. There are no guarantees, cash is required, and prices, like quality, are apt to be low. A minimum inspection of the used cars on display is allowed, but the vehicles cannot leave the display area.

Rental and leased car sales

National rental companies, such as Budget, Hertz, Avis and National sell and lease used vehicles in most major Canadian cities. They are sold after about six months to one year of service with approximately 60,000 to 100,000 km. These rental companies will gladly provide a car's complete history and allow an independent inspection by a qualified mechanic of the buyer's choice, as well as arrange competitive financing without "boosting" the price.

The cars are well maintained, sell for a bit less than the dealer's price (but more than a private sale), and come with a strong guarantee. Rental car companies usually will settle customer complaints out of court so as not to tarnish their image. There are a few risks, however, in buying used cars from the major rental companies. Because the car has been used by many drivers, it is possible that it has been abused. And bigness bears no relation to honesty, either. For example, Hertz, the largest rental agency, bilked its customers and insurance companies out of $15 million in phoney repair charges in the United States.

Repossessions

A repossessed car may be sold by a finance company or bank anxious to recoup its losses. Financing is available, an independent mechanical inspection is usually permitted, and prices can be very reasonable. The biggest problem with repossessed cars is that often they have been abused by their financially troubled owners. Sometimes, the full extent of the abuse cannot be ascertained in one brief garage examination. Before buying a repossessed car, try to find out something about the previous owner and what level of care was taken of the vehicle. A call to the regional office of the manufacturer will usually provide some clues. Financial institutions have been held legally responsible for a car's defects in the past.

Cross-border shopping

There is no iron-clad guarantee you will save money by purchasing a used car in the United States and bringing it into Canada. Safety and pollution control regulations differ considerably between Canada and the United States, and it may be impossible to upgrade your used vehicle to conform to Canadian standards (particularly with cars bought in Europe). Transport Canada also estimates that 15 percent to 20 percent of American cars cannot meet Canadian norms, no matter how they are modified. Ford Thunderbird (1989-93), GM Pontiac Bonneville (1988-91), Honda CRX HF (1985-91), Hyundai Sonata (1989-92) and Mazda 929 (1990-91) are just a few of the cars that are prohibited entry into Canada because they cannot meet our safety and emission control standards.

Check your total costs carefully. Lower U.S. prices do not equal the cost of a higher American dollar and substantial Canadian sales taxes (provincial sales taxes and a gas guzzling surcharge). In a recent study done by the CAA, a 1990 Honda Accord selling for $500 less south of the border ended up costing $3220 more when the currency exchange rate and taxes were included ($14,098 vs. $17,318). The difference was much less with a 1990 Plymouth Voyager ($1121), a VW Jetta ($649) and a Ford Taurus ($134).

Transport Canada has received so many complaints from consumers importing American and European used vehicles that are later rejected as unsafe that it has set up a new program to help importers modify their vehicles to meet Canadian standards. Registrar Systems Ltd. of Toronto will have agents at all major border crossings to assist in collecting duties and taxes, and to enter each vehicle into the company's data base. Within a week, the company will send a letter to the importer listing modifications needed within 60 days to meet federal safety and pollution regulations. Approximately 300 new car dealers across Canada have been appointed to carry out the required safety and pollution control upgrades. Once these repairs are carried out and a $195 to $250 processing fee is paid, the importer gets a certificate allowing the vehicle to be licensed in Canada.

Buyers of American used cars should be wary of vehicles that register in miles instead of kilometers, safety-related defects that have not been corrected because Canada doesn't have a cross-border owner notification system, and engine calibrations set for U.S. emission control regulations. Furthermore, cars that are exported to Canada may have rolled-back odometers.

If you do decide to import a used car from the United States, be careful to check for liens and stolen vehicles. There is little cooperation among provincial registrars and no link-up between U.S. and Canadian registrars, so your chances of getting the required information from them are pretty slim.

Buying the average used car from a private seller in Canada will cost less than one imported from the States. True, there is greater choice south of the border and the car may be in much better condition due to less weather wear, but the differences aren't all that great. That's probably why annual used car imports from the United States have fallen from 135,000 in 1991 to 50,000 units last year. The best bargains may be obtained by using the duty-free provisions of the free-trade agreement to buy recent collectible cars, such as early Ford Mustangs or some of the high-performance Chryslers that were launched in the early 1960s.

Used car imports
Transport Canada's toll-free (within Canada) auto safety hotline has an importer desk that will respond to all questions relating to import regulations, duties and taxes. The primary number is 1-800-333-0510. Other numbers that may be helpful: 1-800-333-0558, 1-613-998-2174 (Ottawa), and 1-514-283-4659 (Montreal).

For registration purposes, importers must show the vehicle's title, registration certificate, sales contract or receipt (if purchased), or a notarized letter showing that the vehicle is a gift.

Table 3

1995 Federal Import Tax				
Origin	Imported From	New	1-15	16-24 Years Old	25+
U.S.	U.S.	2.7%	2.7%	2.7%	0%
Other	U.S.	8.6%	8.6%	8.6%	0%
Mexico	Mexico	2.6%	N/A	2.6%	0%
Other	Other	8.6%	N/A	8.6%	0%

In addition, the GST, a $100 air conditioner tax, and a supplementary tax for vehicles weighing more than 2007 kg must be paid to the federal government.

Note that vehicles 15 years or older are exempt from Canadian safety and pollution regulations.

Models made in the U.S. in the years 1980-84 must carry a U.S. statement of compliance label (found on all vehicles sold in the United States). Vehicles manufactured in 1985 and later have to go through National Registrar Systems Ltd. to ensure that they meet Canadian standards covering bumper strength, seatbelt anchors, child seat tether anchors, a bilingual airbag maintenance label, and a speedometer that registers kilometers, not miles.

Vehicles built after November, 30, 1989 must have daytime running lights.

Financing Choices

No one should spend more than 20 percent of his or her annual gross income for a used car. By keeping the initial cost of a used vehicle low, the purchaser may be able to pay in cash, a key bargaining tool to use in a private sale. Used car dealers are not all that impressed by cash sales, because they lose their kickback from the finance companies based upon the volume and amount of finance business they write up. They also get a commission on the life insurance premium sold with most loans.

In spite of the lower costs involved (vs. a new car purchase), not everyone can pay cash for a used car. If you will need a loan, consider the advantages and disadvantages of the following lending institutions, and get pre-approved for a loan before going shopping.

Credit Unions. The preferred place to borrow money at low interest rates and with easy repayment terms. You will have to join the union or have an account with them before the loan is approved. You will also probably have to come up with a larger downpayment relative to what other lending institutions would require.

Banks. Banks *want* to make small loans to consumers who have average incomes and appear to be financially responsible. Their interest rates are very attractive and can be negotiated downward if you have a good credit history or agree to give them other business. Auto club members can benefit from lower interest rates at some banking institutions recommended by the association. Bank loans are seldom made for more than 36 to 48 months.

Dealer Financing. Dealers can finance the cost of a used car at rates that compete with banks and finance companies because they get substantial rebates from lenders and agree to take back the vehicle if the creditor defaults on the loan. Some dealers mislead their customers into thinking they can get financing at rates three or four percentage points below the prime rate. Actually, the dealer jacks up the base price of the vehicle to compensate for the lower interest charges.

Finance Companies. Although finance companies, with their excessive interest rates, should be the last place to go for a small, short-term loan, the fact remains that these lenders fill a consumer need created by the restrictive policies of other institutions. The advantages of relaxed credit restrictions and quick loans appeal to many people who cannot get financing elsewhere, or who may wish to extend their payments up to 60 months.

Dealer Tricks

Used cars and minivans are subject to the same deceptive sales practices as new cars. Some of the more common tricks involve not identifying the previous owner because the vehicle was used commercially, or because the vehicle had been written off as a total loss from a prior accident. It is also not uncommon to discover that the mileage has been turned back, particularly if the vehicle was part of a company's fleet. All these scams can be thwarted if you demand the name of the vehicle's previous owner as a prerequisite to purchasing it. It would be impossible to list all the dishonest tricks employed in used car sales. As soon as the public is alerted to one scheme, other, more elaborate frauds are used by crooked sellers.

The provinces have stepped in to reimburse buyers who are swindled by setting up industry-financed compensation funds. Ontario and British Columbia, for example, allow claims for $15,000 to $20,000 against registered dealers. The fund protects consumers if the dealership fails to return a trade-in, full payment, deposit or downpayment when the dealer doesn't deliver a vehicle, can't deliver it because of a business failure, is dishonest in his dealings, or fails to provide clear title.

The Ontario law allows a claim payout under one of five categories: 1) the dealer fails to pay a court judgment after 90 days; 2) the consumer has paid for a vehicle but the dealer hasn't delivered it; 3) the dealer has officially gone bankrupt with money owing; 4) the dealer has been convicted of fraud, theft or false pretences (read misleading advertising); 5) the dealer sold an uninsured warranty extension or service plan that goes out of business or refuses to pay a legitimate claim.

The British Columbia fund no longer requires the claimant to get a court judgment to collect up to $20,000 of monies owing. Furthermore, the administration of the B.C. fund is carried out by a board of directors made up of consumers, industry and government officials.

Here are some of the more common fraudulent practices you're likely to encounter:

Failing to declare full purchase price. Used almost exclusively by small, independent dealers and some crooked private sellers, the buyer is told by the salesman that he can save on sales tax by putting in a lower selling price on the contract. But what if the car turns out to be a lemon, or the sales agent has falsified the model year or mileage? Generally nothing will happen because the hapless buyer will only be offered a refund of the fictitious purchase price indicated on the contract. If the buyer takes the seller to court, it is very unlikely that any more than the contract price would be given back. Moreover, the purchaser and seller could be prosecuted for making a false declaration to avoid paying sales tax.

Sales agents posing as private parties ("curbsiders"). Individuals sell about three times as many used vehicles as dealers. Some crooked dealers, though, are using agents to pose as private sellers in order to get a better price for their cars and avoid paying GST and giving a warranty. Once again, this scam is easy to detect if the seller can't produce the original sales contract or a few repair bills. You can also identify a professional car dealer in the want ad section of the newspaper by checking to see if one telephone number is repeated in many different ads.

If you get taken by one of these scam artists, don't hesitate to sue in small claims court both the newspaper carrying the ad and the provincial department responsible for dealer registration. Both parties could be considered negligent for knowingly allowing this rip-off to operate.

Before Ontario passed special legislation, a spokesman for the Ontario Used Car Dealers Association estimated that one car in four was sold illegally by a curbsider. And in Barrie, Ontario, a survey showed that more than 40 percent of the vehicles advertised by so-called private owners were actually dealer cars. Tax officials estimate they lost over $95 million in sales tax revenue annually.

Curbsiders are now moving east and west, having been kicked out of Ontario and Quebec. They buy cars from dealers, auto auctions and junkyards (some have been written off as total losses) at wholesale prices. They then place private classified ads in B.C., Alberta and Maritime newspapers. Most new car dealers get very angry when one of these teams hits town. Unfortunately, they don't get angry enough, because they continue to sell used cars at wholesale prices to curbsiders they know are stealing their business and cheating consumers and tax authorities in their communities.

"Free-exchange" privilege. Dealers get a lot of sales mileage out of this deceptive offer. The dealer offers to exchange any defective vehicle for any other in stock. What really happens, though, is that the dealer will not have any other cars selling for the same price and will thus demand a cash bonus for the exchange, or he may have nothing but lemons in stock.

"Money-back" guarantee. What could be more honest than a money-back guarantee? Dealers using this technique will often charge exorbitant handling charges, rental fees or mechanical repair costs to customers who have bought one of these vehicles and then returned it.

"50/50" guarantee. A 50/50 guarantee means that the dealer will pay one-half the repair costs over a limited period of time. This is a fair offer if the repairs can be done by an independent garage. If not, the dealer can always inflate the repair costs to double their actual worth and write up a bill for that amount. The buyer winds up paying the full price of the warranty repairs. The best kind of used car warranty is 100 percent with full coverage for a fixed term.

"As is" cars. Buying a car "as is" means you are aware of mechanical defects, are prepared to accept the responsibility for any damage or injuries caused by the vehicle, and that all costs to fix it shall be paid by you. The courts have held that the "as is" clause is not a blank check to cheat buyers and must be, therefore, interpreted in light of the seller's true intent. That is, was there an attempt to deceive the buyer by including this clause? Did the buyer really know what the "as is" clause means in terms of his future legal rights? It has also been held that verbal representations—"parole evidence"—made by the seller as to the fine quality of the used car but never written into the formal contract, may also be considered by the court. Generally, Canadian courts ignore "as is" clauses when the vehicle has been misrepresented, when a dealer is the seller, or when the defects are so serious the seller is presumed to have known of their existence.

Odometer tampering. It is often too dangerous for the dealer to turn back the mileage, so independent outfits are hired to pick up the car or visit the dealership and "fix" the odometer, a practice allowed under Canadian law.

Until federal and provincial laws are enforced and convictions result in severe penalties to anyone engaging in this practice (American laws allow citizens to sue for treble damages plus lawyer and court costs), the best protection from this fraud is to demand that the dealer put the mileage figure on the contract and give you the name and address of the previous owner as well as all repair receipts. When dealing with a private seller, it would be smart to demand that the same requirements be met.

Misrepresentation. Used cars can be misrepresented in a variety of ways. A used taxi may be represented as having belonged to a little old lady. A mechanically defective car that has been rebuilt after several major accidents may have sawdust in its transmission to muffle the clunks, heavy oil in the motor to stifle the clanks, and cheap retread tires to eliminate the thumps. These fraudulent practices may lead to the seller being charged with civil or criminal fraud. The best protection against these dirty tricks is to have the vehicle's quality completely verified by an independent mechanic before completing the sale.

Private Sales Scams

A lot of space in this *Guide* has been used to describe how used car dealers cheat uninformed buyers. Of course, private individuals can be dishonest, too, so protect yourself at the outset by keeping the deposit small. After a test drive, you may sign a written agreement to purchase the vehicle, accompanied by a deposit of sufficient value to cover the seller's advertising costs, that is subject to cancellation if the automobile fails inspection.

After you have taken these precautions, watch out for these private seller tricks:

Used cars that are stolen or have finance owing. Bad economic times mean that a lot of used cars are sold without free title because the original auto loan has never been repaid. In Ontario, the Used Vehicle Information Package will alert buyers to any problems with the title, but in other provinces a buyer doesn't have access to this information. Generally, you have to contact the provincial office that registers property and pay a small fee for a computer print-out that may or may not be accurate. You will be asked for the current owner's name and the vehicle's identification number (VIN), found usually on the driver's side of the dashboard or on the ownership.

Both amateur and professional rip-off artists sell cars that haven't been paid for because it's so easy to do and the profits are enormous. They skip town after sticking you with the finance payments. By the time the lender tracks you down, most legal recourse is ineffective. Your best bet may be to buy the car again—from the lender at a discount and take a tax loss.

This racket can be avoided by asking for proof of purchase and payment from any individual who offers to sell a used car for an incredibly low price. Check the sales contract to determine who granted the original loan and call the lender to see if it has been repaid. Place a call to the Ministry of Transport in your province and the insurance agency holding the vehicle policy to ascertain whether the car is registered in the seller's name. Check to find out if a finance company is named as a beneficiary on the auto insurance policy. Finally, call up the original dealer to determine whether there are any outstanding claims.

Stolen cars are almost always sold through private individuals. Car dealers usually can't be fooled and they have insurance to compensate buyers if they inadvertently sell a stolen vehicle.

Choosing the Right Kind of Vehicle

A vehicle's size and styling play an important part in the satisfaction it will give its owner. The principal body sizes and styles and their advantages and disadvantages are listed in Part Three. A full evaluation of the best and worst multipurpose vehicles can be found in the *Lemon-Aid 4X4, Van and Truck Guide.*

Front-wheel drive

It's too bad rear-drives are so hard to find. Although I recommend a number of front-wheel-drive vehicles, I still feel FWD is overrated. Granted, cars with front-wheel drive provide a bit more interior room (eliminating the transmission hump) and claim to provide better fuel economy, but overall servicing costs with rear-drives are likely to be much lower.

Servicing front-wheel drives can be nightmarish. Entire steering, suspension and drivetrain assemblies must be replaced when just one component is defective. In addition, the drivetrain and its components do not lend themselves to the do-it-yourself mechanic.

Parts costs are unbelievable. A new transmission assembly, called a transaxle, can cost about $2000 to repair, compared to $700 for a rear-drive transmission. And keep in mind that transmission, steering or suspension components are almost always damaged in low-speed frontal collisions.

Front-drive constant velocity joints will likely give out after only three years; replacing the joints costs about $600, and the front tires will wear out long before the rear tires need replacing.

Four-wheel drive

Encouraged by the popularity of 4X4 vehicles in North America, many automakers are offering it as an option on their more moderately priced family sedans, pickups and minivans, creating a plethora of overpriced four-wheel drives that promise much more than they actually deliver. Many 4X4 customers have been turned off by high repair costs, fragile mechanical components and government studies showing an increased risk of rollover accidents. They are turning, instead, toward more reliable, front-drive compacts with manual transmissions and better traction tires or two-wheel-drive pickups equipped with winches and large, deep-lugged rear tires. As far as reliability is concerned, American automakers dominate the 4X4 utility vehicle market with Ford's Explorer and Ranger, and Jeep's Cherokee variations.

All-wheel drive
All-wheel-drive and four-wheel-drive vehicles are practically identical. The 4X4 mode must be selected, either manually or electronically, while AWD is always available when needed. Repairs for both systems are costlier than front-drives.

Import or domestic model?
When the Japanese automakers first exported vehicles to Canada in the 1970s, they exported junk cars. But American small cars were junk, too, so the Japanese got a toehold in the North American market. Throughout the 1980s, Japanese quality improved dramatically, with Toyota and Honda leading the pack and Nissan improving slightly. Over the same period, American quality slowly improved to the point that today American quality control is about where the Japanese were in 1980. This fact is confirmed by Consumers Union. CU found that "American cars are aging more gracefully than they used to. The average problem rate for five-year-old models dropped by one-third, from 279 problems per 100 cars in 1980 to 191 per 100 cars in 1990." The quality gap is also narrowing for American new cars because today, according to *Consumer Reports*, "new American cars now experience nearly two and a half times as many problems as Japanese cars, [whereas] the differential was more like three to one in 1980."

This 1988 GM Bonneville's rotten paint job shows why GM's sales have nosedived.

In my *New Car Guide*, the most reliable and durable vehicles are singled out as Japanese makes or American co-ventures—such as the Ford Probe, which is actually a Mazda 626 dropped into a Ford body—

and American "captive imports" such as the Dodge Colt and Eagle Vista that are marketed as American products but are actually foreign in design or manufacture, or both. But, where used vehicles are concerned, American-made rear-drive cars, like the Ford LTD/Crown Victoria/Mercury Grand Marquis, the Lincoln Town Car, the LTD and Marquis V6, and Chrysler's Diplomat/New Yorker V8 are a better choice than imports because their prices are more competitive, they are easy and cheap to service, and they are generally in much better shape. The only problem is that American rear-drives have become an endangered species, with Ford being the only automaker still churning them out in large numbers.

Japanese vehicles hold up fairly well until their fifth year. Then the engine head gasket will probably have to be replaced, the front brakes will need reconditioning, and the rack-and-pinion steering system will likely have to be overhauled. Furthermore, the front-wheel-drive constant-velocity joints will probably need replacing at a cost of about $300 each. Finally, used Japanese-built vehicles are seldom priced reasonably because their owners paid inflated prices when they were new and want to get some of their money back.

South Korean and Taiwanese cars are poor imitations of Japanese vehicles. They don't hold up very well after their third year due to poor quality body construction, cheap and unreliable electrical components, and parts suppliers who put low prices ahead of reliability and durability. This is particularly evident when one looks at the failure-prone Hyundai Excel.

European vehicles are also risky buys. In spite of their high cost, major electrical, suspension and brake failures are commonplace, parts are hard to get, depreciation is incredibly rapid (especially with Audis), and service is usually given with a snarl. Volkswagen, Mercedes, BMW and Porsche models depreciate much more slowly than the others, but their parts are hard to get and service is, as you might expect, unnecessarily expensive. Furthermore, the increased competition from Japanese-built luxury sedans and sports cars has seriously cut into their sales, forcing major layoffs and production cutbacks. Peugeot, Renault and Fiat are gone, and Saab and Jaguar are now owned by GM and Ford where they continue to be a drain on the American automakers' cash reserves.

Eastern European imports have all the parts and service deficiencies outlined for other European vehicles, in addition to their own old, unreliable technology. Their only advantage is a low retail price.

No matter whether you buy domestic or imported, overall vehicle quality has improved a great deal during the past decade. Premature rusting is less of a problem and driveline defects are less common. On the other hand, electrical system failures caused by faulty computer modules, malfunctioning brakes, failure-prone air conditioning and automatic transmissions, and defective fuel systems, suspensions, steering, and exhaust systems are still frequent headaches for the Canadian car owner.

"Beaters" and collectibles
It's getting pretty hard to find a vehicle 10 years old or older that's safe and reliable. Personally, I'd be reluctant to buy any decade-old vehicle from anywhere east of Manitoba. Apart from salt being a real body killer, it's just too easy to fall prey to scam artists who cover up major mechanical or body problems due to accidents or environmental damage.

Still, if you look for one of the following recommended vehicles, avoid the non-recommended ones, take your time, and insist upon an independent checkup, you may find an acceptable "beater" (Canadian expression for an old, beat up-looking vehicle that runs well— most of the time) in the $500 to $1000 range. If you want to take less of a risk and have a bit more money to spend, look up the recommended vehicles found at the beginning of each vehicle category in Part Three.

Some beaters are cheap because they're lemons—unreliable, difficult or expensive to service. Nevertheless, if an independent mechanic says the more common and costly defects have been repaired and if you have the time, knowledge and parts suppliers to do your own maintenance and repairs, you may do all right, but the odds are against you. In the listings below, be wary of trouble areas listed in parentheses.

Acceptable Beaters

Chrysler
Dart, Valiant, Duster, Scamp, Diplomat, Caravelle, Newport, rear-drive New Yorker and Gran Fury (engine electrical, suspension, brakes, body and frame rust plus constant stalling when humidity is high).

Ford
Maverick, Comet, Fairmont, Zephyr, Tracer, Mustang, Capri, Cougar, Thunderbird V6, Torino, Marquis, Grand Marquis, LTD and LTD Crown Victoria (trunk, wheel well and rocker panel rusting, brakes, steering, electrical).

General Motors
Chevette and Acadian (steering and brakes you have to stand on to stop), rear-drive Nova, Ventura, Skylark and Phoenix (suspension); front-drive Nova and Spectrum; Camaro, Firebird, Malibu, LeMans, Century, Regal, Cutlass, Monte Carlo and Grand Prix (suspension, brakes), Bel Air, Impala, Caprice, Laurentian, Catalina, Parisienne, LeSabre, Bonneville, Delta 88 (suspension and brakes).

Toyota (late '80s)
All models, except the LE van (brakes, chassis and body rusting).

"Lemon" Beaters

American Motors
Hornet, Concord, Spirit, Pacer and Eagle 4X4 (faulty engines, transmissions and steering). In the 1970s, American Motors of Canada offered a free TV with each car purchase (a *color* TV for a top-of-the-line model). The TVs worked well.

Audi
Fox and 4000 (engine, transmission and fuel system). Forget about sudden acceleration; any acceleration would be a god-send.

British Leyland
Austin Marina, MG, MGB and Triumph (electrical system, engine, transmission, clutch and chassis rusting).

Chrysler (all years)
Cricket, Omni, Horizon, Volaré/Aspen (engine, brakes, steering chassis rusting); Charger, Cordoba and Mirada (brakes, body and electrical system).

Dacia
All models (engine, transmission, brakes and electrical system). After abandoning the Canadian market about 15 years ago, Dacia is offering franchises to U.S. dealers. America, we feel your pain.

Datsun/Nissan
210, 310, 510, 810, F-10 and 240Z (electrical system, brakes and rusting). The 240Z earned me my first $2-million libel lawsuit from Datsun (now Nissan) after I called the vehicle "a Kamikazi car," after discovering it had serious brake deficiencies. Datsun fixed the brake problem and dropped the lawsuit.

Fiat
Referred to as "fix it again, Tony," all Fiat models and years are known for temperamental fuel and electrical systems and biodegradable bodies. Alfa Romeos have similar problems.

Ford
Cortina, Pinto, Bobcat and Mustang II (electrical, engine and chassis rusting); fire-prone Pinto/Bobcat are mobile Molatov cocktails.

The Cortina was the first "redated" car sold by Ford of Canada. Redating—selling unsold previous year's cars as the following year's model—involved Ford trucks, Datsun 510, Toyota Corolla, and Mazda cars and trucks. Thanks to tough judges across Canada and an efficient small claims court system, the decades-old scam was stopped in its tracks in the early 1980s when the Supreme Court ruled it was a deceptive practice (*Pelletier v. Datsun*).

General Motors

Vega, Astre, Monza and Firenza (engine, transmission, body and brakes); Cadillac Cimarron and Allanté (poor-quality components and overpriced); all front-drives except Toronado and Eldorado (engine, automatic transmission, electronic modules, steering, brakes, rust/paint peeling); Citation, Skylark, Omega and Phoenix (engine, brakes, electronic modules and severe rust canker).

GM bought the rights to the Wankel rotary engine to power its Vega, but couldn't find a way to shoehorn it into the engine compartment. It sold the rights to Mazda and the rest is history.

Stung by this author's criticism that its Vega and Astre were unreliable lemons, GM took a parade of Vegas on a cross-Canada trek and then used the trip in a major ad campaign. Midway through GM's advertising campaign, it was discovered that the Vegas needed a constant resupply of parts and a large contingent of GM engineering staff because of their frequent breakdowns. The Canadian Automobile Protection Association petitioned the federal government to sue GM for false advertising. It did. GM lost and was fined $20,000. (Author's note: That was a sweet time, when automaker deception was easy to detect.)

Hyundai

Pony and Stellar (electrical system, brakes, poor-quality body components, and no parts). Hyundai's first imports into Canada during the early 1980s, these cars were shooting stars that captured lots of sales during their first few years on the market and then crashed once word got around that they were unsafe and unreliable.

Japanese automakers got a toehold in the American market by selling cheap, poor-quality alternatives to the American Big Three in the early 1970s. The Americans stumbled by selling their own not-as-cheap, poor-quality cars. Hyundai's first cars were cheap, poor-quality knock-offs of Japanese cars, but the Japanese have responded by raising quality and trying to cap new car prices inflated by a soaring *yen*. In the end the *yen*, not quality control, will contribute to Hyundai's success or failure.

Innocenti

All models (chassis rusting, unsafe seats and overall poor quality). This Italian econobox was sold principally in Quebec during the late 1970s.

Jaguar

All models (poor body assembly/paint, electrical system and service). Jaguar ownership will teach you quickly why Lucas is called the Prince of Darkness. Incidentally, Lucas supplied many of the electronic components for Operation Desert Storm and, as such, is being sued for $100 million by the United States government for poor-quality parts.

Lincoln

Versailles (electrical system, suspension and rusting).

Renault
(All models) Renault 5, R12, R18/Sportwagon and Fuego (fuel and electrical systems, CV joints and brakes, no parts, and few mechanics); a "separatist's" dream car—poor reliability and expensive parts separate you from your money, moving traffic and friends.

Skoda
120/130 Series: The best of a bad lot of Eastern European imports (Dacia, Lada, Yugo, etc.), the 1983-85 models all sell for less than $500. They are particularly bad buys because parts are unavailable and their low-tech engineering is unreliable. The 1986-89 120 and 130 series' prices vary between $700 and $1000. They are a bit more refined, but they cannot match the high quality of Japanese vehicles or American captive imports.

Volkswagen
Beetle (unsafe front seats, fuel tank placement, wheels and seat tracks); Camper minivan (engine, transmission, fuel system and heater); Rabbit/ Dasher (engine, electrical system, front brakes and cooling system). VW has resurrected the Beetle in Mexico and in other parts of Latin America, but it still remains an unsafe, low-tech small car.

Rabbit: More turkey than Rabbit, VW Rabbits are bizarre creatures. From self-starting Rabbits whenever it rains ("runaway" Rabbits) to fire-bug Rabbits with overheating catalytic converters, these cars are full of surprises. Parts are rare, and the slow and expensive dealer servicing would give anyone nightmares. Buy a more recent Golf or Jetta instead.

Be wary of investing in recent high-performance cars. GM took the Corvette ZR-1 off the market due to poor sales after only four years of production. Although 3000 vehicles were to be produced annually, that figure dropped to fewer than 500 units. Owners who paid $85,307 for a new 1990 ZR-1 now own a car worth about $32,000.

Many cars jump in value on their 20th birthday. Buy an 18- or 19-year-old car, especially a convertible, and it's hard to lose money. Shop the car shows; they are a good place to make contact with wholesalers and restorers. Car clubs also offer a wealth of information and are regularly listed in the "Wheels" section of the *Saturday Toronto Star* and in major American auto magazines like *Auto Week, Car and Driver, Motor Trend* and *Road and Track. Hemmings' Motor News* and *Old Cars Weekly* out of Iola, Wisconsin are two more excellent sources of collector news.

Junkyard bargains
Limited-production older cars that have been off the market for some time present a different problem, because most junkyards, independent parts suppliers and dealers don't stock parts that are older than five years or have a limited clientele. Consumers have been more successful in

scouring Canadian and American "pick and pull" junkyards and dealing with specialized "classic" parts suppliers. These agencies are well known to many provincial car associations, and they usually advertise in special-interest magazines like *Hemmings'* or *Old Car Trader.*

Going under names like U-Pull-It and Pick-N-Pull, self-service auto junkyards are the fastest growing segment of the auto dismantling industry. You can get used parts for about 10 percent of their new retail price, but you must remove the part yourself or pay a mechanic to remove it for you. This gives you the advantage of practising on someone else's car before you have to install the part on your own vehicle. In most cases, if the part fails within 30 days, the self-serve junkyard will allow you to pull another part—as long as you supply the muscle and bring back the part or pay a replacement charge.

Servicing

Servicing has traditionally been the *bête noire* of European car importers in North America, and this has accounted for the demise of some well-engineered vehicles. For example, a model can have the best engineering features in the world, but if the servicing is inadequate, that vehicle will deteriorate quickly and fall into the lemon category. (Fiat, Renault, Dacia and Peugeot all share this problem.) Dealership servicing of most European models is better in cities than in rural areas. One notable exception is Volkswagen, where a large network of independent service agencies has sprouted across the country.

Japanese-built vehicles have relatively few servicing problems. Parts are easily found and available at reasonable prices from independent suppliers, and dealerships are competent and located in major centers. Japanese car servicing costs are often inflated because dealers sell fewer cars with smaller profit margins, and the cars they do sell don't come in that frequently for servicing. Most Japanese vehicles, unlike many European cars, can be repaired anywhere, thus allowing owners to save money by shopping around for the most competitive price.

Parts

Cross-border shopping in the U.S. can save you big bucks (30 percent to 40 percent) on the cost of new parts, and another 20 percent on labor. Without leaving Canada, you can still save from one-third to one-half the cost of a new part by purchasing it from an independent supplier and having the repairs done at an independent garage. Remember, though, car dealers often refuse to install independent supplier parts, claiming they cannot guarantee the job with a part that is not original equipment. Another advantage in buying used is that cars on the market for more than three years have a better selection of independently supplied parts than models recently launched by the automobile manufacturers.

Parts availability

With some European models, you can count on lots of aggravation and expense caused by the unacceptably slow distribution of parts and their high markup. Because these companies have a quasi-monopoly on replacements, there are few independent suppliers one can turn to for help. And auto wreckers, the last-chance repository for inexpensive car parts, are unlikely to carry foreign parts for vehicles older than three years or manufactured in small numbers. Parts supply is hardly a problem, though, with Japanese and domestic cars due to the large number of vehicles produced, the presence of hundreds of independent suppliers, the ease with which relatively simple parts can be interchanged from one model to another, and the large reservoir of used parts stocked by junkyards. Incidentally, when a part is hard to find, the *Mitchell Manual* is a useful guide to substitute parts that can be used among many different models. It's available in some libraries and most auto parts stores.

American cars generally have no problems with parts distribution unless a particular unit has been off the market for some time or a specific component has experienced a high failure rate, like electronic control units that regulate engine, transmission and braking performance. In these cases, though, there are many independent suppliers who can find the missing parts at prices far below dealer cost. Components also can be more easily interchanged on American, Japanese and Korean-made vehicles than on European models.

Purchasing reconditioned parts for large mechanical components, such as motors and transmissions, can offer savings of one-half to two-thirds. There is generally no difference in the quality of reconditioned parts, and they are often guaranteed as long as new ones.

Hard-to-find body panels ("crash parts") are frequently replaced with metal or fiberglass panels made by independent manufacturers. According to the Automobile Protection Association (APA), these parts are less expensive than the originals, are just as durable, and are guaranteed against premature rust-out. Nevertheless, carmakers oppose their use and trot out safety and durability, rather than profit, as their primary motivation.

Car clubs are often helpful sources to find parts that are otherwise unobtainable. Club members trade and sell specialty parts for "high-performance" vehicles, keep a list of where rare parts can be found, and are usually well informed as to where independent parts suppliers are located. Most car enthusiast magazines also list the addresses of auto clubs and suppliers of hard-to-find parts.

Active vs. Passive Safety

Another factor that must be taken into consideration when purchasing a used car is the degree of safety it provides. In establishing evaluation guidelines, the vehicle's mechanical and body components should be examined to determine if they are durable and provide a sufficient degree of active and passive safety.

Active safety components are generally those mechanical systems that help avoid accidents, such as high-performance tires, anti-lock braking systems and specialized suspensions. Advocates of active safety stress that accidents are caused by the proverbial "nut behind the wheel" and believe that safe driving can best be taught through the schools or private driving courses.

The theory of active safety has several drawbacks. First, there is no independent proof that safe driving can be taught successfully. Even if a young driver learns how to master defensive-driving techniques, there is still no assurance that this training will be of any use in an emergency situation.

Second, about 50 percent of all fatal accidents are caused by drivers under the influence of alcohol or drugs. Surely all the high-performance options and specialized driving courses in the world will not provide much protection from impaired drivers who take a bead on your car.

Finally, active safety components get a lot of use—you are likely to need ABS brakes 99 times more often than an airbag—and have to be well maintained to remain effective. ABS-equipped 1985-90 models are risky buys because they were rushed to production and are not as reliable or durable as later designs. They can be expensive to repair because a mechanic will junk the old design and put in a new assembly to make sure you don't come back with other failures. Some early ABS systems were rather crude designs; make sure you can adapt to the excessive pulsation and noise that often occur when the brakes are applied. Also, recent studies show ABS may instill a false sense of security in drivers who are tempted to take extra chances.

Passive safety assumes that the car is going to be involved in an accident some day. When that accident occurs, the vehicle itself provides as much protection as possible to the driver, the car's occupants and other vehicles that may be struck without depending upon the driver's reactions. Passive safety components that have been particularly reliable and durable are safety belts, airbags and vehicles that absorb or deflect crash forces away from the car's occupants.

Seatbelts
Seatbelts provide the best means of reducing the severity of injury arising from low-speed as well as high-speed frontal collisions. A properly adjusted seatbelt is about 42 percent effective in preventing death or severe injury. An airbag by itself is only 21 percent effective because it won't deploy in about half of all fatal collisions, such as rollovers, side impacts or rear-enders. Together, these two safety items are 47 percent effective in preventing death or severe injury. By preventing the ejection of the motorist and occupants from the vehicle, the National Safety Council estimates that seatbelts offer a five times greater chance of accident survival than for an unbelted individual who prefers to be "thrown free."

Seatbelts are not all the same. At best they can be uncomfortable; at their worst they can paralyze or kill. Don't buy any used vehicle that doesn't have three-point belts that include shoulder harnesses and lapbelts that cross the pelvic area. Four years ago, in *Garrett v. Ford*, a Baltimore, Maryland, Federal Court jury rendered a $3.2-million settlement against Ford for installing lapbelts without back seat shoulder harnesses in a 1985 Escort. The lapbelts were designed to cross at the waist instead of the pelvis, and this error contributed to the passenger's paralysis. If shoulder harnesses had been installed, the lapbelts would not have aggravated the injuries. GM, too, was recently hit with a $3-million court judgment by a West Virginia jury which found the company negligent in not equipping a 1978 Oldsmobile Cutlass with lap-shoulder restraints in the rear fold-out seats. A 17-year-old was rendered a paraplegic as a result of the accident (*Johnson v. GM*).

Since 1990, most automakers have offered three-point belts in the rear fold-down seating area as a standard feature. These companies also offer three-point belts for older cars as a $100 option, excluding installation. Incidentally, most automakers will give a free seatbelt extender to occupants who have a bit extra girth.

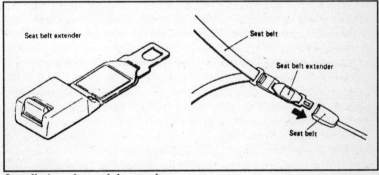

Installation of a seatbelt extender.

Unsafe seatbelts
Over a half million vehicles sold in Canada may have unsafe front and rear seatbelts that are eligible for free repairs under manufacturers' industry recall programs. Transport Canada has alerted U.S. safety investigators that more than 6 million North American cars, minivans, 4X4s and pickups sold by most Japanese firms (Toyota used a different supplier), GM, Ford and Chrysler may have faulty seatbelts that fail to retract, are difficult to latch, or come unbuckled in an accident.

The defect alert targets buckles made by Takata Inc. installed in 600,000 vehicles sold in Canada. Carmakers have received more than 6500 claims for repairing or replacing these buckles and have covered the associated costs through a number of little-known warranty extensions. Transport Canada has recorded 12 failures. In the U.S., 77 reports include 66 consumer complaints and 12 injuries involving Honda Civics.

Honda's seatbelt problems date back to 1970. A confidential dealer service bulletin, issued March 13, 1992, details how Honda extended the base warranty to replace, free of charge, faulty seatbelts found in its 1970-85 cars. Honda models built since 1986 carry a lifetime seatbelt warranty that covers new and used vehicles.

Owners of any Japanese or American-made vehicle with faulty seatbelts should have their dealer repair the buckle or install a new seatbelt assembly at no charge. They may also ask for Transport Canada's assistance through its toll-free hotline if the dealer or automaker refuses to correct the defect for free.

Motorized seatbelts

These front seat restraints run along a channel and cross the shoulder when the ignition is turned on. A lapbelt has to be fastened separately. These automatic belts are set so high above the door frame that they are uncomfortable to wear and a nightmare to adjust. Their most serious shortcoming, however, is that they give the driver a false sense of security, and the separate lapbelt often goes unfastened (the U.S. government says that only 29 percent of people who own cars with motorized seatbelts use the lap portion). This has resulted in a number of accidents where the driver or front passenger has been decapitated or paralyzed by the shoulder belt. Ford lost a $1.3-million lawsuit in Akron, Ohio where the driver of a 1990 Escort was paralyzed in an accident where only the automatic shoulder belt was fastened (*Pflum v. Ford*). Nissan faces a $10-million suit in Newnan, Georgia, from the father of a girl who did not have the lapbelt fastened and who was decapitated by her 1989 Sentra's motorized shoulder harness (*Smith v. Nissan*).

Door-mounted seatbelts

Safety groups have blasted carmakers for this unsafe design which can kill if the door opens in an accident. GM is being sued in the U.S. for $33 million over the inadequate performance of the driver's door-mounted seatbelt on a 1990 Pontiac Sunbird. The driver was killed when the car door opened, rendering the seatbelt inoperative. The suit claims GM was negligent in the design that caused the belt to be undone leaving driver unprotected and unrestrained.

Windowshade design

The Washington-based Institute for Injury Reduction, an industry safety group, says "windowshade" retractor devices on shoulder belts are dangerous. These devices incorporate tension relievers that allow too much slack to be introduced into the harnesses. The belt slackens when you lean forward and remains slack instead of retracting automatically. Usually, a sharp pull will get the belt to retract.

There are more than 100 million cars and trucks on the road that employ the windowshade restraint.

Airbags

About 66 percent of all 1994 model cars and light trucks have airbags;

therefore, your chances of buying an airbag-equipped used vehicle are pretty good. Furthermore, Breed Technologies Inc., a major American airbag manufacturer, plans to market retrofit units at $600 each for drivers who want the extra protection on cars that weren't originally equipped with an airbag. They will be marketed through car dealerships and will fit most 1988-94 cars and trucks.

Don't be unduly concerned about the unit misfiring or failing to deploy due to a vehicle's age. Recently, the American government tested a 15-year-old airbag-equipped Ford and it deployed faultlessly. Of the estimated six million airbag-equipped vehicles now on North American highways, only 60 lawsuits have been filed alleging the device has malfunctioned, and most of these suit were for minor burns. Chrysler is the defendant in most of these lawsuits, because it was the first company to install airbags as a standard feature.

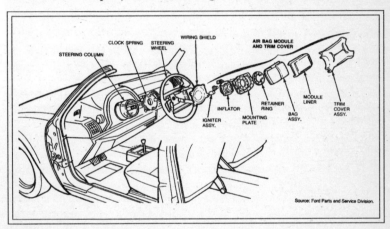

A typical airbag restraint system.

Crashworthiness

Just as with reliability, a vehicle's size doesn't guarantee that you will escape injury in an accident. A 1991 Ford Escort, for example, gives better full-front collision protection than the Mercedes 190E or the Lexus ES 250, two luxury vehicles that are represented as being engineered to crash safely at moderate speeds of about 57 km/h (35 mph).

On the other hand, you can be sure your chances are high of sustaining serious injury or getting killed if you crash an early model multipurpose vehicle (pickup, truck, minivan, van or 4X4 utility vehicle). MPVs made during the 1980s tend to roll over and fail to provide structural integrity to protect occupants. Designed-in safety features required on cars are not yet required on MPVs. Voluntary efforts have paid off, however, and in recent crash tests, the GM Trans Sport and Lumina APV minivans provided good crash protection. The venerable Chrysler Caravan and Voyager minivans haven't done all that well during the last couple of model years.

There are two large Washington-based agencies and one Canadian group that monitor how vehicle design affects crash safety. They are the Insurance Bureau of Canada, the U.S. National Highway Traffic and Safety Administration (NHTSA), and the Insurance Institute for Highway Safety (IIHS), an insurance research group that collects and analyzes insurance claims data. Crash information from these three groups does not always agree because the insurance data looks at all kinds of accidents, while the NHTSA figures relate only to 57 km/h frontal collisions—the equivalent of two cars of equal weight hitting each other head-on while travelling at 57 km/h, or to a car slamming into a parked car at 120 kph (70 mph). Bear in mind that a car providing good injury protection often produces the highest damage claims because its structure, not the occupants, absorbs most of the forces of the collision.

Unsafe designs
Purchasing a used car with the idea that you will be involved in an accident is not unreasonable. According to the IIHS, the average car can be expected to have two accidents over its lifetime. Small domestic subcompacts, like the Colt and Chrysler Omni/Horizon, can do very well in frontal crashes of 57 km/h. Nevertheless, large-sized vehicles, with some exceptions, produce smaller accident injury claims than subcompact and compact vehicles.

Engineering mistakes and shortcuts often are the cause of accidents or the reason why accident injuries are so severe. Flimsy front seats, the absence of rear head restraints in some minivans, dangerous fuel tanks and fuel lines in Ford and GM models, transmissions that pop out of park into reverse in early Fords and the Aerostar, electronic PROM modules that make GM pickups suddenly accelerate, and a high center of gravity that make Jeep, Bronco II and Suzuki Samurai rollovers commonplace are all engineering decisions that put profit ahead of safety.

Exploding gas tanks
Fire-prone fuel tanks have been a problem with GM trucks and rear-drive passenger vehicles for the last two decades. The light truck danger is caused by the side-saddle placement of the truck's tank outside the frame rail of all 1973-87 full-size pickups. Engineering tests, crash data and GM out-of-court settlements all confirm that the danger of fire resulting from a side impact is very real. Furthermore, GM (U.S.) has just settled 39 class-action lawsuits by offering all American owners of the affected trucks a $1000 certificate toward the purchase of any new GM vehicle.

GM engineers warned the company in 1970 that the gas tank placement on many of its rear-drive cars made it vulnerable to puncture during high-speed crashes. GM estimated it would cost $8.59 to $11.59 per vehicle to make a design change that would eliminate the hazard in 1971, but decided the correction was too expensive and would reduce trunk space.

The question was raised again in 1973, prompting GM to do a "value analysis" of fuel tank placement. Edward C. Ivey, the company engineer assigned to the study, subsequently sent a two-page confidential memo to the company predicting 500 people would die annually at a cost to the company of $200,000 each. Ivey then concluded that a design change "would be worth approximately $2.20 per new model auto to prevent a fuel-fed fire in all accidents."

GM felt it wasn't cost effective to invest $8 to $12 for a savings of only $2.20, so it never made the change and is fighting several hundred cases a year brought by burn victims and their relatives.

Faulty computer modules (sudden acceleration, stalling)

Sudden acceleration is an industry-wide problem, despite all the adverse publicity garnered by Audi, due mainly to its inept handling of owner complaints. Experts agree that a defect in the computer module or the cruise control's electronic circuit board can cause a car to jump from idle to full throttle without the gas pedal being depressed. Carmakers have been runaway-proofing their vehicles by installing automatic transmission shift locks since 1990. Many cars now have shift locks that require the driver to depress the brake pedal before shifting from park into drive or reverse.

GM has also been sued repeatedly over its hazardous computer modules. An Alabama jury recently ordered the company to pay $15 million to a youth's parents for a malfunctioning PROM computer chip that caused his 1988 Chevrolet Silverado pickup to stall, leading to his death.

GM documents subpoenaed for the trial disclosed that General Motors was aware of the stalling problem and put a replacement PROM into service in March 1988. It was argued that this action was in effect a "silent recall" and proved GM's negligence. GM maintained the second PROM was actually a "product improvement" unrelated to the stalling problem and that there was no defect that required a customer advisory being issued.

The jurors later learned that confidential GM service bulletins discussed "driveability problems" like sags, hesitations, rolling, surging or rough idles associated with the old computer chip. GM employees testified that service managers would replace the old PROM only if the customer complained of poor engine performance.

Aftermarket computer module chips sold by independent suppliers have also come under fire for not performing as advertised. In an unpublished technical paper submitted to the SAE, EPA chemical engineer Jim Lindner concluded that computer module chips designed to boost fuel economy and lower emissions actually produce the opposite effect: lower gas mileage and higher emissions.

Weak seats

Flimsy front seats leave drivers and passengers vulnerable in accidents.

The seats collapse in low-speed collisions because the mechanisms that hold them upright fail when they are most needed. Failures have been reported among all car lines, except Mercedes-Benz which has a tougher standard than what is required by Transport Canada. All auto seats now meet federal standards, but increased criticism has forced the NHTSA to review its standards.

Court decisions have added to the impetus to make car seats safer. In case , Robert Oakes, a Chicago Camaro owner, recently won a $7-million lawsuit against GM (U.S.) for an accident in which he was rear-ended by a pickup truck. His seat collapsed, throwing him into the back seat, breaking his neck and causing paralysis. General Motors is appealing the decision.

Recalls
More than 200 million unsafe vehicles have been recalled by automakers for the free correction of safety-related defects since American recall legislation was passed in 1966. About one-third of the recalled vehicles never made it back to the dealership for repairs. *Auto Service Monitor*, an American firm that tracks recalls, estimates that there are close to 20 million vehicles still on North American roads that can suddenly careen out of control, explode or fail to stop. This lack of public concern is mostly due to apathy, but carmakers must bear part of the blame because they only send out one recall letter to the first recorded owner of the vehicle. If the owner has moved or has sold the vehicle, he won't be notified and the vehicle won't get fixed.

Options

Most optional equipment on used cars is worth a fraction of its original cost, yet sellers often pretend otherwise. Check out the true value of these options by consulting the options chart in the introduction to Part Three. Remember, extravagantly equipped vehicles hurt your pocketbook in three ways: they inflate the purchase price, they increase the cost of maintenance, and they often consume extra fuel.

Air conditioner
A preferred option of drivers who spend a lot of time in their cars, air conditioning is too risky for buyers of used vehicles going into their fourth year on the market. Air-conditioning units are easy prey for premature corrosion, and you can almost bet the compressor or other expensive components will need overhauling. Allergy sufferers may be seriously affected by molds and other contaminants that can proliferate in the tubing. AC systems on Honda Accords are particularly vulnerable to contamination, prompting the following dealer advisory from Honda:

Evaporator Cleaning

When a car comes in with bad A/C odor, the evaporator must be cleaned. Remove the evaporator assembly and disassemble it. Wash the case halves, the evaporator, and the foam insulators in mild dish soap and water. If the odor was real bad, the foam insulators should be replaced. Don't use bleach or any other type of cleaner/disinfectant; they'll attack the surface coating on the evaporator and make things worse in the long run.

Let the parts dry thoroughly before you reassemble them. Remove any debris from the blower, fresh air intake, and the cowl area.

Remind the customer:

interior deodorizers, perfumes, cigarette smoke generally make A/C odor worse. The key is keeping the evaporator as dry as possible. Use RECIRC when the outside air is humid; FRESH when the outside air is dry. Use the button to turn the A/C off the last few blocks before you reach your destination, but leave the blower on. If necessary, you can use the different ventilation modes to redirect the air to where it's not noticeable.

Air conditioning odours are a common problem.

Automatic cruise control
Notoriously failure prone and expensive to repair, cruise control can lead to driver inattention and can make a vehicle hard to control in a skid.

Battery (heavy-duty)
Most original equipment batteries last for only two winters. The best battery for northern climates is the heavy-duty type which can easily last up to four winters. Consumer groups recommend the Delco Freedom 24-60, Interstate 24-42, Motorcraft Tested Tough BX-24, Energiser and Douglass 24-6000.

Radio
Look for features that make the system easy and safe to operate; for example, radios that automatically seek out stations and cassette decks with automatic reverse eliminate the distraction caused by constant fiddling.

Rustproofing
Do not pay extra for a rustproofed vehicle, and don't waste money rustproofing it yourself. Chances are the warranty isn't transferable or the company has already gone out of business. Just repair what rust damage the vehicle already has, wash it every month, and don't park it in a heated garage during the winter.

Tires
There is no independent Canadian agency that evaluates tire performance

and durability. However, the U.S NHTSA has been rating tires for the past decade, and a number of consumer groups publish lists of tires that provide the best quality/price ratio.

Tire recommendations from the NHTSA and consumer groups are set according to size. For example, Goodyear's Aquatred, the Bridgestone Turanza QL10, and Goodrich's Touring TA are top-rated in both 185/70R14 and 205/70R15 sizes. The Aquatred, however, may not perform all that well on snow. Other 205/70R15 size tires also considered good buys but which perform less well on wet pavement are the Dunlop Axiom, Sears Roadhandler Plus and Michelin XGTA. Some tire brands may be sold under different trade names in Canada, so always ask for the American generic brand name when comparing the NHTSA's ratings.

When shopping for new tires, it is also a good idea to purchase those that provide a road hazard warranty. Under the terms of this guarantee, the tire dealer or manufacturer will provide compensation for any tire that is found to be defective or cannot be repaired.

Be especially vigilant when it comes to the spare tire hidden away in the trunk. Instead of a full-sized spare, you are likely to find a "space saver" spare that is only two-thirds the size of the other four tires. Unfortunately, even if you do get a standard-sized tire, it will probably not fit in the trunk.

The safest choice is four tires of the same size, type and manufacture (although they are the same size, tires from different manufacturers can have different performance quirks). Mixing different sizes and types of tires (bias ply, bias belted and radial) will lead to increased wear on the smaller pair and is said to make the vehicle dangerously unstable at high speeds.

Summer, radial, all-season and snow tires
You should buy summer tires if you plan to do a lot of high-speed, hot-weather driving. They last longer and run cooler than four all-season tires. All-season tires cost between $90 and $150 each. Radial tires make up their extra cost through a longer tread life—up to 40,000 km more than conventional tires—increased gas economy and better high-speed performance. In addition to these advantages, radial tires can also be retreaded more often and are more resistant to punctures than bias-ply tires. According to the Rubber Association of Canada, most car tires sold last year were radials.

All-season tires are a compromise: they will not get you through winter with the same margin of safety as snow tires, according to Transport Canada. They don't provide the same durability on dry surfaces as regular summer tires. In low-to-moderate snowfall areas, these tires are adequate, however, as long as they are not pushed beyond their limits.

Mud or snow tires provide the best traction on snowy surfaces. Traction on wet roads, though, is actually decreased with this type of tire. Tread wear is also accelerated by the use of softer rubber compounds. Beware of wide tires used for winter driving: 70-series or wider tires give poor traction and tend to "float" over snow. Consumers report good performance with Nokia Hakkapellitas snow tires imported from Finland.

Recaps

Buying recapped or remanufactured tires is a great way to save money without sacrificing safety. They sell for one-half to two-thirds the cost of a new tire.

Trailer towing options

The first thing you should do when choosing a vehicle to tow a trailer etc. is to find out if you really need a multipurpose vehicle (4X4, minivan, van or pickup) to handle the trailer's weight. Sometimes, a used passenger vehicle will work just as well and cost much less. There are four towing classes set up by the automakers in ranges from 2000 lbs. to over 5000 lbs.

If you are pulling a trailer that weighs up to 5000 lbs., many passenger vehicles can handle the load as long as they have been outfitted according to the automaker's towing specifications. Pulling a trailer that weighs more will likely require an MPV with a V8 engine and heavy-duty chassis components.

Manual transmissions also have greater clutch wear when trailering than automatics. Unit body (those without a separate frame) and front-drive models are not good choices for trailering, either. Without a frame, the pulling forces are likely to deform the sheet metal on the unit body (convertibles should never be used for towing), and front-drives lose some steering control and traction with all the weight concentrated in the rear.

Additional cooling systems for the radiator, transmission, engine oil and steering are a prerequisite for towing anything over 2000 lbs. Heavy-duty springs and brakes are a big help, too. Separate brakes for the trailer may be necessary to increase your vehicle's maximum towing capacity, and keep in mind that the trailer hitch must have a tongue capacity of at least 10 percent of the trailer's weight; otherwise, it may be unsafe to use.

Check with the trailer manufacturer for an independent assessment of your vehicle's capabilities. Never take the seller's advice as to which equipment is necessary without checking first with the manufacturer of the trailer.

Transmission (5-speed) or overdrive automatic

These relatively expensive options are usually part of a sports package. Either will reduce engine wear and noise and can cut fuel consumption by several tenths of a litre/100 km. A 5-speed manual transmission is standard on most Japanese cars.

Turbocharging

Exhaust gases are used to turn a turbine that compresses air to achieve more power from the engine. What works well for long-hauling diesel trucks creates high repair bills for owners of turbocharged GM, Ford and Chrysler models (bearing burn-outs at 30,000 to 50,000 km and engine failure after hot shutdown.) Engine seizures have also been reported from excessive heat build up and oil deterioration.

Turbos require more frequent changing of oil and oil filters and therefore more maintenance. They need premium gasoline to give the maximum boost in performance, and are far more complicated in their operation than standard motors. Also, they require parts that may not be readily available in most dealerships, or in independent garages for that matter. A good rule of thumb is to stay away from turbocharged used cars. Nevertheless, if you must have a turbocharged engine, remember that the newer water-cooled turbochargers are far more reliable and durable than those that have their central bearings cooled by oil.

Warranties (extended service contracts)

Good for five to ten years, supplementary or extended warranties are sold by automakers and independent agencies to pay for mechanical failures after the basic warranty has expired. They cost between $300 and $1000, and should be purchased only if the vehicle you are buying is off its original warranty, has a poor repair history, or you are reluctant to use the small claims courts. (In Part Three, used car ratings flag which models need extra warranty coverage.)

Sophisticated marketing techniques have been so successful in selling this newest automobile option that the CAA now estimates that 39 percent of all new car buyers purchase an extended service contract from the dealer, although fewer than half actually use it.

Buying a supplementary warranty from a company that is not tied to an automobile manufacturer is risky. Although their warranties are usually backed by an insurance company, it can be quite a hassle getting compensation when the warranty company goes belly up and the insurance company closes its door, too.

About half of the contract's price represents dealer markup. Out of the remainder comes the sponsor's administration costs and profit margin calculated to be another 25 percent. What's left is a minuscule 25 percent of the original amount paid to cover mechanical defects.

Selling Your Car

Private sales

Most people prefer buying from individuals rather than off of used car lots, especially now that the GST doesn't apply to private sales. If you must sell and want to make the most out of the deal, instead of trading in your old car to a dealer for an average 20 percent less than its real value, consider selling it yourself and putting the profits toward another used vehicle of a more recent vintage. Stay away from used car "brokers," though, who promise to sell your car themselves. Sellers have found these operations often close down suddenly and their cars have vanished, or the salesman has sold the vehicle for much more than admitted and pocketed the difference.

When to sell
It doesn't take a genius to figure out that the longer you keep your vehicle, the more money you save. In fact, the Hertz Corporation has estimated that a compactwith standard equipment, driven 10,000 miles and traded each year, costs 9.6 cents more a mile to operate than a comparable compact traded after five years. That same car kept for 10 years and run 10,000 miles a year would cost 10.8 cents less a mile than a similar vehicle kept for five years, and a whopping 20.38 cents less a mile than a comparable compact traded in each year. That would amount to a saving of $20,380 over a 10-year period.

U.S. Department of Transportation (DOT) statistics confirm Hertz's figures and show that ownership cost goes down dramatically after the seventh year.

Shortly after your vehicle's fifth birthday, ask a mechanic to look at it to give you some idea of what repairs and maintenance work it will likely need. Compare the estimated repair costs with what the average annual repair costs would be over the period of time you expect to keep the vehicle. For example, a five-year-old vehicle that will cost $2000 to put in top shape could be a good investment if it has cost you less than $500 annually to maintain up to now and you intend keep it another five years. If you've paid more than $2500 over the past five years and estimated repairs exceed the average $500 annual rate, cut your losses and buy another used vehicle.

Here are some other tips worth reflecting upon:
- Consider whether your car can still be serviced easily. If it is no longer sold, the parts supply is likely to dry up and independent mechanics will be reluctant to repair it. Don't trade for fuel economy alone, either. A more fuel-efficient vehicle may not be as reliable or as comfortable to drive.
- Reassess your needs. Does family growth require a different vehicle? Are you driving less? Are long trips taken less frequently?
- Let your car rust in peace and pocket the savings if its deteriorating condition does not pose a safety hazard or is not too embarrassing.
- If you're in sales and are constantly on the road, it makes sense to trade every few years because mechanical reliability is of prime consideration and the increased depreciation costs are mostly tax deductible.

Selling without fear
By using the following suggestions, you should be able to sell your vehicle quite easily without misleading anyone or losing your time with bargain hunters who "surf" classified ads.

1. Find the "Used Values" listed for your vehicle in Part Three. Select a price somewhere between the high and low figures, taking into consideration mileage, condition and regional price differences. Then, just to be sure you have a fair starting price, look up private classified ads for local market conditions that may deflate or inflate the market value.

FORD — 1987

Fact S.R.P.	Avg. Whsl	Mod. No.	Body Type	Engine	Avg. Retail
ESCORT GL					
*8895	2275	21	2drH/B GL	1.9L-E 4	3225
*9241	2475	25	4drH/B GL	1.9L-E 4	3425
*9741	1975			2.0L-D 4	2925
*9527	2750	28	4dr Wgn. GL	1.9L-E 4	3700
ESCORT GT					
*12078	3825	23	2dr H/B GT	1.9L-EHO	4775
EXP					
10638	3050	17	3dr Lux Cpe	1.9L-EHO	4000
12367	3550	18	3dr Spt. Cpe	1.9L-EHO	4500
MUSTANG LX					
9995	3875	40	2dr Sed. 'LX'	2.3L-E 4	5150
11711	4625			5.0L-EHO	5900
10895	4325	41	2dr H/B 'LX'	2.3L-E 4	5600
12611	5275			5.0L-EHO	6550
17116	7875	44	Convt. 'LX'	2.3L-E 4	9150
18832	8875			5.0L-EHO	10150
MUSTANG COBRA GT					
15731	6575	42	3dr Sed. 'GT'	5.0L-EHO	8075
21019	10375	45	Convt. 'GT'	5.0L-EHO	11875
TEMPO L					
9520	2950	30	2dr Cpe 'L'	2.3L-E 4	4125
9628	3150	35	4dr Sed. 'L'	2.3L-E 4	4325
TEMPO GL					
10087	3250	31	2dr Cpe GL	2.3L-E 4	4425
10187	3450	36	4dr Sed. GL	2.3L-E 4	4625
TEMPO GL SPORT					
11828	3800	33	2dr Spt. GL	2.3L-E 4	4975
11928	4000	38	4dr Spt. GL	2.3L-E 4	5175
TEMPO LX					
11814	4000	32	2dr Cpe. LX	2.3L-E 4	5175
11980	4200	37	4dr Sed LX	2.3L-E 4	5375
TEMPO 4WD					
13569	4300	34	2dr Sed 4WD	2.3L-E 4	5475
13669	4500	39	4dr Sed 4WD	2.3L-E 4	5675
THUNDERBIRD					
14882	4800	60	2dr HT	3.8L-E V6	6300
15486	5100			5.0L-E V8	6600
THUNDERBIRD SPORT					
18734	6325	61	2dr HT Spt.	5.0L-E V8	7825
THUNDERBIRD LX					
18491	6725	62	2dr HT LX	3.8L-E V6	8225
19055	7025			5.0L-E V8	8525
THUNDERBIRD TURBO COUPE					
21357	6775	64	2dr HT Turbo	2.3L-ET 4	8475
TAURUS L					
13575	3725	50	4dr Sed 'L'	2.5L-E 4	5225
14510	3825			3.0L-E V6	5325
15135	4425	55	4dr Wgn 'L'	3.0L-E V6	5925

FORD — 1987

Fact S.R.P.	Avg. Whsl	Mod. No.	Body Type	Engine	Avg. Retail
TAURUS MT5					
15396	3950	51	4dr Sed MT5	2.5L-E 4	5450
16002	4375	56	4dr Wgn MT5	2.5L-E 4	5875
TAURUS GL					
14966	4475	52	4dr Sed 'GL'	2.5L-E 4	5975
15901	4675			3.0L-E V6	6175
16492	5075	57	4dr Wgn 'GL'	3.0L-E 4	6575
TAURUS LX					
19077	5575	53	4dr Sed. 'LX'	3.0L-E V6	7075
19747	5975	58	4dr Wgn. 'LX'	3.0L-E V6	7475
LTD CROWN VICTORIA S					
16291	4950	72	4dr Sed. S	5.0L-E V8	6575
16435	5100			5.8L-2HO	6725
16246	5100	75	Wgn. S	5.0L-E V8	6725
16390	5250			5.8L-2HO	6875
LTD CROWN VICTORIA					
17871	5775	70	2dr Sedan	5.0L-E V8	7400
18015	5975			5.8L-2HO	7600
17384	6025	73	4dr Sedan	5.0L-E V8	7650
17528	6375			5.8L-2HO	8000
LTD CROWN VICTORIA WAGON (NON WOOD GRAIN)					
16716	5625	76	Wgn. (NWG)	5.0L-E V8	7250
16860	5825			5.8L-2HO	7600
18664	6475	77	Wg.LX(NWG)	5.0L-E V8	8100
18808	6675			5.8L-2HO	8300
LTD CROWN VICTORIA LX					
18971	6475	71	2dr 'LX'	5.0L-E V8	8100
19115	6675			5.8L-2HO	8300
19024	6625	74	4dr Sed. 'LX'	5.0L-E V8	8250
19168	6825			5.8L-2HO	8450
LTD COUNTRY SQUIRE WAGON					
17230	6750	78	2St. Cty Sq.	5.0L-E V8	8375
17374	6950			5.8L-2HO	8575
19134	6800	79	Cty Sq. 'LX'	5.0L-E V8	8425
19278	7000			5.8L-2HO	8625
OPTIONAL EQUIPMENT:					
1350	200		Brougham Vinyl RF. (Crn. Vic.)		

FORD — 1986

NOTE: *Model Numbers shown are the 6th & 7th Digits of the VIN No.*
NOTE: *HO in engine column indicates high output engine.*

Fact S.R.P.	Avg. Whsl	Mod. No.	Body Type	Engine	Avg. Retail
ESCORT PONY					
*7362	1250	31	2dr H/B PNY	1.9L-2 4	2175
*8955	850			2.0L-D 4	1775
ESCORT L					
*8034	1500	31	2dr H/B 'L'	1.9L-2 4	2425
*9637	1100			2.0L-D 4	2025

For Provincial Valuations - See Inside Back Cover
* Valuation does not include air conditioning
26

The *Canadian Red Book* is a monthly guide used by most dealers. Most libraries, banks, credit unions and leasing agencies will let you peruse their copy.

2. Don't sell to friends or family. Anything short of perfection, and you spend Saturday nights and Christmas alone.
3. Don't touch the odometer. You may get a few hundred dollars more—and a criminal record.
4. Paint the vehicle. Some specialty shops charge only $300 and give a guarantee.
5. Make minor repairs. This includes a minor tune-up and patching up the exhaust.
6. Clean the vehicle. Use a reconditioning firm ($25 to $50) or spend

the weekend scrubbing the interior and exterior. First impressions are important. Clean the chrome, polish the body and peel off old bumper stickers. Remove cigarette stubs from the ashtrays and clean out the glove compartment. Make sure all personal tools and spare parts have been taken out of the trunk. Don't remove the radio or speakers. The gaping holes will make the vehicle worth much less than the components' cost. Replace missing or broken dash knobs and window cranks.

7. Buy used or recap tires. They're cheap and safe, and some come with a warranty that can be transferred.
8. Let the buyer examine the vehicle. Insist the vehicle be inspected by an independent garage. Accompany the prospect to the garage.
9. Keep important documents handy. Show prospective buyers the sales contract, repair orders, owner's manual and all other documents that indicate how the vehicle has been maintained. Show those repairs carrying a warranty that is still valid.
10. Don't mislead the buyer. If the vehicle was in an accident or some loan payments are outstanding, admit it. Any misleading statements may be used in court against you. It is also advisable to have someone witness the actual transaction (a family member is acceptable) in case a dispute arises.

Signing the contract
First, draw up a bill of sale in duplicate and date it. Identify the vehicle (including the serial number), its price, whether a warranty applies and the nature of the examination made by the buyer.

It's possible the buyer will ask you to put in a lower price than what was actually paid to reduce the retail sales tax. If you agree to this request, don't be surprised when the Minister of Revenue comes knocking. Although the purchaser is the ultimate responsible party, you are an accomplice.

Don't forget to take your licence plates off the car. They are your property and must remain with you.

Summary

In a nutshell, you can avoid high auto ownership costs if you buy— from a private seller—a three-to-five-year-old used American-made vehicle with a good crash rating and some of the original warranty left. This will shave off at least 50 percent of the original purchase price and reduce your insurance premium—with a high enough deductible— by 25 percent. Just before the warranty expires, have a mechanic you trust tell you what needs fixing under warranty and then have the dealer carry out all of the warranty work. If he refuses, sue him and the manufacturer.

Buying any used vehicle involves some risk and haggling over the price isn't that pleasant (a new car purchase isn't any easier). Nevertheless, you can cut your losses considerably if you buy a vehicle recommended in Part Three and become thoroughly familiar with your legal rights outlined in Part Two. You can also keep your risk to a minimum and save money if you follow these steps:

Saving Money and Keeping Safe

1. Keep your vehicle for at least 10 years.
2. Sell to a private party (10% premium).
3. Buy a *Lemon-Aid* recommended rear-drive (parts and service savings).
4. Inspect very carefully Japanese-built vehicles that have reached their fifth year.
5. Buy an extended warranty ($300 to $800 savings).
6. Have repairs done by independent agencies (50% savings).
7. Install used or reconditioned parts (30% to 50% savings).
8. Keep all the previous owners' repair bills to facilitate warranty claims or alert mechanics to what's already been replaced or repaired.
9. Upon delivery, adjust mirrors to eliminate blind spots and adjust head restraints to prevent your head from snapping back in event of a collision. Make sure the spare tire and tire jack haven't been removed from the trunk.
10. Make sure the dealer and automaker have your name in their computer as the new owner of record. Ask for a copy of your vehicle's history stored in the dealer computer.

1992 Ford Crown Victoria: rear-drive and reliable

Part Two

FIGHTING BACK FOR PRINCIPLE AND PROFIT

LOS ANGELES (AP)—Chrysler Corp. may be barred from doing business in California for 10 days as punishment for allegedly selling used cars without telling consumers they were lemons....The California Department of Motor Vehicles accused Chrysler of selling 118 cars without telling buyers the vehicles had been repurchased from consumers because of defects....The proposed penalty would prohibit Chrysler from shipping cars into and within the state.

The Wall Street Journal
March 13, 1995

It's hard to believe, but consumers find it easier to take a used car back to the seller than to return a new one to the dealer. If you find you have purchased a defective used car, you're likely to lose less money and have a more sympathetic court hearing than if you had bought a new

Invest in protest: This angry Honda owner picketed the Alberta Legislature and Honda refunded his money.

"lemon." As well, there is usually still a considerable amount of warranty protection from the unexpired manufacturer's warranty on a used vehicle. The only hurdle, whether you bought new or used, will be proving that the defects existed at the time of purchase and were not caused by abusive driving or inadequate maintenance.

Getting Your Money Back

Generally, a used car contract can be cancelled if the vehicle is unfit for the purpose for which it was bought, if its defects are irreparable, or if it was misrepresented (i.e., wrong model year) at the time it was sold.

In setting aside the contract, the testimony of a mechanic, teacher or some other expert is essential to prove that the defects probably existed when the car was sold and are abnormal and were not caused by poor maintenance or abusive driving. If you wish to allege misrepresentation, it is particularly important to provide evidence in writing and/or witnesses as to a seller's verbal representations (relatives are not excluded).

A lawsuit to cancel the sale must be filed without delay. This "reasonable diligence" rule requires that the buyer file suit when it becomes evident the vehicle has one or more serious defects that prevent it from being used for the purpose intended or was misrepresented by the vendor. If there have been negotiations with the seller, the diligence rule is extended until it's obvious no agreement can be reached. If the seller has been promising to correct the defects or has done some minor repairs while negotiating a final settlement, the delay for filing the lawsuit can be extended for a considerable time.

Warranties

New car warranties are now routinely transferred by automakers to subsequent owners for a small administration fee. These warranties fall into three categories: bumper-to-bumper for a period of three to five years; 10 years (1994 VW vehicles); and powertrain up to 7 years/ 115,000 km (Chrysler products).

Dealers also offer their own limited warranties that vary according to the vehicle purchased. Other important, though little-known warranty programs include "secret" warranty extensions set up by automakers, the emissions and airbag warranty (5 years/80,000 km), seatbelt warranties (5 years/lifetime) and safety recalls where the manufacturer must fix the vehicle free of charge no matter how old it is and compensate the owner for all damages.

Canadian law presumes that car dealers, unlike private sellers, are aware of the defects present in the vehicles they sell. That's why they are paid a commission. Their vehicles are expected to be reasonably durable and merchantable. What is reasonably durable depends upon the price paid, miles driven, the purchaser's driving habits and how well the vehicle was maintained by the new owner. Judges weigh carefully all of these factors in awarding compensation or cancelling a sale.

Private sellers are not expected to give a warranty and they are not

A TYPICAL WARRANTY

	36 months/	60 months/
NEW VEHICLE LIMITED WARRANTY	80,000 km	
MAJOR COMPONENT (DISTRIBUTOR WARRANTY)		100,000 km
SAFETY RESTRAINT SYSTEM		100,000 km
ANTI-PERFORATION		Unlimited kilometrage
EMISSION CONTROL SYSTEM		80,000 km

- The information above is an overview of warranty coverages but not a warranty statement. See page listed for the actual warranty statement.
- Tires are warranty under the separate warranties provided with your Mazda Vehicle.

Warranty coverage varies and is transferable to subsequent owners.

held strictly accountable when major components fail prematurely. But, they are just as responsible as dealers for any misrepresentation they make.

Emissions control warranty

An emissions warranty covers the emissions control system for up to 5 years/80,000 km (Infiniti and Lexus; 6 years/100,000 km). Automakers include it on all vehicles sold in the U.S. and Canada. Unfortunately, the owner's manual doesn't always specify which parts are covered, and dealers and automakers are reluctant to supply the details.

Canada has left the definition of what is covered to the U.S. Environmental Protection Agency (EPA), which has ruled that all major engine and fuel-system components make up the emissions system. The following table, prepared by Ford of Canada, shows which parts make up the emissions system:

EMISSIONS COVERAGE

Under the Emissions Control Systems coverage of this warranty, Ford Motor Company of Canada Limited warrants that your vehicle:

1) is designed, built, and equipped to conform, at the time it was manufactured, with the Emission Regulations under the Canada Motor Vehicle Safety Act.

and

2) is free from defects in factory-supplied materials or workmanship which would cause it to fail to conform to those regulations for a period of five years or 80,000 kilometres, whichever occurs first.

Your Ford of Canada dealer will not charge you to adjust, repair, or replace (including labour and diagnosis) an emissions-related part. If the diagnosis reveals no emissions-related defect, the Emissions Control Systems coverage of this warranty does not apply.

The following list of parts is covered under the Emissions Control Systems coverage of this warranty for 5 years/80,000 kilometres.

- Air/Fuel Feedback Control System and Sensors
- Altitude Compensation System
- Catalytic Converter
- Controls for Deceleration
- Electronic Engine Control Processor
- Electronic Engine Control Sensors and Switches
- Electronic Ignition System
- Exhaust Gas Recirculating (EGR) Valve, Spacer, Plate, and Associated Parts
- Exhaust Manifold

- Exhaust Pipe (Manifold to Catalyst)
- Fuel Filler Cap and Neck Restrictor
- Fuel Injection System
- Fuel Tank
- Fuel Vapor Storage Canister, Liquid Separator, and Associated Controls
- Ignition Coil and/or Control Module
- Intake Air Flow Meter/Temperature Sensor Assembly
- Intake Manifold
- Malfunction Indicator Light System (MIL)
- PCV System and Oil Filler Cap
- Spark Control Components
- Spark Plugs and Ignition Wires
- Throttle Air Control Bypass Valve
- Throttle Body Assembly (MFI)
- TWC Air Control Valve

The emissions-related bulbs, hoses, clamps, brackets, tubes, gaskets, seals, belts, connectors, gasoline fuel lines, and wiring harnesses that are used with the components listed above are also covered by the Emissions Control Systems coverage of this warranty.

Dealer service bulletins listed in Part Three under *Service Tips* often show parts failures that are covered under the emissions warranty. Even though a bulletin may not say so explicitly, any reference to a failure of a component listed in Ford's brochure, or in the EPA's court judgment, is eligible for coverage under the emissions warranty. This secret warranty coverage, for example, would save owners of 1992-93 Ford Tempos, Topaz, Taurus and Sables hundreds of dollars—if they knew about it and had a copy of the bulletin shown below.

Article No.
93-26-6
12/22/93

- BUCKS/JERKS DURING DECELERATION/COASTING - MAF SENSOR CONNECTOR HIGH - RESISTANCE TERMINALS - NEW KIT TO REPLACE MAF CONNECTOR
- HESITATION/STUMBLE - MAF SENSOR CONNECTOR HIGH - RESISTANCE TERMINALS - NEW KIT TO REPLACE MAF CONNECTOR
- MASS AIR FLOW SENSORS - MAF SENSOR CONNECTOR HIGH - RESISTANCE TERMINALS ALTER SIGNAL
- ROUGH IDLE - MAF SENSOR CONNECTOR HIGH - RESISTANCE TERMINALS - NEW KIT TO REPLACE MAF CONNECTOR

FORD:
1992-93 TAURUS, TEMPO
LINCOLN-MERCURY:
1992-93 SABLE, TOPAZ
ISSUE:
Vehicles may exhibit intermittent rough idle, "bucking" or "jerking" (while coasting or decelerating) and/or hesitation during vehicle operation with hot or cold engines. These symptoms may be caused by high resistance across the Mass Air Flow Sensor (MAF) connector terminal-to-terminal interface or the wire-to-terminal crimp. The resistance causes a voltage drop across the connector which alters the A/AF signal, affecting performance.

1992-93 Ford Tempo/Topaz and Taurus/Sable.

In 1989, the EPA accused Chrysler and Ford of billing customers for emissions-related repairs that should have been done for free. Chrysler was fined $660,000 for denying warranty coverage to 66 car owners for replacement of and repairs and adjustments to carburetors, fuel injectors and turbochargers. These owners paid from $22 to $645 to have their cars fixed, even though the repairs fell under warranty. Ford was fined $92,000 for charging for similar repairs. The government had proposed a $230,000 fine for denying the warranty to 23 owners but reduced the amount when Ford agreed to repay over 500 consumers.

EPA investigators had waged a longstanding battle with Ford over the company's charging its customers for repairs covered by the emissions warranty. Each time customers complained to the EPA, Ford refunded the money or agreed to repair the car—but not to change its warranty practice.

This court victory is welcome news for motorists on both sides of the border. It means automakers cannot charge for the repair, replacement or the adjustment of emissions-related parts for 5 years or 80,000 km. If you've paid for repair work that should have been covered by this warranty, contact the automaker and your dealer and ask for a refund. (Don't be shy about mentioning the EPA lawsuit.) It can be refused only if you tampered with the emissions system or if the vehicle was not properly maintained.

Extended warranties
Supplementary warranties for used vehicles are sold by manufacturers and private companies to cover defects after the original warranty has expired. A study conducted by Quebec's Consumer Protection Bureau concluded supplementary warranties for both new and used vehicles are of doubtful value. The study, which polled 18,624 motorists in 1988 (5717 had purchased warranties), found that supplementary warranty holders paid on average only $24 less per year than those without one ($371 vs. $395).

It is often difficult to collect on these warranties because independent companies not tied to the carmakers frequently go out of business. Motorists who had bought these worthless warranties are out of luck unless they make a claim against their dealer and the provincial consumers affairs ministry. If the company's insurance policy won't cover your claim, take the dealer to small claims court and ask for the repair cost and the refund of the original warranty payment.

Secret warranties
Secret warranties have been around since automobiles were first mass produced. They are set up to provide free repairs to fix performance-related defects caused by substandard materials, faulty design or assembly-line errors. In 1975, *Lemon-Aid* exposed Ford's J-67 secret rust warranty that covered the company's 1970-74 models. After first denying that it had such a warranty and throwing this author out of its

annual Toronto auto show, Ford of Canada admitted that it was, indeed, in place, and negotiated a $2.8-million settlement with this author to pay back Ford owners.

Carmakers are reluctant to make these warranty programs public because they feel it would weaken confidence in their product and increase their legal liability. The closest they come to an admission is by sending a "goodwill policy," "product improvement program" or "special policy" service bulletin to dealers. All too often, only motorists who yell the loudest when faced with repairs for defective parts get compensated. Those who hesitate to complain are forced to pay. For example, GM's "Special Policy Adjustment" shown below covers the full costs of transmission repairs on 1991 pick-ups, trucks and vans for 60 months/75,000 miles, yet few owners know about this "secret warranty."

Group Ref.: Special Policy
Bulletin No.: 460601
Date: January, 1994

SPECIAL POLICY
SUBJECT:
SPECIAL POLICY ADJUSTMENT - EXTENDED TRANSMISSION WARRANTY COVERAGE
MODELS:
ALL 1991 CHEVROLET AND GMC TRUCK C/K, R/V, P TRUCKS, AND G VANS EQUIPPED WITH THE HYDRA-MATIC 4L80-E/4L80-EHD AUTOMATIC TRANSMISSION (RPO-MT1)
General Motors has determined that all 1991 Chevrolet and GMC Truck C, K, R, V, P trucks and G vans built with the Hydra-Matic 4L80-E/4L80-EHD automatic transmission may experience premature wear and/or failure requiring repair or unit replacement.
This Special Policy Bulletin has been issued to extend the warranty on all involved vehicles.

SPECIAL POLICY ADJUSTMENT
The warranty on Hydra-Matic 4L80-E/4L80-EHD transmission has been extended from 36 months or 50,000 miles, whichever comes first, to 60 months or 75,000 miles, whichever comes first. The $100 deductible associated with the 36 month/50,000 mile warranty has also been eliminated for this extended warranty period.
Additionally, a customer reimbursement policy has been established. This policy will provide reimbursement for any customer paid 4L80-E/4L80-EHD transmission repair from the date of delivery until 60 months or 75,000 miles, whichever occurs first. The $100 deductible is included in the reimbursement policy.
This "Special Policy Adjustment Bulletin" should be filed in your "Special Policy Adjustment Bulletins" binder furnished to dealers by General Motors.

Paint defects: Free repairs or your money back back—depending on who and what you know.

General Motors, Ford, and Chrysler continue to be plagued by serious paint deficiencies that so far have not been a problem with Japanese and European automakers—the paint whitens and takes on a chalky color, or it peels away prematurely during the first five years of ownership.

Paint flaking, or delamination as it's called in the industry, occurs when the top coat of paint separates from the primer coat, mostly along horizontal surfaces, often as a result of exposure to intense sunlight. When the paint peels, the entire vehicle must be repainted after a new primer resurfacer has been added. For some vehicles, the labor alone can run about 20 hours at a cost of $50 to $75 an hour.

Confidential U.S. dealer service bulletins show us one important benchmark the auto industry uses to accept or reject secret warranty paint claims. They show that, with Corsica and Beretta paint defects, for example, GM lets dealers repaint the entire car at no charge to the owner (up to $650), regardless if it was bought new or used. Interestingly, vehicles as old as six years are still eligible and head office permission isn't required before the work is done.

Ford is more generous than GM (at least in theory), although its dealers first need Oakville's authorization. Ford has been repainting 1983-93 cars, minivans, vans, F-series trucks, Explorers, Rangers and Broncos free of charge for the past five years under a little-known "Owner Dialogue" program. Ford says it discontinued the program in January, but owners who cry foul and threaten small claims action are still getting compensation.

Brandishing some of the same internal dealer bulletins found on the following pages, Ford owners argue convincingly that secret warranty programs are unfair because not everyone has an equal chance of being told they exist. They insist these programs should be used as compensation to owners for the company's factory negligence—not as so-called "goodwill" marketing tools that can be arbitrarily cut off.

Chrysler's paint problems are more recent and more severe. The company's latest paint glitch called "shadowing" produces a blotchy shadow or spotting all over the vehicle. All of Chrysler's 1995 lineup of dark-colored models—except for Jeeps, minivans, and Canadian-made vehicles—are affected. Cars that are kept in a heated garage and then driven in sub-zero temperatures are especially vulnerable.

Chrysler won't be repainting its vehicles with the "shadowing" problem. Instead, the automaker says it will buy back all affected vehicles and sell them at auction as used vehicles—with the paint defect disclosed. Chrysler's other paint deficiencies, affecting older vehicles, include paint cracking and fading between the third and fifth year. The parameters of Chrysler's buyback program or free paint jobs have been reported in automotive trade journals and by owners involved in out-of-court settlements with the company.

The following table based on service bulletins and owner feedback will give you an easier understanding of which vehicles have paint defects, the nature of the defect, and what euphemism is used by the manufacturer to describe the secret warranty program that applies.

TABLE 4

Company	Problem	Solution	Limitations	Euphemism
General Motors All vehicles up to 1994 models (black, blue, red)	"Chalking," whitening	Partial repainting	100% up to 5 years	Special Policy Clearcoat degradation. Bulletin #331708-Nov. 1993
1988-92 trucks vans, 4X4s (blue, grey, silver, black metallic)	Peeling	Full repaint	100% up to 5 years	"Delamin- ation." Bulletin #231054R- Oct. 1992
Corsica/ Beretta	Fading, peeling	Partial repaint- ing	100% up to 3rd year and	Policy Adjustment $650 (U.S.) "Delamin- ation" Bulletin #90334110/ Sept. 1990
Ford 1983-93 trucks, 4X4s, mini- vans, vans, all cars	"Microcheck- ing," hazing, peeling	Full repaint	100% up to 6 years. Program discontinued Jan. 1995.	"Owner Dialogue" Bulletin #93-8-4/ Apr. 1993
Chrysler 1995 vehicles	"Shadowing,"	Buy-back	None	None
1990-94 vehicles (no excep- tions)	"Chalking"	Partial repaint- ing	50/50 after 3rd year; varies	Product "improve- ment"

Getting a refund
If you are refused compensation, keep in mind that secret warranty
extensions are an admission of manufacturing negligence. Try to
compromise with a pro-rata adjustment from the manufacturer. If
polite negotiations fail, challenge the refusal in court on the grounds
that you should not be penalized for failing to make a claim in time
under a secret warranty you never knew existed!

An up-to-date listing of secret warranties and service programs that
offer free repairs for factory defects can be found in Part Three under
the heading *Secret Warranties/Service Tips/Recalls* for specific models.

GM defends policy on peeling paint repairs

DALE JEWETT
Service Editor

National publicity about a problem with
paint peeling off some General Motors cars
is making more work for service departments
at many GM dealerships.

"We hadn't gotten a lot of them before, only
four or five cars a month that needed to be repainted," said Bob Costa, body shop manager
at Biddulph Oldsmobile in Glendale, Ariz. "But
since one of the local TV stations did a story,
we've been taking in three a week, which is the
most we can handle.

"We've got a one-week backlog, but that's
better than some of the local Chevy dealers,
who are making appointments for April," Costa
said.

The Center for Auto Safety touched off the
firestorm of publicity last week when it called
for GM to publicly promise to repaint cars
with factory paint finishes that peel. Several
GM car and truck lines going back to the 1988
model year are affected.

The problem, known as delamination, is not
new. Chevrolet, Pontiac, Oldsmobile, Buick and
GMC Truck dealers were sent service bulletins
in October 1992 that described how to test for
the problem and set warranty labor times for
the repair.

The delamination occurs primarily on hori-
zontal surfaces — hoods, roofs and trunks, said
Chris Race, body shop manager at Good Motor
Co. (Oldsmobile-Cadillac) in Rock Hill, S.C.

He noted that the repair procedures call for
repainting the car from the side moldings up,
about the top two-thirds of the vehicle.

"GM doesn't say anything about painting the
whole car," Race said. "If 75 percent of the
car is peeling, GM is responsible for that. But
if the customer wants the whole car painted,
they should pay for their part."

GM originally acknowledged the problem in
certain Chevrolet and GMC vehicles in September 1990 and said it would cover repairs

for three years. It has since extended coverage
to six years.

But center Director Clarence Ditlow objects
that GM dealers are negotiating repair costs
with customers on a case-by-case basis and
wants GM to notify all owners of the problem.
GM has sold about 30 million cars and trucks
since 1986.

GM spokesman Jack Dinan said the automaker is satisfied with its paint repair policy.
But a recall is not planned.

"You can't put out a blanket notice, it would
be a mess as far as logistics at the dealerships.
Plus you'll always have some people coming in
for a free lunch," Dinan said.

Dealers are empowered to repair flawed paint
jobs that are caused by a factory defect, including covering the $100 deductible that is part of
GM warranties prior to the 1992 model year,
Dinan said. But stone chips and environmental
damage are not covered, he said.

Paint hit list

GM vehicles susceptible to
paint delamination woes:

■ **Buick** — 1988-91 Century; 1988-92 Skylark and
LeSabre.

■ **Chevrolet** — 1988-90 Celebrity; 1988-92 Beretta, Camaro, Corsica and light-duty
trucks and vans.

■ **GMC Truck** — 1988-92
light-duty trucks and vans.

■ **Oldsmobile** — 1988-90
Cutlass Supreme; 1988-91
Cutlass Ciera and Cutlass
Calais; 1988-92 Eighty Eight
and Bravada; 1992 Achieva.

■ **Pontiac** — 1988-91 6000;
1988-90 Grand Prix; 1988-92
Grand Am and Firebird.

*Source: **Automotive News**, January 18, 1993.*

Recall repairs
Vehicles are recalled for one of two reasons: they may be unsafe or they
may not conform to Canadian pollution control regulations. Whatever
the reason, though, recalls are a great way to get free repairs—if you
know which ones apply to you. That's why it's a smart idea to call or visit
a dealership representing the automaker that builds the vehicle

you've just bought, give them your VIN (the vehicle identification number found on the dash, just below the windshield), and have them run it through their computer system ("Function 70" for Chrysler, "CARES" for Ford or "CRIS" for GM). Importers have a similar setup.

Ask for a computer printout of the vehicle's history (have it faxed to you, if you are so equipped) and make sure you're listed in the computer as the new owner of record. If you can't find a cooperative dealer, call the automaker for the information or a reference for a more cooperative dealer in your area.

Auto safety recall campaigns force carmakers to pay the entire cost of fixing a vehicle's safety-related defect. This includes used vehicles and has no cut-off limitation. Recalls may be voluntary or ordered by the U.S. Department of Transportation. Canada has an added twist, however. Transport Canada can only order carmakers to notify owners that their vehicles may be unsafe; it can't force them to correct the problem. Fortunately, most U.S.-ordered recalls are carried out in Canada, and when Transport Canada makes a defect determination on its own, automakers generally comply with both an owner notification and a correction letter.

There have been notable exceptions. In the late 1970s, for example, following this author's Rusty Ford Owners' Association campaign for rust repair compensation, a Transport Canada team of zealous and tough-mided safety investigators sided with the Association and told Ford to notify owners that key suspension components could corrode and lead to steering loss. Ford refused and fought Transport officials many years in court until the Supreme Court ruled that Transport Canada had the authority to force owner notification. By that time, most of the affected cars had been taken off the road; Ford laughed going from the courthouse to the bank, and Transport Canada safety investigators became permanently cynical and demoralized over their lack of clout. Since then, Transport safety defect investigators have nurtured a "nut behind the wheel" mindset that treats public complaints with fear and loathing—leaving much of the investigative legwork to the better staffed and more powerful U.S. National Highway Traffic and Safety Administration. In fact, the recent U.S. recall of nine million cars equipped with defective Takata seatbelt buckles was prompted by Transport Canada alerting the NHTSA in Washington.

Transport Canada's Road and Motor Vehicle Safety Branch does do some things right—or half-right, if you consider its public access telephone service. Two years ago, it set up a toll-free bilingual hotline (1-800-333-0510) to take reports of safety defects and give out recall information. Its small staff was immediately swamped by callers. Now, Paul Marriner, the group's director, says recall information will be refused if the dealer or automaker hasn't been called first. This isn't as radical as it seems, since only the dealer can tell from the vehicle's history if the recall correction was actually done.

Still, Transport Canada has to make just as many call-backs telling people to call their dealer as it would to give them the information in the first place. This wouldn't be necessary if the safety branch would jettison its archaic, inefficient and costly 800 system and put in place an automatic responder that asks callers to speak with their dealers first.

The NHTSA has learned by Transport Canada's errors. It operates a toll-free hot-line that's 100 percent automatic (1-800-424-939 if called within the United States). It will immediately send you a fax with information on recalls applicable to your vehicle, crash ratings for the past decade, and child safety seat regulations. A letter response is sent within three working days. I'm told this setup has cut staff and increased efficiency in Washington. The question is, when will Transport Canada stop blaming the public and emulate the NHTSA by using not cutting-edge, but five-year-old technology that does more for less?

Voluntary recall campaigns are a real problem. They aren't as rigorously monitored as government-ordered recalls, dealers and automakers routinely deny there's a recall (Honda's rusty gas tanks come to mind), and many times the company's so-called "fix" may not correct the hazard.

Take, as an example, Chrysler's recent voluntary recall to strengthen the rear latches on as many as 4.5 million 1984-94 minivans. Independent engineers claim that collisions involving the vehicle's right side could cause the rear door to open, even with the reinforced latch. The culprit is the rear door's remote control solenoid arm that's held in place with a too-weak spring. Striking the latch-mechanism with the palm of one's hand is sufficient force to release the latch.

Ralph Nader's Washington-based Center for Auto Safety reports that Chrysler's 1995 models have the same defect and has called for a government-ordered recall of both the latch and solenoid spring.

Dealer service bulletins

Technical service bulletins are sent to dealers by carmakers to advise them of the latest secret warranties and to help them quickly diagnose and correct factory defects. These bulletins also disclose how much of the repair the dealer can charge back to the manufacturer and which parts are available free of charge. Armed with these bulletins, motorists can use less expensive independent garages to diagnose and repair their vehicles, or to negotiate compensation for defects that the bulletins point out are the manufacturer's fault.

The major problem with these bulletins is that they are difficult to get. Dealers and automakers are reluctant to provide this kind of detailed technical information because it allows customers to second-guess a mechanic's work or to buttress their demands for compensation.

As mentioned before under free emission component repairs, confidential dealer service bulletins pave the road to free repairs because they prove that a part failure is factory related and therefore the repair cost should be paid by the dealer and manufacturer, even if the normal warranty has expired.

These bulletins are also great guides for warranty inspections (especially the final one). They are written by automakers in "mechanic-speak" and remain unedited because service managers relate better to them that way and manufacturers can't weasel out of their obligations by claiming they never wrote such a bulletin.

If your vehicle's warranty has expired, show these bulletins to less expensive independent garages to quickly find the trouble your car is having and order the most recent, upgraded part. Why replace one defective part with another?

Because these bulletins are acquired from U.S. sources, Canadian service managers will sometimes deny, at first, that a bulletin exists when you phone them; however, when shown a copy, they usually find the appropriate Canadian part number or DSB in their files.

The problem and its solution don't change from one side of the border to another. Imagine American and Canadian tourists being towed across the border because each country's technical bulletins differed substantially. Mechanical corrrections would differ in cases where a bulletin were specific for, example, California, or related to a safety or emissions component only used in the U.S. But these cases are rare, indeed.

The best way to get DSB-related repairs carried out is by visiting the dealer and showing him the DSB. Direct his attention to all the tech-speak and codes and ask for the Canadian equivalent. If you're refused help:

- Fax the automaker in Canada a copy of the DSB and ask for the appropriate kit or upgraded part number for Canadians.
- If the dealer and automaker say that Canadians are excluded, ask why Canadians don't have the same rights as Americans.
- Complain to Transport Canada and provincial consumer affairs (see page 59) about being treated as a second-class customer.
- Finally, you could visit an American dealer to have the correction carried out during a vacation trip. Once back in Canada, you can go to small claims court to sue the Canadian automaker and its dealer for your costs (including DSB and fax costs), because they gave you the runaround in the first place.

If you would like to be sent a dealer service bulletin summary for your 1980-95 car, truck, minivan or van, send $10 along with the order form (a photocopy will do) found at the back of this *Guide*.

A computer search will be done and a bulletin summary compiled for your vehicle. After reviewing the summary, you can then order specific bulletins by mail or fax. Each bulletin costs five dollars. Add thrcc dollars for a fax reply. Mail replies take about three weeks; faxes take a few days. I review most bulletins you order, so you don't waste money on duplicates.

What's reasonable durability?
What happens if a part lasts just a little longer than its guarantee? Can you get a refund if the same problem reappears shortly after it has

been repaired? The answer is "yes" to both questions.

Automakers, mechanics and the courts have their own benchmarks as to what's a reasonable period of time or amount of mileage one should expect a part or adjustment to last. The table on page 54 shows what most carmakers consider is reasonable durability as expressed by their original warranties and secret warranties that are often called, "goodwill" or "Special Policy" programs.

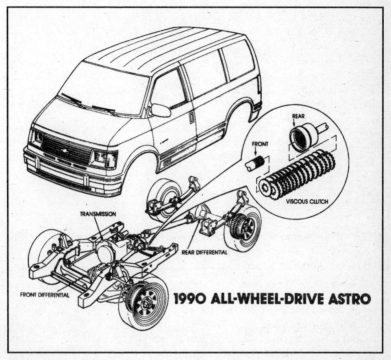

REAR

FRONT

VISCOUS CLUTCH

TRANSMISSION

REAR DIFFERENTIAL

FRONT DIFFERENTIAL

1990 ALL-WHEEL-DRIVE ASTRO

GM's AWD drivetrain isn't very durable and is costly to repair.

TABLE 5

HOW LONG SHOULD PARTS AND SERVICING LAST?

ACCESSORIES
Air conditioner .... 5 years
Cellular phone .... 5 years
Cruise control .... 100,000 km
Power antenna .... 5 years
Power doors, windows .... 5 years
Radio .... 5 years

BODY
Paint peeling .... 5 years
Rust (perforations) .... 7 years
Rust (surface) .... 5 years
Water/wind/air leaks .... 5 years
Vinyl roof .... 5 years

BRAKE SYSTEM
Brake drum .... 120,000 km
Brake drum, turn .... 40,000 km
Brake drum linings .... 35,000 km
Disc brake pads .... 30,000 km
Wheel cylinder,
rebuild .... 80,000 km
Master cylinder,
rebuild .... 100,000 km

ENGINE AND DRIVETRAIN
Constant velocity
joint .... 120,000 km
Differential .... 200,000 km
Engine .... 160,000 km
Radiator .... 5 years/100,000 km
Transfer case .... 150,000 km
Transmission (auto.) .... 120,000 km
Transmission (man.) .... 160,000 km
Transmission
oil cooler .... 120,000 km
Universal joint .... 80,000 km

EXHAUST SYSTEM
Catalytic
converter .... 5 years/80,000 km
Muffler .... 2 years/40,000 km
Tailpipe .... 3 years/60,000 km

FUEL SYSTEM
Carburetor ...... 5 years/120,000 km
Fuel filter .... 2 years/40,000 km
Fuel pump .... 5 years/80,000 km
Injectors .... 5 years/80,000 km

IGNITION SYSTEM
Cable set .... 60,000 km
Electronic
module .... 5 years/80,000 km
Points and condenser ..... 40,000 km
Retiming .... 60,000 km
Spark plugs .... 20,000 km
Tune-up .... 25,000 km

SAFETY COMPONENTS
Airbags......................... life of vehicle
Anti-lock brakes .... 150,000 km
Seatbelts .... life of vehicle

STEERING AND SUSPENSION
Alignment .... 1 year/20,000 km
Ball joints......................... 80,000 km
Power steering... 5 years/80,000 km
Shock absorber . 2 years/40,000 km
Struts.................. 5 years/80,000 km
Tires (radial) ..... 5 years/80,000 km
Wheel bearing ... 3 years/60,000 km

VISIBILITY
Aim headlights .... 20,000 km
Halogen/fog
lights .... 3 years/60,000 km
Sealed beam .... 40,000 km
Windshield
wiper motor .... 80,000 km

Three Steps to a Settlement

Step 1: Informal Negotiations

If your vehicle wasn't properly repaired under warranty, the first thing you should do is give the service manager a written summary of the outstanding problems and stipulate a time period in which they are to be corrected. Send the dealership a copy of your summary and keep a copy along with all your repair records. At the beginning, try to work things out informally.

When negotiating with a dealer personally, speak in a calm, polite manner and try to avoid polarizing the issue. Speak about how "we can work together" on the problem. Support your position with independent garage reports, service bulletins and maintenance records. Let a compromise slowly emerge—don't come in with a hardline set of demands. Don't demand the settlement offer in writing, but make sure you are accompanied by a relative or friend who can confirm the offer in court if it is not honored. Be prepared to act upon the dealer's offer without delay, so that you won't be blamed for it being withdrawn.

Step 2: A Registered Letter or Fax

When polite, informal negotiations fail, send the dealer and automaker a registered letter or fax that asks for compensation for repairs that have been done or need to be done, insurance costs while the vehicle was being repaired, towing charges, supplementary transportation costs like taxis and rented cars, and damages for inconvenience. Make it clear that your next action will be to launch a lawsuit if the problems aren't fixed.

The following sample claim letters or faxes can be helpful in getting compensation for a defective used vehicle and for unsatisfactory repairs. Include a reference in your letter of any court decisions you find in this section that support your claim.

Be well prepared

Used Car Complaint Letter

Without Prejudice:
Date:_____

Name :

Gentlemen,

Please be advised that I am dissatisfied with the following used vehicle, a (state model), for the following reasons:

1. _____
2. _____
3. _____
4. _____
5. _____

In compliance with the provincial consumer protection laws and the "implied warranty" set down by the Supreme Court of Canada in *Donoghue v. Stevenson* and *Longpré v. St-Jacques Automobile*, I hereby request that these defects be repaired, without charge.

This vehicle has not been reasonably durable, and is, therefore, not as represented to me.

Should you fail to repair these defects in a satisfactory manner and within a reasonable period of time, I shall get an estimate of the repairs from an independent source and claim them in court without further delay.

I have dealt with your company because of its honesty, competence and sincere regard for its clients. I'm sure that my case is the exception and not the rule.

A response within the next five (5) days would be appreciated.

Sincerely,

_____
(signed with telephone or fax number)

Repair Complaint Letter

Without Prejudice
Date: _____

Name and address of garage:
Name and address of manufacturer:

Gentlemen,

Please be advised that I am dissatisfied with the repairs to my vehicle (state model and date work done), for the following reasons:

1._____
2._____
3._____
4._____
5._____

I hereby put you formally on notice that I wish either my money refunded or the free correction of these repair deficiencies in compliance with the provincial *Consumer Protection Act* and the implied warranty of your contract.

If you cannot repair my car correctly, I shall get an estimate of the repairs to be made from an independent source and claim that amount in court without further delay.

Should you prefer to refund my money, I feel that the amount of $_____ would be fair.

I have dealt with your company because of its honesty, competence and sincere regard for its clients. I'm sure that my case is the exception and not the rule.

A response within the next five (5) days would be appreciated.

Sincerely,

_____

(signed with telephone or fax number)

Step 3: Launch a Lawsuit

If the dealer agrees to make things right, give him a deadline and then have an independant garage check the repairs. If no offer is made within 10 working days, file suit in small claims court. Make the manufacturer a party to the lawsuit only if a) the original, unexpired warranty was transferred to you; b) your claim falls under the emissions warranty; c) a secret warranty extension, a safety recall campaign or extensive chassis rusting is involved.

There are small claims courts in most counties of each province, and you can make a claim in the county where the problem occurred or where the defendant lives and carries on business. The first step is to make sure your claim doesn't exceed the $3000 to $5000 allowable claim limit. Then you should go to the small claims court office and ask for a claim form. Instructions accompany the form as to how to fill it out properly. Remember, you must identify the defendant correctly. It is a practice of some dishonest firms to change a company's name to escape liability; for example, it would be impossible to sue Joe's Garage (1991) if your contract is with Joe's Garage Inc. (1984).

You are entitled to bring any evidence to court that is relevant to the case, including a written document like a bill of sale or receipt, a contract or a letter. If your car has developed severe rust problems, take a photograph to court. Have the photographer sign and date the photo. You may also have witnesses testify in court (a family member may act as a witness). It is important to discuss a witness's testimony prior to the court date. If a witness cannot attend the court date, he or she can write a report and sign it for representation in court. This situation usually applies to an expert witness, such as an independent mechanic who has evaluated your car's problems.

Be sure to organize your evidence, prepare questions for the witnesses and write down what you want to tell the court.

Involving Other Agencies

Automobile Protection Association

A good place to find an experienced lawyer or expert witness, the APA is a non-profit Canadian motorist protection organization that mediates thousands of complaints annually, mostly for its own members. The group does negotiate class settlements on behalf of motorists across Canada after being alerted to common problems due to the complaints it receives from members and non-members alike. Write to the APA at 292 St-Joseph Blvd. West, Montreal, Quebec H2V 2N7 (tel: 514-273-1733), or at 160 Pears Road, Toronto, Ontario (tel: 416-964-6774).

Center for Auto Safety

Specializing in U.S. auto safety litigation, this Ralph Nader- founded group probes auto safety and consumer protection issues relating to the auto industry. It supplies references of lawyers and experts who have been involved in litigation against automobile manufacturers.

Contact the CFAS at 2001 S. St., N.W., Washington, D.C. (202-328-7700) if you need information additional to that you received from the APA. The Center can give you comprehensive, independent reports on common vehicle defects reported by dissatisfied American car owners and put you in contact with lawyers in your area who have handled cases similar to yours.

Provincial consumer affairs

The wind left the sails of the consumer movement a decade ago, leaving provincial consumer affairs offices understaffed and unsupported by the government. This has created a passive mindset among many staffers who are tired of getting their heads kicked in by business and budget-cutters.

Investigation, mediation and some litigation are the primary areas where consumer affairs offices can be helpful. Strong and effective consumer protection legislation has been left standing in most of the provinces, and resourceful consumers can use these laws and media coverage to prod provincial consumer affairs officials into action. Furthermore, provincial bureaucrats aren't as well shielded from criticism as are their federal counterparts. A call to the local MLA or minister's executive assistant can often get things rolling.

Federal consumer protection is a crock. Although the revised Competition Act has some bite over misleading advertising and a number of other nefarious business practices, reorganized Consumer and Corporate Affairs staffers have been de-fanged and de-gummed.

Choosing the Right Court

You must decide upon the remedy to pursue; that is, whether you want a partial refund or to have the sale cancelled. The amount of the refund is determined by estimating the cost to repair existing problems and adding that to the amount already spent repairing other defects. Don't exaggerate your losses or claim for repairs that are considered routine maintenance.

Generally, if the cost of repairs or the sales contract fall within the small claims court limit, the case should be filed there to keep costs to a minimum and to obtain a speedy hearing. Small claims judgments are not easily appealed. Lawyers are not necessary and in some jurisdictions (Quebec, for example) they are formally excluded. Trials are heard usually within a few months and filing fees are minimal ($25).

If the damages exceed the small claims court limit and there is no way to reduce them, you will have to go to a higher court which will prove costly. Before rushing off to file a lawsuit before a higher court, consider the following ways you can win your case in a higher court and still wind up losing your shirt.

Lawyers' fees can vary between $1000 and $5000 for a simple case that comes to a short trial. These fees must be paid whether the case is won or lost. If you lose, you may have to pay court costs as well.

The first trial will likely not take place for two or three years. Then, even if you win, the judgment is likely to be appealed, thus delaying final judgment another two to four years and boosting each side's legal fees. Once appeals are exhausted and you have won, the judgment will be paid in depreciated dollars supplemented by a low interest rate, if you can collect. Car dealers can avoid judgment by disappearing or closing down and reopening under a new name. It happens quite often and the courts can do little to stop it.

There are practical problems involved in a suit for cancellation of sale. The court requires that the vehicle be "tendered" back to the seller at the time the lawsuit is filed. This means that the plaintiff is without transportation for as long as the case continues, unless the plaintiff purchases another car in the interim. If the plaintiff loses the case, he or she must take back the old car and pay storage fees. One could go from having no car to having two, one of which is a clunker.

For these reasons, try to stay out of higher courts and plead the case yourself if at all possible. In some cases, small claims courts can be used creatively to get as much compensation as would be given by a higher court. For example, the hardship of owning a $6000 lemon can be eased if the owner sues the dealer in small claims court for the maximum to cover repairs, insurance, rental cars, inconvenience, etc., which may total $3000. If the court awards this amount, the car can then be sold without the repairs done for about $3000. The customer, therefore, gets back the $6000 with few legal fees to pay after a delay of only a few months. Furthermore, the car can still be used during the lawsuit, because the plaintiff is not seeking to set the sale aside. If the small claims court rejects such a claim, the car owner has only a $25 filing fee to pay and can still sell the vehicle to reduce his loss.

Trial conduct

On the day of the trial, bring in a mechanic to confirm that defects exist and to estimate the cost to repair them. If the repairs have already been carried out, he can explain what caused the defects and justify his bill for repairing them. This should be done by presenting the defective parts, if possible. He must convince the judge that the defects were present at the time the car was sold and not caused by poor maintenance or abusive driving habits.

When the dealer gets on the stand, ask for the exclusion of all witnesses and try to ferret out the following facts:

- When and from whom was the used car last purchased?
- How much was it bought for?
- What was done to recondition the car and at what cost?
- What was the *Red Book* value of the car when first bought from the previous owner and when sold to the plaintiff?

This line of questioning should show the judge the considerable profits the dealer made by buying the car below the market value, by not spending much to recondition it and by reselling it far above the *Red Book* value.

Before the dealer leaves the stand, get him to confirm whether he or his salesman made any representations, either verbally or through a newspaper ad, extolling the vehicle's qualities. With witnesses excluded, it is quite likely the dealer's witnesses will contradict him when their turn comes to testify. Other witnesses who can help the plaintiff's case are the car's previous owner, who can testify as to its deficiencies when sold, and any co-worker or friend of the plaintiff who can testify as to the level of maintenance on the vehicle and how it was driven, as well as describe the seriousness of the deficiencies.

Do's and don'ts
- Don't sue a car dealer if he has no money, is not bonded, is bankrupt, has changed his company or is willing to negotiate a settlement.
- Don't sign a false sales tax receipt. Crooked car dealers try to get their customers to take a receipt that indicates a selling price far below the price paid.
- Don't threaten or insult the dealer. This will only gain sympathy for him and hurt your own credibility.
- Do complain to the provincial Transport and Consumer Affairs ministries about possible violations of provincial laws.
- Do bring in the RCMP if you suspect the odometer has been tampered with.
- Do contact local consumer groups and the Automobile Protection Association for used car jurisprudence and help in mediating the complaint.
- Do publicize any favorable court judgment as a warning to other dealers and as encouragement for other consumers.

In conclusion, it's obvious that buying a used car from a dealer is a risky affair but, through the skilful use of the courts, it does not have to be a money-losing experience. Remember, do not delay in filing a claim once it's obvious no settlement is forthcoming. A lawsuit should be filed no later than three months after the final registered claim letter has been sent.

Dealers in the courtroom
Lawyers often tell their dealer-clients to settle a small claims case out of court because the cost of defence would be prohibitive and bad publicity could ruin the dealer's business. Also, lawyers know that by urging their clients to settle out of court, they never lose a case.

Sometimes a dealer's lawyer will threaten to sue the plaintiff for libel or slander if the case is taken to court. This is a move to intimidate. No one can be sued for libel or slander merely for exercising his or her rights before the courts. The dealer, though, can be sued for harassment and the lawyer can be cited for unprofessional conduct if the threat is carried out.

The dealer's warranty and the provincial warranty exist independently of each other. The provincial warranty requires that the vehicle be "reasonably durable," of "merchantable quality," and "appropriate for the use intended." These principles are sufficiently broad to allow a judge considerable latitude in awarding compensation.

Collecting Your Winnings

Settlements

You may be asked to sign a document, called a release, which proves that a final settlement has been made. Generally, once you sign the release you cannot sue the other person for that particular debt or injury. If you are the debtor, it is very important that you make sure the other person signs the release when you pay him or her. If you are the creditor collecting on the debt, you must sign the release, but do not do so until you have received the money. Also, do not give up any more rights than you have to. Release the debtor from that particular debt, but do not release him or her from all future debts.

As can be seen from this example, the essential elements of the release are the names of the two people involved, the sum of money that was paid, the nature of the debt (or injury) that was paid off, and the fact that the creditor gives up any present or future rights to sue the debtor on that particular debt.

Sample Settlement Form

I, John Doe, hereby acknowledge the payment of $300 by Jane Smith to compensate me for the defects in the vehicle I bought from her on _____. In accepting this payment, I hereby drop all present and future claims against Ms. Smith arising from the purchase of this vehicle.

_____   _____
Date   **John Doe**

                         _____
                         Jane Smith

Deadbeat defendants

Once you win your case, the real work begins if you are dealing with a professional crook. You may have to garnishee (seize) part of the defendant's bank account or wages, or ask the sheriff to serve a writ of execution. This writ allows the sheriff to demand full settlement plus court costs and, failing that, to seize the defendant's goods to cover the amount of the judgment. But here's the catch. Property that is needed to earn a living (car, tools, machinery, etc.), household goods and anything encumbered by a lien are exempt from seizure.

Professional deadbeats can tell the sheriff that practically everything they own is exempt, and it will take another action before the courts, at the plaintiff's expense, to have the defendant questioned under oath. If he is found to be lying, he can then be sent to jail for perjury or contempt of court—and the small claims judgment will remain unpaid.

A number of provinces are putting winning plaintiffs on a "fast-track" enforcement schedule that takes the time and cost out of collecting judgments.

Helpful Court Decisions

Canadian courts have rendered a number of important decisions in favor of motorists seeking damages from automakers, car dealers, insurance companies and rustproofing firms. By citing relevant cases in your initial claim letter, you may avoid going to court because no dealer or automaker wants to waste time and money defending a position that has been rejected in previous cases. If court can't be avoided, use the following judgments to find out the legal points you should raise, the arguments that will probably be used against you, how much compensation is fair, and how judges in your area have ruled in similar cases.

Court judgments cover typical problems that are likely to arise and have been grouped regionally to reflect the legal peculiarities of each province. Legal principles applying to Canadian and American law are similar; however, Quebec court decisions may be based on legal principles that do not apply outside that province. Therefore, do what most lawyers do: present all the court judgments that may be helpful and let the presiding judge or the defendant's lawyer sort out those that apply.

Additional court judgments can be found in the legal reference section of your city's main public library or at a nearby university law library. Use the following flow chart to look up specific relevant cases. Ask the librarian for help in choosing the legal phrases that best describe your claim.

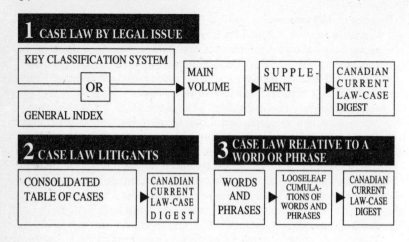

Finding Your Own Jurisprudence

"As Is" clauses

Since 1907, Canadian courts have ruled that a seller can't exclude the implied warranty as to fitness by including such phrases as, "there are no other warranties or guarantees, promises or agreements, than those contained herein." *Sawyer-Massey Co. v. Thibault* (1907), 5 W.L.R. 241.

Tricco v. Haynes (1971), 2 Nfld. and P.E.I.R. 53. A used car sold "as is" and inspected before its purchase later turned out to be a lemon. The court ruled that the selling party would have to take the vehicle back because there was a fundamental breach of warranty by the seller, a private individual.

Thériault v. Roy (1990), 109 N.B.R. (2d) 75. Dealer assured purchaser that used vehicle sold "as is" was in good condition. Three weeks later, the motor failed. Inasmuch as the buyer had complained about excessive oil consumption one day after purchase, the court ruled the seller breached New Brunswick's Consumer Product Warranty and Liability Act. The Act protects buyers with an implied warranty as to durability for a reasonable period of time.

Gillespie v. MacDonald Pontiac Buick GMC Ltd. (1986), 71 N.B.R. (2d) 1. Prior to purchasing a used car, buyer noticed the engine was leaking oil. Seller promised to fix the leak after the vehicle was sold. When customer brought it back, the seller refused to fix the car, claiming it had been sold "as is." The court ruled the seller's promise to repair overruled the "as is" limitation and ordered a refund of the purchase price.

Bedard v. Zelnick Associates Inc., April 15, 1977, Quebec Provincial Court, No. 500-02-026998-760, Judge Decary. This dealer was aware of serious motor and chassis rusting problems with the vehicle when it was sold to the plaintiff. Judgment was in favor of the plaintiff for $2300, including towing costs and repairs, despite the fact that the dealer sold the vehicle "as is—no warranty."

Lauriault v. Guilbeault, May 21, 1981. Quebec Provincial Court (Hull), No. 550-32-142-817. Guilbeault operated a used car lot that sold a used Ford truck as is for $4740. The truck's brakes were defective and, under Quebec's Consumer Protection Act, Article 159, the dealer did not provide "reasonable" service to the plaintiff. The cost of brake repairs—$497.61—was awarded to the plaintiff.

McCann v. B.J.'s Auto Sales, Ontario Provincial Court (Guelph), 1987. Plaintiff McCann bought a used 1977 Thunderbird "as is," without a warranty and without a roadworthiness certificate. A Ford dealer told McCann it would cost her $2200 to put the vehicle in shape to drive. The court found the car was in "deplorable condition," and she was awarded $1000 plus $125 in legal fees.

Adams v. J & D's Used Cars Ltd. (1983), 26 Sask. R. 40 (Q.B.). Shortly after purchase, the engine and transmission failed. The court ruled the inclusion of "as is" in the sales contract had no legal effect. The implied warranty set out in Saskatchewan's Consumer Products Warranties Act was breached by the dealer. The sale was cancelled and all monies refunded.

Damages (punitive)

Bolduc v. Racicot, April 2, 1982, Quebec Provincial Court (Hauterive), No. 655-02-000364-817, Judge Cloutier. Plaintiff was given a verbal estimate of $500 for repairs, but the garage presented a bill for $1255. The court reduced the bill to $900 with the consent of the plaintiff and then awarded another $300 as punitive damages against the garage for failing to provide a written estimate, doing more work than was requested, not guaranteeing the work and not presenting a bill in conformance with the Consumer Protection Act.

Defects (Safety Related)

More than 200 million cars have been recalled since 1966 to correct safety-related defects. Usually, these cars are fixed at no charge. Some used cars, though, may have been defective and never repaired. To find out if your car has been recalled, contact the manufacturer or visit a dealer who can access the manufacturer's computerized recall file.

Under Canadian federal legislation (Canadian Motor Vehicle Safety Act, 1971), car companies do not have to recall their cars or fix them free of charge within a certain period of time. The law stipulates that companies only have to notify owners that their cars can kill them. American legislation requires notification and free correction.

The following successful Canadian lawsuits were brought against automobile manufacturers for safety-related defects.

Axle

Fuller v. Ford of Canada Ltd. (1978), 2 O.R. (2d), 764. This new 1974 Econoline truck had an axle failure that caused an accident. The court held both the manufacturer and seller responsible.

Brakes

Marton Properties v. Northbridge Chrysler Plymouth Ltd., March 2, 1979, British Columbia Supreme Court. Plaintiff's used Chrysler had serious brake defects that warranted cancellation of the sales contract. The court ordered the vehicle returned and the purchase price refunded.

Morschler v. Masser's Garage (1956), 2 D.L.R. (2d), 484. Plaintiff was awarded damages to a third party from a repairer who failed to fix a car's brakes properly.

Phillips v. Ford of Canada and Elgin Motors (1970), 2 O.R., 714. Ford was held responsible for the injuries caused by defective power brakes.

Fires

Brown v. Ford of Canada Ltd. (1979), 27 N.B.R. (2d), 550. Plaintiff's 1977 van suddenly caught fire while under warranty. The court held the manufacturer only partially negligent because the plaintiff's son, who was a mechanic, should have spotted the defect.

La Paix v. Chrysler Canada, April 5, 1982, Quebec Provincial Court, No. 500-02-040677-796, Judge Prenouveau. A new 1976 Volaré suddenly caught fire while the owner tried to start the car. It had only been in use 10 months. Chrysler Canada refused all liability, claiming the fire probably was due to poor starting technique. The court held Chrysler responsible for $4039 in damages after it was proven that the fire was caused by unburned gasoline catching fire in the muffler.

Racine v. Durand Pontiac-Buick and General Motors, December 15, 1977, Quebec Provincial Court, No. 02-015218-774, Judge Lacoste. The plaintiff claimed $700 for a catalytic converter that exploded. General Motors and the dealer claimed the explosion was due to poor maintenance and that the 50,000 mile/5 year emissions warranty on the converter did not cover such maintenance-related defects. The judge disagreed, stating that the catalytic converter exploded due to a defective PCV valve for which General Motors and the dealer had to take responsibility. The fact that the converter could overheat and catch fire whenever the engine was badly tuned caused the judge to suggest that a warning be placed on all General Motors vehicles with the converter. Plaintiff was awarded $700.

Chabot v. Ford Motor Company of Canada Ltd. (1983), 39 O.R. (2d) 162. This case contains an excellent and exhaustive review of manufacturer's liability for vehicles manufactured with defects. It establishes liability for losses arising from a defect while the vehicle is being maintained by the dealer. Although the plaintiff could not prove that a defective part caused a fire, Judge Eberle's presumption that the 1979 F250 truck ignited from some sort of manufacturing defect inferred that the manufacturer was negligent (*re ipsa loquitor*).

The court also ruled that Ford breached a fundamental term of the sale contract by providing an unfit vehicle and also failed to meet its obligations as set by the Manitoba Sale of Goods Act (Ontario Sale of Goods Act R.S.O. 1980 c 462, 5-15).

In his decision, the judge makes a number of interesting and critical observations about the motives and strategy of a large manufacturer like Ford when preparing for a case and presenting expert evidence. In cases where companies try to avoid liability through their own limited warranties or invoke exclusions expressed in the warranty, this judgement confirms *Kravitz v. General Motors* from a common law standpoint. That case struck down these exclusions under Quebec law.

See also:
- *Parent v. Lapointe* (1952), 1 S.C.R., 381.
- *CPR v. Kerr*, 49 S.C.R., 33 at 36.
- *Rioux v. General Motors*, March 9, 1970, C.S.M. 739-005, 6.
- *Zelezen v. Model Auto Sales Ltd.*, November 26, 1971, C.S.M. 722-487, Judge Nichols.
- *Touchette v. Pizzagalli* (1938), S.C.R. 433.
- *Lazanik v. Ford*, June 15, 1965, C.S.M. 623-664, Judge Challies.
- *Gougeon v. Peugeot Canada*, July 20, 1973, Quebec Superior Court, No. 12736, Judge Kaufman.

Parking gear slippage
General Motors v. Colton, October 17, 1980, Quebec Court of Appeal, No. 500-09-000692-772. A 1970 Oldsmobile parked on the plaintiff's inclined driveway rolled back and injured the owner. Judgment was against General Motors for $29,000.

Rusting undercarriage
In *R. v. Ford Motor Company of Canada*, the federal Ministry of Transport successfully pleaded that rusting of the undercarriage of Ford's 1965-1974 mid-sized cars was a safety defect.

McGouey v. Lawson Motors Ltd. (1982), 42 N.B.R. (2d) 225. Seven weeks after buying a used Fiat, the frame collapsed from excessive corrosion. The purchaser was awarded a complete refund of the purchase price and damages.

Steering
Holley v. Ford of Canada, June 18, 1980, Nova Scotia Supreme Court, Judge Cowan. Plaintiff purchased a used 1976 Ford Custom 200 truck that was involved in an accident due to the failure of the steering assembly. The plaintiff was awarded $4100 in damages.

Transmission jumps from park to reverse
McEvoy v. Ford Motor Company et al., Supreme Court of B.C., No. 3841989, September 6, 1989, Judge Hinds.
Mr. McEvoy was killed when his new Ford pickup backed over him after the transmission jumped from Park to Reverse. He had left the engine running and was unloading cargo when the right front wheel crushed his chest. Justice Hinds found Ford 65 percent negligent for the following reasons:

- The RCMP mechanic testified that the gearshift lever could easily be mispositioned into an "unstable Park" position.
- It was determined that Ford was aware of this defect as early as 1971, according to internal company documents presented during the trial.
- Ford had a duty to warn its customers of the hazard caused by the C-6 automatic transmission; the warning in the owner's manual was deemed insufficient.
- Ford and its Canadian distributor had breached their duty to the ultimate consumer.

Wheels
Michel Beauregard v. Goyette Auto and General Motors, July 3, 1982, Quebec Provincial Court, No. 500-05-011478-763, Judge Aronovitch. A new 1975 Ventura had one wheel suddenly lock up that caused the vehicle to go out of control. The plaintiff was awarded $3500.

Defects (Performance Related)

When a used vehicle no longer falls within the limits of the warranty expressed by the manufacturer or dealer, it does not necessarily mean that the manufacturer cannot be held liable for damages caused by defective design. As mentioned before, the manufacturer is always liable for the replacement or repair of defective parts if independent testimony can show that the part was incorrectly manufactured or designed. Usually, the existence of a secret warranty extension or service bulletins will help prove the part has a high failure rate. In addition to replacing or repairing the part that failed, the automaker can also be held responsible for any consequential damages arising from the part's failure. This means loss of wages, supplementary transportation costs and damages for personal inconvenience can be awarded.

Morrison v. Hillside Motors (1973) Ltd. (1981), 35 Nfld. & P.E.I.R. 361. A used car advertised to be in A-1 condition and carrying a 50/50 warranty developed a number of problems. The court decided the purchaser should be partially compensated because of the ad's claim. In deciding how much compensation to award, the presiding judge considered the warranty's wording, the amount paid for the vehicle, the year of the vehicle, its average life, the type of defect that occurred, and how long the purchaser had use of the vehicle before its defects became evident. Although this judgment was rendered in Newfoundland, judges throughout Canada have used a similar approach for more than a decade.

Hachey v. Galbraith Equipment Company (1991), 33 M.V.R. (2d) 242. The plaintiff bought a used truck from the dealer to haul gravel. Shortly afterward the steering failed. Plaintiff's suit was successful because expert testimony showed the truck wasn't roadworthy. The dealer was found liable for damages in breach of the implied condition of fitness for the purpose the truck was purchased as set out in s. 15(a) of the New Brunswick Sale of Goods Act.

Labourdette v. Les Automobiles Racine Ltée., November 20, 1980, Quebec Small Claims Court (Jonquiere), No. 165-32-000466-801, Judge Gagnon. Plaintiff bought a 1978 used car and later found out it had defective brakes, shock absorbers and four different-sized tires made by different companies. The judge awarded the plaintiff $427 for the tires and brake repairs because the dealer exploited the buyer's inexperience, contrary to Article 8 of the Consumer Protection Act, and also failed to respect Articles 159 and 160 of the same Act.

Parent v. Le Grand Trianon and Ford Credit (1982), C.P., 194, Judge Bertrand Gagnon. Nineteen months after paying $3300 for a used 1974 LTD, the plaintiff sued this Ford dealer for his money back because the car was prematurely rusted out. The dealer replied that rust was normal, there was no warranty and the claim was too late. The court held that the garage was still responsible for the following reasons:

- When purchased, the car had been repainted by the dealer to camouflage rust and perforations.
- During the 19 months, the plaintiff and the dealer continued to explore ways the rusting could be stopped.
- It was not until just before the lawsuit that the plaintiff found how bad the rust was.
- Ford and Ford dealers admitted they knew many of their 1970 to 1974 cars had serious premature corrosion problems.

The plaintiff was awarded $1500, representing the cost of rust repairs.

Longpré v. St. Jacques Automobile (1961) C.S., 265. Any salesman is presumed to know the defects present in the merchandise he sells.

Bellerose v. Bouvier (1955), B.R., 175. In this judgment, the court recognized the right of a consumer to ask for a reduction or reimbursement of part of the purchase price if there is a fraudulent representation of part of the transaction. The plaintiff did not have to ask for the contract to be cancelled. See also *Nissan Automobile v. Pelletier* (1974) 503 (reaffirmed by the Supreme Court of Canada). See also *Berube v. Enright,* January 25, 1982, Quebec Provincial Court, No. 500-02-050980-791, Judge Filion.

Beaulieu v. Woodland Auto and Lecavalier Auto Parts, October 4, 1982, Quebec Provincial Court, No. 500-02-020456-815, Judge Filion. The client bought a used 1977 Chrysler Ramcharger. The motor broke down six weeks later. The client paid $1554.41 to repair the engine at the dealer's garage. The motor broke down again 111 days later, and the dealer refused compensation because the 90-day repair warranty was over. Judge Filion awarded $2063.85 to the plaintiff to cover the second motor repair.

Mathieu v. Autos M.L., February 15, 1982, Quebec Small Claims Court (Levis), No. 230-32-000906-817, Judge Bosse. This consumer bought a seven-year-old car with 80,000 km on it. Two months later he spent $441 on motor repairs. Judge Bosse awarded $441 to him because the vehicle "did not withstand normal usage over a reasonable period of time," as prescribed by Articles 37, 38 and 53 of Quebec's Consumer Protection Act.

Beauvais v. Banque Continentale du Canada, August 5, 1982, Quebec Provincial Court (Abitibi), No. 625-32-000172-814, Judge St-Pierre. Plaintiff recovered $500 from small claims court as compensation for a defective repossessed car sold by the bank. The purchase price was $800, but the plaintiff reduced the amount to $500 in order to meet the small claims court limit.

Neilson v. Maclin Motors, 71 D.L.R. (3d), 744. The plaintiff bought a used truck on the strength of the seller's allegations that the motor had been rebuilt and that it had 210 hp. The engine failed. The judge awarded damages and cancelled the contract because the motor had not been rebuilt, it did not have 210 hp and the transmission was defective.

Johnston v. Bodasing Corporation Ltd., Ontario County Court (Bruce), No. 15/11/83, February 23, 1983, Judge McKay. The plaintiff bought a used 1979 Buick Riviera for $8500 that was represented as being "reliable." Two weeks after purchase, the motor self-destructed. Judge McKay awarded the plaintiff $2318 as compensation to fix the Riviera's defects. One feature of this particular decision is that the trial judge found, notwithstanding the fact that the vendor used a standard contract that said there were no warranties or representations, the Sale of Goods Act applied. The judge also accepted the decision in *Kendal v. Lillico* (1969), 2 Appeal Cases, 31, which indicates that the Sale of Goods Act covers not only defects that the seller ought to have detected, but also latent defects that even his utmost skill and judgment could not have detected. This places a very heavy onus on the vendor, and it should prove useful in actions of this type in other common law provinces where laws similar to Ontario's Sale of Goods Act are in force.

Kelly v. Mack Canada, 53 D.L.R. (4th), 476. Kelly bought two trucks from Mack Sales. The first, a used White Freightliner tractor and trailer, was purchased for $29,742. It cost over $12,000 in repairs during the first five months and another $9000 was estimated for future engine repairs. Mack Sales convinced Kelly to trade in the old truck for a new Mack truck. This was done, but shortly thereafter the new truck had similar problems. Kelly sued for the return of all his money, arguing that both transactions were really one.

The Ontario Court of Appeal agreed and awarded Kelly a complete refund because "There was such a congeries of defects that there had been a breach of of the implied conditions set out in the Sale of Goods Act."

Although Mack Sales argued that the contract contained a clause excluding any implied warranties, the court determined that the breach was of such magnitude that the dealer could not rely upon it. The dealer then argued that the client used the trucks, and the depreciation of both should be taken into account in reducing the award. This was refused on the grounds that the plaintiff never had the product he bargained for and in no way did he profit from the transaction. The court also awarded Kelly compensation for loss of income while the trucks were being repaired and the interest on all of the money tied up in both transactions from the time of purchase until final judgment.

Henzel v. Brussels Motors (1973), 1 O.R., 339 (C.C.). The dealer sold this used car while brandishing a copy of the mechanical fitness certificate as proof the car was in good shape. The plaintiff was awarded his money back because the court held the certificate to be a warranty, and it was breached by the car's subsequent defects.

Green v. Holiday Motors (1975), 4 W.W.R., 445. The plaintiff was sold a used car that had been used for drag racing. The seller did not make this fact known. The motor blew up. The judge ruled that the Manitoba Consumer Protection Act allowed damages, in this case $1000.

Friskin v. Chevrolet Oldsmobile, 72 D.L.R. (3d), 289. A Manitoba used car buyer asked that his contract be cancelled because of a chronic stalling problem. The garage owner did his best to correct it. Despite the seller's good intentions, the Manitoba Consumer Protection Act allowed for cancellation.

Fissel v. Ideal Auto Sales Ltd. (1991), 91 Sask. R. 266. Shortly after the vehicle was purchased, the car's motor seized and the dealer refused to replace it although the car was returned on several occasions. The court ruled the dealer had breached the statutory warranties in s.11(4) and (7) of the Consumer Products Warranties Act. The purchasers were entitled to cancel the sale and recover the full purchase price.

Paskiman v. Meadow Ford Sales Ltd. (1983), 28 Sask. R. 241 (Q.B.). Purchaser was assured by seller that used truck's oil leak was minor. After three months of use, the engine seized. The court ruled in favor of the plaintiff because the truck wasn't fit for the purpose intended, not of acceptable quality, and not reasonably durable. Court awarded the purchase price, the cost of repairs, and interest on the bank loans used to buy the truck. On appeal, the plaintiff was held responsible for the loan interest.

Graves v. C & R Motors Ltd., April 8, 1980, British Columbia County Court, Judge Skipp. Plaintiff bought a used car on the condition that certain deficiencies be remedied. They never were, and he was promised a refund. It never arrived, and he brought suit claiming the dealer's deceptive activities violated the provincial Trade Practices Act. The court agreed, concluding that a deceptive act that occurs before, during or after the transaction can lead to the cancellation of the contract.

Defective Diagnosis

Prudent drivers depend upon garages to diagnose correctly the condition of an automobile they plan to purchase or before setting out on a long trip with their own vehicle. The following court decisions show that when this diagnosis is incorrect and leads to financial losses (damages), an automobile owners' association, the garage, or the mechanic can be held responsible for all subsequent repairs, towing fees, damages arising from a lost vacation and the refund of the diagnostic costs.

Chan v. W. Gordon Inc., October 15, 1981, Quebec Provincial Court, No. 02-000002-811, Judge Page. The plaintiff was awarded $300 to cover repairs to a 1973 Volvo that was taken to Gordon's Service Station prior to purchase. The garage mistakenly diagnosed the car as being sound and roadworthy.

McCormick v. Servacar and Esso, February 9, 1981, Quebec Small Claims Court, No. 500-32-008700-801, Judge Prevost. Before purchasing a used 1978 Ford Fairmont, the plaintiff had it checked out by an Esso Diagnostic Clinic. The clinic said the car was in good condition, except for dirty transmission fluid. Ten days after purchasing the car, the transmission was replaced. The court ordered Servacar and Esso to pay the $300 for repairs, reasoning that if it were not for the clinic's incompetence, negligence or lack of experience, the defect could have been detected earlier.

Babcock v. Servacar (1970) 1 O.R., 125. A motorist took a car he was planning to buy to an Ottawa Esso Diagnostic Clinic to determine its condition. He did the recommended repairs and then had serious problems while on vacation. The judge ruled the clinic would have to pay for the repairs and reimburse the diagnostic cost as well because its advertising claims gave rise to a contractual warranty.

Davies v. Alberta Motor Association, Alberta Provincial Court, Civil Division August 13, 1991, Judge Moore. Plaintiff had a used 1985 Nissan Pulsar NX checked out by the AMA's Vehicle Inspection Service prior to buying it. The car passed with flying colors. A month later, the clutch was replaced and numerous electrical problems ensued. At that time, another garage discovered the car had been involved in a major accident, had a bent frame, a leaking radiator and was unsafe to drive. The court awarded the plaintiff $1578.40 plus three years of interest. The judge held that the AMA set itself out as an expert and should have spotted the car's defects. The AMA's defence that it was not responsible for errors was thrown out. The court held that a disclaimer clause could not protect the Association from a fundamental breach of contract.

Delay (In Bringing Lawsuit)

Bouchard v. Vaillancourt (1961), C.S., 171. If the seller has defrauded the consumer, delays for initiating a lawsuit are longer than in cases where fraud is not involved. See also *Ginn v. Canbec Auto* (1976) C.S., 1416; *Lemire v. Pelchat* (1957), R.C.S., 823; *Ennis v. Klassen* 70 D.L.R. (4th), 325.

Estimate Not Given

St. Arnaud v. Art Auto Body, October 7, 1982, Quebec Provincial Court, No. 500-02-050519-805, Judge Prenoveau. Plaintiff asked the garage for an estimate. The vehicle was repaired without the owner's consent, and he was billed $2500. The garage kept the car and sued for its money. The judge ruled the garage illegally retained the vehicle and violated Article 168 of the Quebec Consumer Protection Act by not giving an estimate. The judge cancelled the $2500 bill and ordered the car returned. See also *Gatti v. Gareau* (1981) C.P. 400; *David v. Garage P. Breton (1981)*, C.P., 185. See also *Benoit v. Centre de Voitures Europeennes*, October 20, 1980, Quebec Small Claims Court (St-Francois) No. 450-320001081-801, Judge Roberge.

Estimate (Oral)

Ruscitto v. Automag, June 23, 1981, Quebec Provincial Court, No. 500-02-054-215-806, Judge Robitaille. The plaintiff was given a written estimate for repairs, but the garage owner persuaded him to repaint the vehicle without making another written estimate. Judge Robitaille gave the plaintiff all his money back because the garage owner did not properly note the hour, date and telephone number called to get a verbal authorization as required by Articles 172 and 272 of the Quebec Consumer Protection Act. Judgment was rendered for $579.

Flat-Rate Manuals

Excessive charges
R. v. Birchcliff Lincoln Mercury Ltd., Ontario Court of Appeal, July 7, 1987, 60 O. R. (2d) 610, 220; 220 A. C. 274. This new car dealer advertised a $38 hourly labor charge and then calculated the number of hours using a flat-rate guide that allowed more hours than those actually worked. This was held by the appeal court to be false advertising under the federal Combines Act.

Kesselman v. Chomedy Ford Sales Ltd., September 18, 1975, Quebec Provincial Court, No. 500-02-002113-756, Judge Decary. The plaintiff contested the flat-rate charges for 28.8 hours when the mechanic's clocked time was only 22.8 hours. The Ford dealership raised the defence that the mechanic was following a Ford of Canada flat-rate manual and that was a common practice. The court did not buy this argument. It held the dealer responsible for the excess charges because the customer was never told about the flat-rate method of computing repair time. See also *Quebec Consumer Protection Bureau v. Canadian Tire*.

Gas Mileage Claims

Motorists who fail to get the gas mileage advertised by the manufacturer or dealer can file a criminal complaint for false advertising and initiate a small claims court lawsuit for compensation. There are favorable judgments for each type of claim.

Marchand v. Grondin Auto and Ford Motor Company, October 10, 1975, Quebec Small Claims Court (Thetford Mines), No. 235-32-000387-75-8, Judge Bastien. The owner of a 1974 Bobcat only got 15 miles per gallon, despite Ford's advertising and the dealer's claim that the car would deliver 30. Judge Bastien awarded the plaintiff $310 as compensation for the difference between what was advertised and the car's actual gas mileage. Both Ford and its dealer were judged responsible.

Dubeau v. Ford of Canada and Ventes Mercury Marie Victorin Ltée., November 20, 1980, Quebec Small Claims Court (Longueuil), No. 505-32-001847-806, Judge Langis. In this judgment, Ford was shown to continue its reign as gas-guzzling champ. The plaintiff was promised by the dealer and Ford ads that his new car would get an average of 26 miles per gallon. In fact, it only got 17. Judge Langis forced Ford and the dealer to give the plaintiff $400 for the difference.

Misrepresentation and False Advertising

L.G. Wilson Motors v. Woods (1970), 2 N.B.R. (2d), 581 (S. C.). A safety certification carried out by a provincial inspector doesn't guarantee a used vehicle is safe or that the inspector was competent. The buyer should have made his own inspection. Plaintiff's claim was rejected.

Presley v. MacDonald (1963), 1 O.R. (2d), 619. In this case an Ontario judge ruled that under s. 49(1) of the Highway Traffic Act, the mechanical fitness certificate made the seller half liable for damages caused in a subsequent accident.

Belanger v. Fournier Chrysler Dodge Ltée. (1975), 25 N.B.R. (2d), 673. A used car sold in New Brunswick carried an inspection sticker that the body and mechanical components were in good condition. Actually, the chassis was rusted through, and the police ordered the vehicle off the road. Plaintiff was awarded the purchase price.

Ferraro v. Marsilio, May 15, 1981, Quebec Provincial Court, No. 500-02-026887-807, Judge Thinel. The plaintiff was awarded $3900, representing a refund of the purchase price of a used car that had been misrepresented as being in good condition by the salesman. Actually, the vehicle had been heavily damaged in an accident. The court held that the plaintiff's inexperience had been exploited.

Beliveau v. Duval, November 26, 1973, Quebec Provincial Court, No. 02-046408-72, Judge Casgrain. The plaintiff bought a used Jeep with a spare motor the defendant said could be used if the original engine failed. It did; however, the spare motor was the wrong size. Judgment was awarded against the defendant for misrepresenting the condition of the Jeep and giving false assurances that the spare engine was adequate. Both parties were private individuals.

Gagnon v. Leveille, May 2, 1975, Quebec Provincial Court (Quebec) No. 103-879, Judge Dussault. The plaintiff was told his old motor had been replaced with a new one. Actually, another old motor had been used. The court ordered the plaintiff to pay $1 for the old motor and the defendant to pay $850 for a new one.

Smith v. Marc Patrick Motors and the Canadian Tire Corporation, September 20, 1984, Ontario Small Claims Court (Niagara North), Judge Kingstone. The plaintiff bought a used 1978 Honda Civic that was sold as having a "new" engine. Shortly thereafter the engine failed. Canadian Tire had not put a new engine in the vehicle. Judge Kingstone ordered both defendants to split the cost of the motor repairs ($1000 plus 13 percent interest) for misrepresenting the engine.

Ennis v. Klassen, 70 D.L.R. (4th), 325. Ennis bought a used BMW that was represented as a 1980 733i for $9000. He learned two days later it was really a 1979 BMW 728—a model without fuel injection that was not allowed in Canada because of different federal safety standards. It was also impossible to find parts for this vehicle. He kept the car in his garage for two years thereafter.

Klassen, a private seller, maintained that the lawsuit was tardy, Ennis inspected the vehicle before purchase and that the whole case revolved around innocent misrepresentation.

Manitoba's Court of Appeal disagreed on the grounds that: "The misrepresentation does go to the root of the contract. The plaintiff was led to believe that he was buying a BMW model 733 at a fair retail price for a second-hand vehicle of the advertised model, type and vintage. He received nothing of the kind, and so he may rescind [cancel] the sale."

As for the action being tardy, the Appeal Court also disagreed saying, "The plaintiff no longer used the vehicle, and took immediate steps on the path to rescission." Ennis got a complete refund. See *F & B Transport Ltd. v. White Truck Sales Manitoba Ltd.* (1967), 49 D.L.R. (2d) 670; *Adams v. Canadian Co-Operative Implements Ltd.* (1980), 20 A. R. 533.

Wrong model year
Ginn v. Canbec Auto, Quebec Superior Court (Montreal), No. 500-05-014597-74-4. Relying on expert testimony provided by the APA, the court awarded $10,000 to the purchaser of a 1972 BMW that was fraudulently sold as a 1973 model. The case demonstrates beyond a doubt that car retailers are culpable for the misrepresentation of their products.

Cohen v. Wilson, January 10, 1973, Quebec Provincial Court, No. 409-793, Judge Tormey. The plaintiff was awarded $958, representing the purchase price and repair costs related to a used Land Rover. The vehicle was advertised in the local paper by its owner as being in good condition and as a 1960 model. In fact, the vehicle was in poor shape and was a 1955 model.

In Ontario, two separate, successful lawsuits claimed that Ford systematically cheated consumers by selling 1970 Cortinas as new 1971 models. Each purchaser received $400 in compensation from small claims court. In *Brosseau v. Lewis Motors*, Ottawa-Carleton, and *King v. Paddy Shanahan Ford*, Toronto, the court pointed to deceptive and misleading sales tactics used to sell the Cortinas. See also *Ennis v. Klassen* 70 D.L.R. (4th), 325.

Truck misrepresentation

MacDonald v. Equilease Co. Ltd., January 18, 1979, Ontario Supreme Court, Judge O'Driscoll. Plaintiff leased a truck that was misrepresented as having an axle stronger than it was. The court awarded the plaintiff damages for repairs and set aside the lease.

Seich v. Festival Ford Sales Ltd., (1978), 6 Alta. L.R. (2d), 262. Plaintiff bought a used truck from the defendant after being assured it had a new motor and transmission. It did not, and the court awarded the plaintiff $6400.

Miscellaneous misrepresentation

Beale v. Taylor (1967), 3 All E.R., 253 (C.A.). This time, the seller innocently misrepresented a used car as being in good condition, when it really was two cars welded together. The court ordered the sale set aside.

Bottcher v. Selig, 26 N.S.R. (2d) 347 (C.A.). A used car was represented as only needing a quart of oil every 1000 miles. Plaintiff was awarded damages for serious oil leaks. In addition to misrepresenting the condition of the vehicle, this Nova Scotia court held that the seller's promise was an implied warranty.

Henzel v. Brussels Motors Ltd. (1973), 1 O.R., 339 (C.C.). A used car sold with a mechanical fitness certificate had defective brakes. The court ordered the purchase price refunded.

Hanson and Campbell v. Cornell Chevrolet Oldsmobile Ltd. and Canadian Imperial Bank of Commerce and Weaver (1983), 4 W.W.R. 285. The purchaser of a used car in British Columbia had it seized when he moved to Alberta. He then brought suit against the B.C. dealer who sold him the vehicle, which had a valid chattel mortgage registered against it. The court held that the British Columbia Sale of Goods Act, s.16, protects consumers whether or not the goods remain in the province. The important element is that the contract was agreed to in B.C. As a result, the dealer had to compensate the client for his losses.

Sandilands v. Guelph Datsun 1980 Ltd. (1982), 35 O.R. (2d) 25. The dealer represented a used car as having "good" brakes. Four months after purchase, the vehicle was taken off the road by the Ministry of

Transportation because of defective brakes and rust perforations. The court held that the contract should be cancelled because the dealer's misrepresentation was an "unfair practice" according to Section 4(1)(a) of the Ontario Business Practices Act. It was pointed out that the dealer had given false or misleading information when:

1. He supplied a car equipped with brakes that would not stop in an emergency and without adequate mechanical inspection.
2. He supplied a car that had not had its rust defects repaired, although he had contracted to do so. The stipulation in the contract to provide a full body repair job was supplementary to the safety check.
3. He concerned himself with outfitting a car he knew was not worth making roadworthy.

The dealer was forced to take back the car and pay storage and transport costs.

False Advertising

Dealer posing as a private seller

A recent small claims judgement slammed a practice called "curbsiding" where a professional sales agent sells cars from a residence posing as a private party. Frank Longstaff, lawyer for the plaintiff, tells me a number of other New Brunswickers who fell for this scam, as in the case below, contacted his office after reading about the case in their local paper.

It was held that the defendant's practice of buying used cars wholesale from a dealer and then quickly advertising them for sale to consumers was sufficient to label him a distributor as defined in New Brunswick's Consumer Product Warranty and Liability Act. This made him subject to the act and hence he was required to stand behind any warranty he may have given the purchaser, either orally or in writing, in his advertisement. It also meant, pursuant to sections 10(1) and 12(1) of the act, that he give an implied warranty that the product is "is fit for the purpose" and will be "durable for a reasonable period of time." Previous to this decision, private sellers (curbsiders) had not been subject to the act.

Van Wart v. MacDonald and MacDonald, the Court of Queen's Bench, Trial Division, Judicial District of Saint John, New Brunswick, July 25th, 1994, Judge H. H. McLellan. This 19-year-old bought a 1987 Firefly for $2000 with her parents' assistance after responding to a newspaper advertisement. MacDonald claimed the car belonged to his wife and sold it AS IS, WHERE IS. At trial, it was learned that the vehicle had been bought by MacDonald five days earlier from Brett Chev-Olds for $1200. Brett's sales manager said MacDonald had bought eight cars from him in the past year and that the Firefly purchase was accompanied by a bill of sale stating, THIS VEHICLE IS

JUNK. THERE IS NO EXPECTATION OF DRIVING THIS VEHICLE.
Judge McLellan ordered the car taken back, the $2000 purchase price and sales tax refunded, and payment for plaintiff's lawyer.

False sales prices

R. v. Lanthier and Lalonde, Sessions Court (Montreal). A Montreal Ford dealer was fined $300 for placing ads showing tremendous reductions on new cars sold at prices below the manufacturer's suggested retail price. After criminal charges were laid, it was shown that the advertised savings were lies (judgment on file with Consumer and Corporate Affairs). Several dozen suburban Toronto Chrysler dealers were fined by the federal government for similar deceptions.

Used car sold as new (demonstrator)

Bilodeau v. Sud Auto, Quebec Court of Appeal, No. 09-000751-73, Judge Tremblay. Quebec's Court of Appeal held that a vehicle cannot be sold as new or as a demonstrator if it has ever been rented, leased, sold or titled to anyone other than the dealer. The contract was cancelled.

Leblanc v. Frenette and Chrysler Credit, May 27, 1971, Quebec Provincial Court No. 279-772, Judge Laurier. Plaintiff's new demonstrator was actually a used car that had its odometer rolled back. It had also been in an accident. The court held the dealer responsible and ordered him to refund the purchase price.

False auto auction

Lucie Nopert v. Montreal Motor Vehicle Storage and Sales Corporation and Norman Barmash, President, October 17, 1978, Quebec Small Claims Court, No. 500-32-0003824-788, Judge Durand. This plaintiff received $500 from the court as compensation for a used Triumph she had bought at a fake auto auction run by the defendant.

Taxi sold as private used car

Lessard v. Remi Lavallee Automobiles Inc., June 4, 1975, Quebec Superior Court, No. 16-757, Judge Vallee. The plaintiff was awarded $3200 and the sales contract was cancelled because the buyer had not been told that the vehicle had been used as a taxi.

Information withheld

Girard v. Rond Point Dodge, February 22, 1981, Quebec Provincial Court, No. 500-02-041309-803, Judge Mailloux. This consumer bought a used car that did not have the information ticket required by Article 156 of the Consumer Protection Act. Judge Mailloux interpreted this as a fundamental contravention of the law and, under Article 272 of the Act, cancelled the sale and refunded the plaintiff's money.

Odometer tampering

Odometer tampering is a criminal offence under the federal Weights and Measures Act. The federal government uses the RCMP to investigate all such cases. Many violators have been caught and successfully prosecuted. Nevertheless, the federal law is weak because fines are so low that they practically represent a licence to operate illegally, and an individual can escape prosecution by pleading that the odometer was broken and had to be changed.

Couturier v. Herman, Quebec Small Claims Court (Montreal North), No. 74-2216, Judge Laurier. The seller of this 1967 Oldsmobile turned back the odometer. Judge Laurier awarded $200 to the buyer as compensation for the additional mileage.

Zelezen v. Model Auto Sales, November 26, 1971, Quebec Superior Court, No. 722-487, Judge Nicols. Not only did the judge order the car returned and the purchase price refunded because of odometer tampering, he also ordered the dealer to pay compensation for the plaintiff's injuries from an accident caused by the car's defects.

Henley v. Bob Barnabe, February 15, 1971, Quebec Provincial Court, No. 384-829, Judge Gold. When selling a Datsun, the dealer turned back the odometer and sold the car for the wrong model year. The vehicle had been sold before to another customer who was involved in an accident with it. Judgment was rendered in favor of the plaintiff and the purchase price was reduced by $303.

Delmaire v. Westcoast Honda, British Columbia Small Claims Court (Victoria), August 13, 1986. The plaintiff bought a used 1979 Rabbit "as is" and found the odometer had been turned back. He argued that although he had no proof the dealer was responsible, the dealer was an expert and should have been suspect of the low mileage. The court agreed and awarded $1299 for a rebuilt engine.

Bouchard v. South Park Mercury Sales (1978), 3 W.W.R., 78. The odometer figure written on the contract was incorrect. The dealer pleaded ignorance, but the judge ruled the car's owner should receive damages to compensate for the extra mileage.

Negligence

Repairs

Most provinces have far-reaching legislation that prevents garages from overcharging, charging for shop supplies or refusing to guarantee their work. The Ontario law was enacted in 1990 and is enforced by the Ministry of Consumer and Commercial Relations. Quebec's law has been on the books since 1980, hence the large number of cases cited.

Repairs (causing damage)
Goulet v. Roberval Pontiac Buick, February 11, 1980, Quebec Small Claims Court, No. 155-32-000516-794, Judge Savard. Plaintiff's vehicle was vandalized while being repaired. The court held the garage responsible because the vehicle was under the garage's care.

Proulx v. Salois Automobile, December 6, 1974, Quebec Provincial Court, No. 02-004322-74, Judge Lacourciere. The plaintiff was awarded damages to pay for motor repairs caused by an improperly installed oil filter. The dealer's mechanic was ordered to pay $1000 in damages.

Magloire v. Chomedy Toyota, December 1, 1982, Quebec Provincial Court, No. 500-02-014582-824, Judge Hodge. This Toyota dealer installed a defective oil pump that caused $1494.28 in damages to the motor. Judge Hodge awarded the full amount to the plaintiff.

Repairs (poorly done)
Raiches Steel Works v. J. Clark & Son, 16 N.B.R. (2d), 535. Brakes failed three weeks after being repaired. The judge found the mechanic negligent and awarded damages of $6423.

See also:

- *Acme v. Coziol* (1962) B.R.
- *Gagnon v. Ford Motor Co.* (1974) C.S., 422.
- *Lazanick v. Ford Motor Co.,* June 15, 1965, Quebec Superior Court No. 623504.
- *Chomedy Ford v. Mash,* March 11, 1976, Quebec Provincial Court, No. 500-02-007671-767.

Tremblay v. Au Grand Salon, September 19, 1973, Quebec Provincial Court, No. 02-054410-73, Judge Bousquet. The plaintiff asked that his brakes be checked and paid $30 for the inspection. After the inspection, the brakes failed and an accident ensued. The court held the dealer responsible, although no repairs were done.

Canbec Auto v. de Levo, January 18, 1973, Quebec Provincial Court, No. 03-058009-72, Judge Page. The dealer sued the defendant for money owing on a bill for a general inspection and correction of defects. The car owner refused to pay the bill because the vehicle was still running poorly. Judgment was rendered in favor of the defendant. The court held the garage had an obligation of results, where the repairs would be expected to correct the problems complained of by the car owner.

Sylvain v. Carrosseries d'Automobiles Guy Inc. (1981), C.P. 333, Judge Page. The garage had an obligation of results that the paint job on the plaintiff's car would be satisfactory. It was not. The court held the garage liable for the cost of repainting the car elsewhere.

Berta v. Gold Seal Engine Rebuilders, Ontario Small Claims Court (Toronto), No. C217/83, August 22, 1985, Justice Sigurdson. The plaintiff's engine was improperly repaired. Judge Sigurdson awarded $2047.03 to the plaintiff after hearing the garage's employees testify in a "less than truthful" manner.

Sigurdson v. Hillcrest Service and Acklands (1977), 1 W.W.R., 740. An accident was caused by a defective brake hose. The garage that installed it claimed the parts distributor was responsible. The judge ruled Saskatchewan's Sale of Goods Act held both the garage and distributor responsible.

Premature rusting

Perron v. Vincent Automobile Ltée. (1979), C.P., 166. Plaintiff had the dealer rustproof her new car at a cost of $115. This dealer's warranty said any future rusting would be repaired up to a cost of $115 or the purchase price would be refunded. The dealer interpreted this to mean that $115 would be the total amount that could be claimed while the guarantee was in effect. However, the court agreed with the plaintiff that she could claim up to $115 each time a warranty claim was made.

Rolland v. Chrysler, Ontario Small Claims Court (Lanark), No. 148/79, November, 1979, Judge Thorpe. A couple bought a used 1976 Volaré from a relative. Two years later they found that the vehicle was rusting extensively. The couple sued Chrysler and brought in the first owner as an independent witness. Judge Thorpe awarded the couple $896.17 on the grounds that Chrysler was acutely aware of its body rust problem and was therefore liable, even though there was no contractual lien between the parties.

Secret Warranties

It is common practice for manufacturers to extend their warranties secretly to cover components with a high failure rate. Customers who complain vigorously will get extended warranty compensation in the form of goodwill adjustments.

Desjardins v. Canadian Honda and du Portage Mercury, February 20, 1981, Quebec Small Claims Court (Hull), No.550-32-000933-801, Judge Dagenais. The plaintiff bought a used Honda "as is" from a Ford dealership. One year later the head gasket blew and was repaired free of charge by a Honda dealer under a secret warranty extension and the emissions warranty. Ten months later the head gasket blew again and was repaired without charge. A few months later, the part failed again and was repaired at Honda's expense a third time.

The plaintiff brought suit 22 months after purchase for expenses relating to motor adjustments, rental cars and general inconvenience. Judge Dagenais ruled that Honda Canada and the Ford dealer pay

$281 in damages for having made and sold such a defect-ridden vehicle.

Marielle Signori v. Toyota Canada Ltée. and St-Laurent Toyota Inc., February 18, 1985, Quebec Small Claims Court (Montreal), No. 505-32-002421-841. Judge Gilles Bélanger. In this case, a 1981 Tercel owner forced Toyota Canada to admit that the company had a secret warranty to cover premature brake wear up to two years or 40,000 km.

Summary

Few people like to complain, but if you have no other choice, follow these steps to protect your rights and obtain satisfaction.

1. Hold the dealer and automaker responsible.
2. Compose an effective claim letter.
3. Find out if any secret warranties, emission warranties or recall campaigns cover the cost of repairs.
4. Know what is reasonable maintenance for your vehicle and what is the reasonable durability for a particular part.
5. Get your vehicle's service bulletin history.
6. Use an independent mechanic or teacher as your expert.
7. Find your own jurisprudence.
8. Use arbitration or small claims court to get your money back.

NO: 18-05-94
GROUP: Vehicle Performance
DATE: Apr. 8, 1994
SUBJECT:
Vehicle Shudder During Torque Convertor EMCC Operation
MODELS:

1993 - 1994	(AA)	Acclaim/Spirit/LeBaron Sedan
1993	(AC)	Dynasty/New Yorker/New Yorker Salon
1993	(AG)	Daytona
1993 - 1994	(AJ)	LeBaron Coupe/LeBaron Convertible
1993 - 1994	(AP)	Sundance/Shadow
1993 - 1994	(AS)	Caravan/Voyager/Town & Country
1992 - 1993	(AY)	Imperial/New Yorker Fifth Avenue (Built After MDH 02-08-92)
1993 - 1994	(LH)	Concorde/Intrepid/Vision
1994	(LH)	LHS/New Yorker

NOTE:
THIS BULLETIN APPLIES TO VEHICLES EQUIPPED WITH THE 41TE OR 42LE AUTOMATIC TRANSMISSION.

SYMPTOM/CONDITION:
Light to moderate acceleration shudder during torque converter EMCC (Electronic Modulated Converter Clutch) operation. Most noticeable on smooth roads, or on long, moderate uphill grades (depending on final drive ratio, approximately 28 to 42 MPH). This shudder condition is generally the result of leakage in the transmission front pump caused by a worn pump bushing. It is sometimes accompanied by pump whine and Diagnostic Trouble Code 38 (Torque Converter Control Out of Range).

This bulletin proves transmission shudder is a fequent problem with 1993-94 Chryslers. Dealer can't charge for its correction.

Part Three

USED VEHICLE RATINGS

The Good, the Bad and the Dangerous!

LOS ANGELES (AP) – The policy makers in Detroit are tough, pragmatic businessmen. Market share is their god, and they would spike their mothers going into third to protect market share.

Ed Mullane
President, Ford Dealers Alliance
April 10, 1995

Vehicle Ratings

Before we get into the ratings, we'll look at how vehicles are grouped together, which elements are considered important in our analysis, and how each element is defined.

Vehicles are categorized into the following seven groups based upon size and style: small, compact, mid-size, large/wagons, luxury, sports, and minivans. Trucks, vans and utility vehicles are covered thoroughly in the *Lemon-Aid 4X4, Van and Truck Guide*.

Models are rated on a scale from **Recommended** to **Not Recommended**. Vehicles rated Not Recommended are considered very poor buys (like the GM Astro/Safari), while a Recommended rating designates a car as an excellent choice in its class (the Toyota Previa is a good example). Top-rated vehicles are those that promise their owners relatively trouble-free service. Vehicles that are given an **Above Average** or **Average** rating are good second choices if a recommended vehicle is not your first choice or is too expensive. Cars rated as worse than average are best avoided no matter how low the price; they are likely to suffer from a variety of durability and performance problems that will make them expensive and frustrating to own. Keep in mind, too, that the reliability and quality averages are climbing higher, so a newer vehicle rated as Average is a far better buy than an older model that has an Average rating.

Reliability data is compiled from a number of sources: owner complaints sent to the author by readers who filled out the Readers' Survey found in previous editions of this *Guide*, and survey reports done by auto associations, consumer groups and government organizations. Not all cars sold during the last decade are profiled because of this book's space limitations and that certain models may be relatively rare. Furthermore, vehicles that were sold for a brief period only (a few years) are evaluated but do not carry a Profile table.

Price Analysis

We factor into the selling price the relative availability of a particular vehicle (which could drive up the price of rare models —the '93 Camaro, for example), those models and years that are the best buys, the estimated annual maintenance and repair cost averaged over five years, and alternative vehicles that will give you as much or more for less money. Keep in mind that the annual maintenance cost for a reliable used car hovers around $600.

Technical Data

These tables list engines, horsepower and fuel consumption for each model.

Strengths and Weaknesses

Unlike other auto guides, we try to pinpoint potential parts failures as well as why those parts fail. Complementing the *Service Tips* and *Vehicle Profile* tables, we look at a vehicle's overall road performance and reliability while providing details, for example, as to which part in the electrical or fuel system fails repeatedly, what's wrong with the fuel system, or which body parts are subject to premature rusting. This helps an independent mechanic check out the likely trouble spots before you make your purchase.

Safety Summary/Recalls

Data from independent crash tests, insurance claims statistics, ongoing safety investigations, owner safety-related complaints and safety recalls make up this section.

Vehicles are rated as to how well they performed in U.S. government 57 km/h frontal crash tests. The impact is the same as if two identical vehicles, each traveling at 57 kph, collided head-on. Each test vehicle carries two dummies of average human size and weight, one in the driver's seat and one in the right front passenger seat. Each dummy contains instruments in its head, chest and thigh to measure the forces and impacts that occur during the crash. These measurements form the basis of the "Star Rating" system used by the U.S. NHTSA for the past two years.

Information recorded during the crash tests measures the likelihood of serious injury. Vehicles are classified by the estimated chance of injury for the driver or passenger, and are given a one- to five-star rating by the NHTSA, with five stars indicating the best protection. This *Guide's* safety rating symbols, found in the *Vehicle Profile*, differ slightly. Crash results prior to the 1985 model year are included if more recent tests haven't been carried out. Cars and minivans that are identical but carry different nameplates from the same manufacturer can be expected to perform similarly in these crash tests. *Lemon-Aid* is unique in that it includes estimated head, chest *and* leg trauma as life-threatening factors to determine a model's safety rating.

After rising for four years, the number of North American safety recalls by automakers fell by 45 percent last year with 6.1 million vehicles recalled. This is due to quality improvements on the assembly line and a shaking out of poor-quality suppliers. Most dealers have a telephone hook-up with the manufacturer's computer that tells them instantly which vehicles have been recalled, which have been re-paired, and which ones are covered by secret warranties.

Consumers who wish to report a safety defect or want recall information (only after first being refused information by the dealer for their vehicle) should call Transport Canada toll-free at 1-800-333-0510. This number has not been widely publicized by Transport Canada to avoid their investigators from being swamped by calls for information about recalls that dealers should be handling first.

Both safety and emissions recalls are listed in chronological order. If your vehicle is listed and has not been fixed, the dealer and manufacturer *must* pay for the inspection and correction of the defect, regardless of the vehicle's mileage, model year or number of previous owners. It's not the law. It's general practice.

Secret Warranties/Service Tips/DSBs
It's not enough to know which parts on your vehicle are likely to fail. You should also know which repairs will be done for free by the dealer and carmaker, even though you purchased a used car.

Welcome to the hidden world of secret warranties found in confidential dealer service bulletins (DSBs) or gleaned from owner feedback (see the "all models/years" section). A summary of all the important DSBs for each model year is listed along with selected diagrams. These bulletins target safety-, emissions- and performance-related defects that service managers would have you believe don't exist or are your responsibility. They also list the upgraded parts that will best repair the vehicle you plan to buy or have just bought.

Service bulletins cover repairs that may be eligible for warranty coverage in one or more of the following five categories:

- Emissions warranty (5 years/80,000; Infiniti and Lexus: 6 years/ 100,000 km)
- Safety component warranty (this covers seatbelts and airbags and varies from three years to the lifetime of the vehicle)
- Body warranty (paint: 6 years; rust perforations: 7 years)
- Secret warranty (coverage varies)

GM to cover head gasket on Quad 4

DALE JEWETT
Service Editor

General Motors has extended the powertrain warranty and/or waived the deductible on about 500,000 of its 1987-91 cars equipped with the Quad 4 engine because of problems with a leaking cylinder head gasket.

GM boosted the powertrain warranty coverage from 3 years/50,000 miles to 6 years/60,000 miles on all 1989-91 Quad 4 cars.

In addition, GM waived the $100 deductible on 1987-91 Quad 4 vehicles for up to 6 years/60,000 miles and said it will reimburse customers who paid the deductible to have the engine repaired. Claims for reimbursement must be filed by June 30, according to a letter sent to owners.

Affected car lines are:
■ 1988-91 Buick Skylark.
■ 1990-91 Chevrolet Beretta GTZ.
■ 1987-91 Oldsmobile Cutlass Calais, 1990-91 Cutlass Supreme.
■ 1988-91 Pontiac Grand Am and 1991 Grand Prix.

Symptoms of the problem include white smoke from the exhaust and a loss of engine coolant.

GM attributed the problem to slight movement of the Quad 4's aluminum cylinder head relative to the cast-iron engine block caused by the heating and cooling of the engine. That movement, and corrosion of the head gasket's steel core, may allow coolant to leak into the cylinders.

Dealerships will install a new gasket with a stainless steel core and follow a four-step procedure to tighten the cylinder head bolts.

GM said it has not issued a recall because it doesn't believe that all Quad 4-equipped cars will experience the leaking problem. ■

- Factory defects (depends upon mileage, use and repair cost)
- Service tips (troubleshooting shortcuts and upgraded parts).

Use these bulletins to get free repairs—even if the car has changed hands several times—and to alert an independent mechanic about what defects to look for. They are also great tools for getting compensation from carmakers and dealer service managers long after the warranty has expired by proving that a failure is factory related and therefore not part of routine maintenance.

Many of the bulletins listed in this *Guide* come from American sources and can differ from Canadian bulletins in that the parts numbers may vary somewhat. Nevertheless, the problems and defects they refer to are exactly the same on both sides of the border. Some cars carry more DSBs than others, but this doesn't mean they are lemons. It may be that the bulletins relate to only a small number of vehicles or lists lots of problems that are minor in nature and easily corrected.

By presenting diagnostic shortcuts and listing upgraded parts, these bulletins are invaluable in helping mechanics and do-it-yourselfers troubleshoot problems inexpensively and replace the right part the first time. Auto owners can also use the DSBs listed here to verify if a repair was diagnosed correctly, the right upgraded replacement part was used and the labor costs were fair.

Getting your own bulletins

Dealer service bulletins are tough to get, but dealer mechanics occasionally slip copies to their customers to help them get compensation as long as their involvement is not disclosed. So try your dealer first. Unlike recall campaigns and the emissions warranty, secret warranty coverage is not automatically extended to used cars. It often takes the threat of court action to get even partial compensation. Plaintiffs can obtain copies of these bulletins by sending a subpoena to the manufacturer and dealer through the small claims court.

If you want a personalized DSB for your vehicle, fill out the Bulletin Search/Survey order form in Appendix II. For a $10 fee (this includes computer time and mailing costs), you will receive an exhaustive summary of all DSBs that concern your vehicle. For $5 for each bulletin thereafter, you can then order every DSB listed in the summary that addresses your concerns.

Vehicle Profile
This category covers the various aspects of vehicle ownership at a glance. Included for each model year are details on crashworthiness, repair histories for major mechanical and body components (specific defective parts are listed in the *Strengths and weaknesses* section for each vehicle rated), and evaluations of dealer servicing, parts availability and cost.

Price
Three prices are given for each model year: the vehicle's selling price when new as suggested by the manufacturer, its maximum price used ($\uparrow$), followed by its lowest price used ($\downarrow$). This year, prices have firmed up but are still quite reasonable because improved new car sales are freeing up more used vehicles.

Used vehicle prices are based on private sales as of September 1995. Prices are for the lowest-priced standard model in each category in good condition, with 20,000 km for each calender year, and equipped with a radio and automatic transmission. The original selling price (manufacturer's suggested retail price) is given as a helpful reference point. Sellers overprice some vehicles (mostly Japanese imports, minivans and utility vehicles) in order to get back some of the money *they* overpaid in the first place. This is also particularly true in western provinces.

Prices reflect the auto markets in Quebec and Ontario where the majority of used car transactions take place. Residents in Eastern Canada should add 5 percent, and Western Canadians need to add 10 percent or more to the listed price. Why the higher cost? Less competition and inflated new vehicle prices in these regions. Don't be too disheartened, though; some of what was overpaid will be recouped when you trade in the vehicle later on. Nevertheless, check dealer prices with local private classified ads and add the option values list below to come up with a fairly representative offer:

Model Year	1993	1992	1991	1990	1989	1988
ABS brakes	$900	$700	$500	$400	$300	$300
Air conditioning	900	600	500	400	300	300
AM-FM stereo	200	125	100	75	50	50
Cruise control	225	125	100	75	50	50
Electric 6-way seat	300	175	150	125	100	50
Full vinyl roof	250	125	100	75	50	0
Half vinyl roof	500	200	100	75	50	0
Leather upholstery	700	400	325	225	200	100
Level control (suspension)	250	150	125	100	75	50
Paint protection	50	25	25	0	0	0
Power antenna	125	75	50	50	25	0
Power door locks	300	175	150	125	100	50
Power windows	325	175	150	125	100	50
Rustproofing	50	25	25	0	0	0
T-top roof	1150	600	550	400	300	200
Tilt steering	175	100	75	75	50	50
Wire wheels/locks	275	175	150	125	100	75

It will be easier for you to match the lower used prices if you buy privately. Dealers rarely sell below the maximum prices. They inflate their prices to cover the costs of reconditioning and paying future warranty claims. If you can come within 5 percent to 10 percent of this *Guide*'s price, you will have done well.

NOTE: When reviewing the manufacturer's suggested retail price, keep in mind that the selling price for many 1991-92 new vehicles was less than the 1990 model year. The hidden federal tax on manufactured goods of 13.5 percent was dropped and replaced by the 7 percent Goods and Services Tax.

Reliability and Servicing
This part of the *Vehicle Profile* covers the various aspects of vehicle ownership. Included for each model year are details on reliability, broken down by major components, repair histories for major mechanical and body components (specific defective parts are listed in the *Strengths and weaknesses* section for each model vehicle), and evaluations of dealer servicing, parts availability and cost, crashworthiness, and the availability of important safety features.

The older a car, the greater the chance a major component like the engine or transmission will fail because of mileage and environmental wear and tear. Surprisingly, there is a host of other expensive-to-repair failures that are just as likely to occur in a new vehicle as in an older one. Air conditioners, electronic computer modules, electrical problems, and faulty brakes are the most troublesome components that manifest themselves early in a vehicle's life. Other deficiencies that will appear early due to sloppy manufacturing and a harsh environment include failure-prone body hardware (trim, finish, locks, doors and windows), water leaks, wind noise and paint peeling/discoloration.

The following legend is used in Part Three to show which vehicles are the most reliable, which mechanical and body parts are subject to premature failure, and which automaker's dealers provide the best servicing. Note that the black numbers designate a negative rating.

❶	❷	③	④	⑤
Unacceptable	Below Average	Average	Above Average	Excellent

Crash Safety

Vehicles are rated as to how well they performed in U.S. government 57 km/h frontal crash tests. The impact is the same as if two identical vehicles, each going 57 kph, collided head-on. Vehicles are classified by the estimated chance of injury for the driver or passenger, and are given a one- to five-star rating by the NHTSA, with five stars indicating the best protection. Crashworthiness is shown with the following symbols:

❶	❷	⑤	—
Multiple injuries	One injury	Excellent protection	No data

Safety Features

The availability of key safety features (airbags, anti-lock brakes, and traction control) is shown with the following letters:

O optional   **S** standard   **D** driver side   **P** passenger side
    D/P driver & passenger   — data not available

Note that some safety features that are indicated as standard items may have been dropped by the automaker in Canada in order to keep prices down in the face of a plummeting Canadian dollar.

Small Cars

Ford's 1993 Escort: reliable and inexpensive ($7000).

The proverbial "econobox," this size of car is for city dwellers who want economy at any price. Subcompacts offer excellent gas economy (9.5L/100 km to 5L/100 km—30 to 56 mpg), easy maneuverability in urban areas and a low retail price.

One of the more alarming characteristics of a subcompact's highway performance is its extreme vulnerability to strong lateral winds that may make the car difficult to keep on course. Most of these cars can carry only two passengers in comfort because rear seating is limited. Also, there is insufficient luggage capacity. Engine and road noise are also fairly excessive.

Crash safety is compromised by the small size and light weight of these vehicles. Nevertheless, careful engineering and the addition of standard and optional airbags have made many small cars safer in collisions than some larger cars.

The following used subcompacts are Recommended:

Chrysler Colt/Summit Vista (1990-94)
Ford Escort (1991 and later)
Ford Fiesta (1991-93)
GM Firefly/Sprint/Metro
Honda Civic (1989-94)/CRX
Mazda GLC/323/Protege
Mercury Tracer (1991 and later)
Nissan Altima

Nissan Micra
Nissan NX/Pulsar (1987-94)
Nissan Sentra/Classic (1988-94)
Subaru Chaser (1993-94)
Suzuki Forsa/Swift
Toyota Corolla
Toyota Paseo
Toyota Tercel
VW Golf/Jetta (1993-94)

CHRYSLER/EAGLE

024, Charger, Duster, Expo, Horizon, Omni, TC3, Turismo

Rating: Not Recommended (1983-90). All of these cars are virtually identical and have been off the market for at least five years.

Price analysis: Excellent availability. Lots were sold, but their rapid depreciation and poor reliability make these cars anything but a bargain. Consider buying an extended warranty or expect to pay approximately $600 annually for maintenance and repairs. Other cars worth considering: Chrysler Colt • Ford Escort/Tracer ('91 or later) • Geo Firefly, Sprint or Metro.

Technical Data

ENGINES	Litres/CID	HP	MPG	Model Years
OHV I-4 2 bbl.	1.6/98	64	25-31	1985-86
OHC I-4 2 bbl.	2.2/135	96	23-27	1985-87
OHC I-4 FI	2.2/135	93-96	23-27	1988-90
OHC I-4 2 bbl.	2.2/135	110	22-26	1985-86
OHC I-4T FI	2.2/135	146-148	20-26	1985-87

Strengths and weaknesses: The four-door models are relatively roomy for subcompacts, give excellent fuel economy and can be repaired almost anywhere—which is good because they tend to break down almost everywhere. Overly soft ride and imprecise handling. The 4-speed manual transmission's shift linkage is balky and easily goes out of adjustment. Awkward and outdated controls.

Post-1985 models experience serious problems with the 2.2L engine (see *Service Tips*) in addition to fuel, electrical and ignition system problems that are difficult to diagnose and even harder to repair due to the poor quality of components. The power steering rack develops leaks and the exhaust system rusts quickly. Rapid brake wear and unreliable electronic components, such as dashboard gauges. Air conditioners often malfunction and are expensive to troubleshoot and repair.

All models suffer from premature surface rust with perforations found around rear wheels and the rear hatch. Many owners have complained of severe underbody rusting, affecting safety. All years have such poor body assembly that doors are constantly sticking shut (some owners have had to climb out the windows), locks fall off, handles detach, and water and air leaks are legion.

Safety summary/recalls: A 1979 two-door hatchback performed very well in NHTSA's 57 km/h frontal crash tests. Both the driver and front-seat passenger were well-protected from injury. Subsequent testing of a four-door 1982 Dodge Omni showed the driver would sustain minor injuries, but the front passenger would have been severely or fatally injured. The 1982 test results apply to all four-door models and can be extrapolated to include all model years since.

Recalls: **1985**-Leaking fuel reservoir of 2.2L engine may cause an engine compartment fire. Faulty fuel vapor canister may cause engine to stall during deceleration. **1985-87-Turbo**-Fuel hose connection may leak and cause a fire. **1986**-Battery could rupture during charging. Rear suspension may partially separate from the vehicle causing a sudden loss of control. **1987**-Faulty pressure regulator may leak fuel. **1989-90**-Faulty engine valve cover gasket could leak oil, which could ignite.

Secret Warranties/Service Tips/DSBs

1987-88-An automatic transmission with delayed initial engagement may have low fluid level, a faulty throttle and shift cable, or insufficient front pump pressure. A new pressure plate may be needed (#4377121 for 2.2L, 2.5L and 2.6L engines; #4412412 for 2.2L turbo and 3.0L V6 engines).

• No 2nd or 3rd gear may be due to a faulty 2nd/3rd thrust washer snap ring (#6033348).

• Clutch chatter in reverse may be due to a faulty clutch cable.

• If water leaks from the AC housing, drill three holes in the recirculation housing. Leaks through or around the doors require trim adhesive and gasket sealant.

• FM radio noise may be caused by a faulty SMEC module.

1988-89-2.2L and turbos with automatic transmissions that stall in cold weather can be corrected by installing an upgraded (SMEC) engine controller (#4557522).

1988-90-2.2L and 2.5L EFI engines that run roughly at idle may require a new EGR valve (emissions warranty).

1989-Alternator belt noise may be caused by a misaligned pulley. Install two flat washers.

1989-90-2.2L and 2.5L engine oil leak at valve cover corrected with a new cylinder head cover kit (see *Recalls*).

• 2.2L EFI engines with a spark knock during hot engine idle in drive may need a new engine controller.

1990-Loud clicking or popping when the clutch pedal is depressed signals the need for a new clutch cable adjust spring (#4188653).

All models/years-2.2L, 2.5L and 3.0L V6 engines that surge and buck at 35-55 mph with A413 and A670 transmissions may require driveability kit #4419447. All front-drives with automatic transmissions that have delayed engagement, no Drive or Reverse after start-up should have the front transmission pump replaced. A 10-minute delay when switching AC from defrost to any other mode may be due to a stuck heater check valve. Install a new check valve (#5264270).

Complaint settlement patterns show Chrysler will cover costs related to premature engine head gasket, ring and valve wear up to 5 years/80,000 km under its emissions warranty. Faulty steering assemblies are often fixed free of charge up to 3 years/60,000 km (Ford and GM cover steering repairs two additional years) and the company will pay 100% toward the correction of paint defects during the first 3 years/60,000 km and 50% up to the fifth year of ownership. Surface rust will be corrected free up to 3 years/60,000 km and rust perforations up to 5 years. Water leaks into the vehicle's interior will be corrected without charge during the first year of ownership. These special offers are not voluntarily extended to second owners, but the small claims courts have ruled they should be. It can be argued that Chrysler's 7-year new car warranty is the automaker's own durability benchmark and should be extended to cover earlier models.

Vehicle Profile

	1983	1984	1985	1986	1987	1988	1989	1990
Cost Price ($)								
Omni/Horizon	6600	7000	7397	7397	7295	7795	8550	9500
Charger	7487	7705	7999	8280	8412	—	—	—
Charger 2.2L	8524	8578	9114	9410	12,764	—	—	—
Turismo	7847	7705	7999	8280	8412	—	—	—
Turismo 2.2L	8524	8578	9114	9410	12,764	—	—	—
Used Values ($)								
Omni/Horizon ↑	700	800	1200	1400	1600	2000	2500	3000
Omni/Horizon ↓	500	600	800	1100	1400	1700	2100	2500
Charger ↑	800	1000	1300	1500	1800	—	—	—
Charger ↓	600	800	1100	1300	1600	—	—	—
Charger 2.2L ↑	1000	1300	1600	1900	2200	—	—	—
Charger 2.2L ↓	900	1100	1400	1600	1900	—	—	—
Turismo ↑	900	1000	1300	1500	1800	—	—	—
Turismo ↓	600	800	1100	1300	1600	—	—	—
Turismo 2.2L ↑	1000	1300	1600	1900	2200	—	—	—
Turismo 2.2L ↓	900	1100	1400	1600	1900	—	—	—
Reliability	①	①	①	①	①	①	②	②
Air conditioning	—	—	—	—	①	①	①	②
Body integrity	①	①	①	①	①	①	②	②
Braking system	①	①	①	②	③	③	③	③
Electrical system	①	②	②	②	②	②	②	③
Engines	①	①	①	①	②	①	①	②
Exhaust/Converter	①	①	①	①	②	③	③	③
Fuel system	①	①	①	①	①	①	③	③
Ignition system	②	②	②	②	②	②	②	②
Manual transmission	④	④	④	④	④	④	④	④
— automatic	③	④	④	④	④	④	④	④

Rust/Paint	②	②	②	②	②	②	③	③
Steering	①	①	①	①	①	①	③	③
Suspension	①	①	①	②	②	③	③	④
Dealer Service	①	①	①	①	①	①	①	①
Maintenance	①	①	①	①	①	①	③	③
Parts Availability	②	②	②	②	②	②	②	②
Repair Costs	①	①	①	①	①	①	③	③
Crash Safety	②	②	②	②	②	②	②	②
Safety Features								
Airbag	—	—	—	—	—	—	—	D

Colt, Summit, Vista

Rating: Recommended (1990-94); Average (1989); Mediocre (1985-88). The Summit is cheaper, more practical and more fuel efficient than most other small wagons.

Price analysis: Excellent availability. Try to get a car with a valid Chrysler warranty. Vehicles older than five years are only a bit cheaper and a whole lot more risky. Don't buy an extended warranty. Expect to pay approximately $300 annually for maintenance and repairs. Other small sedans worth considering: Ford Escort/Tracer ('91 or later) • GM Firefly/Sprint • Mazda 323 • Suzuki Forsa/Sprint • Identical U.S.-built Mitsubishi Mirage. Other small wagons: Nissan Multi and Axxess.

Strengths and weaknesses: This well-proven design has accumulated a few problems over the years, but most can be fixed quite easily. Quality control is exceptional. Body construction and assembly are quite good. Stainless-steel exhaust system cuts down replacement costs. Parts are reasonably priced.

These cars are practical and their repair histories are better than most American cars. Although the E and DL models aren't sparkling performers, they remain competitive in the subcompact arena and they can be purchased for a lot less than their Japanese cousins. The 1985-88 Colts don't handle as well or offer as much rear legroom and cargo space as the more rounded, aero-styled contemporary 1989-94 versions. Repairs aren't difficult to perform. Depreciation is more rapid than on other Japanese cars.

Technical Data

ENGINES	Litres/CID	HP	MPG	Model Years
OHV I-4 2 bbl.	1.5/90	68	26-36	1985-88
OHC I-4 FI	1.5/90	75	26-35	1988
OHC I-4 FI	1.5/90	81	24-30	1989-90
OHC I-4 FI	1.5/90	92	23-29	1991-94
OHC I-4T FI	1.6/97	102-105	24-27	1984-88
DOHC I-4T FI	1.6/97	135	21-25	1989
DOHC I-4 FI	1.6/97	113	22-26	1990
DOHC I-4 FI	1.6/97	123	21-25	1991-92
OHC I-4 FI	1.8/110	87-113	22-27	1992-94
OHV I-4 2 bbl.	2.0/122	88	23-27	1985-87
OHC I-4 FI	2.0/122	96	22-26	1988-91
OHC I-4 FI	2.4/155	136	22-25	1993-94

A troublesome turbocharged 1.6L motor was first offered in 1984. The engines on high-mileage cars often burn oil because of worn piston rings. Models equipped with automatic transmissions vibrate badly when idling in gear. Air conditioners are unreliable and expensive to repair. Carburetors can be finicky, too. Many reports of ignition troubles through 1985. Rapid front brake wear. Problems carried over to the 1986 and later models are premature engine and exhaust system wear. Post-'86 LX, Vista and 4X4 models are plagued by similar defects, with the addition of transmission and fuel-system malfunctions.

The five-passenger Colt wagon is a relatively new small version of the minivan. It is similar to the Colt Summit and Nissan Axxess in that it offers the extra versatility of a third seat in back and a tall body. As such, it makes a great car for a small family, while being able to haul small loads to the cottage or wherever. The wagon series is available in 4-wheel drive and uses practically the same mechanical components as the other Colt models. The wagon, like the Colt, should depreciate less rapidly than average. If the wagon's price is too steep, check out the Nissan Axxess which offers similar advantages. The Summit wagon is essentially a wagon version of the Colt 200 and sells at a premium. Front legroom is limited. Even with the seat pushed all the way back, your knees can touch the dash. The 1.8L or 2.4L engines go best with the 5-speed manual transmission. With an automatic, the 2.4L takes a while to change gear, particularly when going uphill.

Colt owners have complained of premature engine piston ring wear on older models. On post-'90 Colts and Summits, the 2.4L head gasket may fail prematurely. Shocks aren't very durable, braking isn't impressive and the front brakes have a short lifespan. Emission components like the oxygen sensor often fail after two years of use. Automatic transmission failures reported by a few owners. Be especially wary of the troublesome 4X4 powertrain on 1989-91 wagons and the 16-valve turbo dropped in 1990. Exhaust system deteriorates prematurely. Surface rust is common as are rust perforations on door bottoms, the front edge of the hood and on the rear hatch.

Owners of 1992-94 models report premature piston ring wear and excessive engine noise caused by carbon buildup on the top of the piston. Front brakes and shock absorbers continue to have a short lifespan. Owners of the 1993 wagon complain of poor heating and defrosting.

Safety summary/recalls: Both the Colt sedan and Vista wagon have been extensively crash tested. A 1985 Colt sedan provided good crash protection for the driver, but the front passenger would have sustained severe leg trauma. A retested 1989 four-door Colt showed that both the driver and passenger would sustain severe leg injuries. An identical '93 four-door Mitsubishi Mirage produced high driver head injury numbers and severe passenger leg injuries.

Tests of a 1986 Vista wagon showed that the driver would sustain fatal head injuries and severe injuries to both legs; the front passenger would receive severe or fatal head injuries. Crash tests of a 1988 Colt wagon have shown that the driver would be fatally injured, but the front seat passenger would escape with minor injuries. A 1992 Colt Vista wagon provided good protection for both the driver and front passenger. The wagon's sliding doors have child-proof door locks. Unfortunately, some Summit wagons may have defective sliding door latches. *Recalls*: None so far.

Secret Warranties/Service Tips/DSBs

1978-89-If engine misses and bucks under hard acceleration or has oil-fouled spark plugs, it could be due to faulty engine jet valves.

1987-88-Front disc brake squeal can be fixed by using a pad kit (#MB 534486).

• A sulphur smell from the exhaust may be due to a faulty catalytic converter on vehicles with 1.5L engines.

1989-90-Cold start driveability problems can be fixed by cleaning engine of carbon deposits and putting in an upgraded valve cover (#MD 118-125).

• Front suspension squeaks: replace both stabilizer bar bushings.

1991-Hard shifting or gear clashing can be corrected by installing an improved 1-2 synchronizer hub and sleeve, 1-2 synchronizer spring, and the 3-4 synchronizer spring on cars equipped with manual transaxles.

1992-Wagon fuel tanks may be slow to fill because in-tank baffle impedes fuel flow. Chrysler will cover the cost of installing an improved tank.

Fuel Tank Slow to Fill

NO.: 14-03-92
GROUP: Fuel
DATE: May 4, 1992
SUBJECT:
Fuel Tank Slow To Fill
THIS BULLETIN APPLIES TO ALL WHEEL DRIVE VEHICLES BUILT PRIOR TO VIN NZ028154.

MODELS:
1992 (B8) Colt Vista/Summit Wagon

SYMPTOM/CONDITION:
Vehicles built prior to VIN NZ028154 may be slow to fill after the fuel tank is half full. This may result in complaints of the fuel filler nozzle frequently shutting off while filling the tank. This condition is caused by the left side of the fuel tank not filling due to a baffle placed in the center of the tank. Installation of a new fuel tank with a relocated fuel leveling pipe will correct this condition.

• Wagons may have excessive wind noise around the upper front door frame.

1992-93-A front-end popping noise means the stabilizer ball joint grease has deteriorated. Add new grease and install an upgraded dust cover to protect the grease from further contamination.

1992-94-Carbon buildup on the piston top can be reduced by adding a bottle of Mopar Fuel Injector Cleanor to a full tank of gas.

• The sliding door may not open from inside due to a faulty connecting door latch rod clip.

1993-Wagons with poor heating/defrosting require upgraded distribution ducts.

All models/years-A common problem with the 1.6L engine is that the exhaust manifold can come loose, causing an exhaust leak. When you first spot the trouble, just tighten the exhaust manifold bolts.

Owners who have gotten free repairs say Chrysler will cover costs related to premature engine head gasket, ring and valve wear up to 5 years/80,000 km under its emissions warranty. Faulty steering assemblies are often fixed free of charge up to 3 years/60,000 km (Ford and GM cover steering repairs two additional years) and the company will pay 100% toward the correction of paint defects during the first 3 years/60,000 km and 50% up to the fifth year of ownership. Surface rust will be corrected free up to 3 years/60,000 km and rust perforations up to 5 years. Water leaks into the vehicle's interior will be corrected without charge during the first year of ownership. These special offers are not voluntarily extended to second owners, but the small claims courts have ruled they should be. Don't forget, Chrysler's 7-year new car warranty is the automaker's own durability benchmark and should be extended to cover earlier models.

Vehicle Profile

	1987	1988	1989	1990	1991	1992	1993	1994
Cost Price ($)								
Colt 100	7869	8526	9098	8672	7723	7820	8745	10,995
Colt 200	—	—	9874	10,181	9195	9380	—	—
Colt Wagon	—	—	—	—	—	12,919	13,146	15,205
Vista Wagon	—	—	13,662	14,850	13,875	—	—	—
Summit Wagon	—	—	—	—	—	12,919	13,600	15,205
Used Values ($)								
Colt 100 ↑	1800	2200	3000	3500	4200	5000	6100	7500
Colt 100 ↓	1100	1400	2100	2800	3300	4000	5000	6500
Colt 200 ↑	—	—	3500	4000	4800	5800	—	—
Colt 200 ↓	—	—	2400	3100	3700	4800	—	—
Colt Wagon ↑	—	—	—	—	—	7700	8800	11,100
Colt Wagon ↓	—	—	—	—	—	6500	7600	9300
Vista Wagon ↑	—	—	4900	6300	7100	—	—	—
Vista Wagon ↓	—	—	3900	5200	5900	—	—	—
Summit Wagon ↑	—	—	—	—	—	7500	8700	11,000
Summit Wagon ↓	—	—	—	—	—	6300	7500	9200
Reliability	2	2	2	3	4	4	4	4
Air conditioning	2	2	2	5	5	5	5	5
Body integrity	2	2	2	2	2	2	3	4
Braking system	2	2	2	2	2	3	4	3
Electrical system	2	2	2	3	3	4	4	5
Engines	2	2	2	3	4	4	4	4
Exhaust/Converter	2	3	3	3	4	4	5	5
Fuel system	3	3	3	4	4	4	5	5
Ignition system	2	3	3	5	5	5	5	5
Manual transmission	2	4	4	5	5	5	5	5
— automatic	2	3	3	3	3	4	2	3
Rust/Paint	2	2	3	3	3	3	4	5
Steering	4	4	4	4	4	5	5	5
Suspension	2	2	2	3	3	3	4	3
Dealer Service	3	3	3	3	3	3	3	3
Maintenance	4	4	4	4	5	5	5	5
Parts Availability	3	3	3	4	4	5	5	5
Repair Costs	2	2	2	3	3	3	5	5
Crash Safety								
Colt Sedan	2	2	1	1	1	1	1	1
Colt Wagon	—	2	2	2	2	2	2	2
Vista Wagon	1	2	2	2	2	5	5	5
Safety Features								
ABS	—	—	—	—	—	—	O	O
Airbag	—	—	—	—	—	—	—	D

FORD

Rating: Recommended (1992-94); Acceptable (1991); Not Recommended (1981-90).

Price analysis: Prices are similar for these small compacts and, since 1991, prices have firmed up, reflecting their increased popularity since they were spun off of the Mazda 323 and Protegé. These are far more reliable subcompacts than Ford produced on its own prior to that time. Expect to pay about $700 annually for maintenance and repairs for pre-'91 models and $300 annually for '91 and later versions. A supplementary warranty would be a good buy for pre-'91 models. In 1987, the Lynx was replaced by the Taiwanese- and Mexican-built Tracer. It's a far better vehicle than the early Escorts, but its relatively high retail price puts it in second place behind its Mazda twin, the 323, which also offers a four-door sedan instead of the Tracer's four-door hatchback. The Tracer wagon's accident repair costs are much lower than average. Other small cars worth considering: Chrysler Colt • GM Firefly/Sprint • Mazda GLC or 323 • Nissan Sentra • Suzuki Forsa.

Technical Data

ENGINES	Litres/CID	HP	MPG	Model Years
OHC I-4 2 bbl.	1.6/98	70-80	25-30	1985
OHC I-4 FI	1.6/98	84	26-30	1985
OHC I-4T FI	1.6/98	120	22-26	1985
OHC I-4 2 bbl.	1.9/114	86	26-30	1985-86
OHC I-4 FI	1.9/114	90	25-31	1987-90
OHC I-4 FI	1.9/114	108-115	21-25	1985-90
OHC I-4D FI	2.0/121	52-58	27-34	1985-87
OHC I-4 FI	1.9/114	88	24-30	1991-95
DOHC I-4 FI	1.8/109	127	23-27	1991-95

Strengths and weaknesses: From 1982 until 1990, these subcompacts were dull performers with an uninspiring interior. They had a terrible reputation for quality and were expensive to repair.

A more powerful 1.9L engine has been available since mid-'85. The Mazda-built 2.0L diesel 4-cylinder (1984-87) is weak, noisy, difficult to service and prone to expensive cylinder head and gasket repairs. Although prices are low, chronic reliability and maintenance woes make pre-1986 Escorts and EXPs terrible used car buys. Parts are easily found but are more expensive than average.

From 1987 until the 1990 model year, quality continued to go downhill. The 1.9L engine used from 1985-90 gives respectable highway performance, but its failure rate is still much higher than average. The radiator and other cooling components, including the fan switch and motor, are failure prone. Carburetors and fuel- injection systems are temperamental. Ignition modules are often defective. Power steering racks fail prematurely. Front and rear wheel alignment is difficult. Exhaust systems rust rapidly.

From 1991 on, these cars have a longer wheelbase making for a more comfortable ride and a bit roomier interior. The 1.9L engine runs more smoothly. Mazda's powerful 127-hp 1.8L 4-cylinder engine equips the GT and Tracer LTS, and overall highway performance and fuel economy are far superior to what previous models offered. Wagon versions are particularly versatile and spacious. Front seats on the Tracer GS and LS are very comfortable, and the cargo area is especially spacious in the wagon. Rear seat room is a bit cramped on all other models. Instrumentation is complete and well laid out on the GS and LS.

The 1991-92 models have registered few owner complaints, except for some reports of air-conditioning and fuel pump failures, minor ignition system glitches, electrical short-circuits caused by corroded fuel pump wiring, engine malfunctions, and a difficult-to-access oil filter.

Confidential dealer service bulletins show the 1993s may have poorly performing AC systems with a slipping clutch at high ambient temperatures; high idle rpm may occur after extended highway cruising; engine lifters may make a metallic ticking sound just after initial startup; the service engine light goes on for no apparent reason; and spark plug knock may occur when accelerating or during highway driving. Bulletins also show fuel pump wiring short-circuits and poor body fits causing wind and water leaks. Owners report that the '93 wagon's base suspension is too soft and that braking is mediocre, and severe wind noise comes from the front passenger door at cruising speeds.

The '94s may have a rough idle, hesitation, excessive fuel consumption, and poor heater output that is likely caused by a thermostat stuck in an open position or opening before it should. Other bulletins note fuel pump wiring short-circuits (see *Service Tips*), defective electric rear window defrosters, and lots of water leaks, rattles and squeaks.

Safety summary/recalls (Escort): NHTSA crash tests of a 1987 Escort hatchback showed that the driver would receive severe leg injuries, while the front seat passenger would escape unscathed. A 1987 Lynx produced similar results.

Ford paid a $3.2-million jury award for the absence of rear shoulder harnesses and improperly designed lapbelts in a 1985 Escort. The lapbelts were designed to cross at the waist instead of the pelvis, and this error contributed to the passenger's paralysis. If shoulder harnesses had been installed, the lapbelts would not have aggravated the injuries.

When Ford switched over to the Mazda-inspired Escort in 1991, there followed a temporary improvement in crashworthiness. NHTSA found that the 1991 two-door Escort gave excellent head and chest protection to both the driver and front seat passenger. Crash tests of a 1993 two-door Escort, however, concluded that the driver and passenger would have severe leg injuries in a 57 km/h frontal collision. Surprisingly, tests of a 1994 Escort wagon with a driver-side airbag posted similar results. Safety problems under investigation are spindle/wheel-bearing failures, faulty fuel-metering jets that cause stalling and diminish engine power, and fires emanating from the steering column of 1990 Escorts. Owners have also complained that the fuel pump may short circuit and cause a fire on '91 models.

Recalls: **1985**-Rocker arm oil leakage could cause a fire. Cars with 1.9L engines may have a faulty throttle lever that may not return to idle. **1985-86**-Prolonged idling may cause a fire from an overheated catalytic converter. Manual gearshift lever may accidentally slip into Neutral in cold weather. **1985-87**-Driver's seat could come loose in an accident. **1986-88**-Fuel line leakage could cause a fire. **1987**-Stainless-steel lug nuts may fracture causing the wheel to fall off. **1988-90**-Exhaust system catalyst on vehicles with 1.9L engines will be replaced to make exhaust emissions conform to Canadian regulations. **1990**-Windshield could come out in a frontal collision. **1991**-Accelerator pedal could stick wide open. Steering column may lock up. **1991-92**-Fuel vapor could escape from a full fuel tank causing a fire. **1993**-Faulty driver's seat could fail in a collision. **1995**-Airbag mounting bolts may be missing or improperly torqued.

Safety summary/recalls (Tracer): NHTSA crash tests of a 1989 four-door Tracer concluded that the driver's left leg would be severely injured, but the front passenger would be unharmed. *Recalls:* **1991**-Fuel vapor could escape from a full fuel tank causing a fire. **1992**-Steering column may lock up.

Secret Warranties/Service Tips/DSBs

Escort

1983-94-Hesitation, a rough idle, or poor heater output may all be caused by a faulty thermostat.

1985-90-An exhaust buzz or rattle may be fixed by installing new clamps to secure the heat shield attachments.

1985-91-Ford's rear window defroster service kit will fix a faulty electric rear window defroster.

1986-89-Hard starting/stalling may be caused by a defective fuel pump or sender assembly.

1987-88-Models with EEC IV experiencing no-starts or hard starts may have a defective TFI module.

1988-Owner notification M59 says any fuel pump malfunction that drains the battery, makes for hard starts or cuts engine performance can be corrected by a free, upgraded fuel pump diode (#E8FZ-14A411-A).

1990-Owner notification B91 allows for the free modification of faulty dealer AC units whose condenser fans rotate backwards.

1991-Factory-related axle problems can cause premature rear tire wear. Ford dealers will cover the cost of replacement after deducting for wear.

1991-Knocking heard after a cold start or when returning to idle speed after freeway driving can be eliminated by installing new engine camshafts after eliminating the possibility of lifter noise.

1991-93-Metallic ticking heard after initial start-up or when returning to idle speed after freeway type driving may be caused by a faulty lifter, low amount of oil in the crankcase, an incorrect oil filter, or oil deterioration. Change the oil and oil filter, purge the air from the system, and if necessary, replace the lifters.

1991-94-Under Service Program #94B55, Ford will install at no charge a fused jumper harness in the fuel pump electrical circuit to prevent stalling, erratic instrument gauge readings and extensive wiring damage caused by water intrusion creating a short-circuit.

Ford Motor Company is providing a no-charge Service Program, Number 94B55, to owners of certain 1991-1994 Escort and Tracer cars.

REASON FOR THIS PROGRAM

We wish to install a fused jumper harness in the fuel pump electrical circuit of your car. The fused jumper harness is designed to prevent erratic instrument gauge readings, engine stalling and extensive wiring damage due to a possible fuel pump/sender wiring harness electrical short circuit. Should a short circuit occur after the jumper is installed, the harness fuse will open preventing a stalled vehicle and damage to the wiring.

NO CHARGE SERVICE

At no charge to you, your dealer will install a fused jumper harness within the fuel pump/sender electrical circuit of your car.

HOW LONG WILL IT TAKE?

The time needed for this service is about one half hour. However, due to service scheduling times, your dealer may need your car for one full working day.

CALL YOUR DEALER

Ask for a service date and if parts are in stock.

If your dealer does not have the parts in stock, they can be ordered before scheduling your service date. Parts would be expected to arrive within a week.

When you bring your car in, show the dealer this letter.

If you misplace this letter, your dealer will still do the work, free of charge.

REFUNDS

If you paid to have this service done before the date of this letter, Ford is offering a full refund. For the refund, please give your paid original receipt to your car dealer.

• A timing belt that's noisy during cold weather can be fixed by installing an upgraded, more rigid belt tensioner.

• A missing or loose front valance panel will be replaced or secured with longer bolts free of charge.

1992-93-A high idle rpm after heavy use may be corrected by installing a new idle air control valve.

Tracer

1988-89-Hesitation, a rough idle, or poor heater output may all be caused by a faulty thermostat.

1991-94-A timing belt that's noisy during cold weather can be fixed by installing an upgraded, more rigid belt tensioner.

All models/years-Owners report Ford has been covering the cost of repairs for premature engine head gasket, ring and valve wear up to 5 years/80,000 km under its emissions warranty. Other components that benefit from Ford "goodwill" warranty extensions: fuel pumps and computer modules that govern engine, fuel injection and transmission functions. If Ford balks at refunding your money for a faulty computer module, threaten to apply the 5 year/80,000 km emissions warranty. Faulty steering assemblies are often fixed free of charge up to 5 years/ 80,000 km. Ford will pay 100% toward the correction of paint defects during the first 5 years/80,000 km and 50% up to the seventh year of ownership in keeping with the policy it adopted to cover pickups and 4X4s. Surface rust will be corrected for free up to 3 years/60,000 km and rust perforations up to 5 years. Water leaks into the vehicle's interior will be corrected without charge during the first year of ownership. All these programs include second owners.

Vehicle Profile

	1987	1988	1989	1990	1991	1992	1993	1994
Cost Price ($)								
Base	7995	8195	9095	9795	10,095	11,195	10,795	12,195
GT	12,078	12,615	13,295	13,101	13,895	15,095	15,472	15,995
Used Values ($)								
Base ↑	1800	2600	2900	3500	4400	6300	7400	9100
Base ↓	1300	1600	1900	2600	3500	5100	6100	7700
GT ↑	2500	3300	4500	5500	6600	9000	10,200	11,300
GT ↓	1900	2500	3500	4500	5600	7200	9000	10,000
Reliability	①	①	②	②	③	④	④	⑤
Air conditioning	①	①	②	②	①	②	②	④
Body integrity	①	①	①	②	②	②	②	③
Braking system	①	①	①	①	②	③	③	④
Electrical system	①	①	①	①	②	③	④	④
Engines	②	②	②	②	③	③	③	⑤
Exhaust/Converter	①	②	②	③	③	④	⑤	⑤
Fuel system	①	①	②	②	③	③	③	③
Ignition system	①	①	②	②	③	④	⑤	⑤
Manual transmission	⑤	⑤	⑤	⑤	⑤	⑤	⑤	⑤
- automatic	①	①	③	③	③	④	⑤	⑤
Rust/Paint	①	①	②	②	③	④	⑤	⑤
Steering	①	①	②	②	③	⑤	⑤	⑤
Suspension	①	①	②	②	③	⑤	⑤	⑤

Dealer Service	①	①	①	①	③	⑤	⑤	⑤
Maintenance	①	①	①	①	③	④	⑤	⑤
Parts Availability	①	①	①	①	⑤	⑤	⑤	⑤
Repair Costs	①	①	①	①	③	⑤	⑤	⑤
Crash Safety								
Escort 2-door	②	②	②	②	⑤	⑤	①	①
Lynx	②	②	②	②	—	—	—	—
Tracer	②	②	②	②	⑤	⑤	①	①
Safety Features								
ABS	—	—	—	—	—	O	O	O
Airbag	—	—	—	—	—	—	—	D

Festiva

Rating: Above Average buy (1993); Average buy (1991-92); Not Recommended (1989-90). Built by Kia in South Korea, the front-drive Ford Festiva is a mini-compact based on the Mazda 121 (not sold in Canada).

Price analysis: Fair availability. Expect to pay about $400 annually for maintenance and repairs. Other small cars worth considering: Chrysler Colt • GM Firefly/Sprint • Mazda GLC and 323 • Nissan Sentra • Suzuki Forsa.

Technical Data

ENGINES	Litres/CID	HP	MPG	Model Years
OHV I-4 2 bbl.	1.3/81	58	34-39	1988-89
OHC I-4 FI	1.3/81	63	32-37	1989-93

Strengths and weaknesses: As far as small commuter cars go, the Festiva offers better reliability and more seating room than most econoboxes except for the Dodge Colt, a car that uses many of the same mechanical components.

The Festiva's small, 1.3L 4-cylinder engine is surprisingly peppy with the manual gearbox. The 4-speed automatic is smooth and precise, but it easily overpowers the small engine. Without power steering, the Festiva's handling is heavy and vague. With power assist, despite some understeering the car's emergency handling is exceptional and sudden stops are short without excessive brake fade. Due to the car's small tires and tall body, cornering under speed produces quite a bit of body roll. The front seats are especially comfortable, but rear seating is compromised by limited room and uncomfortable seats. There is a considerable amount of road and engine noise, and the suspension is a bit firm, producing a choppy ride over uneven terrain.

Owners report poor engine performance accompanied by stalling, hesitation and surging. Body problems include loose door handles, faulty seat anchorages, and premature paint peeling and discoloration. Cruise control, fuel pump, transmission and electrical defects are also commonplace.

Safety summary/recalls: None. *Recalls*: Takata seatbelt failures.

Secret Warranties/Service Tips/DSBs

1988-91-Rattles from door panels are caused by excessive clearance between the door trim panel and the door (DSB 91-12-9).
• Hard cold starting, stalling, rough idle and hesitation upon acceleration can all be traced to sludge in the throttle body or idle air by-pass valve according to DSB 91-10-19. The correction falls under Ford's emissions warranty.
1988-92-A buzz or rattle from the exhaust system may be caused by a loose heat shield. Install worm clamps to secure the heat shield.
1989-Abnormal speed control operation in high ambient temperatures is caused by a short-circuit between the steering wheel slip rings and the brush assembly.
• Sulphur/rotten eggs exhaust smell is caused by incorrect carburetor mixture. Adjust the carburetor idle mixture to reduce carbon dioxide concentration.
• Hesitation and surging may require a new distributor vacuum advance, pulse air orifice and EGR delay valve.
• Exterior door handle breaks off in cold weather. Ford will replace free of charge.
• Seat does not easily move full travel fore and aft. Ford will fix free of charge.
• Stalls when the key is released to the run position due to a defective EEC processor. Ford will replace free of charge (labor included) up to 5 years/80,000 km under the emissions warranty.
• Transmission click, clunk, rattle in Reverse gear caused by the shift lever not fully engaged, resulting in gear damage. Ford will replace, at no charge, the input shaft, Reverse idler gear and idler arm.
• Water and corrosion in the X-07 (C123) wiring connector can cause a dead battery, hard starting, poor idling, inoperative headlights or failure of the automatic transmission throttle kick-down.
• Water may enter timing belt cover causing no-starts, hard starting or poor engine performance. Ford will reseal the cover, but cost is the owner's responsibility.
1989-90-Exhaust system buzz or rattle is likely caused by a loose catalyst or muffler heat shield.
• MTX transmission whine will be corrected by Ford by replacing at no charge the final drive input gear and output shaft up to 5 years/80,000 km.

• Aluminum wheel air leaks will be sealed free of charge (including 0.8 of an hour labor) by Ford under DSB 88-10-4.
• Chrome peeling or moisture inside Ford emblem will be repaired at no cost to the owner.
• Rear brake squeal during light applications is caused by defective rear brake backing plate. Ford will provide free backing plates and spindle nuts and pay the 1.8 hour labor charge to correct this problem. **1990**-Defective door window bracket assembly will be repaired at no cost. **All models/years**-Ford has been repairing for free premature engine head gasket, ring and valve wear up to 5 years/80,000 km under its emissions warranty. Faulty steering assemblies are often fixed free of charge up to 5 years/80,000 km ever since the company was sued by irate Mustang owners a decade ago. Ford will pay 100% toward the correction of paint defects during the first 5 years/80,000 km and 50% up to the seventh year of ownership in keeping with the policy it adopted to cover pickups. Surface rust will be corrected for free up to 3 years/60,000 km and rust perforations up to 5 years. Water leaks into the vehicle's interior will be corrected without charge up to the fifth year of ownership. All these programs include second owners.

Vehicle Profile

	1989	1990	1991	1992	1993
Cost Price ($)					
L	7995	8795	7795	—	8416
Used Values ($)					
L ↑	1800	2800	3500	—	4800
L ↓	900	1900	2600	—	3700
Reliability	①	①	③	③	④
Air conditioning	③	③	④	④	④
Body integrity	②	②	②	②	②
Braking system	②	②	②	②	③
Electrical system	②	②	②	③	③
Engines	③	③	④	④	④
Exhaust/Converter	②	②	②	②	⑤
Fuel system	③	③	④	④	④
Ignition system	③	③	④	④	④
Manual transmission	④	④	④	④	④
— automatic	—	②	③	③	④
Rust/Paint	②	②	②	②	②
Steering	②	③	③	③	⑤
Suspension	④	④	④	④	④
Dealer Service	②	②	②	②	③
Maintenance	③	③	③	③	③
Parts Availability	③	③	③	③	③
Repair Costs	④	④	④	④	⑤
Crash Safety	②	②	②	⑤	⑤

GENERAL MOTORS

Firefly, Metro, Sprint

Rating: Recommended (1992-94); Above Average (1990-91); Average buy (1987-89).

Price analysis: Excellent availability and prices are relatively low. Removal of the manufacturers' tax in 1991 brought down the original selling price by $800 and dropped the 1992 models' original selling price to $200 less than what the 1989 models cost. Expect to pay about $700 annually for maintenance and repairs.

A 1994 survey by the Canadian Automobile Association concluded that GM's servicing was superior to Suzuki's. However, parts sold by GM dealers are more expensive than those sold by a Suzuki dealer. Depreciation is fairly rapid, making these minicars good buys on the used car market. The convertible version packs plenty of fun and performance into a reasonably priced subcompact body. Other small cars worth considering: Chrysler Colt • Ford Aspire or Festiva • Honda Civic • Mazda GLC or 323 • Nissan Sentra • Suzuki Forsa.

Strengths and weaknesses: These cars are tiny—and very economical—3-cylinder, front-wheel-drive hatchbacks. Interior garnishing is decent but plain, and there is plenty of room for two passengers. The Sprint and Firefly, equipped with an automatic transmission, offer the best all-round performance and economy. The turbocharged convertible model is an excellent choice for high-performance thrills in an easy-to-handle ragtop. These little squirts should be considered primarily city vehicles due to their small size, small tires, low ground clearance and average handling. Transmission and differential parts are sometimes hard to find.

Technical Data

ENGINES	Litres/CID	HP	MPG	Model Years
OHC I-3 2 bbl.	1.0/61	46-48	42-55	1985-88
OHC I-3T FI	1.0/61	70	35-39	1987-88
OHC I-3 FI	1.0/61	49-55	36-51	1989-94

Mechanically, the GM-Suzuki partnership has not hurt quality control. These cars have a better-than-average repair history, and body components are well assembled and very durable. The only trouble spots indicated so far concern excessive oil consumption after the fourth year of service, automatic transmission and differential failures around 80,000 km, cooling system, premature brake, clutch and exhaust system wear-out, and minor carburetor malfunctions. Fogging of the side windows and windshield due to inadequate heat distribution is a common complaint.

Confidential dealer service bulletins for 1993 models indicate that hatches vibrate when windows are open and the rear hatch seems to want to open on its own. Push buttons for the lights and wipers tend to fly off the dashboard. Fuel economy is often exaggerated by dealers. Noisy front metallic brake pads, and the front discs warp easily. Poorly performing fuel injection system. The tiny radiator can't stand up to the rigors of the Canadian climate. If not checked, the cooling system will fail eventually, causing great damage to the aluminum engine. Some complaints concerning premature clutch wear, paint peeling, early rusting and sloppy body assembly.

Safety summary/recalls: A 1992 two-door was tested under the Geo Metro label and passed with flying colors; neither the driver nor passenger would be seriously harmed in a collision. Side window defogging is slow and sometimes inadequate. *Recalls*: **1989-93**-Hood may fly up when car is in motion. **1995**-Rear brake drums may have been incorrectly machined leading to sudden wheel separation.

Secret Warranties/Service Tips/DSBs

1986–The push-pull headlight switch will be replaced at no charge under a recall campaign.
1989-92-Stalling or loss of power shortly after starting may be due to high pressure in the hydraulic lifter assemblies.
1991-92-Excessive vehicle vibration when the vehicle is in reverse gear is likely due to poor insulation between the engine/transaxle assembly and the vehicle's chassis. Install upgraded engine mounts.

Vehicle Profile

	1987	1988	1989	1990	1991	1992	1993	1994
Cost Price ($)								
Firefly/Sprint	7208	7580	7995	8395	7765	7765	—	—
Metro	—	—	—	—	—	6999	7995	8995
Used Values ($)								
Firefly/Sprint ↑	1400	1900	2700	3200	3700	4500	—	—
Firefly/Sprint ↓	900	1300	1900	2300	2700	3400	—	—
Metro ↑	—	—	—	—	—	3900	5500	6900
Metro ↓	—	—	—	—	—	3000	4400	6000

Reliability	③	③	③	④	④	⑤	⑤	⑤
Air conditioning	—	—	—	—	—	—	—	—
Body integrity	③	③	③	③	③	③	③	③
Braking system	❷	❷	❷	❷	③	③	③	④
Electrical system	❷	❷	❷	③	③	④	④	⑤
Engines	③	③	④	⑤	④	⑤	⑤	⑤
Exhaust/Converter	❶	❶	③	④	⑤	⑤	⑤	⑤
Fuel system	❷	❷	❷	③	③	③	③	④
Ignition system	③	④	④	④	③	④	④	④
Manual transmission	③	④	④	④	⑤	⑤	④	⑤
— automatic	❷	❷	③	③	④	⑤	④	④
Rust/Paint	③	④	④	④	⑤	⑤	⑤	⑤
Steering	❷	③	④	④	④	⑤	⑤	⑤
Suspension	③	④	④	④	④	⑤	⑤	⑤
Dealer Service	③	③	③	③	④	④	④	④
Maintenance	③	③	③	③	③	③	③	③
Parts Availability	③	③	④	④	④	④	④	④
Repair Costs	③	③	③	③	③	③	③	③
Crash Safety	❶	❶	❶	❶	❶	⑤	⑤	⑤

HONDA

Civic, CRX, del Sol

Rating: Recommended (1993-94); Above Average (1992); Average (1989-91); Below Average buy (1987-88). Can a consumer advocate, sued for liable by Honda for $700,000 in the early 1980s after calling Civics rust heaps with biodegradable engines, still find something nice to say about the company's cars? Sure he can, especially because the Honda lawsuit was tossed out of court and the company improved its cars markedly afterwards.

Price analysis: CRXs are a sportier version of the Civic equipped with a more refined 1.5L and 1.6L engine and stiffer suspension. Fair availability, but prices for recent CRXs are relatively high because the cars are somewhat rare and owners want to recoup what they originally overpaid. Expect to pay about $500 annually for maintenance and repairs. To avoid costly engine repairs, owners must check the engine timing belt every 2 years/40,000 km and replace it every 96,000 km ($300). Other small cars worth considering: Chrysler Colt • Ford Escort/Tracer '91 and later) • Geo Metro and Storm • Mazda GLC or 323 • Nissan Sentra • Suzuki Forsa • Toyota Corolla. The Toyota MR2 rivals the CRX.

Technical Data

ENGINES	Litres/CID	HP	MPG	Model Years
OHC I-4 3 bbl.	1.3/81	60	33-37	1985-87
OHC I-4 3 bbl.	1.5/91	76	27-31	1985-87
OHC I-4 FI	1.5/91	91	28-32	1986-87
OHC I-4 FI	1.5/91	70	32-36	1988-91
OHC I-4 FI	1.5/91	92	28-33	1988-91
OHC I-4 FI	1.6/91	105-108	25-31	1988-91
OHC I-4 FI	1.5/91	70	34-38	1992-95
OHC I-4 FI	1.5/91	92	39-45	1992-95
OHC I-4 FI	1.5/91	102	29-35	1992-95
OHC I-4 FI	1.6/97	125	26-33	1992-95
CRX				
OHC I-4 3 bbl.	1.5/91	58	33-37	1985-87
OHC I-4 3 bbl.	1.5/91	76	27-32	1985-87
OHC I-4 FI	1.5/91	91	36-31	1985-87
OHC I-4 FI	1.5/91	62	37-45	1988-91
OHC I-4 FI	1.5/91	92	29-35	1988-91
OHC I-4 FI	1.6/97	105-108	25-31	1988-91
del Sol				
OHC I-4 FI	1.5/91	102	28-34	1993-95
OHC I-4 FI	1.6/97	125	26-31	1993-95
DOHC VTEC	1.6/97	160	23-27	1994-95

Strengths and weaknesses: The quintessential econobox, Honda Civics have distinguished themselves by providing sports car acceleration and handling with excellent fuel economy and quality control that is better than what American automakers could deliver at the time. CRXs give improved handling at the expense of fuel economy, interior space and a comfortable ride. They also require valve adjustments every 30,000 km. 1984-87 Civics suffer from failing camshafts and prematurely worn piston rings. The 12-valve engine is prone to valve problems and is costly to repair. Early fuel-injection units were also problematic until the system was redesigned in 1988. Manual transmission shifter bushings need frequent replacement, and the automatic version needs careful attention once the 5 year/ 80,000 km point has been reached.

Until 1988, Honda had the market all to itself; then it began enlarging the overall package, making its cars larger and heavier and pricing them aggressively to the point where the company started losing market share to Mazda, Nissan, Suzuki and Toyota. The 1988 redesign improved handling and increased interior room. There isn't a great deal of torque with the 1.6L engine below 3500 rpm, however, and serious generic problems present since the car's debut still continue to plague the later models. First of all, the front brakes continue to wear out quickly and are often noisy when applied causing excessive steering wheel vibration. Premature constant velocity joint and boot wear on all cars is another problem area that needs careful inspection before purchasing. The rack and pinion steering assembly often needs replacement around the five-year mark. There have also been reports of premature clutch wear with 4X4 Civics. Owners of the '93 Civic DX report that shifting into reverse requires shifting into 2nd gear first. Air conditioner condensers frequently fail after a few years. Honda will pick up the approximate $300 cost if you threaten to take the company to court.

A large number of 1988-91 Honda Civics and CRXs have faulty distributor igniters. When the igniter fails, the car stalls, and it may be impossible to restart. The only remedy is to call a tow truck and replace the distributor. Honda will pay for the igniter replacement and all other expenses associated with the towing up to 5 years/80,000 km. This "updated warranty" covers used Hondas and provides retroactive compensation to owners who have paid for the repair even if an independent garage replaced the part. Claims accompanied by receipts will be judged on a case-by-case basis. Owners refused compensation should take their claim to small claims court.

Older Civics are prone to rusting out; simple surface rust rapidly turns into perforations. The underbody is also prone to severe structural damage caused by corrosion that compromises safety; the fuel tank, front suspension and steering components, along with body attachment points, should be examined carefully. If the fuel tank is affected, Honda will replace it without charge if you enlist Transport Canada's help. Since 1988, Hondas are much more resistant to rusting and overall body construction has been vastly improved. All hatchbacks let in too much wind/road noise due to poor sound insulation, and owners complain of water leaking into the trunk area through the rear taillights on the 1990 DX four-door sedan. The two-piece tailgate is a paradise for rattles and is complicated without any reason to be. Metallic paint problems.

Confidential dealer service bulletins show the following problems on the 1993s: excessive steering wheel vibrations, faulty temperature control lever, CD magazine changer in trunk won't eject, water leaks into the footwell, a sticking fuel filler door and noisy window regulators.

On the '94s, the main problem areas are harsh or delayed automatic transmission shifting, excessive steering wheel vibration, a faulty temperature control lever and a sticking fuel filler door.

The 16-valve engine's complexity means dealer servicing is a must. According to the Canadian Automobile Association, parts are a bit more expensive than most other cars in this class.

Safety summary/recalls: The latest crash test of a '95 four-door Civic sedan found the driver and passenger would receive average protection. Owners report that leaky fuel pumps may cause a fire on 1984-85 models.

Optional dual airbags appeared on the 1993 EX. Standard ABS with the 1992 EX and Si. *Recalls*: **1992-94**-The automatic transmission's shift lever position may not match the actual gear that's engaged. **1994**-Passenger-side airbag module may carry a defective inflator.

Secret Warranties/Service Tips/DSBs

Civic/CRX/del Sol

1988-90-A grinding starter motor may have an overrunning clutch assembly. Upgraded assembly (#31207-PM5-LO1, H/C 3690963) available under a "goodwill" program.

• Excessive valve noise will be corrected with a cam holder kit (#04101-PM3-308) provided under a July 7, 1989 "goodwill" program.

• Dashboard cracks at the center bolt hole may be fixed for free under a "goodwill" program.

1988-91-Faulty distributor igniters will be replaced free under a product update program (see *Strengths and weaknesses*).

• New front brake pads that minimize front brake squeal are available for all Civic and CRX models. The pad set is listed under part number #45022-SH3-G11.

• A clicking noise heard while making a left or right turn may be caused by a worn outboard driveshaft joint. It may be repaired for free under a "goodwill" program.

1988-93-A creaking noise coming from the window regulator can be corrected by installing an upgraded regulator spiral spring.

1989-91-An occasional rough idle on cars equipped with an automatic transmission may be caused by inadequate grounding of the throttle angle sensor circuit. Replace the existing ground wire with a revised ground harness (#32105-PM5-315 and H/C 3976487).

• An oil leak around the spark plug well will be corrected with a cam holder kit (#04101-PM3-308) eligible under Honda's "goodwill" program.

• Excessive wear on the inside edge of the front tires is likely due to the front toe being out of adjustment.

1990-Front windshield will be replaced at no charge under a safety recall campaign.

• Front lapbelts that retract too slowly will be fixed for free under Honda's lifetime seatbelt warranty.

• If the horn sounds by itself when the temperature drops, Honda will correct the problem under a "goodwill" program.

1992-A growling noise coming from the wheel area may mean that water has entered the wheel bearing through the hubcap and damaged the bearing. Replacement may be covered under a "goodwill" arrangement.

• A steering wheel shake or body vibration when braking may indicate the rear brake drum hub is crowned, causing excessive runout when the wheel nuts are torqued. Other factors could be a bent rear wheel, overtorqued wheel nuts or excessive rust buildup on the brake rotors.

1992-93-Water leaking into the footwell from under the corner of the dash can be stopped by applying sealer to the seam where the side panel joins the bulkhead
• An abnormally long crank time before the car starts may be caused by a leaking check valve inside the fuel pump.
1993-Poor AM reception or a popping from the speakers is likely due to a poor ground connection between the antenna collar and car body.
1993 Civic del Sol-The automatic transmission's shift lever position may not match the actual gear that's engaged. Dealers will install a new retaining clip.
All models/years-Most Honda DSBs allow for special warranty consideration on a "goodwill" basis even after the warranty has expired or the car has changed hands. Referring to this euphemism will increase your chances of getting some kind of refund for repairs that are obviously related to a factory defect. In small claims court, showing Honda's actual dealer service bulletin will be helpful in getting a negotiated settlement or favorable judgment.
• Honda will repair or replace defective steering assemblies, constant velocity joints and catalytic converters free of charge up to 5 years/ 80,000 km on a case-by-case basis. There is no labor charge or deductible. Used vehicles and repairs carried out by independent garages are not covered by this special program. The converter, however, an emissions component, is almost always automatically covered under the emissions warranty. Seatbelts that fail to function properly during normal use will be replaced for free under Honda's lifetime seatbelt warranty.

Vehicle Profile

	1987	1988	1989	1990	1991	1992	1993	1994
Cost Price ($)								
Civic	7695	8995	8995	9295	8355	9112	10,395	10,595
CRX/del Sol	11,235	12,995	13,895	14,395	12,980	—	16,795	18,595
Si	13,435	14,445	15,695	16,295	14,705	13,320	14,995	16,595
Used Values ($)								
Civic ↑	2400	3100	3600	4300	4900	6000	7000	7700
Civic ↓	1700	2200	2700	3300	4000	5000	6000	6600
CRX/del Sol ↑	4000	5000	6000	7100	7900	—	11,000	12,500
CRX/del Sol ↓	3200	4200	5200	6100	6900	—	9500	11,000
Si ↑	5500	7000	8000	8500	9100	9500	10,500	12,000
Si ↓	4500	6000	6800	7300	7700	8300	9500	11,000
Reliability	②	②	③	③	③	④	⑤	⑤
Air conditioning	①	②	②	③	③	④	④	⑤
Body integrity	①	①	③	③	③	③	③	③
Braking system	②	②	②	②	③	③	④	⑤
Electrical system	②	②	②	②	③	④	④	④

Engines	③	③	③	④	⑤	⑤	⑤	⑤
Exhaust/Converter	❶	❷	❷	❷	③	④	⑤	⑤
Fuel system	❷	❷	③	④	④	④	④	⑤
Ignition system	❷	❷	❷	❷	❷	④	④	④
Manual transmission	③	③	③	③	③	④	④	⑤
— automatic	③	③	③	③	③	④	⑤	⑤
Rust/Paint	❷	❷	③	③	③	⑤	⑤	⑤
Steering	③	③	③	③	④	④	④	④
Suspension	③	③	③	③	④	④	④	④
Dealer Service	⑤	⑤	⑤	⑤	⑤	⑤	⑤	⑤
Maintenance	③	③	③	③	③	⑤	⑤	⑤
Parts Availability	③	③	③	③	③	⑤	⑤	⑤
Repair Costs	③	③	③	③	③	④	⑤	⑤
Crash Safety								
Civic 2-door	⑤	⑤	⑤	⑤	⑤	⑤	⑤	⑤
Civic 4-door	❶	❶	❶	❶	❷	❷	❷	❷
CRX	❶	❶	⑤	⑤	⑤	⑤	—	—
del Sol	—	—	—	—	—	—	—	—
Safety Features								
ABS	—	—	—	—	—	S	S	S
Airbag	—	—	—	—	—	D	D	D/P

HYUNDAI

Excel

Rating: Average (1992-94); Below Average (1988-91); Not Recommended (1987). Replaced by the 1995 Accent. The post-'89 models perform better, but poor quality control and servicing are major handicaps. Don't be taken in by the dirt-cheap prices of early models.

Price analysis: Essentially a Mitsubishi Precis (only sold in the U.S. until late 1993), lots of Excels are on the market but they are generally in poor shape. Interestingly, an '87 model should be less expensive than an '86, just as a '91 is only a bit more expensive than a '90. Expect to pay about $700 annually for maintenance and repairs. To avoid costly engine repairs, check the engine timing belt every 2 years/40,000 km and replace it every 96,000 km ($250). Other small cars worth considering: Chrysler Colt • Ford Escort/Tracer ('91 and later) • Geo Metro and Storm • Honda Civic • Mazda GLC and 323 • Nissan Sentra.

116

Technical Data

ENGINES	Litres/CID	HP	MPG	Model Years
OHC I-4 2 bbl.	1.5/90	68	26-31	1986-89
OHC I-4 FI	1.5/90	81	28-33	1990-94

Strengths and weaknesses: An attractive Korean import that has been marred by quality-control problems and a limited dealer network. Resale prices are low, but these cars are no bargain in the long run. Although overall comfort and handling are passable, the engine is distinctly short on power, and the carburetor provides uneven throttle response, especially when the car is cold, leading to difficult starts. Poor interior ventilation, with chronic window fogging and poor defrosting, is particularly irritating.

On early models, likely problem areas are defective constant velocity joints, water pumps, a leaking head gasket, oil pan gaskets, oil pressure switches, front struts, and heat exchange under dash. Excels made after 1989 are noted for noisy automatic transmissions and engines that fail to start when the weather turns cold or wet. Other problem areas are faulty radiator hoses, alternators, Hyundai radios and wiper motors. Owners have also complained of premature brake wear and temperamental carburetors, electrical problems, poor engine performance, and premature rusting due to poor-quality body parts and paint. Body construction is sloppy, giving rise to wind/water leaks, rattles and breakage. Mufflers last a little over two years.

Confidential dealer service bulletins show the following problems on the 1993s: harsh shifting with the automatic transmission when accelerating or coming to a stop, excessive disc brake noise, engine has difficulty reaching recommended operating temperature (MPI fault code #21), low fuel pressure and wheel cover discoloration. The 1994s have fewer problems reported, but this may be mainly due to the little time they've been in use.

Safety summary/recalls: 1986-89-Excels may have heater core coolant leaks that may cause noxious fumes to enter the passenger compartment according to the NHTSA. *Recalls:* 1986-A defective brake pedal cotter pin may affect braking. 1986-87-Excessive brake fade can be improved by installing upgraded metallic pads. 1986-89-Erratic cruise control operation. Malfunctioning emission control system could cause an engine compartment fire. Insufficient gear lubrication could cause drive wheels to lock. 1988-89-Defective heater stem assembly could allow hot coolant leakage. 1990-Front wheel hub nut lockwasher could crack, allowing too much wheel-bearing free play causing a loss of vehicle control. 1990-94-In frontal crashes, excessive fuel spillage could pose a fire hazard. Dealer will install a spring seat protector. 1994-A short-circuit in the crank-angle sensor could cause sudden stalling.

Secret Warranties/Service Tips/DSBs

1985-86-If the trunk lid won't stay open, add a pair of torsion bar spacers.

1986-88-A faulty fusible link wiring circuit is the likely cause of chronic voltage drop and a discharged battery.

1990-A 5th gear noise can be eliminated by replacing the 3rd and 4th shift forks, synchronizer hub and sleeve.

• Cranking with no spark may be due to a defective noise filter located between the ignition coil and tachometer.

1990-94-A manual transmission that clashes or grinds when shifting from 2nd to 3rd may need a field fix.

1991-Stalling when shifting into gear immediately after starting a cold engine may be corrected by installing a Cold Start Enrichment Kit (#39901-24Q00D).

Vehicle Profile

	1987	1988	1989	1990	1991	1992	1993	1994
Cost Price ($)								
Base	6795	7295	7695	8095	7595	7975	7995	8495
Used Values ($)								
Base ↑	1300	1800	2300	2800	3400	4200	4900	6600
Base ↓	600	900	1500	2000	2500	3200	3900	5500
Reliability	1	2	2	2	2	3	3	3
Air conditioning	1	2	2	2	3	3	3	4
Body integrity	1	2	2	2	2	2	2	2
Braking system	1	2	2	2	2	2	2	2
Electrical system	1	2	2	2	2	2	2	2
Engines	2	2	3	3	3	3	3	3
Exhaust/Converter	3	3	3	3	3	3	3	3
Fuel system	2	2	2	2	3	3	3	3
Ignition system	2	2	2	2	3	3	3	3
Manual transmission	2	2	2	2	2	2	2	2
- automatic	2	2	3	3	3	4	4	4
Rust/Paint	1	2	2	2	2	2	3	3
Steering	2	3	3	3	4	3	4	4
Suspension	2	3	3	3	3	3	3	3
Dealer Service	3	3	3	3	3	3	3	3
Maintenance	2	3	3	3	3	3	3	3
Parts Availability	4	4	4	4	4	4	4	4
Repair Costs	3	3	3	3	3	3	3	3
Crash Safety	2	2	2	1	5	5	5	5

LADA

| Sagona, Samara, Signet |

Rating: Average buy (1993-94); Below Average (1989-92); Not Recommended (1987-88). Not back to the future, but forward to the past: low-tech components (the only car that still uses a carburetor) make for poor reliability but easy, low-cost maintenance — if you are mechanically inclined and can get the parts.

Price analysis: Average availability. Expect to pay about $700 annually for maintenance and repairs if you don't do your own repairs and maintenance or refused an extended warranty. Other small cars worth considering: Chrysler Colt • Geo Metro • Honda Civic • Mazda GLC and 323 • Nissan Sentra Classic.

Strengths and weaknesses: Ladas incorporate a 20-year-old rear-wheel-drive design and use poor-quality body and mechanical components. They are noisy and truck-like on the road. Interestingly, for a car developed in Russia, the Lada is a poor cold weather performer. The dealer network is sparse, and parts are hard to get.

One would expect Ladas to have improved over the years, particularly since the 1987 introduction of the Samara and, later on, the (sporty?) Sagona, but owners of early Ladas swear (something Lada owners do a lot of) that their cars' original problems are nothing compared to the defects present in the 1987-92 versions. It goes without saying that the gap between Lada and, say, a Ford Festiva or Chrysler Colt—both reliable and durable entry-level vehicles—is considerable.

Defective fuel and ignition systems (particularly the ignition control module) and a poorly designed electrical system are the most common problems. Frequent carburetor replacements at $325 plus tax are rendered necessary due to the butterfly shaft warping or corroding because of an inherently defective design. Front brakes need to be replaced often, and transmissions, engine head gaskets, and differentials are not durable, either. Rear window defogger wires corrode easily. Be wary of gas mileage claims. Owners report getting 12 to 15 mpg with the 1500S Signet. Body hardware is extremely fragile and hard to find at reasonable prices. Ladas are poorly rustproofed and paint quality is bad, which translates into rapid surface rusting and sheet metal perforation.

Technical Data

ENGINES	Litres/CID	HP	MPG	Model Years
OHC I-4 2 bbl.	1.3/78	60-65	25-31	1988-95
OHC I-4 2 bbl.	1.5/90	75-83	25-31	1988-95

Safety summary/recalls: These cars have never been crash tested by the U.S. or Canadian governments. *Recalls*: **1986-87**-Signet wagons may have a loose vent hose on the fuel filler pipe. **1988**-Samara models will have the seatbelt buzzer replaced, the headlamp wiper arm adjusted, bumper braces installed and a tab installed to prevent the clutch cable from coming loose. **1988-89**-The emergency brake handle needs to be modified to reduce braking effort. **1988-90**-The glove box latch will be replaced. **1992-93**-Child restraint tether anchorages may not meet Canadian regulations.

Secret Warranties/Service Tips/DSBs: No information available.

Vehicle Profile

	1987	1988	1989	1990	1991	1992	1993	1994
Cost Price ($)								
Signet	4995	7595	7595	7524	7824	—	6980	—
Samara	5995	6495	6995	6954	7235	—	5895	5995
Sagona	—	—	—	—	—	—	—	9295
Used Values ($)								
Signet ↑	800	1500	2300	2700	3300	—	3900	—
Signet ↓	500	900	1300	1800	2400	—	3000	—
Samara ↑	1200	1800	2100	2500	2900	—	3500	4300
Samara ↓	800	1000	1200	1400	1900	—	2800	3500
Sagona ↑	—	—	—	—	—	—	—	6500
Sagona ↓	—	—	—	—	—	—	—	5800
Reliability	①	①	②	②	②	—	③	③
Air conditioning	—	—	—	—	—	—	—	—
Body integrity	①	①	①	①	①	—	③	③
Braking system	①	①	①	①	②	—	③	③
Electrical system	①	①	①	①	①	—	③	③
Engines	②	②	③	③	③	—	③	③
Exhaust/Converter	①	①	①	③	③	—	③	③
Fuel system	①	①	①	①	③	—	③	③
Ignition system	①	①	①	①	②	—	③	③
Manual transmission	③	③	③	③	③	—	③	③
— automatic	②	②	③	③	③	—	③	③
Rust/Paint	①	②	②	②	③	—	③	③
Steering	①	①	③	③	③	—	③	③
Suspension	③	③	③	③	③	—	③	③
Dealer Service	①	①	①	①	①	—	①	①
Maintenance	②	②	②	②	②	—	②	②
Parts Availability	①	①	①	①	①	—	①	①
Repair Costs	①	①	①	①	①	—	③	④
Crash Safety	—	—	—	—	—	—	—	—

MAZDA

323, GLC, Protegé

Rating: Above Average buy (1991-94); Average buy (1987-90).

Price analysis: The 323 is a good small car with a few weaknesses. It is expensive to buy new, which is reflected in high used car prices. Nevertheless, used 323s are priced about $300 less than Escorts and Tracers. Expect to pay about $300 annually for maintenance and repairs. To avoid costly engine repairs, check the engine timing belt every 2 years/40,000 km and replace it every 96,000 km ($250). If you can't find a reasonably priced 323, look for a Mercury Tracer instead— it's a 323 disguised as a Ford. Parts are more expensive than average. Other small cars worth considering: Chrysler Colt • Ford Escort/ Tracer ('91 and later) • GM Firefly/Sprint and Saturn • Nissan Sentra • Suzuki Forsa.

Technical Data

ENGINES	Litres/CID	HP	MPG	Model Years
OHC I-4 FI	1.6/97	82	24-33	1986-94
DOHC I-4T FI	1.6/97	132	19-23	1988-89
OHC I-4 FI	1.8/112	103	24-31	1990-94
DOHC I-4 FI	1.8/112	125	25-28	1990-94

Strengths and weaknesses: The GLC is a peppy performer with a manual transmission hooked to its 1.5L 68-hp base engine. The automatic gearbox produces lethargic acceleration. Handling and fuel economy are fairly good for a car design this old. However, overall durability is not as good as more recent Mazda designs. Retail prices are a bit lower than average, but parts costs are fairly high and parts are relatively rare. Catalytic converters plug up easily and other pollution-control components have been troublesome. Automatic transmission defects, air-conditioner breakdowns and engine oil leaks are also commonplace. Oil leaks in the power steering pump may also be a problem. GLCs rust quickly, especially the rocker panels, door bottoms, the hood and rear hatch. A careful corrosion inspection is a must.

The 323 is longer and heavier than the GLC it replaced. 323s beat the GLC in quality, road performance, roominess and overall value for money spent. The fuel-injected 1.6L engine is a better performer than the 1.5L, but you also get excessive engine and exhaust noise. Stay away from the 3-speed automatic transmission. The car's small engine can't handle the extra burden without cutting fuel economy and performance. Both models are surprisingly roomy, but the Protegé's trunk is surprisingly small for a sedan.

The 1985-89 models offer mediocre reliability. Owners report hard starting in cold weather in addition to automatic transmission problems and electrical-system failures. The engine camshaft assembly and belt pulley often need replacing around 80,000 km. Clutch failure and exhaust-system rust-out are also common. Other areas of concern are constant velocity joint failures, rack and pinion steering wear-out and front brake wear. The front brakes wear quickly due to poor-quality brake pads and seizure of the calipers in their housings. Check for disc scoring on the front brakes. Stay away from models equipped with a turbocharger. Few mechanics want to bother repairing it or hunting for parts. Many reports of premature paint peeling. The Protegé has fared better, but that may be due to its relative short time on the market.

The 1990-93 models are *la crème de la crème*. Nevertheless, owners report problems with weak rear defrosting, rough 2nd gear engagement, engine stalling, a noisy suspension, AC failures, and numerous body defects including wind and water leaks into the interior, paint defects, and power mirror failures. Owners of 1994 models report prematurely worn front brakes, MacPherson struts, and rear shock absorbers, noisy timing chain, clutch squealing, and an off-center steering wheel. Poor fit and paint defects remain a problem.

Safety summary/recalls: Owners report gas tank rust-out on the 1988 models and sudden wheel-bearing failures. ABS and airbags are not available. *Recalls*: **1992-93**-Protegé may not meet regulations relative to child restraint tether anchorages.

Secret Warranties/Service Tips/DSBs

GLC-All models/years-GLCs have MacPherson strut suspensions that use an expensive sealed shock absorber assembly. Canadian Tire prices are much lower.
323, Protegé
1986-Hard starts after long drives may be due to a defective main relay. Install an upgraded moisture-proof relay.
1986-87-Hard starting/rough idle may be due to a corroded solenoid resistor. Put in an upgraded resistor (#E5D318831B).
1986-88-Rear coil spring noise can be fixed by putting in a new spring rubber sheet (#B092280A3).
1990-Cold weather stalling usually requires the replacement of the ECU under the emissions warranty.
• To prevent water damage to the door speakers, order a speaker cover set (#B4Y57696X).
1990-91-Rough idle or vibration in drive may require changing the No. 1 and No. 4 engine mounts and the radiator lower mounts.
1990-92-Noise coming from the front of the car when turning may be due to dirt accumulation in the top strut mount bushing causing

excessive friction. Correct by installing upgraded strut bushings that have a groove to keep dirt from entering the sliding surface.

1990-94-Clutch squealing fixed by installing an upgraded clutch cushioning plate; three-year warranty coverage.

Vehicle Profile

	1987	1988	1989	1990	1991	1992	1993	1994
Cost Price ($)								
323	8150	8640	8940	9650	8845	9250	9435	9965
Protegé	—	—	—	12,260	11,655	12,425	12,675	13,265
Used Values ($)								
323 ↑	1800	2700	3300	4100	4500	5300	6200	7500
323 ↓	1200	1900	2500	3200	3600	4400	5200	6600
Protegé ↑	—	—	—	5900	6500	7500	8500	9700
Protegé ↓	—	—	—	4900	5500	6300	7500	8800
Reliability	③	③	③	③	④	④	④	⑤
Air conditioning	②	③	③	③	④	⑤	⑤	⑤
Body integrity	③	③	③	③	③	③	③	④
Braking system	②	②	②	②	③	③	③	③
Electrical system	③	③	③	③	③	③	④	④
Engines	③	③	③	③	③	④	③	④
Exhaust/Converter	②	②	②	③	③	③	⑤	⑤
Fuel system	③	③	③	③	④	④	⑤	⑤
Ignition system	④	④	④	④	④	④	④	⑤
Manual transmission	④	④	④	④	④	④	④	⑤
— automatic	③	②	②	③	③	④	⑤	⑤
Rust/Paint	②	②	②	②	③	③	③	③
Steering	②	③	③	③	④	④	④	④
Suspension	③	③	③	③	③	③	③	③
Dealer Service	④	④	④	④	⑤	⑤	⑤	⑤
Maintenance	④	④	④	④	④	④	④	④
Parts Availability	②	③	③	③	③	③	③	③
Repair Costs	③	③	③	③	③	③	④	④
Crash Safety								
323	②	②	②	②	②	②	②	②
Protegé	—	—	—	—	⑤	⑤	⑤	⑤

NISSAN/DATSUN

Altima

Rating: Above Average buy (1993-94).

Price analysis: Going into its fourth year on the market, there are few used Altimas available and they are priced unreasonably high. To keep costs down, try to get a car with Nissan's comprehensive standard warranty still in effect. Expect to pay about $300 annually for maintenance and repairs. Look for an Altima with an automatic transmission; the manual is imprecise and not refined enough for pleasurable shifting. Also, a V6 is a prerequisite for the same versatility as the competition coming from the Toyota Camry, Mazda 626 Cronos, the updated Ford Probe or the larger Ford Taurus and Sable.

Strengths and weaknesses: The wheelbase is a couple of inches longer than the Stanza's, and the car is touted by Nissan as a mid-size, but the Altima's interior dimensions put it in the compact league. The small cabin only seats four, and rear seat access is difficult to master due to the slanted roof pillars, inward-curving door frames and narrow clearance.

The base engine gives average acceleration and fuel economy. Good maneuverability around town. No reliability problems reported with the 16-valve powerplant or transmissions. Uncluttered underhood layout makes servicing easy. Parts are easily found from independent suppliers at discount prices. Good body assembly.

Noisy and rough engine performance; this car cries out for a V6 like the one used in the Maxima. The 4-banger has insufficient top-end torque and gets buzzier the more it's pushed. In order to get the automatic to downshift for passing, for example, one has to practically stomp on the accelerator. The 5-speed manual transmission is sloppy. The Altima's sporty handling is way overrated; there's excessive body roll and front-end plow in hard cornering, tires squeal at moderate speeds, and steering is not as precise or responsive as befits a car with performance pretensions. In spite of the car's independent suspension, it gives a busy, uncomfortable ride that is punishing over bumps. Lots of engine, road and tire noise.

Nissan service bulletins show that some 1993s may have a creaking, squeaking or tapping noise coming from the window and door areas; water leaks; electrical system, heater, air-conditioning and defrosting malfunctions; and body/trim deficiencies. 1993-94 bulletin-disclosed problems: no Reverse (automatic), excessive brake and steering wheel vibration, inaccurate fuel gauges and rear suspension noise.

Owners complain of parts shortages and the Canadian Automobile Association reports that parts are more expensive than parts for most other cars in this class.

Technical Data

ENGINES	Litres/CID	HP	MPG	Model Years
DOHC I-4 F	I2.4/146	150	21-26	1993-95

Safety summary/recalls: There have been 53 incidents reported relative to the motorized seatbelt retractors locking up. The U.S. government is investigating. *Recalls*: **1993-94**-Throttle cable may not return to idle.

Secret Warranties/Service Tips/DSBs

1993-Center caps on alloy wheels may not fit properly. Nissan will install upgraded caps (#40315-D9000) under a "goodwill" program.
• A peeling door trim panel is common on cars made during February and March 1993. Correction requires the reapplication of a factory approved adhesive.
• Door and window squeaks can be usually traced to rubber moldings and seals rubbing against metal or glass or other rubber parts. To troubleshoot this type of noise, place a piece of paper between the rubber and other surface where the noise appears to be coming from and road test the vehicle. If the noise goes away, clean the rubber in this area and lubricate by rubbing in a silicone gel lubricant.
• An exhaust rattle during acceleration can be resolved by replacing the pre-muffler assembly with an upgraded muffler assembly-exhaust (#203000-IE860).
• Inadequate defrosting on vehicles made before February '93 can be resolved by carrying out the modifications suggested by Nissan in its NTB93-059 bulletin.
• NTB93-086 is a lengthy Nissan bulletin sent out May 25, 1993 that troubleshoots the Altima's most common water leaks into the interior.
• Poor AC performance is likely caused by the evaporator core freezing the moisture in the air flowing past it. Installing a countermeasure thermal control unit (TCU) will remedy the problem.
• An inoperative AC and heater may have a kinked heater/water valve cable that has damaged the air mix door actuator.
1993-94-No Reverse gear with the manual transmission—install upgrade kit shown on page 125.
• Inaccurate fuel gauge or difficulty in filling fuel tank fixed with upgraded parts.
• Rear suspension rattles or squeaking is likely due to loose suspension mounting nuts.

SERVICE INFORMATION:
Some of the above-referenced vehicles may not engage reverse gear when the selector lever is placed into "R". CONSULT may not detect any malfunction(s). There are no external ATF leaks. The ATF is at the correct level, but is burned.

REPAIR INFORMATION:
Replace the Control Valve Assembly and the Low & Reverse Brake Parts (Dished Plate, Piston, and Retainer), together (as a set), to resolve this incident. Refer to the "AT" Section of the appropriate Service Manual for information concerning disassembly/assembly operations.

CAUTION:
Replacement of the Control Valve Assembly, without changing the Low & Reverse Brake Parts, will cause a secondary incident of N -> R shock.

DESCRIPTION	PART #		
	Altima (U13)	Quest (V40)	Maxima SE(J30)
Control Valve Ass'y.	31705-80X65	31705-80X66	31705-80X68
Low & Reverse Brake Dished Plate	31665-80X02	31665-80X02	31665-80X02
Low & Reverse Brake Piston	31645-80X02	31645-80X02	31645-80X02
Low & Reverse Brake Piston Retainer	31642-80X01	31642-80X01	31642-80X01

Vehicle Profile

	1993	1994
Cost Price ($)		
XE	16,491	17,690
GXE	18,690	19,990
SE	21,190	22,490
Used Values ($)		
XE ↑	13,000	14,500
XE ↓	11,500	13,200
GXE ↑	14,000	16,000
GXE ↓	12,700	14,500
SE ↑	15,800	18,300
SE ↓	14,000	16,800
Reliability	④	④
Air conditioning	③	④
Manual transmission	③	③
Automatic transmission	④	④
Body integrity	③	③
Braking system	③	③
Electrical system	③	④
Engines	④	⑤
Exhaust/Converter	⑤	⑤
Fuel system	③	④
Ignition system	⑤	⑤
Rust/Paint	④	⑤
Steering	③	③
Suspension	③	③
Dealer Service	⑤	⑤
Maintenance	⑤	⑤

Parts Availability	⑤	⑤
Repair Costs	④	④
Crash Safety	⑤	⑤
Safety Features		
ABS	O	O
Airbag	D	D/P

Classic, Sentra

Rating: Recommended (1991-94); Average buy (1988-90); Not Recommended (1987).

Price analysis: Excellent availability. Used prices are exceptionally reasonable, particularly with the Classic entry-level version first offered in 1991. Expect to pay about $300 annually for maintenance and repairs. Other cars worth considering: Chrysler Colt • Ford Escort/Tracer ('91 and later) • Honda Civic and CRX • Mazda 323 and Protegé • Toyota Corolla.

Technical Data

ENGINES	Litres/CID	HP	MPG	Model Years
DOHC I-4D FI	1.7/103	55	32-37	1985
OHC I-4 2 bbl.	1.6/97	69	27-31	1985-86
OHC I-4 2 bbl.	1.6/97	70	26-31	1987
OHC I-4 FI	1.6/97	69	26-32	1987-88
OHC I-4 FI	1.6/97	90	26-31	1989-90
DOHC I-4 FI	1.6/97	110	27-32	1991-94
DOHC I-4 FI	2.0/122	140	23-27	1991-94

Strengths and weaknesses: Most of what ails the Pulsar (see below) ails the Sentra as well, although to a lesser extent because they are the same vehicle except for sheet metal variations. Sentras are not expensive, but maintenance costs on 1983-87 models can wipe out any savings on the purchase price. Until the 1988 models came on stream, the mechanical and body components suffered from poor quality control, making these cars quite unreliable although not that expensive to repair. The 1.5L engine is a disaster with biodegradable valves and head gaskets. A weak starter and ring gear is a common failing. Carburetors were a problem through 1985. Clutches and exhaust systems don't last long. The 1.6L engine is much more reliable, but even there the oil pressure switch may develop a leak that can lead to sudden oil loss and serious engine damage. After 1987, quality improved considerably, yet the vehicle's base price rose only marginally, making it an excellent new or used car buy.

1988-93 Sentras are improved in every respect although they do have their deficiencies, too. Owners report faulty fuel tanks, leaking manual and automatic transmissions, a persistent rotten egg smell, and noisy engine timing chains and front brakes. With the exception of the carburetor and electronic component failures, repairs are relatively simple to perform and parts are relatively easy to find on models made after 1987. The 1993 Sentras that experience hard starts, stalling or poor engine performance may have a faulty alternator. Some manual transmission problems. The '94 models have brake/ steering wheel vibrations, and clutch and exhaust system problems.

Safety summary/recalls: *Recalls:* **1987-88**-Cracked fuel tanks. **1990-91**-Fraying of the front shoulder belts may lead to improper retraction and inadequate protection. **1991-92**-Valve vacuum hose may come loose.

Secret Warranties/Service Tips/DSBs

1982-88-Improved brake pad material will cut brake noise and add to pad durability. Upgraded semi-metallic pads carry the Hitachi HP12 FE designation.
1987-A door hinge popping noise requires upgraded hinge pins (#8040601L02).
1987-88-Insufficient alternator output causing dead batteries can be fixed by installing a 70-amp alternator (#2310-70A0).
• To improve defrosting, install an upgraded center defroster duct (#2780084M00).
1987-90-Manual transmission fluid leaks likely due to insufficient case bolt torque. Install upgraded bolts.
1989-Under the emissions warranty, Nissan will install a free AIV case assembly if the exhaust smells like rotten eggs. It's worth a fight.
• If the trunk lid is hard to close or latch, install an upgraded latch and a softer weatherstrip.
1991-92-Noisy front brakes can be silenced by installing upgraded, non-asbestos front disk brake pads (#41060-63Y90).
• Timing chain rattle may be caused by insufficient oil in the chain tensioner. Correct by replacing the tensioner with a countermeasure part (#13070-53J03).
1991-93-No Reverse gear with manual transmission — install upgrade kit shown above (see Altima).
1991-94-Stiffer trunk torsion bars will help keep the trunk lid from falling.
1993-94-Brake and steering wheel vibrations likely caused by excessive rotor thickness.
1994-Door hinges may have received inadequate rust protection. Nissan will apply a sealer at no charge.

Vehicle Profile

	1987	1988	1989	1990	1991	1992	1993	1994
Cost Price ($)								
Classic/Sentra	9787	10,288	10,889	11,390	8690	8990	9590	10,990
Used Values ($)								
Classic/Sentra ↑	2300	3000	3600	4700	5300	6300	7500	9000
Classic/Sentra ↓	1800	2200	2700	3900	4300	5100	6500	8300
Reliability	2	3	3	3	4	4	4	5
Air conditioning	2	3	4	5	5	5	5	5
Body integrity	2	3	3	3	3	3	3	4
Braking system	2	2	2	2	2	3	3	3
Electrical system	2	2	3	3	3	3	4	4
Engines	4	4	4	4	4	4	5	5
Exhaust/Converter	2	2	2	2	3	4	5	5
Fuel system	2	2	3	3	2	2	3	3
Ignition system	2	3	3	3	3	3	4	4
Manual transmission	3	3	4	4	4	4	5	5
- automatic	3	3	4	4	4	4	5	5
Rust/Paint	2	3	3	3	3	3	3	4
Steering	3	3	3	3	3	4	4	5
Suspension	3	3	3	3	3	4	4	5
Dealer Service	3	3	3	3	3	3	4	5
Maintenance	2	2	3	3	4	4	5	5
Parts Availability	2	3	3	3	3	3	4	5
Repair Costs	2	2	3	3	3	3	5	5
Crash Safety	2	2	2	2	5	5	5	5
Safety Features								
Airbag	—	—	—	—	—	—	O	D

Micra

Rating: Recommended (1991); Average buy (1985-90). The Micra is primarily a commuter car. Body parts are harder to find than generic mechanical components used in a variety of other Nissan vehicles.

Vehicle Profile

	1985	1986	1987	1988	1989	1990	1991
Cost Price ($)							
Base DLX	6455	6556	7587	7988	8289	8599	7590
Used Values ($)							
Base DLX ↑	800	1200	1700	2100	2500	3200	3800
Base DLX ↓	500	800	1300	1600	1900	2500	3200
Reliability	③	③	③	③	③	③	④
Crash Safety	—	—	—	—	—	—	—

NX, Pulsar

Rating: Above Average buy (1992-94); Average buy (1987-91); Not Recommended (1983-86). Stay away from turbo models.

Price analysis: Limited availability. The reworked 1987 Pulsar's new price jumped $4000 over the previous year's version, reflecting the added features and improved performance. 1991-92 models took the NX name and were originally sold for about $3200 less than the 1990 Pulsar, reflecting the savings incurred when the federal government dropped the manufacturers' tax. Expect to pay about $700 annually for maintenance and repairs. Other cars worth considering: Chrysler Colt • Ford Escort/Tracer ('91 and later) • Geo Metro and Storm • Mazda GLC or 323 • Nissan Sentra • Suzuki Forsa • Toyota Tercel. A Honda CRX or Toyota MR2 are better choices than a Pulsar.

Technical Data

ENGINES	Litres/CID	HP	MPG	Model Years
OHC I-4 2 bbl.	1.6/97	69	27-31	1985-86
OHC I-4 FI	1.6/97	69	25-30	1987-88
OHC I-4 FI	1.6/97	90	24-28	1989-90
DOHC I-4 FI	1.6/97	113	22-26	1987
DOHC I-4 FI	1.8/110	125	21-25	1988-89

Strengths and weaknesses: Early Pulsars were not very sporty cars. In fact, considering their bland styling, they weren't even all show and no go, like the unlamented Pontiac Fiero. A Sentra clone, even the turbo models are not appreciably quicker. The rear seat is such a joke that these coupes should be considered only as two-seaters. For 1983-86 models, overall reliability is poor to very poor for the turbos. As with many other Nissans, the 1987-92 models have shown remarkable performance improvement.

Early Pulsars suffer from premature turbocharger failure, early engine wear and difficult-to-diagnose electrical problems. The engine oil pressure switch often leaks. 1983-86 models also have a host of clutch problems and fuel system glitches caused by faulty electronic modules. Manual and automatic transmissions on 1985-86 models are failure prone. The base 1.6L engine is inadequate for the heavier post-1986 model years. All Sentras built before 1991 are prone to premature front brake pad and disc wear and air conditioners that fail. From 1991 on, the only problems reported concern minor AC malfunctions premature front brake and suspension component wear-out and exhaust systems that don't last very long (two years, tops). Complaints of premature rusting and paint peeling are legion on the 1983-90 models. Parts are slightly more expensive than average and sometimes difficult to obtain.

Safety summary/recalls: Standard airbag only on the XE. *Recalls*: 1987-88-Cracked fuel tank inlet pipe.

Secret Warranties/Service Tips/DSBs

1983-88-Improved brake pad material will cut brake noise and add to pad durability. Upgraded semi-metallic pads carry the Hitachi HP12 FE designation.

1987- Hesitation or surging under load may require an upgraded throttle sensor supplied for free under the emissions warranty.

• A door hinge popping noise requires upgraded hinge pins (#8040601L02).

1987-88-Insufficient alternator output causing repeated dead batteries can be fixed by installing a 70 amp alternator (#2310-70A00R).

• Automatic transmission abrupt shifting may be caused by a poorly adjusted throttle wire.

• To improve defrosting, install an upgraded center defroster duct (#2780084M00).

1987-90-Manual transmission fluid leaks likely due to insufficient case bolt torque. Install upgraded bolts.

1991-93-No Reverse gear with manual transmission; install upgrade kit.

1993-Brake and steering wheel vibrations likely caused by excessive rotor thickness.

• Inaccurate fuel gauge or difficulty in filling fuel tank fixed with upgraded parts.

Vehicle Profile

	1986	1987	1988	1989	1990	1991	1992	1993
Cost Price ($)								
Pulsar/NX	9696	13,887	14,878	15,989	16,990	—	—	—
NX	—	—	—	—	—	13,790	13,990	14,990
Used Values ($)								
Pulsar/NX ↑	2800	3700	4800	5900	6500	—	—	—
Pulsar/NX ↓	2200	2800	3900	4700	5500	—	—	—
NX ↑	—	—	—	—	—	7400	9100	10,300
NX ↓	—	—	—	—	—	6200	7600	9200
Reliability	①	①	③	③	③	③	④	④
Air conditioning	—	③	③	③	③	④	④	⑤
Body integrity	①	①	②	②	②	③	③	③
Braking system	①	①	②	③	③	③	③	④
Electrical system	①	①	②	③	③	③	③	④
Engines	②	②	②	④	④	④	④	⑤
Exhaust/Converter	①	①	①	①	②	③	④	④
Fuel system	①	①	②	②	②	③	④	⑤
Ignition system	②	②	③	③	③	③	④	④
Manual transmission	②	②	②	④	④	④	④	⑤
— automatic	②	②	②	④	④	④	④	⑤
Rust/Paint	①	①	②	②	③	③	④	⑤
Steering	③	③	③	③	③	③	④	⑤
Suspension	③	③	③	③	③	③	④	④
Dealer Service	③	③	③	③	③	③	③	③
Maintenance	①	①	②	③	③	③	④	⑤
Parts Availability	①	①	③	③	③	③	③	④
Repair Costs	②	②	②	③	③	③	④	⑤
Crash Safety	①	①	①	①	①	①	①	①
Safety Features								
Airbag	—	—	—	D	D	D	D	D

PASSPORT/ISUZU

I-Mark, Stylus, Optima

Rating: The I-Mark and Stylus compacts are Acceptable buys; they give a lot of value per dollar. The Optima is Not Recommended; a stylish but overpriced wimp.

Vehicle Profile

	1986	1987	1988	1989	1990	1991	1992
Cost Price ($)							
I-Mark XS	—	—	12,108	12,045	13,037	—	—
Optima	—	—	8750	9054	9415	8656	9522
Stylus	—	—	—	—	—	11,865	11,925
Used Values ($)							
I-Mark XS ↑	—	—	2900	3500	4800	—	—
I-Mark XS ↓	—	—	2100	2500	3800	—	—
Optima ↑	—	—	2000	2500	3000	3500	4300
Optima ↓	—	—	1400	1700	2300	2700	3200
Stylus ↑	—	—	—	—	—	5200	6700
Stylus ↓	—	—	—	—	—	4200	5500
Reliability	❶	❶	❶	❶	❷	❷	③
Crash Safety							
I-Mark	❶	❶	❶	❶	⑤	⑤	—
Stylus	—	—	—	—	—	⑤	⑤

SUBARU

Justy

Rating: Above average (1994); Average buy (1991-93); Not Recommended (1988-90).

Price analysis: Average availability and reasonably priced. Although it's hard to believe, the 1992 Justy's suggested retail price was $2000 less than what it sold for in 1988 when it was first launched. Expect to pay about $400 annually for maintenance and repairs. Other small cars worth considering: Chrysler Colt • GM Firefly/Sprint • Mazda GLC and 323 • Nissan Sentra Classic • Suzuki Forsa.

Technical Data

ENGINES	Litres/CID	HP	MPG	Model Years
OHC I-3 FI	1.2/72	66-73	35-41	1988-93

Strengths and weaknesses: The Justy does everything reasonably well for an entry-level Subaru. Both the front-wheel drive and 4X4 models offer a continuously variable transmission (CVT) as an option. The design does away with conventional clutches, torque converters and gears. Instead, the engine's power is transmitted to the driveshaft via a set of pulleys and belts that adjust the engine's power to the messages sent by the gas pedal. CVT increases fuel economy considerably (almost as much as a manual transmission) while making for a simpler and lighter transmission. Smooth and nimble handling with precise and predictable steering. The 4X4 system is a boon for people who often need extra traction and an automatic transmission. Dashboard gauges are simple and the front seats are firm and supportive.

The Justy's engine is anemic, harsh and noisy. There are annoying steering wheel vibrations caused by the rough-running engine. The non-power-assisted steering requires maximum effort when parking. Ride is uncomfortable with a full load. There is some loss of steering stability with hard braking, and cornering at high speeds feels tippy on the 4X4. Larger tires would improve handling. Transmission problems are not easily diagnosed or repaired due to its complicated construction. Front shoulder belts are uncomfortable and rear seatbelts are hard to buckle up. The rear seat is for children only. The heater is insufficient and air distribution is inadequate. Trunk space is less than one would expect.

The Justy's reliability record has been about average from the 1991 model on. There have been some complaints concerning poor engine idling and frequent cold weather stalling, manual and automatic transmission malfunctions, premature exhaust system rust-out, catalytic converter failures and paint peeling. With the exception of the CVT, servicing and repair are made easy due to a very straightforward design. Towing is not recommended.

Safety summary/recalls: *Recalls*: **1988**-The 4X4 solenoid hose/ alternator wiring stay bracket may present a fire hazard.

Secret Warranties/Service Tips/DSBs

1987-90-An exhaust leak or noise may require the installation of a new muffler and upgraded rear exhaust pipe.
1987-91-An exhaust pipe flex joint rattle is corrected with an upgraded part.
1988-If the "check engine" light comes on for no reason, install a new diode harness.
1988-89-2nd gear grind is fixed with an upgraded transmission assembly.
1989-ECVT clutch rattle can be fixed by installing an upgraded clutch control unit (#30522KA091).
1992-Door fabric trim that peels away needs cyanoacrylate glue.

Vehicle Profile

	1988	1989	1990	1991	1992	1993	1994
Cost Price ($)							
Base	9797	7995	7995	8315	7759	7991	10,895
Used Values ($)							
Base ↑	2000	2400	3300	4000	4700	5400	8300
Base ↓	1500	1600	2400	3100	3800	4400	7100
Reliability	②	②	②	③	③	③	④
Air conditioning	—	—	—	—	—	—	—
Body integrity	②	②	②	③	③	③	④
Braking system	②	②	②	③	③	③	④
Electrical system	③	③	③	③	④	④	④
Engines	②	②	②	④	⑤	⑤	⑤
Exhaust/Converter	②	②	③	④	⑤	⑤	⑤
Fuel system	③	③	③	③	④	④	⑤
Ignition system	③	③	③	③	④	④	④
Manual transmission	③	③	③	④	④	④	⑤
- automatic	②	②	③	④	③	③	④
Rust/Paint	②	②	②	③	③	④	④
Steering	③	③	③	③	④	④	④
Suspension	②	②	③	③	④	④	③
Dealer Service	③	③	③	③	③	③	③
Maintenance	④	④	④	⑤	⑤	⑤	⑤
Parts Availability	③	③	③	③	③	③	③
Repair Costs	②	②	②	③	③	④	④
Crash Safety	②	②	②	②	②	②	②

Chaser, DL, GL

Rating: Above Average buy (1994); Average buy (1993); Below Average buy (1987-92). The earlier models aren't recommended because of poor-quality emissions components and the premature wear-out of major mechanical systems (CV joints, steering, etc.).

Price analysis: Excellent availability and reasonably priced. The Chaser is the least expensive of the group, followed by the DL and GL. Expect to pay about $500 annually for maintenance and repairs. The Loyale wagon's accident repair costs are much lower than average. Other small cars worth considering: Chrysler Colt • GM Saturn • Mazda 323 and Protegé • Nissan Sentra • Toyota Corolla.

Technical Data

ENGINES	Litres/CID	HP	MPG	Model Years
OHV F-4 2 bbl.	1.6/97	69	23-30	1985-88
OHV F-4 2 bbl.	1.8/109	73	21-29	1985-89
OHC F-4 2 bbl.	1.8/109	82-84	23-28	1985-87
OHC F-4 FI	1.8/109	90-97	23-28	1984-94
OHC F-4T FI	1.8/109	111-115	20-24	1985-90
OHC F-6 FI	2.7/163	145	17-23	1988-91

Strengths and weaknesses: 1985-87 are the years to avoid. Performance, handling and ride are mediocre. Engine breakdowns and premature clutch and exhaust system wear-out are commonplace. Early hatchbacks came with a weak and growly 1.6L flat-4 cylinder motor; later models have a 1.8L version of the same anemic engine. Expensive catalytic converters are often replaced at the owner's cost before the 5-year emissions warranty has expired. Subaru will reimburse the cost if you raise a fuss. Catalytic converters are often back-ordered for months, but cheap aftermarket systems can be found outside the dealer network.

On 1988 and later models, steering assemblies, CV joints and front brakes are the main problem areas; these parts generally need replacing after three to five years, and Subaru dealers charge the full rate for replacement. All years are susceptible to rapid rusting of the bumpers, door bottoms, the rear hatch and hood. Owners report that the door fabric often peels away. The dealer network is not extensive and few mechanics are familiar with the unusual drivetrain. Towing is not recommended.

Safety summary/recalls: *Recalls*: **1985 XT**-Improper bumper installation could create a fire in a collision. **1985-87 DL/GL/GT**-Rear suspension's inner arms could fail after prolonged exposure to road salt. **1987 DL/GL**-Faulty carburetor components could pose a fire hazard. **1988-91 XT6 and 1989-91-XT**-Power steering failure. **1989-90** -Automatic transmission may engage abruptly causing a sudden lurch into "Reverse."

Secret Warranties/Service Tips/DSBs

1985-87-Continuous exposure to road salt and chemicals may cause corrosion of the rear suspension inner arms that could affect the operation and control of the vehicle. The dealer will check and repair the problem for free.
1985-90-Rear gate door rattling corrected with a plastic sheet buffer.
1987-An overly rich choke condition during cold starts can be corrected

by installing a modified auxiliary choke pull-off spring.

1990-91-A knocking noise from the exhaust flex joint may require the replacement of the exhaust flange gasket with an upgraded gasket (#44022-GA 191).

1992-Door fabric trim that peels away needs cyanoacrylate glue.

All models/years-Owner feedback confirms that defective catalytic converters and steering assemblies will be replaced free of charge up to 5 years/80,000 km.

Vehicle Profile

	1987	1988	1989	1990	1991	1992	1993	1994
Cost Price ($)								
Chaser	—	8989	9495	9969	10,365	—	—	—
XT	—	16,295	25,695	—	—	—	—	—
DL Sedan	—	12,929	13,195	—	—	—	—	—
GL	13,195	14,990	15,275	—	—	—	—	—
Used Values ($)								
Chaser ↑	—	1900	3000	3800	4400	—	—	—
Chaser ↓	—	1200	2300	3200	3700	—	—	—
XT ↑	—	4500	8500	—	—	—	—	—
XT ↓	—	3700	7000	—	—	—	—	—
DL Sedan ↑	—	3100	3700	—	—	—	—	—
DL Sedan ↓	—	2200	2800	—	—	—	—	—
GL ↑	2900	3900	4600	—	—	—	—	
GL ↓	2100	2900	3700	—	—	—	—	
Reliability	②	②	②	②	②	②	③	④
Air conditioning	②	②	②	③	④	④	⑤	⑤
Body integrity	②	②	②	②	③	③	③	④
Braking system	③	③	③	③	③	③	④	④
Electrical system	②	②	②	③	③	③	③	③
Engines	②	②	②	②	②	②	④	⑤
Exhaust/Converter	②	③	③	③	④	④	②	⑤
Fuel system	④	④	④	④	②	②	②	④
Ignition system	②	②	②	②	②	②	④	④
Manual transmission	④	④	④	④	④	④	⑤	⑤
- automatic	②	②	②	②	②	②	③	⑤
Rust/Paint	②	②	②	③	③	③	④	④
Steering	③	③	③	③	③	③	④	④
Suspension	③	③	③	④	④	④	④	④
Dealer Service	③	③	③	③	③	③	③	③
Maintenance	②	②	②	③	③	④	④	④
Parts Availability	③	③	③	③	③	③	③	③
Repair Costs	②	②	②	③	④	④	④	⑤
Crash Safety								
DL Wagon	②	②	②	—	—	—	—	—
GL Sedan	②	②	②	②	—	—	—	—

SUZUKI

Forsa, Swift

Rating: Recommended (1994); Above Average buy (1992-93); Average buy (1987-91).

Price analysis: Good availability and prices are fairly reasonable. The later Swift version has a firmer used car price. Expect to pay about $200 annually for maintenance and repairs. Other small cars worth considering: Chrysler Colt • Geo Metro • Honda Civic • Mazda GLC and 323 • Nissan Sentra.

Technical Data

ENGINES	Litres/CID	HP	MPG	Model Years
OHC I-3 FI	1.0/60	48-55	39-46	1988
OHC I-3T FI	1.0/60	70	35-41	1988
OHC I-4 FI	1.3/76	70	39-46	1989-95
DOHC I-4 FI	1.3/76	100	41-46	1989-94
OHC I-4 FI	1.6/96	92	43-49	1992-95
OHC I-4 FI	1.0/60	55	45-50	1994-95

Strengths and weaknesses: The Swift offers the most fun, reliability and fuel economy per dollar than any other car in its category, particularly when one considers the smoothness of its engine and the quality of the interior. Overall construction and parts quality are above average. Dealer servicing is augmented by the GM dealer body. Secret warranty and service tips may also apply to the Sidekick, Tracker, Firefly and Sprint.

Early 1985-89 models were noted for serious brake deficiencies, poor body construction and engine fuel supply problems. Since then, these cars have improved considerably with only occasional cold starting problems, some premature brake wear and minor body defects reported.

Safety summary/recalls: *Recalls:* **1989-93**-Dealers will reinforce the hood-latch striker plate free of charge to prevent the hood from flying up.

Secret Warranties/Service Tips/DSBs

1989-Transmission oil leaking at the speedometer head requires the replacement of the oil seal and gear case.

1989-90-If you have hard starts or no-starts in cold weather, install Suzuki's cold start harness set (#36690-60A00).

1990-Suzuki will install a trunk lamp and switch for free if it was left out during production.

Vehicle Profile

	1987	1988	1989	1990	1991	1992	1993	1994
Cost Price ($)								
Forsa	7295	6995	—	—	—	—	—	—
Swift	—	—	7995	8495	8835	7395	7495	8995
Used Values ($)								
Forsa ↑	1400	2000	—	—	—	—	—	—
Forsa ↓	900	1200	—	—	—	—	—	—
Swift ↑	—	—	2500	3000	3500	4300	5700	6600
Swift ↓	—	—	1800	2300	2800	3400	4600	5500
Reliability	③	③	③	③	③	④	④	⑤
Air conditioning	—	—	—	—	—	—	—	—
Body integrity	④	④	④	④	③	④	④	⑤
Braking system	❷	❷	❷	③	④	③	❷	④
Electrical system	③	③	③	③	④	④	❷	④
Engines	❷	❷	❷	③	⑤	⑤	⑤	⑤
Exhaust/Converter	❷	❷	❷	③	③	❷	❷	④
Fuel system	❷	❷	❷	④	④	④	⑤	⑤
Ignition system	④	④	④	③	③	③	④	④
Manual transmission	⑤	⑤	⑤	⑤	⑤	⑤	⑤	⑤
- automatic	③	③	④	⑤	⑤	⑤	⑤	⑤
Rust/Paint	❷	❷	❷	③	③	③	③	④
Steering	③	③	④	④	④	❷	④	④
Suspension	③	③	③	③	③	③	③	④
Dealer Service	④	④	④	④	④	④	④	④
Maintenance	❷	❷	❷	③	③	④	⑤	⑤
Parts Availability	④	④	④	④	④	④	④	④
Repair Costs	❷	❷	❷	③	⑤	⑤	⑤	⑤
Crash Safety	—	—	❷	❷	❷	❷	❷	❷

TOYOTA

Paseo

Rating: Recommended (1994); Above Average buy (1992-93).

Price analysis: Average availability but prices are often unreasonably high. Expect to save on the care and feeding of your Paseo—maintenance and repairs should run no more than about $300 annually. Other sporty coupés worth considering: Geo Storm • Hyundai Scoupe • Mazda MX-3.

Technical Data

ENGINES	Litres/CID	HP	MPG	Model Years
OHC I-4 1 bbl.	1.5/89	62-78	26-31	1988-90
OHC I-4 FI	1.5/89	82	25-30	1991-93
OHC I-4 FI	1.5/89	100	23-27	1994-95

Strengths and weaknesses: This baby Tercel's main advantages are a peppy 1.5L 4-cylinder engine, a smooth 5-speed manual transmission, good handling, a supple ride, great fuel economy, and above average reliability. On the other hand, this light little sportster is quite vulnerable to side winds, there's lots of body lean in turns, plenty of engine, exhaust and road noise, limited front headroom and legroom, and very little rear seat space.

Confidential dealer service bulletins show the 1993s may have defective Panasonic tape and CD players, and a radio hum at low volume caused by fuel pump interference.

Safety summary/recalls: There is no crash data for the Paseo but its chassis differs little from the Tercel chassis, so Tercel data should apply. Thick rear pillars reduce rear visibility. *Recalls*: None.

Secret Warranties/Service Tips/DSBs

1992-Low volume radio hum can be corrected by installing spacers (insulators) between the radio chassis and the printed circuit board. **1992-93**-Toyota will improve the shift "feel" on its automatic gearboxes by increasing the C1 accumulator control pressure on cars brought in for this problem.

Vehicle Profile

	1992	1993	1994
Cost Price ($)			
Base	13,338	14,398	14,698
Used Values ($)			
Base ↑		8700	10,000	11,500
Base ↓		7700	8800	10,500
Reliability	④	④	⑤
Crash Safety	❷	⑤	⑤
Safety Features			
ABS	—	O	O
Airbag	—	D	D

Tercel

Rating: Recommended (1993-94); Above Average buy (1991-92); Average buy (1987-90).

Price analysis: Excellent availability. Prices are high but acceptable. The '91 Tercel is the better buy because it offers some savings from a $500 reduction in the original selling price, maximum depreciation in usually the first two years, and only two or three years of wear and tear. Expect to pay about $400 annually for maintenance and repairs. Other small cars worth considering: Chrysler Colt • GM Saturn • Honda Civic • Mazda 323 • Nissan Sentra.

Technical Data

ENGINES	Litres/CID	HP	MPG	Model Years
OHC I-4 1 bbl.	1.5/89	76-78	27-32	1987-90
OHC I-4 2 bbl.	1.5/89	62	28-33	1987-88
OHC I-4 FI	1.5/89	82	25-31	1991-94

Strengths and weaknesses: 1985 Tercels are risky buys. They had serious brake and body problems, numerous electrical faults, including failure-prone horns and premature rusting. Second generation (1985-86) Tercels prices are not inexpensive, but maintenance costs are still quite cheap, and parts are reasonably priced. These models in particular should be checked for door panel and underbody rust damage. Stay away from the troublesome 4X4 versions made from 1984 to 1987.

1987-88 Tercels were further improved through a restyled aero look, a better-performing multivalve, overhead-cam engine, impressive performance with a 5-speed manual gearbox and additional sound insulation. Their main shortcomings were insufficient power when merging into traffic or hill climbing, particularly when shifting from 2nd to 3rd gear with the automatic transmission, cruise control glitches, fuel system malfunctions, excessive engine intake valve carbon buildup, occasional air-conditioner breakdowns, cracked front exhaust pipes and exhaust system/catalytic converter rust-out. All Tercels are plagued by pulsating brakes that wear out much too quickly. Ignition modules are often defective, but Toyota will replace these for free under the 5 year/80,000 km emissions warranty. Owners of the 4-wheel-drive wagon have complained of manual transmission failures and the occasional bug in the transfer case (these repairs are very expensive).

The redesigned 1989-90 versions are roomier, better performing, and above average in quality and reliability (except for some paint peeling and surface rusting). The sunroof is a frill that cuts headroom drastically and causes irritating water leaks and wind noise. Tercels have a great reputation for exemplary durability, but overall performance is not outstanding and the interior is cramped.

1991-93 Tercels are pretty reliable, but they're not perfect. They are the first to be fuel injected, which makes for livelier and smoother acceleration, and interior space feels much larger than it is. Owners report faulty clutch-sleeve cylinders, hard shifting with the automatic transmission, premature brake and suspension component wear-out, brake pulsation, defective CD players, leaking radiators, windshield whistling, and myriad squeaks and rattles.

1987-90 Tercels are rust-prone around the rear wheels, side mirror mounts, along the bottoms of doors and hatches and the rear quarter-panels. Early models have suffered from extensive corrosion of rear suspension components.

Safety summary/recalls: *Recalls*: **1987-90**-Headlights may fail if other than Koito brand is used.

Secret Warranties/Service Tips/DSBs

1987-88-Engines that run on, surge or have flat power spots may need an upgraded carburetor assembly, cold mixture heater temperature switch or engine sub-wire harness.
1989-90-Harsh shifting from 2nd to 3rd on automatics requires a new rubber check ball (#35495-22020).
1990-Fujitsu CD players may scratch disks. The company will repair units and compensate owners.
1991-Poor door speaker sound quality can be corrected by modifying

the way the speakers are installed.
1994-A whistling noise coming from the windshield requires a urethane sealant applied at key points.

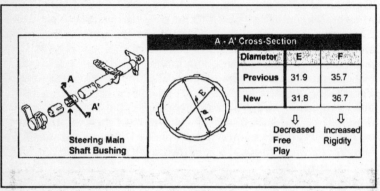

• A steering column with excessive free play or that is noisy may need an upgraded steering main shaft bushing.

All models/years-Older Toyotas with stalling problems should have the engine checked for excessive carbon buildup on the valves before any other repairs are authorized. Faulty cruise control units will be replaced up to 5 years/80,000 km. Interior squeaks and rattles can be fixed with Toyota's kit (#08231-00801).

Improved disc brake pad kits are described in DSB #BR94-004. Another generic Toyota problem: brake pulsation/vibration is fully addressed in DSB #BR94-002 "Cause and Repair of Vibration and Pulsation."

Vehicle Profile

	1987	1988	1989	1990	1991	1992	1993	1994
Cost Price ($)								
S	7998	8198	8598	8798	8258	8798	9098	9618
Used Value ($)								
S ↑	2000	2600	3300	4100	5100	6200	7000	8300
S ↓	1500	2000	2600	3300	4300	5000	5900	7200
Reliability	③	③	③	③	④	④	⑤	⑤
Air conditioning	②	②	③	③	⑤	⑤	⑤	⑤
Body integrity	②	③	③	③	④	④	⑤	⑤
Braking system	①	①	②	②	②	②	②	③
Electrical system	②	③	③	③	④	⑤	⑤	⑤
Engines	④	④	④	④	④	⑤	⑤	⑤
Exhaust/Converter	②	②	②	②	②	④	⑤	⑤
Fuel system	③	③	③	③	④	⑤	⑤	⑤
Ignition system	②	②	③	③	④	④	④	④
- automatic	②	③	④	④	④	⑤	⑤	⑤

Manual transmission	④	④	④	④	④	⑤	⑤	⑤
Rust/Paint	❷	③	③	③	④	④	⑤	⑤
Steering	④	④	④	④	③	④	④	⑤
Suspension	③	③	③	③	③	③	③	④
Dealer Service	③	③	③	③	③	③	③	③
Maintenance	③	④	⑤	⑤	⑤	⑤	⑤	⑤
Parts Availability	③	③	④	⑤	⑤	⑤	⑤	⑤
Repair Costs	③	③	④	⑤	⑤	⑤	⑤	⑤
Crash Safety	⑤	❷	❷	❷	❷	❷	⑤	⑤
Safety Features								
ABS	—	—	—	—	—	—	O	O
Airbag	—	—	—	—	—	—	D	D

Corolla

Rating: Recommended (1993-94); Above Average (1991-92); Average buy (1987-90).

Price analysis: Excellent availability. Selling used for a few thousand dollars more than the entry-level Tercel, a used Corolla commands a high—but acceptable—price. The 1991 Corolla is the better buy because it offers some savings from a $500 reduction in the original selling price due to the dropping of the federal tax on manufactured goods, maximum depreciation (usually the first two years), and only two or three years of use. Newer models are hard to find on the used car market. Expect to pay about $400 annually for maintenance and repairs. Other small cars worth considering: Chrysler Colt • GM Saturn • Honda Civic • Mazda 323 and Protegé • Nissan Sentra.

Technical Data

ENGINES	Litres/CID	HP	MPG	Model Years
OHV I-4 2 bbl.	1.6/97	70-74	24-30	1985-88
DOHV I-4 FI	1.6/97	108-110	22-27	1987-88
OHC I-4D FI	1.8/112	56	27-33	1985
DOHC I-4 2 bbl.	1.6/97	90	25-30	1988-89
DOHC I-4 FI	1.6/97	100-102	22-26	1989-92
DOHC I-4 FI	1.6/97	115-130	23-27	1988-91
DOHC I-4 FI	1.6/97	105	24-29	1993-95
DOHC I-4 FI	1.8/110	105-115	23-28	1993-95

Strengths and weaknesses: Corollas are economical, high-quality, dependable little cars. 1985 and earlier versions may carry the Toyota name and appear to be bargains at first glance, but they are likely to have serious rusting problems and need costly brake, steering and suspension work. Stay away from the 1.8L diesel version; it lacks performance, and parts are not easy to find. 4X4 versions made before 1988 are also risky. Wiper pivot assemblies may seize due to corrosion. Front shocks on rear-wheel-drive models wear out more quickly than average. Exhaust parts are not very durable. Some '85 models have defective ignition modules and the 1.6L engine may develop a leaky oil pressure sending unit which, if left unattended, can cause sudden loss of engine oil and expensive engine damage. Many older Corollas are weakened by extensive rust. If well maintained and not too rusty, these are acceptable buys—despite the high prices they fetch on the used car market.

Post-1987 models are much improved. The two-door models provide sporty performance, especially when equipped with the 16-valve engine. The engines and drivetrains are exceptionally reliable. Front-drive sedans and five-door hatchbacks offer more room than their rear-drive counterparts. The base engine, however, lacks power and is especially deficient in low-end torque making for agonizingly slow merging and passing on the highway. Front and rear suspension struts frequently need replacing. Owners report problems with premature front brake wear, brake vibration, faulty defrosting allowing the windows to fog up in winter, and rusting of body seams, especially door bottoms, side mirror mounts, trunk and hatchback lids, and wheel openings. Underbody corrosion is also common.

From 1990 on, the Corolla's problems are limited to harsh automatic shifting, early front brake pad and strut/shock wear-out, and some interior squeaks and rattles. All cars require regular valve adjustments to prevent serious engine problems.

Confidential dealer service bulletins show the '93s and '94s may have premature brake and suspension wear-out, brake pulsations, defective CD players, and windshield whistling.

Safety summary/recalls: Some owners find the driver's footroom inadequate to safely operate the accelerator, brake and clutch pedals. *Recalls*: **1985-86**-Defective ignition control module could prevent vehicle from starting or provoke frequent stalling. **1993-94**-An unused harness connector for vehicle accessories located under the carpet may cause an electrical short-circuit or fire. **1994**-Seatbelt anchor straps may be faulty.

Secret Warranties/Service Tips/DSBs

1984-Faulty voltage regulator could lead to an overcharged battery and subsequent engine misfiring or stalling. Toyota will replace the regulator free of charge under a recall campaign.
1987-88-Engines that run on, surge or have flat power spots may need an upgraded carburetor assembly, cold mixture heater temperature

switch or engine sub-wire harness.

1988-Rear speaker static could be caused by the wires contacting the rear package tray shelf.

1990-Fujitsu CD players may scratch disks. The company will repair units and compensate owners.

1994-A loose rear seat bolster cover is a common problem says DSB #B094-005.

• Windshield A- pillar wind noise can be stopped by modifying the molding lip.

All models/years-Improved disc brake pad kits are described in DSB #BR94-004. Another generic Toyota problem: brake pulsation/vibration is fully addressed in DSB #BR94-002 "Cause and Repair of Vibration and Pulsation."

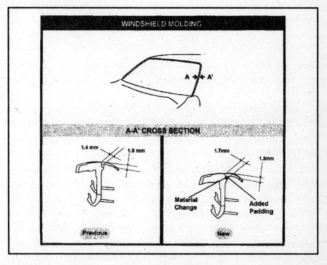

Vehicle Profile

	1987	1988	1989	1990	1991	1992	1993	1994
Cost Price ($)								
Base	10,598	11,688	11,998	12,438	11,948	12,788	14,598	14,798
Used Values ($)								
Base ↑	3500	4300	5200	6000	7700	9000	10,500	12,500
Base ↓	2700	3300	4200	5200	6700	7800	9100	11,100
Reliability	③	③	③	③	④	④	⑤	⑤
Air conditioning	③	④	⑤	⑤	⑤	⑤	⑤	⑤
Body integrity	③	③	③	③	④	④	④	④
Braking system	❶	❷	❷	❷	❷	❷	③	③
Electrical system	❶	❷	❷	③	③	③	④	④
Engines	③	③	④	④	④	④	⑤	⑤
Exhaust/Converter	❷	❷	❷	③	③	④	④	⑤
Fuel system	④	❷	❷	③	③	③	⑤	⑤

Ignition system	2	4	4	4	4	4	5	5
Manual transmission	4	4	4	4	4	4	5	5
- automatic	4	4	3	3	4	4	5	5
Rust/Paint	2	3	3	3	4	4	4	4
Steering	3	3	3	4	4	4	4	5
Suspension	3	3	3	3	3	4	4	5
Dealer Service	3	3	3	3	3	3	5	5
Maintenance	4	4	4	4	4	4	5	5
Parts Availability	4	4	4	4	4	4	5	5
Repair Costs	4	4	4	4	4	4	5	5
Crash Safety	2	2	2	2	2	2	5	5
Safety Features								
ABS	—	—	—	—	—	—	O	O
Airbag	—	—	—	—	—	—	D	D

VOLKSWAGEN

Fox

Rating: Average buy (1990-93); Not Recommended (1987-89).

Price analysis: Average availability. VW's cheapest model, so used prices are very reasonable. The 1991 Fox is the better buy because it offers some savings from a $600 reduction in the original selling price, maximum depreciation (usually the first two years), and only four years of wear and tear. Expect to pay about $600 annually for maintenance and repairs. Other small cars worth considering: Chrysler Colt • Ford Escort/Tracer ('91 and later) • Geo Metro • Honda Civic • Mazda GLC and 323 • Nissan Sentra.

Technical Data

ENGINES	Litres/CID	HP	MPG	Model Years
OHC I-4 FI	1.8/109	81	24-28	1987-93

Strengths and weaknesses: Smooth acceleration with good passing ability. The car handles very well and takes a surprisingly large load. The Fox's old design can't offer the mechanical or interior efficiency that newer cars provide. Other failings on early models are the absence of power steering and an automatic transmission. It's true that these cars are fun to drive and provide lots of extra equipment for the money, but they have a checkered reputation as far as reliability and durability are concerned. To top it all off, servicing has to be done by VW dealers, meaning that repairs cost more than average.

The Fox comes with plenty of standard equipment, but strangely enough power steering is not offered, making parking a chore. The dash is well laid out and has easy-to-read displays. Front seats are very comfortable but headroom is limited. Trunk space is mostly taken up by the spare tire, while the wagon has lots of space for cargo. The fuel-injected engine provides performance and acceleration comparable to the Golf and Jetta. Quick and precise steering complement the Fox's excellent handling. The ride is firm and a bit bouncy but never uncomfortable. The 5-speed manual transaxle has an Overdrive ratio that allows the engine to practically loaf at highway speeds. The 4-speed manual also works well, although the 5-speed makes the best use of the power available. Shifting the 4-speed into Reverse and 1st gear can be difficult. Braking is impressive with little fading after successive stops, but there is excessive front-end plow in sudden stops.

Owners report that engine timing belt, starter motor and brake cylinder failures are common. Other problem areas include electrical, engine cooling and fuel systems, and there are body hardware glitches. The manual transmission shift linkage needs frequent adjustment, and the front brakes, like most VWs, need more frequent servicing than comparable makes. Assembly and paint application quality vary considerably, and interior trim and dashboard controls are easily broken. Towing is not recommended.

Safety summary/recalls: *Recalls*: **1987-89**-Steering wheel shaft nut may be too loose. **1988-91**-Hood may fly open. **1991**-Metal fuel lines may rub against exhaust manifold, posing a fire hazard.

Secret Warranties/Service Tips/DSBs

1987-88-Uneven brake pad wear corrected by new master cylinder made after December 1988.

1988-89-To prevent premature front brake rotor wear, VW proposes upgraded brake pads with a manufacturing code equal to or greater than "1G9."

1988-93-Poor driveability may be caused by a deteriorated oxygen sensor wire shield or ground connection.

1991-1993-If the vehicle loses power, bucks and jerks after several hours of driving, the likely cause may be a faulty mass airflow sensor creating a vibration resonance that sends an intermittent signal to the ECM. This is covered by the emissions warranty.

1993-Wind noise from the top of the door may be fixed by installing a new auxiliary door seal.

• A hard to operate temperature control lever may need a new heater control cable and valve.

All models/years-If the engine fails to crank or the battery is constantly discharged, you may have a loose fastening nut on terminal 30 of the starter motor.

• Water leaking between the sunroof's glass panel and seal can be stopped with VW's Water Management System kit (I swear to God, they call it that) #302877005.

• Install a self-adhesive shim kit (#171698993) to quiet noisy disc brakes.

• Wiper blade chatter and skipping are likely due to a poorly angled wiper arm.

• Wind noise from the outside mirror area or restricted mirror glass adjustment may require a new rubber grommet that seals the opening for the mirror adjustment mechanism.

Vehicle Profile

	1987	1988	1989	1990	1991	1992	1993
Cost Price ($)							
Base	8275	8980	9690	9990	9375	9750	10,042
Used Values ($)							
Base ↑	1700	2300	3100	3700	4500	5300	6000
Base ↓	1100	1600	2200	2800	3600	4300	5000
Reliability	②	②	②	③	③	③	③
Air conditioning	②	②	③	③	③	③	③
Body integrity	③	③	③	③	③	③	③
Braking system	②	②	②	③	③	③	③
Electrical system	②	②	②	③	③	③	③
Engines	②	②	②	③	③	③	③
Exhaust/Converter	②	②	②	③	③	③	⑤
Fuel system	④	②	②	③	③	③	③
Ignition system	②	③	③	③	④	④	④
Manual transmission	④	④	④	④	④	④	⑤
- automatic	④	④	③	③	④	④	⑤
Rust/Paint	②	②	②	③	③	③	③
Steering	③	③	③	④	④	④	④
Suspension	②	③	③	④	④	④	④
Dealer Service	②	②	②	②	②	②	②
Maintenance	④	④	④	④	④	④	⑤
Parts Availability	③	③	③	③	③	③	③
Repair Costs	③	③	③	③	③	③	③
Crash Safety	②	①	②	②	②	②	②

Golf

Rating: Above Average (1993-94); Not Recommended (1987-92).

Price analysis: Good availability. Good used car prices for early 1990s models and do get a more reliable post-'89 Golf or a better-equipped Jetta that still carries some of VW's base warranty. Expect to pay about $400 annually for maintenance and repairs. Insurance rates are higher than average because thieves love stealing VW radios and logo badges from the grille and hatchback. Other small cars worth considering: Ford Escort/Tracer ('91 and later) • Honda Civic • Mazda 323 and Protegé • Nissan Sentra Classic.

Strengths and weaknesses: The Golf is much better executed than the Rabbit and offers very competent performance. The 1.8L gasoline engine is very peppy and the diesel engines (not offered in '88 and '89) are very reliable and economical. Both engines are easily started in cold weather.

Reliability is impressive—for the first five years. Then the engine, ignition fuel and electrical systems start to self-destruct as your wallet gets lighter. Brakes wear out quickly and exhaust-system components are practically biodegradable. Body hardware and dashboard controls are fragile and many owners have reported paint problems. Owners also report that tall drivers who push their seatback prevent the folding of the back seat, making it inconvenient to carry a load on pre-'93 versions.

Although the 1990-93 models are improved a bit, Volkswagen still has lots of quality problems. Owners report electrical short-circuits, heater/defroster resistor and motor failures, leaking transmission and stub axle seals, defective valve pan gaskets, head gaskets, timing belts, steering assemblies, suspension components, alternator pulley, catalytic converters and trim items. Diesel versions are a bit slow to accelerate, and 4th gear can't handle highway speeds above 80 km/h.

The redesigned '94s are much more reliable and safer. Some DSB-disclosed problems: poor driveability, water leaks, trim defects and premature rear tire wear.

Technical Data

ENGINES	Litres/CID	HP	MPG	Model Years
OHC I-4 FI	1.8/109	85-105	23-27	1985-93
DOHC I-4 FI	1.8/109	123	21-25	1987-89
OHC I-4D FI	1.6/97	52	35-42	1985-91
OHC I-4TD FI	1.6/97	68	35-40	1985-86
OHC I-4TD FI	1.6/97	59	35-40	1992
DOHC I-4 FI	2.0/121	134	20-25	1990-92
OHC I-4 FI	2.0L/121	115	22-26	1994-95
DOHC V6 FI2.	8/170	172	18-23	1994-95

Safety summary/recalls: *Recalls*: **Golf-1985**-Faulty brake master cylinder. Front seatbelt retractors on two-door models may not lock properly. **1985-86**-Possibility of excessive fuel spillage in a collision. **1985-87**-Engine may suddenly stall due to a seized fuel pump. **1987**-Loose lug nuts on alloy wheels could cause wheel separation. **1988**-Weak seatbelt retractor pawl. Faulty brake booster. **1988-91**-Engine preheating tube may interfere with braking. **1988-92**-VW will replace the fuel hose and install new spring-type hose clamps. **1993**-Windshield wiper motor may fail. **Golf/Jetta-1985-90**-Hot coolant could escape into the passenger compartment. **1990**-Omission of air ducts could cause brake fluid overheating. **Jetta-1985**-Plastic clip that holds the brake line may be a fire hazard. **1987-89**-Incorrectly contoured brake line could result in brake failure. **1990**-Faulty power steering pump bracket. **1991**-Too short front brake hoses may rupture. **Cabriolet-1985**-Faulty fuel supply hose. **1987-90**-Fuel tank may leak. **1990**-Poorly located airbag harness wire. **1990-91**-A bent water separator panel could cause sudden acceleration. **1990-92**-Faulty fuel hose retaining clamp could be a fire hazard. **1991**-Defective track control arms used to support front wheels leads to wheel misalignment and steering pull to one side.

Secret Warranties/Service Tips/DSBs

1985-87-If the engine fails to crank or the battery is constantly discharged, you may have a loose fastening nut on terminal 30 of the starter motor.
• If the idle fluctuates or hunts for a setting, you may have a vacuum leak in the air shroud injection system; check the O-ring and plastic connecting flange.
• A defective sensor boot screen may be the cause of poor acceleration.
• Install a self-adhesive shim kit (#171698993) to quiet noisy disc brakes.
• Oil leaking under the car may be caused by a defective final drive flange seal. Install repair kit #020498085E.
1985-90-If the engine overheats, the heat exchanger—located underneath the instrument panel—could rupture, spraying hot engine coolant throughout the passenger compartment.
1988-89-Stalling after initial start-up requires ECU replacement.
1988-94-Poor driveability may be caused by a deteriorated oxygen sensor wire shield or ground connection.
1990-VW will provide free plastic wheel covers that mount over the rear wheel housing adjacent to the rear seat under its service action QV program.
• Hard winter starting may require the installation of a new high-energy ignition coil, high tension wires and spark plugs at VW's expense.
1990-91-If the starter motor is noisy or won't engage, try changing the starter motor and torque converter carrier.
1994-Water leaks into the engine bulkhead.

Jetta

Rating: Above Average (1993-94); Not Recommended (1987-92).

Price analysis: Good availability, but used prices are fairly high, reflecting the car's high sticker price. In fact, the removal of the manufacturers' tax only produced a $200 reduction in the original selling price, whereas other models in the same class cut prices two or three times as much. The 1992 Jetta is a better buy than earlier versions because it's priced more reasonably than the Japanese competition and has generous amounts of interior and trunk space. Try to get a Jetta that still carries the comprehensive VW warranty. Expect to pay about $400 annually for maintenance and repairs. Insurance premiums are high; radio theft has been a major problem. Other small cars worth considering: Ford Escort/Tracer ('91 and later) • Honda Civic • Mazda 323 and Protegé • Nissan Sentra.

Strengths and weaknesses: Jettas provide slightly more comfort and better road performance than their hatchback counterparts. The 1.6L 4-cylinder found on early Jettas was surprisingly peppy and the diesel engine is very economical although quite slow to accelerate. Diesels have a better overall reliability record than gasoline models and are popular as taxis. Jettas are far more reliable than the Rabbit but they, too, suffer from rapid body deterioration and some mechanical problems after their fourth year in service. For example, on post-'88 Jettas, starters often burn out because of their vulnerability to engine heat, sunroofs leak, door locks jam, window cranks break and windows bind. Owners also report engine head gasket leaks, water pump and heater core breakdowns (the heater core will be replaced free under a recall campaign). It's axiomatic that all diesels are slow to accelerate, but VW's 4th gear can't handle highway speeds above 80 km/h. Engine noise is deafening when shifting down from 4th gear.

Problems on 1990-93 versions include electrical short-circuits, vacuum hose mis-routing, defective steering assemblies, suspension components, catalytic converters and trim items. The redesigned '94s are much more reliable and safe. DSB-disclosed problems include poor driveability, water leaks, trim defects, and premature rear tire wear.

Safety summary/recalls: NHTSA crash tests carried out on a '95 Jetta showed the driver and passenger would have average protection. The identical '94 version can be expected to produce similar results.

Secret Warranties/Service Tips/DSBs

1985-87-A rough idle or misfire under partial load may be due to ignition sparks jumping from the plug wires to the noise suppression shield or the cylinder head.
• Oil leaking under the car may be caused by a defective final drive flange seal. Install repair kit #020498085E.
1985-90-If the engine overheats, the heat exchanger—located underneath the instrument panel—could rupture, spraying hot engine coolant throughout the passenger compartment.
1988-89-Stalling after initial start-up requires ECU replacement.
1988-94-Poor driveability may be caused by a deteriorated oxygen sensor wire shield or ground connection.
1990-VW will replace faulty fuel pumps free of charge under service

action campaign QW.
• Hard winter starting may require the installation of a new high-energy ignition coil, high tension wires and spark plugs at VW's expense.
1992-94-Poor 2.8L engine performance or a rough idle may be due to a misrouted EVAP vacuum hose.
1994-Water leaks into the engine bulkhead.

Scirocco

Rating: Not Recommended (1986-89).

Price analysis: Not easily found. The Scirocco has been one of VW's most expensive compacts. Used, these cars are subject to such rapid depreciation that they can be bought for almost as much as a fully equipped Jetta, a car that has a new-car price of about $5000 less. Expect to pay about $800 annually for maintenance and repairs. Insurance premiums are high; thieves just love VW radios. Other small cars worth considering: Ford Escort and Tracer ('91 and later) • Honda Civic • Mazda 323 and Protegé • VW Golf or Jetta.

Technical Data

ENGINES	Litres/CID	HP	MPG	Model Years
OHV I-4 FI	1.8/109	85	23-27	1988-89
DOHC I-4 FI	1.8/109	123	21-25	1988-89

Strengths and weaknesses: This car is fun to drive, mainly because of its nimble handling, strong, responsive engine, and tight steering. Post-'85 Sciroccos are fairly reliable, but parts are in short supply, and repair costs are higher than average.

This is a slightly more comfortable car, but don't expect to get more than four people to ride in it at one time. Electrical short-circuits, chronic fuel-supply problems, premature front brake wear and fragile body parts are common.

Safety summary/recalls: *Recalls*: **1985**-A loose connection where the fuel supply hose attaches to the gas tank mounted fuel pump could be the cause of chronic stalling and hard starting. **1985-87**-The fuel pump may fail when ambient temperatures rise. **1988**-Faulty fuel filter.

Secret Warranties/Service Tips/DSBs

1985-86-If the engine is hard to start in cold weather, install a ground strap (#533971235) from the battery to the transmission housing.

1985-87-Oil leaking under the car may be caused by a defective final drive flange seal. Install repair kit #020498085E.

1985-88-Install a self-adhesive shim kit (#171698993) to quiet noisy disc brakes.

All models/years-VW will replace defective catalytic converters, steering assemblies and suspension components free of charge on a case-by-case basis.

Vehicle Profile

	1987	1988	1989	1990	1991	1992	1993	1994
Cost Price ($)								
Golf	11,835	11,490	11,950	10,950	10,270	10,710	10,710	12,600
Jetta	12,670	12,550	13,645	13,400	12,615	13,140	13,140	15,370
Scirocco	16,370	16,900	18,280	—	—	—	—	—
Used Values ($)								
Golf ↑	2500	3300	4000	4600	5700	6800	8200	9700
Golf ↓	1700	2300	3000	3600	4600	5600	7400	8800
Jetta ↑	3600	4500	5600	6400	7500	8800	9900	11,500
Jetta ↓	2500	3500	4600	5300	6400	7400	8800	10,300
Scirocco ↑	4000	5200	6400	—	—	—	—	—
Scirocco ↓	3000	4200	5400	—	—	—	—	—
Reliability	①	①	①	②	②	②	④	④
Air conditioning	②	②	②	④	④	⑤	⑤	⑤
Body integrity	①	①	①	①	①	①	③	③
Braking system	②	②	②	②	③	③	③	③
Electrical system	①	①	①	①	①	①	③	③
Engines	③	③	③	③	③	③	⑤	⑤
Exhaust/Converter	①	②	③	③	④	④	⑤	⑤
Fuel system	①	②	③	③	③	③	④	④
Ignition system	②	③	③	③	③	④	④	④
Manual transmission	④	④	④	④	⑤	⑤	⑤	⑤
- automatic	②	③	④	④	④	⑤	⑤	⑤
Rust/Paint	②	②	③	③	④	④	⑤	⑤
Steering	③	③	③	③	③	④	⑤	⑤
Suspension	②	③	③	③	③	③	④	④
Dealer Service	②	②	②	③	③	③	③	③
Maintenance	②	②	②	③	③	③	⑤	⑤
Parts Availability	②	②	②	③	③	③	③	④
Repair Costs	②	②	②	③	③	③	④	⑤
Crash Safety								
Golf	②	②	②	②	②	②	②	③
Jetta	②	②	②	②	②	②	②	③
Scirocco	②	②	②	—	—	—	—	—
Safety Features								
ABS	—	—	—	—	—	—	—	O

COMPACT CARS

1993 Plymouth Acclaim: cheap, fairly reliable, excellent warranty and easy to repair.

A compact car is a trade-off between size and fuel economy, offering more room and comfort but a bit less fuel economy (11.5L/100 km to 9.6L/100 km—25 to 30 mpg) than a subcompact. It is the best car for combined city and highway driving.

Compacts are popular because they combine the advantages of a subcompact with those of a larger car. The trunk is usually large enough to meet average baggage requirements and the interior is spacious enough to meet the needs of the average family (seating four persons in comfort and five in a pinch).

Crash safety is fair to good, but many North American-built cars, particularly some of the newer GM models, offer insufficient protection to the driver and passengers. Airbags, fortunately, have been available on many North American-built compacts since 1991.

The following used compacts are recommended:

Chrysler Spirit/Acclaim
Honda Accord (1990-93)
Nissan Stanza (1989-92)
Toyota Corolla
Toyota Camry
Volvo 850
Volvo 900 series

1993 Volvo 240: a Swedish orphan.

ACURA

Integra

Rating: Not Recommended due to outrageously high prices (1994); Above Average buy (1990-93); Acceptable buy (1986-89).

Price analysis: Limited availability and prices are stiff on recent models. Expect to pay about $400 annually for maintenance and repairs. To avoid costly engine repairs, check the engine timing belt every 2 years/40,000 km and replace it every 96,000 km ($250). Other compact cars worth considering: Ford Probe • Honda Accord • Nissan Stanza • Toyota Camry • Volvo 850.

Technical Data

ENGINES	Litres/CID	HP	MPG	Model Years
DOHC I-4 FI	1.6/97	113-118	24-28	1986-89
DOHC I-4 FI	1.7/102	160	22-26	1992-93
DOHC I-4 FI	1.8/112	130-160	23-27	1990-93
DOHC I-4 FI	1.8/112	142	23-29	1994-95
DOHC I-4 FI	1.8/109	170	22-28	1994-95

Strengths and weaknesses: A Honda spin-off, early Integras (1986-89) came with lots of standard equipment and are a pleasure to drive, especially when equipped with a manual transmission. The high-revving 1.7L powerplant growls when pushed and lacks guts (read torque) in the lower gears. The 4-speed automatic saps the base engine's power considerably. Engine and tire noise are intrusive at highway speeds. The car corners well and is more agile than later 1990-93 models. Its hard-riding characteristic can be reduced a bit by changing the shocks and wide tires. The front seats are very comfortable, but they are set a bit low, and the side wheel wells leave little room for your feet. Rear seat room is very limited, especially on the three-door version.

A large number of 1989-90 Integras have faulty distributor igniters. When the igniter fails, the car stalls and it may be impossible to restart. The only remedy is to call a tow truck and have a garage replace the distributor. Honda will pay for the igniter replacement and all other expenses associated with the towing up to 5 years/80,000 km. This "updated warranty" covers used Integras and provides retroactive compensation to owners who have paid for the repair even if an independent garage replaced the part. Claims accompanied by receipts will be judged on a case-by-case basis.

Overall, assembly and component quality are good but not exceptional, as can be seen from the *Service Tips* list.

For model years 1990 to 1993, the 1.8L engine is smoother running but delivers the same maximum horsepower as the 1.7L it replaced. Surprisingly, overall performance has been toned down and is seriously compromised by the 4-speed automatic gearbox. Interior design is more user-friendly, front seating is roomier than with previous years, but reduced rear seating is still best left to small children.

Mechanical reliability is impressive, but that's the case with most Hondas that sell for far less, and many mechanical components are so complex that self-service can pretty well be ruled out. The front brakes may require more attention than usual. Surprisingly, what Integras give you in mechanical reliability they take away in poor quality control of body components and accessories. Water leaks, excessive wind noise, low-quality trim items and plastic panels that deform easily are all commonplace. Owners also report severe steering shimmy, excessive brake noise, premature front brake pad wear-out and radio malfunctions.

In the 1994 model year, the Integra was dramatically restyled for a more aerodynamic profile and a few more horses out of the venerable 1.8L 4-banger through variable valve timing. The '94s and '95s also offer a smoother ride than previous versions. Overall, there are too few improvements for the high prices late-model Integras command.

Dealer service bulletins show that steering wheel shimmy, fit and finish deficiencies and malfunctioning accessories continue to be problems. Owners also complain of premature front brake wear. Squeaks and rattles frequently crop up in the door panels and hatches.

The sedan's frameless windows often have sealing problems.

Safety summary/recalls: Crash tests of a 1990 and 1993 four-door Integra concluded that both driver and passenger would have suffered severe leg trauma. Furthermore, according to the U.S. Highway Loss Data Institute, 1989-91 Integras have collision losses 37 percent higher than average. In a related safety field, Integras are under investigation in the U.S. for fuel tank overpressurization which results in fuel spewing out when the cap is removed. Anti-lock brakes became a standard feature on the GS in 1990. *Recalls*: **1986-87**-An upgraded contact unit retainer needs to be attached to the front windshield wiper assembly. **1987-88**-Acura will repair or replace defective heaters for free. **1994**-Automatic transmission retaining clip may show wrong gear.

Secret Warranties/Service Tips/DSBs

1986-87-Defective bearings cause steering-knuckle clunk.
• Seat track rattle can be stopped by retorquing the seat track bolts or installing a new seat track.
1986-89-A faulty fuel pump check valve or fuel pressure regulator may be the cause of hard starts. Correct with an improved fuel pressure regulator (#16740-PG7-663) or fuel pump (#16700-PG7-663).
• Low battery charge or a dead battery likely due to excessive drain. Correct with Acura Charge Kit A or B.
1986-91-A creaking sound coming from the window regulator while raising or lowering the window may require the replacement of the regulator spiral spring.
1987-Excessive front brake squeal can be reduced by adding pad shims, resurfacing both discs (for shudder), replacing the brake pads, applying Molykote M77 and checking lug nut torque.
• A noisy rear power window can be fixed by installing a 4mm flat washer in the power window regulator.
1988-If dash brightness varies with engine speed, install an upgraded brightness controller (#35150-SD2-902).
1988-89-A faulty distributor igniter will be replaced free under a product update program.
• An upshift engine surge from 2nd to 3rd gear in cold weather may require that the transmission's second orifice control valve be replaced.
1990-Damaged teeth in the window regulator drive may be the reason why a rear window goes up only part way.
• If the sunroof deflector won't sit right, it's probably deformed. Install an upgraded deflector seal (#70511-SK7-003).
• Water in the spare tire well is likely caused by a hole in the melt sheet sound insulation.
1990-91-Door mirror vibration, rattle and wind noise will be fixed with EPT sealer under Acura's "goodwill" program.
• Front door vertical glass scratches mean the fiber pads on the outer

glass stabilizers are contaminated with dirt.

• A hum or whine coming from the upper windshield molding can be corrected by resealing the molding.

• DSB 91-015 is an excellent trouble-shooting guide to the myriad squeaks and rattles in the dash, front doors, hatch, steering shaft and sunroof.

1990-93-Poor AM radio reception is likely caused by a poor ground connection between the antenna collar and car body.

1992-A faulty oil pressure switch will be replaced free under a product update program.

1994-Slow electric window operation on three-door models is due to window misalignment.

• Rear hatch rattles are usually caused by a poorly adjusted striker.

• Lots of troubleshooting bulletins dealing with in-dash cellular phone problems.

• Moonroof chattering is likely caused by poorly lubricated lifters and sliders.

• Power door locks that cycle from locked to unlocked require a new power door lock control unit. Acura is silent as to who pays if the car or contents are stolen. Lawyers say Acura would be 100% responsible.

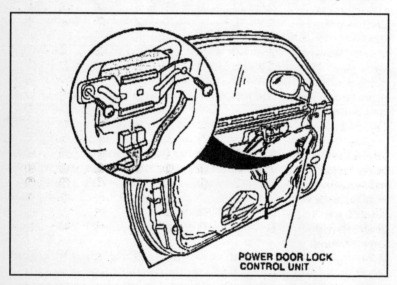

POWER DOOR LOCK
CONTROL UNIT

1994-95-Partially open window rattles may be caused by excess clearance between the window guide pin and center sash guide, or the glass run channel has come out of the center channel.

• A hard-to-close rear hatch may also be caused by a poorly adjusted striker or hardening of the rubber stops.

All models/years-Severe and persistent steering wheel shimmy due to an imbalanced wheel/tire/hub/rotor assembly will be fixed for free on a case-by-case basis under a "goodwill" program.

Acura will repair or replace defective steering assemblies, constant velocity joints and catalytic converters free of charge up to 5 years/ 80,000 km on a case-by-case basis. The converter, however, an emissions component, is almost always automatically covered.

Vehicle Profile

	1987	1988	1989	1990	1991	1992	1993	1994
Cost Price ($)								
LS	16,895	16,895	17,795	18,795	17,560	18,495	20,155	22,095
RS	13,695	14,195	14,995	15,995	14,800	15,495	16,250	17,655
Used Values ($)								
LS ↑	3800	5000	6500	7400	10,000	12,500	15,500	18,000
LS ↓	3000	4000	5400	8000	11,000	11,700	13,000	16,000
RS ↑	3000	4400	6000	7500	9300	11,000	13,000	15,000
RS ↓	2400	3400	4500	6000	7700	9200	11,200	13,500
Reliability	④	④	④	⑤	⑤	⑤	⑤	⑤
Air conditioning	❷	❷	③	④	④	⑤	⑤	⑤
Body integrity	③	③	③	③	③	③	③	③
Braking system	③	③	③	③	③	③	③	④
Electrical system	③	③	③	③	③	③	④	④
Engines	④	④	④	④	④	④	⑤	⑤
Exhaust/Converter	③	③	④	④	⑤	⑤	⑤	⑤
Fuel system	③	③	③	③	④	④	⑤	⑤
Ignition system	④	④	④	④	④	④	⑤	⑤
Manual transmission	⑤	⑤	⑤	⑤	⑤	⑤	⑤	⑤
- automatic	④	④	④	④	④	⑤	⑤	⑤
Rust/Paint	③	③	③	④	④	⑤	⑤	⑤
Steering	③	③	③	④	④	④	④	④
Suspension	③	③	③	④	④	④	④	④
Dealer Service	③	③	③	③	③	③	③	④
Maintenance	③	③	③	④	④	⑤	⑤	⑤
Parts Availability	④	④	④	④	④	④	⑤	⑤
Repair Costs	③	③	③	③	④	⑤	⑤	⑤
Crash Safety	❶	❶	❶	❶	❶	❶	❶	❶
Safety Features								
ABS	—	—	—	S	S	S	S	S
Airbag	—	—	—	—	—	—	—	D
Traction control	—	—	—	—	—	—	—	O

Vigor

Rating: Above Average buy.

Price analysis: A spin-off of the Honda Accord sedan, the 5-cylinder Vigor only went through three model years (1992-94). Due to its high cost and the absence of a more economical, smoother and easier-to-repair 6-cylinder powerplant, most buyers choose the cheaper Accord instead. Resale value has remained high due to the car's reputation for reliability and speculation from collectors. Expect to pay about $400 annually for maintenance and repairs. Accord parts can be used for most maintenance chores. Body panels and engine components, however, are more difficult to find. Other compact cars worth considering: Ford Probe • Honda Accord • Infiniti G20 sedan • Nissan Stanza • Toyota Camry • Volvo 850.

Technical Data

ENGINES	Litres/CID	HP	MPG	Model Years
OHC I-5 FI	2.5/152	176	19-23	1992-94

Strengths and weaknesses: This compact has power to spare, handles well, and has an impressive reliability/durability record. On the other hand, owners report that lots of engine, tire and road noise intrude into the passenger compartment at highway speeds, the engine and transmission lack smoothness, and the brakes aren't easy to modulate. The suspension is firm but not unpleasant, rear legroom is limited, and there have been some complaints of fit and finish deficiencies. Vigors are also notoriously thirsty—for premium fuel.

Safety summary/recalls: Although equipped with a standard driver's side airbag (dual airbags arrived with the 1993 models) and ABS, NHTSA crash tests of an airbag-equipped '92 Vigor concluded that the driver would suffer serious chest injuries and the passenger would sustain severe head trauma. *Recalls*: **1992**-Inadequate venting may allow moisture to build up in the distributor cap and prevent the engine from starting. Correction involves installing a distributor kit.

Secret Warranties/Service Tips/DSBs

1992-DSB 92-034 goes into great detail on ways to silence the Vigor's many squeaks and rattles.

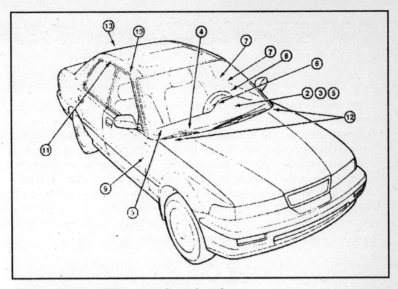

Points of origin of Vigor squeaks and rattles.

1992-93-Poor AM reception is probably due to a poor ground connection between the antenna collar and car body.
All models/years-Excessive steering wheel shimmy is likely due to an imbalance of the wheel/tire/hub/rotor assembly in the front end.

Vehicle Profile			
	1992	1993	1994
Cost Price ($)			
LS	26,600	28,450	29,300
Used Values ($)			
LS ↑	17,000	19,000	22,600
LS ↓	14,200	16,000	19,700
Reliability	⑤	⑤	⑤
Dealer Service	③	③	③
Maintenance	③	③	③
Parts Availability	③	③	③
Repair Costs	③	③	③
Crash Safety	❶	❶	❶
Safety Features			
ABS	S	S	S
Airbag	D	D/P	D/P

CHRYSLER/EAGLE

Aries, Reliant

Rating: Not Recommended (1983-89).

Price analysis: Excellent availability and prices are depressed due mainly to the fact that the car was dropped after the 1989 model year. Expect to pay about $500 annually for maintenance and repairs. Other compact cars worth considering: Chrysler Spirit/Acclaim • Honda Accord • Nissan Stanza • Toyota Camry • Volvo 850.

Technical Data

ENGINES	Litres/CID	HP	MPG	Model Years
OHC I-4 2 bbl.	2.2/135	96	23-27	1985
OHC I-4 2 bbl.	2.6/156	101	20-25	1985
OHC I-4 2 FI	2.2/135	93-97	22-27	1986-89
OHC I-4 2 FI	2.5/153	96-100	21-26	1986-89

Strengths and weaknesses: A low selling price, uncomplicated mechanical components and a roomy interior made these cars attractive buys when new, but once in service they quickly deteriorated. Don't make a final decision on purchasing an Aries or Reliant unless you have done a careful mechanical and body inspection. These cars are both frustrating and costly to own. They use dirt-cheap, low-tech components that tend to break down frequently. Luckily, they cost little to repair.

Manual transmission shifters are imprecise and balky. All cars have a problem with idle shake caused by the transverse-mounted 4-cylinder engine, as well as driveability problems, especially in cold or damp weather. The "gutless" 2.2L Chrysler-built 4-cylinder motor is a bit more reliable than the 2.6L Mitsubishi engine, which has a tendency to self-destruct. It also suffers from premature timing belt guide and piston ring wear, as well as leaky camshaft oil plugs. The 2.2L powerplant has multiple problems, the main ones being a weak cylinder head gasket and timing belt failures. The turbocharged version often requires expensive repairs. The MAP sensor fails frequently and is no longer covered under the emissions warranty.

Best powertrain choices are either the fuel-injected 2.2L or 2.5L engine. Although the engine reliability record is poor, parts are plentiful at reasonable cost. Some transaxle and front suspension components wear out quickly, and power-steering rack seals develop leaks. Front brake rotors warp and rust, and hand brake cables seize.

Carbureted engines are renowned for stalling and poor driveability. Exhaust systems, wheel bearings and air-conditioning components are not durable. The 5-speed manual transmission has a troublesome clutch. Water infiltration around the windshield and into the trunk are common. Surface rust due to chipped paint is frequent. More serious corrosion generally starts along the trunk line and along the edges of the rear wheel wells. Perforations tend to develop along the bottom door edges, around the windshield and on the floor. Front doors stick when opened wide and make loud creaking and cracking noises when they are closed.

Safety summary/recalls: NHTSA crash tests of a 1985 four-door Reliant concluded that the front seat passenger would be well-protected, but the driver would suffer severe leg injuries. *Recalls*: **1985**-Fuel leak at seam and inlet hose connection. **1985-87**-A free fuel regulator hose will be put on vehicles equipped with a 2.2L turbocharged engine. **1989**-Possibility of engine oil leakage means owners can get a new engine valve cover gasket cover.

Secret Warranties/Service Tips/DSBs

1987-A surging of the lockup torque converter on cars with 2.5L and 3.0L engines can be fixed with driveability kit (#4419447).
1987-88-Harsh or abrupt shifting into Drive may mean the rear clutch disks need changing.
• If the manual transmission fails to engage 2nd or 3rd gear, consider replacing the second and third thrust washer snap ring (#6033348).
1987-89-2.2L and 2.5L engines with an erratic low idle and/or no fast idle with fault code 25 may require that the throttle body wiring harness be tie-wrapped and positioned away from the valve cover edge.
1988-Engine stalling in cold weather may require a new SMEC module (#4557522).
1988-89-A power-steering gear hissing noise may mean the lower steering column coupling is defective.
1988-90-2.2L and 2.5L engines running roughly at idle may need a new EGR valve.
1989-90-2.2L engine knock may require a new engine controller module (#4557518).
• Surging or bucking at 35 to 55 mph with A413 or A670 automatic transmission can be fixed with driveability kit (#4419447).
All models/years-A rotten egg odor coming from the exhaust is probably the result of a malfunctioning catalytic converter that has exceeded the emissions warranty's five-year coverage. Ask for a pro-rated refund. Chrysler has been repairing for free premature engine head gasket, ring and valve wear on its 2.2L and 2.6L engines up to 5 years/80,000 km under its emissions warranty. Again, it's now too late to get a full refund, but you can always try to get Chrysler and the dealer

to pay half the cost.

The 2.6L Mitsubishi engine balancer chains frequently wear out prematurely and often cause serious damage (up to $1500) to the engine's internal components. The problem can be prevented by adjusting the chain every 24,000 km, changing the oil every three months or 5,000 km, and by using SAE 5W-30 motor oil rated for both gas and diesel.

Vehicle Profile

	1983	1984	1985	1986	1987	1988	1989
Cost Price ($)							
Base	7438	7727	7883	8142	8999	9785	11,353
Used Values ($)							
Base ↑	600	900	1300	1700	2300	2800	3300
Base ↓	300	500	700	1000	1300	1700	2100
Reliability	②	②	②	②	③	③	③
Air conditioning	②	②	②	②	②	②	②
Body integrity	②	②	②	②	②	②	③
Braking system	②	②	②	②	②	③	③
Electrical system	②	③	③	③	③	③	③
Engines	②	②	②	②	③	③	③
Exhaust/Converter	②	②	②	②	②	②	③
Fuel system	②	②	②	②	②	②	③
Ignition system	②	②	②	②	②	③	③
Manual transmission	②	②	—	—	—	—	—
- automatic	③	④	④	④	④	④	④
Rust/Paint	②	②	②	②	②	③	③
Steering	②	②	②	②	③	③	③
Suspension	②	②	②	②	②	②	③
Dealer Service	③	③	③	③	③	③	③
Maintenance	③	③	④	④	④	④	④
Parts Availability	③	③	③	③	③	③	③
Repair Costs	③	③	③	③	③	③	③
Crash Safety	②	②	②	②	②	②	②

Acclaim, LeBaron, Spirit

Rating: Recommended (1991-94); Not Recommended 1989-90). These front-drives are a better choice than the Aries/Reliant due to their recent vintage and more refined engines and suspension.

Price analysis: Excellent availability and prices are very reasonable. Expect to pay less than average (about $400 annually) for maintenance and repairs. Other compact cars worth considering: Honda Accord •

Nissan Stanza • Toyota Camry • Volvo 850.

Technical Data

ENGINES	Litres/CID	HP	MPG	Model Years
DOHC I-4T FI	2.2/135	224	17-23	1991-92
OHC I-4 FI	2.5/153	100	22-28	1989-95
OHC I-4 FI	2.5/153	150-152	19-23	1989-92
OHC V6 FI	3.0/181	141-142	18-24	1989-95

Strengths and weaknesses: Although it still uses an outdated design, Chrysler improved assembly quality and backed these cars with a strong base warranty, transferable to second owners. Furthermore, the ease with which the Spirit and Acclaim can be repaired and the low cost of most replacement parts add to their attractiveness as relatively inexpensive five-passenger, fuel-efficient used cars. The 100-hp 2.5L 4-cylinder engine and 3-speed automatic are models of ruggedness.

Acceleration is adequate with the standard 4-cylinder engine, and quite fast and smooth with the 150-hp Chrysler-bred 2.5L turbo. Try to find a car with sport or heavy-duty suspension.

Cylinder head gaskets on the 2.5L engine, front suspension, brakes, fuel system and air conditioning are all prone to rapid wear. The Mitsubishi-built V6 has generated complaints about premature oil leaks and fuel system problems. The Ultradrive A604 4-speed automatic transmissions (renamed the 41TE in 1992) were found early in production to have poor shifting, internal fluid leakage leading to clutch burn-out, and sudden 2nd gear lockup. The problem first becomes apparent when the transmission tries to engage 3rd and 4th gears simultaneously, causing either clutch failure or sticking in 2nd gear. Between 1989 and July 1991, Chrysler tried 28 different changes to resolve the Ultradrive's clutch failures, 2nd gear lockup, and excessive shifting on hills. 41TE automatic transmissions on 1992-95 models are also failure prone.

The air conditioner switches on and off continuously. Windshield wiper and interior fan motors, the speedometer-sending unit and MAP sensor, the steering rack, bushings and front stabilizer bar all often need replacing. Owners report that the steering wheel's vinyl coating rubs off on hands and clothing and the plastics used in the seats and dash area give off vapors that collect as a film on inside window surfaces.

1989-92 LeBarons are more high-tech, but overall road performance and reliability are just as disappointing. The ride is rough and vibrations and rattles are constant. Automatic transmission torque convertors frequently malfunction. The front suspension is particularly trouble prone, and electrical bugs and major computer module failures are common. Wheel bearings, fuel pumps and rear window motors tend to wear out prematurely.

1991-92-Oil leaks and oil pump failures are common, rear brakes are noisy, the heating, air-conditioning and ventilation systems often malfunction, and electrical components (notably electronic modules) are not very durable. Paint and assembly quality are also below par, characterized by body hardware and trim that rust out, break or fall off.

1993-94-Confidential dealer service bulletins indicate that the 41TE transaxle tends to buzz in Reverse and is noisy when shifting. Transmission fluid leaks from the transaxle vent. Other problems include poor AC compressor performance and AC evaporator freezing. Squeaks are common from the strut mount area while turning and the windshield washer nozzles freeze up. Other problems designated in bulletins are acceleration shudder with cars equipped with automatic transmissions, carbon buildup on pistons, stalling while accelerating after a cold start, malfunctioning radios, faulty speedometers, condensation inside the headlights, a faulty serpentine belt, and a stiff accelerator pedal.

All model years have fragile body hardware and sloppy body assembly. Many owners report water infiltration, especially around the windshield and into the trunk. Surface rust is common, especially around the windshield, door bottoms and the rear lip of the trunklid.

Safety summary/recalls: NHTSA crash tests of a 1989 four-door Spirit concluded that the driver would sustain severe or fatal chest injuries in a 57 km/h frontal crash, while the passenger would receive serious leg injuries. A retested '93 Acclaim and '94 Spirit showed a slight improvement: no head trauma, but the driver and passenger would sustain serious leg injuries. A 1987 LeBaron two-door was tested with equally unimpressive scores: the driver would have severe or fatal chest and leg injuries, while the passenger would sustain severe leg trauma. The LeBaron convertible fared just as badly: a 1990 version transmitted crash forces strong enough to cause severe or fatal head injuries to the driver and serious leg injuries to the passenger. The front wheels tend to lock prematurely in heavy braking on all three cars. According to the Washington-based Center for Auto Safety, engine fires due to fuel and oil leaks from 1978-90 front-drive Chrysler's have generated hundreds of complaints. Rear brake lockup and master cylinder failures on 1978-92 models are also common, according to the CFAS. *Recalls*: **1989-90**-Possibility of engine oil leakage means owners can get a new engine valve cover gasket cover. **1991**-Front disc brake caliper guide pin bolts may be too loose. Both airbag front impact sensors may be improperly mounted. Outboard front seatbelts may not latch properly. **1992**-Faulty steering column shaft coupling bolts. **1994**-Seatbelt assembly may fail in an accident. **1990 LeBaron**-Airbag inflator module may be defective.

Secret Warranties/Service Tips/DSBs

1989-Leaking fuel injectors are a common problem that Chrysler once fixed free of charge (TSB No. 18-11-89).

• A power-steering gear hissing noise may mean the lower steering column coupling is defective.

• If the AC heater check valve freezes, install a new vacuum control check valve (#5264270).

• Models with 3.0L engines that lose power may need a new throttle body base gasket.

• 3.0L engines that burn oil, stall or lack power may have excessive sludge accumulation in the left bank (front) rocker cover baffle oil drain hole. Replace the left rocker cover and PCV valve. Clean the PCV valve and MAP sensor hose.

• 2.5L turbo engines that lose power may need Chrysler driveability kit (#4419460), or during hot weather a new vacuum connector (#5277577).

1989-90-A604 automatic transmissions with excessive upshifting/downshifting require a new A604 controller (#4557585).

• Rough idling may require the replacement of the EGR valve.

1989-91-A604 automatic transmissions with 1-2 upshift shudder may need the 2-4 clutch replaced.

1989-93-3.0L engines that burn oil or produce a smokey exhaust at idle can be fixed by installing snap rings on the exhaust valve guides and replacing all of the valve guide stems or the cylinder head.

1990-Excessive alternator belt noise can be stopped by retorquing the mounting bracket and/or installing washers to align the alternator pulley.

• A604 automatic transmissions that limp or fail to shift require the replacement of the PRNDL and Neutral safety switch.

1990-91-Surging or bucking at 35 to 55 mph with A413 or A670 automatic transmission can be fixed with driveability kit (#4419447).

• 2.2L and 2.5L engines with oil leaks at the valve cover need a new cover.

1990-92-A loud clicking or popping occurring when the clutch pedal is depressed signals the need for a new clutch cable spring (#4188653).

• Erratic idle speeds occurring after deceleration from a steady cruising speed can be corrected by replacing the idle air control motor with a revised motor.

1990-94-Harsh automatic shifts can be tamed by installing the following revised parts: kickdown, accumulator, reverse servo cushion springs and the accumulator piston.

1991-Customer Satisfaction Notifications #499 and #521 set out Chrysler's free repair commitment to correct engine oil pump failure. The carmaker will install a revised oil pump and intermediate shaft.

1991-92-Engines with a rough idle and stalling following a cold start may require a new Single Board Engine Controller (SBEC).

1991-93-The serpentine belt may come off the pulley after driving through snow. Install an upgraded shield, screw and retainers.

1991-94-Engines that stall following a cold start may need an upgraded Park/Neutral/start switch.

1991-95-Poor AC performance while the AC blower continues to operate is likely due to the evaporator freezing because the powertrain control module (PCM) isn't properly disengaging the AC clutch via the relay.

1992-If the heater and ventilation system changes to the defrost mode during acceleration, trailer towing or hill climbing, the installation of a revised vacuum check valve should cure the problem.

• Long crank times, a rough idle and hesitation may be corrected by replacing the intake manifold assembly.

• An oil leak in the oil filter area may be corrected by installing a special oil filter bracket gasket (#MD198554).

• A low-frequency moan or groan coming from the rear brakes can be reduced by installing an upgraded rear disk pad set (#4423667).

1992-93-Rough idling after a cold start with 2.2L and 2.5L engines can be corrected by installing an upgraded powertrain control module (PCM).

• Some 41TE transaxles may produce a buzzing noise when shifted into Reverse. This problem can be corrected by replacing the valve body assembly or valve body separator plate.

• A deceleration shudder can be eliminated by replacing the powertrain control module with an upgraded version.

1993-A fuel pump check valve failure can cause startup die-out, reduced power or erratic shifting.

1993-94-Acceleration shudder may be caused by automatic transmission front pump leakage.

• Improved automatic shifting can be had by installing an upgraded transmission control module.

1994-95-Poor AC performance is likely due to defective compressor suction or discharge lines.

All models/years-A rotten egg odor coming from the exhaust is likely the result of a defective catalytic converter that should be replaced free under the 5 year/80,000 km emissions warranty. If the dealer stonewalls your request for a refund, go directly to small claims court.

Chrysler will pay 100% toward the correction of paint defects during the first 3 years/60,000 km and 50% up to the fifth year of ownership—far less than the 6 years/60,000 *miles* GM covers. Water leaking into the vehicle's interior will be corrected without charge up to the fifth year of ownership.

An excessive effort required to disengage Park may mean a new Park rod assembly is required (#4431530). Headlight condensation requires installing vents in the headlight assemblies.

Vehicle Profile

	1989	1990	1991	1992	1993	1994
Cost Price ($)						
Acclaim/Spirit	13,354	13,650	12,425	12,605	13,575	14,100
LeBaron Sedan	—	14,860	13,485	16,720	16,720	16,760
Convertible	18,870	20,065	21,785	20,395	21,715	22,400
Used Values ($)						
Acclaim/Spirit ↑	4000	4600	5300	7000	9200	11,600
Acclaim/Spirit ↓	2500	3200	3900	5500	7700	10,000
LeBaron Sedan↑	4400	—	7100	8500	9700	12,700
LeBaron Sedan ↓	3300	—	5700	6900	8100	10,300
Convertible ↑	6900	8000	10,000	12,000	13,300	18,000
Convertible ↓	5400	6500	8500	10,300	11,800	16,000
Reliability	②	③	③	④	④	④
Air conditioning	②	③	③	③	③	③
Body integrity	❶	❶	③	③	③	③
Braking system	②	②	③	③	③	④
Electrical system	②	②	③	③	④	④
Engines	②	②	③	③	④	④
Exhaust/Converter	②	④	④	⑤	⑤	⑤
Fuel system	③	③	③	③	③	④
Ignition system	③	③	④	④	④	④
Manual transmission	⑤	⑤	⑤	⑤	⑤	⑤
- automatic	②	②	②	②	②	③
Rust/Paint	②	②	④	④	④	④
Steering	②	③	③	⑤	⑤	⑤
Suspension	②	②	③	③	③	④
Dealer Service	③	③	④	④	④	④
Maintenance	③	③	④	⑤	⑤	⑤
Parts Availability	④	④	⑤	⑤	⑤	⑤
Repair Costs	③	③	③	③	④	⑤
Crash Safety						
Spirit/Acclaim	❶	❶	❶	❶	❷	❷
LeBaron Convertible	❶	❶	❶	❶	❶	❶
LeBaron 2-door	❶	—	❶	❶	❶	❶
Safety Features						
ABS	—	—	O	O	O	O
Airbag	—	—	O	O	D	D

Shadow, Sundance

Rating: Average buy (1993-94); Not Recommended (1987-91). Remaining relatively unchanged since their debut, these models are risky buys due to their serious mechanical and body problems. The 1993 and 1994 models are the best of a bad lot.

Price analysis: Excellent availability and prices are very reasonable. Prices for a new 1991 and 1992 model dropped a whopping $2600 and $2300 compared to the 1990 version after the federal manufacturers' tax was removed. Expect to pay about $500 annually for maintenance and repairs. Other compact cars worth considering: Chrysler Spirit/ Acclaim • Honda Accord • Nissan Stanza • Toyota Camry • Volvo 850.

Technical Data

ENGINES	Litres/CID	HP	MPG	Model Years
OHC I-4 FI	2.2/135	93-96	22-25	1987-94
OHC I-4 FI	2.2/135	146	18-22	1987-88
OHC I-4 FI	2.2/135	174	18-22	1990
OHC I-4 FI	2.5/153	96-100	19-24	1988-94
OHC I-4T FI	2.5/153	150-152	18-22	1989-91
OHC V6 FI	3.0/181	142	18-24	1992-94

Strengths and weaknesses: Fairly rapid depreciation makes these cars relatively inexpensive to buy. They are better built than other Chryslers in their class, but they still have many of the same mechanical and body weaknesses Chrysler owners have suffered with throughout the years. On the other hand, finding cheap replacement parts is no problem.

On early models, the turbocharged engine is not very reliable and can be quite expensive to repair. The fuel-injection system can be temperamental and the MacPherson struts leak or wear out prematurely. Front brakes are particularly prone to rapid wear and parking brake cables need more frequent service than normal. Convertible tops on the 1991 Shadow tend to leak profusely and non-metallic paint chips easily.

Owners of 1989-92 models report that cylinder head, oil pan gaskets and rear crankshaft seal are prone to leaking, the air conditioning compressor rarely lasts more than two years, windshield wiper fluid often freezes in hoses, and the power-steering assembly seldom lasts longer than five years. Fortunately, the assembly isn't that expensive to replace. The upgraded '92 41TE automatic transmission is problematic, engine head gaskets often need replacing, oil leaks and oil pump failures are common, rear brakes are noisy, the heating, air-conditioning and ventilation systems often malfunction, electrical components (notably electronic modules) are not very durable and excessive suspension vibrations are common. Body assembly is sloppy, paint discolors or peels prematurely, door moldings fall off and doors freeze shut.

Confidential dealer service bulletins covering the 1993-94s indicate that the 41TE automatic transaxle shifts poorly, leaks transmission fluid from the transaxle vent, tends to buzz in Reverse and is often noisy when shifting. Squeaks are common from the strut mount area while the car is turning. Other problems designated by bulletins are acceleration shudder with cars equipped with automatic transmissions, stalling upon acceleration after a cold start, erratic idling with the car in Reverse, a squeaking manual shifter, carbon buildup on the pistons, excessive intake valve deposits, a rattling speed control switch, faulty speedometers and malfunctioning radios.

Safety summary/recalls: A 1987 two-door Sundance crash tested by the U.S. government provided poor chest and leg protection for the driver and good protection for the front seat passenger. A retested '93 Shadow showed some improvement: only the driver's legs would have been seriously injured. According to the Center for Auto Safety, engine fires due to fuel and oil leaks from 1978-90 front-drive Chryslers have generated hundreds of complaints. Rear brake lockup and master cylinder failures on 1978-92 models are also common, according to the CFAS. American safety researchers are investigating reports of seatback failures on 1991-92 models. Rear visibility is limited. *Recalls*: **1987 Turbo**-Possibility of fuel leak at supply hose/pressure regulator/fuel rail connections. **1987 Shelby**-Parking brake may be faulty. **1988**-Front passenger seatbelt retractor may be faulty, compromising child safety seat protection. **1988-89**-Automatic shoulder restraint system may malfunction in a collision. **1989-91**-Possibility of engine oil leakage means owners can get a new engine valve cover gasket cover. **1991**-Front disc brake caliper guide pin bolts may be too loose. **1991 Shadow**-Both airbag front impact sensors may be improperly mounted. Outboard front seatbelts may not latch properly. **1992**-Faulty steering column shaft coupling bolts.

Secret Warranties/Service Tips/DSBs

1987-Driveline shudder on vehicles with 2.2L turbo engines may need a new intermediate driveshaft bearing mounting (#4504007).
1987-88-If the manual transmission fails to shift into Reverse, install a pull-up ring service kit (#4443404).
1987-89-Exhaust system heat may scorch or melt carpet. Install a heat shield kit (#4549356).
1989-Leaking fuel injectors are a common problem.
• A power-steering gear hissing noise may mean the lower steering column coupling is defective.
• 2.5L turbo engines that lose power may need Chrysler driveability kit (#4419460), or during hot weather a new vacuum connector (#5277577).
1989-90-Rough idling may require the replacement of the EGR valve.
• Squeaking from the exhaust flex joint requires a revised exhaust manifold-to-exhaust pipe sealing ring.
• ES models equipped with a manual 5-speed have defective radiator cradles that can't support the increased torque of the more powerful engine. The '91 versions were given stronger cradles.

1990-Excessive alternator belt noise can be stopped by retorquing the mounting bracket and/or installing washers to align the alternator pulley.

1990-91-Surging or bucking at 35 to 55 mph with A413 or A670 automatic transmission can be fixed with driveability kit (#4419447).

• 2.2L and 2.5L engines with oil leaks at the valve cover need a new cover.

1990-92-A loud clicking or popping occurring when the clutch pedal is depressed signals the need for a new clutch cable adjust spring (#4188653).

• Erratic idle speeds occurring after deceleration from a steady cruising speed can be corrected by replacing the idle air control motor.

1991-93-The serpentine belt may come off the pulley after driving through snow. Install an upgraded shield, screw and retainers.

1991-94-Engines that stall following a cold start may need an upgraded Park/Neutral/start switch.

• Poor AC performance while the AC blower continues to operate is likely due to the evaporator freezing because the powertrain control module (PCM) isn't properly disengaging the AC clutch via the relay.

1992-If the heater and ventilation systems change to the defrost mode during acceleration, trailer towing or hill climbing, the installation of a revised vacuum check valve should cure the problem.

• Long crank times, rough idle and hesitation may be corrected by replacing the intake manifold assembly.

• A thumping noise coming from the rear of the vehicle during light acceleration or braking may be remedied by replacing the fuel level sending unit and seal included in the Sending Unit Package (#4723105).

1992-93-A buzzing heard when the 41TE automatic transmission shifts into Reverse can be fixed by replacing the valve body assembly or the valve body separator plate.

• A deceleration shudder can be eliminated by replacing the powertrain control module with an upgraded version.

• 3.0L engines that burn oil or produce a smokey exhaust at idle can be fixed by installing snap rings on the exhaust valve guides and replacing all of the valve guide stems or the cylinder head.

• Engines that stall following a cold start may need an upgraded Park/Neutral/start switch (see following page).

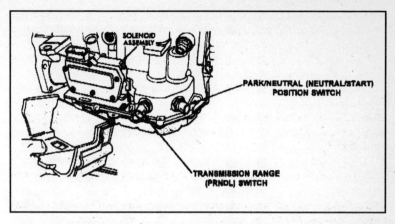

1992-94-Rough idling after a cold start with 2.2L and 2.5L engines can be corrected by installing an upgraded powertrain control module (PCM).

• Harsh automatic shifts can be tamed by installing the following revised parts: kickdown, accumulator, reverse servo cushion springs and accumulator piston.

1993-A fuel pump check valve failure can cause startup die-out, reduced power or erratic shifting.

1993-94-Acceleration shudder may be caused by automatic transmission front pump leakage.

• Improved automatic shifting can be had by installing an upgraded transmission control module.

1994-95-Poor AC performance is likely due to defective compressor suction or discharge lines.

All models/years-A rotten egg odor coming from the exhaust is likely the result of a malfunctioning catalytic converter covered up to 5 years/80,000 km under the emissions warranty. If you exceed these limits, try to get a pro-rated refund. Water leaks into the vehicle interior will be corrected without charge up to the fifth year of ownership.

Vehicle Profile

	1987	1988	1989	1990	1991	1992	1993	1994
Cost Price ($)								
Shadow/Sundance	9402	9795	10,150	11,650	8995	9295	10,750	11,170
Duster V6	—	—	—	—	—	11,400	11,400	14,000
Used Values ($)								
Shadow/Sundance ↑	2000	2500	3000	3800	4300	5500	7500	9200
Shadow/Sundance ↓	1200	1700	2100	2700	3000	4100	6100	7700
Duster V6 ↑	—	—	—	—	—	6600	7900	10,000
Duster V6 ↓	—	—	—	—	—	5200	6600	8600

Reliability	❶	❷	❷	❷	③	③	③	③
Air conditioning	—	❷	❷	❷	❷	❷	❷	❷
Body integrity	❷	③	③	③	③	③	③	③
Braking system	❶	❶	❷	❷	③	③	③	④
Electrical system	❶	❶	❷	❷	③	③	④	④
Engines	❶	❷	③	③	③	③	③	④
Exhaust/Converter	❷	③	③	④	⑤	⑤	⑤	⑤
Fuel system	❶	❷	③	③	❷	③	③	③
Ignition system	❶	❷	③	③	❷	③	④	⑤
Manual transmission	③	③	③	④	④	⑤	⑤	⑤
- automatic	❷	❷	❷	❷	❷	❷	❷	③
Rust/Paint	❷	③	③	③	③	④	④	④
Steering	❷	❷	❷	③	③	③	④	④
Suspension	❷	❷	③	③	④	⑤	⑤	⑤
Dealer Service	③	③	③	③	③	③	③	③
Maintenance	❶	❷	❷	❷	③	⑤	⑤	⑤
Parts Availability	⑤	⑤	⑤	⑤	⑤	⑤	⑤	⑤
Repair Costs	❷	③	③	③	③	④	⑤	⑤
Crash Safety	❶	❶	❶	❶	❶	❶	❷	❷
Safety Features								
ABS	—	—	—	—	—	—	O	O
Airbag	—	—	—	—	O	O	D	D

2000GTX

Rating: An Above Average buy (1991-93). A reliable Japanese-built sedan that was discontinued in 1994.

Price analysis: Limited availability and fairly expensive. Expect to pay about $500 annually for maintenance and repairs. Other compact cars worth considering: Ford Probe • Honda Accord • Nissan Stanza • Toyota Camry • Volvo 850.

Strengths and weaknesses: The 2000GTX has a competitive price, modern styling and high-performance options that put it on par with such benchmark cars as the Honda Accord and Toyota Camry. The base engine provides uninspiring yet adequate performance, but this car is distinguished by the high-performing optional powerplant. The 16-valve version is smooth and powerful, but it must be revved higher than normal for maximum power. The manual transmission and clutch are exceptionally smooth. Handling is acceptable in all situations. Excellent braking with anti-lock brakes, but mediocre without. The ride is firm but fairly comfortable on most roads, especially with the adjustable suspension. Front seat gives good driver position. Comfortable seating for four. Exceptionally clear and well-placed gauges and controls. Interior room is generous for four people and can carry a fifth passenger in a pinch (in the literal sense). Plenty of headroom even with a sunroof. Interior has a lot of little storage areas. Low trunk sill makes for easy loading. Excellent soundproofing.

The 8-valve 2.0L engine has been around for a while without any major reliability or durability problems. A stainless-steel exhaust system cuts down replacement costs. Parts are reasonably priced and easily found. Body assembly and finish are first-rate.

The automatic transmission shifts abruptly at times, and it will hesitate between 3rd and 4th gears occasionally in city driving. The steering is a bit imprecise, but the electronically controlled steering is an unnecessary and expensive gimmick.

High-tech and complicated components may cause problems as the vehicle ages. Some reports of automatic transmission failures around the 60,000-km mark. The front brakes need more attention than average. The underhood area is cluttered with wires and hoses.

Safety summary/recalls: NHTSA crash tests of an '89 four-door Galant, a car identical to the 2000GTX, concluded that the driver would sustain severe leg trauma. The airbag-protected passenger only had a 10 percent to 20 percent chance of serious injury. Data for the driver was inconclusive. *Recalls*: N/A.

Secret Warranties/Service Tips/DSBs:

No data available.

Vehicle Profile

	1991	1992	1993
Cost Price ($)			
Sedan	14,226	14,549	15,230
4X4	20,926	24,514	—
Used Values ($)			
Sedan ↑	5800	7400	9000
Sedan ↓	4500	5900	7500
4X4 ↑	9300	11,200	—
4X4 ↓	7900	9600	—
Reliability	④	④	④
Air conditioning	④	④	④
Automatic transmission	⑤	⑤	⑤
Body integrity	③	③	③
Braking system	③	③	③
Electrical system	③	③	④
Engines	⑤	⑤	⑤
Exhaust/Converter	⑤	⑤	⑤
Fuel system	③	③	③
Ignition system	③	③	③
Rust/Paint	⑤	⑤	⑤

Steering	③	③	④
Suspension	④	④	④
Dealer Service	③	③	③
Maintenance	③	③	③
Parts Availability	③	③	③
Repair Costs	③	③	③
Crash Safety	❷	❷	❷
Safety Features			
ABS	—	—	O

Medallion

Rating: The 1988 and 1989 models are Not Recommended.

Price analysis: Limited availability. Used prices are unbelievably low ($1,500 - 1988; $2200 - 1989) now that the Medallion has been taken off the market. Expect to pay about $900 annually for maintenance and repairs. Other compact cars worth considering: Chrysler Spirit/Acclaim • Honda Accord • Nissan Stanza • Toyota Camry • Volvo 850.

Strengths and weaknesses: The Medallion is a European import spawned by Chrysler's acquisition of AMC/Renault. Its best points are comfort and responsiveness evident during highway cruising, much in the European tradition. Its worst side is that no one has the parts or patience to repair it. Add to that poor reliability and expensive parts and you get a recipe for lots of expensive repairs and lost time. Towing is not recommended.

Information is sketchy, but most owner complaints focus on the car's front brakes, electrical system, engine malfunctions and body hardware. In March of 1988, Chrysler issued five Customer Satisfaction Notifications outlining the following special warranty coverage for specific factory problems:

#8801-Replacement of front brake pads to reduce excessive noise.

#8802-Replacement of the AC pressure hose with a more durable hose.

#8803-Replacement of the electronic control module (ECU) for smoother shifting and engine performance.

#8804-Installation of an oxygen sensor module kit on vehicles equipped with a manual transmission to improve engine performance.

#8805-Install improved windshield molding (all models) that won't loosen and secure the rear door panel trim with adhesive to prevent loosening of panels.

Safety summary/recalls: NHTSA crash tests on a 1988 four-door Medallion showed that the driver would sustain severe or fatal head trauma and the passenger would receive massive leg injuries. A subsequent test of a 1989 four-door Medallion showed that the driver and the front seat passenger would sustain massive leg injuries. *Recalls*: **1988-89**-On vehicles equipped with air conditioning, the fuse block wiring may overheat and cause an engine fire. Chrysler will replace the fuse block.

Monaco, Premier

Rating: Not Recommended (1988-92).

Price analysis: Another auto orphan spawned by the AMC, Renault and Chrysler corporate merger. Limited availability, and used prices are a bit higher than the car merits. Expect to pay over $1000 annually for maintenance and repairs. Other compact cars worth considering: Chrysler Spirit/Acclaim • Honda Accord • Nissan Stanza • Toyota Camry • Volvo 850.

Technical Data

ENGINES	Litres/CID	HP	MPG	Model Years
OHV I-4 FI	2.5/150	111	20-25	1988-89
OHC V6 FI	3.0/182	150	18-24	1988-92

Strengths and weaknesses: When the car runs, it runs well with the accent on comfort and handling. Unfortunately, the Premier doesn't run all that often. As with its older sister, the Medallion, the Premier's failings are many, including the electrical system, engine, transmission, fuel supply (chronic fuel pump freezing), air conditioning, steering, suspension and brakes. Parts and competent servicing are hard to find. Body hardware does not stand up very well to the rigors of Canada's climate.

By taking the Premier off the market, Chrysler hasn't put its troubles to rest. There are still a lot of irate owners who won't simply go away. One Chemainus, B.C. owner of a 1988 Premier had this to say: "We have had electrical chips go while driving in the desert and had overnight expenses due to repairs done in Phoenix—150 miles away. We drove on tires that wore excessively on our long trips and have been without the car for periods of up to four days. We've had the engine stop dead just before crossing a narrow bridge. We have struggled financially and mentally with the lack of quality and general unreliability of the Eagle Premier."

Safety summary/recalls: NHTSA crash tests on a 1989 four-door Premier concluded that the driver would sustain massive leg injuries. Safety experts in the U.S. are investigating 875 reports of ABS brake failures on 1990-91 models and engine fires believed to be caused by an overheated plastic air cleaner on the 1991-92s. *Recalls:***1988**-Brake master cylinder may have been misassembled. Automatic transmissions hooked to a 4-cylinder engine may fail prematurely. **1988-90**-Front brake hose may be misrouted. **1989-91**-A misrouted rear brake tube may leak fluid. Faulty oxygen sensors will be replaced at no charge under an emissions recall campaign. **1989-92**-Heater coolant may scald front passengers. **1990**-Lower intermediate steering shaft may separate. **1991**-Battery main feed wiring may short circuit, creating a fire hazard. **1991 ABS**-Faulty high-pressure hose may leak brake fluid.

Secret Warranties/Service Tips/DSBs

1988-89-An intermittent no-start condition can be remedied by replacing the crank position sensor (CPS) under the emissions warranty.

1988-91-Engine knocking, stalling and surging can be corrected by installing a revised engine controller (ECU).

1988-92-Cold engine no-starts and low engine compression signals the need to install upgraded engine rocker arm assemblies.

1989-90-Rear wheel brake squeal can be reduced by installing a Rear Disk Brake Package #4423662.

1991-92-If the heater blows cold air, it may be necessary to replace the Powertrain Control Module.

• Fuel pump noise, erratic transmission shifting or engine power loss may signal the need to replace the fuel pump module.

• An engine that hesitates and surges can be corrected by installing a new Single Board Engine Controller.

Vehicle Profile

	1988	1989	1990	1991	1992
Cost Price ($)					
LX	17,000	17,815	21,695	18,860	19,800
Used Values ($)					
LX ↑	3500	4300	4700	6100	7500
LX ↓	2400	3100	3400	4600	6000
Reliability	②	②	②	③	③
Air conditioning	①	①	②	②	③
Body integrity	①	②	②	②	③
Braking system	①	②	②	②	②
Electrical system	①	②	②	②	②
Engines	②	③	③	③	③
Exhaust/Converter	③	③	④	④	⑤
Fuel system	②	②	②	②	③
Ignition system	②	②	③	③	③

Manual transmission	③	③	④	④	④
- automatic	②	②	②	③	③
Rust/Paint	③	③	③	③	④
Steering	❶	②	③	③	③
Suspension	❶	②	③	③	③
Dealer Service	❶	❶	❶	❶	❶
Maintenance	❶	❶	❶	❶	❶
Parts Availability	❶	❶	❶	❶	❶
Repair Costs	❶	❶	❶	❶	❶
Crash Safety	❷	❷	❷	❷	❷
Safety Features					
ABS	—	—	—	S	S

FORD

Tempo, Topaz

Rating: Not Recommended (1985-94).

Price analysis: Excellent availability and prices are generally soft, except for the 4X4 version (1990 and later) which is overvalued. Expect to pay about $800 annually for maintenance and repairs—a good reason to snag a Tempo with some of Ford's warranty left. Other compact cars worth considering: Chrysler Spirit/Acclaim • Honda Accord • Nissan Stanza • Toyota Camry • Volvo 850.

Technical Data

ENGINES	Litres/CID	HP	MPG	Model Years
OHV I-4 FI	2.3/141	86-100	22-26	1985-94
OHC I-4D FI	2.0/121	52	33-37	1985-86
OHV V6 FI	3.0/182	130-135	21-24	1992-94

Strengths and weaknesses: Although bargain prices are tempting, you can lose your shirt from frequent and excessive repair costs. Overall quality control on these cars has been much worse than the industry average. On the plus side, repairs are straightforward and the parts supply is ample, except for the Mazda diesel engine.

These cars are riddled with design and manufacturing bugs. Engines, transmissions, electrical systems, electronic modules, fuel pumps, power steering, suspension components and the cruise control all tend to fail prematurely. The 2.0L Mazda diesel engine is unreliable and does not deliver traditional diesel durability.

The 2.3L gas engine is not much better. Cylinder head gaskets tend to leak and the engine's cooling, fuel and ignition systems are plagued by a multitude of breakdowns. Stalling and hard starting are often caused by a malfunctioning catalytic converter. If the car still won't start, mechanics advise owners to tap the solenoid switch behind the battery. The starter motor is weak, and the oil pan gasket tends to leak. There are many complaints of prematurely worn front axles and leaking seals. The air conditioning fails frequently and is expensive to repair. Heater noise often signals the need to change the heater motor. Power-steering rack seals deteriorate quickly. Suspension components, such as tie-rod ends and strut bearings, need replacement almost annually. Shocks, for example, last barely 20,000 km. Front brakes wear out almost as quickly and rotors are easily damaged. Body components are substandard and poorly assembled on all models and all years.

Confidential dealer service bulletins show the 1993s may have poorly performing AC systems caused by a slipping clutch at high ambient temperatures and power-steering units may also be noisy. The '94s appear to be more problematic. Bulletins show they may have a malfunctioning electric rear window defroster, rough idle, hesitation, excessive fuel consumption and poor heater output. Poor automatic transmission shifting is due to a misaligned valve body gasket. Noise in radio speakers is caused by a defective fuel pump.

The front door seal is torn every time the seatbelt doesn't retract properly, the car's air dam often works loose, and the hood cable release mechanism tends to jam. Paint peeling and premature rusting are common. Radio reception is mediocre. The 4X4 models are particularly unreliable, with most of the complaints centering on the driveline, electrical and fuel systems. Parts are plentiful, but they cost more than the North American average.

Safety summary/recalls: NHTSA crash tests of a 1985 Tempo GL showed that the driver and passenger would sustain severe or fatal head injuries. In a test of a '93 Tempo, both the driver and passenger would sustain serious leg injuries. The '94 model performed slightly better, although both of the driver's legs would have been seriously injured. Owners report the daytime driving lights and dome light fail frequently. One Pickering, Ontario owner of a '91 Tempo says, "The car will stall in all weather conditions and in all driving conditions. The engine failure is most apparent when decelerating or stopping after exiting from highways. The car frequently, and dangerously, stalls in the midst of lefthand turns. There is absolutely no warning. The car engine dies and there is occasionally some difficulty reigniting the engine."

Recalls: **1985**-Rear suspension control arm bolts may fail. 2.3L engine stalling, hesitation, and hard starting due to faulty ignition module. **1985-86**-Manual shift lever may accidentally slip into Neutral gear. **1986**-Sudden acceleration on cars with 2.3L engines may be due to a defective electronic control module. **1987**-Again, a faulty 2.3L engine electronic control module may cause high idling, loss of power and stalling. **1987 Tempo**-Stainless-steel lug nuts may cause stud failure/wheel separation. **1988**-Faulty throttle sensor could cause unintended acceleration. **1990**-Fan motor could overheat and cause engine damage.

Secret Warranties/Service Tips/DSBs

1983-90-Buzzing or humming coming from the fuel pump when the engine is shut off, a low battery, and hard or no-starts signal the need to install an upgraded fuel pump relay (#F19Z-9345-A).

1984-86-Surging and bucking during acceleration likely due to a loose intake manifold damaging the gasket.

• Poor heater performance with 2.3L engines may require an upgraded thermostat (#E73Z-8575-A).

1984-87-2.3L engines with Duraspark II ignition may have starting problems. Correct with a new module (#D9UZ-12A199-A).

• Hard starting/stalling caused by defective TFI modules that link a vehicle's distributor to its microprocessor and signal the plugs.

1984-88-Coolant and oil leaks that have plagued 2.3L and 2.5L HSC engines can be stopped by installing an improved cylinder head gasket (#E83Z-6051-A).

• Inoperative power door locks require an upgraded retainer clip assembly (#E8AZ-5421952-A).

1985-92-An exhaust buzz or rattle may be fixed by installing new clamps to secure the heat shield attachments.

1985-91-The in-tank fuel pump is the likely cause of all that radio static you hear. Squelch the noise by installing an electronic noise RFI filter (#F1PZ-18B925-A).

1986-94-Ford offers an upgraded wiper motor service kit for wiper motor malfunctions.

1987-Rough idle or stall at idle may be caused by a shorted 12A581 wire harness.

• No power on acceleration, stalling or high engine idle may require the replacement of the EEC IV processor.

• Warping around the defroster opening requires a new instrument panel pad (#E73Z-5404320-A).

1987-88-All models with EEC IV experiencing no-starts or hard starts probably have a faulty TFI module.

• A steering wheel clunk or looseness can be corrected by putting in an upgraded steering wheel bolt and washer (#M804385-S100).

1987-94-Loss of Reverse gear in cold weather may be due to defective inner and outer Reverse clutch piston seals. Install the upgraded seals indicated by the bulletin on the following page.

```
Article No.
94-24-8
11/28/94
TRANSAXLE - ATX - NO REVERSE IN EXTREME COLD CONDITIONS - SERVICE TIP
FORD:
1987-94 TEMPO
LINCOLN-MERCURY:
1987-94 TOPAZ
ISSUE:
Some vehicles may exhibit the lack of reverse in extreme cold conditions. This could be caused by the inner and outer reverse
clutch piston seals adhering to the adjacent surfaces and separating when the piston moves.
ACTION:
Replace the inner and outer reverse clutch piston seals with the revised material seals if service to the transaxle is required.
The revised seals are identified with an axial white stripe on the inside diameter. Verify gasket and seal kit contain the white
stripe on the inner diameter of the reverse clutch seals. If the kit does not contain the newer seals, discard the seals and
obtain the revised seals.
```

PART NUMBER	PART NAME	CLASS
F43Z-7D403-A	Reverse Clutch Piston Inner Seal	A
F43Z-7D404-A	Reverse Clutch Piston Outer Seal	A

• A rusty catalytic converter inlet pipe flange will be replaced free of charge with a stainless-steel flange under the emissions warranty.

1988-Loss of AC when switching between AC and Max-AC can be fixed by installing an upgraded fan controller (#E83Z-8B658-A).

1988-89-Loose or missing air deflector may cause engine overheating. Install new deflector.

• Engine bucks, jerks, hesitates and stumbles. Install upgraded engine fan controller (#E932-88658-A).

1988-92-Cold hesitation when accelerating, rough idle, long crank times and stalling may all signal the need to clean out excessive intake valve deposits. These problems also may result from the use of fuels that have low volatility, such as high octane, premium blends.

1989-90-Owner Notification #B90: cooling fans on AC may loosen; replace with upgraded fan (#F03Z-8600-B).

1988-94-A speaker whine or buzz caused by the fuel pump can be stopped by installing an electronic noise RFI filter.

1990-Loss of AC cooling may be due to a cracked spring lock connector. Put in a new discharge manifold and discharge hose.

1990-93-Noise heard from the power-steering pump may be caused by air in the system.

1990-94-If the rear view mirror detaches from the windshield, use Ford's mirror attachment kit.

1992-93-The air-conditioner clutch may slip during high ambient temperature conditions. This is likely caused by an improper air gap adjustment between the clutch plate and hub assembly. Set the gap between 0.35 and 0.85 mm.

• An inoperative air conditioner may be due to a faulty cool fan relay (#E93Z-8Z658-A).

All models/years-If the transmission seems erratic in shifting from

2nd gear to 3rd, or downshifting from 3rd to 2nd, at speeds approximating 38 km/h, a newly designed governor spring will have to be installed. A rotten egg odor coming from the exhaust is the result of a malfunctioning catalytic converter.

Two components that benefit from Ford "goodwill" warranty extensions are fuel pumps and computer modules that govern engine, fuel injection, and transmission functions. If Ford balks at refunding your money for a faulty computer module or fuel pump, apply the 5 year/80,000 km emissions warranty.

Ford will pay 100% toward the correction of paint defects during the first 5 years/80,000 km and 50% up to the seventh year of ownership in keeping with the policy it adopted to cover pickups. Water leaking into the vehicle's interior will be corrected without charge up to the fifth year of ownership.

Vehicle Profile

	1987	1988	1989	1990	1991	1992	1993	1994
Cost Price ($)								
L	9520	9794	10,695	11,695	10,695	—	—	—
GL	10,087	10,697	11,536	12,547	11,395	11,295	9995	10,995
LX	11,814	12,208	12,751	13,497	12,295	12,995	10,775	11,195
4X4	—	—	14,864	15,607	14,195	—	—	—
Used Values ($)								
L ↑	1700	2200	2700	3500	4300	—	—	—
L ↓	800	1300	1700	2300	3300	—	—	—
GL ↑	2200	2900	3500	4000	4700	5900	6900	8600
GL ↓	1400	1800	2300	2900	3600	4500	5600	7200
LX ↑	2800	3700	4200	4800	5500	6400	7700	9600
LX ↓	1800	2500	3000	3700	4300	5100	6300	8200
4X4 ↑	—	—	4700	5600	6500	—	—	—
4X4 ↓	—	—	3500	4400	5600	—	—	—
Reliability	①	①	①	①	②	③	③	③
Air conditioning	①	②	②	②	②	②	②	②
Body integrity	②	②	②	③	③	③	③	③
Braking system	①	①	②	③	③	③	③	③
Electrical system	②	②	①	①	②	②	②	②
Engines	①	①	①	①	②	②	③	③
Exhaust/Converter	①	①	①	①	③	③	③	③
Fuel system	①	①	①	①	②	②	②	②
Ignition system	①	①	①	②	②	②	③	③
Manual transmission	④	④	④	④	④	④	⑤	⑤
- automatic	②	②	②	②	②	③	③	③
Rust/Paint	①	②	②	③	③	③	③	④
Steering	①	①	②	②	③	③	③	③
Suspension	①	①	①	①	②	②	②	③

Dealer Service	①	①	①	②	②	②	②	②
Maintenance	①	①	①	②	③	③	③	③
Parts Availability	⑤	⑤	⑤	⑤	⑤	⑤	⑤	⑤
Repair Costs	①	①	①	①	①	③	③	③
Crash Safety	①	①	①	①	①	①	①	①
Safety Features								
Airbag	—	—	—	—	—	—	—	O

GENERAL MOTORS

Beretta, Corsica, Tempest

Rating: Not Recommended (1987-94).

Price analysis: Lots are available at reasonably prices. The Corsica is the entry-level model, followed in price by the Tempest and Beretta. The 1991 and 1992 models carried substantially reduced prices after the federal manufacturer's tax was dropped. Expect to pay about $700 annually for maintenance and repairs. Other compact cars worth considering: Chrysler Spirit/Acclaim • Honda Accord • Nissan Stanza • Toyota Camry • Volvo 850.

Technical Data				
ENGINES	Litres/CID	HP	MPG	Model Years
OHV I-4 FI	2.0/121	90	22-27	1987-89
OHV I-4 FI	2.2/133	95-120	21-25	1990-95
DOHC I-4 FI	2.3/138	170-180	19-25	1990-94
OHV V6 FI	2.8/173	130	19-25	1987-89
OHV V6 FI	3.1/191	135-160	18-24	1990-94

Strengths and weaknesses: These L-bodies are worse cars than the J-bodies (Cavalier, Skyhawk, Firenza, J2000, 2000 and Sunbird) they were intended to replace. The anemic, failure-prone and expensive-to-repair 2.0L 4-cylinder engine with its faulty computer modules is a major disappointment. Modest inclines require shifting into low gear. Owners report frequent no-starts and stalling with all engine variations, due mainly to temperamental electronic modules, particularly in conjunction with multi-port fuel-injection systems. Fuel system and ignition glitches are legion and the cruise control operation is erratic. Servicing is made difficult by the tight engine compartment. The V6 engine is seriously weakened by air conditioning and the automatic transmission's poor quality control. The lockup on the automatic engages and disengages constantly. The 5-speed manual performs better but it, too, is unreliable, being handicapped by long clutch pedal travel and a tendency to stall at light throttle. Owners report some instances where it has shifted into Reverse rather than 1st gear. Steering is vague, and components are unreliable. Braking is terrible, and the front brakes rust and wear out quickly. The standard suspension offers poor ride control on bumpy roads, produces excessive body roll in turns and is characterized by imprecise handling, especially at highway speeds. The sport suspension option (standard on some models) offers better handling and a firmer but comfortable ride. Shock absorbers often begin leaking before 50,000 km and the replacement of the suspension struts is sometimes an annual affair. Electrical components often short circuit. Owners report that the windshield wiper motor fails frequently.

1990-92 models also have more than their share of performance problems and factory-related defects. Braking is still scary, even with ABS, and cornering is a white-knuckle affair. The 2.2L engines have a "piston scuffing" problem and the Quad 4 engine's head gaskets fail prematurely. Hard starting, stalling and engine surging are common, and AC operation is erratic.

Confidential dealer service bulletins covering the 1993 models show the 2.2L engine frequently hesitates and stalls and the 3T40 automatic transmission may lose Reverse gear or slip in Reverse. Bulletins also show the '94s and '95s may lose engine coolant due to a faulty surge tank cap, the power steering may lead or pull, Quad 4 engines continue to perform poorly, and V6-equipped models may experience excessive 2nd gear vibrations caused by a defective hub shaft bearing and sleeve assembly. Problems specific to the 1994 models include AC leaks, excessive noise, and insufficient cooling, automatic transaxle gear whine, harsh upshifts and premature front brake wear.

For all years, overall body assembly is poor, water leaks, squeaks and rattles are legion, and paint problems abound. Body parts are generally poor quality and often break, deform, fall away or corrode prematurely. Adding insult to injury, body parts are also unreasonably expensive to replace. There are also frequent reports of side window disengagement, water leaking through the rear windows, and rattles coming from loose parts in the door-locking mechanism.

GM announced in the January 18, 1993 edition of *Automotive News* that Corsica and Beretta paint peeling would be covered for six years under a special extended warranty. This change in GM's policy was first communicated to American dealers on October 16, 1992 in a series of letters and bulletins sent to each division's dealers.

Amazingly, GM Canada weasels out of paying many claims for paint repairs by ignoring the *Automotive News* article or by pretending that the extended warranty applies only to the U.S.

186

Safety summary/recalls: Crash tests of a 1988 four-door Corsica concluded that only the driver would sustain severe or fatal leg injuries. A test of a 1988 two-door Beretta GT showed even less crash protection; both the driver and passenger would have sustained massive leg injuries. A 1991 airbag-equipped two-door Beretta and four-door Corsica were subsequently tested and passed with flying colors: both the driver and passenger would have escaped serious injury. Crash tests of a 1994 four-door Corsica concluded that the passenger would suffer massive head injuries and that the driver would sustain severe injuries to both legs. There have been many reports of rear-wheel lockup and sudden brake loss on non-ABS equipped models and ABS brake performance hasn't been impressive. 1990-91 models with throttles that stick in open or closed position and leaking fuel filters are being probed by Transport Canada. *Recalls*: **1987-88**-Hood could fly up. Front door hinge breakage requires the installation of upgraded hinges (#10092242-3). **1988-89**-Front shoulder belt retractors may fail in a collision. **1989**-Dealers will install free front seatbelt latch plate and buckle. Fuel tank could leak. Dealers will replace both front seat frames, if found defective. **1989 Corsica**-Steel wheel fracture could cause wheel separation. **1991**-Loose steering wheel nut may cause steering wheel separation. **1992**-Faulty brakelight switch. **1992-93**-Dealers will install a redesigned intake manifold gasket on vehicles with rough-running 2.2L engines. **Models with 2.3L Quad 4 engines-1988-89**-Vehicles may have a cracked fuel-hose feed, causing a fuel leak. **1990**-Faulty ignition coils that cause engine misfiring will be replaced under an emissions recall campaign.

Secret Warranties/Service Tips/DSBs

1987-89-AC refrigerant loss may be corrected by installing a new valve and cap seal.
• No 1st gear/and or slips in 1st may mean you need new forward clutch piston seals.
• Poor AM/FM reception caused by poor contact on the female terminal of the antenna coaxial cable lead.
1987-Erratic idle and 2.0L engine surging require the replacement of the PROM.
1987-88-Brake pulsations may be caused by unevenly worn brake rotors. Install upgraded, reduced diameter caliper slide pins (#18016164).
• A rotten egg odor can be stopped by replacing the catalytic converter. Independents sell the part for half what the dealer charges.
• Difficult cold starts with 2.0L engines may require a new drop-in manifold deflector plate (#10112342).
• High accelerator pedal effort or inoperative cruise control may require a new throttle body actuating linkage.
• Rear speaker ignition noise calls for the installation of a separate

jumper cable harness.

1987-89-Free emissions warranty replacement of the port fuel injector on 2.8L engines.

• Excessive 2.0L engine knock may signal a need for tighter fitting pistons.

1987-90-GM will repaint cars with paint blemishes at no cost to owners under a special policy adjustment.

1987-91-Vehicles equipped with the 3T40 automatic transmission may experience slippage in manual Low or Reverse. Install Service Package #8628222; it includes a Low/Reverse clutch release spring (#8664961) and clutch retainer and snap ring (#656/657).

1988-Erratic performance of the window motor may call for a replacement brush package (#22094719).

• 2.0L engine valve train noise can be reduced by adjusting or replacing the rocker arms.

• Lack of heat in the rear may require upgraded floor heater outlets.

• Corsica bumpers or facias that warp or sag near the license plate will be fixed free.

1988-95-A binding or popping noise coming from the front door glass when the glass is rolled down means the regulator arm stabilizer plate is misadjusted.

1988-89-Product Campaign #89C06 provides for the free rewiring of a faulty 2.0L engine coolant switch.

• 2.0L engines that fail to run or stall in cold weather probably need a new PROM.

• Door rattles can be corrected by installing upgraded anti-rattle clips (#16608794)

1989-Product Campaign #89C16 provides for the free replacement of the 5-speed manual transmission.

• Occasional 2.8L engine stalling may require the replacement of the MEMCAL.

1989-90-If the wiper starts in high speed only, install service package #22063283.

1989-91-A power-steering shudder, moan or vibration signals the need for a "tuned" power-steering return hose and/or high-expansion pressure hose between the steering pump and gear.

1990-Engine piston scuffing may cause cold engine knock. GM DSB 90-433-6A recommends a partial engine replacement.

1990-91-No-starts, stalling and rough running may be caused by a DIS ignition wiring short-circuit.

• Poor starting may be caused by the spring in early starter drives compressing too easily. Install an upgraded starter motor drive assembly (#10473700).

• Engine overheating or poor AC performance may be due to an inoperative engine cooling fan.

1990-92-Poor braking may be due to excessive corrosion of the front disc brake caliper bolt bore.

1991-94-A crunching noise coming from the right side of the dash when turning the steering wheel can be silenced by installing a new steering grommet on the right side.

• Water leaking onto the right front carpet from a gap between the air inlet screen and windshield can be stopped by applying a urethane sealing strip as show in the diagram below.

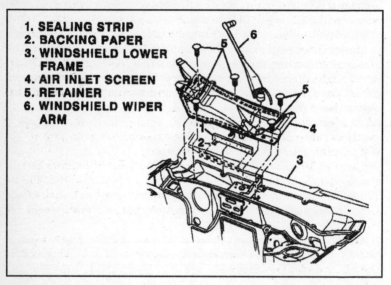

1. **SEALING STRIP**
2. **BACKING PAPER**
3. **WINDSHIELD LOWER FRAME**
4. **AIR INLET SCREEN**
5. **RETAINER**
6. **WINDSHIELD WIPER ARM**

1992-Chafing of the engine harness wires can cause hard starting, engine surging, stalling in gear, the display of the "Service Engine Soon" warning and an inoperative temperature gauge.

• Engine hesitation or roughness, particularly at idle, may be corrected by installing a new lower intake manifold gasket (#10103647).

1992-93-No Reverse or slipping in reverse can be corrected by installing an upgraded Low/Rev. clutch return spring and spiral retaining ring.

1992-94-Front brake linings can be made to last longer by replacing the front brake pads with new 8100 lining compound (#18022600).

1994-Insufficient AC cooling may be due to a leak at the low charge primary port seal.

• Automatic transaxle gear whine may be eliminated by installing a redesigned transaxle final drive assembly.

• A squeaking noise heard when going over bumps, accelerating, or shifting can be stopped by replacing the exhaust manifold pipe seal.

• Harsh automatic transmission upshifts can be corrected by installing an upgraded accumulator valve in the control valve body.

• Loss of Drive or erratic shifts may be caused by an intermittent short to ground on the A or B shift solenoid or an electrical short-circuit in the transaxle.

• Knocking from the accessory drive belt tensioner requires an upgraded replacement.

2.3L Quad 4 engine

1990-91-Head gasket leaks are a problem covered by a secret warranty extension. The first sign of trouble is a loss of power caused by combustion gases mixing with coolant. This is followed by a cloud of steam and coolant loss through the exhaust system. If these warnings are ignored, cylinder bore scoring, a warped cylinder head and piston seizure will likely result as the engine continues to overheat. Up to 6 years/60,000 miles, GM will replace the head gasket with an improved version and carry out a new multi-step head-bolt tightening procedure at no cost to the owner. The deductible will be also refunded. Others who bought their cars used or had repairs done at an independent garage are eligible for this free repair and a refund if the engine has already been fixed.

All models/years-A rotten egg odor coming from the exhaust is probably caused by a malfunctioning catalytic converter covered by GM's 5 year/80,000 km emissions warranty.

General Motors will repair defective steering assemblies free of charge up to 5 years/80,000 km and pay half the cost up to 100,000 km. There is no labor charge or $100 supplementary warranty deductible. Used vehicles and repairs carried out by independent garages are covered by this special program.

Don't forget to hold GM responsible for paint defects up to 6 years/60,000 *miles* (see GM's internal dealer memo sent to U. S. dealers in this *Guide* under Bonneville).

Vehicle Profile

	1988	1989	1990	1991	1992	1993	1994
Cost Price ($)							
Beretta	12,448	13,098	14,099	12,698	12,998	12,999	15,300
Beretta GT	14,150	14,998	16,498	15,398	14,898	14,998	—
Beretta GTZ	—	—	19,498	18,298	18,298	18,398	18,398
Corsica LT	11,239	12,298	12,298	12,098	12,698	12,998	15,698
Corsica LTZ	—	14,898	17,399	—	—	—	—
Tempest	11,528	12,798	13,500	12,396	—	—	—
Used Values ($)							
Beretta ↑	3700	4600	5200	6100	7700	9000	11,000
Beretta ↓	2700	3300	4000	4900	6300	7600	9500
Beretta GT ↑	3900	5800	7000	7800	9400	10,500	—
Beretta GT ↓	2900	4600	5700	6500	8000	9100	—
Beretta GTZ ↑	—	—	8200	8900	10,700	12,500	—
Beretta GTZ ↓	—	—	6900	7600	9300	10,500	—
Corsica LT ↑	3300	4000	4800	5900	7300	8600	10,800
Corsica LT ↓	2500	3200	3700	4700	5900	7200	9300
Corsica LTZ ↑	—	6100	7100	—	—	—	—
Corsica LTZ ↓	—	5100	5800	—	—	—	—
Tempest ↑	3100	3800	4900	5700	—	—	—

Tempest ↓	2100	2700	3700	4500	—	—	—
Reliability	①	①	②	②	②	②	②
Air conditioning	②	②	②	②	②	②	②
Body integrity	②	②	②	②	②	②	②
Braking system	①	①	①	①	①	②	②
Electrical system	①	①	②	②	③	③	③
Engines	①	①	②	②	②	③	③
Exhaust/Converter	②	②	③	③	③	④	④
Fuel system	①	①	②	②	③	③	③
Ignition system	①	②	②	②	③	③	③
Manual transmission	②	②	③	③	③	④	④
- automatic	②	②	②	②	②	②	②
Rust/Paint	①	②	②	②	②	②	②
Steering	①	②	②	③	③	④	④
Suspension	①	②	②	③	③	④	④
Dealer Service	②	②	②	②	③	③	③
Maintenance	③	③	③	③	③	③	③
Parts Availability	⑤	⑤	⑤	⑤	⑤	⑤	⑤
Repair Costs	①	①	②	②	②	②	③
Crash Safety							
Corsica 4-door	②	②	②	⑤	⑤	⑤	①
Beretta 2-door	①	①	①	⑤	⑤	⑤	⑤
Safety Features							
ABS	—	—	—	—	S	S	S
Airbag	—	—	—	D	D	D	D

Saturn

Rating: Above Average Buy (1994); Average buy (1992-93). Almost as good as the Japanese competition.

Price analysis: Reasonable availability but fairly expensive. Expect to pay about $400 annually for maintenance and repairs. The Geo Storm, Honda Civic LX and Toyota Corolla perform well and offer better quality for about $1500 more. They don't match the Saturn for interior room, however. Other compact cars worth considering: Chrysler Spirit/Acclaim • Honda Accord • Nissan Stanza • Toyota Camry • Volvo 850.

Technical Data

ENGINES	Litres/CID	HP	MPG	Model Years
OHC I-4 FI	1.9/116	85	27-33	1991-94
OHC I-4 FI	1.9/116	100	27-35	1995
DOHC I-4 FI	1.9/116	123	23-29	1991-95

Strengths and weaknesses: Conceived as an all-American effort to beat the Japanese in the small car market, the Saturn compact is a better car than the other GM home-grown compacts we have learned to be wary of over the past 20 years. Nevertheless, the car has had a surprising number of serious body and mechanical problems that GM has covered under its base warranty. Second owners aren't treated as generously.

Overall, these are competitively priced, roomy and comfortable small cars. Handling is nimble for both two-door coupes and four-door sedans. Powered by a 4-cylinder aluminum engine, and a multi-valve variation of the same powerplant in the coupe, these cars are remarkably fuel efficient with the base engine hooked to a manual transmission.

The double-cam, multi-valve 1.9L powerplant is no neck-snapper, but it does a decent job in most situations when coupled to a manual transmission that is precise and easily shifted. The rack and pinion steering is fairly precise and predictable, while the suspension gives a firm, but not harsh, ride.

The base, single-cam engine gives barely adequate acceleration times (12.2 seconds to reach 60 mph) with the manual transmission. This time is increased to a near glacial 13.7 seconds with the 4-speed automatic gearbox that robs the engine of what little power it produces. Another generic problem affecting all model years is stalling and hard starting. The 5-speed manual transmission sometimes has trouble going into Reverse, and with the automatic, there is lots of gearbox shudder when the kickdown is engaged while passing.

Dealer service bulletins indicate that three major quality problems are likely to crop up: malfunctioning automatic transmissions, electrical short-circuits, and numerous wind and water leaks. On early models, the doors were poorly fitted, rear seats had to be lowered a half inch to give much needed headroom, engine mounts were changed to reduce vibrations, the shifter mechanism on the manual transmission was unreliable and the reclining front seats were recalled because they could suddenly slip backward. Rear headroom is a bit tight and owners report that the headliner in the rear tends to sag.

Confidential dealer service bulletins covering the 1993 models show the AC may emit foul odors and the trunk lock assembly may be defective. The '94s may have malfunctioning cruise control assemblies, engine knocking, rough running, hard starting, and stalling, malfunctioning window cranks, paint spotting (white paint only), suspension/body noises, floor board rattles, inoperative electrically controlled door locks, and radio static when the power windows are operated.

Safety summary/recalls: A 1991 Saturn SL2 crash-tested by the U.S. government failed to prevent possible serious head injury to the front occupant; the driver would have sustained only minor injuries. A retested 1993 SL2 showed both the driver and front passenger would receive severe leg injuries. The 1994's test results were worse: serious leg injuries to driver and passenger in addition to severe head trauma to the passenger. The U. S. government is probing reports of cruise control failures on 1993-95 Saturns. The optional ABS brakes, while effective, take what seems to be a long time to grip the discs. *Recalls*: **1991**-Seatback recliners will be strengthened at no charge. **1991-92**-The seatbelt retractor may not retract the belt fully. **1991-93**-Faulty trunk lock assemblies will be replaced. GM dealers will install at no charge a fusible link wiring harness to prevent an engine fire. **1992**-Automatic shift lever may show the wrong gear. **1993**-Sudden brake loss may be caused by a faulty brake booster housing. Positive battery terminal could contact starter solenoid creating a fire hazard. The windshield wiper and brake booster assemblies will be inspected and replaced if necessary at no charge under two separate safety recalls.

Secret Warranties/Service Tips/DSBs

1991-Engine misses, surges or backfires may be caused by a poor ground at the electronic distributorless ignition (DIS). Install another DIS module.
• Headlamps that stay on when the switch is turned off can be fixed by installing an upgraded switch.
• Loose door trim panels can be refastened by installing upgraded retainers on both doors.
• Wind noise from the front and rear doors may be caused by insufficient sealing under the mirror patch gasket, missing sealer at certain locations (for example, the door frame to door assembly at the beltline), insufficient contact of the secondary seals to door openings, or the glass run channels not sealing to the glass at the upper corners.
1991-92-Some owners of 1991 and 1992 models have reported excessive noise and vibration levels coming from the steering wheel, seat and floor pan. Saturn officials say the noise and vibration may be caused by:
• preloaded powertrain mounts (1991)
• preloaded engine strut cradle bracket (1992)
• improperly positioned or worn exhaust system isolators and muffler band clamp/block (1991-92)
• lower cooling module grommets, improper positioning of wiring harnesses and upper cooling system module grommets (1991-92)
• improper routing of AC hoses or hood release cable and air inlet snorkel (1991-92)
• debris in accessory drive belt pulleys (1991)
• improper adjustment of hood stop(s) (1991-92)
• PCV or brake booster check valve noise (1991)
• DOHC (LLO) automatic transaxle mount assembly replacement (1991)
• malfunction of the engine's electrical or fuel systems (1991-92).
1991-94-Rough running or surging after a cold start may signal the need to clean carbon or fuel deposits from the engine's intake valves. (see diagram on next page)

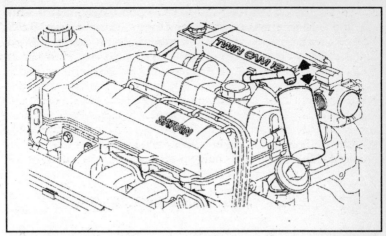

• The many causes of hard-to-crank windows are covered in DSB 94-T-19.

• Inoperative electric door locks may have been shorted by water contamination. Since the design and positioning of the power door lock relay allows this to develop, Saturn is accepting claims on a case-by-case basis.

• Water leaks into the front footwell and at the front upper door frame are treated in depth in two DSBs published in August and November 1994.

• Whistling noises are also treated in two different bulletins published in June and October 1994.

1991-95-Erratic cruise control operation can be corrected by replacing the cruise control module assembly.

• If the engine stalls within five minutes after starting, or when coming to a stop, or is difficult to restart, the oil viscosity or engine's hydraulic lifters may be at fault.

• Engine squealing after a cold start can be corrected by installing an upgraded belt idler pulley assembly.

1992-An engine that stalls, hesitates or surges during light acceleration may require new PCM calibrations.

• Harsh Reverse engagement can also be corrected by new PCM calibrations.

1993-94-A popping noise coming from the base of the lefthand A-pillar, hinge pillar, and engine compartment is caused by a slight flexing in the area were the three are joined together.

1994-White Saturns may have yellow stains or spotting along the fenders, fender extension or quarter panel. If so, the company will change the affected part and repaint the area at no charge to the owner.

• Saturns equipped with manual transmissions may find the transaxle stuck in two gears due to a defective shift control housing.

1994-95-Excessive engine knocking can be corrected by changing the clearance between the piston pin and connecting rod bushing.

All models/years-A rotten egg odor coming from the exhaust is likely the result of a malfunctioning catalytic converter that you can get replaced free of charge under GM's 5 year/80,000 km emissions warranty. Remember, GM says it's responsible for paint defects up to six years or 60,000 miles (see GM internal document in the Bonneville section).

Vehicle Profile

	1992	1993	1994
Cost Price ($)			
SL	9895	10,995	11,595
SL1	11,080	12,350	12,825
SL2	13,865	15,095	14,510
SC	14,620	15,840	13,895
Used Values ($)			
SL ↑	7100	8200	9500
SL ↓	6000	7000	8600
SL1 ↑	8000	9300	10,200
SL1 ↓	6700	7900	9300
SL2 ↑	9300	10,900	11,500
SL2 ↓	7800	9400	10,800
SC ↑	10,700	12,000	12,500
SC ↓	9200	10,200	10,800
Reliability	③	③	④
Air conditioning	③	③	⑤
Automatic transmission	③	④	④
Body integrity	③	③	③
Braking system	③	④	④
Electrical system	③	③	③
Engines	③	③	③
Exhaust/Converter	⑤	⑤	⑤
Fuel system	④	⑤	⑤
Ignition system	④	⑤	⑤
Rust/Paint	③	③	④
Steering	⑤	⑤	⑤
Suspension	④	④	④
Dealer Service	④	④	④
Maintenance	③	③	④
Parts Availability	⑤	⑤	⑤
Repair Costs	④	④	④
Crash Safety			
SL2	❷	❶	❶
Safety Features			
ABS	O	O	O
Airbag	—	D	D
Traction control	—	—	O

Cavalier, Cimarron, Firenza, J2000, Skyhawk, Sunbird

Rating: Average buy (1992-94); Not Recommended (1984-91).

Price analysis: Although the Cavalier and Sunbird have serious reliability problems, anyone who is mechanically inclined can easily fix them at little cost by picking up parts from independent suppliers. These cars are particularly unforgiving, however, if maintenance schedules aren't followed to the letter, as one photographer from the *Ottawa Citizen* and Cavalier owner knows all too well. A Cadillac Cimarron is worth little more than a Cavalier, which costs half as much new. The fully equipped Cavalier Z24 and convertibles have a remarkably low rate of depreciation, unlike other Cavalier models. Z24 convertible prices are listed until the RS convertible appeared in 1992. Base Sunbirds usually cost a few hundred dollars more than a practically identical Cavalier, but the Cavalier's sportier versions often cost more than the Sunbird equivalent. The base Sunbird became the LE in 1989. Expect to pay about $700 annually for maintenance and repairs. Other compact cars worth considering: Chrysler Spirit/Acclaim • Honda Accord • Nissan Stanza • Toyota Camry • Volvo 850.

Technical Data				
ENGINES	Litres/CID	HP	MPG	Model Years
OHV I-4 FI	2.0/121	85-90	21-25	1985-89
OHV I-4 FI	2.2/133	95-120	21-25	1990-94
OHV V6 FI	2.8/173	120-130	19-23	1985-89
OHV V6 FI	3.1/173	135-140	19-23	1990-94
	Sunbird			
OHC I-4 FI	1.8/109	82-84	24-27	1985-86
OHC I-4T FI	1.8/109	150	20-24	1985-86
OHV I-4 FI	2.0/122	88	21-26	1985
OHC I-4 FI	2.0/121	96-111	22-26	1987-94
OHC I-4T FI	2.0/121	165	19-24	1987-90
OHV V6 FI	3.1/191	140	18-22	1991-94

Strengths and weaknesses: Snappy road performance (with the right engine and transmission hook-up) has been marred by abysmally poor reliability. The basic versions are lackluster performers. The 2.L 4-cylinder engine gets overwhelmed by the demands of passing and merging. On top of that, major reliability weaknesses afflict all J-body mechanical and body components. Engine, transmission, electronic module and brake failures are common throughout all model years. 2.0L engine blocks crack, cylinder heads leak and the turbocharged version frequently needs expensive repairs. Oil leakage from the rear crankshaft seal is common. Oil filters on all model years tend to wear out quickly.

For the 1986-87 model years, improvements simply changed the nature, not the frequency, of breakdowns. Power-steering rack and front suspension components are not durable. Consider replacing the original components with front gas struts and rear cargo coil springs to improve handling and durability. Owners also report that a change to high-octane fuel can help improve engine performance, and reduce knocking and engine run on. The cooling, exhaust, ignition and fuel systems have had more than the average number of problems. The manifold heat shield tends to be noisy. Front brakes wear out quickly, and the rear brakes tend to lock the rear wheels in emergency stops (one cause being the seizure of the rear brake adjusters). The optional 2.8L V6, with a 3-speed automatic transmission, is the best highway performer, but intake manifold gasket failures, premature head gasket wear and transmission malfunctions compromise driving pleasure.

For 1990 and later versions, a base 2.2L 4-cylinder and optional 3.1L replaced the failure-prone 2.0L and 2.8L powerplants. The newer engines already have a checkered reputation highlighted by reports of hard starting, stalling and surging. Air-conditioning and hood latch failures, seatbelt defects, and a plethora of body deficiencies are also commonplace. Door bottoms and wheelhousings are particularly vulnerable to rust perforation. Premature paint peeling and cracking, discoloring and surface rust have been regular problems since these cars were introduced. Amazingly, GM Canada customer relations people deny this is a defect and insist upon blaming the problem on acid rain or road debris (phenomena that prey upon GM products).

Confidential dealer service bulletins covering the 1993 models confirm the following problems: 3.1L engines hesitate or stall, no Reverse or slipping in Reverse with 3T40 automatic transmissions and rear brake squawk. For 1994s, problems include lots of body fit deficiencies, premature front brake wear, faulty ignition switches, and electrical short-circuits.

Safety summary/recalls: NHTSA crash tests of a 1986 four-door Cavalier found only the passenger would suffer serious leg injuries. A 1990 version was judged to cause serious leg trauma to the driver. A year later, a 1991 four-door Cavalier was crash tested and neither the driver nor passenger would have been injured. Unfortunately, the '93 and '94 Cavaliers didn't do as well; the driver would have had both legs severely injured. Tests of a 1987 and 1990 four-door Sunbird also concluded that the driver would sustain serious leg trauma. The Cavalier data applies also to the Firenza, Skyhawk and Cimarron. Engine fires have been reported with 1983 and 1984 models while electrical wire harness short-circuits create a fire hazard with 1988-91 models. This last problem is believed to be caused by the engine cooling fan drawing too much current. *Recalls*: **1983-84** The floor pan anchor on cars with a manually adjusted driver's seat could break, permitting the driver's seat to tip rearward suddenly and causing a potential loss of vehicle control. A free reinforcing bracket is available under this safety recall. Models with 2.0L engines may suddenly accelerate due to a kinked accelerator control cable. A recall campaign has been launched to fix the defect. **1985**-Air cleaner plastic trim could catch fire. **1986**-Defective headlight switch can cause headlights to flicker or fail. **1987**-Possibility the fuel feed/return lines will crack, leaking fuel. Parking brake lever may fail, allowing the vehicle to roll away unexpectedly. Cars with 2.0L engines may have a frozen accelerator cable that would cause sudden acceleration. **1989**-Free inspection and replacement of the fuel tank which could leak fuel. **1991**-Cracked front-door shoulder belt guide loops could pull loose in an accident. Front door frames that anchor the seatbelt housing could collapse in an accident, resulting in seatbelt failure. **1992**-The hood could open suddenly, blocking the driver's view. Install a new secondary hood latch spring. **1993**-Faulty rear brake hoses could cause brake failure. **1992-93**-Dealers will install a redesigned intake manifold gasket on vehicles with rough-running 2.2L engines. **1994**-Loose drive-axle spindle nuts may cause steering knuckle tire-wheel assembly to separate from the axle. **Sunbird-1988**-Inoperative backup lights due to a short-circuit will be fixed free of charge. **1992-93**-Vehicles equipped with 2.0L engines may have defective throttle-cable assemblies that could stick open in cold weather and cause the vehicle to accelerate.

Secret Warranties/Service Tips/DSBs

1985-88-Premature brake lining wear may be caused by a misadjusted cruise control cutoff or brake light switch. Both switches can keep the brake pedal engaged without you knowing it.

1985-89-No 1st gear and/or slips in 1st may mean you need new forward clutch piston seals.

1985-90-Exhaust boom or moan can be corrected by installing a mass dampener (#10137382).

• Noise from rear springs requires the installation of upgraded rear spring insulators (#22555689).

1986-87-Erratic idle and 2.0L engine surging require the replacement of the PROM or TCC solenoid. Another possible cause is a defective mass air flow sensor.

1987-88-Difficult cold starts with 2.0L engines may require a new drop-in manifold deflector plate (#10112342).

• A sagging headliner needs service package #22541347.

1987-90-A rattle or buzz from the instrument panel may require a new, upgraded brake booster check valve (#18012017).

1988-Occasional 2.8L engine stalling may require the replacement of the MEMCAL.

1988-89-2.0L engines that run poorly or stall in cold weather probably need a new PROM.

- 2.0L engine valve train noise can be reduced by adjusting or replacing the rocker arms.

1988-94-Water leaks at the front upper door frame are treated in depth in a DSB issued in October 1994.

1989-Product Campaign 89C16 provides for the free replacement of the 5-speed manual transmission.

1990-Heater and AC blower noise can be reduced by replacing the blower assembly.

1990-91-Poor starting may be caused by the spring in early starter drives compressing too easily. Install an upgraded starter motor drive assembly (#10473700).

1991-94-A crunching noise coming from the right side of the dash when turning the steering wheel can be silenced by installing a new steering grommet on the right side.

1992-94-Front brake linings can be made to last longer by replacing the front brake pads with new 8100 lining compound (#18022600).

1993-94-Excessive engine vibrations at idle or a clunk upon acceleration are likely due to a defective engine mount.

1994-A squeaking noise heard when going over bumps, accelerating, or shifting can be stopped by replacing the exhaust manifold pipe seal.

- A hard-to-adjust temperature control may require a new temperature cable.

- Water leaks into the front footwell are treated in depth in a December 1993 DSB.

Cavalier

1985-88-Brake pulsations may be caused by unevenly worn brake rotors. Install upgraded, reduced diameter caliper slide pins (#18016164).

1986-92-Vehicles equipped with the 3T40 automatic transmission may experience slippage in manual Low or Reverse. Install service package #8628222 which includes a Low/Reverse clutch release spring (#8664961) and clutch retainer and snap ring (#656/657).

1987-Models equipped with 2.0L engines that are hard to start, stall frequently, idle poorly and surge at low speed may have EGR valve damage. The PROM module MEMCAL (memory calibrations) also may have to be changed.

1987-88-Engine stalling in Reverse or Drive with the THM 125C automatic transmission may mean you need an upgraded auxiliary valve body filter (#8664921).

- Poor AC cooling may be caused by a faulty pressure switch O-ring seal (TSB 87-18-1B).

1988-Insufficient interior cooling at idle may require a new PROM (#16086125) to regulate the cooling fan.

1991-94-The ignition switch may not return to the "run" position after the vehicle is started. This may cause the accessories to fail to operate. Retorque the ignition switch mounting screws.

1992-Engine hesitation or roughness, particularly at idle, may be corrected by installing a new lower intake manifold gasket (#10103647).

1992-94-A loose horn pad may only require stronger horn pad clips.
1.8L engine
1985-86-Rough idling, loss of power and engine surging may be caused by a defective heat shield that allows the TPS module to overheat. Replace the TPS and install a new heat shield (#17111750).
All models/years-A rotten egg odor coming from the exhaust is likely caused by a malfunctioning catalytic converter covered by the 5 year/80,000 km emissions warranty. Squeaking front brakes can be silenced by replacing the semi-metallic front brake linings with quieter linings (#123214 24). The new linings will be 20% less durable (TSB 86-5-20).

General Motors will repair defective steering assemblies free of charge up to 5 years/80,000 km and pay half the cost up to 100,000 km. GM also says its vehicles with rust/paint peeling problems will be repainted free of charge up to six years (confirmed by GM internal dealer memo found in the Bonneville section). If the dealer balks or starts stonewalling your claim, slip the GM document under his nose.

Vehicle Profile

	1987	1988	1989	1990	1991	1992	1993	1994
Cost Price ($)								
Cavalier	8551	9150	10,948	10,999	10,998	10,598	10,498	10,998
Z24	12,840	13,498	13,998	15,648	14,998	15,798	14,798	17,298
Z24/RS Conv.	17,392	13,498	20,398	—	—	18,400	18,098	20,298
Sunbird/LE	9158	9969	11,148	11,550	11,398	11,398	10,498	11,498
Sunbird GT	12,905	12,870	12,882	15,648	14,998	15,398	14,998	—
Firenza	11,226	12,154	—	—	—	—	—	—
Skyhawk	11,538	12,557	—	—	—	—	—	—
Used Values ($)								
Cavalier ↑	2200	2900	3400	4000	4700	6100	7100	8700
Cavalier ↓	1600	2000	2200	2600	3400	4800	5800	7300
Z24 ↑	3800	4800	5500	6100	7000	10,200	10,900	12,500
Z24 ↓	2500	3500	4100	4900	5800	8800	9500	11,500
Z24/RS Conv. ↑	5100	6300	7200	—	—	10,700	11,800	15,300
Z24/RS Conv. ↓	4200	5300	6000	—	—	9000	10,100	15,000
Sunbird/LE ↑	2500	3000	3200	4000	4900	6400	7300	9000
Sunbird/LE ↓	1500	2000	2200	3000	3900	5100	6000	7500
Sunbird GT ↑	3800	3900	4900	6000	7100	8500	9400	—
Sunbird GT ↓	2500	2700	3700	5000	5800	7500	8500	—
Firenza ↑	2800	4000	—	—	—	—	—	—
Firenza ↓	2100	2900	—	—	—	—	—	—
Skyhawk ↑	2300	3200	—	—	—	—	—	—
Skyhawk ↓	1700	2200	—	—	—	—	—	—
Reliability	❶	❶	❶	❶	❷	❸	❸	❸
Air conditioning	❸	❸	❸	❸	❸	❸	❸	❹
Body integrity	❶	❶	❶	❶	❷	❷	❷	❷
Braking system	❶	❶	❶	❶	❷	❷	❷	❷

200

Electrical system	①	①	①	①	②	②	②	②
Engines	②	②	②	③	③	③	③	③
Exhaust/Converter	②	②	②	③	③	③	④	④
Fuel system	①	①	①	①	③	③	③	④
Ignition system	②	②	②	②	②	③	③	④
Manual transmission	③	③	③	③	③	③	④	④
- automatic	②	②	②	②	②	③	③	③
Rust/Paint	②	②	②	②	②	②	③	③
Steering	②	②	②	②	②	②	③	③
Suspension	①	①	①	①	②	②	③	③
Dealer Service	②	②	②	②	③	③	③	④
Maintenance	②	②	③	③	③	③	③	③
Parts Availability	⑤	⑤	⑤	⑤	⑤	⑤	⑤	⑤
Repair Costs	①	①	①	①	②	③	③	③
Crash Safety								
Cavalier 4-door	②	②	②	②	⑤	⑤	❷	❷
Firenza	②	②	—	—	—	—	—	
Skyhawk	②	②	—	—	—	—	—	
Sunbird 4-door	②	②	②	②	⑤	⑤	❷	❷
Safety Features								
ABS	—	—	—	—	—	S	S	S

Achieva, Calais, Grand AM, Skylark, Somerset

Rating: Below Average buy (1993-94); Not Recommended (1987-92). The '92 Achieva replaced the Calais; except for styling, it's practically identical to the others.

Price analysis: Easy to find and prices are generally quite reasonable. Don't pay extra for cars equipped with the Computer Command Ride; the difference between sport and soft modes isn't all that discernable. The Skylark's price depreciates more rapidly than the Grand AM's, but the Achieva's low initial cost from 1992-94 makes it a bargain—if only it were more reliable. Try to get a vehicle with some time remaining on the original warranty, or buy an extended warranty. Expect to pay about $800 annually for maintenance and repairs. Other cars worth considering: Chrysler Spirit/Acclaim • Ford Taurus and Sable • Honda Accord • Nissan Stanza • Toyota Camry • Volvo 850.

Technical Data

Calais, Grand AM, Somerset

ENGINES	Litres/CID	HP	MPG	Model Years
OHC I-4T FI	2.0/121	165	18-22	1987-89

DOHC I-4 FI	2.3/138	150-160	22-26	1988-91
DOHC I-4 FI	2.3/138	180	21-25	1990-91
OHV I-4T FI	2.5/151	92-98	22-25	1985-88
OHV I-4T FI	2.5/151	110	21-25	1989-91
OHV V6 FI	3.0/181	125	18-21	1985-87
Skylark				
OHV V6 FI	3.3/204	125	19-24	1989-91
OHC I-4 FI	2.3/138	115-120	21-25	1992-94
OHC I-4 FI	2.3/138	150	22-26	1995
OHC V6 FI	3.1/191	155	20-25	1994-95
OHC V6 FI	3.3/204	160	19-23	1992-93
Achieva				
OHC I-4 FI	2.3/138	115-120	21-25	1992-94
DOHC I-4 FI	2.3/138	150-160	20-24	1992-95
DOHC I-4 FI	2.3/138	170-190	20-24	1992-94
OHC V6 FI	3.1/191	155	20-25	1994-95
OHC V6 FI	3.3L/204	160	19-23	1992-93

Strengths and weaknesses: There is little to recommend in these cars. More reliable and reasonably priced family haulers and sporty sedans are available from other domestic automakers. These cars ride and handle fairly well and share chassis components with the failure-prone J-bodies. This explains why engine, transmission, brake and electronic problems are similar. Body squeaks and rattles are so abundant, GM has published a six-page troubleshooting DSB that pinpoints the noises and lists fixes (see *Service Tips*).

The 2.5L 4-cylinder engine doesn't provide much power and has a poor reliability record. Avoid the Quad 4 and 3.0L V6 engine with SFI (sequential fuel injection) because of their frequent breakdowns and difficult servicing. If you have a blown head gasket or other problems with the Quad 4, keep in mind that GM has a secret warranty covering its defects (again, see *Service Tips*). Poor engine cooling and fuel-system malfunctions are common; diagnosis and repair are more complicated than average. The engine computer on V6 models has a high failure rate, and the oil pressure switch often malfunctions. The electrical system is gremlin-plagued. Seals in the power-steering rack deteriorate rapidly. Front brake discs need more frequent replacement than average. Paint defects are common; consequently, surface rust may occur sooner than expected.

Confidential dealer service bulletins covering the 1993 models confirm the following problems with Achievas and other cars equipped with 2.3L and 3.1L V6 engines: they won't continue running after a cold start, the converter seal leaks on 4T60E automatic transmissions, front door windows may be hard to roll up and seal poorly, intermittent electrical problems, stalling when decelerating, hard starting, faulty Reverse gear on 3T40 automatic transmissions, rear brake squawk and faulty windshield washers.

Skylarks and Grand AMs have the same deficiencies plus the following problems: clunking from the driver's side on turns and the 2.3L engine stalling or missing.

GM bulletins confirm the following 1994 model problems: V6-equipped models may experience excessive 2nd gear vibration caused by a defective hub shaft bearing and sleeve assembly, loss of engine coolant likely caused by faulty surge tank caps, power steering may lead or pull, and a faulty automatic transmission fluid level indicator could give false readings. A poorly running 2.3L Quad 4 engine can often be traced to a moisture-contaminated or corroded ECM connector. Correction requires the re-sealing of the engine harness pass-through.

Safety summary/recalls: Crash tests of a 1987 four-door Skylark, Calais, and Grand AM were disappointing: the driver would sustain massive chest and leg trauma, while the passenger would have severe leg injuries. A 1987 two-door Grand AM and Somerset did a bit better: only the driver was judged to have had severe leg injuries. A retested '87 four-door Grand AM did very well; neither the driver nor passenger would have been seriously injured. Of the more recent models tested, the 1991 four-door Calais and two-door Grand AM turned in an impressive score; both the driver and passenger were judged to have escaped serious injury. Unfortunately, the '93 four-door Grand AM and Skylark didn't do as well; the driver was judged to have sustained serious head injuries and the passenger would have received head and leg injuries. *Recalls*: **1985**-A faulty throttle return spring on 2.5L engines could lead to sudden acceleration. **1985-86**-Door pillar cracks. **1986**-Erratically operating headlights. **1987**-The fuel feed or return hose could leak. **1990**-The fuel feed or return hose could leak. **1991**-Power windows could short-circuit and remain in the down position or start an electrical fire. **2.3L Quad 4 engine-1987-90**-Faulty ignition coils that cause engine misfiring will be replaced under an emissions recall campaign. **1988-89**-It's possible a cracked fuel hose feed could leak.

Secret Warranties/Service Tips/DSBs

1982-88-Interior water leaks are likely due to plugged AC evaporator drain hoses.
1982-90-Noise from rear springs requires the installation of upgraded spring insulators (#22555689).
1985-88-A 3.0L engine whine heard in the interior can be silenced by installing a new right rear engine mount.
1986-A front seatback rattle on the Grand AM requires a new pivot bolt and bushing.
1987-88-Knocking or rattling coming from the timing chain requires a noise kit (#12337434).
• Frequent stalling when shifting from Neutral or Park into Drive or Reverse may be caused by a sticking torque converter clutch

(TCC) solenoid.

• Poor braking can be corrected by installing improved brake pads (#18015497). See DSB 88-5-2.

• A sagging headliner needs service package #22541347.

1987-90-A rattle or buzz from the instrument panel may require an upgraded brake booster check valve (#18012017).

• Squealing or squeaking brake noise can be reduced by installing improved brake pads (#12321424).

1988-89-An upgraded front engine mount (#22538994) will silence engine rattles.

1989-An inoperative power window may be due to a short-circuit in the wiring harness; fix the short and replace the window switch.

1989-90-Poor cold engine performance will be corrected with a new MEMCAL.

1991-94-A crunching noise coming from the right side of the dash when turning the steering wheel can be silenced by installing a new steering grommet on the right side.

1992-93-A front-end engine knock troubleshooting chart is found in DSB 306001.

1992-94-Front brake linings can be made to last longer by replacing the front brake pads with new 8100 lining compound (#18022600).

• The ignition switch may not return to the "run" position after the vehicle is started. This may cause the accessories to fail to operate. Retorque the ignition switch mounting screws.

• Corrosion of the ECM connectors can lead to a host of driveability problems (DSB 338109A).

• DSB 431007 is an excellent troubleshooting guide to finding and correcting squeaks and rattles. It contains six charts that show noise sources and remedies. Two of the charts are found on the following pages.

1994-Gear whine with the 4T60E automatic transaxle can be stopped by replacing the final drive and updating the PCM calibration.

• Insufficient AC cooling may be due to a leak at the low charge primary port seal.

• Loss of Drive or erratic shifts may be caused by an intermittent short to ground on the A or B shift solenoid or an electrical short-circuit in the transaxle.

• A front-end clunking noise when driving over rough roads may require the repositioning of the diagonal radiator support braces.

2.3L Quad 4 engine

1987-91-Head gasket leaks are a problem covered by a secret warranty extension. The first sign of trouble is a loss of power caused by combustion gases mixing with coolant. This is followed by a cloud of steam and coolant loss through the exhaust system. If these symptoms are ignored, cylinder bore scoring, a warped cylinder head, and piston seizure will likely result as the engine continues to overheat. Up to 6 years/60,000 miles, GM will replace the head gasket with an improved version and carry out a new multi-step head-bolt tightening procedure

COMPONENT/CAUSE	CORRECTION
INTERIOR (continued)	
Rear Folding Seat - (1992-94 Buick, Olds, Pontiac)	
1. Rattle at upper right or left corners of rear folding seat.	1. Adjust rear seat lock striker, refer to "Lock Striker Alignment" in Section 10-10 of the Service Manual. Labor Operation: C7400 Use published labor operation time.
Rear Window Panel Trim - (1992 Oldsmobile)	
1. Rattle between rear window panel trim and rear speakers or rear window panel trim and metal stand-offs below rear window.	1. Remove rear window panel trim, refer to Page 1 in Section 10-8 of the Service Manual. Attach 25mm x 75mm x 4mm foam tape to all four stand-offs below rear window and top back edge of each rear speaker. Labor Operation: C4240 Use published labor operation time.
Steering Column - (1994 Buick, Olds, Pontiac)	
1. Rubbing noise when turning steering wheel during cold, ambient temperatures. Noticeable at top of steering column.	1. Refer to Page 13 in Section 3F-4 of the Service Manual. 2. Remove column jacket bushing assembly. 3. Wipe steering column shaft and bushing clean. 4. Remove burrs if present. 5. Install column jacket bushing assembly WITHOUT lubrication. Labor Operation: E7820 Use published labor operation time.
DOOR	
Center Door Trim Area - (1992-94 Buick, Olds, Pontiac)	
1. Creak noise between armrest and map pocket.	1. Refer to Bulletin #331049.
Power Window Regulator Wires - (1992-94 Buick, Olds, Pontiac)	
1. Buzz or rattle at forward top area of left front door caused by wires contacting the door inner metal or power window regulator.	1. Wrap foam tape around wires at area of contact. Labor Operation: C3358 Use published labor operation time.
Power Window Switch Wires - (1993-94 Oldsmobile)	
1. Buzz or rattle at left front door power window switch between power window switch wires and plastic cup.	1. Wrap foam tape around wires at area of contact. Labor Operation: N2145 Use published labor operation time.
Power Window Wiring Harness - (1993-94 Buick, Olds, Pontiac Sedan)	
1. Buzz or rattle at forward area of left front door caused by a stick/slip condition from the taped wires inside split seamless conduit. The conduit is between the door inner metal and the power window motor. NOTE: The exterior of the conduit is wrapped with tape.	1. Remove door panel, refer to Section 10-8 in the Service Manual. 2. Peel water deflector to access wire harness conduit. 3. Remove tape from conduit. 4. Remove conduit. 5. Remove tape from wire harness. 6. Install conduit. 7. Tape conduit on the outside only. Labor Operation: T3439 Labor Time: 0.8 hr

at no cost to the owner. The deductible will be also refunded. Owners who bought their cars used or had repairs done at an independent garage are eligible for this free repair and a refund if the engine has already been fixed.

1988-89-Power loss in cold weather can be corrected by installing ventilation kit (#12339306).

• A whistle or whine coming from the engine is likely caused by a noisy oil pump. Replace it with an improved oil pump (#22538689).

• The engine wiring harness may be cut by constant rubbing on the alternator. This will cause a rough-running engine, inoperative air

COMPONENT/CAUSE	CORRECTION
BODY	
Power Antenna - (1992 Buick)	
1. Rattle between right rear quarter panel and power antenna body.	1. Attach foam tape to antenna body at area of contact. Labor Operation: C4540 Use published labor operation time.
Rear Fascia - (1992-94 Buick)	
1. Squeak or rattle between rear fascia and stud for deck lid latch or body just under deck lid opening.	1. Attach closed cell foam on fascia and area of contact. Labor Operation: T3440 Labor Time: 0.2 hr
Tail Panel Reinforcement - (1994 Buick, Olds, Pontiac)	
1. Creak between tail panel reinforcement and body. Noticeable during body twist occurred by a sloped driveway.	1. Pry tail panel reinforcement away from body at the area of contact. Refer to Figure 6. Labor Operation: T3441 Labor Time: 0.2 hr
UNDERBODY	
Fuel Tank - (1992-94 Buick, Olds, Pontiac)	
1. Creak between fuel tank and fuel tank straps on right or left side. Noticeable during body twist occurred by a sloped driveway.	1. Remove fuel tank. Install one additional fuel tank insulator, P/N 22524101, on top of existing insulators for both right and left side of fuel tank. Labor Operation: L1260 Use published labor operation time.
Park Brake Cable - (1993 Buick, Olds, Pontiac)	
1. Slapping at left rear between parking brake cable and rear axle. Noticeable behind left front seat.	1. Attach a 21" (53cm) tie strap around the front park brake cable and axle. In addition, the strap must be routed under the left park brake cable and ABS wires. Refer to Figure 7. Labor Operation: T3442 Labor Time: 0.2 hr
Park Brake Cable - (1992-93 Pontiac, Olds, Buick)	
1. Squawk or chirp at left rear between park brake cable and guide loop. Noticeable behind left front seat.	1. Using pliers, squeeze the outboard portion of the guide loop enough to provide a slight interference fit. Labor Operation: T3443 Labor Time: 0.2 hr
Rear Axle Bushing - (1993-94 Buick, Olds, Pontiac)	
1. Creak or squawk at rear axle bushing. Noticeable during body twist occurred by a sloped driveway.	1. No permanent fix available yet, but applying silicone lubricant to the rear axle bushing will temporarily eliminate noise. Labor Operation: T3444 Labor Time: 0.2 hr
UNDERHOOD	
Engine Mount Strut - (1992-93 Buick, Olds, Pontiac)	
1. Squawk between engine mount strut rubber insert and housing.	1. Refer to Bulletin #336102R
Hood Flange - (1993-94 Buick, Olds, Pontiac)	
1. Creak between the two flanges just inboard and rearward of right hood hinge. Noticeable during body flex or during steering while vehicle is stopped.	1. Spread two flanges apart at contact. Refer to Figure 8. Labor Operation: T3445 Labor Time: 0.2 hr

conditioner/alternator, the illumination of the check engine light, failure of the ECM module and excessive white smoke (DSB 88-8-11). 2.5L engine

• Excessive oil consumption may be caused by one or more damaged intake valve guides (TSB 88-6-81). The correction of the defect should be covered up to 5 years/80,000 km under GM emissions warranty.

• Hard starting and engine pinging can be fixed by the free installation of a new PROM module (#16121217) TSB 88-6E-11.

• Frequent engine overheating caused by a defective thermostat; replace it with an upgraded part (#3059793).

206

All models/years-A rotten egg odor coming from the exhaust may be the result of a malfunctioning catalytic converter covered by the 5 year/80,000 km emissions warranty. Stand your ground if GM or dealer says you must pay.

General Motors will repair defective steering assemblies free of charge up to 5 years/80,000 km and pay half the cost up to 100,000 km. GM has had a serious rust/paint peeling problem with all its domestic-made vehicles. Faced with this, GM has set up a substantial slush fund to compensate owners. Original owners will get 100% compensation for paint peeling/surface rusting up to six years (see GM's internal dealer memo found under Bonneville).

Vehicle Profile

	1987	1988	1989	1990	1991	1992	1993	1994
Cost Price ($)								
Achieva S	—	—	—	—	—	15,098	15,298	16,698
Calais S	13,034	13,785	14,298	15,899	14,298	—	—	—
Grand AM	12,241	12,970	14,098	15,099	13,698	13,698	14,898	15,798
Skylark	13,619	14,512	15,196	16,199	14,598	16,350	15,298	16,398
Somerset	13,501	—	—	—	—	—	—	—
Used Values ($)								
Achieva S ↑	—	—	—	—	—	7500	9500	10,900
Achieva S ↓	—	—	—	—	—	6300	7900	9100
Calais S ↑	3000	3500	4400	5000	5900	—	—	—
Calais S ↓	1800	2200	2800	3300	4200	—	—	—
Grand AM ↑	3200	3800	4600	5800	6400	8000	10,000	13,000
Grand AM ↓	2300	2800	3300	4100	4700	6500	8900	11,500
Skylark ↑	2700	3700	4400	5300	6300	8100	10,000	12,600
Skylark ↓	1700	2100	2700	3600	4600	6200	8300	10,600
Somerset ↑	2700	—	—	—	—	—	—	—
Somerset ↓	1800	—	—	—	—	—	—	—
Reliability	②	②	②	②	②	②	②	②
Air conditioning	③	③	③	③	③	③	④	④
Body integrity	②	②	②	②	②	②	②	②
Braking system	②	②	②	②	②	③	③	③
Electrical system	②	②	②	②	②	②	②	②
Engines	②	②	②	③	③	③	③	③
Exhaust/Converter	②	②	②	②	③	③	③	④
Fuel system	②	②	②	②	③	③	③	③
Ignition system	②	②	②	②	③	③	③	③
Manual transmission	③	③	③	③	③	④	⑤	⑤
- automatic	②	②	②	②	②	②	②	②
Rust/Paint	②	②	②	②	③	③	③	③
Steering	②	②	③	③	③	④	⑤	⑤
Suspension	②	②	③	③	③	⑤	⑤	⑤
Dealer Service	②	②	②	②	③	③	④	④

Maintenance	③	③	③	③	③	③	④	④
Parts Availability	③	③	③	③	④	④	⑤	⑤
Repair Costs	❶	❶	❶	❶	❷	❷	③	③
Crash Safety								
Calais 4-door	❶	❶	❶	❶	⑤	⑤	⑤	⑤
Grand Am 4-door	⑤	⑤	⑤	⑤	⑤	⑤	❶	❶
Grand Am 2-door	❷	❷	❷	❷	⑤	⑤	⑤	⑤
Skylark 4-door	❶	❶	❶	❶	❶	❶	❶	❶
Somerset 2-door	❷	—	—	—	—	—	—	—
Safety Features								
ABS	—	—	—	—	O	S	S	S
Airbag	—	—	—	—	—	—	—	D

HONDA

Accord

Rating: Recommended (1992-93); Above Average buy (1990-91); Average buy (1988-89); Not Recommended (1986-87).

Price analysis: Average availability but prices are fairly high. The 1991 has the best price and depreciation ratio. Its original selling price dropped $1600 when the federal manufacturer's tax was dropped. Try to get an Accord with some time remaining on the original warranty. Expect to pay about $400 annually for maintenance and repairs. To avoid costly engine repairs, check the engine timing belt every 2 years/ 40,000 km and replace it every 96,000 km ($250). Other cars worth considering: Chrysler Spirit/Acclaim • Nissan Stanza • Toyota Tercel and Camry • Volvo 850.

Technical Data

ENGINES	Litres/CID	HP	MPG	Model Years
OHC I-4 2 bbl.	2.0/119	98	24-28	1986-89
OHC I-4 FI	2.0/119	110-122	23-28	1986-89
OHC I-4 FI	2.2/132	125-130	23-27	1990-93
OHC I-4 FI	2.2/132	140-145	23-27	1991-95
OHC V6 FI	2.7/163	170	20-24	1995

Strengths and weaknesses: Surprisingly, this has not always been a great car; early versions were beset with premature rusting, frequent engine camshaft and crankshaft failures, and severe front brake problems. Engines on the 1980-86 models leak or burn oil and blow their cylinder head gaskets easily. Carbureted models suffer from driveability problems through 1986. Improved with every makeover, the 1991-92 Accords presently have one of the best reliability and crash safety records in the business. The 1990-92 improvements included additional passenger and luggage space. From 1986 to 1989, the brakes, automatic transmission (particularly the 2-4 clutch assembly), rack and pinion steering, suspension (coils are practically biodegradable) and electrical system become the major problem areas. Water pumps and alternators are also replaced about every three years. Corrosion problems are still present on pre-1988 Accords. Rapid front brake wear and frequent brake rotor replacements are common. The automatic transmission shifts a bit harshly upon hard acceleration. Shock absorbers go soft quickly, and replacement prices are often beaten by independent suppliers.

The exhaust system tends to wear out quickly. Accords are susceptible to paint chipping, flaking and premature surface rust. If left untreated, sheet metal perforations develop unusually quickly. Especially vulnerable spots are front fender seams, door bottoms, and areas surrounding side view mirrors and door handles, rocker panels, wheel openings, windshield posts, the front cowl, trunk and hatchback lids.

1988-93 models are likely to have prematurely worn automatic transmissions, constant velocity joints, and power-steering assemblies. Poor quality control in the choice of body trim and assembly leads to numerous air and water leaks. A careful underbody inspection is a prerequisite to buying any Honda, particularly in view of the fact that body repairs are outrageously expensive on Accords.

Confidential dealer service bulletins show the following problems on the 1993s: poor radio reception on the AM band, excessive steering wheel vibrations, CD magazine changer in trunk won't eject and noisy window regulators.

The 1994s have faulty door weatherstripping that bunches up and slides in the channel and excessive wind noise emanating from the outside mirror. One Red Deer, Alberta *Lemon-Aid* reader wrote: "We returned the car to the dealer several times (at least six) to have the doors adjusted to reduce wind noise affecting my 1994 Accord LX sedan. They were finally able to reduce the noise a small amount. The treatment we received from the dealer (T&T Honda Calgary) was exemplary. A letter written to Honda Canada explaining our dissatisfaction with the car resulted in a response letter with very definite 'screw you' overtones."

Other problems noted in the Accord DSBs: buzzing when the turn signals are activated, a clunking noise from the door glass and instrument panel creaking, damaged door handle seals, faulty fuel filler doors, rattling moonroof deflectors, outside mirror wind noise, power door locks that unlock themselves, difficulty in closing the trunk lid, and lots of water leaks and wind noise.

Mechanical parts are easy to find, and most are no more expensive than average. Emission control components are another story, however. Owners report that Honda frequently charges for parts that should be replaced for free under the 5 year/80,000 km emissions warranty and that those charges are far in excess of what other carmakers ask. One Richmond Hill, Ontario, owner of a 1991 Accord complained that the car's oxygen sensor would have cost him $450, while the same part costs $50 to $100 when bought from other carmakers.

Safety summary/recalls: NHTSA crash tests have judged the 1986 four-door Accord would provide excellent protection for the driver and passenger, but the 1987 two-door Accord's driver would sustain severe leg injuries. The '91 and '93 airbag-equipped versions were judged to offer excellent protection to the driver and front seat passenger. Safety probers believe a faulty ignition control module may be the cause of chronic stalling on 1990 Accords. Passengers complain that the rear seatbelts are awkward and difficult to fasten. Dashboard indicator lights need a dimmer switch; their brightness is distracting. *Recalls:* **1982-87-**Road salt may cause the fuel filler/and or breather pipe to rust through, resulting in fuel leakage and fire hazard. **1990-91-**Defective crank pulleys connected to the drive generator and power-steering pump could fail, preventing the battery from recharging. **1991-**Power window malfunctions. The module may overheat and cause a fire. One symptom of this defect is the window may go down by itself and stay down. **1991-93-**Faulty rear seatbelts won't pull out if the car is parked on a steep incline. **1994-**Faulty tire stems may lead to sudden air loss.

Secret Warranties/Service Tips/DSBs

1986-88-Interior water leaks when parked uphill require the sealing of the cowl area, wheelhouse and door frame seam.
1986-89-If the engine hesitates under light acceleration, install an ignition coil kit.
• Premature battery failure can be corrected by installing a rear defogger switch/timer assembly and a cover kit to protect the battery from high temperatures.
1988-89-Power-steering moan can be fixed by replacing the control valve.
• Steering wheel vibration at idle can be fixed by replacing the rear engine mount and installing a vibration clip.
1988-93-Creaking coming from the window regulator can be corrected by installing an upgraded regulator spiral spring.
1990-Delay after shifting into Drive can be corrected by adjusting the cable (87-040).
• A right rear suspension clunking noise can be fixed with a new spring silencer tube.
• An interior roaring noise can be silenced by installing blind body

plugs (#95550-15000) in the door rocker panels.

• If the front inside door handle doesn't work, check for a loose or broken actuator rod clip.

• Moaning when the steering wheel is turned may mean the steering pump outlet hose orifice has slipped out of position or the outlet hose is faulty.

• Water leaks behind dashboard require sealing near windshield locating blocks and frame panel seams in the cowl.

• Whistling from the front of the car is likely caused by poor hood sealing.

1990-91-A faulty automatic transmission countershaft nut will be replaced free under a product update program.

• A new distributor body and kit will help cars that have a starting problem.

1990-93-Poor AM reception or a popping noise from the speakers is likely due to poor ground connection between the antenna collar and car body. Correct by improving the ground connection and tightening the antenna assembly mounting nuts in the proper sequence.

1992-A faulty oil pressure switch will be replaced free under a product update program.

1994-Damaged door handle seals will be replaced for free under a "goodwill" warranty. Doors may also lock themselves.

ELECTRICAL
Issue Date
JUNE 24, 1994
Power Door Locks Cycle From Unlocked to Locked
SYMPTOM
When unlocking the doors with either the master power lock switch or the door key, the door locks cycle several times from the unlocked to the locked position.
PROBABLE CAUSE
The driver's door lock actuator is faulty.
VEHICLES AFFECTED
1994 Accord LX and EX models only
● Japan production:
    4-Door - thru VIN JHMCD5...RC072220
● Ohio production:
    2-Door - thru VIN 1HGCD7...RA024565
    4-Door - thru VIN 1HGCD5...RA081047
    Wagon - thru VIN 1HGCE1...RA003328
CORRECTIVE ACTION
Replace the driver's side door lock actuator with the parts listed under PARTS INFORMATION.
1.   Remove the driver's door panel as described in section 20 of the Service Manual.

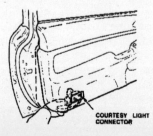

**COURTESY LIGHT
CONNECTOR**

All models/years-Steering wheel shimmy is a frequent problem taken care of in DSB 94-025. Honda will repair or replace defective steering assemblies, constant velocity joints and catalytic converters free of charge up to 5 years/80,000 km on a case-by-case basis.

Vehicle Profile

	1987	1988	1989	1990	1991	1992	1993	1994
Cost Price ($)								
EXi/EX	16,945	18,200	20,285	19,895	17,975	18,695	20,545	21,495
LX	14,625	15,495	15,695	16,695	15,095	15,690	17,195	18,695
Used Values ($)								
EXi/EX↑	6000	7500	8500	9400	10,700	12,300	14,800	17,700
EXi/EX↓	5000	6500	7500	8000	9300	10,700	13,200	16,000
LX↑	5000	6600	7400	8000	8900	10,700	12,500	15,200
LX↓	4000	5200	6000	6900	7800	9200	11,300	13,600
Reliability	2	3	3	4	5	5	5	5
Air conditioning	3	3	4	4	4	4	4	4
Body integrity	1	3	3	3	3	3	3	4
Braking system	2	2	2	3	4	4	5	5
Electrical system	2	4	4	4	4	4	5	5
Engines	3	4	4	4	5	5	5	5
Exhaust/Converter	2	2	2	2	4	4	5	5
Fuel system	2	4	4	4	5	5	5	5
Ignition system	2	3	3	4	5	5	5	5
Manual transmission	4	5	5	5	5	5	5	5
- automatic	2	2	2	3	4	5	5	5
Rust/Paint	1	2	2	2	3	3	4	5
Steering	2	2	2	3	3	3	4	5
Suspension	3	3	3	4	5	5	5	5
Dealer Service	5	5	5	5	5	5	5	5
Maintenance	3	3	4	4	5	5	5	5
Parts Availability	4	4	4	4	5	5	5	5
Repair Costs	2	3	4	4	5	5	5	5
Crash Safety								
2-door	2	2	2	2	5	5	5	5
4-door	5	5	5	5	5	5	5	5
Safety Features								
ABS	—	—	—	—	S	S	S	S
Airbag	—	—	—	—	—	D	D/P	D/P

HYUNDAI

Elantra

Rating: Average buy (1991-94).

Price analysis: Limited availability and reasonably priced. Expect to pay about $600 annually for maintenance and repairs. An automatic transmission requires the new 1.8L powerplant. Other cars worth considering: Chrysler Spirit/Acclaim • GM Saturn SL • Nissan Sentra and Stanza • Toyota Camry and Corolla • Volvo 850.

Technical Data

ENGINES	Litres/CID	HP	MPG	Model Years
DOHC I-4 FI	1.6/97	113	22-29	1992-93
DOHC I-4 FI	1.8/110	124	21-27	1993-94

Strengths and weaknesses: This conservatively styled sedan is only marginally larger than the Excel. The 16-valve 1.6L 4-cylinder is smooth, efficient and adequate when mated to the 5-speed manual transmission. It produces 32 more horses (113 hp) than the Excel. Ride and handling are also quite good due mainly to the Elantra's longer wheelbase and more sophisticated suspension.

The 4-speed automatic transmission robs the base engine of at least 10 horses. Brakes are difficult to modulate. Conservative styling makes the Elantra look a bit like an underfed Accord. The car is available only as a four-door hatchback. Interior room is limited. Headroom is a bit tight for tall drivers.

Owners report that body deficiencies, harsh shifting with the automatic transmission, and oil leaks, and brake defects are the most frequent problems.

Confidential dealer service bulletins don't show many serious defects. For example, problems on the 1993s harsh shifting with the automatic transmission when accelerating or coming to a stop, excessive disc brake noise, engine has difficulty reaching recommended operating temperature (MPI fault code #21), low fuel pressure, oil leaks between the oil filter and mounting bracket, and wheel cover discoloration. The 1994 model has the following deficiencies: excessive front brake noise and premature wear, rear speaker whine, harsh automatic transmission engagement, and slow windshield defrosting and defogging.

Safety summary/recalls: A 1992 Elantra performed very poorly in NHTSA 57 km/h crash tests; both the driver and front passenger would have sustained severe or fatal head and leg injuries. A retested '94 showed the driver would sustain serious leg injuries; the passenger would receive serious or fatal head and leg trauma. *Recalls:* N/A.

Secret Warranties/Service Tips/DSBs

1991-92-A harsh shift when coming to a stop or upon acceleration may be due to a misadjusted accelerator switch TCU.

1992-Oil leaking between the oil filter and mounting bracket may be due to a mounting surface on the bracket that's too wide. Correct by replacing the bracket.

1992-94-Hyundai has a field fix for manual transaxle gear clash/grind (DSB 9440-004).

1994-Rear speaker whine can be stopped by installing an improved noise reduction filter.

All models/years-Hyundai has a new brake pad kit (#58101-28A00) that the company says will eliminate squeaks and squeals during light brake application. Hyundai also suggests one replace the oil pump assembly if the engine rpm increases as the automatic transmission engages abruptly upon a cold start.

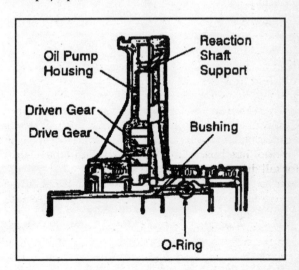

Vehicle Profile

	1991	1992	1993	1994
Cost Price ($)				
GL	10,595	10,795	11,295	11,795
GLS	11,795	11,995	12,795	13,695
Used Values ($)				
GL ↑	5300	6200	7200	8600
GL ↓	4100	4800	5800	7100
GLS ↑	5800	6700	8000	9600
GLS ↓	4800	5700	6800	8100
Reliability	④	④	④	④
Air conditioning	④	④	⑤	⑤
Automatic transmission	③	③	③	③
Body integrity	③	③	③	③
Braking system	③	③	③	③
Electrical system	③	③	③	③
Engines	③	④	⑤	⑤
Exhaust/Converter	⑤	⑤	⑤	⑤
Fuel system	③	③	③	③
Ignition system	④	④	③	③
Rust/Paint	④	④	⑤	⑤
Steering	④	⑤	⑤	⑤
Suspension	④	⑤	④	④
Dealer Service	⑤	⑤	⑤	⑤
Maintenance	③	③	③	③
Parts Availability	⑤	⑤	⑤	⑤
Repair Costs	④	④	④	④
Crash Safety	—	❶	❶	❶

Sonata

Rating: Average buy (1993); Not Recommended (1989-92). The 1994 model year was skipped and the 1995s were launched in April 1994.

Price analysis: Easy to find and prices are low to average. Be wary of the 1989's low price; it reflects the serious quality-control deficiencies present in the first-year series. Expect to pay about $700 annually for maintenance and repairs. If you are brave enough to risk buying a used Sonata, get one with some time remaining on the original warranty. Other cars worth considering: Chrysler Spirit/Acclaim • Honda Accord • Nissan Stanza • Toyota Camry • Volvo 850.

Technical Data

ENGINES	Litres/CID	HP	MPG	Model Years
OHC I-4 FI	2.0/122	128	19-24	1992-94
OHC I-4 FI	2.4/143	110-116	20-25	1989-91
OHC V6 FI	3.0/181	142	18-22	1990-94

Strengths and weaknesses: Overall reliability has been about average from 1989-92 while the 1993s seem to be moderately improved. Nevertheless, that may only be because they haven't been off warranty long enough to generate the traditional complaints. Another year will give us a clearer picture. These cars are rated as below average buys this year because of their poor crash rating, barely average parts supply, and the uncertain future of the parent company in Canada. Remember, the threat to pull out of Quebec and Hyundai's sudden dropping of the failure-prone Pony and Stellar models that subsequently left thousands of owners in the lurch.

Most complaints concern sloppy body assembly, cheap interior and exterior trim components, rusting and paint peeling, air-conditioning breakdowns, automatic transmission malfunctions (fluid leakage, in particular), electrical short-circuits, excessive brake vibration and assorted engine problems, including the timing belt, chronic oil leaks and cooling-system defects. Owners also complain of excessive engine noise that goes away once the car reaches cruising speed. Some complaints of long waits for parts.

Confidential dealer service bulletins show the following problems on the 1993s: harsh shifting with the automatic transmission when accelerating or coming to a stop, excessive disc brake noise, engine has difficulty reaching recommended operating temperature (MPI fault code #21), DOHC timing belt noise, low fuel pressure and oil leaking between the oil filter and mounting bracket.

Safety summary/recalls: NHTSA crash data for the 1989 four-door Sonata indicate that the driver would sustain severe or fatal head injuries and the passenger would receive massive leg trauma. Reports of electrical fires on the 1989-90 models. Emergency handling leaves lots to be desired. A Charlottetown, P.E.I. owner of a '93 Sonata reports, "One other thing I found out to my panic is that the car is not very stable. I almost lost control once when I had to cut the wheel sharply to avoid a collision. I wasn't travelling especially fast at the time and weather and highway conditions were ideal. The car rocked and swerved violently and would not respond to any corrective measures I tried. It was just pure luck that I managed to keep it on the road or avoid colliding with other vehicles." *Recalls*: N/A.

Secret Warranties/Service Tips/DSBs

1989-If the cruise control shifts the transmission out of Overdrive, the throttle control cables probably need adjusting.
• Stiff heater controls are likely due to bent cables.
1989-90-Vibrations caused by excessive hub and brake disc run-out require a new hub, machining of the disc or new brake discs.
• Cold start stalling with the 2.4L engine can be fixed by installing start enrichment kit #39901-326000D.
• Engine oil drain plug leaks are likely caused by a faulty gasket or incorrect gasket installation.
1990-Difficult shifts into 4th gear require a new transmission restrict ball assembly.
1992-Oil leaking between the oil filter and mounting bracket may be due to a mounting surface on the bracket that's too wide. Correct by replacing the bracket.
1992-93-Hyundai has a field fix for manual transaxle gear clash/grind (DSB 9440-004).

NO	PART NAME	PART NUMBER	QTY KIT 1	KIT 2
1	GEAR ASSY-3RD SPD	43260-34030	1	1
2	GEAR ASSY-4TH SPD.	43280-34030	1	1
3	HUB & SLEEVE-SYNCHRONIZER (3RD & 4TH)	43360-34020		1
4	FORK SHIFT (3RD & 4TH)	43861-34030	1	1
5	RAIL SUB ASSY-SHIFT (3RD & 4TH)	43820-34020	--	1
6	RAIL SUB ASSY-SHIFT (3RD & 4TH)	43820-34005	1	--
7	GUIDE OIL	43135-34010	1	1
8	SPRING-SYNCHRONIZER (3RD & 4TH)	43387-34002	2	2
9	RING-SYNCHRONIZER (3RD & 4TH)	43374-34001	2	2
10	KEY SYNCHRONIZER	43373-34005	3	3
11	PIN-SPRING	43842-21000	1	1

All models/years-Harsh shifting when coming to a stop or upon initial acceleration is likely caused by a misadjusted accelerator pedal switch TCU. If a harsh shift on vehicles equipped with an automatic transmission is experienced going into 2nd and 4th gear, a faulty air exhaust plug may be the culprit.

Vehicle Profile

	1989	1990	1991	1992	1993
Cost Price ($)					
Base	12,990	13,198	12,595	13,095	13,495
Used Values ($)					
Base ↑	5000	6000	6900	8000	9300
Base ↓	3800	4700	5500	6500	7800
Reliability	③	③	③	③	③
Air conditioning	⑤	⑤	③	③	④
Body integrity	❷	❷	❷	❷	❷
Braking system	③	③	③	③	③
Electrical system	③	③	③	③	④
Engines	⑤	⑤	⑤	⑤	⑤
Exhaust/Converter	③	③	④	④	⑤
Fuel system	④	③	⑤	⑤	④
Ignition system	④	④	④	⑤	⑤
Manual transmission	④	④	④	③	③
- automatic	③	③	③	③	③
Rust/Paint	③	③	③	③	③
Steering	③	③	④	④	④
Suspension	③	③	③	④	④
Dealer Service	③	③	③	③	③
Maintenance	⑤	⑤	⑤	⑤	⑤
Parts Availability	❷	❷	❷	❷	❷
Repair Costs	③	③	④	⑤	⑤
Crash Safety	❶	❶	❶	❶	❶
Safety Features					
ABS	—	—	—	O	O

MAZDA

626/Cronos, MX-6, Mystère

Rating: Average Buy (1991-94); Not Recommended (1985-90).

Price analysis: Average availability but prices are a bit higher than average. Pay a bit more if the original Mazda warranty is still in effect. Expect to pay about $300 annually for maintenance during the warranty period and $500 annually thereafter. Stay away from Mazda dealers, if possible; owners report high servicing/parts costs. According to the CAA, parts for the 626 cost twice as much as other cars in its class. The electronically controlled shock absorbers have not been durable and they cost a lot to replace. Mazda suggests changing the engine timing chain after 100,000 km. Other cars worth considering: Chrysler Spirit/Acclaim • Honda Accord • Nissan Stanza • Toyota Camry • Volvo 850.

Technical Data

ENGINES	Litres/CID	HP	MPG	Model Years
OHC I-4 2 bbl.	2.0/122	84	22-27	1985
OHC I-4 FI	2.0/122	93	22-26	1986-87
OHC I-4T FI	2.0/122	120	19-24	1986-87
OHC I-4D FI	2.0/122	61	30-35	1985
OHC I-4 FI	2.2/133	110	22-26	1988-92
OHC I-4T FI	2.2/133	145	18-23	1988-92
DOHC I-4 FI	2.0/122	118	22-27	1993-95
DOHC V6 FI	2.5/153	164	19-24	1993-95

Strengths and weaknesses: Although far from being high-performance vehicles, these cars ride and handle especially well and still manage to accommodate four people in comfort. The earlier models had a bit more interior room than post-1987 models. Electronically adjustable shock absorbers on the 1983-85 coupes and touring sedan became optional in 1986. The five-door hatchback touring sedan offers lots of sports and luxury extras as well.

Four-wheel steering was part of the sedan's equipment in 1988, but it was added exclusively to the MX-6 a year later. Wise buyers should pass over this option and look instead for anti-lock brakes and airbags on 1992 LG and GT versions. The manual transmission is a better choice because the automatic robs the engine of much-needed horsepower.

A mid-sport and mid-compact hybrid, the MX-6/Mystère is a coupe version of the 626. It has a more sophisticated suspension, more horsepower and better steering response than its sedan alter ego. The 1993 model gained a base 2.5L 165-hp V6 powerplant. Overall reliability and durability are on par with the 626.

Mazda 626/MX-6 reliability was initially mediocre until 1984, then it improved in the car's middle years, and now it's declining again. Fortunately, the newer models have a strong, comprehensive factory warranty that protects subsequent purchasers. The original rear-drive is a good compact sedan marred by steady deterioration of mechanical and body components as it ages. Newer front-wheel-drive models are doing better. Air-conditioning malfunctions, poor body assembly (leaks and paint problems), automatic transmission malfunctions, and premature exhaust system rust-out are commonplace, particularly on 1987-88 versions. The steering rack is failure prone prior to 1988.

Newer 626s still generate complaints concerning automatic transmission failures and jerky downshifts when the 4-cylinder is at full throttle (corrected on the 1994s). The automatic transmission on turbo-equipped models is particularly troublesome. Shocks and struts are expensive to replace. MacPherson strut defects are common, especially when the model is equipped with the electronic adjustment feature. Front and rear brakes are troublesome and often need replacing within 2 years/24,000 km. The exhaust system will rarely last more than two years, and wheel bearings fail repeatedly within the same period.

Door and hatch locks often freeze up, the headliner rattles, and metal surrounding the rear wheel wells is prone to rust perforation, as are hood, trunk and door seams. The underbody and suspension components should be examined carefully for corrosion damage.

Confidential dealer service bulletins show the 1993s may have door glass that rattles, a vibrating hood, water leaking into the trunk and an engine that misses during hard cornering. Problems with the '94s include air conditioning defects, head gasket leaks, automatic transmission malfunctions, excessive engine hydraulic lifter noise, brake vibration, premature wear-out of the front brakes, the steering gear may produce a clunking noise or be off center, the door glass pulls out of its track, inside rearview mirrors fall off the windshield, the driver's side power seat may not work, and reports of lots of wind noise around the side mirrors and A-pillars of both model years.

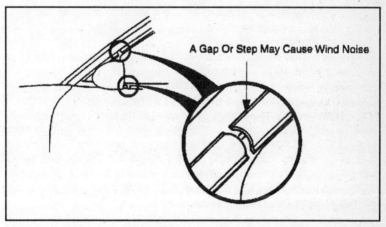

A Gap Or Step May Cause Wind Noise

Safety summary/recalls: Crash tests of a 1987 four-door 626 have shown that the driver and passenger would have severe leg injuries. Retested 1993 and '94 four-doors performed similarly. The driver and passenger would have sustained serious injuries to both legs. Secondary hood latches may malfunction and allow the hood to fly up (1983-87 models). Transport Canada is investigating this defect (S3328210-20). U.S. NHTSA safety investigators are looking into complaints of door handles falling off and doors opening accidentally when windows are lowered (1988-91 models). Daytime driving lights may not shut off when weather is hot. *Recalls*: **1979-82**-The free replacement of suspension components, including the idler arm, is authorized under recall #17510. **1986**-Throttle may stick open due to a defective nylon rotor. **1986-87**-Ignition switch failure results in faulty wipers, washer, engine fan, heater blower, and air-conditioner compressor. **1988**-Automatic shoulder belt may break. Floor mat could interfere with gas pedal. Rear brake shoe may separate from wheel cylinder piston. Band flexing may cause fuel tank leak. **1988-91**-Mazda will replace door handles with handles that are more durable.

Secret Warranties/Service Tips/DSBs

1986-Hard starting requires a new moisture-proof relay (DSB 038-87/15).

1986-87-Rough idle after a cold start requires the installation of repair kit #8AG113SPX.

1988-Engine piston slap requires an upgraded vacuum set (#F26218V35).

1989-Engine stalling in temperatures below zero requires the replacement of the ECU.

1993-94-Freezing door and hatch lock cylinders are addressed in DSB 021/94.

• Headliner rattles can be fixed by using Mazda's fastener kit.

• The driver's side power seat may not work if the wiring harness touches the seat frame.

• A clunking noise coming from the steering gear is caused by excessive backlash in the steering gear assembly.

All models/years-Non-turbo models that have a rough engine idle after a warm restart may have fuel vaporizing in the distribution pipe due to high underhood temperatures. To eliminate this problem, the emission control unit has been redesigned to allow higher fuel pressure at lower temperatures (DSB 023/87R). Excessive rear brake squealing can be reduced with improved brake pads (DSB 015/89-11). Excessive vibrations felt in the brake pedal, steering wheel, floor or seat when applying the brakes can be fixed by installing a redesigned brake assembly. Mazda says it's not a warrantable item. Lawyers say it is.

Vehicle Profile

	1987	1988	1989	1990	1991	1992	1993	1994
Cost Price ($)								
626/Cronos	13,975	15,330	15,980	16,840	15,215	15,595	17,395	18,725
MX-6	—	15,650	16,250	16,990	15,540	15,825	19,375	20,695

Used Values ($)

626/Cronos ↑	3900	4800	5800	7100	8100	8900	11,700	13,500
626/Cronos ↓	2900	3800	4600	5700	6600	7300	10,100	12,000
MX-6/Mystère ↑	—	5800	6400	7200	8000	8800	13,000	15,000
MX-6/Mystère ↓	—	4300	4900	5700	6500	7200	11,500	14,000
Reliability	②	②	②	②	③	③	③	③
Air conditioning	②	②	③	③	②	②	③	③
Body integrity	③	③	④	④	⑤	⑤	③	③
Braking system	③	③	④	④	③	③	③	③
Electrical system	③	③	③	③	③	④	⑤	⑤
Engines	④	④	④	④	⑤	⑤	③	③
Exhaust/Converter	⑤	⑤	⑤	⑤	③	④	⑤	⑤
Fuel system	④	④	④	③	④	④	④	⑤
Ignition system	④	④	④	④	④	⑤	⑤	⑤
Manual transmission	④	④	④	④	④	⑤	⑤	⑤
- automatic	③	③	③	③	③	③	③	③
Rust/Paint	③	③	③	③	③	③	④	④
Steering	③	③	③	③	④	④	⑤	⑤
Suspension	⑤	③	③	④	④	④	④	④
Dealer Service	②	②	②	②	②	④	④	④
Maintenance	②	②	②	②	③	③	③	③
Parts Availability	③	③	③	③	⑤	⑤	⑤	⑤
Repair Costs	②	②	②	②	②	④	④	④
Crash Safety								
626 4-door	❶	❶	❶	❶	❶	❶	⑤	❶
Safety Features								
ABS	—	—	—	—	—	O	O	O
Airbag	—	—	—	—	—	—	D	D/P

NISSAN

Stanza

Rating: Recommended (1991-92). Above Average (1989-90); Not Recommended (1985-88).

Price analysis: Average availability and reasonably priced. Expect to pay about $400 annually for maintenance during the warranty period and $600 annually thereafter. Other cars worth considering: Chrysler Spirit/Acclaim • Honda Accord • Nissan Sentra • Toyota Camry • Volvo 850.

Technical Data

ENGINES	Litres/CID	HP	MPG	Model Years
OHC I-4 FI	2.0/120	97	23-27	1985-89
OHC I-4 FI	2.4/146	138	20-25	1990-92

Strengths and weaknesses: Late-model Stanzas are roomy, reasonably priced, four-passenger compacts that offer peppy performance and good fuel economy with the added versatility of 4-wheel drive. Overall reliability and rust/paint have been good during the past six years. Except for some starting difficulties, transmission malfunctions and a biodegradable exhaust system, no major problems have been reported on 1987-92 Stanzas.

Automatic transmission vibrates annoyingly when car is idling in gear, clutches are noisy and steering wheel vibrations are frequent. Power antenna malfunctions. Front brakes wear out prematurely. Surface rust complaints are common for all years; wheel openings, the front edge of the hood, rear hatch and door bottoms are especially prone to rust perforation. Parts are more expensive than the compact average, but this is offset somewhat by the Stanza's reasonable resale price.

Safety summary/recalls: Crash tests of a 1984 four-door Stanza concluded that driver and passenger would have had severe or fatal head injuries. A 1990 four-door did much better. Both the driver and passenger were judged to have been well-protected. Only the GXE came with a standard limited-slip differential. *Recalls*: **1986 Wagon 2X4**-Cover fuel filler pipe for increased accident protection.

Secret Warranties/Service Tips/DSBs

1982-88-Improved brake pad material will cut brake noise and add to pad durability. Upgraded semi-metallic pads carry the Hitachi HP12 FE designation.
1986-Cruising vibrations can be reduced by installing upgraded engine mount insulators.
1986-88-Reverse gear grind with manual transmissions requires a new input shaft (#32280-39E25 or E26).
• A slipping or erratic shift means you probably need new brake servo accumulator seals.
1987-Front brake squeal can be reduced by installing pad kit #41060-32E94.
1987-89-Trunk lid torsion bars won't fall off if you install a torsion bar spacer (#84449-D4060) provided free by Nissan.
1989-92-Clutch shudder and steering wheel vibration can be eliminated by checking brake rotor thickness or installing an

upgraded pressure plate release lever.

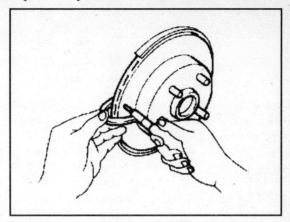

1990-Starting in D4 or delayed downshifting requires a new valve body separator plate.

1990-91-Starting difficulties can often be traced to an ECU connector not fully seated in the ECU.

1990-92-Clutch whine or screech in cold temperatures requires the installation of an upgraded clutch disc.

All models/years-A rotten egg sulphur smell may be caused by a defective catalytic converter. It will be replaced free of charge under the emissions warranty up to 5 years/80,000 km. Customer feedback confirms that Nissan will also replace the constant velocity joints and power-steering assembly free of charge up to 5 years/80,000 km.

Vehicle Profile

	1987	1988	1989	1990	1991	1992
Cost Price ($)						
Base	13,687	14,288	15,089	15,690	15,290	15,290
Used Values ($)						
Base ↑	2800	4500	5500	6300	7300	9000
Base ↓	2200	3500	4800	5100	6100	7700
Reliability	②	③	③	③	④	④
Air conditioning	③	④	④	④	⑤	⑤
Body integrity	②	②	③	③	③	③
Braking system	②	②	③	③	③	③
Electrical system	②	②	③	③	③	③
Engines	②	③	④	④	④	④
Exhaust/Converter	②	②	②	③	③	③
Fuel system	②	③	③	③	③	③
Ignition system	③	③	③	③	③	③
Manual transmission	④	④	④	④	④	④
- automatic	②	③	③	③	③	③

Rust/Paint	❷	❷	③	③	③	③
Steering	❷	③	③	④	④	④
Suspension	❷	③	③	③	③	④
Dealer Service	④	④	④	④	④	④
Maintenance	③	③	③	③	③	④
Parts Availability	④	④	④	④	④	④
Repair Costs	③	③	③	③	③	④
Crash Safety						
Stanza 4-door	❶	❶	❶	⑤	⑤	⑤
Safety Features						
ABS	—	—	—	O	O	O
Airbag	—	—	—	—	—	—
Traction control	—	—	—	S	S	S

SUBARU

Legacy, Loyale

Rating: Average buy (1993-94); Below Average buy (1990-92).

Price analysis: Limited availability and reasonably priced, except for the 4X4s. Recent Legacy models depreciate rapidly. Pay a bit more if the original Subaru warranty is still in effect. Expect to pay about $600 annually for maintenance and repairs during the warranty period and $800 annually thereafter. Other cars worth considering: Chrysler Spirit/Acclaim • Honda Accord • Nissan Sentra or Stanza • Toyota Camry • Volvo 850.

Technical Data

ENGINES	Litres/CID	HP	MPG	Model Years
		Legacy		
OHC flat-4 FI	2.2/135	130	19-25	1990-94
OHC flat-4T FI	2.2/135	160	17-22	1991-94
		Loyale		
OHC flat-4 FI	1.8/109	90-97	23-28	1985-94
OHC flat-4T FI	1.8/109	111-115	19-24	1985-90
OHC flat-6 FI	2.7/163	145	17-23	1988-91

Strengths and weaknesses: These are sluggish cars whose bland styling masks their solid, dependable performance with recent models. The availability of a proven 4-wheel drive powertrain in a compact family sedan and wagon makes them appealing for special uses. Subarus can be a good used car choice if maintained carefully and the body has not begun to rust. In spite of their reputation for dependability, Subarus are not trouble free. Engine, clutch and driveline defects are common.

Through 1994, premature exhaust system rust-out, automatic transmission (front seals, especially) and clutch breakdowns are the more common complaints. Brakes require frequent attention. Shock absorbers, constant velocity joints and catalytic converters often wear out prematurely. Other problems that appear over many model years include starter and ignition relay failures and front-end suspension noises. Parts shortages have been common and prices are slightly higher than average.

Bodies are particularly rust prone. Fenders, door bottoms, rocker panels, wheel openings, bumpers and supports, rear quarter-panels, tailgate, trunk lid and hood are particularly rust prone. The underbody and chassis components should be examined very carefully for corrosion damage. Towing is not recommended.

Safety summary/recalls: Crash tests of a 1990 four-door Legacy concluded that the driver would sustain severe or fatal head and leg injuries, while the passenger would suffer massive leg trauma. NHTSA crash tests of an airbag-equipped 1993 Legacy concluded that both the driver and passenger would be well-protected. A retested '94 showed the driver sustaining serious injuries to both legs. *Recalls*: **1989-90 Loyale**-Automatic transmission may engage abruptly causing a sudden lurch into "Reverse." **1990 Loyale with 3AT transmission**-Vehicle may jump into gear from "Park." **1990-93 Loyale**-Five-speed manual transmission may suddenly seize. **1989-93 Legacy**-Frost may build up in the manual transmission dipstick vent causing transmission oil leakage and eventual wheel lockup. **1990-91**-Faulty defroster. Help! Door may not open from the inside. Automatic transmission may engage abruptly causing a sudden lurch into "Reverse." **1990-93 4X4**-Cold weather or high humidity may cause the manual transmission to seize. **1993**-Top of fuel tank may leak.

Secret Warranties/Service Tips/DSBs

1990-91 Loyale-A knocking noise from the exhaust flex joint may require the replacement of the exhaust flange gasket with an upgraded gasket (#44022-GA 191).
1991-Weak, noisy AM reception can be corrected by installing a modified antenna feeder cable (#86324AA040).
• Banging over bumps is likely caused by the struts, strut mounts, brake cable clamps on trailing arms or the rear defogger condenser hitting the quarter panel.
• A "popping" noise heard when going over small bumps may be caused by the front stabilizer bar bushing clamps.
1991-92-Ignition relay failure is the likely cause of no-starts.

1992-Door fabric trim that peels away needs cyanoacrylate glue.

1992-94-The heater mode door actuator may be culprit causing an annoying clicking in the heater area.

1993-Legacys may have a headliner droop that is addressed in a March 1994 DSB.

1994-Squeaking from the torque converter is addressed in a June 1993 DSB.

All models/years-A rotten egg sulphur smell may be caused by a defective catalytic converter. It will be replaced, after a bit of arguing, free of charge up to 5 years/80,000 km. The company will replace the constant velocity joints and power-steering assembly for half price up to 5 years/80,000 km.

Vehicle Profile

	1987	1988	1989	1990	1991	1992	1993	1994
Cost Price ($)								
Legacy	—	—	—	15,849	16,482	16,888	16,888	19,995
Legacy 4X4	—	—	—	17,349	18,042	18,969	—	22,695
Loyale	—	—	—	12,549	13,050	11,899	12,781	—
Loyale 4X4	—	—	—	13,749	14,299	12,909	—	—
Wagon 4X4	15,425	15,210	15,595	—	—	—	—	14,995
Used Values ($)								
Legacy ↑	—	—	—	6400	7400	10,500	12,000	14,400
Legacy ↓	—	—	—	5100	6100	9000	10,600	12,800
Legacy 4X4 ↑	—	—	—	7500	8500	11,200	—	—
Legacy 4X4 ↓	—	—	—	6300	7100	9700	—	—
Loyale ↑	—	—	—	4700	5300	6400	7600	—
Loyale ↓	—	—	—	3800	4300	5300	6400	—
Loyale 4X4 ↑	—	—	—	5000	5900	7100	—	—
Loyale 4X4 ↓	—	—	—	3800	4900	6000	—	—
Wagon 4X4 ↑	3000	4100	5100	—	—	—	—	—
Wagon 4X4 ↓	2200	3100	4000	—	—	—	—	—
Reliability	②	②	②	②	③	④	④	⑤
Air conditioning	③	④	④	④	④	⑤	⑤	⑤
Body integrity	②	②	②	②	③	③	③	③
Braking system	②	②	③	③	③	③	③	④
Electrical system	②	③	③	③	③	④	⑤	⑤
Engines	②	③	③	④	⑤	⑤	⑤	⑤
Exhaust/Converter	②	②	②	③	④	⑤	⑤	⑤
Fuel system	③	③	③	③	④	④	④	④
Ignition system	②	②	②	②	③	③	④	⑤
Manual transmission	③	③	③	③	④	⑤	⑤	⑤
- automatic	②	②	③	③	③	③	⑤	⑤
Rust/Paint	②	②	②	③	③	③	④	④
Steering	②	②	③	③	④	④	⑤	⑤
Suspension	②	②	③	③	③	③	⑤	⑤

Dealer Service	②	②	②	②	③	③	③	③
Maintenance	②	②	②	②	③	③	④	④
Parts Availability	②	②	②	②	③	③	③	③
Repair Costs	②	②	②	②	③	③	③	③
Crash Safety								
Legacy								
4-door, 2X4, 4X4	—	—	—	❶	❶	❶	⑤	❶
Safety Features								
ABS	—	—	—	—	—	—	—	O
Airbag	—	—	—	—	—	—	D	D

VOLKSWAGEN

Passat

Rating: Not Recommended (1991-93). VW skipped the 1994 model year.

Price analysis: Rapid depreciation but availability is limited. Be wary of any Passat sold as a 1994; all '94s were carried over from the 1993 model year. Expect to pay about $500 annually for maintenance and repairs during the warranty period and $800 annually thereafter—all the more reason to buy a car with the original warranty. Insurance rates are higher than average because these cars are targeted for theft for their radios, wheels and VW badges—or the entire car! Other cars worth considering: Chrysler Laser and Talon • Ford Probe • Toyota Celica GTS • Camry V6 • Volvo 850.

Technical Data

ENGINES	Litres/CID	HP	MPG	Model Years
DOHC I-4 FI	2.0/121	134	19-24	1990-94
OHC V6 FI	2.8/170	172	17-22	1993-95

Strengths and weaknesses: The base drivetrain uses a 2.0L engine and other mechanical parts borrowed from the Golf, Jetta and Corrado. The car's long wheelbase and squat appearance give the Passat a massive, solid feeling, while its styling makes it look sleek and clean. It comes fairly well appointed.

As far as overall performance goes, the Passat is no slouch. The multivalve 4-cylinder engine is adequate, and handling is superior to most of the competition. The 2.8L V6 provides lots of power when revved.

The 5-speed manual transmission gear ranges are too far apart; there's an enormous gap between 3rd and 4th gear. The 4-speed automatic isn't as smooth as it should be and has generated a host of reliability complaints. Problems with the front brakes, MacPherson struts, and fuel and electrical systems as the car ages. Interior trim and controls are fragile. Parts and service are more expensive than average and the dealers do not always provide excellent work. This problem is likely to worsen now that VW Canada has closed down and won't be around to provide much-needed technical support and parts.

Owners have complained that the transmission pops out of 3rd gear, and when this happens they have been left in darkness when going from driving lights to highway high beams. The back of the car is a dirt and grime collector.

Confidential dealer service bulletins show the 1993s have AC expansion)valve noise, faulty ABS warning lights, excessive diagonal tire wear and frequent windshield wiper failures.

Safety summary/recalls: Crash data for the 1993 shows the driver would likely sustain severe head and trauma to both legs from a frontal collision at 57 km/h; the front passenger would have serious injuries to both legs. *Recalls*: **1993**-Axle may separate from struts causing loss of vehicle control.

Secret Warranties/Service Tips/DSBs

1990-A flickering alternator warning light and squealing V-belt during wet conditions can be corrected by installing a new splash shield.

1990-91-If the radiator fan stays on high speed with the ignition off, discharging the battery, replace the fan's high-speed relay with part number #321-919-505A.

1991-93-AC expansion valve noises require the installation of an upgraded expansion valve.

• Poor driveability may be caused by magnetic interference due to a deteriorated oxygen sensor wire shield or improper oxygen sensor wire shield ground connection. Replace the 025 wire with an upgraded component, or tighten the ground connection as necessary. (See diagram p. 229).

1992-94-Poor 2.8L engine performance or a rough idle may be due to a misrouted EVAP vacuum hose or an improperly routed positive crankcase ventilation hose causing a vacuum leak.

1993-If the ABS warning light won't go out, a faulty start switch/lock is the likely culprit.

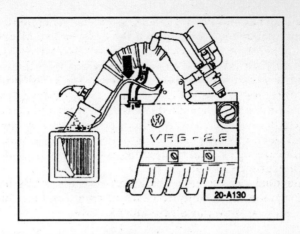

20-A130

Vehicle Profile

	1991	1992	1993
Cost Price ($)			
CL	18,995	19,790	21,525
Used Values ($)			
CL ↑	9500	12,400	15,000
CL ↓	7800	10,700	13,500
Reliability	③	③	③
Air conditioning	❷	④	④
Automatic transmission	❶	❶	❶
Body integrity	③	③	③
Braking system	③	③	③
Electrical system	❷	❷	③
Engines	⑤	⑤	⑤
Exhaust/Converter	⑤	⑤	⑤
Fuel system	③	③	③
Ignition system	③	③	③
Rust/Paint	⑤	⑤	⑤
Steering	④	⑤	⑤
Suspension	③	③	③
Dealer Service	③	③	③
Maintenance	⑤	⑤	⑤
Parts Availability	③	③	③
Repair Costs	③	③	⑤
Crash Safety	❶	❶	❶
Safety Features			
ABS	O	O	O

VOLVO

240 Series

Rating: Average buy (1989-93); Below Average buy (1985-88).

Price analysis: Average availability and reasonably priced. Expect to pay about $300 annually for maintenance and repairs during the warranty period, and $500 annually thereafter. The 240's accident repair costs are much lower than average. Other cars worth considering: Chrysler Spirit/Acclaim • Honda Accord • Nissan Sentra or Stanza • Toyota Camry • Volvo 850.

Technical Data

ENGINES	Litres/CID	HP	MPG	Model Years
OHC I-4T FI	2.1/130	162	17-21	1985
OHC I-4 FI	2.3/141	111-114	19-23	1985-93
OHC I-6D FI	2.4/145	80	25-29	1985

Strengths and weaknesses: Volvos mirror the quality-control problems manifested by Saab, the other Swedish automaker, except for the fact that Volvo styling is more bland than bizarre and earlier models are just as troublesome as post-1985 versions. The 240 is the cheapest entry-level version and is a solid and spacious car. Unfortunately, it doesn't live up to Volvo's advertising as an automotive longevity wonder. Reliability, in fact, is a bit below average if one factors in the Japanese competition, and repair costs are outrageously high. The 1989-93 cars are the best of a bad lot.

The V6 is an honest, though imperfect, engine. Avoid the turbocharged 4-cylinder engine and failure-prone air-conditioning systems. Diesels suffer from cooling system breakdowns and leaky cylinder head gaskets. The brakes need frequent and expensive service for all model years, and exhaust systems are notorious for their short lifespan. The GL and GLE suffer from occasional electrical bugs. Volvos are fairly rust prone, and the front and rear wheel openings are especially susceptible to perforation. The lower edge of the side cargo window on station wagons rusts prematurely, as does the lower tailgate lip.

Confidential dealer service bulletins address the following deficiencies affecting models over the past few years: hard cold starting, electronic module defects, excessive brake and cruise control noise, knocking sway bar bushings, and leaking sunroofs.

Safety summary/recalls: NHTSA crash tests of a 1979 244 four-door Volvo concluded that the driver would sustain severe or fatal head trauma and the passenger would have massive head and chest injuries. An '82 two-door DL, '85 four-door DL, and '85 DL wagon were judged to give poor protection to the driver's legs. When a 1992 and '93 airbag-equipped four-door were crash tested, both the driver and front seat passenger were judged to have been well-protected.

The heated driver's seat has come under fire (no pun intended) for being a fire hazard: owners have complained that the seat's wiring may short-circuit. American safety agencies are looking into incidents of accidental airbag deployment on 1991s. *Recalls*: **1985-86**-A low-speed frontal collision could lead to unintended sudden acceleration. **1986-87**-Erratic cruise control operation caused by voltage drop. **1992**-Ball joint and strut may separate leading to loss of vehicle control.

Secret Warranties/Service Tips/DSBs

1988-90-Brake pulsation, a common problem, is addressed in DSB 51/111.
• If you're having problems starting your Volvo on cold mornings, see DSB 23/135 and 23/21A.
1989-93-To improve cold starting, Volvo will install an improved fuel injection control module for free under the emissions warranty. Under another program, Volvo will replace the MFI EPROM to improve cold starting and idle quality.
1990-93-Noise coming from the cruise control vacuum pump can be stopped by modifying the pump bracket mounting.
1991-93-Under Service Campaign 62, Volvo will replace the sway bar bushing at no charge. The bushing can pull away from the retainers and create a knocking noise. Volvo says the problem isn't safety related.
All models/years-The April 1993 DSB chart below lists front and rear brake pad kits that have been specially developed to eliminate brake noise.

Braking system	Brake pad P/N	Type of pad	Remark
Girling, front	271739-5	DB861EE	Kit includes four rubber-coated anti-squeal shims
ATE, front	270165-4	DB861EE	
Girling, rear	270164-7	DB862EE	
ATE, rear	271702-3	DB862EE	Kit includes four rubber-coated anti-squeal shims and four stainless steel shims

Vehicle Profile

	1986	1987	1988	1989	1990	1991	1992	1993
Cost Price ($)								
240 DL	17,515	17,930	18,965	20,330	21,915	19,620	21,890	24,270
240 GL	19,810	—	—	—	—	—	—	—
Used Values ($)								
240 DL ↑	4700	6100	7700	8700	10,200	11,000	13,200	15,800
240 DL ↓	3500	4900	5800	6700	8100	9100	11,400	13,600
240 GL ↑	5500	—	—	—	—	—	—	—
240 GL ↓	4600	—	—	—	—	—	—	—
Reliability	③	③	③	③	③	③	③	④
Air conditioning	②	②	②	③	④	④	④	④
Body integrity	③	③	③	③	③	③	③	④
Braking system	①	①	①	②	②	③	④	④
Electrical system	①	①	①	③	③	③	②	③
Engines	③	③	③	③	③	③	③	④
Exhaust/Converter	②	②	②	②	③	③	④	⑤
Fuel system	①	①	①	②	②	②	③	③
Ignition system	④	④	④	④	③	③	④	⑤
Manual transmission	③	③	③	③	③	③	③	④
- automatic	④	④	④	④	③	③	③	④
Rust/Paint	②	②	④	④	④	④	④	⑤
Steering	④	④	④	④	④	⑤	③	④
Suspension	④	④	④	④	④	②	③	③
Dealer Service	③	③	③	③	③	③	③	③
Maintenance	③	③	③	③	③	③	③	③
Parts Availability	③	③	③	③	③	③	③	③
Repair Costs	②	②	②	②	②	②	②	③
Crash Safety	②	②	②	②	②	②	⑤	⑤
Safety Features								
ABS	—	—	—	—	—	O	S	S
Airbag	—	—	—	—	D	D	D	D

MID-SIZE CARS

Ford Taurus/Sable 1986-88 models were dogs, but this 1993 is a great buy.

These cars stress comfort and good highway performance. Gas consumption is high in city driving unless a 4-cylinder engine is chosen. However, a smaller powerplant compromises highway performance and reduces resale value. In the case of Ford, the V6 engine is the most reliable choice.

Intermediates offer consumers an interior that can seat six (but five in comfort) and provide lots of space for luggage. High-speed performance is not spectacular, but the vehicle is effortless to drive. Gas consumption on the highway is moderate (about 12L/100 km) and is a plus that attracts a lot of buyers. Intermediates are ill-suited to urban driving where parking may be a problem and gas consumption suffers from stop-and-go conditions. Crash safety is fair to good, but increased size does not always mean better protection.

The following used mid-sized cars are recommended:

Ford Sable/Taurus (1991-94)
Toyota Camry/Wagon
Toyota Tercel/Wagon

Chrysler's Concorde, Intrepid and Vision are pretty—and pretty bad.

CHRYSLER

600, Caravelle

Rating: Not Recommended (1985-89).

Price analysis: Lots available at reasonable prices. Expect to pay about $800 annually for maintenance and repairs. Convertible models are grossly overpriced with their mediocre performance and poor quality. Other mid-size cars worth considering: Ford Taurus/Sable • Toyota Tercel and Camry • Volvo 850.

Technical Data				
ENGINES	Litres/CID	HP	MPG	Model Years
OHC I-4 2 bbl.	2.6/156	101	18-24	1985
OHC I-4 FI	2.2/135	100	19-24	1986-88
OHC I-4T FI	2.2/135	146	18-22	1985-88
OHC I-4 FI	2.5/153	100	19-24	1986-88

Strengths and weaknesses: These low-tech cars depreciate quickly, but their bargain price doesn't make up for high maintenance costs and low quality. Mechanical parts and competent service are never hard to find, mainly because these models use identical parts and all have similar failings. Body parts, however, may be in short supply.

The base Mitsubishi-built engines are a major source of mechanical woes and, when turbocharged, can cost a small fortune to repair. There are no best powertrain or transmission choices. The Dodge 600ES, a specialty model available in 1985, had a standard 5-speed manual transmission that is inconvenient to use and unreliable. Carbureted models exhibit chronic driveability problems. The exhaust system, front brake rotors, parking brake cable, shock absorbers and MacPherson struts need frequent replacement. Low-quality air conditioning components have frequent and costly breakdowns.

Safety summary/recalls: Crash tests have shown that the 1985 four-door Caravelle produced serious leg injuries to the driver. *Recalls*: **1985**-Driver's seat frame may be weakened by fatigue cracks. **1985-86**-Seatback may have excessive rearward movement. **1985-87 Turbo**-Supply hose fuel leakage may create a fire hazard. **1986 600**-Overloaded instrument panel resistor may cause a fire.

Secret Warranties/Service Tips/DSBs

1987-Surging of the lockup torque converter on cars with the 2.5L engine can be fixed with driveability kit (#4419447).
1987-88-The electronic module (MAP) frequently malfunctions.
1987-89-Exhaust system heat may melt carpet. Install free heat shield kit (#4549356).
1988-No Reverse gear requires a new 3rd and 4th clutch sleeve.
• Oil in the air cleaner housing requires a new crankcase vent nipple.
• If accelerator pedal freezes in idle position, install adapter kit (#4419456).

Vehicle Profile

	1987	1988	1989
Cost Price ($)			
600	12,651	13,800	—
Caravelle	12,463	13,740	—
Salon	13,282	14,635	15,485
Used Values ($)			
600 ↑	2100	3000	—
600 ↓	1200	1700	—
Caravelle ↑	2000	2900	—
Caravelle ↓	1100	1700	—
Salon ↑	2400	3200	4300
Salon ↓	1600	2400	3200
Reliability	❶	❶	③
Air conditioning	❶	❷	❷
Automatic trans.	❷	❷	❷

Body integrity	❷	❷	❸
Braking system	❶	❶	❶
Electrical system	❷	❷	❷
Engines	❶	❷	❷
Exhaust/Converter	❷	❷	❷
Fuel system	❶	❶	❶
Ignition system	❶	❷	❷
Rust/Paint	❷	❸	❸
Steering	❶	❶	❶
Suspension	❶	❶	❶
Dealer Service	❸	❸	❸
Maintenance	❸	❸	❸
Parts Availability	❸	❸	❸
Repair Costs	❸	❸	❸
Crash Safety			
600	❷	❷	—
Caravelle	❷	❷	—
Salon	❷	❷	—

Dynasty, Fifth Avenue, Imperial, New Yorker

Rating: Not Recommended (1988-93).

Price analysis: Lots available at reasonable prices. These cars depreciate quickly, but their bargain price doesn't make up for high maintenance costs and low quality. Expect to pay about $300 annually for maintenance and repairs during the warranty period and $1000 annually thereafter—all the more reason to buy a car with the original warranty. Imperial body parts are rare and costly. The '94 LHS New Yorker is a completely different car from previous New Yorkers. Other mid-size cars worth considering: Ford Taurus/Sable • Toyota Tercel and Camry • Volvo 850.

Technical Data

ENGINES	Litres/CID	HP	MPG	Model Years
OHC I-4 FI	2.5/153	96-100	20-24	1986-93
OHC I-4 2 bbl.	2.6/156	101	19-24	1985
OHC I-4T FI	2.2/135	146	18-23	1985-88
OHC V6 FI	3.0/181	136-141	17-22	1988-93
OHV V6 FI	3.3/201	164	17-22	1990-93

Strengths and weaknesses: These relatively fuel-efficient, four-door sedans handle and ride like the average mid-size car popular two decades ago. When compared to large rear-drives equipped with V6 or V8 engines, they cannot tow as much weight, their unit-body construction makes for a noisier ride, and long-term reliability is way below average.

The base 2.5L engines are a major source of mechanical woes and, when turbocharged, can cost you a small fortune to repair. Owners complain of substandard piston rings, faulty oil seals and a failure-prone timing-chain mechanism that can lead to severe engine damage unless it is checked and adjusted frequently. The Mitsubishi 3.0L V6 engine, offered since 1988, has generated complaints concerning oil leaks, electronic malfunctions and fuel-system problems. Chrysler's 3.3L V6, available since 1989, is more reliable. The electronic 4-speed automatic has elicited a number of complaints concerning erratic and noisy shifting. The A604 automatic transmission is a nightmare and Chrysler is replacing it by the ton, paying the warranty deductible and compensating consumers for consequential damages. Front suspension components and brakes wear out quickly. The electrical system is bug-plagued; the electronic dashboard should be avoided. Air conditioning malfunctions occur all the time accompanied by the freezing up of the evaporator. Windshield wiper motor short-circuits often lead to unnecessary motor replacement. Erratic horn operation and leaky radiators are reported. Knobs and levers break very easily. Front seats lack lower-back support, and the middle passenger is punished by the hard edges of the split seat and folded armrest. Mediocre heating—when the Dynasty accelerates, there is not enough engine vacuum to operate the actuators to maintain a consistent heat range. No ducts to distribute warm air to the rear. When going over bumps, these cars shake and rattle like old taxicabs. Many owners report water infiltration, especially around the windshield and into the trunk. Surface rust is common, especially around the windshield, door bottoms and the rear lip on the trunklid.

Safety summary/recalls: Crash tests have shown that the 1985 New Yorker four-door produced serious leg injuries to the driver. An '88 New Yorker and Dynasty four-door did even worse: the driver would have had severe or fatal chest and leg injuries, while the passenger would sustain severe leg trauma. A 1991 four-door Dynasty protected the driver and gave inconclusive results concerning the front passenger. A '93 airbag-equipped Dynasty showed the driver would sustain serious injury to the right leg; the passenger was judged to have been well-protected. Tests of an airbag-equipped 1990 Imperial concluded that the passenger would sustain severe or fatal head injuries. U.S. safety experts are investigating 875 reports of ABS brake failures on 1990-91 models and are also looking into fuel line leaks at the fuel pump connection on the 1992-93 models. Airbags and ABS were optional on the 1991 New Yorker and Dynasty and standard features on the Imperial. *Recalls*: **1989-90 Dynasty/all 1990s**-Dealer will install a free bypass valve to prevent automatic transmission damage in cold

238

weather. **1990-91 ABS**-High-pressure hose may leak. **1991**-Faulty front outboard seatbelt latch. **1992**-Faulty steering column shaft coupling bolts. **1990 Fifth Avenue**-Airbag may be defective on cars with a grey interior. **1991 Fifth Avenue**-Front disc brake caliper guide pin bolts may be too loose. Short-circuit in the heater blower motor may cause a fire in the cowl area.

Secret Warranties/Service Tips/DSBs

1988-93-3.0L engines that burn oil or produce a smokey exhaust at idle can be fixed by installing snap rings on the exhaust valve guides and replacing all of the valve guide stems or the cylinder head.
1990-93-Harsh automatic shifts can be tamed by installing the following revised parts: kickdown, accumulator, reverse servo cushion springs and the accumulator piston.
• Cold startup piston knocking noise can be eliminated by replacing the piston and connecting rod assembly.
1991-92-Engines with a rough idle and stalling following a cold start may require a new single board engine controller (SBEC).
1991-93-Poor AC performance while the AC blower continues to operate is likely due to the evaporator freezing because the powertrain control module (PCM) isn't properly disengaging the AC clutch via the relay.
• Engines that stall following a cold start may need an upgraded Park/Neutral/start switch.
• The serpentine belt may come off the pulley after driving through snow. Install an upgraded shield, screw and retainers.
1992-If the heater and ventilation system change to the defrost mode during acceleration, while towing a trailer or climbing a hill, the installation of a revised vacuum check valve should cure the problem.
• Long crank times, a rough idle and hesitation may be corrected by replacing the intake manifold assembly.
• A vehicle that is hard to start may have a corroded ECT/sensor connector.
1992-93-Some 41TE transaxles may produce a buzzing noise when shifted into Reverse. This problem can be corrected by replacing the valve body assembly or valve body separator plate.
• A deceleration shudder can be eliminated by replacing the powertrain control module with an upgraded version.
• Rough idling after a cold start with 2.2L and 2.5L engines can be corrected by installing an upgraded powertrain control module (PCM).
1993-Acceleration shudder may be caused by automatic transmission front pump leakage.
• For improved automatic shifting, install an upgraded transmission control module.
• A fuel pump check valve failure can cause startup die-out, reduced power or erratic shifting.
All models/years-Defective valve springs on the 3.3L V6 engine will be

replaced free of charge (DSB R#466). Excessive air conditioner noise with 3.3L engine (DSB 24-8-89). A-604 automatic transmission clutch slippage (DSB 21-09-90) is a common failure that affects most model years where the transmission was used. A rotten egg odor coming from the exhaust is probably caused by a malfunctioning catalytic converter covered under the 5 year/80,000 km emissions warranty.

Faulty steering assemblies are often fixed free of charge up to 3 years/60,000 km (Ford and GM cover steering repairs two extra years). Water leaks into the vehicle interior will be corrected without charge up to the fifth year of ownership.

Vehicle Profile

	1988	1989	1990	1991	1992	1993
Cost Price ($)						
Dynasty	15,000	15,865	16,715	15,575	16,505	16,910
Fifth Avenue	25,300	26,235	25,180	—	—	—
Imperial	—	—	38,200	34,415	35,915	35,915
New Yorker	21,000	21,000	25,180	25,600	21,910	21,755
Used Values ($)						
Dynasty ↑	3500	4500	6000	7000	7800	11,300
Dynasty ↓	2600	3300	4500	5500	6200	9700
Fifth Avenue ↑	5700	6800	8800	—	—	—
Fifth Avenue ↓	3900	5500	7400	—	—	—
Imperial ↑	—	—	10,700	13,600	16,900	21,000
Imperial ↓	—	—	8700	11,600	14,700	19,000
New Yorker ↑	5500	6400	8500	8500	9400	12,000
New Yorker ↓	4300	4800	6700	7700	7600	10,200
Reliability	①	①	①	①	①	①
Air conditioning	①	①	①	①	②	②
Automatic transmission	②	②	①	①	①	①
Body integrity	②	②	②	②	②	②
Braking system	①	①	①	②	②	③
Electrical system	②	②	②	②	③	③
Engines	①	①	①	②	②	②
Exhaust/Converter	②	②	②	⑤	⑤	⑤
Fuel system	①	①	③	③	③	③
Ignition system	①	①	②	②	②	③
Rust/Paint	②	③	③	③	③	③
Steering	①	①	①	②	②	③
Suspension	①	①	①	②	③	③
Dealer Service	②	②	②	②	②	②
Maintenance	②	②	②	②	②	②
Parts Availability	③	③	③	③	③	③
Repair Costs	③	③	③	③	③	③
Crash Safety						
Dynasty	①	①	①	②	②	②

Imperial	—	—	❷	❷	❷	❷
New Yorker	❶	❶	❶	❶	❶	❶
Safety Features						
ABS	—	—	—	O	O	O
Airbag	—	—	—	O	O	O

Lancer, LeBaron GTS

Rating: Not Recommended (1985-89).

Price analysis: Limited availability and prices are relatively low. Expect to pay about $800 annually for maintenance and repairs. Other mid-size cars worth considering: Ford Taurus/Sable • Toyota Tercel and Camry • Volvo 850.

Technical Data

ENGINES	Litres/CID	HP	MPG	Model Years
OHC I-4 FI	2.2/135	93-99	20-23	1985-89
OHC I-4T FI	2.2/135	146	18-23	1985-88
OHC I-4T FI	2.2/135	174	17-22	1987-89
OHC I-4 FI	2.5/153	96-100	18-23	1986-89
OHC I-4T FI	2.5/153	150	18-23	1989

Strengths and weaknesses: These cars suffer from many of the same problems as the Aries and Reliant K-cars and their 1989 replacements, the Spirit and Acclaim. Road performance is sedate with the standard engines and suspension, and snappy with turbocharging. The interior will seat five comfortably and offers all the advantages of the hatchback design. The manual transmission is balky and its clutch has a poor durability record. Turbo models are risky buys at all times although parts are widely available and relatively inexpensive.

Head gaskets are prone to leaks on all engines. Shock absorbers, MacPherson struts and brakes wear out quickly. Front brake rotors are prone to rusting and warping. The electrical system is troublesome, with the distributor pickup and computer modules malfunctioning constantly, causing stalling and hard starting. Air-conditioning components have a short lifespan. Body hardware is fragile.

Safety summary/recalls: Crash tests of a 1985 Lancer and '85 LeBaron GTS two-door concluded that the driver would sustain severe or fatal head injuries. *Recalls*: **1985**-Seatbelt may be missing. Driver's seat frame may be weakened by fatigue cracks. **1985-86**-Seatback may have excessive rearward movement. **1985-87 Turbo**-Supply hose fuel leakage may create a fire hazard. **1987 Shelby**-Parking brake may malfunction. **1989**-Original brake pads fail due to excessive corrosion. Engine valve cover gasket may leak oil creating a fire hazard.

Vehicle Profile

	1985	1986	1987	1988	1989
Cost Price ($)					
Lancer	10,297	11,169	11,927	12,710	13,795
LeBaron GTS	10,671	11,550	12,290	13,075	16,222
Used Values ($)					
Lancer ↑	1200	1800	2500	3500	4200
Lancer ↓	700	1300	1700	2300	3000
LeBaron GTS ↑	1500	2100	2900	3800	5500
LeBaron GTS ↓	900	1500	2000	2500	4300
Reliability	②	②	②	②	②
Air conditioning	②	②	②	②	②
Body integrity	②	②	②	②	③
Braking system	①	①	①	①	②
Electrical system	①	①	①	①	②
Engines	①	①	①	①	②
Exhaust/Converter	②	②	②	③	③
Fuel system	②	②	②	②	②
Ignition system	②	②	②	②	②
Manual transmission	③	③	③	③	③
- automatic	③	③	③	③	①
Rust/Paint	①	①	①	③	③
Steering	②	②	②	②	②
Suspension	①	①	①	②	③
Dealer Service	②	②	②	②	②
Maintenance	②	③	③	④	④
Parts Availability	②	②	②	②	③
Repair Costs	②	②	②	②	②
Crash Safety	②	②	②	②	②

Concorde, Intrepid, LHS, New Yorker, Vision

Rating: Below Average buy (1993-94). These vehicles would be unacceptable if they didn't carry Chrysler's now discontinued seven-year powertrain and body warranty.

Price analysis: Since most leases run at least three years, there should be quite a few used units available for sale at prices a bit higher than normal. Other mid-size cars worth considering: Ford Taurus/Sable • Toyota Tercel and Camry • Volvo 850.

Technical Data

ENGINES	Litres/CID	HP	MPG	Model Years
	Intrepid, Vision			
OHV V6 FI	3.3/201	153-161	18-23	1993-95
OHC V6 FI	3.5/215	214	17-21	1993-95
	Concorde, New Yorker, LHS			
OHV V6 FI	3.3/201	153-161	18-23	1993-95

Strengths and weaknesses: These aerodynamic front-wheel-drives are Chrysler's mid-size flag bearers. They are roomy, fuel efficient and highly maneuverable. The base engine is a 3.3L 153-hp 6-banger, but 70 percent of buyers choose the optional 3.5L for the 61 extra horses. Both engines provide plenty of low-end torque and acceleration that blows the Camry and Accord away with a 0-to-60 time of 8.9 seconds. Good or better handling and steering response than the Taurus. Independent suspension also maximizes control, reduces body roll and provides lots of suspension travel, so you don't get bumped around on rough roads.

A perusal of dealer service bulletins and comments from car rental agencies and owners tells me these cars continue to have many serious "first-series" deficiencies, including lots of interior noise, uneven fit and finish, poor-quality trim items that break or easily fall off, exposed screw heads, faulty door hinges that make the doors rattle and hard to open, windows that come off their tracks or are misaligned and poorly sealed, power window motor failures and steering wheel noise when the car is turning. The automatic climate control system operates erratically, blowing cold air when it's set for warm and warm air when it's set for cool. Servicing the ventilation system requires the removal of instrument panel because the AC ducts are molded into the plastic panel.

The shift console needs lighting, radio and climate controls are too small, the trunk release is hidden in the glove compartment, the hood release is found on the floor, the rearview mirror is too narrow, and the fuel filler door needs a lock. The trunk has a high decklid, making for difficult loading and unloading, and there is no inside access by folding down the rear seat as in the Camry.

The 4-speed LE42 automatic transmission is a spin-off of Chrysler's failure-prone A604 version and is problematic. Owners report glitches in the computerized transmission's shift timing and computer malfunctions causing driveability problems (stalling, hard starts and surging).

Confidential dealer service bulletins indicate that 1993 models' AC operates erratically, the ATC (automatic temperature control) works poorly in warm weather, an ominous clicking noise comes from the passenger compartment and the 3.3L engine emits a ticking sound when cold. Hard starting and long crank times when the engine is hot. Ignition noise on the AM band and malfunctioning AC ducts that blow different temperatures of air.

Bulletins applicable to the '94s address acceleration shudder and faulty engine timing belts. The transmission wiring harness bracket may break, transmission wires may short circuit, floor shifter knob may stick, and the radio often "locks up."

Leaks and noise continue to be Chrysler's nemesis with the same defects carried over from previous model years. Bulletins show AC refrigerant leaks, heater/AC housing water leaks and moisture in headlamps. Excessive engine noise is likely caused by carbon buildup on the top of the pistons, engine mount rattles, transmission clicks and clunks, and fuel line rattles caused by a faulty fuel rail assembly. Squeaking front or rear brakes require upgraded brake linings. A-pillar wind noise, rattling C-post appliqué or poor fit of the appliqué to the back glass, front hub clicks and clunks, B-pillar and rear spring rattles. The upper strut mount squeaks. Excessive road noise from the front wheels and rear seat require reduced tire pressure and adding foam/sealer insulation to the front upper load beam or the C-pillar.

Upscale LHS and New Yorker versions haven't escaped Chrysler's notorious poor-quality body components and sloppy assembly.

Apart from the above-mentioned problems, internal service bulletins for these cars indicate they are likely to have faulty fuel pumps causing stalling, reduced power or erratic transmission shifting, radio lockups, water leaks coming from the heater-AC housing and moisture in headlamps. Bulletins report excessive road noise from the front wheels and the rear seat require reduced tire pressure and adding foam/sealer insulation to the front upper load beam or the C-pillar, a noisy AC compressor, a squeaking or creaking noise coming from the rear window while traveling at slow speeds over rough roads, and a high-pitched whistling noise caused by a defective idle air control motor.

Safety summary/recalls: NHTSA 57 km/h crash tests have concluded that a 1994 New Yorker would provide mediocre crash protection to both the driver and front seat passenger; serious leg injuries would be sustained. A test of a '93 Intrepid produced serious injuries to the passenger's legs. Standard dual airbags and optional ABS (standard on the Concorde) and traction control.

Headlights are too dim for safe motoring and some owners report they sometimes cut out completely. This problem also affects 1994 versions. Defrosting is inadequate on some '93s, allowing ice and moisture to collect at the base of the windshield. Chrysler has a fix for these two problems that requires the installation of a new headlight lens and small foam pads into the defroster outlet ducts.

Non-ABS brakes perform poorly, resulting in excessively long stopping distances that exceed other cars in this class. The overhead digital panel is distracting and forces you to take your eyes from the road. The emergency brake pedal catches pant cuffs and shoe laces as you enter or exit. A high rear window sill obstructs rear visibility. These cars have safety-related peculiarities you wouldn't believe. The owner of a '93 Intrepid recounts his unique experience in these words: "I started having trouble getting the key out of the ignition after I shut the car off. This happened on a Saturday afternoon. I called the dealer and was told I was pretty much out of luck until a mechanic was available on Monday. If I had been smart, I would have left the keys in the ignition and prayed some stupid thief would steal the car. I finally had to call a friend who works at Transport Canada-Road Safety here in Ottawa. He had the answer—you have to smack the gearshift lever from right to left to so the internals under the button on the gearshift lever pop out. Lo and behold, this worked. Nifty feature on a $27,000-plus car. I still have to do this to this day, especially during colder weather.... The power remote locks would not work and the driver's side door could not even be unlocked with the key (some rod was broken). The only way I could get into the car was to unlock the passenger door with the key and crawl across the front seat.... Who is the brainiac who decided the location of the horn button? The horn is impossible to locate in an emergency."*Recalls*: **1993**-Dealers will re-route the wiring harness to prevent shorting. **1994**-Faulty transmission wiring may allow car to start when not in Park position. **1993 Intrepid and Vision**-Defective lower control arm washers may cause loss of steering.

Secret Warranties/Service Tips/DSBs

1993-If the stainless-steel exhaust system becomes rust spotted, Chrysler will replace it free with an improved system.
• A fuel pump check valve failure can cause startup die-out, reduced power or erratic shifting.
1993-94-Acceleration shudder may be caused by automatic transmission front pump leakage.
• A-pillar wind noise requires sealing the upper load beam and A-pillar, or sealing the roof rail body seam.
• AC belt rollover requires the installation of a revised AC belt and idler pulley.
• Exchange the base body control module (BCM) for an upgraded version if dash instruments and gauges suddenly quit working.
• Upgraded disc brake linings will help reduce front or rear squeaking noises.
• AM radio static affecting distant stations requires the installation of a supplemental engine suppression strap to the left side of the engine.
• Engine mount rattles signal the need to replace the engine mounts (always in pairs).
• Cold startup piston knocking noise can be eliminated by replacing the piston and connecting rod assembly.
• No-starts, poor engine performance and loud noises when attempting

to start this requires installing a snubber over the timing belt tensioner plunger. This applies only to the 3.5L engine.

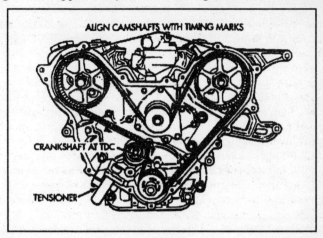

• Replace the fuel rail assembly to reduce fuel system rattling near the passenger side instrument panel.

• Dealers will exchange small head restraints for larger ones free of charge.

• A heater AC housing that leaks water into the passenger compartment can be plugged by enlarging the right plenum drain hole.

• Rear disc brake noise can be stopped by installing upgraded rear disc brake adapters.

• Rear glass rattling is likely caused by a loose backlight.

• Excessive rear road noise can be reduced by indexing the spring to the upper strut mount. In cases where indexing doesn't work, it may be necessary to replace the rear upper strut mounts with revised mounts.

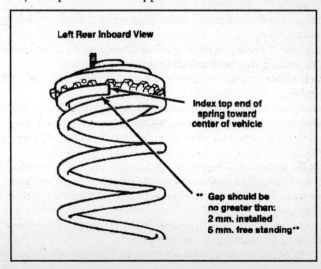

• A transmission buzz or rattle can be stopped by replacing the transfer chain snubber and attaching screws.

• If water leaks or dust accumulates inside the trunk, try sealing the quarter panel to outer wheel house panel seam.

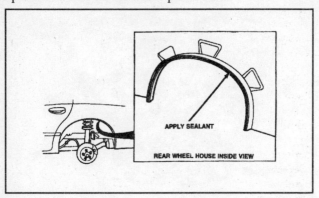

APPLY SEALANT

REAR WHEEL HOUSE INSIDE VIEW

1994-Harsh, erratic or delayed transmission shifts can be corrected by replacing the throttle position sensor (TPS) with a revised part.

1994-95-The intermittent or total loss of air conditioning can be corrected by installing a revised AC pressure transducer.

All models/years-A rotten egg odor coming from the exhaust is probably caused by a malfunctioning catalytic converter covered by Chrysler's original warranty *and* the emissions warranty. Don't take no for an answer. Same advice goes for all of the squeaks and rattles, water and wind leaks that afflict these vehicles. Don't let Chrysler or the dealer pawn these problems off as maintenance items. They are all factory related and should be covered for at least 5 years/80,000 km.

Vehicle Profile

	1993	1994
Cost Price ($)		
Concorde	20,425	22,590
Intrepid	17,555	19,170
LHS	—	35,020
New Yorker	—	29,990
Vision	18,450	21,485
Used Values ($)		
Concorde ↑	16,000	18,600
Concorde ↓	14,200	16,700
Intrepid ↑	14,000	16,400
Intrepid ↓	12,400	14,600
LHS ↑	—	29,500
LHS ↓	—	27,800
New Yorker ↑	—	26,500
New Yorker ↓	—	24,500

Vision ↑	14,000	17,000
Vision ↓	12,400	15,200
Reliability	➋	➋
Air conditioning	➊	➋
Automatic transmission	➊	➋
Body integrity	➊	➊
Braking system	➌	➌
Electrical system	➊	➊
Engines	➍	➍
Exhaust/Converter	➍	➍
Fuel system	➌	➌
Ignition system	➋	➋
Rust/Paint	➎	➎
Steering	➎	➎
Suspension	➋	➋
Dealer Service	➍	➍
Maintenance	➌	➌
Parts Availability	➎	➎
Repair Costs	➎	➎
Crash Safety		
Concorde	➋	➋
Intrepid	➋	➋
LHS	—	➋
New Yorker	—	➋
Vision	➋	➋
Safety Features		
ABS	O	O
Airbag	D/P	D/P
Traction control	O	O

FORD

Sable, Taurus

Rating: Recommended (1991-94). Not Recommended (1986-90).

Price analysis: Excellent availability and reasonably priced. Expect to pay about $300 annually for maintenance and repairs during the warranty period and $600 annually thereafter. Other mid-size cars worth considering: Toyota Tercel and Camry • Volvo 850.

Technical Data

ENGINES	Litres/CID	HP	MPG	Model Years
OHV I-4 FI	2.5/153	88-90	21-25	1986-90
OHV I-4 FI	2.5/153	105	21-25	1991
OHV V6 FI	3.0/182	140	20-24	1986-95
DOHC V6 FI	3.0/182	220	18-24	1989-95
DOHC V6 FI	3.2/192	220	17-23	1993-95
OHV V6 FI	3.8/232	140	20-24	1988-95

Strengths and weaknesses: The best-performing engine and transmission for all driving conditions are the V6 3.8L and 4-speed Overdrive automatic introduced with the 1988 models. Two caveats, however; the automatic transmission is slow to shift, an annoying drawback if you need to rock the car out of a snowbank and fairly dangerous if you need to pull onto a busy roadway. The other problem with the 3.8L is that acceleration is not exactly sparkling; the wagon takes quite a while to get up to speed. The 3.0L V6 that equips most of the late-model cars offers similar acceleration and good highway performance combined with above-average fuel economy. The transmission is a bit sluggish, though, when downshifting from Overdrive to 3rd gear while climbing steep hills. The turning radius is unusually large, making parking a chore.

The problem-plagued 1986-90 models are the object of multiple safety-related recalls, secret warranties and service adjustments. The 4-cylinder engine is a dog which no amount of servicing can change. It's slow, noisy, prone to stalling and surging, and actually consumes more gas than the V6.

The 3.0L engine is noted for cylinder head bolt failures and piston scuffing, characterized by hard starting, stalling, excessive engine noise and poor fuel economy. Changing the oil filter and spark plugs is particularly difficult and messy. Transmission cooler lines leak, heater hoses blow and fuel gauge sending units often malfunction. Brakes need constant attention. In front, they are noisy, tend to wear out prematurely, require a great deal of pedal effort and are hard to modulate. Master cylinders need replacing around 60,000 km.

1989-92 models have been known for defective ignition modules and oxygen sensors, causing rough running, chronic stalling, hard starting and electrical system short-circuits. Other problem areas are an automatic transmission that is slow to downshift, hunts for Overdrive and gives jerky performance, malfunctioning heaters that are slow to warm up and don't direct enough heat to the floor (particularly on the passenger side), a defective heater core that cost big bills to replace (buy from an independent supplier), and prematurely worn rack and pinion steering assemblies. Front suspension components also wear out quickly and body/trim items are fragile on all cars.

Other electrical components like windshield wipers, fuel pumps and the rear defroster interfere with radio reception. The automatic antenna often sticks and the electronic dash gives inaccurate readings. Owners report that electrical short-circuits that illuminate the "Check Engine" light, cause flickering lights and engine surging are frequently misdiagnosed and customers end up paying for the unnecessary replacement of the alternator, voltage regulator or battery, in addition to unnecessary tuneups. The speedometer is noisy and often inaccurate in cold weather.

Confidential dealer service bulletins show the 1993 models may have poorly performing air-conditioning systems caused by a slipping clutch at high ambient temperatures, a growling AC FX-15 compressor, fuel odors in the passenger compartment, noisy power-steering units, inoperative power door locks, underhood squeaks, chirps and knocks, wind noise coming from front door windows, intermittent long cranks or no-starts and a service engine light that has a mind of its own and may go on for no apparent reason.

1994 model bulletins designate a faulty 3.8L engine rocker arm assembly as responsible for squeaking, chirping and knocking noises. A rough idle, hesitation, excessive fuel consumption and poor heater output are likely caused by a malfunctioning thermostat stuck in an open position or opening before it should. Defective fuel pumps are targeted as responsible for extraneous noise in radio speakers. Other bulletins mention faulty electric rear window defrosters and inadequate AC operation caused by a faulty cold engine lockout switch and hose assembly.

Over the past seven years, there have been frequent complaints of paint defects and premature paint peeling. One Toronto 1990 Sable owner found pin-point rust spots during the first year of ownership and had the entire car repainted at Ford's expense. Unfortunately, the problem didn't go away. "I have recently noticed continued paint defects causing the car to rust prematurely, specifically under the front edge of the hood.... I maintain that the sealer and paint were improperly applied when the car was manufactured and that this is a defect that the Ford Motor Company should correct."

This *Lemon-Aid* reader is right and that's why this year's *Guide* has a comprehensive list of DSBs and other secret warranty documents that will help other readers get their cars, minivans, trucks and 4X4s repainted for free by Ford.

Paint adherence is particularly poor on plastic components, weld joints and the underside, even with mud guards. Owners also report that water leaks into the trunk through the taillight assembly and 1986-95 versions produce an annoying sound of fuel sloshing when accelerating or stopping.

Safety summary/recalls: Crash tests of a 1986 four-door Taurus have shown that the driver and passenger would sustain severe or fatal chest and leg trauma. Tests of a 1990 four-door showed that the driver would suffer severe leg trauma. In a 1991 Taurus wagon, neither the driver nor passenger was judged to have been seriously injured. A retested '93 and '94 dual airbag-equipped Taurus produced serious leg injuries to the driver and passenger.

Canadian investigators are looking into steering failures caused by premature corrosion of the steering assembly on 1986-92 models and steering lockup up while turning due to a defective turn-signal lever on 1988 and '89s. U.S. safety investigators are probing incidents of power-steering fluid leakage and 3.8L engine fires on 1988-90 models. Other probes have shown that the polycast wheels may crack and separate from 1986-93 and broken tie-rods may lead to loss of steering control on 1987-93 models. Airbags are also coming under close scrutiny from NHTSA investigators; they are looking into reports of injuries from dash trim panels flying apart when the airbag is deployed on the 1992 Taurus/Sable.

Owners report that airbag sensors often fail around 80,000 km (a $200 repair), the daylight running lights (DLR) module fails after two years (replaced at no charge) and the center console automatic transmission shift has no ignition lock. With the key removed, the car can be shifted out of Park. Seatbelts are sometimes difficult to latch on 1989 models. The floor-mounted gearbox is poorly designed, requiring the driver to press a thumb button to put the car into Neutral. This makes it too easy to hit Reverse or Park by mistake. Wagon rear visibility is limited, and occupants sitting on the optional rear-facing third seat can't get out on their own; the door needs to be unlocked from the outside. Reports of serious corrosion of the torque arm bushing eyelet hole. ABS has been a standard feature beginning with the 1990 SHO version and optional on other models. *Recalls*: **1986-** Ignition key can be removed when the ignition switch isn't locked. Faulty cooling fan motor resistor may cause air conditioner to malfunction. Misrouted battery wire may lead to premature radiator leakage. **1986 wagons-**Improperly tempered right quarter tinted window. **1986-87 wagons-**Sudden rear window breakage. **1986-87-**Faulty spring-lock fuel line coupling is a fire hazard. **1986-91-**The front brake rotors may snap as a result of corrosion. Under Recall Campaign #C90S19, Ford will replace them free without time, mileage or ownership limitations. Reimbursement will be made to owners who have previously paid for this repair. **1986-92 wagons-**Rear storage compartment is a hazard to children because it can't be opened from the inside. Owners should deactivate the slam-down latching mechanism with a screwdriver until a dealer installs a replacement mechanism. **1986-93-**Vehicles may have detached body mounts at the rear corners of the car's subframe. This defect could allow the subframe to drop and make steering difficult. The mounts will be inspected and a reinforcement plate installed with new attaching bolts. **1987-**Lower steering shaft may separate. A defective rear spindle assembly could separate and cause loss of vehicle control. **1988 3.0L-**Faulty air conditioner compressor shaft seal. **1988 3.8L-**Power-steering pump pulley may fail causing loss of power steering and other accessories. **1988-89**-Misrouted power seat switch could cause an electrical fire. **1988-90**-Engine mount failure could lead to engine surges, stuck throttle or power-steering hose failures. **1989-90**-End release seatbelt buckles on rigid mountings may not latch or unlatch properly. **1992 wagon**-Liftgate could open while vehicle is in motion. **1993 ABS**-Rear-drive controllers installed in error.

Secret Warranties/Service Tips/DSBs

1986-87-Ford will replace defective gas tanks that warp and cause the car to appear to have run out of fuel. Owners may experience engine stalling or stumbling and see their fuel gauge stuck on empty.

• Hard starting or stalling on vehicles equipped with EEC IV and certain TFI modules may be caused by moisture entering at the upper righthand mounting hole of the module.

• Faulty catalytic converters that produce a rotten egg smell should be replaced with #E7DZ-5F250-B.

• Abnormal front brake wear may be caused by an improperly adjusted rear height sensor brake proportioning valve (DSB 87-2-9).

• Higher than normal engine rpm at idle may be caused by defective throttle position sensors.

1986-88-Coolant and oil leaks that have plagued these models can be stopped by installing an improved cylinder head gasket (#E83Z-6051-A).

• Cracked plastic or metal door handles require upgraded handles.

1986-89-A great deal of tailgate rusting occurs around the bottom horizontal window sill, usually after the third year. Ford will assume part of the repair cost on a case-by-case basis.

• A glove compartment rattle may require rerouting the AC vacuum hoses.

• If the accessories frequently cut out, install a new ignition switch wire harness.

1986-90-Extended or no 3-4 shift may require a reassembled direct clutch piston and spring retainer.

• No shifts, harsh shifts or extended shifts may be due to faulty oil pump body and valve body check balls.

• AC evaporator water leaks onto the carpet require a new core and seal assembly (#E9DZ-19860-A).

• Poor AM radio reception may be caused by interference from the heated windshield system.

1986-91-Poor forward shifting may require a new clutch piston.

• Engine knocking at idle may require the installation of a new, thicker thrust plate to reduce camshaft end play.

• The in-tank fuel pump is the likely cause of all that radio static you hear. Squelch the noise by installing an electronic noise RFI filter (#F1PZ-18B925-A).

1986-92-A buzz or rattle from the exhaust system may be caused by a loose heat shield catalyst.

1986-94-A squeak or chirp coming from the blower motor can be stopped by installing an upgraded blower motor with improved brush-to-commutator friction.

• A rear suspension clunk or rattle when a wagon goes over a bump may be caused by a loose rear tension strut. Retorque the body attaching fastener.

• A speaker whine or buzz caused by the fuel pump can be stopped by installing an electronic noise RFI filter.

1986-95-A cracked forward clutch piston may cause forward/reverse problems. Install improved clutch piston.

• Premature wear on the inner edges of the rear tires calls for the installation of Ford's rear suspension adjustable camber kit. Ford will pay the cost for one year.

1987-A rough idle on vehicles equipped with electronic fuel injection (EFI) may be caused by loose injector electrical terminals.

1988-Air conditioners with shaft seal leaks will be fixed free of charge without any time or mileage limitation (DSB ON M68).

1988-89-Harsh downshifts may require a new 1990 level pump and main control assembly.

1988-91-The fist-size hydraulic engine mounts on cars equipped with a 3.8L V6 engine may deteriorate, causing a vibrating noise when the transmission is engaged or during acceleration. The problem is covered by Ford for 6 years/100,000 km (60,000 miles).

1988-92-Cold hesitation when accelerating, rough idle, long crank times and stalling may all signal the need to clean out excessive intake valve deposits.

1989-93-A persistent fuel odor in the interior when the AC is running signals the need to install a new auxiliary vapor tube service kit and relocate the vapor tube near the rear bumper.

1990-93-Noise coming from the power-steering pump may be caused by air in the system. Purge the system.

1991-93-Growling from the FX-15 AC compressor can be eliminated by installing a new compressor rubber damped disc and hub assembly.

1991-95-A sloshing noise from the fuel tank when accelerating or stopping requires the installation of an upgraded tank. Cost is covered under the emissions warranty.

PART NUMBER	PART NAME	CLASS
F4DZ-9002-A	Fuel Tank (16 Gallon)	A
F4DZ-9002-B	Fuel Tank (18 Gallon)	A
E6DZ-9417-A	O-Ring Gasket (For Pump/Sender)	R

1992-A 3.0L engine that stalls or idles roughly after a cold start may require a new EEC IV processor installed under the emissions warranty. **1992-95**-A corroded solenoid may be the cause of starter failures. Replace the corroded connector with a service wiring and connector assembly.

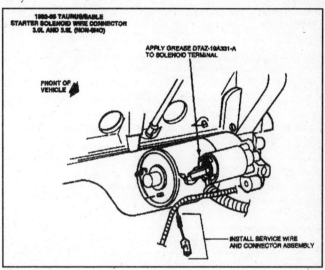

1993-94-Faulty catalytic converters that produce a rotten egg smell will be replaced for free under the emissions warranty.

• An inoperative AC blower probably needs an improved cold engine lockout switch and hose assembly.

• Stalling or hard starts in high ambient temperatures or high altitudes may be due to fuel tank contamination damaging the fuel pump. Ford will pay for a fuel tank flush and new fuel pump/sender and in-line fuel filter until May 31, 1997 under Service Program 94B48. (See internal document on following page.)

1994-95-A thumping or clanking noise heard from the front brakes signals the need to machine the front disc brake rotors. Ford will pay for this repair under its base warranty.

All models/years-A rotten egg odor coming from the exhaust probably means you have a faulty catalytic converter. Vehicles equipped with 3.0L engines where piston scuffing is evident (hard starting/stalling/excessive engine noise/poor fuel economy) may be eligible for free engine repairs or replacement on a case-by-case basis. On other engines, Ford has been repairing for free premature engine head gasket, ring and valve wear up to 5 years/80,000 km under its emissions warranty. Other components that benefit from Ford "goodwill" warranty extensions: fuel pumps and computer modules that govern engine, fuel injection and transmission functions. If Ford balks at refunding your money for a faulty computer module, apply the 5 year/80,000 km emissions warranty.

Overview of Program 94B48

June, 1994.

TO: All NAAO Export Sales North American Ford and Lincoln-Mercury Dealers

SUBJECT:

Owner Notification Program 94B48 - Certain 1993-1994 Taurus (Except Flex-Fuel), Sable and Continental Cars - Fuel Tank Contamination

OASIS	- Yes
OWNER LIST	- Yes
PARTS RETURN	- NO
PROGRAM TIMING	- 1993-1994 Taurus, Sable and Continental cars are eligible for this program through May 31, 1997 regardless of mileage.
	(After May 31, 1997, a vehicle is still eligible for this program if it is within the time and mileage limitations of the basic warranty coverage).

AFFECTED VEHICLES

Certain 1993 and 1994 Taurus (except flex-fuel), Sable and Continental cars built from December 1, 1992 through October 8, 1993.

REASON FOR THIS PROGRAM

Fuel pump components on some of these cars may experience premature wear. This condition is caused by excess amounts of metallic weld spatter contaminants (from tank manufacturing process) remaining in the fuel tank and entering the fuel pump. The effect on vehicle operation may include one or a combination of the following driveability symptoms:

Lack of power/fuel starvation, resulting in hesitation, stumbling and/or stalling in hot weather, above 90 degrees F (or warm weather in the spring or fall when high volatility "winter gasoline" is available).

Stalls at low vehicle speed or idling in high ambient temperatures above 90 degrees F and/or at high altitudes.

No start condition after stalling or shortly after an extended drive in hot weather above 90 degrees F.

SERVICE ACTION

To correct this condition, the fuel tank is to be flushed with water and the fuel pump/sender and in-line fuel filter replaced.

REFUNDS

Only for owner-paid repairs made before the date of the Owner Letter or after the date of the Owner Letter if an emergency repair was made away from the selling dealer.

Faulty steering assemblies are often fixed free of charge up to 5 years/80,000 km. Ford will pay 100% toward the correction of paint defects during the first 5 years/80,000 km and 50% up to the seventh year of ownership in keeping with the policy it adopted to cover pickups. Water leaks into the vehicle interior will be corrected without charge up to the fifth year of ownership. All of these programs include second owners.

Vehicle Profile

	1987	1988	1989	1990	1991	1992	1993	1994
Cost Price ($)								
Sable GS	15,678	16,995	17,955	19,187	17,895	18,995	19,470	20,995
LS Wagon	19,388	20,578	22,332	23,550	22,096	23,550	23,570	24,196
Taurus L/GL	13,575	14,845	15,780	16,876	16,495	17,495	18,195	19,295
Taurus LX	19,077	19,290	20,381	21,534	20,095	21,195	22,595	23,495
L Wagon	15,135	14,845	17,270	18,429	17,595	18,895	—	—
GL Wagon	—	—	—	—	—	—	18,196	19,296
Used Values ($)								
Sable GS ↑	3500	4600	5200	6400	8200	9900	12,000	14,500
Sable GS ↓	2700	3000	3600	4800	6600	8100	10,100	12,600
LS Wagon ↑	4700	5900	6800	8100	11,000	12,500	14,700	17,900
LS Wagon ↓	3800	4300	5200	6400	9300	10,600	12,800	15,900
Taurus L/GL ↑	3000	4100	4800	6100	7500	9600	11,600	14,300
Taurus L/GL ↓	2000	2600	3200	4500	6000	7800	9800	12,400

LX ↑	4300	5300	6000	7600	10,000	11,500	13,600	16,500
LX ↓	3200	3700	4400	5900	8300	9600	11,700	14,500
L Wagon ↑	3700	4100	4700	5800	7900	9400	—	—
L Wagon ↓	2500	3100	3500	4200	6300	7600	—	—
GL Wagon ↑	—	—	—	—	—	—	12,600	15,300
GL Wagon ↓	—	—	—	—	—	—	10,800	13,400
Reliability	②	③	③	③	③	④	④	④
Air conditioning	①	②	②	②	②	③	③	③
Automatic trans.	②	②	③	③	③	④	④	④
Body integrity	②	②	②	②	③	③	③	③
Braking system	①	②	②	②	③	③	③	③
Electrical system	②	②	②	③	③	③	③	③
Engines	②	③	③	③	③	④	④	⑤
Exhaust/Converter	②	③	③	③	⑤	⑤	⑤	⑤
Fuel system	②	②	③	③	③	④	④	④
Ignition system	②	③	③	③	③	③	③	④
Rust/Paint	②	②	②	②	③	③	③	③
Steering	①	②	③	③	③	④	④	④
Suspension	①	③	③	③	④	⑤	⑤	⑤
Dealer Service	③	③	③	③	③	④	④	④
Maintenance	②	②	②	②	③	④	④	④
Parts Availability	④	④	⑤	⑤	⑤	⑤	⑤	⑤
Repair Costs	①	②	②	③	④	④	④	⑤
Crash Safety	①	⑤	⑤	②	⑤	⑤	①	①
Safety Features								
ABS	—	—	—	O	O	O	O	O
Airbag	—	—	—	D	D	D	D	D/P

GENERAL MOTORS

6000, Celebrity, Century, Ciera

Rating: Not Recommended (1982-94).

Price analysis: Lots available at reasonably prices. The 1991 Century, Ciera and 6000 price and depreciation ratio is excellent. Expect to pay about $500 annually for maintenance and repairs during the warranty period and $1000 annually thereafter—all the more reason to buy a car with the original warranty. Other mid-size cars worth considering: Ford Taurus/Sable • Toyota Tercel and Camry • Volvo 850.

Technical Data

ENGINES	Litres/CID	HP	MPG	Model Years
OHV I-4 FI	2.2/133	110-120	21-25	1993-95
OHV I-4 FI	2.5/151	92-110	19-24	1985-92
OHV V6 2 bbl.	2.8/173	112	18-24	1985-86
OHV V6 FI	2.8/173	125	18-24	1987-88
OHV V6 2 bbl.	3.0/181	110	17-24	1985
OHV V6 FI	3.1/191	160	18-25	1994-95
OHV V6 FI	3.3/204	160	18-24	1989-93
OHV V6 FI	3.8/231	125	16-21	1985
OHV V6 FI	3.8/231	150	17-22	1986-88
OHV V6D FI	4.3/262	85	23-28	1985

Strengths and weaknesses: Popular with fleet buyers and car rental agencies, these cars are comfortable family sedans and wagons that have suffered from a host of serious mechanical deficiencies over the years. Handling and other aspects of road performance vary considerably depending on the suspension and powertrain chosen. The 2.5L 4-cylinder engine suffers from engine-block cracking and a host of other serious defects. The 2.8L V6 engine has not been durable, either; it suffers from premature camshaft wear and leaky gaskets and seals—especially the intake manifold gasket. A 4-speed automatic has been optional on a number of models but is prone to failure. The 3-speed automatic transmission is weak and the 4-speed automatic frequently malfunctions.

From 1986 to the present, quality control hasn't improved much. 4T60 automatic transmissions have had frequent problems with Reverse gear in 1987 to 1990 models. Temperamental and expensive-to-replace fuel systems (including the in-tank fuel pump) afflict all models/years causing chronic stalling, hard starting and poor fuel economy (use the emissions warranty to get compensation). Fuel-system diagnosis and repair for the 3.0L V6 (Buick and Oldsmobile) are difficult and the electronic controls are often defective. Air conditioners frequently malfunction and the cooling system is prone to leaks.

Prematurely worn power-steering assemblies are particularly commonplace. Brakes are weak and need frequent attention; front brake rotors warp easily, excessive pulsation is common and rear drums often lock up. Shock absorbers and springs wear out quickly. Rear wheel alignment should be checked often. Electric door locks frequently malfunction. Premature and extensive surface rust due to poor paint application, delamination and defective materials is common for all years.

Confidential dealer service bulletins covering the 1993 models confirm the following problems on vehicles equipped with 3.3L V6 engines: converter seal leaks on 4T60E automatic transmissions, faulty speedometers, loss of power, unexpected downshifts, defective cruise control, stalling when decelerating or extended cranking and faulty Reverse gear on 3T40 automatic transmissions. The Buick Century may also experience brake drag and loss of power.

Bulletins applicable to the '94s show that a front-end squeak may require the replacement of the exhaust manifold pipe springs with dampers and vehicles equipped with the 3.1L V6 may have a faulty throttle return spring that could lead to unintended acceleration. Other problems addressed are excessive noise or vibrations caused by defective rear transmission mounts, engine wiring harnesses may melt, water-contaminated door lock relays could cause a fire in the door pillar, exhaust moan may occur, temperature gauges could give false readings, and fuel pumps may fail prematurely.

Safety summary/recalls: NHTSA crash tests of a 1986 two-door and four-door Century found that the driver and passenger would be well-protected. The Celebrity, Ciera and 6000 posted identical results. The front passenger in a 1991 four-door Century would not have been as fortunate: crash forces would have caused severe or fatal head trauma. A 1993 four-door Century was retested two years later with similar results; the driver sustained severe head and leg trauma. The '94 version was judged to seriously injure the driver's right leg. Drivers report that the head restraints don't stay up. An optional driver-side airbag was added to the '93 Special. *Recalls*: **1983-87**-Fuel system on 2.5L engine may leak fuel, creating a fire hazard. Some wagons were recalled due to poor braking performance. **1985**-Throttle on V6 engines may stick open causing sudden acceleration. Misrouted clutch cable could cause fluid leakage from the brake master cylinder. **1986**-Defective headlight switch can cause headlights to flicker or fail. **1988**-GM will repair a leaking fuel feed hose on vehicles with 2.8L engines. Dealer will inspect and repair the front suspension. The lower arm bracket could develop cracks and cause the disengagement of the lower control arm, resulting in steering loss. **1990-91**-A short-circuit in the six-way power seat or power recliner that could set the seat on fire. **1992**-Automatic 4-speed transmissions were recalled because they performed poorly or remained in Reverse while indicator showed Neutral. Wagons may have erratically operating interior lights and sudden tailgate opening. **1992-93**-Dealers will install a redesigned intake manifold gasket at no charge on vehicles with rough running 2.2L engines. **1993**-Defective right front brake hoses. **1986 Century**-Cars with 2.8L engines could have underhood fire due to misrouted wiring. **1994 Century**-Sudden acceleration may occur when the 3.1L primary accelerators spring binds. Water leakage into the power door lock may cause a short-circuit fire.

Secret Warranties/Service Tips/DSBs

1981-87-Stalling when shifting into Reverse or Drive may require a new solenoid and conduit assembly.

1982-88-Brake pulsations caused by unevenly worn brake rotors need upgraded, reduced diameter caliper slide pins (#18016164).

1983-87-2.8L engines with automatic transmissions may click or knock because of a cracked flexplate assembly found in the crankshaft and transmission converter area.

1984-87-The automatic transmission may have a delayed 2-3 upshift. This problem is likely caused by a leaking 3rd clutch seal. A thicker seal (#8646991) will correct the problem.

1984-89-No 3rd gear may require a new thrust bearing assembly.

1984-90-Frequent loss of Drive with 440-T4 transmissions likely caused by a misadjusted 1-2 band stop unit.

1986-90-Vehicles equipped with the 3T40 automatic transmission may experience slippage in manual Low or Reverse gears. Install service package #8628222 which includes a Low/Reverse clutch release spring (#8664961) and clutch retainer and snap ring (#656/657).

1988-89-If 2nd gear fails, install an upgraded intermediate servo cover/servo oil ring.

1986-87-Serious stalling problems with these cars can usually be traced to a defective PROM module or a malfunctioning TCC solenoid. Ask your dealer to consult GM DSB 87-T57B when checking the solenoid and DSB 87-T-40A for data on tracking PROM malfunctions. Another possible cause is a defective mass air flow sensor.

• Excessive oil consumption may be caused by one or more damaged intake valve stem seals.

1987-A rotten egg odor coming from the exhaust means you need a new catalytic converter (#25104019) (DSB No. 88-92-6F).

1987-88-Poor engine performance troubleshooting shortcuts are detailed in DSB No. 88-T-47B.

1987-89-An AC growl on cars equipped with 2.8L engines may be silenced by a new compressor mounting brace and muffled hose assembly.

• Excessive idle noise may require the installation of an improved tensioner assembly and belt.

1987-90-A rattle or buzz from the instrument panel may require a new, upgraded brake booster check valve (#18012017).

1988-Faulty O-ring may cause 2.8L engine oil cooler leaks (SG39/9-6B).

• If there is a delay in the automatic transmission shifting from Neutral into Drive, chances are you require a new clutch housing (#8664982) and thrust washer (#8664762).

1988-89-Power-steering shudder on 2.8L-equipped cars requires a new power-steering hose and pipe assembly.

1989-90-Poor cold engine performance will be corrected with a new MEMCAL (#16138174).

1989-93-Vehicles equipped with a 3300 or 3800 engine that experience stalling upon deceleration or hard starts may need a new air control motor (IAC).

1990-Door lock rods that fall off need an upgraded inside handle to lock rod.

1991-An erratic oil pressure gauge that reads high may signal the need for a new oil pressure sender.

1992-93-A front-end engine knock troubleshooting chart is found in DSB 306001.

1993-94-An exhaust moan at idle is likely due to the catalytic converter assembly and intermediate pipe assembly flange flexing.

1994-Loss of Drive or erratic shifts may be caused by an intermittent short to ground on the A or B shift solenoid or an electrical short-circuit in the transaxle.

• A front-end clunking noise when driving over rough roads may require the repositioning of the diagonal radiator support braces.

• Knocking from the accessory drive belt tensioner requires an upgraded replacement.

1994-95-DSB 43-81-29 troubleshoots cruise controls that fail to engage.

1991-92 Ciera-Uncomfortable front seat shoulder belts will be replaced at no charge with an improved '93 belt and retractor.

1994-Loss of Drive or erratic shifts may be caused by an intermittent short to ground on the A or B shift solenoid or an electrical short-circuit in the transaxle.

• Knocking from the accessory drive belt tensioner requires an upgraded replacement.

All models/years-A rotten egg odor coming from the exhaust is probably the result of a malfunctioning catalytic converter. 3.8L V6 engines have a history of low oil pressure caused by a failure-prone oil pump. A temporary remedy is to avoid low viscosity oils and use 10W-40 in the winter and 20W-50 for summer driving. Spark knock on the 2.5L engine can be fixed with the installation of a new PROM module (#12269198; DSB 804-5812) under the emissions warranty coverage. THM 44C-T4 automatic transaxles with V6 engines are particularly failure prone due to pinched or kinked vacuum lines that cause oil starvation.

General Motors will repair defective steering assemblies free of charge up to 5 years/80,000 km and pay half the cost up to 100,000 km. The automaker has had a serious rust/paint peeling problem with all its domestic-made vehicles for the last decade. Faced with this, GM has set up a substantial slush fund to compensate owners. Original owners will get 100% compensation for paint peeling/surface rusting up to six years. Although GM and many of its dealers try to weasel out of this commitment, they can't deny the existence of GM's internal dealer memo that confirms this fact (see the Bonneville section of this *Guide*).

Vehicle Profile

	1987	1988	1989	1990	1991	1992	1993	1994
Cost Price ($)								
6000	13,015	14,547	15,941	16,899	15,798	—	—	—
Celebrity	12,730	14,074	15,341	16,991	—	—	—	—
Century	14,019	15,178	17,758	18,899	17,498	17,798	17,298	20,398
Ciera S	14,357	15,586	16,398	17,299	16,198	16,398	17,298	20,598
Used Values ($)								
6000 ↑	2800	4000	4800	5600	6800	—	—	—
6000 ↓	1900	2500	3200	3900	5100	—	—	—
Celebrity ↑	2600	3400	4400	5900	—	—	—	—
Celebrity ↓	1800	2000	3000	4500	—	—	—	—
Century ↑	2800	3600	4300	5600	6900	8900	10,700	14,700
Century ↓	2100	2700	2700	3800	5200	7000	8800	12,700
Ciera S ↑	3200	4200	5100	6000	6700	8600	10,600	13,400
Ciera S ↓	2100	2700	3400	4300	5000	6700	8700	11,400
Reliability	2	2	2	2	2	2	3	3
Air conditioning	2	2	2	2	2	3	3	3
Automatic trans.	2	2	2	2	2	2	2	2
Body integrity	2	2	2	2	2	2	2	2
Braking system	2	2	2	2	2	2	2	2
Electrical system	2	2	2	2	2	2	2	2
Engines	2	2	2	3	3	3	3	3
Exhaust/Converter	2	2	2	3	3	4	5	5
Fuel system	2	2	2	2	2	2	3	3
Ignition system	2	2	2	2	2	2	3	4
Rust/Paint	2	2	2	2	2	2	2	2
Steering	2	2	2	2	2	3	3	3
Suspension	2	2	2	2	2	2	2	3
Dealer Service	2	2	2	2	2	2	2	2
Maintenance	3	3	3	3	3	3	3	3
Parts Availability	5	5	5	5	5	5	5	5
Repair Costs	2	2	2	2	2	2	2	2
Crash Safety								
6000	5	5	5	5	5	—	—	—
Celebrity	5	5	5	5	—	—	—	—
Century 2-door	2	2	2	2	2	2	2	2
Century 4-door	5	5	5	5	5	2	1	2
Ciera	5	5	5	5	5	5	5	5
Safety Features								
ABS	—	—	—	—	—	—	O	S
Airbag	—	—	—	—	—	—	—	D

TOYOTA

Camry

Rating: Recommended (1990-94); Above Average (1987-89); Average buy (1985-86).

Price analysis: Limited availability and fairly expensive. Expect to pay about $300 annually for maintenance and repairs during the warranty period and $400 annually thereafter. According to the Canadian Automobile Association, parts are more expensive than most other cars in this class (alternator and ignition module, for example). Other cars worth considering: Toyota Tercel • Ford Taurus/Sable • Volvo 850.

Technical Data

ENGINES	Litres/CID	HP	MPG	Model Years
OHC I-4 FI	2.0/122	92-95	25-29	1985-86
OHC I-4TD FI	1.8/112	73	27-33	1985
OHC I-4TD FI	2.0/121	79	27-33	1986
DOHC I-4 FI	2.0/122	115	24-29	1987-91
DOHC V6 FI	2.5/153	156	16-22	1988-91
DOHC I-4 FI	2.2/132	125-135	22-27	1992-95
DOHC V6 FI	3.0/180	185-188	17-23	1992-95

Strengths and weaknesses: The Camry is an excellent family car buy because of its spacious, comfortable interior, good fuel economy, and impressive reliability and durability. Furthermore, Camry repair costs are reasonable and parts availability is excellent.

1987 to 1993 models have few problems, although they're far from perfect. Main areas of concern are failure-prone cylinder head gaskets, suspension and electrical system failures, defective starter drive and ring gear, premature brake wear, and some paint peeling and rusting. Mufflers last only two years on earlier models and sunroofs are rattle prone (probably a factory defect since rattles affect many sunroofs that are seldom used). All models require extensive periodic front brake maintenance; the pads wear quickly and the rotors warp easily and often. Brake pulsation is a common problem initially covered by a secret warranty and now the subject of several recent DSBs that propose a variety of remedies (see *Service Tips*). Front suspension bushings wear out quickly, leading to clunking and squeaking noises when going over bumps or when stopping quickly. There is also the so-called "Camry chop" (exceptionally rough rides when passing over uneven roadways) reported by owners of 1992-94 models. Cruise-control failure is frequent on all years. Owners of the 1992 Camry have reported that there is a chronic drone noise along with a vibration felt from the floor and gas pedal which occurs mostly when the automatic transmission changes from 2nd to 3rd gear at 1800 to 2000 rpm.

Confidential dealer service bulletins show that the 1993 models may have defective CD players and faulty engine-control modules that cause hard starts when the engine is hot and stalling when driving downhill. The radio/tape player doesn't play tapes very well and often malfunctions when in Reverse mode. One Calgary, Alberta, Camry owner replaced five units—and Toyota still refuses to refund his money. Not surprisingly, more and more owners say customer service has declined.

1994 models reportedly have problems with excessive wind noise coming from the front windshield, back doors and sunroof. Routine servicing is complicated by inaccessible spark plugs.

1992-94 model body problems include excessive wind noise coming from the front windshield, back doors and sunroof. Older Camrys have trim items that rust and fall off, door handles that pull away, and mufflers with a two-year life span. No reports of rust perforation problems, but weak spots are door bottoms, rear wheel openings and trunk and hatchback edges. Complaints concerning premature rusting on cars painted white. Toyota generally corrects these paint/rust deficiencies for free.

Safety summary/recalls: Crash tests of an '87 four-door concluded the car offered poor protection to the driver and passenger; both would suffer severe leg injuries. Subsequent crash tests of a 1992 airbag-equipped four-door Camry concluded that the driver and passenger would remain unharmed. *Recalls*: **1987**-Liquid spilled on console could short out the automatic seatbelt motor. **1987-89**-Front seatbelt guides that stay retracted will be changed. **1987-90**-Malfunctioning power door locks. **1991**-Dealers will replace faulty electrical components in Fujitsu Ten radios to eliminate the chance of fire. **1988 station wagon**-Original equipment jack may collapse.

Secret Warranties/Service Tips/DSBs

1985-86-A failure to start when parked facing downhill requires a modified fuel pump filter (#23220-16190).
1985-94-Toyota will give a seatbelt extender to anyone who needs the extra length.
1987-Inadequate windshield defrosting will be improved with an air deflector plate.
1987-88-Excessive front brake squeaking can be silenced with upgraded brake pads (#04491-32290).
1987-90-Engine ping, surging or jerk can be fixed with an upgraded ECU.

1987-91-A front inner shoulder belt guide is available to keep the belt away from the neck and face. This free accessory is covered under the seatbelt warranty.

1988-Poor engine performance in cold weather can be improved with an upgraded ECU.

• Harsh 2-3 shifts may require the replacement of worn valve body rubber check balls.

1988-89-Hard starting may require a new cold start time switch.

1989-90-A rattling sunroof will be silenced with an upgraded sliding mechanism, new cables and shoes.

• Wind noise coming from the upper windshield molding requires sealant injected underneath the molding.

1992-Noisy rear brakes can be silenced by installing upgraded brake pads identified by the letter "N" stamped on the part number label.

1992-93-Upgraded brake rods will reduce front brake groan/grind (see table)

1994-A steering column clicking noise calls for the replacement of the steering main shaft assembly and steering column tube assembly.

• Rear window wind noise can be stopped by replacing the front centering type bolt with a non-centering type bolt with washer.

All models/years-Owner feedback over the last decade and dealer service who wish to remain anonymous tell me that Toyota has a secret warranty that will pay for replacing front disc brake components that wear out before 2 years/40,000 km. If you are denied this coverage, threaten small claims court action. A decade-old brake pulsation/vibration problem is fully described and corrective measures detailed in DSB #BR94-002, issued February 7, 1994. Sometimes only the parts are covered, so the owner pays for labor. To reduce front brake squeaks on ABS-equipped vehicles, ask the dealer to install new, upgraded rotors (#43517-32020).

MODEL	FROM VIN #	P/D
JAPAN BUILT V6	JT2VK####PO210848	5/93
US BUILT V6	4T1VK####PU103224	7/93
JAPAN BUILT 4 CYL.	JT2SK####RD188032	8/93
US BUILT 4 CYL.	4T1SK####RU329745	9/93

Vehicle Profile

	1987	1988	1989	1990	1991	1992	1993	1994
Cost Price ($)								
Base Coupe	—	—	—	—	—	—	—	19,238
Base Sedan	14,418	15,548	16,198	16,658	16,048	17,948	18,778	20,138
LE	16,728	17,938	18,798	19,248	18,648	20,998	23,058	24,918
4X4	—	20,338	18,688	19,718	19,488	—	—	—
Wagon V6	—	—	—	25,988	23,568	26,008	27,668	29,708
Used Values ($)								
Base Coupe ↑	—	—	—	—	—	—	—	16,700
Base Coupe ↓	—	—	—	—	—	—	—	14,600
Base Sedan ↑	4800	6200	7100	8300	9600	12,600	14,800	17,200
Base Sedan ↓	3700	4700	5600	7600	7900	10,800	12,800	15,100
LE ↑	6600	7800	8900	9900	11,000	14,900	17,300	19,900
LE ↓	5200	6300	7400	8200	9400	13,000	15,300	17,700
4X4 ↑	—	8500	9600	9100	10,900	—	—	—
4X4 ↓	—	7000	8100	7500	9200	—	—	—
Wagon V6 ↑	—	—	—	11,400	12,600	16,700	19,100	22,500
Wagon V6 ↓	—	—	—	9700	10,800	14,800	17,400	21,000
Reliability	④	④	⑤	⑤	⑤	⑤	⑤	⑤
Air conditioning	③	④	④	④	⑤	⑤	⑤	⑤
Body integrity	③	③	③	④	④	④	④	④
Braking system	❷	❷	❷	❷	❷	③	③	③
Electrical system	③	③	③	④	④	④	⑤	⑤
Engines	③	③	④	④	④	⑤	⑤	⑤
Exhaust/Converter	❷	❷	❷	④	④	④	⑤	⑤
Fuel system	③	③	③	③	④	④	③	⑤
Ignition system	③	③	③	③	④	④	④	⑤
Manual transmission	④	④	④	④	⑤	⑤	⑤	⑤
- automatic	❷	③	③	③	⑤	⑤	④	④
Rust/Paint	③	④	④	④	④	④	④	④
Steering	③	③	③	③	③	③	⑤	⑤
Suspension	❷	③	③	④	④	④	⑤	⑤
Dealer Service	④	④	④	④	④	④	④	④
Maintenance	④	④	④	⑤	⑤	⑤	⑤	⑤
Parts Availability	⑤	⑤	⑤	⑤	⑤	⑤	⑤	⑤
Repair Costs	⑤	⑤	⑤	⑤	⑤	⑤	⑤	⑤
Crash Safety	❶	❶	❶	❶	❶	⑤	⑤	⑤
Safety Features								
ABS	—	—	—	—	—	O	O	O
Airbag	—	—	—	—	—	D	D	D/P

LARGE CARS/WAGONS

These are excellent cars for extensive highway driving for motorists who can write off relatively high gasoline consumption and maintenance and insurance premiums.

The term "large car" is relative. It designates vehicles with a wheelbase of more than 285 cm (114 inches) that weigh about 1600 kg (3200 lbs.). But now that the carmakers have shortened most of the wheelbases of their large cars, reduced weight and switched to front-wheel drive, existing definitions may no longer be accurate indicators of a car's size. Some large cars, like some Cadillacs, are bucking this trend, however, and remain long and heavy.

Owners have to pay a considerable amount of money for these vehicles, but large cars offer considerable comfort and stability at high speeds. Large cars also depreciate slowly, can seat six adults comfortably, and make excellent cars for families that take motoring vacations.

These vehicles generally incur less damage from front, rear and side collisions, although recent U.S. government crash tests show some smaller cars absorb frontal crash forces better.

The following used large cars are recommended:

Chrysler Fifth Avenue (RWD)
Chrysler Caravelle/Dodge Diplomat
Ford LTD Crown Victoria/Marquis
Ford Thunderbird/Cougar (1993-94)
Mercury Marquis/Grand Marquis

Ford's '93 Crown Victoria and Grand Marquis are land yachts, but cops, retirees and chauffered politicians love 'em.

STATION WAGONS (Full-Size)

If passenger and cargo space and car-like handling are what you want, a large station wagon may not be the answer—a used minivan, van, light truck or compact wagon can fill the same need for less cost and will probably still be around a decade from now. Popular wagons like the Caprice and Roadmaster (scheduled to be axed in '96) that you could cram a Little League team into are an endangered species, losing out to the van and minivan craze. (See *Lemon-Aid 4X4, Van and Truck Guide.*)

Some of the disadvantages associated with large station wagons are the difficulty in keeping the interior heated in winter, atrocious gas consumption, sloppy handling and poor rear visibility. Exterior road noise also is a frequent problem, because the vehicle's interior has a tendency to amplify normal road noise. Rear hatches tend to be rust prone. Crash safety is variable.

No full-sized station wagons are recommended.

GM's 1992 Cutlass Cruiser is a "Leave It to Beaver" flashback that proves not all large rear-drives are good buys.

CHRYSLER

Caravelle Salon, Diplomat, Fifth Avenue (RWD), Gran Fury

Rating: Recommended (1988-89); Average buy (1986-87); Not Recommended (1984-85). Reasonably reliable and simple to repair throwbacks to a time when land yachts ruled the highways.

Price analysis: Limited availability and prices are lower than average. Expect to pay about $800 annually for maintenance and repairs. Other cars worth considering: Ford LTD Crown Victoria, Mercury Marquis or Grand Marquis.

Technical Data

ENGINES	Litres/CID	HP	MPG	Model Years
OHV V8 2 bbl.	5.2/318	140	15-19	1985-89

Strengths and weaknesses: Both the 6- and 8-cylinder engines will run practically forever with a minimum of care. Repairs and maintenance are simple. The fuel-efficient "slant 6" powerplant was too small for this type of car and was changed to a gas-guzzling, though smooth and reliable, V8 after 1983. Handling is vague and sloppy, and emergency braking is often accompanied by rear-wheel lockup.

Overall reliability is average, but inexpensive parts are available anywhere. Carburetor, ignition, electrical system, brake and suspension (premature idler arm wear) problems predominate. It's a good idea to adjust the torsion bars frequently for better suspension performance. Front door locks and exterior chrome trim pieces fall off, chip paint and promote premature rusting. Surface rust is very common. Doors, windshield pillars, the bottoms of both front and rear fenders and trunk lid rust through more quickly than average.

Safety summary/recalls: *Recalls*: **1985**-Driver's seat frame may be weakened by fatigue cracks. **1985-86**-Seatbacks on power bucket or 50/50 seats may have a sudden rearward movement. **1985-87 turbo**-Supply hose fuel leakage may cause a fire. **1986 600**-Electronic instrument panel resistor may overload and result in a fire. **1988 with cruise control**-Misrouted fusible link wires may cause an underhood fire. **1988-89 Diplomat**-Steering wheel may separate.

Secret Warranties/Service Tips/DSBs

1985-90-Excessive 3.9L, 5.2L or 5.9L engine tappet noise requires upgraded tappets (#4636794).
• 5.2L engine vapor locking diagnosis and repair (18-09-88).
1986-87-The erratic operation of the right rear door lock requires a revised lock motor (#4467252).
1988-Engine die-out during cold start or rough running during warm-up requires an upgraded ESA/EFC module and EGR valve.
• Diplomats require a filter jumper harness (#4414708) to correct low- speed engine bucking and surging.
1988-89-To prevent auxiliary oil cooler freeze-up, install an oil cooler bypass connector (#4401013).

Vehicle Profile

	1984	1985	1986	1987	1988	1989
Cost Price ($)						
Caravelle Salon	10,893	11,299	12,181	13,282	14,635	15,485
Diplomat	10,893	11,299	12,181	13,282	14,635	15,485
N.Y. 5th Avenue	16,557	17,261	18,116	19,376	20,895	22,075
Used Values ($)						
Caravelle Salon ↑	1100	1600	2300	3000	3700	4400
Caravelle Salon ↓	700	1100	1700	2000	2400	3200
Diplomat ↑	1100	1600	2300	3000	3700	4300
Diplomat ↓	800	1200	1800	2100	2500	3300
N.Y. 5th Avenue ↑	2000	2700	3500	4500	5700	6800
N.Y. 5th Avenue ↓	1500	2200	2600	3200	3900	5000
Reliability	③	③	③	③	④	④
Air conditioning	❶	❶	❷	❷	❷	③
Automatic transmission	③	③	③	④	④	④
Body integrity	❷	❷	③	③	③	⑤
Braking system	❶	❶	❷	③	③	③
Electrical system	❶	❶	❷	③	③	③
Engines	④	④	④	④	④	④
Exhaust/Converter	❷	③	③	③	③	④
Fuel system	❷	❷	❷	③	③	④
Ignition system	❷	❷	③	③	③	③
Rust/Paint	❷	❷	❷	❷	④	⑤
Steering	❷	❷	③	③	④	④
Suspension	❷	❷	③	③	③	③
Dealer Service	④	④	④	④	④	④
Maintenance	④	④	④	④	④	④
Parts Availability	④	④	④	④	④	④
Repair Costs	④	④	④	④	④	④
Crash Safety	—	—	—	—	—	—

Safety Features

Airbag	—	—	—	—	D	D

FORD

LTD Crown Victoria, Grand Marquis

Rating: Recommended˙ (1992-94); Above Average buy (1987-91); Average buy (1985-86).

Price analysis: Excellent availability and reasonable prices when compared to the used prices of other large cars. The 1992 Crown Victoria and Marquis combine the most refinements, highest depreciation, lowest base price and least wear and tear. Expect to pay about $300 annually for maintenance and repairs during the warranty period and $800 annually thereafter. According to the Canadian Automobile Association, Crown Victoria parts are more expensive than most other cars in this class. Other cars worth considering: Chrysler Caravelle Salon, Diplomat, Gran Fury, Fifth Avenue (rwd).

Technical Data

ENGINES	Litres/CID	HP	MPG	Model Years
OHC I-4 1 bbl.	2.3/140	88	17-22	1985
OHV V6 FI	3.8/232	120	16-21	1985-86
OHV V8 FI	5.0/302	140-165	15-18	1985-91
OHC V8 FI	4.6/281	190-210	17-22	1992-95

Strengths and weaknesses: Built in Ontario, these cars are especially suited for people who need lots of room or who prefer the safety blanket provided by road-hugging and gas-guzzling weight. Handling is mediocre, but it's about average for cars this size. Both the 4.6L and 5.0L V8s provide adequate, though sometimes sluggish, power with most of their torque found in the lower gear ranges. The fuel pump, sender, fuel filter and fuel-hose assemblies are failure prone. Many complaints of EEC IV ignition module malfunctions causing hard starting and frequent stalling. A small number of differential failures have been reported occurring around 50,000 km with the 1987 model. Brakes, shock absorbers and springs wear out more quickly than they should on 1987-92 models.

Confidential dealer service bulletins show the '93s may have poorly performing AC systems caused by a slipping clutch at high ambient temperatures, ticking, pinging or popping when the AC clutch cycles, and a noisy FX-15 AC compressor. Other items include premature front brake rotor wear and vibrations when braking, noisy power-steering units, inoperative or malfunctioning cellular phones, and power door locks that may not work.

'94 Crown Victoria and Grand Marquis service bulletins address transmission shudder under light to moderate acceleration, radio speaker noise caused by a faulty fuel pump, and defective electric rear window defrosters.

Some complaints of rust perforations around the windshield, trunk and lower body areas, but they concern cars that have a lot of years and mileage. Parts are plentiful and maintenance is a cinch. Overall, these cars are not as reliable as Japanese luxury vehicles, but they are the best of the domestic crop.

Safety summary/recalls: Crash tests of a 1994 Crown Victoria concluded that both the driver and passenger would sustain serious leg trauma. Transport Canada is investigating reports of the throttle linkage sticking on models equipped with the 5.0L engine on 1985-90 models. Owners have reported that seatbelts aren't long enough and are difficult to adjust, particularly on 1991 models. The NHTSA is looking into reports of fuel line leakage near the fuel filter on 1992 models. Ford has received 19 complaints of reduced power-steering assist during high-speed maneuvers with 1992-93 Crown Victoria police cars. Lawsuits have been filed and the NHTSA is also involved. Reports of hoods suddenly flying up, shattering the windshield, while 1992-93 vehicles are in motion. Some complaints of poor traction on ice, hard-to-see shift indicator, and instrument panel washes out in sunlight. *Recalls*: **1984**-Seatbelt anchors may not meet federal regulations. **1987**-Faulty fuel-injection tube assembly may cause fuel leakage and create a fire hazard. **1987-88 station wagons/dual-facing rear seats**-Faulty automatic seatbelt retractors. **1991**-Car may roll away even though automatic transmission lever says its in the "Park" position. **1992-93**-A short-circuit could cause a front seat fire.

Secret Warranties/Service Tips/DSBs

1980-91-A refrigerant or chemical smell coming from the AC is likely caused by the clutch cycling pressure switch drifting downward, causing the evaporator core temperature to drop too low.
1983-90-Buzzing or humming coming from the fuel pump when the engine is shut off, a low battery, and hard or no-starts signal the need to install an upgraded fuel pump relay (#F19Z-9345-A).
1984-87-Stalling and no-starts on vehicles equipped with EEC IV and TFI modules may be caused by water entering the upper righthand mounting hole of the TFI module.
1985-90-An exhaust buzz or rattle may be fixed by installing new clamps to secure heat shield attachments.
• Inoperative rear window defroster can be fixed by repairing the

pigtail connections/grid line breaks with a service kit.

1985-91-Faulty door latches cannot be adjusted and must be replaced.

• An inoperative electric rear window defroster (heated backlights) may need a special defroster service kit.

1985-92-A buzz or rattle from the exhaust system may be caused by a loose heat shield catalyst.

1986-88-Reduce front brake squeal by installing upgraded pads (#E8AZ-2001-B).

1986-90-Poor radio reception can be fixed by preventing electrical interference from the heated windshield charging system.

1986-94-A speaker whine or buzz caused by the fuel pump can be stopped by installing an electronic noise RFI filter.

1987-Ford will replace the steering assembly for free if the steering centerlink is defective (#SR-87S23).

• Faulty fuel-injection tube assembly may cause fuel leakage and create a fire hazard. Ford will fix the unit free of charge.

1987-88-Hard starting/stalling is likely caused by defective TFI modules that link a vehicle's distributor to its microprocessor and signal the plugs.

1987-90-Excessive oil consumption is likely caused by leaking gaskets, poor sealing of the lower intake manifold, defective intake and exhaust valve stem seals, or worn piston rings. Install new guide mounted valve stem seals for a more positive fit and new piston rings with improved oil control.

• An unusual engine metal-to-metal noise may be caused by the flexing of the torque converter. Install six new flywheel bolts with reduced head height to provide additional clearance.

1988-91-The intermittent loss of the AC may be due to a defective suction accumulator (#E6VY-19C836-A). Change the accumulator, install a larger AC liquid line and a new 1992 condenser (#F2AZ-19712-A).

1989-Hard cold start, hesitation, stalls during idle or deceleration: correct by removing excessive sludge deposits or an oil film from the throttle body bore and plate, or the idler air bypass valve.

1989-90-Program B89 provides for the free inspection and replacement of the Overdrive gear and installation of a repair kit (#E9AZ-7L22B-A)

• No Overdrive or an extended 3-4 shift may require a new Overdrive band, transmission separator plate kit, overhaul kit and reverse drum.

• Harsh or rough shifting may be caused by sticking control valves.

• Poor AM radio reception due to ignition static can be improved by securing the antenna ground connection.

• Ford will replace for free defective fuel-pump sender assemblies.

1990-Excessive transmission noise, delayed shifts or no engagements may be due to thrust washer metal particles that have plugged the filter or burnt clutch plates.

• Install a new "service only" EEC IV processor to correct driveline clunk when the throttle is closed.

• If the AC blower won't change speed, consider installing a new switch assembly. If the blower sometimes cuts out, look for a loose connection at the variable-blower speed control.

• If the front seats move in their tracks or make noise, Ford will install, free of charge, new seat tracks and a memory track on the driver's side.

• A sluggish speed control response can be remedied by installing a new EEC IV processor.

• A loose or wobbly steering wheel requires putting in a new bearing tolerance ring service kit (#F0DZ-3L539-D).

1990-91-Fuel pump whining can be reduced by adding tank insulation material.

1992-Premature brake wear and seizure due to overheating can be corrected by installing air scoops to cool the brakes.

1992-94-A moan or loud noise coming from the engine compartment of cars equipped with the 4.6L engine can be corrected by installing a new air idle bypass tube and resonator assembly.

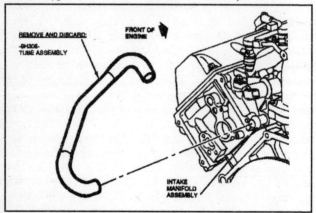

1990-93-Noise heard from the power-steering pump may be caused by air in the system. Purge the system.

• Brake pedal and steering vibration when braking can be reduced by installing improved brake rotors (#F1VY-1125-A) and linings (#F3AZ-2001-A).

1992-94-Automatic transmissions with delayed or no forward engagement, or a higher engine rpm than expected when coming to a stop, are covered in DSB 94-26-9.

• A hum from the air suspension system can be corrected by replacing the compressor isolators with upgraded parts.

1991-93-The air-conditioner clutch may slip during high ambient temperature conditions. This is likely caused by an improper air gap adjustment between the clutch plate and hub assembly. Set the gap between 0.35 and 0.85 mm.

All models/years-Two components that benefit from Ford "goodwill" warranty extensions are fuel pumps and computer modules that govern engine, fuel-injection and transmission functions. If Ford balks at refunding your money for a faulty computer module, threaten to apply the 5 year/80,000 km emissions warranty. A rotten egg odor coming from the exhaust is likely the result of a malfunctioning catalytic converter—not your fellow passengers. Get Ford to replace the converter under its 5 year/80,000 km emissions warranty.

Faulty steering assemblies are often fixed free of charge up to 5 years/80,000 km. Ford will pay 100% toward the correction of paint defects during the first 5 years/80,000 km and 50% up to the seventh year of ownership in keeping with the policy it adopted to cover pickups. Water leaks into the vehicle interior will be corrected without charge up to the fifth year of ownership. All of these programs include second owners.

Vehicle Profile

	1987	1988	1989	1990	1991	1992	1993	1994
Cost Price ($)								
Crown S/LTD	16,291	17,643	18,990	20,828	19,795	22,095	23,195	22,495
Marquis GS	18,685	20,224	21,407	23,406	21,795	23,995	24,595	23,795
Used Values ($)								
Crown S/LTD ↑	3300	4500	6000	7500	9200	11,200	12,500	15,800
Crown S/LTD ↓	2200	2800	4300	5800	7500	9500	10,700	13,800
Marquis GS ↑	4700	5900	6700	9200	9500	13,200	15,400	18,100
Marquis GS ↓	4000	4200	5000	7400	7800	11,200	13,500	16,500
Reliability	④	④	④	④	④	⑤	⑤	⑤
Air conditioning	❶	❷	❷	❷	③	④	④	⑤
Automatic trans.	③	③	③	④	④	④	⑤	⑤
Body integrity	③	④	④	④	④	④	④	④
Braking system	❶	❷	❷	❷	③	③	④	⑤
Electrical system	❶	④	④	④	④	④	④	④
Engines	④	④	④	④	④	④	④	⑤
Exhaust/Converter	④	④	④	④	③	③	③	⑤
Fuel system	❶	❷	❷	③	③	③	③	④
Ignition system	❶	❷	③	③	③	③	③	④
Rust/Paint	③	④	④	④	④	④	④	④
Steering	③	③	③	③	③	③	③	③
Suspension	❶	❷	❷	③	③	③	④	⑤
Dealer Service	④	④	④	④	④	④	④	⑤
Maintenance	③	③	③	③	③	③	④	④
Parts Availability	⑤	⑤	⑤	⑤	⑤	⑤	⑤	⑤
Repair Costs	④	④	④	④	④	④	④	⑤
Crash Safety	—	—	—	—	—	—	—	❷
Safety Features								
ABS	—	—	—	O	O	O	O	O
Airbag	—	—	—	D	D	D	D	D/P
Traction control	—	—	—	—	—	—	—	O

Cougar, Thunderbird

Rating: Recommended (1993-94); Average buy (1989-92); Not Recommended (1985-88).

Price analysis: Excellent availability and reasonable prices when compared to the used prices of other cars in the same category. The 1991 models combine the highest depreciation, lowest base price and least wear and tear. Expect to pay about $300 annually for maintenance and repairs during the warranty period and $700 annually thereafter. Parts are cheap and plentiful. Other cars worth considering: Chrysler Caravelle Salon, New Yorker/Fifth Avenue (rwd) • Ford LTD Crown Victoria, Mercury Marquis or Grand Marquis.

Technical Data

ENGINES	Litres/CID	HP	MPG	Model Years
OHC I-4 FI	2.3/140	45-155	21-25	1985-86
OHC I-4 FI	2.3/140	190	18-24	1987-88
OHV V6 FI	3.8/232	120-140	16-21	1985-88
OHV V8 FI	5.0/302	140-150	15-18	1985-88
OHV V6 FI	3.8/232	140	17-22	1989-95
OHV V6 FI	3.8/232	210-230	15-21	1989-95
OHC V8 FI	4.6/281	205	17-22	1994-95
OHV V8 FI	5.0/302	200	17-22	1991-93

Strengths and weaknesses: These are no-surprise, average-performing two-door luxury cars that have changed little over the years. Nevertheless, they offer more performance and greater reliability than GM rear-drives. Handling and ride are far from perfect, with considerable body lean and rear-end instability when taking curves at moderate speed.

The reliability of non-turbocharged 1989-94 models has been average to better than average. Stay away from the turbocharged 4-cylinder engine. True, it offers lots of power, but excessive noise and expensive repairs are the price you pay. Front suspension components wear out quickly as do power steering rack seals. A faulty carburetor design, especially on 6-cylinder engines, causes poor driveability, high gas consumption and stalling. Owners of recent models have complained of EEC IV ignition module defects, electrical system bugs, parking brake cables that seize and steering pump hoses that burst repeatedly (one Winnipeg owner of a '94 Cougar wrote that he replaced the hose twice in the same year), transmission shudder in Overdrive during cold weather, numerous squeaks and rattles, faulty heater fans and failure-prone power window regulators.

Confidential dealer service bulletins show the '93s may have poorly performing AC systems caused by a slipping clutch at high ambient temperatures, AC cooling may be insufficient at idle, the AC compressor may moan from idle to 1500 rpm, power-steering units may be noisy and power door locks may not work. Models equipped with 3.8L engines may also have lots of underhood squeaks and chirps coming from the power-steering pump.

Other bulletins show the 1994s could have faulty 3.8L engine rocker arm assemblies that may cause squeaking, chirping and knocking. Other problems include a rough idle, hesitation, excessive fuel consumption and poor heater output that are likely caused by a thermostat sticking in an open position or opening before it should. Transmission shudders under light to moderate acceleration; there may be extraneous noise in radio speakers caused by a malfunctioning fuel pump, electric rear window defrosters may fail prematurely, and the floor ducts tend to leak water. Moon roofs are also plagued by excessive wind noise and buffeting.

Safety summary/recalls: Crash tests of an 1989 Thunderbird concluded that both the driver and passenger were likely to sustain severe or fatal injuries. A '91 version was judged to give excellent crash protection to both the driver and passenger. A retested '94 produced serious injuries to the driver's left leg. There are some complaints of defective hood latches on 1989-90 models that allow hoods to fly up suddenly when the cars are in operation. Transport Canada is investigating reports of a sticking throttle linkage on 1985-92 models. The U.S. government is looking into 13 reports of seatbelt buckle failure and feul-line ruptures. Standard ABS first appeared on the 1989 Super Coupe. *Recalls:* **1989**-Rear suspension wheel knuckles.

Secret Warranties/Service Tips/DSBs

1980-88-Inoperative power door locks require an upgraded retainer clip (#E8AZ-5421952-A).
1982-91-A refrigerant or chemical smell coming from the AC is likely caused by the clutch cycling pressure switch drifting downward, causing the evaporator core temperature to drop too low.
1983-90-Buzzing or humming coming from the fuel pump when the engine is shut off, a low battery, and hard or no-starts signal the need to install an upgraded fuel-pump relay (#F19Z-9345-A).
1984-87-Stalling and no-starts on vehicles equipped with EEC IV and TFI modules may be caused by water entering the upper righthand mounting hole of the TFI housing.
• A vehicle that bucks or jerks during deceleration probably needs a new MAP sensor (#E5SZ-9F479-A).
1984-88-Poor radio reception, including whining and buzzing, may be caused by electrical noise emanating from a faulty fuel pump.

1985-91-Ford will replace free of charge faulty door latches that function improperly and cannot be adjusted.

1985-92-A buzz or rattle from the exhaust system may be caused by a loose heat shield catalyst.

1987-A rough idle, too rich mixture or stalling may signal that the MAP sensor wires are grounding out.

• A rough idle on vehicles equipped with electronic fuel injection may be caused by loose injector electrical terminals.

• Hesitation on acceleration, erratic idle and no-starts on vehicles equipped with a 3.8L engine may require a new throttle position sensor (TPS) with a date code after 6L17A.

1987-88-Hard starting/stalling caused by defective TFI modules that link a vehicle's distributor to its microprocessor and signal the plugs. Modules will be replaced for free, without prior ownership limitations, up to 5 years/80,000 km.

• Excessive oil consumption is likely caused by leaking gaskets, poor sealing of the lower intake manifold, defective intake and exhaust valve stem seals or worn piston rings. Install new guide mounted valve stem seals for a more positive fit and new piston rings with improved oil control.

• Erratic automatic shifting may require a new 3-4 shift solenoid and sleeve/screen assembly.

1988-Delayed Reverse engagement may require a new service separator plate.

1988-92-Cold hesitation when accelerating, rough idle, long crank times and stalling may require cleaning out excessive intake valve deposits.

1989-A fuel gauge that sticks in the full position may need a new fuel pump float assembly.

• Door handles that pinch fingers require new caps and latch remote control assemblies.

• A loose instrument panel requires stronger, upgraded panel clips.

1989-90-Harsh, rough 3-4 and 4-3 shifts may be caused by sticking control valves.

• Excessive suspension vibration and steering wheel shake when braking indicate uneven front brake rotor wear.

• Braking pulsation or shudder can be reduced by installing service kit #F1SZ-2001-A.

1989-91-Poor radio reception can be improved by changing the antenna cable.

1989-94-Water dripping from the floor ducts when the AC is working requires a relocated evaporator core.

1990-93-Noise heard from the power-steering pump may be caused by air in the system.

1991-94-A rear-end clunk when turning may be caused by insufficient installation torque on the rear axle wheel hub retainer nut.

1992-94-A moan or loud noise coming from the engine compartment of cars equipped with the 4.6L engine can be corrected by installing a new air idle bypass tube and resonator assembly.

1992-95-A corroded solenoid may be the cause of starter failures. Replace the corroded connector with a service wiring and connector assembly.

• An exhaust moan or vibration can be eliminated by installing an exhaust system damper and rear frame support damper.

1993-94-A squeak or chirp coming from the blower motor can be stopped by installing an upgraded blower motor with improved brush-to-commutator friction.

1994-Automatic transmissions with delayed or no forward engagement, or a higher engine rpm than expected when coming to a stop, are covered in DSB 94-26-9.

• Erratic heater/air conditioning operation may be caused by a shorted wire on the blend door actuator jumper harness.

• Ford will replace the cluster mask, lens and the instrument panel finish panel to reduce glare from the instrument panel cluster.

• A no-crank condition in cold weather may be due to water freezing in the starter solenoid. Replace with an upgraded service starter motor assembly.

• Hesitation or stumble with vehicles equipped with a 3.8L engine may be fixed by installing an upgraded PCM (powertrain control module) that allows for poor fuel quality.

1994-95-A thumping or clacking heard from the front brakes signals the need to machine the front disc brake rotors. Ford will pay for this repair under its base warranty.

All models/years-Ford's "goodwill" warranty extensions cover fuel pumps and computer modules that govern engine, fuel injection and transmission functions. If Ford balks at refunding your money for a faulty computer module, say you wish to have the 5 year/80,000 km emissions warranty applied either by the company or by the courts. There's nothing like a small claims court action to focus an automaker's attention.

Same advice applies if you notice a rotten egg odor coming from the exhaust. It's likely the result of a malfunctioning catalytic converter—not last night's sumptuous helpings of *fèves au lard.*

Faulty steering assemblies are often fixed free of charge up to 5 years/80,000 km. Ford will pay 100% toward the correction of paint defects during the first 5 years/80,000 km and 50% up to the seventh year of ownership in keeping with the policy it adopted to cover pickups. Water leaks into the vehicle interior will be corrected without charge up to the fifth year of ownership. All of these programs include second owners.

Vehicle Profile

	1987	1988	1989	1990	1991	1992	1993	1994
Cost Price ($)								
Cougar	15,899	16,856	19,165	20,052	18,295	19,395	19,650	21,395
T-bird	14,882	15,913	17,780	18,670	17,495	18,795	19,695	21,895
Used Values ($)								
Cougar ↑	3500	5100	6400	7900	9200	11,100	14,000	16,300
Cougar ↓	2700	3600	4900	6300	7600	9400	12,300	14,300
T-bird ↑	3500	4700	6100	7400	8700	10,500	13,500	15,000
T-bird ↓	2800	3200	4700	5900	7200	9000	11,700	14,000
Reliability	③	③	③	③	③	③	④	④
Air conditioning	②	②	②	②	②	②	③	③
Body integrity	②	②	②	②	②	②	③	③
Braking system	②	②	②	②	②	②	③	③
Electrical system	②	②	②	②	②	②	③	③
Engines	④	④	④	④	⑤	⑤	⑤	⑤
Exhaust/Converter	②	②	③	③	③	④	⑤	⑤
Fuel system	②	③	③	③	③	③	④	④
Ignition system	②	③	③	③	④	④	⑤	⑤
Manual transmission	—	—	—	—	—	—	—	—
- automatic	④	④	③	③	③	③	⑤	⑤
Rust/Paint	②	②	②	②	②	②	③	③
Steering	②	②	②	②	③	③	③	③
Suspension	②	②	②	③	③	④	④	④
Dealer Service	④	④	④	④	④	④	⑤	⑤
Maintenance	④	④	④	④	④	④	④	④
Parts Availability	⑤	⑤	⑤	⑤	⑤	⑤	⑤	⑤
Repair Costs	③	③	③	③	③	③	③	③
Crash Safety	—	—	❶	❶	⑤	⑤	⑤	❷
Safety Features								
ABS	—	—	—	—	—	—	—	O
Airbag	—	—	—	—	—	—	—	D/P
Traction control	—	—	—	—	—	—	—	O

GENERAL MOTORS

Bonneville, Cutlass Supreme, Delta 88, Grand LeMans, Grand Prix, LeSabre, Lumina, Monte Carlo, Regal

Rating: Front-drives are Not Recommended (1988-94); rear-drives are Average buys (1984-87).

Price analysis: Excellent availability and reasonable prices when compared to the used prices of other rear-drive models in the same category. The 1991 models combine the highest depreciation, lowest base price and least wear and tear. The front-drives are especially reasonably priced after 1991. Expect to pay about $500 annually for maintenance and repairs during the warranty period and $900 annually thereafter—all the more reason to buy a front-drive with the original warranty. The LeSabre's accident repair costs are much lower than average. Other cars worth considering: Chrysler Caravelle Salon, New Yorker/Fifth Avenue (rwd) • Ford LTD Crown Victoria, Mercury Marquis or Grand Marquis.

Technical Data

ENGINES	Litres/CID	HP	MPG	Model Years
OHC I-4 FI	2.2/133	110	21-24	1993
OHC I-4 FI	2.5/151	110	20-23	1990-92
OHV V6 2 bbl.	3.8/231	110	18-21	1985-87
OHV V6 FI	3.0/181	125	18-22	1986
OHV V6 FI	3.8/231	150-165	16-21	1986-91
OHV V6 FI	3.8/231	170	17-22	1992-95
OHV V6 FI	4.3/262	140	17-22	1987
OHV V8 4 bbl.	5.0/305	150-165	16-18	1985-87
DOHC I-4 FI	2.3/138	160	21-24	1990-91
OHV V6 FI	2.8/173	130	18-23	1988-89
OHV V6 FI	3.1/191	140-160	17-22	1989-95
OHV V6T FI	3.1/191	205	15-19	1989-90
DOHC V6 FI	3.4/207	200-210	16-21	1991-95

Strengths and weaknesses: *Rear-drives*: The rear-drives are competent and comfortable cars, but they definitely point to a time when handling was not a priority and fuel economy was unimportant. Their overall reliability isn't impressive, but at least repairs are easy, defects are obvious, and any independent garage can service them. Models equipped with diesel engines or with the turbocharged gas V6 should be approached with extreme caution. These cars have a higher incidence of repairs than average, but parts are inexpensive and all mechanical work is very easy to perform.

Original-equipment shock absorbers and springs are not durable and electrical malfunctions increase proportionally with extra equipment. The AC module and condenser and wheel bearings (incredibly expensive) also have short lifespans. The 4-speed automatic transmission available in later models is not reliable. Surface rust caused by poor paint quality and application is common. The rear edge of trunk lids, roof areas above doors, and the windshield and windshield posts rust through easily.

Front-drives: The front-drives are a different, less reliable and more expensive to repair breed of car, with a considerable number of mechanical and electrical deficiencies directly related to their front-wheel-drive configuration. Nevertheless, acceleration is adequate, fuel economy is good, and they are better handling than their rear-drive cousins—except in emergencies when their non-ABS brakes lock up and directional stability is the first to go. The front-drive's many design and manufacturing weaknesses make for unimpressive high-speed performance, mediocre interior comfort, a poor reliability record and expensive maintenance costs. That's why most fleets and police agencies use rear-drives. They've seen the rear-drive advantages in safety and operating costs.

These aren't driver-friendly cars. Many models have a dash that is replete with confusing push-buttons and gauges. The digital display panel which shows speed, oil pressure, temperature and other information may freeze and not light up when the temperature reaches -18°C. Drivers must wait at least ten minutes for their car to warm up sufficiently before this vital information is displayed. The keyless entry system often fails, the radio's memory is frequently forgetful, and the fuel light comes on when the tank is below the 1/2 fuel level mark. The electronic climate control frequently malfunctions and owners report that warm air doesn't reach the driver-side heating vents. Servicing, especially for the electronic engine controls, is complicated and expensive.

Other major problem areas are the engine, automatic transmission, leaking and malfunctioning AC systems due mainly to defective AC modules, faulty electronic modules, rack and pinion steering failure, bursting steering hoses on 1991 models, weak shocks, excessive front brake pad wear and seizure of the rear brake calipers rear brake/wheel lockup, myriad electrical failures requiring replacement of the computer module (a $500 to $750 repair if the 5 year/80,000 km emissions warranty has expired), leaking oil pan and suspension struts.

Owners report that 3.8L engines won't continue running after a cold start, the exhaust system booms, 3T40 automatic transmissions may have faulty Reverse gears and the instrument panel may pop or creak.

Confidential dealer service bulletins covering the show the following generic problems: AC hisses from the instrument panel and it becomes too warm on extended idle, poor heat distribution, the 3.8L engine stalls after a cold start, door speakers buzz and the converter seal leaks on 4T60E automatic transmissions.

The Lumina's engine is buzzy and anemic, giving out only 140 hp with the V6; the instruments and steering column shake when the car is travelling over uneven road surfaces; lots of road and wind noise comes through the side windows due to an inadequately sound-proofed chassis. Seating isn't very comfortable due to lack of support caused by low-density foam, knees-in-your-face low seating, and the ramrod-straight rear backrest. The ride is acceptable with a light load, but when fully loaded the car's back end sags and the ride deteriorates.

Service bulletins covering the 1993 and 1994 LeSabre provide remedies for stalling and hard starts, whistling when the AC is in recirculate mode, rattling when the car passes over bumps, and a wavy rear fascia lower edge.

GM dealer service bulletins covering the '94 Olds 88 and Bonneville confirm the following problems: AC hisses from the instrument panel and it becomes too warm on extended idle, poor heat distribution, the 3.8L engine won't continue running after a cold start, door speakers buzz, converter seal leaks on 4T60E automatic transmissions, and 3T40 automatic transmissions have faulty Reverse gears.

Body assembly is notoriously poor and is no doubt one of the main reasons why GM has lost so much market share over the past decade. Premature paint peeling and rusting, water and dust leak into the trunk and squeaks, rattles, wind and road noise are all too common. Accessories are also problem-plagued with defective radios, power antenna, door locks, cruise control, and alarm systems leading the pack.

Safety summary/recalls: According to the U.S. Highway Loss Data Institute, 1989-91 Regals had collision losses 6 percent below average, 1989-91 Grand Prix models produced collision losses 9 percent lower than average, the Cutlass Supreme's losses were 13 percent below average, and the Lumina registered claims losses that were a surprising 23 percent below the norm.

Crash tests of 1984-87 rear-drives were disappointing: both the driver and passenger would sustain serious or fatal injuries. Tests of the 1988 and 1989 front-drive Regals showed an improvement; the cars offered excellent crash protection to the driver and front seat passenger. A '92 two-door Regal also provided excellent crash protection. A 1992 and '93 dual airbag-equipped four-door Bonneville passed the same test with flying colors; both the driver and front passenger would have escaped serious injury.

Crash tests found that a 1988 four-door Olds 88 driver would have sustained moderate injuries, while the front seat passenger would have been only slightly injured. In a subsequent test, a 1990 two-door Olds 88 and Buick LeSabre posted excellent scores in protecting both the driver and passenger from injury.

NHTSA investigators are looking into reports of damaged fuel lines caused by their sagging beneath the vehicle on 1991-92 Olds 88 models, and some 1992 88s may have a misaligned PRNDL indicator that allows shifting from Park to Reverse with the engine running. Reports of the driver's seat breaking from its moorings. ABS on the 1990 Cutlass Supreme is tough to modulate; it doesn't always engage quickly enough or it's sometimes too sensitive. Wheels that may crack and fracture, leading to wheel failure and loss of control, is another potential safety defect being investigated on 1990-91 Luminas. The motorized seatbelt may stick in its track on the 1990 LeMans. Safety is compromised and visibility hindered by the driver-side window frame, small side-view mirrors and obtrusive side rear roof pillars. Dual airbags became standard with the 1992 Bonneville. *Recalls*: **1986-**

Faulty headlight switch may cause erratic operation of lights. **1987**-A recall will fix 200-4R transmissions that engage the wrong gear or start in gear. **1988**-Three separate recalls will correct faulty tie-rod nuts or lower control arms that could cause steering loss, a faulty transmission cable that indicates the wrong gear, and a leaking left front brake hose. Parking brake cable may separate from the left rear brake caliper. **1989-90**-Faulty brake lights. **1988-91**-Faulty front shoulder belt guide loop. **1992**-Four-speed automatic transmissions that slip in Reverse, lock in Reverse when indicator shows "Neutral," or generally perform poorly are eligible for free recall repairs. **1993**-The seatback may suddenly recline. **1991 Regal**-The fuel-feed hose on vehicles with 3.8L V6 engines may leak fuel. Dealers will install a new fuel-feed hose. **1990 models with the 2.3L Quad 4 engine**-Faulty ignition coils that may cause engine misfiring will be replaced under an emissions recall campaign. **1991 Olds 88 and 1992 LeSabre and Bonneville**-Parking brakes may not hold well enough, allowing the car to roll when the brake is on. **1994-95 Olds 98**-Headlight switch may not work.

Secret Warranties/Service Tips/DSBs

Rear-Drives
1986-87-A malfunctioning voltage regulator is a common problem leading to poor battery performance. Install an upgraded voltage regulator (#1116423) to correct the problem.
1987-88-An engine surge at 45 to 55 mph may be due to a defective PROM. Install upgraded PROM (#16139524).
Front-Drives
1980-89-First gear malfunctions with the THM 125C transmission may require new forward clutch piston seals (#8631986).
1984-89-No 3rd gear with the automatic 440-T4 transmission means a new thrust bearing assembly should be installed.
1985-89-Wind noise around the doors can be cured by using several kits mentioned in DSB 89-286-10.
1986-87-Serious stalling problems can usually be traced to a defective PROM module or a malfunctioning TCC solenoid. Ask your dealer to consult GM DSB 87-T57B when checking the solenoid and DSB 87-T-40A for data on tracking PROM malfunctions.
• A rotten egg sulphur smell may be caused by a defective catalytic converter.
1986-88-Models with anti-lock brakes may have defective hoses. A GM service bulletin advises dealers to replace the flexible hoses with rigid pipes.
• The NHTSA is investigating 892 complaints that the brakes either fail or the pedal goes to the floor when pressed.
• 3.8L V6 engines have a history of low oil pressure caused by a failure-prone oil pump. A temporary remedy is to avoid low viscosity oils and

use 10W-40 in the winter and 20W-50 for summer driving.

• Slow or inadequate heating may require the installation of a new heater outlet duct (#52452131).

1986-89-Excessive rear suspension noise can be cut by replacing the variable-rate rear coil spring.

1986-90-A chirp or squeal from the engine compartment may mean the AC and crankshaft pulleys are misaligned.

1987-Frequent engine stalling may require that a different PROM be put in the ECM (DSB 87-6-17A).

1987-88-If there is insufficient heat flow on the driver's side, the likely cause is a kinked heat distribution floor duct. Insufficient heat flow throughout the car's interior may be caused by an improperly positioned heater air (max heat) door.

1987-89-If the engine constantly stalls and won't restart, consider replacing the fuel pump and installing a fuel-sender kit.

1988-If heat output is low, the lack of a gasket under the thermostat may be the cause. Without this gasket, the engine cannot warm up properly and the heater air is only lukewarm. Install the missing gasket (DSB 88-6-30).

• Poor engine performance diagnostic shortcuts are detailed in DSB No. 88-T-47B.

1988-89-Poor FM reception can be improved by installing an RFI suppressor harness (#25027405).

• If your door hinge breaks, GM will replace it for free up to ten years under a special policy.

• Rattles in the front door require the installation of anti-rattle clips.

• Rear suspension thud noise may be reduced by replacing the strut assemblies.

1988-93-Vehicles equipped with a 3300 or 3800 engine that stalls when decelerating or is hard to start may need a new air-control motor (IAC).

1989-Constant stalling with the 2.8L engine may be fixed by installing a new service MEMCAL.

1989-90-Hard cold starts may require a new MEMCAL.

1990-Sunroof failures may be due to static electricity blowing the sunroof's electric module. Install a plastic button switch.

1990-92-Vehicles equipped with a 3.1L or 3.4L engine that are hard to start when cold or stall chronically may need new engine calibrations or an upgraded MEMCAL module.

1990-94-An engine ticking at idle can be traced to rattling piston pins that must be replaced with upgraded parts.

1991-94-Loss of Drive or erratic shifts may be caused by an intermittent short to ground on the A or B shift solenoid or an electrical short-circuit in the transaxle.

• Harsh automatic transmission upshifts can be corrected by installing an upgraded accumulator valve in the control valve body.

• A scraping noise or high effort when opening the front doors can be fixed by bending the door's lower check ear.

1992-94-A front-end engine knock troubleshooting chart is found in DSB 306001.

Steps	Description	Labor Operation	Labor Time
1/2	Knock Noise Diagnosis	J0005	0.2 Hour
3	Replace Accessory Drive Belt	J0667	Use published time
4	Knock Noise Diagnosis	J0005	0.5 Hour
4	Replace Power Steering Pump	E9050	Use published time
5	Check Clearances w/Gaging Plastic and Replace Number One Main Bearing	J1150	Use published time

• Water leaking from the doors into the passenger compartment has a number of causes and remedies says DSB 431003.

1993-94-Knocking from the accessory drive belt tensioner requires an upgraded replacement.

• Owners who complain of automatic transmission low-speed miss, hesitation, chuggle or skip may find relief with an improved MEMCAL module that GM developed to remedy the problem.

1991-92 LeSabre-Premature front brake caliper bolt bore corrosion can be fixed by changing the rubber bushings and honing out the bores.

1991-94-A scraping noise or high effort when opening the front doors can be fixed by bending the door's lower check ear.

• Water leaking from the doors into the passenger compartment has a number of causes and remedies (DSB 431003).

1992-A metallic rattle coming from the rear of the vehicle when the deck lid is closed can be cured by installing a new heat shield bumper.

1992-94-Loss of Drive or erratic shifts may be caused by an intermittent short to ground on the A or B shift solenoid or an electrical short-circuit in the transaxle.

1990 Lumina-Instrument panel pad separation will be fixed free of charge by GM under a Special Policy Adjustment detailed in a May 17, 1991 dealer letter.

• Vehicles equipped with a 3.1L engine may exhibit piston scuffing which produces cold engine knock at low ambient temperatures. GM recommends a partial engine replacement rather than changing the pistons.

1990-91-Late transaxle upshifts may be fixed by resetting the TV cable.

1991-94-A front-end clunking noise when driving over rough roads may require the repositioning of the diagonal radiator support braces.

1994-Excessive brake pedal effort when cold can be fixed by installing upgraded brake pads.

1994-95-A steering wheel clicking or scrubbing noise when turning can be fixed by installing an upgraded wire protector shield.

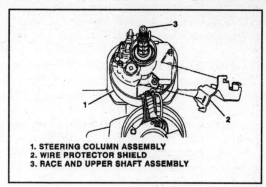

1. STEERING COLUMN ASSEMBLY
2. WIRE PROTECTOR SHIELD
3. RACE AND UPPER SHAFT ASSEMBLY

1990-91 Lumina and Regal with 3.1L V6 engine-If the starter makes a grinding noise or won't engage the engine, the fault may be a weak starter spring. Replace the starter motor drive assembly with #10473700.
• A defective sending unit will cause a display of high oil pressure or erratic readings. Replace the old pressure sender with #25605389.
• High brake pedal effort can be corrected by replacing the original pads with modified parts.
1990-92-Vehicles equipped with the 3T40 automatic transmission may experience slippage in manual Low or Reverse. Install service package #8628222 which includes a Low/Reverse clutch release spring (#8664961) and clutch retainer and nap ring (#656/657).
1991 Lumina-Poor starting may be caused by the spring in early starter drives compressing too easily. Install an upgraded starter motor drive assembly (#10473700).
• A clunk or snapping noise coming from the front door glass may be caused by a defective stop bumper.
• A leaking or noisy AC compressor requires changing the placement of the reservoir and the reservoir hose clip.
• An annoying exhaust moan or boom requires the installation of a new damper (#10199232).
1991-92 Lumina-A delayed shift between Drive and Reverse is likely caused by a rolled or cut input clutch piston outer seal.
1991-94-Loss of Drive or erratic shifts may be caused by an intermittent short to ground on the A or B shift solenoid or an electrical short-circuit in the transaxle.
1992-93-No Reverse or slipping in Reverse can be corrected by installing an upgraded Lo/Rev clutch return spring and spiral retaining ring.
1991-94 Regal-Loss of Drive or erratic shifts may be caused by an intermittent short to ground on the A or B shift solenoid or an electrical short-circuit in the transaxle.
1992-Front door wind noise and water leaks can be fixed by replacing the run channel retainer and adding sealer between the retainer and the door frame.

2.3L Quad 4 engine
1990 models-Faulty ignition coils that cause engine misfiring will be replaced under an emissions recall campaign.

1990-91-Head gasket leaks are a problem covered by a secret warranty extension. The first sign of trouble is a loss of power caused by combustion gases mixing with coolant. This is followed by a cloud of steam and coolant loss through the exhaust system. If these warnings are ignored, cylinder-bore scoring, a warped cylinder head and piston seizure will likely result as the engine continues to overheat. Up to 6 years/60,000 miles, GM will replace the head gasket with an improved version and carry out a new multi-step head-bolt tightening procedure at no cost to the owner. The deductible will be also refunded. Others who bought their cars used or had repairs done at an independent garage are eligible for this free repair and a refund if the engine has already been fixed.

All models/years-A rotten egg odor coming from the exhaust is probably caused by a malfunctioning catalytic converter covered by the 5 year/80,000 km emissions warranty. General Motors will repair defective steering assemblies free of charge up to 5 years/80,000 km and pay half the cost up to 100,000 km.

GM has had a serious rust/paint peeling problem with all its domestic-made vehicles. Original owners will get 100% compensation for paint peeling/surface rusting up to six years says this October 16, 1992 internal letter (see page 288) sent to all GM divisions.

Vehicle Profile

	1987	1988	1989	1990	1991	1992	1993	1994
Cost Price ($)								
Bonneville	15,995	18,377	19,976	21,300	20,098	22,898	23,498	25,298
Delta 88	17,350	19,525	21,198	22,599	21,298	22,250	23,098	25,598
Grand Prix	13,765	15,938	18,450	20,299	18,098	17,598	18,498	22,098
LeSabre	17,042	19,357	21,253	22,599	21,298	23,198	23,997	25,498
Lumina	—	—	—	17,399	16,098	15,998	17,798	19,898
Monte Carlo	13,520	16,136	—	—	—	—	—	—
Regal	14,290	16,398	19,498	20,899	18,998	19,398	20,006	21,898
Supreme	14,241	16,879	18,595	20,399	18,798	18,398	18,858	21,398
Used Values ($)								
Bonneville ↑	3800	5000	5900	7400	9700	13,900	16,800	19,900
Bonneville ↓	2500	3300	4200	5500	7900	11,900	14,700	17,800
Delta 88 ↑	4100	5100	6300	8700	10,200	13,000	15,200	18,500
Delta 88 ↓	2900	3300	4400	6800	8300	11,000	13,100	16,400
Grand Prix ↑	4300	5700	6500	7300	9700	11,100	12,400	16,300
Grand Prix ↓	3600	4200	4800	5600	8000	9200	10,500	14,200
LeSabre ↑	4100	5100	6100	8700	10,600	13,500	16,100	19,200
LeSabre ↓	3000	3200	4300	6800	8700	11,400	14,100	17,100
Lumina ↑	—	—	—	5300	6000	7900	9800	12,400
Lumina ↓	—	—	—	3900	4600	6300	8200	10,700

Monte Carlo ↑	4000	5300	—	—	—	—	—	—
Monte Carlo ↓	2700	3800	—	—	—	—	—	—
Regal ↑	4400	5600	6400	8000	9700	11,500	13,500	18,200
Regal ↓	3200	4000	4700	6300	8000	9600	11,600	16,200
Supreme ↑	4400	5300	6300	8300	9900	11,700	13,000	16,100
Supreme ↓	3200	4200	4600	6600	8300	9800	11,200	14,100
Reliability	③	②	②	②	②	②	②	③
Air conditioning	②	②	②	②	②	②	②	②
Automatic trans.	①	①	①	①	①	①	②	②
Body integrity	①	①	①	①	①	①	②	②
Braking system	①	①	①	①	①	①	②	②
Electrical system	①	①	①	①	①	①	①	①
Engines	②	②	②	②	②	②	③	③
Exhaust/Converter	②	②	②	②	②	③	④	④
Fuel system	②	②	②	②	②	②	③	④
Ignition system	②	②	②	③	③	③	③	④
Rust/Paint	①	①	①	①	①	①	②	③
Steering	②	②	②	②	②	②	③	③
Suspension	②	②	②	②	②	②	②	③
Dealer Service	③	③	③	③	③	③	③	③
Maintenance	③	③	③	③	③	③	③	③
Parts Availability	④	④	④	④	④	④	④	④
Repair Costs	②	②	②	②	②	②	③	③
Crash Safety								
Bonneville 4-door	—	—	⑤	⑤	⑤	⑤	❶	❶
Delta 88 2-door	—	—	—	—	⑤	⑤	⑤	⑤
Delta 88 4-door	—	—	②	②	②	②	❶	❶
Grand Prix 2-door	②	②	②	②	②	②	②	❶
Grand Prix 4-door	—	—	②	—	❶	❶	❶	❶
LeSabre 2-door	—	—	—	—	②	②	②	②
Lumina 4-door	—	—	—	—	⑤	⑤	②	②
Monte Carlo	②	②	②	②	—	—	—	—
Regal 2-door	②	②	⑤	⑤	⑤	⑤	⑤	⑤
Regal 4-door	②	②	⑤	⑤	—	—	⑤	❶
Supreme 2-door	②	②	②	②	②	②	②	②
Supreme 4-door	—	—	②	②	❶	❶	❶	❶
Safety Features								
ABS	—	—	O	O	O	S	S	S
Airbag	—	—	—	—	—	D/P	D/P	D/P
Traction control	—	—	—	—	—	—	—	O

288

PONTIAC DIVISION
General Motors Corporation
One Pontiac Plaza
Pontiac, Michigan 48340-2952

October 16, 1992

TO: All Pontiac Dealers

SUBJECT: Partners in Satisfaction (PICS)
Dealer Authorization

Pontiac continually reviews the Warranty Management System to ensure that Warranty Administration achieves its purposes, including high levels of customer satisfaction with after sale treatment.

Following a recent review, Pontiac has decided to provide dealers authorization for cases involving <u>paint repairs</u> for vehicles up to six (6) years from the date of delivery, without regard for mileage. This is a change from the current PICS dealer self-authorization which allows paint repair goodwill adjustments to be made up to 6 years/60,000 miles. Dealers who have a deductible override capabilities may also waive deductibles as they see appropriate on this type of repair.

Paint repairs are only to be authorized beyond the warranty period by the Dealership <u>Service Manager</u> on a case-by-case basis as with any other goodwill policy adjustment.

Assistance should only be considered for cases involving evidence of a defect in materials or workmanship by the manufacturer. Assistance should not be considered for conditions related to wear and tear and/or lack of maintenance (such as fading, stone chips, scratches, environmental damage, etc.).

Please contact your Zone representative if you have specific questions.

Perry S. White

Perry S. White
Director of Service/
Customer Satisfaction

98 Regency (FWD), Electra, Park Avenue

Rating: Average Buy (1994); Below Average buy (1991-93); Not Recommended (1985-90).

Price analysis: Excellent availability but fairly expensive. Most of the 1991 models combine the highest depreciation, lowest base price and least wear and tear. Expect to pay about $500 annually for maintenance and repairs during the warranty period and $1000 annually thereafter— all the more reason to buy a car with the original warranty. Other cars worth considering: Chrysler Caravelle Salon, New Yorker/Fifth Avenue (rwd) • Ford LTD Crown Victoria, Mercury Marquis or Grand Marquis.

Technical Data

ENGINES	Litres/CID	HP	MPG	Model Years
98 Regency (fwd), Electra, Park Avenue				
OHV V6 2 bbl.	3.0/181	110	15-20	1985
OHV V6 FI	3.8/231	125-150	17-20	1985-87
OHV V6 FI	3.8/231	165	17-20	1988-90
OHV V6D FI	4.3/262	85	20-23	1985
98, Toronado				
OHV V6 FI	3.8/231	140-170	18-22	1986-94
OHV V6 FI	3.8/231	205	18-21	1995
OHV V6 FI*	3.8/231	205-225	17-21	1992-95

*supercharged

Strengths and weaknesses: These attractive, luxurious cars are billed as six-seaters, but only four passengers can ride in comfort. Although the 1989-93 models were improved, they have compiled the worst repair history among large cars. Main problem areas are the engine, automatic transmission, fuel system, brakes, the electrical system (including defective PROM and MEMCAL modules), starters and alternators, and badly assembled, poor-quality body hardware. The 3.0L V6 engine is inadequate for cars this heavy and the 3.8L has been a big quality disappointment. Stay away from the failure-prone diesel engine. Underhood servicing is complicated. Automatic transmission and engine computer malfunctions are common. The fuel-injection system is temperamental. Window mechanisms are poorly designed. The power-steering assembly is failure prone. Frequent electrical failures. Front brake pads and rotors require frequent replacement. Shock absorbers leak or go soft very quickly. Extensive surface corrosion has been a problem because of poor and often incomplete paint application at the factory. Overall, these cars are expensive to buy and operate.

GM dealer service bulletins show the 1993 models have 3.8L engines that frequently stall when decelerating or lead to extended cranking, and they often stall after a cold start. Other problems include excessive front-end vibration when passing over bumps and whistling when the AC is in recirculate mode. The '94s have lots of DSBs for automatic transmission and heater/AC problems.

Safety summary/recalls: NHTSA crash tests of a 1985 four-door Park Avenue concluded that the driver would sustain severe or fatal head and leg injuries. An '88 Park Avenue and Olds 98 Regency were tested; once again the driver was judged to have severe head injuries and the passenger would have sustained serious leg trauma. When the 1990 Olds 98 was tested, only the passenger would have sustained serious leg injuries.

NHTSA investigators are looking into reports of damaged fuel lines damaged by sagging under the vehicle on 1991-92 Olds 98 models. *Recalls*: **1986**-Faulty headlight switches that cause erratic operation of the lights are covered by a recall. Power-steering hose leaks could cause an underhood fire. ABS may suddenly fail due to fluid leaking from system. **1987**-A faulty fusible link could cause an underhood fire. Some throttle cables may not return to idle position. **1991 Park Avenue and Olds 98**-Parking brakes may not hold well enough, allowing the car to roll when the brake is on. A safety recall specifies a free correction of this problem. **1994-95 Olds 98**-Headlight switch may not work.

Secret Warranties/Service Tips/DSBs

1985-87-THM 440-T4 transaxles may experience a delayed upshift. This problem is likely caused by a leaking 3rd clutch seal. A thicker seal (#8646991) will correct the problem.
1985-92-A loss of power when making a righthand turn may be due to a fuel pump and strainer assembly slightly mispositioned on the tank sending unit. Correct by replacing the fuel-pump strainer with part #25121783.
1986-Poor automatic transmission performance can be traced to a defective 3-4 throttle-valve spring (DSB 86-7440-8A).
• An irritating buzz in the radio's AM band when accelerating is likely caused by a defective electronic vacuum regulating valve on the 3.8L engine (DSB 86-9-8).
1986-87-Serious stalling problems with the 3.8L engine and electronic fuel injection likely caused by a defective PROM module or a malfunctioning TCC solenoid. Ask your dealer to refer to DSB 87-T57B when checking the solenoid and DSB 87-T-40A or DSB 86-6E-19A for data on tracking PROM malfunctions.
• If your car won't start, don't change the battery. The culprit may be a defective voltage regulator (a common problem). GM's upgraded voltage regulator (#1116423) is far more reliable (DSB 87-6D-6A).
• A rotten egg odor coming from the exhaust is the result of a

malfunctioning catalytic converter.

1986-88-Models with anti-lock brakes may have defective hoses. GM will replace them with rigid pipes.

• 3.8L V6 engines have a history of low oil pressure caused by a failure-prone oil pump. A temporary remedy is to avoid low-viscosity oils and use 10W-40 in the winter and 20W-50 for summer driving.

• DSB 88-6C-5 says unusually noisy fuel pumps can be silenced by installing a new fuel-sending kit, a fuel pump kit and pulsator (#25093316, 25116296 and 25094266).

1987-Warm air from the heater is blown into the driver's face unless a redesigned heater outlet (#100023900) is installed.

1988-A common cause of poor engine performance (unsteady idle speed, no starts and stalling) is a vacuum leak at the PCV valve (DSB 88-6E-21).

• Radio speakers within both doors can be ruined by water seepage if the screws securing the outside mirrors and moldings are loose (DSB 88-9-8).

1988-93-Vehicles equipped with a 3800 engine that stalls upon deceleration or is hard to start may need a new air-control motor (IAC).

1991-94-Harsh automatic transmission upshifts can be corrected by installing an upgraded accumulator valve in the control valve body.

1991 Park Avenue and Olds 98-Corrosion of the outside door handle screws can be prevented by using upgraded screws.

1991-92-Fuel line fasteners may fail, allowing fuel to spill onto the roadway. Transport authorities are investigating.

1991-94-Loss of Drive or erratic shifts may be caused by an intermittent short to ground on the A or B shift solenoid or an electrical short-circuit in the transaxle.

• A scraping noise or high effort when opening the front doors can be fixed by bending the door's lower check ear.

• Water leaking from the doors into the passenger compartment has a number of causes and remedies (DSB 431003).

1991-92 Olds 98-NHTSA investigators are looking into reports of damaged fuel lines caused by their sagging beneath the vehicle.

1994-Inadequate heating, ventilation, and AC operation is addressed in DSB 431219.

1993-94-Owners who complain of automatic transmission low speed miss, hesitation, chuggle or skip may find relief with an improved MEMCAL module that GM developed to remedy the problem.

All models/years-A rotten egg odor coming from the exhaust is probably caused by a malfunctioning catalytic converter and is covered by GM's 5 year/80,000 km emissions warranty. The THM 44C-T4 automatic transaxles on front-drive models equipped with V6 engines are particularly failure prone due to pinched or kinked vacuum lines that result in low oil pressure.

For the past decade, GM has had a serious rust/paint peeling problem with all its domestic-made vehicles. Original owners will get

100% compensation for paint peeling/surface rusting up to six years (see Bonneville rating). Don't let GM or its dealers deny your right to a free paint job. Use the Bonneville letter, if necessary.

Vehicle Profile

	1987	1988	1989	1990	1991	1992	1993	1994
Cost Price ($)								
Electra	21,349	—	—	—	—	—	—	—
Olds 98 Regency	21,755	24,984	26,498	29,490	27,795	28,798	29,298	34,498
Park Avenue	23,609	26,564	28,298	29,994	29,995	30,898	31,798	33,798
Used Values ($)								
Electra ↑	3900	—	—	—	—	—	—	—
Electra ↓	2900	—	—	—	—	—	—	—
Olds 98 Regency ↑	4900	6200	7800	11,400	14,000	17,500	19,900	24,700
Olds 98 Regency ↓	3800	4000	5700	9300	11,900	15,200	17,800	22,300
Park Avenue ↑	5100	6400	8500	11,400	14,500	17,800	21,200	25,100
Park Avenue ↓	3800	4500	6400	9300	12,400	15,500	18,900	22,700
Reliability	②	②	②	②	②	②	②	③
Air conditioning	②	②	②	②	②	②	③	③
Automatic trans.	②	②	②	②	③	③	③	③
Body integrity	①	①	①	①	①	①	①	①
Braking system	②	②	②	②	③	③	③	③
Electrical system	②	②	②	②	②	②	②	②
Engines	②	②	②	②	③	③	③	③
Fuel system	①	②	②	②	②	②	③	③
Ignition system	②	②	②	②	③	③	③	③
Rust/Paint	①	①	①	①	①	②	③	③
Steering	①	①	①	①	①	②	②	③
Suspension	②	②	②	②	②	③	③	③
Dealer Service	②	②	②	③	③	③	③	③
Maintenance	②	②	②	③	③	③	③	③
Parts Availability	④	④	④	④	④	④	④	④
Repair Costs	②	②	②	②	②	③	③	③
Crash Safety								
Electra Park Avenue	②	①	①	②	②	②	②	②
Olds 98	—	—	—	②	②	②	②	②
Safety Features								
ABS	O	O	O	O	S	S	S	S
Airbag	—	—	—	—	D	D	D	D/P
Traction control	—	—	—	—	—	—	—	O

Caprice, Custom Cruiser, Electra, Estate Wagon, LeSabre, Roadmaster, Safari Wagon

Rating: Below Average buy (1993-94); Not Recommended (1985-90).

Price analysis: Excellent availability and reasonable prices when compared to the used prices of other rear-drive wagons. The 1991 Caprice combines the highest depreciation, lowest base price and least wear and tear. Expect to pay about $400 annually for maintenance and repairs during the warranty period and $700 annually thereafter—all the more reason to buy a car with the original warranty. Other vehicles worth considering: any of the recommended minivans.

Technical Data

ENGINES	Litres/CID	HP	MPG	Model Years
OHV V6 FI	4.3/262	130-140	18-21	1985-88
OHV V8 4 bbl.	5.0/305	150-170	14-17	1985-88
OHV V8 FI	5.0/305	170	15-16	1989-90
OHV V8 4 bbl.	5.0/307	140	14-17	1987-90
OHV V8D FI	5.7/350	105	22-25	1985
OHV V8 FI	4.3/265	200	18-22	1994-95
OHV V8 FI	5.0/305	170	16-20	1991-93
OHV V8 FI	5.7/350	180	16-23	1992-93
OHV V8 FI	5.7/350	260	17-23	1994-95

Strengths and weaknesses: These cars are large, comfortable and easy to maintain. The trunk is spacious. Overall handling is acceptable, but expect a queasy ride from the too-soft suspension. Gas mileage is particularly poor. In spite of the many generic deficiencies inherent in these rear-drives, the LeSabre has scored highest among this group for overall reliability and durability.

On all cars, engine problems include crankshaft and head gasket failures, cracked cylinder heads, injection-pump malfunctions and oil leaks. Engine knocking is a common V8 problem which is hard to correct inexpensively due to the various possible causes that have to be eliminated. Cars equipped with the 5.7L diesel V8 should be approached with caution. All V8s suffer from premature camshaft wear and the 350 cu. in. V8s often fall prey to premature valve guide wear caused by a faulty EGR valve. The 4-speed automatic transmission was troublesome until 1987. Burnt-out clutches and malfunctioning torque converters are quite common.

The 1991-92 models have shown the following deficiencies: prematurely worn suspension components, especially shock absorbers and rear springs; serious electrical problems, poor paint quality and application, and excessive surface rusting (door bottoms, windshield posts and roof panels are especially vulnerable); wagons have a rust problem around cargo area side windows; hubcaps on later models tend to fly off. Parts are available anywhere at reasonable prices.

Confidential dealer service bulletins covering the '93s show the following problems: buzzing at idle coming from the 4L60E automatic transmission along with a misadjusted shift linkage, causing loss of Reverse or lack of power in 2nd gear. Other DSB-addressed problems include noisy power-steering units, intermittent cruise control operation, extreme temperature difference when the AC is put in a bi-level mode, and inoperative AC compressors.

The '94s may exhibit excessive oil consumption, faulty door-mounted radio speakers, poor AC performance, inadequate interior air flow, improperly adjusted automatic transmission shift linkage leading to a burnt-out Low/Reverse clutch and increased rpms with downshifts.

Safety summary/recalls: Tests of a 1989 Caprice concluded that the driver would sustain serious or fatal head injuries. 57 km/h crash tests of an airbag-equipped (driver's side) 1991 four-door Caprice found that the passenger would suffer severe or fatal head injuries. Follow-up tests of a '93 and '94 demonstrated that the driver would have received serious injuries to both legs and the passenger would have sustained severe head trauma. Transport Canada officials are investigating reports that sudden acceleration and speed control problems may be due to sticking throttle control cables on cars with 4.3L engines. The 1991 models equipped with a police package may have a defective ball joint assembly that could compromise steering control if it fails. *Recalls*: **1985**-Leaking fuel feed and return pipe may cause a fire. Cars equipped with a 4.3L engine could have a battery cable short that creates a fire hazard. **1985-88**-Faulty cruise control could lead to sudden acceleration. **1987**-Cars equipped with 200-4R automatic transmission could start up in gear, or engage the wrong gear. **1989**-GM will inspect and replace the AC condenser inlet pipe. **1991**-Seatbelts malfunction due to defective shoulder belt guide loop. **1991-92**-Rear seatbelts that are uncomfortable will be changed for free by GM. Corrosion could prevent the hood from latching properly, make it hard to open or cause it to fly open. **1992**-A rattling front door lock rod can be silenced by installing a corrective kit (#10222731). The 4.3L engine fuel feed and return pipes may leak. **1994**-A leaking oil cooler inlet hose is a fire hazard. Fractured wheel studs may allow wheel to separate from car. **1994-95**-Accelerator pedal may stick.

Secret Warranties/Service Tips/DSBs

1985-88-The 307-cid V8 is the most reliable and durable engine in this lineup. In 1985-86, it was plagued by camshaft/lifter problems due to the small lifter bore to cam lobe offset. The problem was rectified in

1987 when GM adopted roller-lifters. The engine's aluminum intake manifold and gasket can be eaten away by extensive corrosion in each of the four corners where they contact a coolant port; serious coolant leaks result. Flush the radiator yearly and use a good quality antifreeze to extend the life of these components.

1982-91-Hydramatic 4L60/700R4 automatic transmission may have no upshift or appear to be stuck in 1st gear. The probable cause is a worn governor gear. It would be wise to also replace the retaining ring.

1982-93-Vehicles equipped with a Hydramatic 4L60 transmission that buzzes when the car is in Reverse or at idle may need a new oil pressure regulator valve.

1986-87-A rotten egg sulphur smell may be caused by a defective catalytic converter.

1986-92-A loss of power when making a righthand turn may be due to a fuel pump and strainer assembly slightly mispositioned on the tank sending unit.

1987-91-Different types of tailpipe smoke signal the need for different repairs. **1987** cars with V8 engines that emit blue or bluish white smoke may require a valve seal kit (#12511890); **1987-88** models with port fuel injection that emit black smoke after long starter cranks may have fuel leaking into the engine from the injectors; **1987-88** models with throttle body injection and port fuel injection that emit white or bluish smoke and have normal oil consumption likely have poor sealing between the intake manifold joint and the cylinder head.

1988-89-Insufficient AC cooling upon light acceleration can be corrected by installing a new service PROM (16122177).

1988-92-Hydramatic 4L60/700R4 automatic transmission may click or whine in 3rd or 4th gear. There may also be a rattle from the rear of the transmission. Correct by installing five new fiber plates in the Low and Reverse clutch. The new plates have a different groove configuration preventing gear vibration.

1989-Excessive 5.0L engine knocking when cold can be remedied by installing an upgraded PROM (#16148142).

• Stalling or hard starting may be due to a disconnected fuel-pump coupler.

1989-91-If the transmission won't go into Reverse or is slow to shift into Reverse, GM suggests that the Reverse input clutch housing be changed.

1991-Caprices with warped or wavy front door lower reveal moldings will be fixed free by GM.

• Poor windshield defrosting can be corrected by installing a revised defroster grille.

• A poor-running 5.0L or 5.7L engine may require an EGR valve kit and PCV valve in addition to a new PROM.

• Poor starting may be caused by the spring in early starter drives compressing too easily. Install an upgraded starter motor drive assembly (#10473700).

• If the rear brakes click when they are applied, install new countermeasure brake drums (#1244646) on both wheels.

1992-A rattling front door lock rod can be silenced by installing a corrective kit (#10222731).

• Oil leaks from the rear of a 5.0L or 5.7L engine may be caused by insufficient sealing around the camshaft plug. Replace the plug and reseal.

1994-Excessive oil consumption is likely due to delaminated intake manifold gaskets. Install an upgraded intake manifold gasket kit.

• GM campaign 94C15 will adjust at no charge a misadjusted automatic transmission shift linkage that could, if left alone, burn out the Low/Reverse clutch.

Roadmaster

1991-If the starter makes a grinding noise or won't engage the engine, the fault may be a weak starter spring. Replace the starter motor drive assembly with part #10473700.

• Front doors that won't stay open on an incline or are hard to open need an improved hold-open door spring.

1991-92-If the instrument panel glares in the windshield, GM will refinish the instrument panel to correct the problem free of charge.

1992-If water leaks into the trunk from the fixed mast antenna, install an upgraded antenna base (#25610633) and bezel (#25609129).

• Another cause of water leaking into the trunk is missing washers on the opera lamp bezel mounted in the sail panel area.

• If the front seat doesn't have enough upward travel, GM will provide a special kit (#12520796) to raise it.

• A chuggle or shudder at 70 km/h on vehicles equipped with a 5.7L engine may be corrected by installing a new torque converter assembly which has a 280-ft.-lb. damper.

1994-Excessive oil consumption is likely due to delaminated intake manifold gaskets. Install an upgraded intake manifold gasket kit.

• Poor AC performance can be improved by replacing the temperature control cable.

• Delayed automatic transmission shift engagement is a common problem addressed in DSB 47-71-20A.

• Increased RPM when downshifting a Caprice equipped with a 4.3L engine may need a recalibrated transaxle.

• Overall sluggish engine performance may also require a recalibrated engine.

All models/years-A rotten egg odor coming from the exhaust is usually the result of a malfunctioning catalytic converter covered by the 5 year/80,000 km emissions warranty. For over a decade, GM has had a serious rust/paint peeling problem with all its domestic-made vehicles. Under a secret warranty, original owners will get 100% compensation for paint peeling/surface rusting up to six years. This practice is confirmed by GM in a special internal memo sent to its dealers (see Bonneville section). The intake manifold is often corroded and costs over $500 to replace. Go to an independent repair facility where parts are cheaper.

Vehicle Profile

	1987	1988	1989	1990	1991	1992	1993	1994
Cost Price ($)								
Caprice	14,212	15,750	18,487	20,128	19,698	20,298	20,806	22,500
Caprice wagon	14,485	18,717	20,248	21,347	20,398	21,598	22,138	24,985
Cruiser wagon	17,485	21,265	23,348	25,116	25,098	25,350	—	—
Electra wagon	21,830	—	—	—	—	—	—	—
LeSabre wagon	17,768	—	—	—	—	—	—	—
Roadmaster	—	—	—	—	—	25,398	26,298	29,798
Road. wagon	—	—	—	—	—	26,150	27,398	31,798
Safari wagon	17,008	19,566	21,317	—	—	—	—	—
Used Values ($)								
Caprice ↑	2900	3900	5200	6000	7300	10,500	11,800	16,000
Caprice ↓	2000	2800	3800	4400	5700	8500	10,000	13,900
Caprice wagon ↑	4800	5900	6600	8500	8100	11,200	12,800	18,000
Caprice wagon ↓	3600	4200	4900	6800	6400	9300	11,000	16,000
Cruiser wagon ↑	5300	6500	7500	9600	12,200	14,500	—	—
Cruiser wagon ↓	4300	5000	5600	7700	10,300	12,000	—	—
Electra wagon ↑	4900	—	—	—	—	—	—	—
Electra wagon ↓	3800	—	—	—	—	—	—	—
LeSabre wagon ↑	4800	—	—	—	—	—	—	—
LeSabre wagon ↓	3700	—	—	—	—	—	—	—
Roadmaster ↑	—	—	—	—	—	14,700	17,400	20,400
Roadmaster ↓	—	—	—	—	—	12,600	15,300	18,300
Road. wagon ↑	—	—	—	—	—	14,500	17,400	21,100
Road. wagon ↓	—	—	—	—	—	12,500	15,300	19,000
Safari wagon ↑	5300	6700	7500	—	—	—	—	—
Safari wagon ↓	4500	5000	5700	—	—	—	—	—
Reliability	②	②	②	②	②	②	③	③
Air conditioning	②	②	②	②	②	②	②	②
Automatic trans.	①	①	①	①	①	①	②	②
Body integrity	②	②	②	②	②	②	③	③
Braking system	③	③	③	③	③	③	③	③
Electrical system	②	②	②	②	②	②	②	③
Engines	③	③	③	③	③	③	③	③
Exhaust/Converter	②	②	②	②	②	③	④	④
Fuel system	③	③	③	③	③	③	③	③
Ignition system	③	③	③	③	③	③	④	④
Rust/Paint	②	②	②	②	②	②	③	③
Steering	②	②	②	②	②	③	④	④
Suspension	②	②	②	②	②	②	③	③
Dealer Service	⑤	⑤	⑤	⑤	⑤	⑤	⑤	⑤
Maintenance	③	③	③	③	③	③	③	③
Parts Availability	⑤	⑤	⑤	⑤	⑤	⑤	⑤	⑤
Repair Costs	②	②	②	②	②	②	③	③

Crash Safety

Caprice	❷	❷	❷	❷	❷	❷	❶	❶
Safety Features								
ABS	—	—	—	S	S	S	S	S
Airbag	—	—	—	D	D	D	D	D/P

LUXURY CARS

Used luxury cars are attractive buys because they project a flashy image that can be bought at a 50 percent discount. True, they can be bargains if their selling price is reasonable, independent servicing is available and used parts can be found. But on the downside, they are complicated to service and the cost for new parts can be horrendous. For example, a 1990 Audi 100 power-steering pump's total cost with taxes included would be $852; for a Mercedes 190 about $1100.

The luxury car niche has been traditionally dominated by American and German automakers. During the past decade, however, buyers have gravitated toward Japanese models. This shift in buyer preference has forced GM, Ford and Chrysler to downsize and adopt front-drive. This has also forced GM to drop its rear-drive Caprice, Roadmaster and Fleetwood.

Smart buyers can get around high prices for Japanese imports in two ways: they can target fully equipped used models such as Toyota Camry and Cressida, Honda Accord, Nissan Maxima and Mazda 929 that offer the same equipment, reliability and performance as Lexus, Infiniti and Acura models but for much, much less. Consumers can also buy hybrid Japanese vehicles sold under American automaker badges, like the Dodge Stealth and Ford Probe.

There are few used American luxury cars that can stand up to a six-year-old Japanese or German vehicle. Chrysler's rear-drive New Yorker and Ford's Crown Victoria/Mercury Grand Marquis and Lincoln Town Car are the most reliable, reasonably priced competitors. The discontinued Imperial is more show than go and the recently relaunched front-drive New Yorker and its LHS variant are unremarkable and seem to have serious reliability problems as can be seen by the numerous dealer service bulletins intercepted by the author. GM's Cadillacs aren't even in the running.

The following used luxury cars are recommended:

Chrysler New Yorker/Fifth Avenue (RWD)
Ford LTD, Crown Victoria/Mercury Grand Marquis
Lexus ES 250
Lexus LS 400
Lincoln Town Car
Mazda 929
Mercedes-Benz 260
Mercedes-Benz 300 series
Nissan Maxima
Toyota Cressida
Volvo 850
Volvo 900 series

The '93 Volvo 850 combines impressive reliability, comfort and understated luxury.

ACURA

Legend

Rating: Above Average buy (1990-94); Acceptable (1989); Not Recommended (1986-88).

Price analysis: Limited availability and fairly expensive; don't let the Acura nameplate fool you into paying more than the Legend merits. The '90 sedan combines the highest depreciation, lowest base price and least wear and tear. Resale value is high on all Legend models, but especially so with the coupe. Shop instead for a cheaper 1989 base Legend with the coupe's upgraded features. Repair costs are higher than average. Expect to pay about $300 annually for maintenance and repairs during the warranty period and $700 annually thereafter. Other luxury cars worth considering: BMW 300 and 500 series • Chrysler New Yorker/Fifth Avenue (RWD) • Ford LTD Crown Victoria, Marquis or Grand Marquis • Lexus ES 250 or ES 400 • Mazda 929 • Mercedes-Benz 300 series • Nissan Maxima • Toyota Cressida and Camry V6.

Technical Data

ENGINES	Litres/CID	HP	MPG	Model Years
OHC V6 FI	2.5/152	151	19-25	1986-87
OHC V6 FI	2.7/163	161	18-24	1987-90
OHC V6 FI	3.2/196	200	18-24	1991-95
OHC V6 FI	3.2/196	230	17-24	1994-95

Strengths and weaknesses: 1986-90-Early Legends were upscale, enlarged Accords that were unimpressive performers with both 6-cylinder powerplants. Dependability, acceptable road handling and a spacious interior are the car's main advantages. In spite of occasional clutch malfunctions, the 5-speed manual gearbox is the transmission of choice. The automatic shifts harshly and its lockup torque converter is constantly cutting in and out, reducing both performance and fuel economy. An overly soft suspension gives the car a bouncy ride and it easily bottoms out when the vehicle is loaded or traversing rough roads. Front-end components get noisier as time passes. Long-term durability is better than average with the only problems centered around body hardware and accessory equipment malfunctions, notably poor radio performance.

1991-94-The 3.2L V6 is by far a better performer than the 2.5L and 2.7L engines that equipped earlier models. Ride quality is improved, power steering is more responsive, and rear seating is more spacious. Automatic shifting is still rough, especially during acceleration. Owners report that suspension struts soften quickly, minor electrical problems occur occasionally, radio reception is poor, and brake service is too frequent. The windshield-washer pump frequently malfunctions on the '91 and '92 versions. Dealer service bulletins show the 1993 models may have faulty trunk-mounted CD changer magazines. The '94s are shown to have lots of body panel fit problems, poor radio reception, steering wheel shimmy, faulty power-steering speed sensors, and door glass scratches.

Safety summary/recalls: A dual airbag-equipped 1991 four-door Legend was tested; the driver was judged to have sustained serious chest trauma but the passenger would have been well-protected. A '94 was retested and, again, the driver was judged to have sustained serious injury to the right leg. 1986-88 Legends have one of the highest sudden acceleration accident rates reported by owners, and 1986-87 Legends are under investigation for fuel tank overpressurization which results in fuel spewing out when the cap is removed. Inadvertent airbag deployment on the 1992-93 models is also being probed. Anti-lock brakes became standard on the '88 model (L and LS versions) and became a standard feature on all '93 models. On the '91 LS, an additional airbag for the front passenger was added. L models were so equipped in 1992 and sedans in 1993. *Recalls:* **1991-**A faulty automatic transmission shift cable will be replaced free of charge. **1991-92-**Vehicles may not have an igniter for the passenger-side airbag.

Secret Warranties/Service Tips/DSBs

1986-87-Transmission shudder during up/downshifts may require the replacement of the 2nd-4th clutch plate, 2nd gear needle bearing and thrust washer.

1986-88-Excessive brake squeal may require new shims (front brakes) or new pads (rear brakes).

• An alternator that is slow to charge may require an upgraded pulley and belt (#06310-PL2-A00).

1987-A rear quarter-window water leak can be fixed by realigning the window.

• An upgraded ECU module will improve cold starts.

1988-No automatic transmission upshift past 2nd gear may require the replacement of the secondary valve body separator plate, solenoid filter and ECU.

1988-90-Erratic fuel and temperature gauges can be fixed by replacing the circuit board and deburring the washer.

1990-Water collects in the spare tire well: diagnosis and repair DSB 89-021.

• Security system control unit malfunction: diagnosis and repair DSB 90-002.

1991-Power-steering pump noise while turning when the car is cold can be corrected by replacing the power-steering pump control valve.

• Poor AM radio reception or interference from the car's electrical equipment may be due to a poor ground connection between the antenna collar and car body.

• The lower dashboard cover may not fit snugly against the dashboard, leaving a gap. Correct by installing a clip.

• Wind noise from the door glass may be caused by the glass not scaling properly at the rear of the door.

• If the ashtray won't stay in when it's pushed closed, try straightening the latch spring.

• Vibrating door mirror glass can be fixed by installing a new actuator bracket and mounting screw.

1991-92-Wind noise from the front door glass may be caused by the run channel not sealing against the glass. Correct by adjusting the glass engagement and reinforcing the channel.

• Static on the AM radio band is likely caused by a faulty Bose amplifier or poor antenna grounding due to loose mounting nuts.

• If the remote audio volume controls cause static or operate erratically, change the volume control motor inside the audio unit.

• Poor AC performance is often caused by a misadjusted heater valve cable.

1991-93-A poorly functioning cellular phone may have a shorted wire at the strain relief grommet.

• Engine knocking after a cold startup is likely due to carbon buildup in the piston ring land.

1991-94-To prevent the lower bumper face from pulling loose, Acura will reinforce the mounting points and reverse the overlap of the lower bumper face and the splash shield.

• Power-steering speed sensor failures are covered under Acura's "goodwill" warranty (DSB 94-018).

1992-A faulty oil pressure switch will be replaced free under Acura's product update program.

All models/years-Acura will repair or replace defective steering assemblies, constant velocity joints and catalytic converters free of charge up to 5 years/80,000 km on a case-by-case basis. There is no labor charge or deductible. Used vehicles and repairs carried out by independent garages are not covered by this special program. The converter, however, an emissions component, is almost always automatically covered under the emissions warranty. To avoid costly engine repairs, check the engine timing belt every 2 years/40,000 km and replace it every 96,000 km.

Steering wheel shimmy can be reduced by rebalancing the wheel/tire/hub/rotor assembly in the front end. Poor radio reception or interference is addressed in DSB 94-011, issued August 30, 1994. The automaker will install air intake screens, for free, to keep debris away from the blower motor. Vertical scratches on the door glass is due to the window making contact with the molding's metal clips. Acura will replace the window for free. Seatbelts that fail to function properly during normal use will be replaced for free under the company's lifetime seatbelt warranty.

Like Honda, most Acura DSBs allow for special warranty consideration on a "goodwill" basis even after the warranty has expired or the car has changed hands. Referring to this euphemism will increase your chances of getting some kind of refund for repairs that are obviously factory defects.

Vehicle Profile

	1987	1988	1989	1990	1991	1992	1993	1994
Cost Price ($)								
LS	26,995	29,895	31,995	33,295	38,540	42,360	44,655	50,000
Used Values ($)								
LS ↑	7000	8900	10,600	16,600	21,000	25,000	33,000	39,000
LS ↓	5500	6400	8100	13,600	18,000	22,000	30,000	36,000
Reliability	③	③	④	④	⑤	⑤	⑤	⑤
Air conditioning	❷	④	⑤	⑤	⑤	⑤	⑤	⑤
Body integrity	③	③	③	③	③	③	③	③
Braking system	③	③	③	③	④	④	④	⑤

Electrical system	③	③	③	③	③	③	③	⑤
Engines	❷	④	④	④	④	⑤	⑤	⑤
Exhaust/Converter	④	④	④	⑤	⑤	⑤	⑤	⑤
Fuel system	④	④	④	④	④	④	⑤	⑤
Ignition system	③	③	③	④	④	④	⑤	⑤
Manual transmission	③	③	❷	④	⑤	⑤	⑤	⑤
- automatic	❷	③	③	③	③	③	④	④
Rust/Paint	❷	❷	④	④	⑤	⑤	⑤	⑤
Steering	④	④	④	④	④	⑤	⑤	⑤
Suspension	❷	③	③	④	④	⑤	⑤	⑤
Dealer Service	③	③	③	③	③	③	③	③
Maintenance	③	③	③	④	④	⑤	⑤	⑤
Parts Availability	③	③	③	③	③	❷	⑤	⑤
Repair Costs	③	③	③	③	③	③	⑤	⑤
Crash Safety	⑤	⑤	⑤	⑤	❷	❷	❷	❷
Safety Features								
ABS	—	S	S	S	S	S	S	S
Airbag	—	—	D	D	D/P	D/P	D/P	D/P

AUDI

80, 90, 100, 200, 4000, 5000, Coupe, Quattro, V8 Series

Rating: Not Recommended (1984-94).

Price analysis: Excellent availability but fairly expensive. Expect to pay about $700 annually for maintenance and repairs during the warranty period and $1000 annually thereafter—all the more reason to buy a car with the original warranty. Other luxury cars worth considering: BMW 300 and 500 series • Chrysler New Yorker/Fifth Avenue (rwd) • Ford LTD Crown Victoria, Marquis or Grand Marquis • Lexus ES 250 or ES 400 • Mazda 929 • Mercedes-Benz 300 series • Nissan Maxima • Toyota Cressida and Camry V6 • Volvo 850.

Technical Data

ENGINES	Litres/CID	HP	MPG	Model Years
OHC I-5 FI	1.8/109	102	22-25	1985-87
OHC I-5T FI	2.1/131	140	17-23	1985
OHC I-5 FI	2.2/136	115	20-24	1985-87
OHC I-5T FI	2.2/136	158-162	17-23	1986-91
DOHC I-5T FI	2.2/136	217	17-23	1991

DOHC I-5T FI	2.2/136	227	17-23	1992-95
OHC I-5 FI	2.3/141	130	18-23	1987-91
OHC V6 FI	2.8/169	172	20-25	1992-95

Strengths and weaknesses: These cars are attractively styled, handle well, are comfortable to drive and provide a spacious interior. The newer 80 and 90 series are much improved, but they still have a worse-than-average reliability record. Unfortunately, all Audis are handicapped by mechanical and electrical components that don't stand up to the rigors of driving in Canada. Furthermore, the dealer body isn't strong enough to adequately service these vehicles. Volkswagen's decision to transfer its administrative operations to the United States only means servicing will become even more hit or miss.

80, 90 and 100 series
Launched in 1988, these entry-level Audis share the same wheelbase, front-drive and 4X4 componentry. Equipped with an efficient, but wimpish 2.0L 4-cylinder (dropped in 1991) or the more powerful 2.3L 5-cylinder engine, four-wheel disc brakes and galvanized body panels, these small sedans are leagues ahead of Audi's mid-1980s vehicles. The 1991 models are clearly a better choice; they use an improved 4-speed automatic transmission hooked to a more powerful engine. 1992 was basically a carryover year where unsold '91 models were recycled.

Dealer service bulletins show the '93 Audi 100s may have misaligned deck lids that are hard to close, steering columns that make a scraping noise, squeaking and rattling coming from the front seats and inside of the B-pillar, excessive wind noise because of poor window sealing, and smearing, chattering wiper blades. The 1992-94 100 series and 1993-94 90s have quirky AC systems that often malfunction and have to be constantly readjusted. The fresh air fan for the same model years will suddenly go into high-speed operation without reason.

5000
Renamed the 100 and 200 in 1989, these sedans have had a terrible repair record. The diesel engine is a nightmare as are turbocharged gasoline engines coupled to automatic transmissions. Front-drive mechanicals are unreliable and very complex to troubleshoot. Steering racks are not durable and engine cooling and electrical systems require frequent repair. Front brake rotors and calipers wear out very quickly and exhaust-system components have a short lifespan. Other common problems are electrical short-circuits in the rear lights, air-conditioning failures, hot starting difficulties and leaking transmission seals. The tops of front fenders and the front edge of the hood and rear-wheel housings are susceptible to rust perforations. Furthermore, a common body problem is the persistent poor alignment of lower side moldings. Resale value is much lower than average, and owners sucked into buying one because of its bargain-basement price face frequent and outrageously expensive

"routine" servicing that is anything but routine.

4000

Gasoline engines require constant and expensive adjustments, the cooling and electrical systems are weak, front brakes require frequent and expensive servicing, and the front MacPherson struts don't last long. Additionally, exhaust-system parts rust through quickly and the fuel-injection system needs constant adjusting. Door panel trim peels away from the body on 1988-89 models. Parts and service are outrageously expensive and not easily available. Later models have fewer complaints, probably due to their comprehensive base warranty.

Safety summary/recalls: Crash tests of a 1980 four-door 4000 concluded that driver would suffer severe or fatal head and chest trauma, while the passenger would have serious leg injuries. A 1981 four-door 5000 produced inconclusive results, but the 1985 models' test scores indicated that the driver would have sustained severe or fatal head trauma. When an '89 four-door 100 was tested, researchers concluded that both the driver and passenger would be well-protected. An airbag-equipped '91 four-door Audi 100 performed similarly. Transport Canada is probing fuel tank leaks on 1985-87 models. *Recalls:* **1984-90-80, 90, 4000**-Dealers will fix leaky or cracked brake hoses. **1985-86**-Defective idle stabilizer valve on the 5-cylinder version with automatic transmission may cause the vehicle to surge and buck. **1985-91**-Evaporation of the differential oil could result in bearing and gear failure sapping power from the front wheels or locking them up. **1986**-Rear or right front seatbelt locks may malfunction. **1990**-Faulty steering lock bolts may block steering wheel movement. A faulty idle control module may cause erratic or increased idle speed. **1990 Quattro**-Faulty front seatback hinges. **1984-85 5000, 100, 200 Quattro, V8**-A faulty idle control module causing erratic or increased idle speed will be fixed for free. **1984-86**-Audi will install a transmission/brake interlock. **1984-88**-Audi will install a vent line valve or modify the fuel filler neck to prevent fuel vapor ignition on Turbo models. **1984-89 Turbo and Quattro**-Hardened fuel injector seals allow fuel to leak on the engine. **1985-86**-Misadjustment of the fuel distributor may cause fuel vapors to collect in the air filter and ignite if the engine backfires. Defective idle stabilizer valve on the 5-cylinder version with automatic transmission may cause the vehicle to surge and buck. **1985-91**-An extension of the previous recall to prevent bearing and gear failure sapping power from the front wheels or locking them up. **1986**-Malfunctioning rear or right front seatbelt locks. **1992 100 series**-Audi will modify the brake vacuum booster system to improve brake pedal assist.

Secret Warranties/Service Tips/DSBs

80, 90, 4000
1984-90-Rear crankshaft seals that leak oil require a new Bruss seal (#068-1030-0516).
1987-89-Distorted injector O-rings require new Viton injectors.
1988-90-Leaking water pumps require a new sealing gasket.
5000, 100, 200 Quattro, V8
1984-85-Hesitation during cold take-off can be caused by a too lean fuel mixture. Install a pressure gradient switch kit (#447-998-217).
• Exhaust manifold leakage causing by a warped manifold and broken exhaust studs is a common problem addressed in DSB 89-03/26.
1984-88-Broken radiator neck a common problem (DSB 90-02/19).
• Poor AC cooling likely caused by a broken fresh air/recirculation servo mount due to a defective or shifted recirculation air flap seal.
1986-87-Rear brake calipers could bend and overheat, causing poor stopping or a partial loss of braking ability.
1986-88-Excessive brake noise is a common problem that is addressed in DSB 88-03/46. Brake pads must have anti-vibration material; if not, replace them.
1991-92-A clacking noise occurring whenever the vehicle passes over a bump is caused by plastic-to-plastic contact between the door lock latch and the door wedge.
1992-94-DSB 94-09 troubleshoots common AC problems.
• DSB 94-05 recommends replacing the fresh air fan with an upgraded part.
All models/years-Defective catalytic converters that cause a rotten egg smell will be replaced free of charge under the 5 year/80,000 km emissions warranty.

Vehicle Profile

	1987	1988	1989	1990	1991	1992	1993	1994
Cost Price ($)								
80	—	—	—	—	—	27,995	—	—
90	—	31,575	32,300	34,850	32,920	—	28,450	—
90S/4X4	—	38,660	39,150	39,700	37,065	—	38,750	35,250
4000	26,325	—	—	—	—	—	—	—
Used Values ($)								
80 ↑	—	—	—	—	—	11,500	—	—
80 ↓	—	—	—	—	—	9100	—	—
90 ↑	—	7000	8300	10,000	11,800	—	16,000	—
90 ↓	—	4900	6100	7700	9400	—	14,000	—
90S/4X4 ↑	—	8100	9200	11,500	13,900	—	18,000	24,000
90S/4X4 ↓	—	5800	7000	9100	11,500	—	16,000	21,500
4000 ↑	2800	—	—	—	—	—	—	—

4000 ↓	2100	—	—	—	—	—	—	—
Reliability	①	②	①	①	②	—	③	③
Air conditioning	②	①	①	①	①	—	②	②
Body integrity	④	④	④	④	④	—	④	④
Braking system	②	②	②	②	①	—	②	②
Electrical system	①	①	①	①	①	—	②	②
Engines	①	①	①	①	②	—	③	③
Exhaust/Converter	②	②	②	②	①	—	⑤	⑤
Fuel system	①	①	②	②	⑤	—	④	④
Ignition system	①	②	②	②	①	—	③	③
Maintenance	①	①	①	①	②	—	③	③
Manual transmission	③	③	③	③	③	—	④	⑤
- automatic	②	②	②	④	④	—	⑤	⑤
Rust/Paint	②	②	①	④	④	—	④	④
Steering	②	②	②	③	③	—	③	③
Suspension	②	②	③	③	③	—	③	③
Dealer Service	①	①	①	①	③	—	③	③
Parts Availability	②	②	②	②	③	—	③	③
Repair Costs	①	①	①	①	③	—	③	③
Crash Safety								
80	—	—	②	②	②	—	—	—
4000	①	—	—	—	—	—	—	—
Safety Features								
ABS	—	—	—	—	—	—	S	S
Airbag	—	—	—	—	D	—	D	D/P

Vehicle Profile

	1987	1988	1989	1990	1991	1992	1993	1994
Cost Price ($)								
100	—	—	39,100	41,200	38,915	—	37,600	48,250
100Q	—	—	43,250	43,850	40,945	—	—	—
200	—	—	46,250	48,600	45,365	—	—	—
200TQ	—	—	49,900	51,740	48,295	—	—	—
5000	31,400	38,375	—	—	—	—	—	—
5000Q	44,725	46,125	—	—	—	—	—	—
V8	—	—	70,800	66,560	—	69,900	73,050	—
Used Values ($)								
100 ↑	—	—	9100	12,700	14,700	—	18,400	31,500
100 ↓	—	—	6500	10,200	12,100	—	15,600	25,000
100Q ↑	—	—	9800	13,200	16,100	—	—	—
100Q ↓	—	—	7200	10,700	13,600	—	—	—
200 ↑	—	—	9500	13,300	17,000	—	—	—
200 ↓	—	—	7000	10,600	14,300	—	—	—
200TQ ↑	—	—	10,300	14,700	18,900	—	—	—
200TQ ↓	—	—	7800	11,900	16,100	—	—	—
5000 ↑	5500	7000	—	—	—	—	—	—

5000 ↓	4200	5000	—	—	—	—	—	—
5000Q ↑	6700	8200	—	—	—	—	—	—
5000Q ↓	5500	6600	—	—	—	—	—	—
V8 ↑	—	—	18,700	21,000	—	29,000	51,100	—
V8 ↓	—	—	15,200	18,000	—	25,000	44,000	—
Reliability	①	①	①	①	②	—	③	③
Air conditioning	②	③	③	③	③	—	③	③
Body integrity	④	④	④	④	④	—	④	⑤
Braking system	②	②	②	②	②	—	③	③
Electrical system	①	①	①	①	①	—	②	③
Engines	①	①	①	①	②	—	④	⑤
Exhaust/Converter	②	②	②	②	③	—	⑤	⑤
Fuel system	①	①	②	②	②	—	③	③
Ignition system	①	②	②	②	③	—	③	③
Manual transmission	④	④	④	④	—	—	⑤	⑤
- automatic	②	②	②	④	④	—	⑤	⑤
Rust/Paint	②	②	③	④	④	—	④	⑤
Steering	②	②	②	③	③	—	④	④
Suspension	②	②	③	③	③	—	⑤	⑤
Dealer Service	①	①	①	①	③	—	③	③
Maintenance	①	①	①	①	②	—	③	③
Parts Availability	②	②	②	②	③	—	③	③
Repair Costs	①	①	①	①	③	—	③	④
Crash Safety								
100	—	—	⑤	⑤	⑤	—	⑤	⑤
5000	②	②	—	—	—	—	—	—
Safety Features								
ABS	—	—	—	—	—	—	S	S
Airbag	—	—	—	—	—	—	D/P	D/P

BMW

3 Series, 5 Series

Rating: **3 Series**: Above Average buy (1989-94); Average buy (1984-88). **5 Series**: Recommended (1992-94); Average buys (1986-91) with a reputation that far exceeds what they actually deliver.

Price analysis: Limited availability. Prices fluctuate wildly and most of the time they are very unrealistic. Resale value is good and has appreciated with the threat (now dropped) of U.S. tariffs on Japanese luxury cars. Expect to pay about $500 annually for maintenance and repairs during the warranty period and $800 annually thereafter—all the more reason to buy a BMW with the original warranty. The 525i and 535i's accident repair costs are much higher than average. Other luxury cars worth considering: Chrysler New Yorker/Fifth Avenue (rwd) • Ford LTD Crown Victoria, Marquis or Grand Marquis • Lexus ES 250 or ES 400 • Mazda 929 • Mercedes-Benz 300 series • Nissan Maxima • Toyota Cressida and Camry V6 • Volvo 850.

Technical Data

ENGINES	Litres/CID	HP	MPG	Model Years
OHC I-4 FI	1.8/108	101	23-28	1985
OHC I-4 FI	1.8/108	101	23-28	1985
DOHC I-4 FI	1.8/110	134	23-27	1991-93
DOHC I-4 FI	1.8/110	138	23-27	1991-95
OHC I-6FI	2.5/152	168	18-24	1988-93
DOHC I-6FI	2.5/152	189	18-24	1992-95
OHC I-6 FI	2.7/164	121	20-26	1985-87

Strengths and weaknesses: **1984-91**-The 318's lethargic engine is seriously compromised by an automatic transmission; the 325e is more pleasant to drive and delivers lots of low-end torque. Both cars are fun to drive as long as one is mindful of the fact the rear end is unstable on slippery pavement. The 3 series offers average reliability. However, whenever a problem arises, repair costs are particularly high due to the small number of dealers, BMW's control of the parts market and the acquiescence of affluent owners. All body styles in the 3 series are cramped in the rear and have much less interior room than the 5 series. Towing is not recommended.

The electrical system is the source of most complaints. The automatic transmission is not durable and front brakes require frequent attention. Owners also report chronic surging at idle and a rotten egg smell from the exhaust (all models/years).

Door seams, rocker panels, rear wheel openings and fender seams are particularly rust prone. 1985 BMWs were poorly rustproofed and deteriorated very quickly, especially along the door bottoms and within the front and rear wheelwells. Check the muffler bracket for premature wear, and weather seals and door adjustments for leaks.

1992-94-Peppy 6-cylinder acceleration only with high revs. City driving requires lots of manual gear shifting characterized by an abrupt clutch. Confidential dealer service bulletins confirm the 1993 3 series has poorly performing and noisy AC, the cellular phone interferes with FM radio reception, doors don't close easily, accelerator pedal buzz and vibration, excessive engine-compartment noises, flickering odometer display and backlighting, leaking radiator expansion tank seals, a rough idle caused by a loose or broken carbon canister, a rotten egg odor coming from the exhaust, excessive brake vibrations caused by Jurid brake pads, defective reverse switch pins, and malfunctioning power windows.

Bulletins show the 1994 3 series could have coolant leakage from the timing case profile gasket, a binding/sticking ignition leading to starter failures, sagging convertible headliners, water leaking into the driver's side footwell and into the E-box area flooding the DME control module, self-activating emergency flashers, flickering instrument lighting and a rotten egg smell caused by faulty catalytic converters.

5 series owners report numerous electrical and fuel glitches, faulty turn signal indicators, starter failures, self-activating emergency flashers, exhaust rotten egg odors and excessive steering wheel/brake vibration.

Safety summary/recalls: NHTSA crash tests of an '85 318i two-door concluded that the driver would sustain severe or fatal head and chest injuries. Tests of a '90 325i two-door indicated that the driver was judged to sustain severe or fatal trauma to the head area . Results for a '92 airbag-equipped 325i four-door showed that both the front passenger and driver would have escaped serious injury. A retested '93 was judged to have produced serious injuries to the driver's legs. U.S. government researchers are looking into reports of airbags failing to deploy or deploying inadvertently on all 1991-93 models. *Recalls*: **1984**-Sudden acceleration may be caused by a faulty engine on 318i models. Sudden acceleration on 318i models may also be caused by a defective idle control valve. A binding heater control valve can cause the solenoid to malfunction, resulting in an instrument panel fire. **1984-91**-Leaks caused by a cooling-system malfunction will be corrected at no charge. **1985-86**-Supporting plates will be installed to reinforce the steering column. **1985-90**-Fuel-pump relay failures causing no-starts require a new relay replaced free under the emissions warranty. **1986-87**-Faulty center-mounted brake light switch needs to be replaced. **1988 325iX**-A bent oil dipstick tube could prevent the throttle from returning to idle when the accelerator is released. **1991-92 318**-Ice buildup moving into the throttle housing can lead to increased idle speed or impaired deceleration. **1991 318/325**-Erratic wiper operation caused by electrical short-circuit. **1991 318i/325is**-The knee booster will be relocated so it won't interfere with the steering column's absorption of crash forces. **1991 325i**-Faulty windshield wiper switch ground screw. **1991 325ix**-If the transfer case is leaking at the weep hole, it signals the need to revise the depth of the inner seal. Repair is covered under BMW's emissions warranty. **1992**-On 318 versions, a faulty cooling system may spray hot water in the interior.

Secret Warranties/Service Tips/DSBs

3 Series
1984-88-Door wiring short-circuits may cause erratic window, mirror and central locking malfunctions.
1986-89-A cracked intake manifold purge valve is a common problem.
1990-Engine oil cap may break and pieces could fall into the engine.

Replace the cap.

1990-91 vehicles with E34 and M50 engines-Cylinder head cover leaks require a new, upgraded cover (11-12-1-722-385 or 11-12-738-171 for later models).

1990-93-Vehicles equipped with Jurid 506 brake pads may exhibit a steering vibration. Replace the old pads with upgraded pads.

1992-If the heater blower performs erratically, chances are the blower resistor unit needs replacing.

1993-94-Emergency flashers may self-activate due to a defective crash control module. This problem affect all BMWs. Replace with an upgraded module.

1994-A starter motor failure may be caused by a faulty steering lock and electrical switch.

• A sagging convertible headliner requires reinforced plastic clips that hold the headliner bracket to the bow.

• Water intrusion into the driver's footwell area and the subsequent corrosion of the X13 and X14 connectors can be prevented by sealing off the hood's mounting flange just inboard of the left gas strut.

• Water leaks into the E-box can be prevented by installing an improved capacity air intake drain hose in the right side drain in addition to installing another drain hose.

5 Series

1989-A fusible link could fail, shorting out all electrical power.

1990-93-Change the Jurid 506 brake pads (see above).

1991-Inoperative power accessories may require the installation of a Reinshagen general module (version 5.2 or later).

1993-94-Emergency flashers may self-activate (see above).

1994-If the audible turn signal indicator fails its probably because residue left from the manufacturing process is causing the armature relay to stick.

• Starter motor failures (see above).

All models/years-BMW says an exhaust rotten egg smell is due to fuel impurities and cannot be resolved by changing the catalytic converter. The company says it won't pay for any converters replaced for this reason. BMW may be the only automaker to take this position which blames its customers' choice of fuel instead of BMW's own engineering.

Vehicle Profile (3 Series)

	1987	1988	1989	1990	1991	1992	1993	1994
Cost Price ($)								
318i 2-door	—	—	—	—	25,187	26,900	29,510	27,980
318i 4-door	—	—	—	—	23,271	25,700	28,430	26,900
Convertible	—	—	—	—	31,682	33,270	34,760	—
325E	27,120	28,500	—	—	—	—	—	—
325i	33,660	36,300	32,500	34,270	32,336	38,800	39,750	38,200
Convertible	43,900	45,800	41,500	43,150	40,654	42,365	45,780	52,900

Used Values ($)

318i 2-door ↑	—	—	—	—	12,900	14,900	16,600	19,100
318i 2-door ↓	—	—	—	—	10,300	12,200	13,900	16,300
318i 4-door ↑	—	—	—	—	11,900	14,000	15,800	18,300
318i 4-door ↓	—	—	—	—	9300	11,400	13,100	15,500
Convertible ↑	—	—	—	—	16,000	19,000	23,600	—
Convertible ↓	—	—	—	—	13,400	16,400	21,800	—
325E ↑	7000	8800	—	—	—	—	—	—
325E ↓	5500	6600	—	—	—	—	—	—
325i ↑	9400	10,700	11,600	15,000	18,000	21,600	24,300	29,200
325i ↓	7400	8300	9000	12,300	15,400	18,900	21,600	26,400
Convertible ↑	10,000	12,500	14,700	18,000	20,000	24,000	31,000	39,000
Convertible ↓	8500	9700	12,100	15,000	18,000	21,100	26,000	34,700
Reliability	③	③	③	③	③	④	④	④
Air conditioning	❷	❷	③	③	④	④	④	⑤
Body integrity	③	③	③	③	③	③	③	④
Braking system	③	③	③	③	③	③	③	③
Electrical system	❷	❷	③	③	③	③	③	④
Engines	❷	③	④	④	④	⑤	⑤	⑤
Exhaust/Converter	❷	❷	③	③	③	③	③	③
Fuel system	③	③	③	③	③	③	③	④
Ignition system	❷	③	③	③	③	④	④	④
Manual transmission	③	③	③	③	④	⑤	⑤	⑤
- automatic	③	③	③	③	③	④	⑤	⑤
Rust/Paint	③	③	③	③	④	④	⑤	⑤
Suspension	④	④	④	④	④	④	⑤	⑤
Dealer Service	③	③	③	③	③	③	④	④
Maintenance	❷	❷	❷	❷	❷	③	③	③
Parts Availability	③	③	③	③	③	③	③	③
Repair Costs	❷	❷	❷	❷	❷	❷	③	③
Crash Safety								
318i 2-door	—	—	—	—	❶	❶	❶	❶
325i	—	—	—	❷	❷	⑤	❷	❷
325i Convertible	—	—	—	⑤	⑤	⑤	⑤	⑤
Safety Features								
ABS	S	S	S	S	S	S	S	S
Airbag	—	—	—	—	—	D	D	D/P
Traction control	—	—	—	—	—	—	—	S

Vehicle Profile/5 Series

	1987	1988	1989	1990	1991	1992	1993	1994
Cost Price ($)								
525i	—	—	52,600	47,900	45,200	47,830	51,210	49,750
528E	31,480	42,200	—	—	—	—	—	—
535i	46,140	50,700	64,400	55,130	52,150	54,760	58,520	—

Used Values ($)

525i ↑	—	—	16,000	18,600	20,800	24,400	28,700	33,900
525i ↓	—	—	12,500	14,800	17,200	20,700	25,000	31,000
528E ↑	6200	7800	—	—	—	—	—	—
528E ↓	4300	5200	—	—	—	—	—	—
535i ↑	9200	11,000	16,100	18,600	20,800	24,400	31,400	—
535i ↓	7300	8700	12,500	14,800	17,200	20,700	27,700	—
Reliability	③	③	③	③	④	⑤	⑤	⑤
Air conditioning	③	④	④	④	⑤	⑤	⑤	⑤
Body integrity	③	③	③	③	③	③	③	③
Braking system	③	③	③	③	③	③	③	③
Electrical system	❷	❷	③	③	③	③	③	③
Engines	③	③	④	④	④	⑤	⑤	⑤
Exhaust/Converter	❷	❷	③	③	③	③	③	③
Fuel system	③	③	③	③	③	③	④	④
Ignition system	❷	③	③	③	③	④	④	④
Manual transmission	③	③	③	③	④	⑤	⑤	⑤
- automatic	③	③	③	③	③	④	⑤	⑤
Rust/Paint	③	③	③	③	④	④	④	④
Suspension	④	④	④	④	④	④	⑤	⑤
Dealer Service	③	③	③	③	③	③	④	④
Maintenance	❷	❷	❷	❷	❷	③	④	④
Parts Availability	③	③	③	③	③	③	③	③
Repair Costs	❷	❷	❷	❷	❷	③	③	④
Crash Safety	—	—	—	—	—	—	—	—
Safety Features								
ABS	S	S	S	S	S	S	S	S
Airbag	—	—	—	—	—	D	D	D/P
Traction control	—	—	—	—	—	—	—	S

GENERAL MOTORS

Reatta

Rating: Average buy. A smooth-running, comfortable and quiet Riviera, disguised as a luxury sports car.

Price analysis: Limited availability and fairly expensive. This luxury two-seater was only on the market from 1988-91. The '90 and '91 models have the highest collector potential, particularly the convertibles. Parts are easily found except for body panels which have to be specially ordered at premium prices.

Strengths and weaknesses: This front-wheel-drive luxury coupe and convertible combines lots of luxury with a checkered repair history.

GM improved the quality somewhat with its 1991 models, but then discontinued production. The 1988-89 cars were replete with the same low level of quality control that affected the Riviera.

Design and manufacturing defects include chronic fuel injection, engine computer and electrical-system defects. The electronic cathode ray tube on the instrument panel which the driver touched to operate the accessories was taken from the Riviera and is awkward to use and dangerously distracting. The automatic transmission is subject to costly failures, shock absorbers wear out quickly and the front brakes aren't very durable and perform poorly. Surface rust and poor paint quality are the most common body complaints on all years.

Safety summary/recalls: NHTSA researchers crash tested an '86 two-door Riviera and Toronado and concluded that only the passenger would sustain severe leg trauma. These results can be extrapolated to the Reatta. *Recalls*: See Riviera data.

Secret Warranties/Service Tips/DSBs

See Riviera data.

Vehicle Profile

	1988	1989	1990	1991
Cost Price ($)				
Coupe	37,995	39,998	40,631	35,598
Convertible	—	—	49,289	43,898
Used Values ($)				
Coupe ↑	9400	11,000	15,000	19,900
Coupe ↓	6900	8300	11,800	16,700
Convertible ↑	—	—	18,500	22,500
Convertible ↓	—	—	16,000	20,000
Reliability	②	③	③	③
Automatic transmission	②	②	②	②
Body integrity	③	③	③	③
Braking system	②	②	②	③
Electrical system	②	②	②	②
Engines	③	③	③	④
Exhaust/Converter	②	②	②	②
Fuel system	②	③	③	③
Ignition system	③	③	③	③
Rust/Paint	②	②	②	②
Steering	②	②	③	③
Suspension	②	③	③	③
Dealer Service	③	③	③	③
Maintenance	③	③	③	③
Parts Availability	④	④	④	④
Repair Costs	④	④	④	④
Crash Safety	②	②	②	②

Riviera, Toronado

Rating: Average buy (1992-93); Not Recommended (1986-91). GM skipped the '94 model year and introduced an all-new '95 version.

Price analysis: Limited availability and fairly expensive. Expect to pay about $400 annually for maintenance and repairs during the warranty period and $800 annually thereafter. Mechanical parts are easy to find but body panels have to be ordered from GM at a premium. Other luxury cars worth considering: BMW 300 or 500 series • Chrysler New Yorker/Fifth Avenue (rwd) • Ford LTD Crown Victoria, Marquis or Grand Marquis • Lexus ES 250 or ES 400 • Mazda 929 • Mercedes-Benz 300 series • Nissan Maxima • Toyota Cressida and Camry V6 • Volvo 850.

Technical Data

ENGINES	Litres/CID	HP	MPG	Model Years
OHV V6 FI	3.8/231	140-170	17-23	1986-93

Strengths and weaknesses: The redesigned 1986-89 cars managed to keep the same low level of quality control with multiple design and manufacturing defects, including serious fuel injection, engine computer and electrical-system defects. One particularly poor design was the complex Graphic Control Center which used an oversensitive video screen and small pushbuttons. It's both distracting and expensive to repair. The automatic transmission is notoriously failure prone and brakes wear out prematurely and perform poorly. Surface rust and poor paint quality are the most common body complaints on all years. The dashboard control screen (Riviera) is awkward to use and dangerously distracting. Shock absorbers wear out quickly, and the diesel engine seldom runs properly.

The 1990 through 1993 models offer lots of luxury with a checkered repair history. GM improved the quality over the years but generic deficiencies affecting the automatic transmission, engine, computer modules, suspension, and fit and finish make these cars less than luxury from a quality control standpoint.

Safety summary/recalls: NHTSA crash tests of an '86 two-door Riviera and Toronado concluded that only the passenger would sustain severe leg trauma. Seatbelts that jam when the seatbelt retractor malfunctions on '92 Toronados are currently being investigated. *Recalls*: **1986-87**-The power-steering pump hose may leak, creating the possibility of an engine fire. **1989**-ABS brakes may fail due to a faulty brake line. **1990**-Faulty transmission cable may indicate wrong gear is engaged. **1990-93**-Front shoulder belt may stick in retractor. Misaligned rear seatbelt shoulder retractor assemblies. **1992**-Possible steering loss due to the disengagement of the steering shaft.

Secret Warranties/Service Tips/DSBs

1984-87-THM 440-T4 transaxles may experience a delayed 2-3 upshift. This problem is likely caused by a leaking 3rd clutch seal. A thicker seal (#8646991) will correct the problem.

1986-87-Serious stalling problems with these cars can usually be traced to a defective PROM module or a malfunctioning TCC solenoid. Ask your dealer to consult GM DSB 87-T57B when checking the solenoid and DSB 87-T-40A for data on tracking PROM malfunctions. Another possible cause is a defective mass air flow sensor.

• If the engine won't start, check the oil pressure sensor switch wiring harness. It may be hitting the engine drive belt and shorting out, causing the fuel pump to become inoperative (DSB-87-8-6).

• If the car shudders whenever the transmission shifts from 1st to 2nd gear, you may need a new set of 2nd gear clutch plates (DSB 87-7440-7A).

• Excessive brake noise can be reduced by installing improved front (#12321440) and rear (#12321441) brake assemblies.

1986-88-If the power-steering whines or is hard to turn, the likely cause is a defective power-steering reservoir (noise) or flow control valve (hard steering), according to DSB 88-3-8A.

1986-90-The belt accessory drive may chirp or squeal. The root cause of this condition is misaligned pulleys.

1987-88-A heavy clunk upon acceleration or when shifting is likely caused by loose or missing front engine mount bracket bolts (DSB 88-6-4A).

1988-A common cause of poor engine performance (unsteady idle speed, no starts and stalling) is a vacuum leak at the PCV valve (DSB 88-6E-21).

• 3.8L engines have weak valve spring caps. DSB 88-6-20 suggests that new, stronger valve spring caps (#255605) should be installed.

• If the engine won't turn over, check the wiring harness for a short-circuit caused by passing too close to the exhaust system heat shield (DSB 87-6E-9).

1989-90-A wiper motor that starts in high speed only may need a new park switch assembly (#22063283).

• Engine oil pan leaks with 3300 or 3800 V6 engines require an engine oil pan gasket kit (#12350268).

• Stalling from a cold start and a chuggle at 70 km/h require a new MEMCAL.

1990-91-A revised headrest guide loop will be installed on Rivieras if the shoulder belt rides uncomfortably on the neck.

1990-93-An engine ticking at idle can be traced to rattling piston pins that must be replaced with upgraded parts.

1991-92-A noisy power antenna should be replaced by GM's upgraded antenna which has a lower viscosity oil in the upper motor bearing and a revised plastic shim washer.

1991-93-Loss of Drive or erratic shifts may be caused by an intermittent short-circuit to ground on the A or B shift solenoid or an electrical short-circuit in the transaxle.

1992-93-Harsh automatic transmission upshifts can be corrected by installing an upgraded accumulator valve in the control valve body.

1992-93-A front-end engine knock troubleshooting chart and extensive diagnostic tips are found in DSB 306001.

1990-92 Toronado and Trofeo-A body mount creak that occurs whenever the vehicle passes over a bump may be due to one or more of the body mounts being mispositioned in the frame. Correct by installing a new lower insulator.

• Chronic wind noise coming from the front door window can be corrected by reinstalling the run channel retainer.

• A shake or vibration in the front end when going over smooth roads may be caused by an internal leak in the engine mount. Correct by installing an upgraded mount (#22113021).

1990-93-An engine ticking at idle can be traced to rattling piston pins that must be replaced with upgraded parts.

1991-92-Harsh automatic transmission upshifts can be corrected by installing an upgraded accumulator valve in the control valve body.

All models/years-For over a decade, GM has had a serious rust/paint peeling problem with all its domestic-made vehicles—running the gamut from its cheapest to most expensive cars. Instead of fixing the problem, GM has set up a secret slush fund to pay off customers who scream the loudest. Original owners will get 100% compensation for paint peeling/surface rusting up to six years (confirmed by GM's internal letter to dealers found in the Bonneville section of this *Guide*). A rotten egg odor coming from the exhaust is likely the result of a malfunctioning catalytic converter covered by GM's 5 year/80,000 km emissions warranty. It doesn't take much screaming to get coverage.

Vehicle Profile

	1987	1988	1989	1990	1991	1992	1993
Cost Price ($)							
Riviera	27,338	30,940	32,898	33,514	29,698	29,898	30,790
Toronado	26,679	29,570	30,989	32,817	29,698	28,799	—
Trofeo	—	33,029	34,798	36,241	32,698	31,998	—
Used Values ($)							
Riviera ↑	5200	6500	8100	11,100	14,300	17,800	21,300
Riviera ↓	3900	4500	6100	8900	12,100	15,500	19,000
Toronado ↑	5400	6500	8300	11,100	14,500	18,200	—
Toronado ↓	3800	4400	6200	9100	12,500	15,900	—

Trofeo ↑	—	7000	8900	12,000	15,500	19,600	—
Trofeo ↓	—	5100	6700	9800	13,300	17,200	—
Reliability	②	②	③	③	③	③	④
Air conditioning	③	③	③	④	④	④	④
Automatic trans.	②	②	②	③	③	③	③
Body integrity	②	③	③	③	③	⑤	⑤
Braking system	②	②	②	②	③	③	③
Electrical system	②	②	②	②	②	③	③
Engines	④	③	③	③	④	④	④
Exhaust/Converter	③	④	④	④	⑤	⑤	⑤
Fuel system	②	②	③	③	③	③	③
Ignition system	③	③	③	③	③	③	③
Rust/Paint	④	④	④	④	④	④	④
Steering	②	③	③	③	④	④	④
Suspension	②	②	③	③	③	③	④
Dealer Service	③	③	③	③	③	③	③
Maintenance	③	③	③	③	③	③	③
Parts Availability	③	③	③	③	③	③	③
Repair Costs	③	③	③	③	③	④	④
Crash Safety	②	②	②	②	②	②	②
Safety Features							
ABS	—	—	—	—	S	S	S
Airbag	—	—	—	D	D	D	D

Allanté, Eldorado, Seville

Rating: Not Recommended (1985-94).

Price analysis: Average availability and fairly expensive. Expect to pay about $500 annually for maintenance and repairs during the warranty period and $900 annually thereafter—all the more reason to buy a Cadillac with the original warranty. Other luxury cars worth considering: BMW 300 or 500 series • Chrysler New Yorker/Fifth Avenue (rwd) • Ford LTD Crown Victoria, Marquis or Grand Marquis Lexus ES 250 or ES 400 • Mazda 929 • Mercedes-Benz 300 series • Nissan Maxima • Toyota Cressida and Camry V6 • Volvo 850.

Technical Data

ENGINES	Litres/CID	HP	MPG	Model Years
OHV V8 FI	4.1/249	130	16-21	1986-87
OHV V8 FI	4.5/273	155	16-21	1988-89
OHV V8 FI	4.5/273	180	16-20	1990
OHV V8 FI	4.9/300	200	16-20	1991-93
DOHC V8 FI	4.6/279	270-300	16-20	1993-95

Strengths and weaknesses: These cars are luxury lemons. Even though most use the same mechanical components with the same deficiencies as the Riviera and Toronado models, they are far more failure prone due to the complexity of their different luxury features.

The 4.1L V8 is best avoided. It's fuel thirsty and overpowered by the Eldorado's weight. These cars have generic deficiencies that fall into the same categories: poorly calibrated and failure-prone engines, transmissions, fuel and ignition systems, a multiplicity of electrical short-circuits, and sloppy body assembly using poor-quality components.

Specifically, engines and fuel systems often produce intermittent stalling, rough idling, hesitation and no-starts, the overdrive automatic is prone to premature failure, oil pumps fail frequently, front brakes and shock absorbers wear out quickly, paint is often poorly applied, fades or peels away prematurely, fragile body hardware breaks easily, and there are large gaps between sheet metal panels and doors that are poorly hung and not entirely square. Other body problems include cracking of front outside door handles, door rattles (Eldorado), poor bumper fit, loose sun visor mounting, rear taillamp condensation, fading and discoloring appliqué mouldings (Seville), interior window fogging, "creaking" body mounts, water leaking into trunk from license plate holder (Eldorado), noisy roof panels and seatback lumbar motors, and a creaking noise at the upper front door hinge areas.

GM dealer service bulletins show that '93 models equipped with 3.8L or 4.9L engines may be hard to start, frequently stall, lose power and may not maintain the cruise control set speed. Other problems confirmed by GM: condensation in the taillamps, radio static and excessive front-end vibrations when passing over bumps, faulty engine oil pumps (Allanté only), transmission gear whine and rear suspension noise. Eldorados may also have squeaks and squealing after a cold start and warped windshield and rear-window molding.

Bulletins applicable to the '94s show the following problems: erratic shifting, engine accessory belt noise, an AC hissing noise, rear suspension noise, condensation dripping from the heater duct, poor heat distribution (driver's feet get cold), an inoperative cruise control or brake/transmission interlock, engine oil leaks, doors won't stay open on slight grades, noisy fuel pumps, faulty engine oil pumps, 4.6L engines may run roughly, miss, surge or hesitate, and parking brake binds.

Safety summary/recalls: Researchers crash tested an '86 two-door Eldorado and concluded that only the passenger would sustain severe leg trauma. Crash tests of a 1980 Seville concluded that the driver would have sustained severe leg injuries. A retested airbag-equipped '92 Seville gave excellent crash protection to both the driver and passenger. The 1994 Seville's airbags are coming under close scrutiny from NHTSA investigators; they are looking into reports of injuries from dash trim panels flying apart when the airbag is deployed. Owners report that the throttle may stick in the open or closed position. Dealers will modify the throttle control cable to secure it in place. Drivers also complain that the shoulder belt chafes the neck and the Eldorado's wide rear pillars obstruct the driver's view to the right rear. *Recalls:* See comments on Riviera and Toronado.

Secret Warranties/Service Tips/DSBs

1990-94 A rear suspension squawk can be eliminated by installing upgraded stabilizer shaft insulators.

1993 DSB 476506 gives lots of tips on fixing 4.6L engines that run roughly, miss, surge or hesitate.

1993-94 Accessory drive belt noise may require the installation of an upgraded serpentine belt.

• DSB 476003 goes into great detail troubleshooting the various engine oil leaks afflicting 1993-94 models.

• Noisy fuel pumps can be silenced only by installing an upgraded fuel pump under warranty.

• Poor heat distribution (driver's feet get cold) can be fixed by replacing the floor outlet assembly.

1994 Condensation dripping from the heater duct requires the installation of a watertight dam in the HVAC case.

• An inoperative cruise control or brake/transmission interlock may signal a misadjusted stoplamp switch assembly.

• A binding parking brake may need a new park brake vacuum release switch.

Vehicle Profile

	1987	1988	1989	1990	1991	1992	1993	1994
Cost Price ($)								
Allanté	77,475	81,235	83,178	88,857	69,998	74,198	71,998	—
Eldorado	34,278	37,388	40,498	42,935	39,198	39,840	40,998	46,498
Seville	37,899	41,175	44,450	46,856	42,598	42,640	44,488	49,998
Used Values ($)								
Allanté ↑	13,000	16,000	19,700	28,000	36,000	39,000	44,000	—
Allanté ↓	11,000	14,000	18,100	24,300	33,000	37,000	40,000	—
Eldorado ↑	6700	8100	10,400	14,200	17,600	23,000	26,000	31,100
Eldorado ↓	5500	5300	7500	11,000	14,300	19,800	22,600	27,500
Seville ↑	9000	11,000	13,500	15,000	16,900	23,400	26,600	34,000
Seville ↓	7000	8000	10,500	12,000	13,600	20,000	25,100	30,000
Reliability	②	②	②	②	②	②	②	②
Air conditioning	②	②	③	③	④	④	④	④
Automatic trans.	②	②	②	②	②	③	③	④
Body integrity	②	②	②	②	③	③	③	③
Braking system	②	②	②	②	③	③	③	③
Electrical system	②	②	②	②	②	②	②	③
Engines	③	③	③	③	③	③	③	②

Exhaust/Converter	②	②	②	②	③	③	④	④
Fuel system	②	②	②	③	③	③	③	③
Ignition system	②	②	③	③	③	③	③	③
Rust/Paint	②	②	②	②	③	③	③	③
Steering	②	②	②	②	②	④	④	④
Suspension	②	②	②	②	②	②	③	③
Dealer Service	③	③	③	③	③	③	③	③
Maintenance	②	②	②	②	②	②	③	③
Parts Availability	③	③	③	③	③	③	③	③
Repair Costs	②	②	②	②	②	③	③	③
Crash Safety								
Eldorado	②	②	②	②	②	②	②	②
Seville	❶	❶	❶	❶	❶	⑤	⑤	⑤
Safety Features								
ABS	O	O	O	O	S	S	S	S
Airbag	—	—	—	D	D	D	D/P	D/P
Traction control	—	—	—	—	—	—	—	S

Concours, DeVille, Fleetwood (FWD)

Rating: Below Average buy (1990-94); Not Recommended (1985-89).

Price analysis: Limited availability and fairly expensive. The 1991 models combine the highest depreciation, lowest base price and least wear and tear. Expect to pay about $500 annually for maintenance and repairs during the warranty period and $900 annually thereafter. Somewhat surprisingly, the DeVille's accident repair costs are much lower than average. Other luxury cars worth considering: BMW 300 or 500 series • Chrysler New Yorker/Fifth Avenue (rwd) • Ford LTD Crown Victoria, Marquis or Grand Marquis • Lexus ES 250 or ES 400 • Mazda 929 • Mercedes-Benz 300 series • Nissan Maxima • Toyota Cressida and Camry V6 • Volvo 850.

Technical Data

ENGINES	Litres/CID	HP	MPG	Model Years
OHV V8 FI	4.1/249	130	16-20	1985-87
OHV V6D FI	4.3/262	85	21-25	1985
OHV V8 FI	4.5/273	155	15-19	1988-89
OHV V8 FI	4.5/273	180	15-19	1990
OHV V8 FI	4.6/279	270-275	16-20	1994-95
OHV V8 FI	4.9/300	200	16-20	1991-95

Strengths and weaknesses: Better handling and almost as comfortable as the old series, these cars are not worth considering because of dismal reliability and overly complex servicing. Many were sold with optional anti-lock brakes. The 4.1L aluminum V8 and 4-speed automatic transmission suffer from a variety of terminal maladies, including oil leaks and excessive noise. The electrical system and related components are temperamental. The suspensions go soft quickly and the front brakes wear out after 18 months/20,000 km. The digital fuel-injection and engine-control systems are very difficult to diagnose and repair. Poor body assembly characterized by premature paint peeling and rusting, excessive wind noise in the interior, and fragile trim items.

Bulletins confirm that the 1993 Cadillacs may have buzzing or whining 4L60 automatic transmissions, fuel tank popping during startup, a noisy cooling fan, a moaning power-steering assembly, rattles from the rear strut area, rear quarter-panel gaps, squeaks and squealing after a cold start, and whistling when the AC is in a recirculate mode.

Bulletins applicable to the '94 models (except Fleetwood) show the following problems: erratic shifting, engine accessory belt noise, an AC hissing noise, condensation dripping from the heater duct, poor heat distribution (driver's feet get cold), an inoperative cruise control or brake/transmission interlock, parking brake binding, engine oil leaks, doors won't stay open on slight grades, rear compartment water leaks, noisy fuel pumps, faulty engine oil pumps, 4.6L engines may run roughly, miss, surge or hesitate, and harsh Concours suspension performance.

Other service bulletins show the '93 Fleetwoods have noisy transmissions, power-steering units and cooling fans, the AC bi-level mode produces extreme temperature differences, instrument panel squeaks and rattles, rusting at the rear side door window molding and water leaks into the passenger side of the front compartment.

The 1994 Fleetwoods and Broughams may have instrument panel displays that are too dim. GM installed an upgraded cluster in mid-1994. Intermittent loss of power door locks, power seats, and mirrors is likely due to a short-circuit in the door lock circuit.

Safety summary/recalls: NHTSA crash tests of an '88 DeVille concluded that the driver would have received severe head injuries, and the passenger would have sustained serious leg trauma. When a 1990 DeVille was tested, only the passenger was judged to have sustained serious leg injuries. An airbag-equipped 1991 DeVille was judged to provide excellent driver and passenger protection. However, when a '93 and '94 DeVille were tested, the driver suffered serious leg injuries one year, and the passenger, the next year. NHTSA investigators are looking into reports of fuel lines damaged when they sag under 1991-92 models. *Recalls*: **1986**-Faulty headlight switch. **1986-87**-Anti-lock brake fluid may leak onto the pump motor and cause partial or complete loss of front or rear braking. **1994**-Engine oil cooler inlet hoses may be too close to the steering gear, causing it to leak, creating a fire hazard. **1994-95-**Accelerator pedal may stick.

Secret Warranties/Service Tips/DSBs

1988-93-If a fuel tank pop noise occurs upon startup, install a new, revised tank pressure control valve (#17089068).

1989-90-Excessive interior road noise can be reduced by installing a dampening kit (#25600885).

1991-94-Loss of Drive or erratic shifts may be caused by an intermittent short to ground on the A or B shift solenoid or an electrical short-circuit in the transaxle.

• A front-end clunking noise when driving over rough roads may require the repositioning of the diagonal radiator support braces.

1992-An exhaust rattle can be reduced by installing a larger volume muffler assembly.

1993-94-Accessory drive belt noise may require the installation of an upgraded serpentine belt.

1994-An AC hissing noise can be caused by a damaged, mislocated or missing refrigerant orifice O-ring.

• Condensation dripping from the heater duct requires the installation of a watertight dam in the HVAC case.

• An inoperative cruise control or brake/transmission interlock may signal a misadjusted stoplamp switch assembly.

• DSB 476003 goes into great detail troubleshooting the various engine oil leaks afflicting '94 models.

• Doors that won't stay open on slight grades require upgraded door springs.

• Noisy fuel pumps can be silenced only by installing an upgraded fuel pump under warranty.

• DSB 476506 gives lots of tips on fixing 4.6L engines that run roughly, miss, surge or hesitate.

• A binding parking brake may need a new park brake vacuum release switch.

• Poor heat distribution (driver's feet get cold) can be fixed by replacing the floor outlet assembly.

• Rear compartment water leaks are addressed in DSB 311510.

• A rear suspension squawk can be eliminated by installing upgraded stabilizer shaft insulators. (see table below).

Year	Series	Suspension Option	P/N
1990-1991	E	FE1	3545378
	E	FE2	3545380
1992-1994	E	FE1	3545376
	E	FE2	3545378

1994 Concours-Harsh suspension performance can be alleviated by installing upgraded struts, rear shocks, and recalibrating the RSS module.
• Rear compartment water leaks (see 1994 DeVille).
All models/years-Defective catalytic converters that cause a rotten egg smell in the interior will be replaced free of charge under the 5 year/80,000 km emissions warranty.

GM has had a serious rust/paint peeling problem with all its domestic-made vehicles. Original owners will get 100% compensation for paint peeling/surface rusting up to six years (see Bonneville entry).

Vehicle Profile

	1987	1988	1989	1990	1991	1992	1993	1994
Cost Price ($)								
DeVille	28,692	32,716	35,998	39,107	36,598	37,388	39,685	41,998
Concours	—	—	—	—	—	—	—	49,498
Fleetwood	29,794	33,640	37,698	40,827	37,598	37,389	—	—
Used Values ($)								
DeVille ↑	5000	6700	8500	11,500	14,500	18,500	22,000	28,300
DeVille ↓	3800	4600	5900	8500	11,500	15,200	18,900	24,800
Concours ↑	—	—	—	—	—	—	—	32,300
Concours ↓	—	—	—	—	—	—	—	29,000
Fleetwood ↑	6500	8000	10,900	13,100	17,500	22,000	—	—
Fleetwood ↓	5500	6500	8100	10,200	14,500	19,100	—	—
Reliability	②	②	②	③	③	③	③	③
Air conditioning	②	②	③	③	④	④	④	④
Automatic trans.	②	③	③	③	③	③	②	④
Body integrity	②	②	②	③	③	③	③	③
Braking system	②	②	②	②	②	③	③	③
Electrical system	②	③	③	③	③	③	③	③
Engines	②	②	②	③	③	③	③	④
Exhaust/Converter	③	③	③	③	③	③	④	④
Fuel system	②	②	②	②	②	③	③	③
Ignition system	②	②	②	②	②	③	③	③
Rust/Paint	③	③	③	③	③	③	④	④
Steering	②	②	②	②	②	③	④	④
Suspension	②	②	②	②	②	③	③	④
Dealer Service	②	③	③	③	③	③	③	③
Maintenance	②	③	③	③	③	③	③	③
Parts Availability	③	③	③	④	④	④	④	④
Repair Costs	③	③	③	③	③	③	③	③
Crash Safety	②	①	①	②	②	②	②	②
Safety Features								
ABS	O	O	S	S	S	S	S	S
Airbag	—	—	—	D	D	D	D	D/P
Traction control	—	—	—	—	—	O	O	O

DeVille, Fleetwood (RWD)

Rating: Average buy (1990-94); Below Average buy (1986-89); Not Recommended (1985).

Price analysis: Limited availability and fairly expensive. Expect to pay about $500 annually for maintenance and repairs during the warranty period and $700 annually thereafter. The DeVille's accident repair costs are much lower than average. Other rear-drive luxury cars worth considering: Chrysler New Yorker/Fifth Avenue (rwd) • Ford LTD Crown Victoria, Marquis or Grand Marquis • Mazda 929 • Mercedes-Benz 300 series • Nissan Maxima • Toyota Cressida and Camry V6 • Volvo 850.

Technical Data

ENGINES	Litres/CID	HP	MPG	Model Years
OHV V8 FI	4.1/249	135	13-16	1985
OHV V8 FI	5.0/305	170	15-19	1991-92
OHV V8 4 bbl.	5.0/307	140	15-18	1986-90
OHV V8 FI	5.7/350	175-185	13-17	1990-93
OHV V8 FI	5.7/350	260	14-17	1994-95
OHV V8D FI	5.7/350	105	20-23	1985

Strengths and weaknesses: The quintessential land yacht, these cars emphasize comfort over handling with their powerful engines and large chassis. On '85 models, lots of coolant and oil leaks afflict the 4.1L aluminum V8, the diesel engines self-destruct, and the 200-series automatic transmission taken from the Chevette is a disaster. From 1990 to 1994, the most serious problem areas are the fuel-injection system which frequently malfunctions and costs an arm and a leg to repair, automatic transmissions which shift erratically, a weak suspension, computer module glitches, and poor body assembly and paint defects. From a reliability/durability standpoint, these rear-drives are only slightly better made than their front-drive counterparts.

GM dealer service bulletins show the Fleetwoods have noisy power-steering units and cooling fans, the AC bi-level mode produces extreme temperature differences, instrument panel squeaks and rattles, rear quarter-panel gaps, rusting at the rear side door window molding and water leaks into the passenger side of the front compartment.

Safety summary/recalls: NHTSA crash tests of a 1985 four-door DeVille concluded that the driver would sustain severe or fatal head and leg injuries. An '88 DeVille was tested; once again the driver was judged to have received severe head injuries, and the passenger would have sustained serious leg trauma. When a 1990 DeVille was tested, only the passenger was judged to have sustained serious leg injuries. An airbag-equipped '91 DeVille was judged to provide excellent driver and passenger protection. NHTSA investigators are looking into reports of fuel lines damaged when they sag in 1991-92 models. *Recalls*: **1984-88**-A sticking throttle could lead to sudden acceleration. **1986**-Vehicles with a 5.0L engine could also have a sticking throttle. **1987**-Cars equipped with an automatic transmission could start in gear or engage the wrong gear. **1993**-Passenger-side airbag may have a defective igniter.

Secret Warranties/Service Tips/DSBs

All models/years-Defective catalytic converters that cause a rotten egg smell in the interior will be replaced free of charge under the 5 year/ 80,000 km emissions warranty.

GM has had a serious rust/paint peeling problem with all its domestic-made vehicles. Faced with this, GM has set up a substantial slush fund to compensate owners. Original owners will get 100% compensation for paint peeling/surface rusting up to six years (GM's own internal documents confirm this in the Bonneville section of this *Guide*).

Vehicle Profile

	1987	1988	1989	1990	1991	1992	1993	1994
Cost Price ($)								
Brougham	29,866	34,061	37,781	39,816	37,298	37,488	39,988	41,798
Used Values ($)								
Brougham/Fleet ↑	5200	6700	8100	10,500	13,800	17,800	22,200	27,200
Brougham/Fleet ↓	3800	4300	5200	7700	10,900	14,900	19,500	23,800
Reliability	③	③	③	③	③	③	③	③
Air conditioning	③	③	③	③	③	③	③	④
Automatic trans.	②	②	②	②	②	②	③	③
Body integrity	②	②	②	②	③	③	③	③
Braking system	③	③	③	③	③	③	③	③
Electrical system	②	②	②	②	②	②	②	②
Engines	③	③	③	③	③	③	③	③
Exhaust/Converter	②	②	②	②	②	③	③	④
Fuel system	②	②	②	②	③	③	③	③
Ignition system	③	③	③	③	③	③	③	③
Rust/Paint	③	③	③	③	③	③	③	③
Steering	③	③	③	③	③	④	④	④
Suspension	②	②	②	③	③	③	③	③
Dealer Service	②	③	③	③	③	③	④	④
Maintenance	②	③	③	③	③	③	③	③
Parts Availability	③	③	④	④	④	④	④	④
Repair Costs	④	④	④	④	④	④	④	④

Crash Safety	❷	❶	❶	❷	⑤	⑤	⑤	⑤
Safety Features								
ABS	O	O	S	S	S	S	S	S
Airbag	—	—	—	D	D	D	D	D/P
Traction control	—	—	—	—	—	S	S	S

INFINITI

G20, J30, Q45

Rating: Above Average buys.

Price analysis: Hard to find and very expensive. A fully equipped Maxima, Accord, Camry or 929 are better buys. In fact, a fully equipped Maxima, Taurus or Sable will provide dual airbags, comparable highway performance and reliability and impressive crashworthiness for about half the price. Expect to pay about $200 annually for maintenance and repairs during the warranty period and $400 annually thereafter. The Q45's accident repair costs are much higher than average.

Strengths and weaknesses: By emphasizing sporty handling, the Infiniti takes an opposite tack to Lexus, which puts the accent on comfort and luxury. Still, the Infiniti comes fully equipped and offers owners the prestige of driving a comfortable, reliable and nicely styled luxury car. One serious weakness, however, is the 1993 airbag-equipped J30's poor crash rating—all the more surprising when one considers that the 1992 Nissan Maxima passed the NHTSA 57 km/h crash tests with flying colors.

G20
The least expensive Infiniti, the G20 is a front-drive luxury sports sedan that uses a base 2.0L 140-hp, 16-valve, twin-cam, 4-cylinder powerplant to accelerate smoothly, albeit noisily, through all gear ranges. It does this while delivering 24 miles to a gallon of gasoline. Dual airbags came on line midway through the 1993 model year, and ABS is standard. Towing capacity is 1000 pounds. Cruise control is a bit erratic, particularly when traversing hilly terrain. The automatic transmission is silent and engine power is reduced automatically when shifting. Steering is precise and responsive under all conditions. However, the rear end tends to swing out sharply following abrupt steering changes. Early Infinitis rode a bit too firmly, leading to a softening of the suspension on the '94 model. Now drivers say the suspension tends to bounce and jiggle occupants whenever the car goes over uneven pavement or the load is increased.

Overall, however, the Infiniti models are not as refined as the Lexus in interior space, drivetrain or convenience features. Owners have complained that the engine's lack of low-speed torque means it has to work hard above 4000 rpm—while protesting noisily—to produce brisk engine response in the higher gear ranges. The automatic transmission shifts roughly, particularly when passing (a problem corrected with the '94 models), the power steering needs more assist during parking maneuvers, and the dealer-installed fog lamps cost an exorbitant $500 to replace. Poorly thought-out control layout is best exemplified by the hard-to-reach heat/vent controls, an armrest-mounted trunk and filler release that's inconvenient to operate, and center console-mounted power window switches that are hard to find while driving. Tall drivers will find legroom insufficient. The trunk is spacious, but its small opening is limited by the angle of the rear window. The temporary service tire is an anomaly for this class of vehicle.

J30

Resembling the 929 Serenia, the rear-drive, four-door J30 is sized and priced midway between the G20 and the top-of-the-line Q45. It uses a modified version of the Nissan 300ZX's 3.0L 210-hp V6 engine. Although the J30 is replete with important safety features and accelerates and handles well, its engine is noisy, passenger and cargo room have been sacrificed to styling, and fuel economy hovers around 16 mph in the city.

The J30 comes with a standard airbag, ABS and traction control, and has changed very little over the years—meaning there's no reason to choose a more recent model over a much cheaper older version. Consider buying an Acura Legend, Lexus ES 300 or a fully equipped Accord, Maxima, 929, Cressida or Camry.

Q45

This luxury sedan provides performance while its chief rival, the Lexus ES 400, provides luxury and quiet. Faster and more glitzy than other cars in its category, the Q45 uses a 32-valve, 278-hp, 4.5L V8 tire-burner not frequently found on a Japanese luxury compact. It accelerates faster than the Lexus—going from 0-to-60 mph in 7.1 seconds without a hint of noise or abrupt shifting. Unlike the base G20, though, the Q45's engine supplies plenty of upper-range torque as well. The suspension was softened in '94, but the car still rides much more firmly than its Lexus counterpart. The 4-wheel steering is precise, but the standard limited-slip differential is no help in preventing the car's rear end from sliding out on slippery roads, due mainly to the original equipment "sport" tires designed mainly for 130-mph Autobahn cruising. There's not much footroom for passengers and cargo room is disappointing. Fuel economy is nonexistent. ABS is standard but a passenger-side airbag wasn't available before 1994.

Owners report excessive wind noise around the A-pillars, sunroof wind leaks, tire thumping noise, cellular telephone echoing, faulty CD players and a popping sound coming from the radio.

Safety summary/recalls: Crash tests of a 1993 airbag-equipped J30 concluded that both the driver and passenger would sustain serious leg injuries. *Recalls*: N/A.

Secret Warranties/Service Tips/DSBs

G20
1990-A side door clunk noise requires new weatherstrips.
1991-An intermittent slip of the sunroof motor requires the installation of an improved motor assembly.
• Noisy shifting from 2-3 requires the installation of a countermeasure input shaft and an improved high clutch assembly with less free play.
• Reverse gear blocking can be corrected by installing an improved Reverse idle gear set.
1991-92-If the engine's timing chain rattles, install an upgraded chain tensioner (#13070-53J03).
• If the air conditioner emits a stale odor or blows out small white flakes, Infiniti will install an improved evaporator core that should correct the problem.
1991-94-Condensation may prevent the CD player from reading the CD. Only recourse is to wait until optic sensor dries (10 to 20 minutes, and longer for trunk-mounted players).
All models/years-Vehicles with sunroofs may have wind noise coming from the sunroof area caused by a small pinhole in the body sealer at the rear C-pillar.
Q45
1990-An idle vibration felt through the steering, floor and seat can be corrected by idle adjustments.
• Air and wind noise coming from the windshield, dash or A-pillar may be corrected by resealing the problem areas.
• The following noises require the following repairs according to DSB #ITB90-039: valve ticking—replace valves/guides; front engine block knocking—replace tensioners; tapping from valves during warm-up—replace pivot/rocker; tapping from valves at all times—check cam bearings.
1990-91-Front suspension clicking may require that the shock absorber upper bushing be regreased.
• A driveline vibration or drone at moderate speeds can be eliminated by installing a new balance propshaft assembly.
1991-Reports of transmission overheating and failures have forced Infiniti to extend the warranty to 7 years/160,000 km to compensate owners whose transmissions have insufficient cooling and filtration. Furthermore, the company will install an external cooler and filter at no charge.

All models/years-Erratic operation of the power antenna requires that the antenna rod be replaced.

	Vehicle Profile			
	1991	**1992**	**1993**	**1994**
Cost Price ($)				
G20	24,300	25,275	23,440	26,440
J30	—	—	41,500	45,000
Q45	50,840	54,000	59,500	72,000
Used Values ($)				
G20 ↑	12,000	14,100	16,200	18,900
G20 ↓	9700	11,700	13,800	16,400
J30 ↑	—	—	27,800	32,000
J30 ↓	—	—	24,700	28,800
Q45 ↑	26,200	32,400	38,700	47,800
Q45 ↓	22,600	28,600	34,900	43,800
Reliability	⑤	⑤	⑤	⑤
Air conditioning	❷	④	⑤	⑤
Automatic transmission	③	③	③	⑤
Body integrity	③	③	③	③
Braking system	⑤	③	④	④
Electrical system	③	③	④	④
Engines	⑤	⑤	⑤	⑤
Exhaust/Converter	③	③	⑤	⑤
Fuel system	③	③	④	④
Rust/Paint	③	③	⑤	⑤
Steering	❷	③	④	④
Suspension	③	③	⑤	⑤
Dealer Service	⑤	⑤	⑤	⑤
Maintenance	③	③	③	③
Parts Availability	④	④	④	④
Repair Costs	④	④	④	④
Crash Safety				
J30	❷	❷	❷	❷
Safety Features				
ABS	S	S	S	S
Airbag	D/P	D/P	D/P	D/P
Traction control	S	S	S	S

JAGUAR

XJ, XJS and Convertible

Rating: Not recommended.

Price analysis: Fairly rare and very expensive. Expect to pay about $700 annually for maintenance and repairs during the warranty period and $1000 annually thereafter—all the more reason to buy a Jaguar with its original manufacturer's warranty. Other luxury cars worth considering: BMW 500 series • Chrysler New Yorker/Fifth Avenue (rwd) • Ford LTD Crown Victoria, Marquis or Grand Marquis • Lexus ES 250 or ES 400 • Mazda 929 • Mercedes-Benz 300 series • Nissan Maxima • Toyota Cressida and Camry V6 • Volvo 850.

Strengths and weaknesses: None of the Jaguars listed below is an impressive performer, and as far as reliability and overall quality are concerned, companies like Lincoln, Volvo, Mercedes-Benz and BMW build better cars. Furthermore, the new benchmark cars for luxury and reliability are the Nissan Infiniti and Toyota Lexus. There is no reason—except for nostalgia and the need to look prosperous—to purchase any Jaguar.

Jaguar is owned by Ford but all of its cars are made in England. These rear-drives are offered as a 2-door coupe, 2-door convertible and 4-door sedan. Two engines are offered: a 4.0L 243 hp 6-cylinder and a 6.0L V12 unleashing 365 horses hooked to an electronic automatic transmission—made by GM. There's very little interior room, fuel economy is very low, the quality of servicing is spotty and—the biggest surprise of all—crashworthiness is lacking. Fortunately, ABS is standard and a passenger-side airbag was added in 1994.

Safety summary/recalls: N/A. *Recalls*: N/A.

Secret Warranties/Service Tips/DSBs

XJS
1990-91-Noisy AC blower motors require the installation of an upgraded motor.
• Frequent short trips can discharge the original equipment battery (Varta DIN 55). Install a Varta DIN 66 battery.
• Oil or coolant leaks from the rear of the engine or engine oil/coolant contamination may be caused by a leak in the cylinder head rear cover. Correct by installing the appropriate gasket (EBC 2568).
• Wind noise coming from the front doors is likely caused by the inner waist seals not contacting the door glass.
1991-94-Automatic transmission fluid leaks may be due to a blocked

transmission vent pipe.

• Engine power loss and stalling is addressed in DSB 18-38.

1994-Automatic transmission oil cooler leaks require the pipes replacement and the removal of the tie straps.

• Cylinder head gasket erosion requires an upgraded gasket and resurfacing of the cylinder head.

• Oil leaking from the generator bracket bolts requires the application of Loctite.

• AM band noise requires the re-routing of the antenna cable.

CONDITION	CHANGE	INTRO. VIN
Resistance build-up across Mass Air Flow Sensor connector	MAFS and harness connector pins gold plated	Sedan: 699043 XJS: 192404
EMS ground stud loose (Sedan only)	Tightening process assured	Sedan: 691370
HT tracking across ignition coil tower (Sedan only)	Ignition coil cover fitted	Sedan: 688765
Water ingress to ECM connector (Sedan only)	ECM drip shield fitted Plenum drain modified	Sedan: 683199 Sedan: 681967
EMS relay contacts contaminated	Cleanliness assured	Relay date code 183

All models/years-AC control panel vibrations and malfunctions require the installation of a service kit.

Vehicle Profile

	1987	1988	1989	1990	1991	1992	1993	1994
Cost Price ($)								
XJ	49,000	60,665	64,300	67,595	53,790	59,900	69,500	72,000
XJS	51,500	61,375	69,990	72,895	65,590	63,100	67,500	72,001
XJS convertible	58,900	69,375	84,750	87,895	78,990	89,300	76,000	87,000
Used Values ($)								
XJ ↑	9000	10,800	12,500	14,000	16,200	26,000	39,600	49,500
XJ ↓	6700	7700	8700	10,000	12,200	21,900	35,200	43,000
XJS ↑	11,000	13,200	14,300	18,000	24,400	30,000	40,000	49,000
XJS ↓	8500	9500	10,500	14,000	22,000	25,600	35,000	44,000
XJS convertible ↑	11,000	13,200	19,800	23,600	30,700	40,700	51,000	60,000
XJS convertible ↓	8000	9500	16,000	19,600	26,500	36,200	45,000	55,000
Reliability	❶	❶	❶	❷	❷	❷	❸	❸
Crash Safety	❶	❶	❶	❶	❶	❶	❶	❶
Safety Features								
ABS	—	—	—	—	S	S	S	S
Airbag	—	—	—	—	D	D	D	D

LEXUS

ES 250, ES 300, LS 400, SC 400

Rating: Recommended (1991-93). Reliable but overpriced.

Price analysis: Limited availability and fairly expensive. Used prices will soar if the U.S. taxes new Japanese luxury cars next year. Expect to pay about $300 annually for maintenance and repairs during the warranty period and $500 annually thereafter. A fully equipped Legend, Accord, Maxima, Camry, Taurus or Sable will provide airbags, comparable highway performance and reliability at far less cost.

Strengths and weaknesses: Like the Acuras and Infinitis, Lexus models all suffer from some electrical, body, trim and accessory deficiencies confirmed by confidential dealer service bulletins.

ES 250

The ES 250's 32-valve V8 engine gives exceptional, smooth acceleration and gets 19 mpg. The 4-speed Overdrive transmission makes subtle changes by reducing the engine power just before shifting. Trailers up to 2000 lbs. can be towed by cutting out overdrive. One of the best-riding front-drive cars money can buy, seating offers plenty of support and a comfortable driving position that can be automatically adjusted for two drivers. Braking and handling, though, are not very impressive.

ES 300

Resembling a LS 400 dressed in sporty attire, the ES 300 was launched in 1992 to fill the gap between the ES 250 and the LS 400. In fact, the ES 300 has many of the attributes of the LS 400 sedan for much less money. A five-passenger sedan based on the Camry, it comes equipped with a standard 3.0L, 24-valve engine that produces 181 horsepower coupled to either a 5-speed manual or 4-speed electronically controlled transmission. Unlike the Infinitis, the ES 300 accelerates smoothly and quietly, while averaging about 20 mpg in mixed driving. The suspension is soft and steady. Passenger and cargo room is plentiful with lots of legroom and headroom (except on sunroof equipped versions). ABS is standard, but a second airbag was only available on the '94 model.

LS 400

The Lexus flagship, the LS 400 rear-drive outclasses all other luxury sedans in reliability, styling and function. The base engine is a 242-hp 4.0L V8 that provides smooth, impressive acceleration and superior highway passing ability at all speeds. Its transmission is smooth and efficient. The suspension gives an easy ride without body roll or front-end plow during emergency stops, thereby delivering a major comfort advantage over other luxury compacts. There is an absence of engine and wind noise. Parts are reasonably priced. ABS and dual airbags are standard.

Owners have complained that the brakes don't inspire confidence due to their mushy feel and average performance. Furthermore, there's limited rear footroom under the front seats, and the rear middle passenger has to sit on the transmission hump. This car is a gas guzzler that thirsts for premium fuel.

Safety summary/recalls: NHTSA crash tests of a 1991 airbag-equipped Lexus ES 250 four-door have concluded that the driver and passenger would be well-protected. When a '94 GS 300 was tested, researchers concluded the passenger would sustain serious right leg injuries. *Recalls:* **1990 Lexus 400-**Cruise control may not return to its former position. Prolonged illumination of the center-mounted brake light.

Secret Warranties/Service Tips/DSBs

ES 250
1990-To reduce front brake squeaks, Lexus has changed the rotors (#43517-32020).
1990-91-Front brake squeaking can be reduced by using revised brake pads (#04491-32390).
1991-Cellular telephone antenna wind noise can be eliminated by installing a newly designed antenna.
• A cruise control that cancels after setting needs a filter circuit added to the cruise control ECU.

ES 300
1992-Inaccurate fuel gauges require an improved indicator needle.
1992-93-Sun visor rattles can be fixed by using the Lexus Squeak and Rattle Repair Kit.
• Rear brake squeaks can be reduced by using upgraded rear brake pads.
• Rear stabilizer bar bushing noise can be eliminated by installing upgraded bushings.
1993-Problems with hot start or poor engine performance when going downhill require the installation of an upgraded ECM.
• Front seat headrest rattles can be corrected by installing an improved headrest support.

SC 300/SC 400
1992-Popping from the Nakamichi radio has been eliminated with an upgraded model containing improved volume control resistors.
• To increase the durability of the leather material on the front seat outer side bolsters, install specially developed internal protector sheets between the bolster padding and outward seat frame on both driver and passenger sides.

LS 400

1990-Front brake popping can be corrected by installing a modified pad support plate and applying new adhesive.

• Moonroof wind noise may be corrected by realigning the roof panel.

• A rattling glove box door may be fixed by installing a felt washer on the check arm pivots at the side of the glove box door. A small piece of felt should also be glued to the through holes.

• Faulty cruise control assemblies will be replaced with an improved assembly (SSC 901).

• Warped center high-mounted stoplamp housings will be replaced free under a goodwill program (SSC 902).

1990-91-Hard rear door opening effort may be reduced by modifying the rear door check arm.

• To prevent transmission clicking when shifting from N to D or R, reduce the depth of the flange yoke assembly.

• Reduce side door wind noise by installing revised weatherstrips.

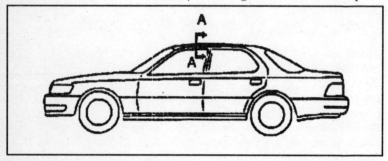

• To improve retention of the rear decklid trim cover, the trim clips should be changed.

• To improve the side mirror operation, the ECU must be changed.

• Windshield upper molding noise requires that the molding be changed and a thicker adhesive tape applied.

• AC groaning can be eliminated by reducing the expansion valve flow rate and adding an O-ring to the EPR piston.

1991-Cellular telephone antenna wind noise can be eliminated by installing a newly designed antenna.

Vehicle Profile

	1991	1992	1993	1994
Cost Price ($)				
ES 250	29,300	—	—	—
ES 300	—	34,400	37,300	41,300
GS 300	—	—	54,700	57,800
LS 400	57,000	63,000	67,200	71,100
SC 400	—	57,000	61,000	64,600
Used Values ($)				
ES 250 ↑	14,300	—	—	—

ES 250 ↓	11,800	—	—	—
ES 300 ↑	—	20,200	25,500	31,700
ES 300 ↓	—	17,500	22,800	28,900
GS 300 ↑	—	—	36,700	42,900
GS 300 ↓	—	—	33,700	39,800
LS 400 ↑	32,300	39,500	47,800	55,000
LS 400 ↓	28,500	35,000	43,600	50,600
SC 400 ↑	—	35,000	43,000	51,000
SC 400 ↓	—	31,000	39,900	47,000
Reliability	⑤	⑤	⑤	⑤
Air conditioning	④	⑤	⑤	⑤
Automatic transmission	④	⑤	⑤	⑤
Body integrity	④	④	⑤	⑤
Braking system	③	③	③	④
Electrical system	③	③	③	④
Engines	④	④	⑤	⑤
Exhaust/Converter	⑤	⑤	⑤	⑤
Fuel system	④	④	⑤	⑤
Ignition system	④	⑤	⑤	⑤
Rust/Paint	⑤	⑤	⑤	⑤
Steering	④	⑤	⑤	⑤
Suspension	④	⑤	⑤	⑤
Dealer Service	⑤	⑤	⑤	⑤
Maintenance	④	④	④	④
Parts Availability	④	④	④	④
Repair Costs	④	④	④	④
Crash Safety				
ES 250	⑤	—	—	—
GS 300	—	—	—	❷
Safety Features				
ABS	S	S	S	S
Airbag	D/P	D/P	D/P	D/P
Traction control	—	S	S	S

LINCOLN

Continental, Mark VII, Mark VIII, Town Car

Rating: Above Average buy (1993-94); Not Recommended (1986-92).

Price analysis: Limited availability and prices are on the high side. Expect to pay about $500 annually for maintenance and repairs during the warranty period and $900 annually thereafter—all the more reason to shop around for a Lincoln with some of the original warranty left. The Mark VII's accident repair costs are much higher than average. Other luxury cars worth considering: BMW 300 and 500 series • Chrysler New Yorker/Fifth Avenue (rwd) • Ford LTD Crown Victoria, Marquis or Grand Marquis • Lexus ES 300 or LS 400 • Mazda 929 • Mercedes-Benz 300 series • Nissan Maxima • Toyota Cressida and Camry • Volvo 850.

Technical Data

ENGINES	Litres/CID	HP	MPG	Model Years
OHV V8 FI	5.0/302	140-200	14-19	1985-95
OHV V8 FI	5.0/302	225	14-20	1988-92
OHC 1-6TD FI	2.4/149	115	22-27	1985
Town Car				
OHC V8 FI	4.6/281	190-210	14-17	1991-95

Strengths and weaknesses: These large luxury cruisers are proof that quality is not proportional to the money one spends. Several designer series offer all the luxury options anyone could wish for, but the two ingredients most owners would expect to find—high quality and consistent reliability—are sadly lacking, especially when it comes to the automatic transmission, electrical system, brakes, body hardware and fit and finish.

These cars are not lemons (at least the later models aren't), but they don't offer the kind of trouble-free driving one would normally expect in a new vehicle selling for over $40,000. The automatic-levelling air-spring suspension system makes for a a stiff ride (especially on early models), while still allowing the Continental to "porpoise" due to its heavy front end. The anemic V6 powertrain is poorly suited to a car of this heft. The engine hesitates in cold weather and the automatic transmission shifts roughly due to malfunctioning computer modules.

Major mechanical defects affect the engine (frequent flywheel replacements) transmission, ABS brakes, electrical, suspension, and steering systems, and electronic modules. The mass of electrical gadgets increases the likelihood of problems as the cars age. For example, automatic headlight doors fail frequently, and the electronic antenna seldom rises to the occasion. The computerized dashboard is particularly failure prone.

Most reliability complaints concern the 1985-92 models. Owners report transmission fluid leakage due to misplaced bolts and rough up-shifting caused by a defective valve body. The air conditioning and heating sometimes work in reverse order. You often get heat when opening the AC and air conditioning frequently comes on when the heater is engaged. Side windows on 1988 and 1989 models tend to fog up when carrying a few passengers. Persistent wind noise caused by defectively designed outside rearview mirrors and air leaks from the driver's door are commonplace.

Confidential dealer service bulletins show the '93 models may have poorly performing AC systems caused by a slipping clutch at high ambient temperatures and the AC FX-15 compressor may growl, the service engine light may go on for no apparent reason, and A-pillars may make cracking noises in cold weather. Power-steering units may be noisy and power door locks may not work. Frequent underhood squeaks, chirps and knocks are also mentioned. Premature wear on the inner edge of the rear tires can be corrected by a new camber kit.

Other bulletins show the 1994 models may have faulty 3.8L engine rocker arm assemblies that could cause squeaking, chirping and knocking. Other problems mentioned in these internal bulletins: inadequate AC operation caused by a faulty cold engine lockout switch and hose assembly and faulty electric rear window defrosters.

Safety summary/recalls: NHTSA crash tests of a '79 Continental concluded that the driver and the front seat passenger would not sustain serious injury. An '82 version was judged to produce collision forces sufficient to cause severe leg injuries to the driver and passenger. *Recalls*: **1986-87**-Vehicle may have detached body mounts at the rear corners of the car's subframe. This defect could allow the subframe to drop and make steering difficult. The mounts will be inspected and a reinforcement plate installed.

Continental (front-drive)
When the Continental went front-drive in 1988, it made a bad situation worse. The frequency and cost of repairs increased considerably and parts became more difficult to find. The automatic transmission continued to malfunction, particularly on 1988 models, electrical components became even less reliable, stopping performance was compromised by premature brake wear and rear wheel lockup, and body hardware continued to be secondclass.

Safety summary/recalls: From a safety perspective, the '91 model is the best buy. NHTSA crash tests of an '89 Continental concluded that the driver and the front seat passenger would sustain serious leg injuries. An airbag-equipped '91 Continental did remarkably better: both the driver and passenger were well-protected. Retested '93 and '94 versions didn't do as well: the driver sustained serious right leg injuries and the passenger had injuries to both legs. NHTSA safety investigators are looking into reports of power-steering fluid leakage and 3.8L engine fires on 1988-90 models. *Recalls*: **1988**-Body mounts will be inspected and a reinforcement plate installed. **1988-93**-Recall campaign #92-166 covers the cost of repairs needed to correct advanced front subframe fastener corrosion.

Lincoln Town Car
The rear-drive Lincoln Town Car is the best of a bad lot. Nevertheless,

until the '93 model year, it's still afflicted by the Lincoln's generic problems: transmission, AC, and electrical glitches and body hardware deficiencies. Nevertheless, thanks to its rear-drive configuration, it is relatively inexpensive to repair.

Service bulletins show the '94 Town Car may have a rough idle, hesitation, excessive fuel consumption and poor heater output that are likely caused by a thermostat sticking in an open position or opening before it should. Other problems include transmission shudder under light-to-moderate acceleration, noise in radio speakers caused by fuel pump malfunctions, and faulty electric rear window defrosters.

Safety summary/recalls: NHTSA crash tests of an '84 Town Car were disappointing: both the driver and passenger were judged to have sustained severe or fatal head injuries. Tests of a 1990 version concluded that the driver would sustain serious leg injuries; passenger results were inconclusive. An airbag-equipped '91 Town Car did much better: both the driver and passenger were well-protected. Retested '93 and '94 versions showed the driver's left leg would be seriously injured. Transport Canada and U.S. investigators are looking into steering failures caused by premature corrosion of the steering assembly on 1988-92 models and reports of the throttle linkage sticking on 1985-90 Town Cars equipped with 5.0L engines. One incident of "sudden acceleration" has been reported by the owner of a 1992 Town Car. Transport Canada is looking into the complaint. Although Ford promoted standard dual airbags on its 1990 Town Car, a supplier shortage didn't allow the dual airbags to come on line until the '92 model year. *Recalls:* **1990-**If the front seats move in their tracks or make noise, Ford will install new seat tracks and a memory track on the driver's side.

Secret Warranties/Service Tips/DSBs

Continental
1983-90-Buzzing or humming from the fuel pump when the engine is shut off, a low battery, and hard or no-starts signal the need to install an upgraded fuel pump relay (#F19Z-9345-A) in Continentals and Mark VIIs and Town Cars.
1984-94-A hum from the air suspension system can be corrected by replacing the compressor isolators with upgraded parts.
1985-91-An inoperative electric rear window defroster (heated backlights) needs a rear window defroster service kit.
• Squeaking from beneath the car can be stopped by installing two new bushing insulators.
1988-90-Hard cold start, hesitation, stalling during idle or when decelerating may be corrected by removing excessive sludge deposits or an oil film from the throttle body bore and plate, or the idler air bypass valve.

- High effort during wide turns at highway speeds signals the need to install a new power-steering short rack.
- The intermittent loss of the AC may be due to a defective suction accumulator (#E6VY-19C836-A). Change the accumulator, install a larger AC liquid line and a new 1992 condenser (#F2AZ-19712-A).

1988-91-Groaning power windows require that a Teflon lubricant (D2AZ-19590-A) be applied to the window regulator sliding surface mechanism.

- The in-tank fuel pump is the likely cause of all that radio static you hear. Stop the noise by installing an electronic noise RFI filter (#F1PZ-18B925-A).

1988-94-A squeak or chirp coming from the blower motor can be stopped by installing an upgraded blower motor with improved brush-to-commutator friction.

1988-94-A cracked forward clutch piston may cause forward/reverse problems. Install improved clutch piston.

- A speaker whine or buzz caused by the fuel pump can be stopped by installing an electronic noise RFI filter.

1989-A rough idle or lean fuel flow may require the installation of deposit resistant injectors under the emissions warranty.

1989-93-A persistent fuel odor in the interior when the AC is running signals the need to install a new auxiliary vapor tube kit and relocate the tube near the rear bumper.

1990-93-Noise heard from the power-steering pump may be caused by air in the system. Purge the system.

1991-Delayed transaxle 3-2 downshifts may require a new, more durable spring retainer clip (#F1DZ-7F194-A).

1991-94-A sloshing noise from the fuel tank when accelerating or stopping requires the installation of an upgraded tank. Cost is covered under the emissions warranty.

1992-94-A corroded solenoid may be the cause of starter failures. Replace the corroded connector with a service wiring and connector assembly.

1993-94-An inoperative AC blower probably needs an improved cold engine lockout switch and hose assembly.

- A slipping/sticking service brake pedal requires the installation of an improved brake booster.
- Stalling or hard starts in high ambient temperatures or high altitudes may be due to fuel tank contamination damaging the fuel pump. Ford will pay for a fuel tank flush and new fuel pump/sender and in-line fuel filter until May 31, 1997 under Service Program 94B48.

1994-95-A thumping or clacking heard from the front brakes signals the need to machine the front disc brake rotors. Ford will pay for this repair under its base warranty.

Mark VII, Mark V

1985-92-An exhaust buzz or rattle may be caused by a loose heat shield catalyst.

1986-90-The in-tank fuel pump is the likely cause of radio static. Install an electronic noise RFI filter (#F1PZ-18B925-A).

1993-94-A squeak or chirp coming from the blower motor can be stopped by installing an upgraded blower motor with improved brush-to-commutator friction.

• Automatic transmissions with delayed or no forward engagement, or a higher engine RPM than expected when coming to a stop are covered in DSB 94-26-9.

• A speaker whine or buzz caused by the fuel pump can be stopped by installing an electronic noise RFI filter.

Town Car

1983-90-A buzzing or humming from the fuel pump when the engine is shut off, a low battery, and hard or no-starts signal the need to install an upgraded pump relay (#F19Z-9345-A).

1985-91-An inoperative electric rear window defroster (heated backlites) may be caused by bond separation of the pigtail terminal to bus bar or broken grid lines. Install a rear window defroster service kit.

1985-92-A buzz or rattle from the exhaust system may be caused by a loose heat shield catalyst.

1986-88-Reduce front disc brake squeal by installing upgraded pads (#E8AZ-2001-B).

1987-90-Excessive oil consumption is likely caused by leaking gaskets, poor sealing of the lower intake manifold, defective intake and exhaust valve stem seals or worn piston rings. Install new guide mounted valve stem seals for a more positive fit and new piston rings with improved oil control.

1989-90-No Overdrive or an extended 3-4 shift may require the installation of a new Overdrive band, transmission separator plate kit, overhaul kit and reverse drum.

1990-A no-start condition may be caused by a defective Neutral start switch.

• A pull to the right when braking can be corrected by installing a new brake pad and lining kit (#F1VY-20001-A).

1990-92-Brake pedal and steering vibration when braking can be reduced by installing improved rotors (#F1VY-1125-A) and linings (#F3AZ-2001-A).

1990-94-A hum from the air suspension system can be corrected by replacing the compressor isolators with upgraded parts.

1992-94-Automatic transmissions with delayed or no forward engagement, or a higher engine rpm than expected when coming to a stop, are covered in DSB 94-26-9.

• A moan or hooting noise coming from the engine compartment of cars equipped with the 4.6L engine can be corrected by installing a new air idle bypass tube and resonator assembly.

1993-94-A speaker whine or buzz caused by the fuel pump can be stopped by installing an electronic noise RFI filter.

All models/years-Stalling at idle, poor fuel economy and inadequate heating can all be traced to the thermostat being stuck in a partially open position (DSB 86-17-12). A rotten egg odor coming from the exhaust is the result of a malfunctioning catalytic converter.

Two components that benefit from Ford's "goodwill" warranty extensions are fuel pumps and computer modules that govern engine, fuel injection, and transmission functions. If Ford balks at refunding your money for a faulty computer module, apply the 5 year/80,000 km emissions warranty. Ford will pay 100% toward the correction of paint defects during the first 5 years/80,000 km and 50% up to the seventh year of ownership in keeping with the policy it adopted to cover pickups. Water leaks into the vehicle interior will be corrected without charge up to the fifth year of ownership. All of these programs include second owners.

Vehicle Profile

	1987	1988	1989	1990	1991	1992	1993	1994
Cost Price ($)								
Mark VII/V	33,200	38,825	40,437	42,313	38,895	41,010	43,968	47,995
Used Values ($)								
Mark VII/V ↑	6100	7600	9700	12,700	16,400	20,700	27,400	31,300
Mark VII/V ↓	4500	5400	6800	9800	13,300	17,300	23,900	27,700
Reliability	②	②	②	②	②	③	④	④
Air conditioning	②	②	②	②	③	③	③	③
Automatic trans.	③	③	③	③	③	③	③	③
Body integrity	②	②	②	②	③	③	③	③
Braking system	②	②	②	②	②	②	③	④
Electrical system	②	②	②	②	②	②	③	③
Engines	③	④	④	③	③	④	④	⑤
Exhaust/Converter	②	②	②	③	④	④	④	⑤
Fuel system	②	③	③	③	③	③	③	④
Ignition system	③	③	③	③	③	③	③	④
Rust/Paint	③	③	③	③	④	④	④	⑤
Steering	③	②	②	③	④	④	④	⑤
Suspension	②	②	②	②	③	④	④	④
Dealer Service	③	③	③	③	④	④	④	④
Maintenance	③	③	③	③	③	③	③	④
Parts Availability	④	④	④	④	④	④	④	④
Repair Costs	③	④	④	④	④	④	④	④
Crash Safety								
Continental	①	—	—	—	—	—	—	—
Safety Features								
ABS	S	S	S	S	S	S	S	S
Airbag	—	—	—	D	D	D/P	D/P	D/P

Vehicle Profile

	1988	1989	1990	1991	1992	1993	1994
Cost Price ($)							
Continental	38,320	41,003	42,550	38,495	37,895	38,842	40,295
Used Values ($)							
Continental ↑	8200	9400	12,100	15,000	18,600	22,200	25,900
Continental ↓	6500	7500	9000	11,800	15,100	18,700	22,300
Reliability	2	2	2	2	2	3	3
Air conditioning	2	2	2	2	2	3	3
Automatic transmission	2	2	2	2	3	3	3
Body integrity	2	2	2	2	3	3	3
Braking system	2	2	2	2	2	3	3
Electrical system	2	2	2	2	2	2	3
Engines	3	3	3	4	4	4	4
Exhaust/Converter	3	3	4	4	5	5	5
Fuel system	3	3	3	3	3	3	3
Ignition system	3	3	3	3	3	4	4
Rust/Paint	2	2	3	4	4	4	4
Steering	2	2	3	3	4	4	4
Suspension	2	2	2	2	3	4	4
Dealer Service	2	2	2	3	3	4	4
Maintenance	2	2	3	4	4	4	4
Parts Availability	2	2	3	3	3	3	3
Repair Costs	2	2	3	4	4	4	4
Crash Safety	1	1	1	5	5	1	1
Safety Features							
ABS	S	S	S	S	S	S	S
Airbag	—	—	—	D	D	D/P	D/P

Vehicle Profile

	1987	1988	1989	1990	1991	1992	1993	1994
Cost Price ($)								
Town Car	32,331	35,043	36,656	41,109	37,195	37,695	38,637	43,295
Used Values ($)								
Town Car ↑	6500	7200	9300	11,900	14,600	21,400	23,900	28,000
Town Car ↓	4400	5200	6500	9000	11,700	18,200	21,700	23,000
Reliability	3	3	3	3	3	3	4	4
Air conditioning	2	2	2	2	3	3	3	3
Automatic trans.	3	3	3	2	3	4	4	4
Body integrity	3	2	2	3	3	3	3	3
Braking system	3	3	3	3	3	3	4	5
Electrical system	2	2	2	2	3	3	3	3
Engines	4	4	4	4	4	4	4	4
Exhaust/Converter	2	2	2	2	3	4	4	5

Fuel system	③	③	③	③	③	③	③	③
Ignition system	③	③	③	③	③	③	③	③
Rust/Paint	③	③	③	③	③	③	④	⑤
Steering	③	③	③	③	④	④	③	③
Suspension	③	③	③	③	③	③	④	④
Dealer Service	③	③	③	③	③	③	④	④
Maintenance	③	③	③	③	③	③	④	④
Parts Availability	④	④	④	④	④	④	④	④
Repair Costs	④	④	④	④	④	④	④	④
Crash Safety	❶	❶	❶	❷	⑤	⑤	❷	❷
Safety Features								
ABS	S	S	S	S	S	S	S	S
Airbag	—	—	—	D	D	D/P	D/P	D/P
Traction control	—	—	—	S	S	S	S	S

MAZDA

929

Rating: Recommended (1994); Above Average buy (1991-93); Average buy (1988-90).

Price analysis: Average availability and reasonably priced. Expect to pay about $200 annually for maintenance and repairs during the warranty period and $500 annually thereafter. Other luxury cars worth considering: BMW 300 series • Chrysler New Yorker/Fifth Avenue (rwd) • Ford LTD Crown Victoria, Marquis or Grand Marquis • Lexus ES 250 or ES 400 • Mercedes-Benz 300 series • Nissan Maxima • Toyota Cressida • Volvo 850.

Technical Data

ENGINES	Litres/CID	HP	MPG	Model Years
OHC V6 FI	3.0/180	158	17-21	1988-91
DOHC V6 FI	3.0/180	190-195	17-22	1990-95

Strengths and weaknesses: The key word for the 929 is understatement: the engine is unobtrusive, the exterior is anonymous and the interior is far from flashy. In spite of its lack of pizazz and imprecise power steering, the 929 will accelerate and handle curves as well as the best large European sedans. The 929 has proven to be fairly reliable.

The car's main drawbacks are its limited interior room and trunk space. The driver's seat doesn't have enough rear travel for tall drivers and headroom is tight. Owners report some problems with premature disc brake wear, electrical glitches, exhaust system rust-out, electronic shock absorber durability, particularly with the 1989 and '90 models, and fit ad finish deficiencies.

Shocks are very expensive to replace. Manual transmission is not offered, and the automatic's many settings can be confusing. Furthermore, the transmission's lockup feature frequently cuts in and out. The rear end sometimes wants to slide out a bit on slippery surfaces, and the front end bounces around on bumpy roads. The optional automatic adjusting suspension does little to improve the car's ride or handling.

Safety summary/recalls: Crash tests of an '88 929 concluded that the driver would sustain severe leg trauma. The fuel tank is vulnerable in a rear-end collision, and there is no shift lock to prevent sudden acceleration. NHTSA safety investigators are looking into complaints of 1988-89 door handles falling off and allowing the doors to open accidently when the windows are lowered. ABS is optional since 1989 (standard on the '90 929S). *Recalls*: **1988-91**-Mazda will replace door handles with handles that won't break as easily.

Secret Warranties/Service Tips/DSBs

1988-Changing the front disc plates will prevent brake chatter.
1988-89-Rough idling or stalling in temperatures below zero can be fixed by using regular unleaded fuel and replacing the ECU (#JEY618881R).
• Insufficient alternator output may require switching to a 70-amp alternator.
• Chronic rear brake squeal can be eliminated by installing upgraded rear pads (#HF392648ZA).
1988-91-Cold engine piston slapping requires replacement pistons to fix the problem.
• Constant brake pulsation or shudder is likely caused by an uneven rotor surface or excessive rotor run-out.
• Hard shifting after cold weather starts can be corrected by installing upgraded synchronizer rings and clutch hub assemblies.
1989-To provide a better ride, Mazda has modified the bushing assembly to reduce shudder and make for a more comfortable ride. The new assembly part is #H260-34-230C.
1988-92-Valve train noise occurring just after startup may be caused by air trapped in the hydraulic lash adjuster. Correct by installing redesigned rocker arm shafts that promote better oil flow.
1990-A power seat that won't adjust up or down smoothly likely has a broken gear in the seat motor. Correct by replacing the power unit.
1990-91-Difficult starts in hot weather can be corrected by installing an upgraded cold start thermo-switch (#JE27-18-870).

1992-94-Freezing door and hatch lock cylinders are addressed in DSB 021/94.

All models/years-DSB 006/94 covers all the possible causes and remedies for excessive vibrations when braking.

• Split or warped door trim should be replaced with an upgraded and reinforced trim panel.

• Water intrusion into the lock actuator connectors may cause the unintended operation of the rear defroster.

Vehicle Profile

	1988	1989	1990	1991	1992	1993	1994
Cost Price ($)							
Sedan	27,538	31,888	32,708	31,158	35,238	38,550	40,295
Used Values ($)							
Sedan ↑	6600	8300	11,700	13,700	20,000	22,800	28,500
Sedan ↓	5000	6200	9600	11,500	17,700	20,500	26,000
Reliability	②	③	③	④	⑤	⑤	⑤
Air conditioning	④	④	⑤	⑤	⑤	⑤	⑤
Automatic transmission	③	③	③	④	④	⑤	⑤
Body integrity	②	②	②	②	②	②	③
Braking system	②	②	②	②	②	②	②
Electrical system	②	②	②	②	④	④	④
Engines	②	③	③	④	⑤	④	④
Exhaust/Converter	②	②	②	③	③	④	⑤
Fuel system	③	③	③	④	③	④	④
Ignition system	②	③	④	⑤	⑤	⑤	⑤
Rust/Paint	③	③	③	③	⑤	⑤	⑤
Steering	③	③	③	③	④	⑤	⑤
Suspension	②	②	②	③	④	⑤	⑤
Dealer Service	③	③	③	④	④	④	④
Maintenance	③	④	④	④	④	⑤	⑤
Parts Availability	⑤	⑤	⑤	⑤	⑤	⑤	⑤
Repair Costs	③	③	③	④	⑤	⑤	⑤
Crash Safety	②	②	②	②	②	②	②
Safety Features							
ABS	—	O	S	S	S	S	S
Airbag	—	—	—	—	D/P	D/P	D/P

MERCEDES-BENZ

190E 2.3, 190E 2.6, 190D, C220, C280

Rating: Above Average buy (1994); Average buy (1993); Below Average buy (1986-92). Although these cars are above average in reliability and comfort, they are way overpriced and overrated.

Price analysis: Limited availability and fairly expensive. Parts supply and servicing have become problematic now that the 190 series has been off the market for almost three years. The '94 models were renamed the C-class and gained interior room and more powerful engines. Expect to pay about $900 annually for maintenance and repairs. Other luxury cars worth considering: BMW 300 and 500 series • Chrysler New Yorker/Fifth Avenue (rwd) • Ford LTD Crown Victoria, Marquis or Grand Marquis • Lexus ES 250 or ES 400 • Mazda 929 • Nissan Maxima • Toyota Cressida • Volvo 850.

Strengths and weaknesses: The standard 2.6L 6-cylinder motor is a real powerhouse in this small car, and its power is used effectively when coupled to the 5-speed manual transmission. The 4-speed automatic is a big disappointment it requires a lot of throttle effort to downshift and prefers to start out in 2nd gear. The '94 versions add much-needed horsepower, but the manual 5-speed transmission that would set those extra horses free is discontinued. Rear seat room is limited and there's lots of road noise intrusion into the passenger compartment.

The 190's reliability is a notch below that of other Mercedes. Owners report frequent problems with brakes, air-conditioning and electrical systems, and fit and finish.

Safety summary/recalls: Crash tests of a 1990 190E four-door have concluded that the driver would sustain severe leg injuries. An airbag-equipped 1991 190E 2.6 four-door showed, surprisingly, that the driver would probably have sustained severe or fatal chest injuries. *Recalls*: N/A.

Secret Warranties/Service Tips/DSBs

1989-92-Excessive oil consumption may be corrected by replacing the valve stem seals with upgraded Viton seals.
1990-91-A jerking that occurs when driving downhill with the cruise control engaged can be corrected by installing a relay to disable the deceleration fuel shut-off switch.
All models/years-Excessive engine valve train noise may be caused by

a stretched timing chain. After 48,000 km, the camshaft and timing chain drive should be checked carefully, especially if excessive noise is heard.

Vehicle Profile

	1987	1988	1989	1990	1991	1992	1993	1994
Cost Price ($)								
190E 2.3	37,400	41,425	—	—	36,700	38,150	38,050	—
190E 2.6	42,950	47,610	45,900	46,950	43,500	45,250	45,050	—
190D 2.5	37,401	41,426	43,900	—	—	—	—	—
C220	—	—	—	—	—	—	—	34,350
C280	—	—	—	—	—	—	—	47,650
Used Values ($)								
190E 2.3 ↑	9000	11,400	—	—	16,600	19,600	23,000	—
190E 2.3 ↓	7500	9600	—	—	13,600	16,300	20,000	—
190E 2.6 ↑	9800	12,800	14,800	17,600	20,600	24,200	28,500	—
190E 2.6 ↓	8500	10,200	12,000	14,500	17,600	21,000	25,300	—
190D 2.5 ↑	8800	9700	11,500	—	—	—	—	—
190D 2.5 ↓	7600	7400	8700	—	—	—	—	—
C220 ↑	—	—	—	—	—	—	—	25,000
C220 ↓	—	—	—	—	—	—	—	21,800
C280 ↑	—	—	—	—	—	—	—	35,000
C280 ↓	—	—	—	—	—	—	—	31,000
Reliability	②	②	③	③	③	③	④	⑤
Air conditioning	②	②	②	②	③	③	④	④
Automatic trans.	②	②	③	③	③	④	④	⑤
Body integrity	③	②	③	③	③	③	③	④
Braking system	②	②	②	②	②	②	③	④
Electrical system	②	②	②	②	③	③	③	④
Engines	②	②	③	③	③	③	③	⑤
Exhaust/Converter	②	③	③	③	④	④	④	⑤
Fuel system	②	②	②	②	③	③	④	⑤
Ignition system	②	②	③	③	③	④	⑤	⑤
Rust/Paint	③	④	④	③	③	④	④	⑤
Steering	②	②	②	③	④	④	⑤	⑤
Suspension	②	②	②	②	②	③	④	⑤
Dealer Service	②	②	②	②	②	②	②	⑤
Maintenance	③	③	③	③	③	③	③	⑤
Parts Availability	③	③	③	③	③	③	③	⑤
Repair Costs	③	③	③	③	③	③	③	⑤
Crash Safety	②	②	②	②	②	②	②	—
Safety Features								
ABS	—	—	S	S	S	S	S	S
Airbag	—	—	—	—	D	D/P	D/P	D/P
Traction control	—	—	—	—	—	—	—	O

260E, 300E, 300CE, 300D, E300, E320, E420, E500

Rating: Recommended buy (1993-94); Above Average buy (1988-92); Below Average buy (1985-87).

Price analysis: Limited availability and very expensive. The '94 models are referred to as E-class with the entry-level model a 300 diesel. This—and BMW to a lesser extent—is the carline that's likely to profit the most if U.S. tariff threats are carried out against new Japanese luxury imports. A 20 percent increase in used values is likely by the end of the year. Expect to pay about $700 annually for maintenance and repairs during the warranty period and $900 annually thereafter. Fuel economy (except for the diesels) is nonexistent. The SL series' accident repair costs are much higher than average. Other luxury cars worth considering: BMW 300 and 500 series • Chrysler New Yorker/Fifth Avenue (rwd) • Ford LTD Crown Victoria, Marquis or Grand Marquis • Lexus ES 250 or ES 400 • Mazda 929 • Nissan Maxima • Toyota Cressida or Camry wagon • Volvo 850.

Strengths and weaknesses: These cars are ideal family sedans. They are reliable, depreciate slowly and provide all the interior space the pre-94 190 series leaves out. Their only shortcomings are a high resale value that murders bargain hunters and a weak dealer network that limits parts distribution and makes servicing by independent garages almost impossible. The 300 series offers a traction-control system that prevents wheelspin upon acceleration—somewhat like ABS in reverse.

Another interesting feature is a 24-valve 220-hp high-performance version of the in-line 6-cylinder engine that powers the 300 series. All this has its price, though. If, ironically, you would like to drive one of these cars but are of an economical frame of mind, choose the 260E; it offers everything the 300 does but for much less. The 300CE is a coupe version, appealing to a sportier crowd, while the 300TE is the station wagon variant.

Owners report problems with the engine's cooling and electrical systems, AC malfunctions around the three-year mark, and body hardware glitches.

Safety summary/recalls: A 1984 300SD four-door was crash tested by the NHTSA and didn't fare very well; the driver was judged to have sustained severe or fatal chest and leg injuries. A crash-tested '94 C220 was judged to produce serious injuries to the driver's left and right leg and the passenger's right leg. *Recalls*: N/A.

Secret Warranties/Service Tips/DSBs

1987-92-Excessive brake vibrations can be reduced by installing upgraded Jurid 226 front brake pads.

1988-90-A gurgling heater core noise can be silenced by Mercedes' "gurgling kit."

1987-90-A cruise control that surges or maintains speed that's 4 to 6 km above the set speed may have a faulty amplifier or reference resistor gasket.

1990-91-Excessive exhaust noise between the exhaust manifold flange and rear muffler may be caused by a leak at the O$_2$ sensor or the clamped joints. If this is not the cause, change the catalytic converter.

Vehicle Profile

	1987	1988	1989	1990	1991	1992	1993	1994
Cost Price ($)								
260E	49,175	54,925	57,400	—	—	—	—	—
300E	44,800	60,950	66,400	59,900	64,700	67,275	68,050	55,995
300CE	—	71,750	75,500	81,900	76,800	79,800	80,800	—
300D	54,700	—	—	—	—	58,551	58,550	—
E300D	—	—	—	—	—	—	—	55,995
E320 4-door	—	—	—	—	—	—	—	58,895
E420	—	—	—	—	—	—	—	71,000
E500	—	—	—	—	—	—	—	108,000
Used Values ($)								
260E ↑	13,000	15,800	18,300	—	—	—	—	—
260E ↓	10,500	12,300	14,700	—	—	—	—	—
300E ↑	13,000	17,500	19,500	27,000	30,000	34,700	40,300	46,400
300E ↓	11,500	13,500	15,300	22,700	25,700	30,200	35,800	41,800
300CE ↑	—	19,500	22,500	30,500	34,000	39,700	46,300	—
300CE ↓	—	15,500	18,500	26,000	29,700	35,200	41,800	—
300D ↑	12,500	—	—	—	—	31,000	36,000	—
300D ↓	11,000	—	—	—	—	27,700	33,000	—
E300D ↑	—	—	—	—	—	—	—	46,400
E300D ↓	—	—	—	—	—	—	—	41,700
E320 4-door ↑	—	—	—	—	—	—	—	50,000
E320 4-door ↓	—	—	—	—	—	—	—	45,800
E420 ↑	—	—	—	—	—	—	—	60,000
E420 ↓	—	—	—	—	—	—	—	54,000
E500 ↑	—	—	—	—	—	—	—	N/A
E500 ↓	—	—	—	—	—	—	—	N/A
Reliability	②	③	③	③	③	③	⑤	⑤
Air conditioning	②	③	③	③	③	④	⑤	⑤
Automatic trans.	②	③	③	③	③	④	⑤	⑤
Body integrity	②	③	③	③	③	③	④	④
Braking system	②	②	②	②	②	③	③	④
Electrical system	②	②	②	②	③	③	⑤	⑤
Engines	②	③	③	③	③	③	⑤	⑤
Exhaust/Converter	③	③	③	③	③	③	⑤	⑤
Fuel system	②	②	②	③	③	③	③	⑤

Ignition system	③	③	③	③	⑤	⑤	⑤	⑤
Rust/Paint	④	④	④	④	④	④	④	④
Steering	③	③	③	③	③	③	④	④
Suspension	❷	❷	❷	❷	③	③	⑤	⑤
Dealer Service	❷	③	③	③	③	③	③	③
Maintenance	③	③	③	③	③	③	⑤	⑤
Parts Availability	④	④	④	④	④	④	④	④
Repair Costs	③	③	③	③	③	③	⑤	⑤
Crash Safety								
300SD	❶	❶	❶	❶	❶	❶	❶	❶
C220	—	—	—	—	—	—	—	❶
Safety Features								
ABS	—	—	S	S	S	S	S	S
Airbag	—	—	—	—	D	D/P	D/P	D/P
Traction control	—	—	—	—	—	—	—	O

NISSAN

Maxima

Rating: Recommended (1992-94); Above Average buy (1985-91).

Price analysis: Good availability and fairly inexpensive. Expect to pay about $200 annually for maintenance and repairs during the warranty period and $400 annually, thereafter—surprisingly little for a luxury car. Other luxury cars worth considering: BMW 300 and 500 series _ Chrysler New Yorker/Fifth Avenue (rwd) • Ford LTD Crown Victoria, Marquis or Grand Marquis • Lexus ES 250 or ES 400 • Mazda 929 • Mercedes-Benz 300 series • Toyota Cressida and Camry wagon • Volvo 850.

Technical Data

ENGINES	Litres/CID	HP	MPG	Model Years
OHC V6 FI	3.0/181	152	17-23	1985-88
OHC V6 FI	3.0/181	160	18-24	1989-94

Strengths and weaknesses: These front-wheel drive sedans are very well equipped and nicely finished, but cramped for their size. Although the trunk is spacious, only five passengers can travel in a pinch (pinch, in the literal sense). The 6-cylinder engine, borrowed from the 300ZX, offers sparkling performance. Parts are fairly expensive, but mechanical reliability is better than average. Early Maximas are less expensive to buy, but more costly to maintain.

Minor electrical and front suspension problems afflict early Maximas. Brakes need frequent attention in all years. Newer models have a weak automatic transmission and ignition-system malfunctions. Owners report that the V6-equipped Maxima is particularly hard to start in cold weather due to the engine's tendency to "flood" easily. The engine is flooded by the cold start system unless it's left running for ten minutes. If the engine is shut off before that time, the only way to get the car started again is to replace the spark plugs. Replacement of the spark plugs and fuel-injection components only brings temporary relief. The cruise-control unit is another problematic component on more recent Maximas. When it is engaged at moderate speeds, it hesitates or "drifts" to a lower speed, acting as if the fuel line was clogged. It only operates correctly at much higher speeds than needed. Incidentally, a new fuel filter will *not* correct the problem, say owners. Additionally, warped manifolds are routinely replaced under a "goodwill" warranty. There may be a connection between the manifold's early wear-out and the cruise control malfunction. Presently, Nissan engineers are said to be looking into the problem. In the meantime, insist that Nissan's "goodwill" remain in effect until the problem is resolved.

Aluminum wheels corrode quickly and are easily damaged by road hazards. Many reports of surface rust and paint problems. Earlier Maximas suffer from rapid rust perforation on the sunroof, door bottoms, rear wheel wells, front edge of the hood and bumper supports. The underbody also should be checked carefully for corrosion damage. Premature wear-out of the muffler is a frequent problem covered by Nissan's "goodwill" warranty, where the company and dealer contribute 50 percent of the replacement cost.

Safety summary/recalls: Crash tests of an '85 Maxima four-door determined that the driver would sustain severe or fatal head, chest, and leg injuries. The passenger would also have had severe or fatal head injuries. A 1989 Maxima was tested and only the passenger was judged to have sustained severe or fatal leg injuries. The 1992 Maxima passed with flying colors. There have been 548 complaints of leaks in the fuel-injection system and 300 reports of engine fires caused by leaks on models built in the late 1980s. Nissan says owners should inspect injector hoses and connecting hoses every few years. *Recalls*: **1992-93**-Dealers will install a new airbag sensor so that the airbags won't inadvertently deploy whenever the car passes over a speed bump. **1993-94**-Loose wheel nuts on aluminum wheels could allow the wheel to fall away.

Secret Warranties/Service Tips/DSBs

1985-87-Off-idle hesitation or backfire may be due to excessive engine valve deposits.
• Door hinge noise can be eliminated by installing upgraded hinge pins.
• Improved brake pad material will cut brake noise and add to pad durability. Upgraded semi-metallic pads carry the Hitachi HP12 FE designation.
• Reverse gear grind with automatic transmissions can be stopped by installing a Reverse gear kit.
• A front inner shoulder belt guide will be provided free of charge to keep the belt away from the neck and face.
1985-91-Excessive brake noise can be corrected with upgraded front and rear pads, caliper pins and baffle plates.
1989-Insufficient heating may be caused by air bubbles trapped in the heater core.
• Ice-induced heater motor failure requires a new blower (#27200-85E02).
1989-91-Starting difficulties can often be traced to a connector not fully seated in the ECU.
1989-92-Nissan has developed a variety of brake pads to respond to a number of customer complaints regarding excessive noise when braking.
• Clutch shudder can be eliminated by installing an upgraded a pressure plate release lever.
All models/years-Defective catalytic converters that cause a rotten egg smell will be replaced free of charge under Nissan's 5 year/80,000 km emissions warranty. Vehicles with rust/paint peeling problems will be repainted free of charge up to 5 years/80,000 km. DSB BR94-002 looks at the many causes and remedies for excessive brake/steering wheel vibrations.

Vehicle Profile

	1987	1988	1989	1990	1991	1992	1993	1994
Cost Price ($)								
Base	22,987	24,988	28,989	26,900	22,790	23,190	24,690	25,690
Used Values ($)								
Base ↑	6100	7800	9100	10,400	12,500	15,400	17,900	20,500
Base ↓	4800	5800	7100	8300	10,200	13,000	15,600	18,000
Reliability	③	③	③	④	④	⑤	⑤	⑤
Air conditioning	③	③	④	④	⑤	⑤	⑤	⑤
Body integrity	③	③	③	③	③	④	④	④
Braking system	③	③	③	③	③	③	④	④
Electrical system	❷	❷	❷	④	④	④	④	④

Engines	④	④	④	④	④	⑤	⑤	⑤
Exhaust/Converter	❷	❷	③	③	③	③	⑤	⑤
Fuel system	③	③	④	④	④	④	④	④
Ignition system	❷	③	④	④	③	④	④	④
Manual transmission	❷	❷	❷	③	③	③	⑤	⑤
- automatic	❷	③	③	③	④	④	⑤	⑤
Rust/Paint	❷	③	③	③	④	④	⑤	⑤
Steering	③	③	③	④	④	④	⑤	⑤
Suspension	③	③	③	④	④	④	⑤	⑤
Dealer Service	④	④	④	④	④	④	⑤	⑤
Maintenance	③	③	③	③	④	④	⑤	⑤
Parts Availability	③	④	④	④	④	④	⑤	⑤
Repair Costs	③	③	③	③	④	④	⑤	⑤
Crash Safety	❶	❷	❷	❷	❷	⑤	⑤	⑤
Safety Features								
ABS	—	—	O	O	O	O	O	O
Airbag	—	—	—	—	—	—	D	D

SAAB

900 and 9000

Rating: Not Recommended (1985-94).

Price analysis: Limited availability and reasonably priced. Servicing is inadequate and will probably get much worse in the future. Already parts are costly and not easy to find outside major urban areas. Expect to pay about $500 annually for maintenance and repairs during the warranty period and $800 annually thereafter—a good reason to shop around for a Saab with some of GM's original warranty left. This may be easier said than done. Saab owners tend to keep their vehicles for a long time, which makes finding a recent used one difficult. Other luxury cars worth considering: BMW 300 and 500 series • Chrysler New Yorker/Fifth Avenue (rwd) • Ford all-dressed Taurus or Sable, LTD Crown Victoria, Marquis or Grand Marquis • Lexus ES 250 or ES 400 • Mazda 929 • Mercedes-Benz 300 series • Nissan Maxima • Toyota Cressida and Camry wagon • Volvo 850.

Technical Data

ENGINES	Litres/CID	HP	MPG	Model Years
		900		
OHC I-4 FI	2.0/121	110	21-24	1985-88
DOHC I-4T FI	2.0/121	160-175	20-25	1985-94
DOHC I-4 FI	2.0/121	128	21-26	1986-90

DOHC I-4 FI	2.1/129	140	20-25	1991-94
DOHC I-4 FI	2.3/140	150	19-24	1994-95
DOHC I-4T FI	2.3/140	185	20-25	1995
DOHC V6 FI	2.5/152	170	18-23	1994-95
	9000			
DOHC I-4 FI	2.0/121	125-130	20-23	1987-90
DOHC I-4T FI	2.0/121	160-165	19-22	1986-90
DOHC I-4 FI	2.3/140	150	19-22	1990-94
DOHC I-4 FI	2.3/140	170	19-23	1995
DOHC I-4T FI	2.3/140	200-225	17-20	1990-95
DOHC V6 FI	3.0/180	210	17-20	1995

Strengths and weaknesses: These Swedish-built luxury cars don't offer the refinement and ride comfort of most other cars in their class. They do combine, however, excellent handling and great interior ergonomics without all the bells and whistles found with domestic luxury breeds. Unfortunately, Saabs don't live up to the Swedish reputation for exceptional reliability and are quirky in design. Generally, the 900 and 9000 series have similar deficiencies affecting the engine cooling and electrical systems, brakes, automatic transmission and body hardware. The 9000 is assembled with greater care, but owner reports only show a marginal improvement in overall reliability and durability.

Turbos produce much stronger acceleration and better handling than other 9000s without compromising their overall reliability. Nevertheless, they should be approached with caution, because owner abuse or poor maintenance can lead quickly to turbocharger deterioration. Air conditioners and exhaust-system parts have a short lifespan, and leaky seals and gaskets are common. Rust perforations tend to develop along door bottoms and the rocker panels. The underbody, especially the floor, should be inspected for corrosion damage on older models.

Safety summary/recalls: Crash tests of a 1982 Saab 900 four-door found that the passenger would likely have severe or fatal head and chest injuries. An '88 900S two-door produced disappointing crash test results: the driver would have severe leg injuries and the passenger would sustain severe or fatal head and leg injuries. An '86 Saab 9000 four-door performed just as badly: the driver would have severe or fatal chest injuries, the passenger would sustain massive head injuries. A 1987 and 1993 airbag-equipped four-door Saab 9000 provided good injury protection, except for the driver's right leg injuries in the '93 crash test. Safety authorities have opened three investigations of the 900: on the 1988 model, the possibility that the driver-side bucket-seat bracket may fail, causing the seatback to suddenly fall backward; leaking fuel pumps on '90 versions; and reports that the fuel tank can be damaged by the in-tank fuel gauge and release vapor or fuel in

1990-91 models. 1986-91 Saab 9000s have had 35 reports of passenger compartment fires. *Recalls*: **1989 900**-Recall #274 provides for the free replacement of the fuel filter. **1994**-Front seats may not lock properly. **1994 hatchbacks**-Fatigue cracks could allow seat to suddenly fold backwards. **1985 900 Turbo**-Flexible fuel hose may leak. **1986 900 Turbo**-Steering shaft could pull out of joint. **1986-87 Turbo 900**-Fuel hose may rupture. **1987-88 Turbo 900**-Wiring harness may chafe creating a fire hazard. **1988 Turbo 900**-Front lower control arm may fail. **1989 Turbo 900**-Leaking fuel filter may create a fire hazard. Heater fan resistor may overheat. **1993 Turbo 900**-Front brakes very vulnerable to salt and slush which compromise braking. **1986 9000**-Wiring harness may short circuit creating a fire hazard. **1986-90**-Fire may ignite in console area. **1988**-Faulty cruise control may lead to unintended acceleration. **1988-89**-Fluid leakage may compromise braking effectiveness. **1988-90**-Fire may erupt in the backup light circuit. **1989**-Leaking fuel filter may create a fire hazard. **1991**-Car may be started in gear. **1992-93**-Dealers will install a new fuel-filler and fuel filler vent hose to prevent fuel leakage. Vehicles equipped with an engine oil cooler may catch fire in a collision. **1993**-Brake lights may operate erratically.

Secret Warranties/Service Tips/DSBs

900
1987-Uncomfortable seatback angle can be remedied with kit #4052866.
1986-88-Free adjustment and latches for the convertible top under a service campaign.
1987-88-Wiring harness chafing diagnosis and repair (DSB 12/88-1098).
1988-Radio rattling can be reduced by installing extra felt padding.
• Recall No. 272 provides for the free replacement of the lower control arm attachment bolts.
1988-91-Cold weather starting problems may be fixed with service kit #8819070.
1989-A new fuel pump feed hose and clamp may correct a no-start, stalling or power loss condition.
1990-91-A new valve and O-rings will correct starting problems caused by a sticking fuel pump check valve.
1993-94-Binding ignition switch contacts can lead to electrical failures.
1994-A-pillar wind noise is addressed in DSB 08194-0486.
• DSB 88/94-0480 lists the causes and remedies of AC malfunctions.

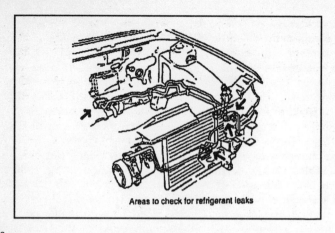

Areas to check for refrigerant leaks

9000

1992-94–A noisy climate control unit may have excess pressure building up at the fresh air intake.

1993-94–A stuck shift lever may be caused by a blown #3 fuse. A faulty sun visor/vanity mirror causes the short-circuit.

Vehicle Profile

	1987	1988	1989	1990	1991	1992	1993	1994
Cost Price ($)								
900	18,725	21,050	23,995	25,495	24,965	24,965	26,715	27,000
9000	31,495	34,525	36,895	36,995	33,680	31,795	33,875	35,000
Used Values ($)								
900 ↑	5200	7700	9200	11,100	13,000	16,100	19,500	23,000
900 ↓	4200	5800	7300	9000	10,900	13,900	16,100	17,000
9000 ↑	7500	9500	11,200	13,000	14,500	18,500	23,000	27,000
9000 ↓	6300	7700	8700	10,500	9000	16,500	20,500	22,000
Reliability	②	②	②	②	②	②	③	③
Air conditioning	②	②	②	③	③	③	③	③
Body integrity	②	②	②	②	②	③	②	③
Braking system	②	②	②	②	②	②	②	②
Electrical system	②	②	②	②	②	②	②	②
Engines	③	③	③	③	③	③	④	④
Exhaust/Converter	②	②	②	②	②	③	③	④
Fuel system	③	③	③	②	②	②	③	③
Ignition system	②	②	②	③	③	③	④	⑤
Manual transmission	②	③	③	③	③	③	⑤	⑤
- automatic	②	②	②	②	②	②	③	③
Rust/Paint	②	②	②	③	③	③	③	⑤
Steering	③	③	③	⑤	⑤	⑤	⑤	⑤
Suspension	③	③	③	③	③	③	③	③
Dealer Service	①	①	①	①	①	①	②	②

Maintenance	❶	❶	❶	❶	❶	❶	❷	❷
Parts Availability	❶	❶	❶	❶	❶	❶	❷	❷
Repair Costs	❷	❷	❷	❷	❷	❷	❷	❷
Crash Safety								
900	❷	❷	❶	❶	❶	❶	❶	❶
9000	⑤	⑤	⑤	⑤	⑤	⑤	❷	❷
Safety Features								
ABS 900	—	—	—	S	S	S	S	S
Airbag	—	—	—	D	D	D	D	D/P
Traction control	—	—	—	—	—	—	—	S
ABS 9000	—	S	S	S	S	S	S	S
Airbag	—	—	—	D	D	D	D	D/P
Traction control	—	—	—	—	—	S	S	S

TOYOTA

Cressida

Rating: Recommended (1989-92); Above Average buy (1985-88).

Price analysis: Good availability and reasonably priced. The price for a good used Cressida is likely to be very high, but 1990-92 models represent a bargain when depreciation and quality improvements are taken into account. Expect to pay about $300 annually for maintenance and repairs during the warranty period and $400 annually thereafter. Other luxury cars worth considering: BMW 300 and 500 series • Chrysler New Yorker/Fifth Avenue (rwd) • Ford LTD Crown Victoria, Marquis or Grand Marquis • Lexus ES 250 or ES 400 • Mazda 929 • Mercedes-Benz 300 series • Nissan Maxima • Toyota Camry V6 • Volvo 850.

Technical Data

ENGINES	Litres/CID	HP	MPG	Model Years
DOHC I-6 FI	2.8/168	156	17-23	1985-88
DOHC I-6 FI	3.0/180	190	16-23	1989-92

Strengths and weaknesses: The Cressida offers an excellent combination of performance, comfort and luxury. There is little to fault when it comes to overall reliability, and the engine is a model of smooth power. Surprisingly, the newer models are not as reliable and trouble free as the pre-1987 versions. This is due primarily to quality cutbacks in body and electronic components.

Two exceptions are premature front brake wear and excessive pulsation/vibration, both frequent complaints throughout the decade. Air-conditioning glitches and electrical short-circuits are commonplace. Exhaust-system parts rust quickly. These problems aside, Cressidas have shown themselves to be exceptionally reliable and repair costs have also been exceptionally reasonable, with good parts distribution.

Safety summary/recalls: NHTSA crash tests of an '85 Cressida four-door concluded that both the driver and passenger would sustain serious leg injuries. An 1989 two-door showed similar results. A '91 version performed very well: both the driver and passenger were well-protected. *Recalls*: N/A.

Secret Warranties/Service Tips/DSBs

1985-86-A 1-2 shift clunk can be fixed by installing upgraded parts listed in DSB 12-19-86.
1985-87-Excessive brake noise can be reduced with upgraded front and rear brake pads.
1985-88-Starter/ring gear clash can be corrected with an upgraded starter assembly (#28100-62011 or 62021).
1989-Speaker static when the power mirror is activated requires a noise filter in the power-mirror circuit.
1990-Toyota will replace at no charge Fujitsu players that scratch CDs.
1992-Panasonic CD players that skip or won't play were upgraded as of 6/93.
All models/years-Inoperative Panasonic cassette players may have defective gears controlling the tape head. Replace with a model using upgraded gears used after 11/91. Panasonic CD player have a similar problem with the optical pick-up and guide pins. Use CD player units made after 2/92. Moldings that fall off and faulty cruise control components will be fixed at no charge. Older Toyotas with stalling problems should have the engine checked for excessive carbon buildup on the valves before any more extensive repairs are authorized. The brake pulsation/vibration problem is fully outlined and corrective measures detailed in DSB #BR94-002, issued February 7, 1994.

Vehicle Profile

	1985	1986	1987	1988	1989	1990	1991	1992
Cost Price ($)								
Base	19,998	23,228	25,968	27,538	31,888	32,708	31,158	35,238
Used Values ($)								
Base ↑	4700	6000	7200	8200	10,500	11,600	14,800	18,100
Base ↓	3400	4800	5900	6800	8500	9500	12,400	15,700
Reliability	③	③	③	③	③	③	④	④
Air conditioning	❶	❶	❶	❷	❷	❷	③	③

Body integrity	②	②	②	②	③	③	③	③
Braking system	②	②	②	②	②	②	③	③
Electrical system	②	②	③	③	③	③	③	③
Engines	④	④	④	④	④	④	④	④
Exhaust/Converter	②	②	②	②	②	②	②	③
Fuel system	③	③	③	④	④	④	④	④
Ignition system	②	②	③	③	③	③	③	④
Manual transmission	③	③	③	③	—	—	—	—
- automatic	③	④	④	④	④	③	③	③
Rust/Paint	③	③	③	③	③	③	③	③
Steering	③	③	③	③	③	④	④	④
Suspension	①	①	①	②	③	③	③	④
Dealer Service	④	④	④	④	④	④	④	④
Maintenance	④	④	④	④	④	④	④	④
Parts Availability	③	③	③	③	③	③	③	③
Repair Costs	④	④	④	④	④	④	④	④
Crash Safety	①	①	①	①	①	①	⑤	⑤
Safety Features								
ABS	—	—	—	—	O	S	S	S

VOLVO

700 Series

Rating: Above Average buy (1992); Average buy (1991); Not Recommended (1986-90).

Price analysis: Limited availability and fairly expensive. Expect to pay about $800 annually for maintenance and repairs. Parts are sometimes hard to find. Other luxury cars worth considering: BMW 300 and 500 series • Chrysler New Yorker/Fifth Avenue (rwd) • Ford LTD Crown Victoria, Marquis or Grand Marquis • Lexus ES 250 or ES 400 • Mazda 929 • Mercedes-Benz 300 series • Nissan Maxima • Toyota Cressida and Camry wagon • Volvo 850.

Technical Data

ENGINES	Litres/CID	HP	MPG	Model Years
OHC I-4 FI	2.3/141	114	20-24	1985-92
DOHC I-4 FI	2.3/141	153	20-24	1989-91
OHC I-4T FI	2.3/141	157-162	19-24	1985-92
OHC V6 FI	2.8/174	134-145	17-22	1985-90
OHC 1-6TD FI	2.4/145	108	24-29	1985-86
DOHC 1-6 FI	2.9/178	181-201	18-22	1992

Strengths and weaknesses: The 700 series is more spacious, luxurious, and expensive than the 240 series. Its standard engine and transmission perform well, and it's more crashworthy than the 240 series.

On the downside, the 700 series suffers from the same generic brake, electrical, engine cooling, air conditioning and body problems as its cheaper cousin. Brakes tend to squeak or grind, wear rapidly and require expensive service. Exhaust systems usually need replacing after two years.

Owners complain of hard cold starts on 1987-89 models. Power windows fail to operate because of dirt getting into the mechanism or the wiring short-circuits. Air-conditioning units that emit a musty odor or fail to work properly when the car is idling are a common problem. Body and interior trim pieces are fragile— dashboard cracks often appear after the third year. The windshield wiper motor malfunctions after two years. Some complaints of sunroof rattles, premature surface rust (the paint chips easily) and rusted-out exhaust systems.

Safety summary/recalls: NHTSA crash tests of an '88 740 GLE four-door concluded that the driver would sustain serious leg injuries. A '91 740 four-door gave excellent crash protection to the driver and passenger. U.S. safety agencies are looking into incidents of inadvertent airbag deployment on 1991 models. *Recalls:* **1985**-Water pump pulley may be defective. **1985-87**-Possible engine wiring harness short-circuit. **1985-88**-On vehicles with B230F engines driveshaft could separate from the transmission. **1986 wagons**-Tailgate can be opened from inside the vehicle while locked. **1988**-Headlight switch may short circuit. **1989-90**-Fuel may seep from fuel tank. Cars are eligible for new fuel tanks . This correction is set out in a Volvo dealer bulletin that can be obtained from Transport Canada. **1992-93**-Faulty front seatbelts could detach from anchors.

Secret Warranties/Service Tips/DSBs

1987 (740) models-Popping from the radio is a frequent complaint addressed in DSB 39/106.

1988-90-Brake pulsation, a common problem, is addressed in DSB 51/111.

• If you're having problems starting your Volvo on cold mornings, see DSB 23/135 and 23/21A.

1989-90-Service Campaign No. 54 calls for the free installation of a cable harness.

1989-93-To improve cold starting, Volvo will install an improved fuel injection control module gratis, under the emissions warranty. Under another program, Volvo will replace the MFI E PROM to improve cold starting.

1990-91-AM band radio interference will be stopped with kit #3533250-1.

1992-Volvo Special Service Campaign No. 59 provides for the free replacement of AC pressure switches and harness, the Regina fuel control units, and Rex ignition control units. These repairs are to be carried out regardless of vehicle mileage or number of previous owners.

1992-94-A decrease in idling speed when the AC engages can be corrected by installing a capacitor kit.

All models/years-Check the valve cover nuts at every servicing interval to prevent oil leakage.

Vehicle Profile

	1986	1987	1988	1989	1990	1991	1992
Cost Price ($)							
740 GL	—	—	—	25,995	26,420	23,175	—
740 GLE	22,905	24,040	26,960	30,675	33,085	—	—
745	—	—	—	—	—	—	30,345
760 GLE	29,190	31,955	39,485	41,415	43,995	—	—
780 GLE	—	—	49,980	51,730	53,740	41,945	—
Used Values ($)							
740 GL ↑	—	—	—	9800	11,000	12,600	—
740 GL ↓	—	—	—	7700	8800	10,300	—
740 GLE ↑	5900	7200	8700	11,800	12,700	—	—
740 GLE ↓	5000	6100	7200	9500	10,400	—	—
745 ↑	—	—	—	—	—	—	16,000
745 ↓	—	—	—	—	—	—	13,600
760 GLE ↑	7300	9100	11,200	14,800	17,000	—	—
760 GLE ↓	6200	7600	8600	12,000	14,000	—	—
780 GLE ↑	—	—	14,300	16,300	18,000	22,300	—
780 GLE ↓	—	—	11,500	13,300	15,000	19,200	—
Reliability	3	3	3	3	3	3	4
Air conditioning	1	1	1	2	2	3	4
Body integrity	2	2	2	2	2	2	3
Braking system	1	1	1	1	1	1	2
Electrical system	1	1	1	1	1	1	2
Exhaust/Converter	1	1	1	2	3	4	4
Fuel system	3	3	3	3	3	3	4
Ignition system	3	3	4	3	3	3	3
Manual transmission	3	3	3	3	3	3	4
- automatic	2	2	4	3	3	3	4
Rust/Paint	3	3	3	3	3	3	4
Steering	3	3	3	3	3	3	3
Suspension	3	3	3	3	3	3	4
Dealer Service	3	3	3	3	3	3	3
Maintenance	3	3	3	3	3	3	3
Parts Availability	3	3	3	3	3	3	3
Repair Costs	2	2	2	3	3	3	3

364

Crash Safety	❷	❷	❷	❷	❷	⑤	⑤
Safety Features							
ABS	—	S	S	S	S	S	S
Airbag	—	—	—	—	D	D	D

850

Rating: Recommended (1993-94).

Price analysis: Limited availability and fairly expensive. New, these cars are reasonably priced, but their depreciation is so slow that used bargains are rare. Parts are less expensive than other cars in this class, according to the CAA. Expect to pay about $500 annually for maintenance and repairs during the warranty period and $400 annually thereafter. Other luxury cars worth considering: Acura Legend • Mazda 929 • Nissan Maxima GX • Toyota Camry. A fully equipped Taurus or Sable wagon would save you $6,000, is very reliable, performs just as well and is easier to repair.

Technical Data

ENGINES	Litres/CID	HP	MPG	Model Years
DOHC I-5 FI	2.4/149	168	20-27	1993-95
DOHC I-5T FI	2.3/192	222	19-25	1994-95

Strengths and weaknesses: Bland but practical to the extreme with plenty of power, good handling and plenty of capacity. The wagons use the same base powerplant hooked to a 5-speed manual or optional 4-speed electronic automatic. Both the wagon's and sedan's ride deteriorate progressively as the road gets rougher and passengers are added. Passenger space, seating comfort and trunk and cargo space are unmatched by the competition. Braking on dry and wet pavement is also exemplary.

So far, the 850 has escaped the traditional AC, electrical system and brake problems and body hardware deficiencies that afflict its predecessors. Owners complain that seatbelts are uncomfortable and there's insufficient rear travel for the front seats. One Edmonton, Alberta owner of a '94 GLT sedan complains that the rear suspension makes a clunking noise when the brakes are applied. Volvo dealer says it's normal. I don't think so.

Confidential dealer service bulletins show the following problems on the 1993 models: faulty engine accessory mounting brackets, electrical short-circuits, water contamination of the accessory drive belt, and poor radio reception on the FM band.

Safety summary/recalls: When a '94 850 was crash tested, researchers estimated that both of the driver's legs and the passenger's left leg would be seriously injured. **Recalls**: N/A.

Secret Warranties/Service Tips/DSBs

1993-A jerking sensation while accelerating may be caused by electrical interference between the RPM sensor wiring and the secondary ignition system.

• Accessory drive belt noise due to water infiltrating into the system can be corrected by installing a special right front fender liner extension made by Volvo to fix the problem.

• Headlamp wiper and washer motors may cause radio interference on the FM band. Eliminate this noise by installing suppressed wiper motors and a suppressor between the washer pump and the existing wiring.

• Under Service Campaign 62, Volvo dealers will install at no charge an improved engine accessory mounting bracket.

1993-94-Steering column spring noise can be silenced by using upgraded bolts to secure the upper bracket to the airbag retaining plate.

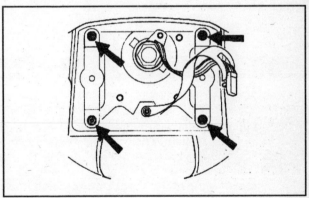

All models/years-Check the valve cover nuts at every servicing interval to prevent oil leakage.

Vehicle Profile

	1993	1994
Cost Price ($)		
GLT	29,950	29,095
Used Values ($)		
GLT ↑	19,000	22,000

GLT ↓	17,000	19,500
Reliability	⑤	⑤
Air conditioning	⑤	⑤
Automatic transmission	⑤	⑤
Body integrity	④	④
Braking system	⑤	⑤
Electrical system	④	④
Engines	⑤	⑤
Exhaust/Converter	⑤	⑤
Fuel system	④	④
Ignition system	④	④
Rust/Paint	④	④
Steering	⑤	⑤
Suspension	⑤	⑤
Dealer Service	④	④
Maintenance	⑤	⑤
Parts Availability	④	④
Repair Costs	⑤	⑤
Crash Safety	—	❶
Safety Features		
ABS	S	S
Airbag	D/P	D/P
Traction control	O	S

900 Series

Rating: Recommended (1991-94).

Price analysis: Limited availability and fairly expensive. Repair and maintenance costs are a bit higher than average. Expect to pay about $600 annually for maintenance and repairs during the warranty period and $800 annually thereafter—making it a good idea to shop around for a 900 with some of the Volvo warranty left. Other luxury cars worth considering: BMW 300 and 500 series • Chrysler New Yorker/Fifth Avenue (rwd) • Ford LTD Crown Victoria, Marquis or Grand Marquis • Lexus ES 250 or ES 400 • Mazda 929 • Mercedes-Benz 300 series • Nissan Maxima • Toyota Cressida.

Technical Data

ENGINES	Litres/CID	HP	MPG	Model Years
OHC I-4 FI	2.3/141	114	20-24	1991-95
OHC I-4T FI	2.3/141	162	19-24	1991-95
DOHC 1-6 FI	2.9/178	201	18-22	1991-95

Strengths and weaknesses: These flagship rear-drive sedans and wagons have a much better reliability record than the 240 and 700 series and are on a par with the 850 over the past four model years. Both the 940 and 960 offer exceptional roominess and comfort and are capable of carrying six people in comfort. The wagon provides lots of cargo space and manages to do it in great style.

Dealer service bulletins show the following problems on the 1993 models: hard starting and stalling caused by low fuel volatility, excessive vibrations when idling on vehicles equipped with an automatic transmission, and whistling from the bulkhead and wiper-well cover panel.

Safety summary/recalls: These cars have not been crash tested, but they come with reinforced sides that Volvo claims exceed federal regulations. American safety agencies are looking at inadvertent airbag deployment on 1991 models. The '93 960 model offers standard dual airbags. *Recalls:* **1989-90-**Fuel may seep from fuel tank. **1991 Turbo-**Throttle may jam . Child Car Seat may not conform to federal safety standards. 1992-93-Front seatbelts may detach from anchorage.

Secret Warranties/Service Tips/DSBs

1989-93-To improve cold starting, Volvo will install an improved fuel-injection control module free of charge, under the emissions warranty. Under another program, Volvo will replace the MFI E PROM to improve cold starting.
1992-Volvo Special Service Campaign No. 59 provides for the free replacement of AC pressure switches and harness, the Regina fuel control units and Rex ignition control units. These repairs are to be carried out regardless of vehicle mileage or number of previous owners.
1992-94-A decrease in idling speed when the AC engages can be corrected by installing a capacitator kit.
All models/years-Check the valve cover nuts at every servicing interval to prevent oil leakage.

Vehicle Profile

	1991	1992	1993	1994
Cost Price ($)				
940 GLE	27,885	33,275	29,995	26,995
Wagon	28,565	33,900	30,995	27,995
940 SE	33,775	—	—	—
Wagon SE	34,455	—	—	—
960	—	40,986	43,045	35,495

368

Used Values ($)

940 GLE ↑	15,300	18,000	19,500	21,000
940 GLE ↓	12,500	15,000	17,000	19,000
Wagon ↑	15,700	18,900	21,000	22,500
Wagon ↓	13,000	16,500	19,000	20,500
940 SE ↑	17,000	—	—	—
940 SE ↓	14,500	—	—	—
Wagon SE ↑	17,700	—	—	—
Wagon SE ↓	15,500	—	—	—
960 ↑	—	22,000	25,000	29,500
960 ↓	—	20,000	23,000	27,000
Reliability	⑤	⑤	⑤	⑤
Air conditioning	④	⑤	⑤	⑤
Automatic transmission	⑤	⑤	⑤	⑤
Body integrity	④	④	④	④
Braking system	④	④	④	④
Electrical system	③	③	③	③
Engines	⑤	⑤	⑤	⑤
Exhaust/Converter	⑤	⑤	⑤	⑤
Fuel system	④	④	⑤	⑤
Ignition system	④	④	⑤	⑤
Rust/Paint	⑤	⑤	⑤	⑤
Steering	⑤	⑤	⑤	⑤
Suspension	⑤	⑤	⑤	⑤
Dealer Service	④	④	④	④
Maintenance	④	④	④	④
Parts Availability	④	④	④	④
Repair Costs	⑤	⑤	⑤	⑤
Crash Safety	—	—	—	—
Safety Features				
ABS	S	S	S	S
Airbag	O	O	D/P	D/P

SPORTS CARS

Speed is essential for that sports car feeling, and the average model, like the Mazda Miata, should be able to go from 0-to-60 mph under ten seconds and top 80 mph at the end of one-quarter mile. Luxury sports sedans like the Infiniti Q45 and Lexus LS 400 have produced exceptional acceleration times of 60 mph in less than eight seconds and have exceeded 90 mph after one-quarter mile. Nevertheless, most sports cars, or "high-performance vehicles" as they are euphemistically named, sacrifice reliability, fuel economy, interior space and a comfortable suspension for speed, superior road handling and attractive styling. Sports cars come with a whole slew of expensive high-performance packages mainly because they are not very sporty in their basic form.

There are some exceptions, however. Toyota's MR2, for example, gives good fuel economy without sacrificing speed due to its light weight and powerful base engine; it's far more reliable than the average automobile and, best of all, it isn't that expensive.

Unlike the Japanese offerings, American-made sports cars are not very reliable or durable. The Mustang is the best of a bad lot, and GM's Camaro/Firebird models are more often in the repair shop than on the road. The less said about the unlamented Pontiac Fiero, the better.

The following used sports cars are recommended:

Chrysler Laser/Talon 4X4   Mazda MX-3, Precidia
Chrysler Stealth   Mazda Miata, MX-5
Ford Mustang (1993-94)   Mazda RX-7
Ford Probe   Nissan 240SX
GM Camaro/Firebird (1993-94)   Toyota MR2
Honda Prelude   Toyota Celica
Honda CRX

Mazda's '93 MX-3: a pocket rocket that doesn't need NASA's budget.

CHRYSLER

Daytona, Laser

Rating: Below Average buy (1990-93); Not Recommended (1984-89).

Price analysis: Excellent availability and fairly inexpensive. Expect to pay about $500 annually for maintenance and repairs during the warranty period and $800 annually thereafter—good enough reason to shop around for a recent model with some of Chrysler's warranty left. Parts are expensive and hard to find now that Chrysler has taken these cars off the market. Other sports cars worth considering: Chrysler Stealth or Laser/Talon 4X4 • Ford Mustang or Probe • Honda Prelude or CRX • Mazda MX-3, Miata or RX-7 • Nissan 240SX • Toyota Celica and MR2.

Technical Data

ENGINES	Litres/CID	HP	MPG	Model Years
OHC I-4 FI	2.2/135	96	19-24	1985-86
OHC I-4T FI	2.2/135	149	18-23	1985-88
OHC I-4T FI	2.2/135	174	17-21	1987-90
DOHC I-4T FI	2.2/135	224	17-21	1992-93
OHC I-4 FI	2.5/153	100	19-24	1986-93
OHC I-4 FI	2.5/153	152	17-21	1989-92
OHC V6 FI	3.0/181	141	17-21	1990-93

Strengths and weaknesses: The high-performance Daytonas—the Turbo Z, Pacifica and Shelby Z—can run with the best of them, for a little while, and then the service bills start piling up. Without the failure-prone turbocharged engine and sport suspension, these coupes provide mediocre handling and acceleration.

All engines are troublesome. If not maintained meticulously from the very beginning, the turbocharger is likely to fail around the 80,000-km mark and cause serious damage to the engine and your wallet. Fuel system problems are common on all versions, requiring the frequent replacement of electronic computer modules under the 5 year/80,000 km emissions warranty. The manual transmission has a sloppy shift linkage and heavy clutch that doesn't stand up to hard use. Models loaded with electrical accessories have a higher failure rate than stripped-down versions. Electronic instrument panels and other electrical items are temperamental. The body is particularly poorly assembled and water/wind leaks are common.

Safety summary/recalls: NHTSA crash tests of an '84 Daytona two-door determined that both the driver and passenger would be well-protected. An '89 Daytona two-door was crash tested with similar results. An airbag-equipped 1991 version turned in the lowest figures of all, signifying that both the driver and passenger would be unharmed. *Recalls*: **1985**-Fatigue cracks could allow seat to suddenly move backwards. **1985-87 Turbo**-Fire hazard caused by fuel supply hose leak. **1987-89**-Exhaust system heat may melt carpet. Install free heat shield kit #4549356. **1989-90**-Leaking cylinder heads and gaskets will be replaced free of charge under Recall No. 467. **1990**-Airbag may be defective on cars with a grey interior. **1991**-Front disc brake caliper guide pin bolts may be too loose. **1992**-Faulty steering column shaft coupling bolts. **1992-93**-Dealers will install additional bolts to better secure the dash panel. Inadequate spot welds attaching the front rails to the dash panel could cause structural damage, including door-opening interference and sheet metal cracking.

Secret Warranties/Service Tips/DSBs

1987-89-An erratic idle and difficulty in reaching a fast idle with the 2.2L or 2.5L are addressed in DSB 18-18-88.

1988-Intermittent rough running at idle may require an upgraded EGR.

1989-Leaking fuel injectors are a common problem.

• Corrosion of the oxygen sensor connector is a common problem no longer covered by the emissions warranty.

• Notification #445 says leaky manual transmission flywheel attachment bolts will be replaced at no charge.

1989-90-Defective valve stem seals are the likely cause of high oil consumption with 2.2L and 2.5L engines (DSB HL-49-89C).

1990-92-Erratic idle speeds occurring after deceleration from a steady cruising speed can be corrected by replacing the idle air control motor with a revised motor.

1991-92-Engines with a rough idle and stalling following a cold start may require a new single board engine controller (SBEC).

1992-If the heater and ventilation system change to the defrost mode during acceleration, trailer towing or hill climbing, the installation of a revised vacuum check valve should cure the problem.

• Long crank times, a rough idle and hesitation may be corrected by replacing the intake manifold assembly.

• A leak in the oil filter area may be corrected by installing a special oil filter bracket gasket (#MD198554).

1992-93-Some 41TE transaxles may produce a buzzing noise when shifted into Reverse. Replace the valve body assembly or valve body separator plate.

All models/years-A rotten egg odor coming from the exhaust is probably caused by a defective catalytic converter that's covered by the

5 year/80,000 km emissions warranty. Faulty steering assemblies are often fixed free of charge up to 3 years/60,000 km (Ford and GM cover steering repairs two additional years.) Water leaks into the vehicle interior will be corrected without charge up to the fifth year of ownership.

Vehicle Profile

	1986	1987	1988	1989	1990	1991	1992	1993
Cost Price ($)								
Daytona	—	11,642	10,995	11,475	12,425	11,900	12,370	12,855
Turbo	13,940	—	—	—	—	—	—	—
Pacifica	—	15,930	16,385	—	—	—	—	—
Z (Shelby)	—	15,409	15,935	16,788	18,575	—	—	—
ES	—	—	—	13,155	14,250	13,675	14,200	14,745
IROC	—	—	—	—	—	15,585	16,150	16,735
Laser	11,255	—	—	—	—	—	—	—
Used Values ($)								
Daytona ↑	—	2600	3300	3900	4500	5400	6500	7600
Daytona ↓	—	1600	2100	2800	3300	4200	5200	6200
Turbo ↑	2600	—	—	—	—	—	—	—
Turbo ↓	1800	—	—	—	—	—	—	—
Pacifica ↑	—	3000	4200	—	—	—	—	—
Pacifica ↓	—	2200	3100	—	—	—	—	—
Z (Shelby) ↑	—	3600	4900	6500	7800	—	—	—
Z (Shelby) ↓	—	2500	3800	5300	6500	—	—	—
ES ↑	—	—	—	4500	5400	6500	7600	9000
ES ↓	—	—	—	3400	4100	5300	6200	7600
IROC ↑	—	—	—	—	8800	10,100	12,100	
IROC ↓	—	—	—	—	7500	8600	9900	
Laser ↑	1700	—	—	—	—	—	—	—
Laser ↓	1200	—	—	—	—	—	—	—
Reliability	③	③	②	②	③	③	③	③
Air conditioning	①	①	①	②	③	③	③	③
Body integrity	②	②	②	②	②	②	②	③
Braking system	②	②	②	②	③	③	③	④
Electrical system	②	②	②	②	②	②	②	③
Engines	③	③	②	②	③	③	③	③
Exhaust/Converter	②	②	②	④	④	④	④	⑤
Fuel system	②	②	②	②	②	②	③	④
Ignition system	③	②	③	③	③	③	③	③
Manual transmission	②	②	③	③	③	③	④	⑤
- automatic	③	③	③	③	③	③	③	③
Rust/Paint	②	②	②	②	③	③	④	④
Steering	③	③	②	②	③	③	③	③
Suspension	③	③	②	②	②	③	③	③
Dealer Service	②	②	②	②	②	②	②	②

Maintenance	❷	❷	❷	❷	❷	❷	❷	❷
Parts Availability	❷	❷	❷	❷	❷	❷	❷	❷
Repair Costs	❷	❷	❷	❷	❷	❷	❷	❷
Crash Safety								
Daytona	⑤	⑤	⑤	⑤	⑤	⑤	⑤	⑤
Safety Features								
ABS	S	S	S	S	S	S	S	S
Airbag	—	—	—	—	D	D	D	D

Laser, Talon 4X4

Rating: Recommended (1993-94); Above Average buy (1990-92).

Price analysis: Average availability and fairly expensive. According to the Canadian Automobile Association (CAA), parts are a bit more expensive than other cars in this class. Expect to pay about $300 annually for maintenance and repairs during the warranty period and $400 annually thereafter. Other sports cars worth considering: Chrysler Stealth • Ford Mustang or Probe • Honda Prelude or CRX • Mazda MX-3, Miata or RX-7 • Nissan 240SX • Toyota Celica, MR2 and Supra.

Technical Data

ENGINES	Litres/CID	HP	MPG	Model Years
OHC I-4T FI	1.8/107	92	22-26	1990-94
DOHC I-4 FI	2.0/122	135	21-25	1990-94
DOHC I-4T FI	2.0/122	195	17-23	1990-94

Strengths and weaknesses: These Mitsubishi-made sporty cars combine high performance, low price and reasonable durability. The base 1.8L engine is adequate, and the suspension is comfortable although a bit soft. The optional 16-valve, turbocharged 2.0L comes with a firmer suspension and gives more horsepower for the dollar than most other front-drive sports coupes and without the turbo lag. The 5-speed manual is the gearbox of choice. Torque steer makes the car appear to try to twist out of your hands when all 195 turbocharged horses are unleashed. The 4-speed automatic transmission cuts into the Laser's highway performance. Overall handling is impressive with the 4X4 system giving sure-footed foul weather stability.

Excellent ergonomics highlighted by a wrap-around dash that makes the good, old-fashioned analog gauges easy to read and controls easy to adjust. Dashboard air vents provide excellent ventilation. Lots of small storage spaces. Quiet riding, rattle-free construction. On the downside, the driving position may be set too low for some drivers, rear room is limited and seats are a bit hard.

Mitsubishi products have an above-average reliability record as over a decade of Colts have shown. Nevertheless, some problems remain, notably with the 1.8L engine, electrical system, driveline vibrations, brakes, and fit and finish. A stainless-steel exhaust system prevents rust damage. Dealers have had some trouble servicing these high-tech vehicles adequately.

DSBs address the following '94 model problems: turbocharger bolts may be poorly torqued (Chrysler will retorque them for free—DSB JE-41-89), excessive engine noise caused by carbon buildup on the top of the pistons, excessive driveline vibration, rear brake squeak and standard brakes that often lock up or require long stopping distances.

Safety summary/recalls: A 1990 Mitsubishi Eclipse two-door (identical to the Laser and Talon) was crash tested by the NHTSA at 57 km/h: the driver was judged to have sustained serious leg injuries. A '91 Eclipse was judged to offer excellent protection for both the driver and passenger. A retested '93 Eclipse was shown to produce serious driver leg injuries. U.S. safety researchers are looking into reports of hood latch failures on 1990-93 models. Standard brakes often lock up or require long stopping distances. Choose the optional ABS system. The absence of airbags and ABS on the Laser, a small, shallow trunk with a high sill and head restraints that block rear visibility are three deficiencies that compromise comfort and safety on these cars. *Recalls*: **1990**-Sunroof glass may detach from roof. Poor windshield retention during a collision. **1990 Laser**-Headlight wiring harness may short, causing the lights to fail. **1990 Talon**-Early production oxygen sensors that couldn't withstand the turbo engine's high temperatures will be replaced for free under an emissions recall.

Secret Warranties/Service Tips/DSBs

1990-92-Vehicles equipped with a 1.8L engine may produce excessive exhaust noise due to leakage from the center exhaust pipe at the submuffler.

1991-92-Tappet/lash adjuster noise is a common problem that DSB 09-53-91 covers.

Laser

1990-If the automatic seatbelt makes a clunking sound, replace the rubber stopper.

• To correct transmission case gasket leaks, use gasket kit #MD730803.

Talon

1990-Turbocharger bolts may be poorly torqued. Chrysler will retorque them for free (DSB JE-41-89).

• Warping of the headliner molding will be fixed by installing an improved molding.

• If the headlights won't retract when the switch is turned off, replace the passing control relay, heat shrink tube and tie straps.

• Hard shifting/gear clash can be prevented by installing a modified 1-2 synchronizer sleeve, spring and 3-4 spring.

1990-91-A loose rear-quarter trim panel may require new clips.

1990-94-Driveline vibrations on smooth roads can be eliminated by installing upgraded engine and transmission mounting brackets.

1992-94-Rear brake squeaks can be silenced with a Mitsubishi shim kit.

All models/years-A rotten egg odor coming from the exhaust may be the result of a malfunctioning catalytic converter that's covered by the 5 year/80,000 km emissions warranty. Faulty steering assemblies are often fixed free of charge up to 3 years/60,000 km (Ford and GM cover steering repairs two additional years.) Water leaks into the vehicle interior will be corrected without charge up to the fifth year of ownership.

Vehicle Profile

	1990	1991	1992	1993	1994
Cost Price ($)					
Laser	14,300	13,000	13,735	14,145	15,000
RS	15,300	14,900	15,820	16,310	16,800
Talon	16,300	15,505	16,205	14,475	16,000
Talon TSI	19,500	18,100	19,365	19,365	19,975
Used Values ($)					
Laser ↑	5900	6900	8000	10,000	11,700
Laser ↓	4400	5400	6600	8500	10,100
RS ↑	6300	7500	9200	11,000	12,700
RS ↓	4800	6000	7600	9700	11,100
Talon ↑	6500	7500	8900	10,300	11,900
Talon ↓	4800	6100	7200	8800	10,700
Talon TSI ↑	9000	10,500	12,700	13,900	15,000
Talon TSI ↓	7500	9000	11,100	12,000	13,800
Reliability	③	③	③	⑤	⑤
Air conditioning	④	④	⑤	⑤	⑤
Body integrity	②	②	②	③	③
Braking system	②	③	③	③	④
Electrical system	②	②	②	③	④
Engines	②	②	②	④	⑤
Exhaust/Converter	③	③	③	④	⑤
Fuel system	④	④	④	④	⑤
Ignition system	④	④	④	④	⑤
Manual transmission	③	③	③	④	④
- automatic	③	③	④	⑤	⑤
Rust/Paint	④	④	④	④	⑤
Steering	④	④	④	④	⑤
Suspension	④	④	④	④	⑤
Dealer Service	③	③	③	③	③
Maintenance	③	③	③	③	③

Parts Availability	③	③	③	③	③
Repair Costs	③	③	③	④	⑤
Crash Safety	❷	⑤	⑤	❷	❷
Safety Features					
ABS	—	S	S	S	S
Airbag	—	—	—	D/P	D/P

Stealth

Rating: Recommended (1991-94). A serious, reasonably priced sports car that's as much go as show.

Price analysis: Limited availability and fairly expensive. Repair and maintenance costs are significantly lower than average. Expect to pay about $300 annually for maintenance and repairs during the warranty period and $400 annually thereafter. Other sports cars worth considering: Chrysler Laser/Talon 4X4 • Ford Mustang or Probe • Honda Prelude or CRX • Mazda MX-3, Miata or RX-7 • Nissan 240SX • Toyota Celica and MR2.

Technical Data

ENGINES	Litres/CID	HP	MPG	Model Years
OHC V6 FI	3.0/181	164	18-23	1991-94
DOHC V6 FI	3.0/181	222	18-23	1991-94
DOHC V6T FI	3.0/181	320	18-23	1991-94

Strengths and weaknesses: An impressive highway performer with a good reliability record. The base V6 engine accelerates well and provides more than enough power for all driving conditions. Twin turbo power on the R/T Turbo is awesome and rivals engine performance with sports cars selling for far more. Power steering is crisp and predictable and provides just the right amount of road feel. Standard disc brakes work very well, but the ABS is particularly impressive in stopping the car in a short distance without any loss of steering stability or fading after repeated application. The manual and automatic transmissions shift impeccably.

Mitsubishi products have a reliability record above average in spite of the Stealth's obvious teething problems. Four-wheel-steering kicks in when the car reaches 30 mph, adding to the Stealth's high-speed stability, particularly when cornering. The stainless-steel exhaust system prevents rust damage.

Where the Stealth disappoints is in its limited driver headroom (a Ford Probe problem, too), confusing and hard-to-find interior instrumentation and controls, hard-to-service engine compartment, and mediocre quality control when it comes to body hardware, fit and finish. The Stealth is not a car for short drivers, either they may have trouble seeing over the hood or reaching the clutch pedal. When the seat is moved forward, they may be unable to see overhead lights. Rear seating is very cramped as is the norm with most sports cars. The dash control that adjusts exhaust system sound is more gimmick than innovation. The Turbo's excessive weight taxes fuel economy. The small engine compartment means some of the simplest jobs will require special tools and take an inordinate amount of time to carry out.

Dealer service bulletins and a small number of owner complaints show the first-year (1991) Stealth had an unusually large number of factory defects that were corrected in the second year. For example, owners report frequent gearbox and fit problems, including drivetrain noise, grinding noise when shifting, gear clash, hard shifting into all gears, difficulty shifting into Reverse, door glass rattling, excessive wind noise along door glass, water leaks and sluggish window operation. Other problems reported by owners and confirmed by dealer service bulletins: cruise-control failure due to improper wiring connection, noisy engine lash adjuster, power transfer unit and viscous coupling failure, 1st to 2nd gear clash, faulty exhaust manifold nuts, noisy steering column, rear suspension tapping noise, and faulty turn signals.

Safety summary/recalls: Crash tests of a '93 Stealth concluded that the driver's and passenger's two legs would be seriously injured. *Recalls*: N/A.

Secret Warranties/Service Tips/DSBs

1991-94-Rear cargo cover rattling or failure to stay in the holder requires a new clip.
1994-Door glass weatherstripping may pull out requiring the installation of upgraded weatherstripping.
All models/years-A rotten egg odor coming from the exhaust is probably the result of a malfunctioning catalytic converter that's covered by the 5 year/80,000 km emissions warranty.

Vehicle Profile

	1991	1992	1993	1994
Cost Price ($)				
Base	20,458	21,908	—	—
ES	22,204	25,435	26,695	—
RT	32,080	33,176	36,115	30,965
RT Turbo	42,235	38,820	42,235	48,015

Used Values ($)

Base ↑	9500	11,700	—	—
Base ↓	8300	10,800	—	—
ES ↑	10,800	12,900	14,900	—
ES ↓	9800	12,200	13,900	—
RT ↑	15,500	17,500	21,000	22,500
RT ↓	13,700	16,000	20,000	21,000
RT Turbo ↑	21,700	24,000	27,500	31,000
RT Turbo ↓	19,500	22,500	25,000	28,500
Reliability	③	④	⑤	⑤
Air conditioning	④	⑤	⑤	⑤
Body integrity	❷	❷	❷	❷
Braking system	③	④	④	④
Electrical system	❷	❷	③	③
Engines	⑤	⑤	④	④
Exhaust/Converter	③	⑤	⑤	⑤
Fuel system	④	④	⑤	⑤
Ignition system	④	④	⑤	⑤
Manual transmission	③	③	③	③
- automatic	③	③	③	③
Rust/Paint	❷	❷	③	④
Steering	⑤	⑤	④	④
Suspension	⑤	⑤	④	④
Dealer Service	③	③	③	③
Maintenance	③	③	③	③
Parts Availability	③	③	③	③
Repair Costs	③	③	③	③
Crash Safety	—	—	❶	❶
Safety Features				
ABS	O	O	S	S
Airbag	D	D	D/P	D/P

FORD

Mustang

Rating: Recommended (1993-94); Not Recommended (1985-92). All 4-cylinder versions should be shunned.

Price analysis: Excellent availability and reasonably priced. Expect to pay about $400 annually for maintenance and repairs during the warranty period and $700 annually thereafter. Other sports cars worth considering: Chrysler Laser/Talon 4X4 and Stealth • Ford Probe • Honda Prelude or CRX • Mazda MX-3, Miata or RX-7 • Nissan 240SX • Toyota Celica and MR2.

Technical Data

ENGINES	Litres/CID	HP	MPG	Model Years
OHC I-4 1 bbl.	2.3/140	88	18-21	1985-86
OHC I-4 FI	2.3/140	88	19-23	1987-90
OHC I-4 FI	2.3/140	105	20-24	1991-93
OHC I-4T FI	2.3/140	155-205	17-20	1985-86
OHV V6 FI	3.8/232	120	16-19	1985-86
OHV V6 FI	3.8/232	145	19-24	1994-95
OHV V8 4 bbl.	5.0/302	210	13-16	1985
OHV V8 FI	5.0/302	165-225	13-17	1985-95

Strengths and weaknesses: Rear-wheel-drive Mustangs remain popular because they offer sporty styling and high-performance thrills for less money than GM's Camaro and Firebird, the Mustang's main domestic competitors. Unfortunately, the 1993 Mustang fell behind its GM competition when the Camaro and Firebird were radically restyled that year, gaining additional safety features, a more rigid, dent-resistant body, better body fit and finish, and a more powerful base engine.

The Mustang has never been a very reliable car. The first Mustang, launched in 1964 and now worth more than $25,000, always had serious rusting, electrical and suspension problems. Guess what? Thirty-one years later, Mustangs still have electrical systems and electronic modules that are constantly breaking down, and the base suspension and front brakes wear out quickly.

The less said about the infamous 2.3L 4-cylinder engine, the better. The V6 and V8 engines are reasonably reliable, but the V8 has the performance and reliability edge. Turbocharged models are not recommended because of frequent and expensive mechanical break-downs. If you want high-performance action, you will have to pay a premium and be prepared for some monstrous repair bills. Sport trim models feature an upgraded suspension and wheel package that improves handling considerably, and the SVO rivals many expensive sports cars in performance but commands a very high resale price.

Common problems with most models are failure-prone 4-cylinder engines, manual transmission malfunctions, worn-out power-steering assemblies, prematurely worn front suspension components and temperamental carburetors. Troublesome EEC IV ignition modules have produced many stalling and hard starting complaints. Hood and trunk lid edges are prone to rust perforation.

Confidential dealer service bulletins show the following problems on the '93 models: air conditioning odors, minor surface damage to bumper covers and noisy power steering. The '94 models have these deficiencies: a faulty 3.8L engine rocker arm assembly that causes squeaking, chirping or knocking. Rough idle, hesitation and excessive fuel consumption, poor heater output likely caused by a thermostat stuck in an open position or opening before it should, transmission shudder under light-to-moderate acceleration, noise in radio speakers caused by the fuel pump and a faulty electric rear window defroster.

Safety summary/recalls: Crash tests of an '84 convertible concluded that the passenger would likely sustain severe or fatal head and leg trauma, while the driver would receive serious leg injuries. A 1987 Mustang LX was tested and figures show that only the driver would suffer serious leg injuries. A 1990 convertible produced disappointing results: both the driver and passenger would likely have severe leg injuries. An airbag-equipped '91 Mustang did much better: both the driver and passenger were judged to have been well-protected. A '93 convertible, though, was judged to have injured both driver's legs and the passenger's left leg. A retested '94 convertible differed only slightly: the driver's right and passenger's left leg would have been seriously injured. An additional safety note: regularly equipped Mustangs, like most rear-drive Fords, don't handle sharp curves very well. Under moderate speed, the rear end swings out suddenly and the car tends to spin. Furthermore, the car loses traction easily on wet roads and braking is barely adequate. There have been some reports of sudden acceleration with 1986-88 models and complaints that the fuel line's proximity to the rear exhaust pipe is a fire hazard on 1989-91 Mustangs equipped with a 5.0L engine. Transport Canada is investigating reports of the throttle linkage sticking on 1985-90 models equipped with the 5.0L engine. Daylight running light modules last about 18 months. *Recalls*: **1985**-Defective ignition module. Faulty plastic sleeve in front safety belt tongue assembly. Power brake booster could come apart. **1986-87**-Fuel line coupling may leak fuel. **1991**-Vehicle could roll away with shift lever in the Park position.

Secret Warranties/Service Tips/DSBs

1979-84-According to Ford DSB 86-18-1, published September 11, 1986, floor fatigue cracks could cause the front seats to become loose, rock or sag and allow water or fumes to enter the passenger compartment. Ford, if pushed, will pay half the repair costs for the installation of floor pan reinforcement panels. Over 11,300 claims have been paid by Ford. If the company balks at providing compensation, get the federal Ministry of Transport's Vehicle Safety Branch involved.
1980-88-Inoperative power door locks need an upgraded retainer clip assembly (#E8AZ-5421952-A).
1982-86-Wind noise and water leaks with T-roofs and convertibles are usually caused by misaligned doors. Install door alignment kit #E72Z-6123042-A or -B.
1982-90-An unusual engine metal-to-metal noise may be caused by the flexing of the torque converter. Install six new flywheel bolts with

reduced head height to provide additional clearance.

1984-85-Front seatbelt buckles may break and separate from the belt webbing. Ford dealers will correct this defect by replacing the buckle free of charge. This policy was confirmed in the September 28th, 1992 edition of *Automotive News.*

1984-87-Stalling and a no-start condition on vehicles equipped with EEC IV and TFI modules may be caused by water entering the upper righthand mounting hole of the TFI module housing.

1985-Water may leak through a faulty seal in the cowl area and short circuit the engine.

• Stalling at idle, poor fuel economy and poor heater performance may all be caused by the thermostat stuck in a partially open position (DSB 86-17-12).

1985-90-An exhaust buzz or rattle may be fixed by installing new clamps to secure the heat shield.

1985-91-Ford will replace free of charge faulty door latches that function improperly and cannot be adjusted.

• An inoperative electric rear window defroster (heated backlights) may be caused by bond separation of the pigtail terminal to bus bar or broken grid lines. Install a rear window defroster service kit.

1985-92-A buzz or rattle from the exhaust system may be caused by a loose heat shield catalyst.

1986-91-The in-tank fuel pump is the likely cause of all that radio static you hear. Stop the noise by installing an electronic noise RFI filter (#F1PZ-18B925-A).

1987-Faulty fuel-injection tube assemblies may cause fuel leakage and create a fire hazard. Ford will fix the unit free of charge.

• A rough idle on vehicles equipped with electronic fuel injection may be caused by loose fuel injector electrical terminals.

1987-88-Hard starting/stalling may be caused by defective TFI modules.

1987-90-Excessive oil consumption is likely caused by leaking gaskets, poor sealing of the lower intake manifold, defective intake and exhaust valve stem seals, or worn piston rings. Install new guide-mounted valve stem seals for a more positive fit and new piston rings with improved oil control.

1988-Delayed Reverse engagement may require a new separator plate.

1988-92-Cold hesitation when accelerating, rough idle, long crank times and stalling may all signal the need to clean out excessive intake valve deposits. These problems also may result from the use of fuels that have low volatility, such as high octane, premium blends.

1989-90-Harsh, rough 3-4 and 4-3 shifts may be caused by improper TV pressure or sticking control valves.

1990-Excessive transmission noise, delayed shifts or no engagements may be due to thrust washer metal particles that have plugged the filter or burnt out the clutch plates.

1990-92-Speedometer may indicate higher than actual speed in cold weather. Replace the speedometer head.

1990-93-Noise heard from the power-steering pump may be caused by

382

air in the system. Purge the system.

1990-94-A speaker whine or buzz caused by the fuel pump can be stopped by installing an electronic noise RFI filter.

1991-A rough idle or lean fuel flow may require the installation of deposit resistant injectors under the emissions warranty.

1992-Windshield wiper failures are being investigated by safety authorities.

1994-Automatic transmissions with delayed or no forward engagement, or a higher engine rpm than expected when coming to a stop are covered in DSB 94-26-9.

• A cracked cowl top vent grille should be replaced with an upgraded version.

• A driveline "boom" can be silenced by replacing the rear upper control arms.

• A noisy fuel pump needs to be replaced by an improved "guided check valve" fuel pump.

• A binding or sticking hood needs a readjustment of the hood bumpers or latch.

• Models with laser red paint may have serious paint "decay" problems requiring a repainting of the entire body.

• A ticking or tapping sound coming from the engine at idle can be silenced by installing an improved fuel hose/damper assembly.

1994-95-A thumping or clacking heard from the front brakes signals the need to machine the front disc brake rotors. Ford will pay for this repair under its base warranty.

• Loose rocker panel mouldings require new retaining clips.

All models/years-A rotten egg odor coming from the exhaust is likely the result of a malfunctioning catalytic converter that's covered by the 5 year/80,000 km emissions warranty.

Ford's "goodwill" warranty extensions cover fuel pumps and computer modules that govern engine, fuel injection and transmission functions. If Ford balks at refunding your money for a faulty computer module, apply the 5 year/80,000 km emissions warranty.

Faulty steering assemblies are often fixed free of charge up to 5 years/80,000 km ever since the company was sued by irate Mustang owners a decade ago. Ford will pay 100% toward the correction of paint defects during the first 5 years/80,000 km and 50% up to the seventh year of ownership in keeping with the policy it adopted to cover pickups. Water leaks into the vehicle interior will be corrected without charge up to the fifth year of ownership.

Vehicle Profile

	1987	1988	1989	1990	1991	1992	1993	1994
Cost Price ($)								
LX/Coupe	9995	10,595	11,418	12,195	11,295	12,095	10,995	15,595
Convertible	17,116	18,971	20,117	20,937	19,195	19,995	20,495	24,995

Cobra GT	15,731	17,383	18,109	18,659	16,895	17,995	18,995	20,295
Used Values ($)								
LX/Coupe ↑	2300	3200	3900	4100	4700	6000	7000	12,700
LX/Coupe ↓	1700	2100	2600	2800	3400	4700	5700	11,200
Convertible ↑	4800	5500	6300	7100	8500	11,000	12,900	17,900
Convertible ↓	3500	4300	5000	5800	7200	9600	11,500	16,000
Cobra GT ↑	5000	6200	7200	8500	10,000	11,400	12,500	20,375
Cobra GT ↓	3900	4700	5700	7000	8500	8900	9900	17,900
Reliability	②	②	②	③	③	③	④	⑤
Air conditioning	①	①	①	②	④	⑤	⑤	⑤
Body integrity	①	①	①	②	②	②	②	③
Braking system	③	③	③	③	③	②	②	③
Electrical system	①	①	①	①	①	②	③	④
Engines	③	③	③	③	④	④	④	④
Exhaust/Converter	②	②	③	③	③	③	④	⑤
Fuel system	②	②	③	③	③	③	④	⑤
Ignition system	③	③	③	③	③	④	④	④
Manual transmission	③	③	③	③	③	④	⑤	⑤
- automatic	②	②	③	③	③	④	④	④
Rust/Paint	①	①	①	①	①	①	②	③
Steering	②	②	③	③	③	③	④	⑤
Suspension	②	②	③	③	③	③	④	⑤
Dealer Service	③	③	③	③	④	④	⑤	⑤
Maintenance	④	④	④	④	④	④	⑤	⑤
Parts Availability	④	④	④	④	④	④	⑤	⑤
Repair Costs	④	④	④	④	④	⑤	⑤	⑤
Crash Safety								
Base	②	②	②	②	⑤	⑤	⑤	⑤
Convertible	①	①	①	①	①	①	①	①
Safety Features								
ABS	—	—	—	—	—	—	—	S
Airbag	—	—	—	D	D	D	D	D/P

Probe

Rating: Recommended (1992-94); Average buy (1989-91).

Price analysis: Depreciation has been very low, and buyer demand for used Probes is quite strong making these cars a bit hard to find and fairly expensive. Maintenance and repairs should cost about $400 annually during the warranty period and $700 annually thereafter—a good reason to get a Probe with some of Ford's original warranty left. Other sports cars worth considering: Chrysler Laser/Talon 4X4 and Stealth • Ford Mustang • Honda Prelude or CRX • Mazda MX-3, Miata or RX-7 • Nissan 240SX • Toyota Celica and MR2.

Technical Data

ENGINES	Litres/CID	HP	MPG	Model Years
OHC I-4 FI	2.2/133	110	20-26	1989-92
OHC I-4T FI	2.2/133	145	19-23	1989-92
OHV V6 FI	3.0/182	140-145	17-23	1990-92
DOHC I-4 FI	2.0/122	118	21-27	1993-95
DOHC V6 FI	2.5/153	164	19-23	1993-95

Strengths and weaknesses: Essentially a Mazda 626 disguised as a Ford. Mazda's mechanicals are above reproach; Ford's body and chassis work are disappointing. Despite gobs of torque, the GT doesn't give the muscle-car performance found in the more brutish and less refined 5.0L Mustang GT. Performance is sapped considerably by the automatic transmission. Early models are beset by severe "torque steer," a tendency for the chassis to twist when the vehicle accelerates. Nevertheless, overall handling is precise and predictable on all models without a sacrifice in ride quality, which is a bit on the hard side.

The Probe's overall mechanically reliability is very good, but, like its Mustang cousin, body assembly is a big letdown. Paint quality and rust protection are pretty good, though. The turbocharged engine has been relatively trouble free, but owners have complained of frequent stalling and stumbling with the base 2.2L powerplant. Front brakes are known to wear out very quickly and produce excessive vibrations when applied. The underhood layout is crowded, making for high routine maintenance costs.

For 1993, model refinements included two new Mazda-designed engines that gave the car a small horsepower boost, more interior room, all-disc brakes on the GT and the elimination of torque steer.

The car is essentially a 2+2 with the rear reserved for children or cargo. The interior is short on headroom for tall drivers (especially with a sunroof), but cargo room is increased with the folding rear seatbacks. Multiple squeaks and rattles, wind and water leaks, and cheap interior appointments are the most common body complaints. The digital readouts are distracting and often incorrect.

Confidential dealer service bulletins show the 1993 models may have poorly performing 4EAT automatic transmissions that produce harsh 3-2 downshifts and the "service engine" light may go on for no apparent reason.

Safety summary/recalls: Crash tests of a 1989 Probe concluded that both the driver and front passenger would be well-protected. A retested '91 confirmed the earlier score, but a '93 airbag-equipped version showed that the driver's two legs would have been seriously injured. A retested 1994 Probe was shown to produce serious leg injuries to the driver and passenger. The driver's motorized shoulder belt is literally a pain in the neck. It rides high on the neck, fails to retract properly, tangles easily, and often hangs too loose. It also requires that the driver attach the lapbelt separately. *Recalls:* **1985**-A defective ignition may make 2.3L engines hard to start. Defective plastic sleeve in front seatbelt tongue assembly. Power brake booster could come apart (except police/taxi). **1986-87**-Fuel line coupling could leak fuel. **1991**-Vehicle could roll away with shifter in Park position. **1991 GL**-A safety recall specifies a free fix of welds that anchor the front shoulder belt retractors. **1993**-A faulty rear hatch strut may cause the hatch to drop without warning. A Ford recall will replace the rivets that have undersized heads on the strut pivot pins.

Secret Warranties/Service Tips/DSBs

1989-2.2L engines with hairline cracks in the cylinder head must have the head replaced.
• Hard cold starts or chronic stalling may require a cold stall pressure regulator kit (#900809A).
• No-starts/low battery mean you may need a new alternator pulley and belt kit (#E92Z-10344-D).
1989-90-An exhaust buzz or rattle may be fixed by installing new clamps to secure the heat shield.
1989-91-Constant fogging and moisture condensation on the interior windows and windshield signal the need to adjust the recirculation/fresh control cable.
1989-92-A buzz or rattle from the exhaust system may be caused by a loose heat shield catalyst.
1989-94-A no-start condition, or inoperative heater or lamps, may be caused by water and corrosion in the wiring connector, or a short-to-ground at splice 102 (circuit 9).
1990-Faulty 3.0L V6 engine control modules will be replaced at no charge under an emissions recall.
1990 GT-Service Program No. 96 provides for the free rerouting of the wiring harness and hose clamp to prevent transmission failure.
1990-91-Rear disc brake squeal can be corrected by installing revised brake pads (#E92Z-2200-A).
• Taillight condensation can be prevented by installing a new outer lens kit.
• Engine knocking at idle may require the installation of a thicker thrust plate.
• The in-tank fuel pump is the likely cause of all that radio static you hear. Squelch the noise by installing an electronic noise RFI filter (#F1PZ-18B925-A).
1990-94-A speaker whine or buzz caused by the fuel pump can be stopped by installing an electronic noise RFI filter.
1993-94-A clunk or knock from the steering assembly when turning is likely due to insufficient yoke plug (pinion) preload.

• Wind/water leaks require the readjustment of the front door glass as outlined in DSB 994-5-4.

• Inoperative power door locks may have a corroded wiring harness connection.

• Frozen door locks, a common problem, are addressed in DSB 94-8-6.

• A ticking noise coming from the 2.0L engine's hydraulic lash adjusters can be stopped by a longer oil pump control plunger that prevents air from passing through to the oil pump.

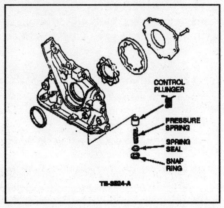

1994-A loose air dams skirt can be secured by replacing the factory installed grommets with aftermarket license plate nuts, screws and washers.

• A rough idle affecting 2.0L engines could be caused by spark leakage from a damaged number 1 or number 2 spark plug wire.

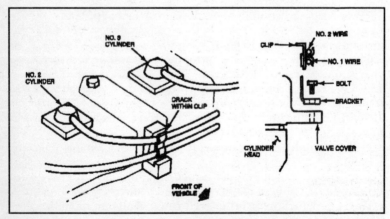

All models/years-A rotten egg odor coming from the exhaust is probably the result of a malfunctioning catalytic converter that's covered by the 5 year/80,000 km emissions warranty.

Two components that benefit from Ford "goodwill" warranty extensions are fuel pumps and computer modules that govern engine, fuel injection, and transmission functions. If Ford balks at refunding your money for a faulty computer module, apply the 5 year/80,000 km emissions warranty. Faulty steering assemblies are often fixed free of charge up to 5 years/80,000 km. Ford will pay 100% toward the correction of paint defects during the first 5 years/80,000 km and 50% up to the seventh year of ownership in keeping with the policy it adopted to cover pickups. Water leaks into the vehicle interior will be corrected without charge up to the fifth year of ownership.

Vehicle Profile

	1989	1990	1991	1992	1993	1994
Cost Price ($)						
GL	14,298	14,972	13,795	14,795	15,165	16,495
GT	19,903	21,760	19,895	17,795	18,240	20,195
Used Values ($)						
GL ↑	5300	6700	7600	9400	10,900	12,400
GL ↓	4300	5100	6000	8400	9100	10,600
GT ↑	8200	9400	10,600	12,200	13,500	15,200
GT ↓	6600	7800	8900	10,400	11,800	13,300
Reliability	③	③	③	③	④	④
Air conditioning	②	②	②	②	③	③
Body integrity	①	①	①	①	①	①
Braking system	①	①	①	①	①	②
Electrical system	①	①	①	①	①	③
Engines	③	③	③	⑤	⑤	⑤
Exhaust/Converter	②	②	③	⑤	⑤	⑤
Fuel system	③	③	③	⑤	④	⑤
Ignition system	③	③	③	⑤	⑤	⑤
Manual transmission	③	③	③	④	⑤	⑤
- automatic	③	③	③	④	③	④
Rust/Paint	④	④	④	⑤	⑤	⑤
Steering	③	③	③	③	④	④
Suspension	③	③	③	④	④	④
Dealer Service	④	④	④	⑤	⑤	⑤
Maintenance	②	②	③	④	④	⑤
Parts Availability	⑤	⑤	⑤	⑤	⑤	⑤
Repair Costs	②	②	③	③	④	⑤
Crash Safety	⑤	⑤	⑤	⑤	①	①
Safety Features						
ABS	O	O	O	O	O	O
Airbag	—	—	—	—	D	D

GENERAL MOTORS

Camaro, Z28, IROC-Z, Firebird, Trans Am

Rating: Recommended (1993-94); Below Average buy (1991-92); Not Recommended (1985-90).

Price analysis: Excellent availability and reasonably priced. Pre-'93 prices are dropping fast, now that the reworked 1993 Camaro and Firebird have hit the used-car lots. Don't look for leftover '93 models, though. GM sent almost all of that year's production to the U.S. The 1992 models combine the highest depreciation, lowest base price and least wear and tear. And best of all, there are many available. Expect to pay about $500 annually for maintenance and repairs during the warranty period and $800 annually, thereafter—plenty of reason to shop around for a model with some of the GM warranty left. Other sports cars worth considering: Chrysler Laser/Talon 4X4 and Stealth • Ford Mustang or Probe • Honda Prelude or CRX • Mazda Miata, MX-3 or RX-7 • Nissan 240SX • Toyota Celica and MR2.

Technical Data

ENGINES	Litres/CID	HP	MPG	Model Years
OHV I-4 F	I2.5/151	88	19-22	1985-86
OHV V6 FI	2.8/173	135	17-22	1985-89
OHV V6 FI	3.1/191	140	17-22	1990-92
OHV V8 4 bbl.	5.0/305	150-190	14-16	1985-87
OHV V8 FI	5.0/305	195-230	16-19	1985-87
OHV V8 FI	5.0/305	170	16-19	1988-92
OHV V8 FI	5.7/350	225-245	15-18	1987-92
OHV V6 FI	3.4/207	160	18-23	1993-95
OHV V8 FI	5.7/350	275	15-19	1993-95

Strengths and weaknesses: Brute power combined with brutal repair charges, the Camaro and Firebird's overall performance varies a great deal depending on the engine, transmission and suspension combination on each particular car. Base models don't accelerate the way sporty cars should, and handling is compromised by poor wet road traction, minimal comfort, and a suspension too soft for high-speed cornering and too bone-jarring for smooth cruising. The Z28, IROC-Z and Trans Am provide smart acceleration and handling, at the expense of fuel economy.

1984-92-The puny and failure-prone 2.5L 4-cylinder powerplant was the standard engine up to 1987. Trans Ams offered three more reliable engines: the Buick 3.8L (231 cu. in.) V6, a 4.3L (265 cu. in.)

Oldsmobile V8 and the Buick 5.0L (301 cu. in.) V8. The turbocharged V8 offered on some Trans Am models should be viewed with caution because of many durability problems.

Camaro flat seats don't offer as much support as the better-contoured Firebird seats. 1982 and later cars have had chronic fuel-system problems, especially on the Cross-Fire and multi-port fuel-injection controls. Automatic transmissions, especially the 4-speed, are not durable. The standard 5-speed manual gearbox has a stiff shifter and heavy clutch. Clutches fail frequently and do not stand up to hard use. The 2.8L V6, used through 1989, suffers from leaky gaskets and seals and premature camshaft wear. The larger 3.1L 6-cylinder has fewer problems. Electrical problems and malfunctioning dash gauges are common. Exhaust parts rust quickly. Dual outlet exhaust systems on V8 engines are expensive to replace. Front suspension components and shock absorbers wear out very quickly.

On pre-1993 models, like its Mustang rival, body hardware is fragile, poor paint quality and application are common and lead to premature rusting, and squeaks and rattles are legion. Body integrity is especially poor on cars equipped with a T-roof. Areas particularly vulnerable to rusting are the windshield and rear wheel openings, door bottoms and rear quarter panels. The assorted add-on plastic body parts found on sporty versions promote corrosion by trapping moisture along with road salt and grime.

1993-94 These cars are much better overall performers with a more powerful, reliable base engine, increased body rigidity that hushes some of the squeaks and rattles so prevalent with previous years, a redesigned, easier-to-read dash, a bit more rear headroom and additional standard safety features.

Not all is perfect, however. Owners report that the base engine is noisy, fuel economy is practically nonexistent, the air conditioner malfunctions, front brakes and MacPherson struts wear out quickly, servicing the fuel injection system is an exercise in frustration, and body problems just won't go away. Yes, body defects are still a major problem in spite of the millions of dollars GM spent to redesign the car in 1993. These cars are still afflicted by door rattles, misaligned doors and hatch, a sticking hatch power release, and poor fit and finish. Owners also complain that the steering wheel is positioned too close to the driver's chest, the low seats create a feeling of claustrophobia, visibility is limited by wide side pillars, and trunk space is sparse with a high liftover.

Dealer service bulletins show the 1994 models may have poor radio reception and require an upgraded antenna bracket assembly (#10257131, #10257133 for Pontiac). A rough-running A/C compressor on V8-equipped vehicles requires an upgraded compressor pulley.

Safety summary/recalls: Crash tests of an '83 Camaro and Firebird concluded that both the driver and front passenger would be well-protected. Tests of an '87 Camaro showed similar results. An airbag-equipped '91 version produced identical findings, as did a '94 model. NHTSA investigators are looking into reports of fuel leaks on 1992 models. *Recalls*: **1985**-Shoulder seatbelt may not retract. **1985-86**-For vehicles with rear disc brakes and manual transmissions, the parking brake adjuster may not hold the vehicle when parked on an incline. **1985-90**-Defective seatbelt buckle assemblies may not latch. **1986**-Faulty push-pull headlight switch. **1988**-GM will inspect and repair the power-steering pump support brace and mounting bracket. **1988-89**-Fuel feed hoses may leak on vehicles equipped with a 2.8L V6 engine. **1989 convertible**-Rear seatbelts may be too long. **1990**-Fuel return hoses may leak on vehicles equipped with a V8 engine. **1991**-Poor windshield retention in an accident. Defective seatbelt latchplates will be fixed for free. Defective front seats. **1991-92**-Fuel filler neck may leak. **1992**-The automatic transmission shift control cable may separate and hamper shifting. **1994**-Fuel line on V8-equipped cars may leak fuel into the engine compartment.

Secret Warranties/Service Tips/DSBs

1982-88-Rear brake self-adjusters may not work properly. Install a revised cone-clutch adjuster.

1982-91-T-top roof leaks may be caused by spot weld burn in the rear hatch gutter between the hinge attachment points.

1982-93-Vehicles equipped with a Hydramatic 4L60 transmission that buzzes when the car is in Reverse or idle may need a new oil pressure regulator valve.

1984-87-Left side cowl leaks can be plugged by sealing the wiper transmission mounting area.

1985-87-Hard starting or reduced acceleration may require a no-charge replacement of the catalytic converter.

1985-88-A long crank time with the 5.7L engine may be due to a faulty cold start injector, fuel pump clutch valve, fuel pressure regulator, or the fuel injector leaking pressure and shutting down.

1985-89-Vehicles equipped with 4.3L, 5.0L or 5.7L engines and an automatic transmission may have a starter and flexplate that don't mesh properly. This results in grinding and clashing similar to what one would hear if the key was turned while the engine was already running. The problem can be corrected by installing an upgraded starter drive assembly (#10456422).

1985-91-Hydramatic 4L60/700R4 automatic transmission may have no upshift or appear to be stuck in 1st gear. The probable cause is a worn governor gear. It would be wise also to replace the retaining ring.

1986-Faulty headlight switch may cause erratic operation of lights. GM will fix the contact free of charge.

1987-88-If cold weather makes your THM 200-4R automatic transmission difficult to downshift from 2nd to 1st gear, the likely cause is a defective 1-2 throttle valve spring (#8634619) in the valve body (DSB 88-164-7A).

1987-89-Different types of tailpipe smoke signal the need for different repairs. **1987** cars with V8 engines that emit blue or bluish white smoke may require a valve seal kit; **1987-88** cars with port fuel injection that emit black smoke after long starter cranks may have fuel leaking into the engine from the injectors; **1987-88** models with throttle body injection and port fuel injection that emit white or bluish white smoke and have normal oil consumption likely have poor sealing between the intake manifold joint and the cylinder head.

1988-91-Center instrument panel squeaks or popping may require refitting and an additional hole drilled.

1988-91 convertibles-If water leaks under rear seat cushions, drill holes in the quarter-rocker inner extension for drainage.

1989-If the rear brakes moan when backing up or turning with the brakes slightly applied, a redesigned caliper mounting plate may be needed (DSB 89-162-5).

• Knocking from a cold 5.0L engine requires that the PROM module be replaced (DSB 89-284-6E).

• No-start or stalling may be caused by a disconnected fuel pump coupler.

1989-90-Campaign 90-C-11 provides for free convertible top latch handles.

• Damaged front seatback trim will be replaced, free of charge, along with the rear seat shoulder belt guide loops.

1990-Cold start stalling with the 3.1L engine can be corrected by replacing the MEMCAL under the emissions warranty.

1993-94-DSB 431028 covers all the aspects relative to securing loose door outer panels.

• A loose, rattling instrument panel or upper trim panel requires new dual lock riveted fasteners.

• Noisy windshield wipers can be silenced by modifying the upper edge of the mounting bracket or the crank arm.

• Poor heater performance may be caused by a loose heater core to heater case seal.

• Rear brake squeal can be silenced by installing upgraded disc brake pads.

1994-Excessive oil consumption is likely due to delaminated intake manifold gaskets. Install an upgraded intake manifold gasket kit.

• Delayed automatic transmission shift engagement is a common problem addressed in DSB 47-71-20A.

• Install a new "flash" PROM to cure erratic increases in engine rpm or start/stall/hesitation upon acceleration with automatic transmission equipped cars.

Engines

2.5L-Spark knock can be fixed with the free installation of a new PROM module (#12269198). Frequent stalling may require a new MAP sensor (DSB 90-142-8A).

3.8L V6-These engines have a history of low oil pressure caused by a failure-prone oil pump. A temporary remedy is to avoid low viscosity oils and use 10W-40 in the winter and 20W-50 for summer driving.

1990-91-Stalling on deceleration or at stops requires a new MEMCAL that refines idle speed control and throttle follower operation.

1991-Poor starting may be caused by the spring in early starter drives compressing too easily. Install an upgraded starter motor drive assembly (#10473700).

• Power windows that pop when operated may need a revised window motor (#22121553).

• Defective seatbelt latchplates will be fixed for free under a recall campaign.

• Defective front seats will be fixed for free under a recall campaign.

1992-The automatic transmission shift control cable may separate and hamper shifting. A safety recall campaign ensures the problem will be repaired at no charge.

• Oil leaks from the rear of a 5.0L or 5.7L engine may be caused by insufficient sealing around the camshaft plug. Replace the plug and reseal.

All models/years-A rotten egg odor coming from the exhaust is probably the result of a malfunctioning catalytic converter that's covered by the 5 year/80,000 km emissions warranty. For over a decade, GM has had a serious rust/paint peeling problem with all its domestic-made vehicles. Faced with this, the automaker has set up a substantial slush fund to compensate owners. Original owners will get 100% refunds for correcting paint peeling/surface rusting up to six years.

Vehicle Profile

	1987	1988	1989	1990	1991	1992	1993	1994
Cost Price ($)								
Camaro/RS	12,395	14,473	15,799	16,898	15,298	14,298	15,998	16,498
Z28	16,250	17,085	18,650	20,698	19,098	18,998	19,898	20,498
IROC Convertible	—	24,532	25,550	29,498	24,998	—	—	—
Firebird	12,716	14,179	15,998	16,898	15,698	14,798	15,168	17,198
Trans Am	16,605	18,376	19,998	21,638	19,898	20,998	23,265	24,500
Used Values ($)								
Camaro R/S ↑	3100	4000	5000	6000	6900	8400	10,700	11,900
Camaro R/S ↓	2200	2900	3500	4400	5600	6700	9000	10,500
Z28 ↑	5300	6700	7700	9100	10,700	11,700	14,800	16,500
Z28 ↓	4000	4900	5900	7300	8900	9800	12,900	14,900
IROC Convertible ↑	—	9500	10,700	12,200	13,900	—	—	—
IROC Convertible ↓	—	7800	8900	10,400	12,100	—	—	—
Firebird ↑	3200	4100	4700	6000	6800	8700	11,000	12,800
Firebird ↓	2100	2600	3200	4400	5300	7000	9200	11,800
Trans Am ↑	5700	6800	7800	9400	11,100	12,600	16,000	19,000
Trans Am ↓	4400	5200	6000	8600	9300	10,700	14,000	16,500

Reliability	❶	❶	❶	❷	③	③	④	④
Air conditioning	❶	❷	③	③	③	④	⑤	⑤
Body integrity	❶	❶	❶	❶	❶	❶	❶	❶
Braking system	❶	❶	❶	❶	③	③	③	⑤
Electrical system	❶	❶	❶	❶	❶	❶	③	④
Engines	❶	❷	③	③	③	③	④	④
Exhaust/Converter	❶	❶	③	③	③	③	④	④
Fuel system	❶	❶	❷	❷	❷	❷	④	④
Ignition system	❶	③	❷	③	❷	❷	④	④
Manual transmission	❷	③	③	③	④	④	⑤	⑤
- automatic	❷	③	③	③	③	④	⑤	⑤
Rust/Paint	❶	❶	❶	❷	❷	❷	③	④
Steering	❷	③	③	③	③	③	③	④
Suspension	❶	❷	❷	❷	❷	③	③	④
Dealer Service	❷	❷	③	③	③	③	④	④
Maintenance	③	③	③	③	③	③	④	④
Parts Availability	❷	❷	④	④	④	④	④	④
Repair Costs	③	③	③	③	③	③	④	④
Crash Safety	⑤	⑤	⑤	⑤	⑤	⑤	⑤	⑤
Safety Features								
ABS	—	—	—	—	—	—	S	S
Airbag	—	—	—	D	D	D	D/P	D/P

Corvette

Rating: Average buy (1994); Not Recommended (1980-93).

Price analysis: Limited availability and fairly expensive. Expect to pay about $600 annually for maintenance and repairs during the warranty period and $1000 annually thereafter, making it imperative that you shop around for a Corvette with some of the base warranty unexpired. The convertible's accident repair costs are much higher than average. Other sports cars worth considering: Chrysler Laser/Talon 4X4 and Stealth • Ford Mustang or Probe • Honda Prelude or CRX • Mazda Miata, MX-3 or RX-7 • Nissan 240SX • Toyota Celica and MR2.

Technical Data

ENGINES	Litres/CID	HP	MPG	Model Years
OHV V8 FI	5.7/350	225-245	17-26	1988-93
OHV V8 FI	5.7/350	300	17-26	1994
OHV V8 FI	5.7/350	405	17-24	1988-93
DOHC V8 FI	5.7/350	375	17-24	1990-93

Strengths and weaknesses: Corvettes made in the late 1960s and early 1970s are Above Average buys due mainly to their value as collector cars and uncomplicated repairs. Parts for these older cars are often more easily found through collectors' clubs than many high-tech components used today. The Corvette's overall reliability has declined as its price and complexity have increased over the years. This is due in large part to GM's "updating" its antiquated design with high-tech, complicated add-ons, rather than coming up with something original. Consequently, the car has been gutted and then retuned using failure-prone electronic circuitry and miles of emissions plumbing in order to become a fuel efficient, user friendly, high-performance vehicle. Unfortunately, the Corvette has missed these goals by a large margin.

The electronically controlled suspension systems have been glitch-plagued over the past several years. Servicing the different sophisticated fuel-injection systems is not easy—even (especially) for GM mechanics. The noisy 5.7L engine frequently hesitates and stalls, there's lots of transmission buzz and whine, and excessive noise from the rear tires, wind whistling through the A- and C-pillars, and the all-too-familiar fiberglass body squeaks continue to be unwanted standard features throughout all model years. The electronic dash never works quite right (speedometer lag, for example).

On the other hand, Corvette ownership does have its positive side with more recent models. For example, the ABS vented disc brakes, available since 1986, are easy to modulate and fade-free. The standard European-made Bilstein FX-3 Selective Ride Control suspension can be preset for touring, sport or performance. Under speed, an electronic module automatically varies the suspension setting—finally curing these cars of their all-too-familiar oversteer, wheelspinning, breakaway rear ends and other nasty surprises that would suddenly appear with earlier Corvettes.

Summary of shortcomings: If you're planning to buy a used Corvette, don't buy any model made before 1992—and make sure you get some of GM's original warranty or a supplementary warranty with later models! The frequency of repairs and high repair costs are outrageous on all but the more recent versions. Although older cars are likely to be junked or already restored, here are some of the things that can put a large dent in your wallet if they haven't been fixed already.

1977-83-Major mechanical failings affect the air conditioning, transmission, clutch, shift linkage, camshaft lifters and rear half-shaft soft yokes, carburetor, steering, rear brakes, starter and electrical system, including the lights. As far as body assembly goes, the major deficiencies are poor panel fits, faulty and fragile interior/exterior parts and trim items, quirky instruments, cheap upholstery and defective window lifts. Owners also complain of poor quality of workmanship/shoddy assembly causing a cacophony of squeaks and rattles, poor dealer servicing, unavailable and expensive parts, and excessive labor charges. No crashworthiness data is available before 1984.

1984-94-Incredibly difficult to service. One *Lemon-Aid* reader had a faulty engine bearing at 16,000 km and spent $2500 to remove the engine. It takes half a day to change the spark plugs on the passenger side. Likely mechanical problem areas are the emission-control system (injectors, computer-controlled sensors, fuel injection, and engine gaskets), engine and drivetrain failures, air conditioning, ignition/distributor, Bosche radio malfunctions, and frequent wheel alignments. Fragile body hardware, poor fit and finish, and wind/road noise/water intrusion into the interior are still a major weakness. Owners complain of faulty controls and window lifts and defective paint (base coat comes through the finish), interior/exterior parts and trim, glass and weatherstripping, instruments, lights, door locks, upholstery and carpeting. The only bright spot is that the '92 and later models are much improved with problems affecting mostly the electronic and electrical system, body hardware, fit and finish, suspension and air conditioning.

Safety summary/recalls: Crash tests of an '84 Corvette have shown that the driver and passenger would be well-protected. Although frontal crash protection is excellent, the Insurance Institute for Highway Safety found that fatality rates from all kinds of crashes involving Corvettes during 1985-89 was the highest of any car. *Recalls*: **1990**-Inoperative parking brakes will get a new brake lever assembly. The fuel feed and return line connectors may leak fuel.

Secret Warranties/Service Tips/DSBs

1982-91-Hydramatic 4L60/700R4 automatic transmission may have no upshift or appear to be stuck in 1st gear. The probable cause is a worn governor gear. It would be wise to also replace the retaining ring. **1982-93**-Vehicles equipped with a Hydramatic 4L60 transmission that "buzzes" when the car is in Reverse or idle may need a new oil pressure regulator valve.
1984-The cruise control vacuum solenoid valve may malfunction when engaged, resulting in unexpected engine acceleration. A GM dealer will modify the mechanism, if the solenoid causes the problem, at no cost to the owner.
1985-If your Corvette lacks power or shudders when traveling under 41 mph, chances are that the PROM module is defective. Replace it with an upgraded PROM (#1227805).
1987-A persistent poor idling or stalling problem may be a signal that the PROM is malfunctioning. Remember, the PROM is often called a MEMCAL, and the part number varies according to the kind of Corvette you drive (DSB 87-278-6E).
1987-89-Revised cylinder head gaskets provide better sealing (DSB 89-283-6A).
1988-Faulty window lift motors that operate erratically or fail may

need a new brush replacement package (#22094719).

1988-89-A special GM policy will cover repainting costs on white cars that have yellowed (DSB 89-136-10).

• The rear wheel tie-rod end could fracture. GM will replace any defective tie-rod assembly free of charge.

• No-start, hard start, long cranks and engine surge may be caused by defective MAF relays.

1990-91-Engine wiring short-circuits may be caused by an abraded electrical harness at the mounting clamp just below the oil pressure sensor.

1992-5.7L engines may develop leaks at the oil filter area. GM Campaign 92COS will cover the cost of repairs.

• 5.7L engines may backfire excessively when shifting from 1st to 2nd gear with the throttle wide open. Correct by changing the MEMCAL module.

• Oil leaks from the rear of a 5.0L or 5.7L engine may be caused by insufficient sealing around the camshaft plug. Replace the plug and reseal.

1994-Excessive oil consumption is likely due to delaminated intake manifold gaskets. Install an upgraded intake manifold gasket kit.

• Delayed automatic transmission shift engagement is a common problem addressed in DSB 47-71-20A.

All models/years-A rotten egg odor coming from the exhaust is probably caused by a defective catalytic converter that's covered by the 5 year/80,000 km emissions warranty. Clearcoat paint degradation, whitening, and chalking, long a problem with GM's other cars, is also a serious problem with the fiberglass bodied Corvette, says DSB 331708. It, too, is covered by a secret warranty up to six years.

Vehicle Profile

	1987	1988	1989	1990	1991	1992	1993	1994
Cost Price ($)								
Base	37,453	41,636	44,850	47,425	42,798	40,398	41,398	43,398
Convertible	44,317	47,744	50,698	53,623	48,398	48,098	48,298	50,498
ZR-1	—	—	—	—	—	76,998	78,898	—
Used Values ($)								
Base ↑	10,000	11,900	15,400	18,700	22,800	28,000	31,700	36,000
Base ↓	8000	9200	12,400	15,700	19,800	24,000	27,700	33,000
Convertible ↑	13,000	15,000	18,700	22,100	26,000	31,600	34,000	37,000
Convertible ↓	11,500	12,500	15,700	19,100	22,000	27,600	31,000	34,000
ZR-1 ↑	—	—	—	—	—	43,000	51,000	—
ZR-1 ↓	—	—	—	—	—	33,000	41,000	—
Reliability	②	②	②	②	②	③	③	④
Air conditioning	②	③	③	③	③	③	③	③
Body integrity	①	②	②	②	②	②	②	②
Braking system	④	③	③	③	③	③	④	④

Electrical system	①	②	②	②	②	②	②	③
Engines	③	③	③	②	②	③	③	③
Exhaust/Converter	②	②	②	②	③	③	④	④
Fuel system	①	②	②	②	②	②	③	③
Ignition system	①	②	②	②	②	②	③	④
Manual transmission	②	②	②	③	③	③	④	④
- automatic	②	③	③	①	③	③	③	③
Rust/Paint	②	②	②	③	③	③	④	④
Steering	②	②	②	②	③	③	④	④
Suspension	①	②	②	②	②	③	④	④
Dealer Service	③	③	③	③	③	④	④	④
Maintenance	②	②	②	②	②	③	④	④
Parts Availability	②	②	②	③	③	③	③	③
Repair Costs	①	②	②	②	②	③	③	③
Crash Safety	⑤	⑤	⑤	⑤	⑤	⑤	⑤	⑤
Safety Features								
ABS	S	S	S	S	S	S	S	S
Airbag	—	—	—	—	D	D	D/P	D/P
Traction control	—	—	—	—	—	—	S	S

Fiero

Rating: Not Recommended (1984-88). A real fire-trap.

Price analysis: Average availability and fairly cheap—for a reason. No one wants these orphaned lemons. Expect to pay about $900 annually for maintenance and repairs—if you're lucky. Other sports cars worth considering: Chrysler Laser/Talon 4X4 or Stealth • Ford Mustang or Probe • Honda Prelude or CRX Mazda Miata, MX-3 or RX-7 Nissan 240SX • Toyota Celica and MR2.

Technical Data

ENGINES	Litres/CID	HP	MPG	Model Years
OHV I-4 FI	2.5/151	98	21-25	1985-88
OHV V6 FI	2.8/173	140	19-23	1985-88

Strengths and weaknesses: This rear-engined two-seater may seem like an inexpensive alternative to a real sports car, but it is disappointing in all respects. Performance is weak with the 2.5L engine, the vehicle is unstable on slippery surfaces and the reliability record has been dismal. Repair and maintenance costs are higher than average. Due to a poor reputation, resale has become difficult—especially for 4-cylinder Fieros.
  Cars equipped with the 2.5L 4-cylinder have experienced cracked

engine blocks. The V6 engine has a better overall reliability record, but it's still a headache. The cooling system has been troublesome on all Fieros, which can lead to overheating and extensive engine damage. Electronic engine controls are temperamental; the throttle position sensor (TPS) requires frequent replacement. Clutches wear out quickly and are frequently defective. Front brake rotors score and warp easily, and the parking brake cables seize after only a few winter months. Electrical accessories are unreliable. Door window mechanisms often go out of adjustment. Body integrity is poor and complaints about body hardware are frequent. The aluminum wheels are easily damaged by corrosion and road hazards.

The Fiero is a sports car to avoid at all costs. Even if you put the odds on your side by purchasing a 6-cylinder, low-mileage Fiero at a bargain-basement price, chances are you will lose your shirt through high maintenance and insurance costs. Don't expect to make money through the Fiero's attractive styling pushing up its value on the used car market. Everybody knows these cars are lemons and there is absolutely no chance their value will increase over the years. Towing is not recommended.

Safety summary/recalls: Crash tests of an '84 Fiero concluded that the driver and front seat passenger would have been well-protected. *Recalls*: **1984-86**-Parking brake may fail due to a faulty adjuster in the rear disc assembly. **1985-86**-For vehicles with a manual transmission, the parking brake adjuster may not hold vehicle when parked on an incline. **1985-88**-Possibility of connecting rod failure leading to engine compartment fire. Lots of other problems that could create a fire hazard, including defective PCV grommet oil leaks, transmission oil cooler leaks, fuel rail leaks, coolant leaks, rocker cover oil leaks and poor maintenance on V6-equipped cars.

Secret Warranties/Service Tips/DSBs

1984-Replacement of the TCS switch wire will correct poor idling.
1984-86-2.5L engine block/cylinder head cracking.
1985-86-A prematurely worn-out clutch is likely caused by the master cylinder not releasing fully, causing constant wear of the clutch plate. The master cylinder push-rod bushing is the likely culprit.
• A loud engine knock could be caused by a defective timing gear assembly. The cam, thrust plate and crank gear may have to be replaced (DSB 86-6-64).
• Transmission slippage upon acceleration may be caused by a loss of oil pressure due to a defective oil strainer seal. Replace the seal (DSB 86-7-10).
1985-87-If your Fiero has a noisy rear end (a clunk or click when going over small bumps), the likely cause is the rear spring coils hitting against each other.

1985-88-A 2.8L engine that fails to run at closed throttle may have excess residue accumulated inside the throttle body bore.

1986-A constant stalling problem when a warm engine is restarted (with the 2.5L engine) may signal the need for a new PROM module (#16085998).

1986-87-Clutch failures on V6 Fieros with automatic transmissions may be caused by a broken spring finger or bent release fork.

1987-Hard starting or pinging with a 2.5L engine requires a new, upgraded PROM, fuel sender, pulsator and fuel pump (DSB 88-6-334).

• A number of Fieros were manufactured with defective engine exhaust valve stems (2.5L). This may explain the engine's rough idling, excessive noise and hesitation upon acceleration. Install oversize valves or, if this doesn't work, replace the cylinder head and all exhaust valves.

1987-88-If the engine stalls when shifting to Reverse or Drive, replace the auxiliary valve body filter.

Vehicle Profile

	1984	1985	1986	1987	1988
Cost Price ($)					
Base	10,200	10,874	11,410	12,000	13,548
Used Values ($)					
Base ↑	700	1100	1700	2100	2600
Base ↓	500	800	1300	1600	1800
Reliability	❶	❶	❶	❶	❷
Crash Safety	⑤	⑤	⑤	⑤	⑤

HONDA

Prelude

Rating: Recommended (1992-94); Above Average buy (1988-92); Average buy (1985-87).

Price analysis: Limited availability and fairly expensive. According to the CAA, parts are a bit more expensive than other cars in this class. Expect to pay about $300 annually for maintenance and repairs during the warranty period and $500 annually thereafter. To avoid costly engine repairs, check the engine timing belt every 2 years/40,000 km and replace it every 96,000 km ($250). Other sports cars worth considering: Chrysler Laser/Talon 4X4 and Stealth • Ford Mustang or Probe • Honda CRX • Mazda Miata, MX-3 or RX-7 • Nissan 240SX • Toyota Celica and MR2.

Technical Data

ENGINES	Litres/CID	HP	MPG	Model Years
OHC I-4 2X1 bbl.	1.8/113	100	20-25	1985-87
OHC I-4 FI	2.0/119	110	20-25	1985-87
OHC I-4 2X1 bbl.	2.0/119	105	19-24	1988-90
DOHC I-4 FI	2.0/119	135	19-24	1988-91
DOHC I-4 FI	2.1/125	140	18-23	1991
OHC I-4 FI	2.2/132	135	21-26	1992-95
DOHC VTEC	2.2/132	190	20-24	1993-95
DOHC I-4 FI	2.3/138	160	21-25	1992-95

Strengths and weaknesses: Unimpressive as a high-performance sports car, the Prelude delivers a stylish exterior, legendary reliability and excellent resale value, instead. Don't expect to find any bargains.

1985-87-First-generation Preludes were described as luxury sporty cars but didn't offer much of either. They should be inspected carefully for engine problems and severe underbody corrosion, particularly near the fuel tank. Noisy front brakes, premature disc warpage, high oil consumption and worn engine crankshaft/camshaft lobes are the main problem areas with these models. They are also prone to extensive surface rust and perforations around wheel openings, door bottoms, trunk lids, fenders, rear taillights and bumper supports.

1983-87-Preludes have problems with corrosion on key chassis members, suspension components and the fuel tank.

1988-91 models offer more and smoother engine power, excellent handling and improved reliability. There are some generic complaints that continue to crop up, including rapid front brake wear, scored and warped front brake rotors, some automatic transmission failures, defective constant velocity joints, premature exhaust system rust-out and a warping hood.

1992-94 models are afflicted by fewer, but all-too-familiar glitches, including minor electrical problems, body and accessory defects, brake squealing, and prematurely warped front brake rotors. Most independent mechanics are ill-equipped to service these cars because they have gotten increasingly more complicated to repair during the past three years.

Confidential dealer service bulletins show the following problems on the '93 models: poor radio reception on the AM band, excessive steering wheel vibrations, CD magazine changer in trunk won't eject and noisy window regulators. DSBs covering the '94 models mostly concern body and accessory deficiencies, including buzzing in the driver's door, cup holders that don't stay closed, fuel filler doors that won't stay open, cellular phone troubleshooting, and noise from the driver's seat track. Steering wheel shimmy continues to be a problem.

Safety summary/recalls: NHTSA crash tests of a 1984 Prelude two-door concluded that the driver and front seat passenger would have been well-protected. A 1990 two-door Prelude did not do as well: the driver was judged to have sustained severe or fatal head trauma. A '93 model passed with flying colors. Standard dual airbags were added to the '92 Si and adopted on all 1994 versions. ABS became standard with the 1991 Si and was optional with other models. *Recalls*: **1978-85**-Severe chassis corrosion around fuel tank and body seams prompted Honda to provide free chassis repairs, suspension/steering component and fuel tank replacement under a "silent" recall campaign. **1983-87**-Road salt may cause the fuel filler/and or breather pipe to rust through, resulting in leaks. A recall campaign has been organized to fix this defect. **1988**-Rusting of the coil spring support could cause loss of control. Power-steering hose leaks may cause a fire.

Secret Warranties/Service Tips/DSBs

1988-Windshield may suddenly crack due to defective lower rubber spacers.

1988-89-A power-steering moan signals the need for a new control valve (#53647-SF1-305).

1988-90-If water leaks onto the speaker housing and grill, apply sealer to the outside mirror, replace the damaged speaker and install a plastic sheet around the back of the speaker housing.

1988-93-Poor AM reception or popping from the speakers is likely due to a poor ground connection between the antenna collar and car body. Correct by improving the ground connection and tightening the antenna assembly mounting nuts in the proper sequence.

• Creaking from the window regulator can be corrected by installing an upgraded regulator spiral spring.

1990-Defective AC compressor pickup sensors are a common problem.

1992-Rattling from the front of the car when driving over rough surfaces that goes away with light brake application can be corrected by installing new front brake pad retainers.

All models/years-Steering wheel shimmy can be reduced by rebalancing the wheel/tire/hub/rotor assembly in the front end. Seatbelts that fail to function properly during normal use will be replaced for free under Honda's lifetime seatbelt warranty.

Honda will also repair or replace defective steering assemblies, constant velocity joints and catalytic converters free of charge up to 5 years/80,000 km on a case-by-case basis. There is no labor charge or deductible. Used vehicles and repairs carried out by independent garages are not covered by this special program. The converter is almost always covered under the emissions warranty.

Most Honda DSBs allow for special warranty consideration on a "goodwill" basis for most problems even after the warranty has expired or the car has changed hands.

Vehicle Profile

	1987	1988	1989	1990	1991	1992	1993	1994
Cost Price ($)								
Base/SR	15,495	18,395	19,250	19,455	17,575	16,550	26,195	27,300
2.0L Si	17,895	20,295	21,580	22,155	22,190	19,650	—	—
VTEC	—	—	—	—	—	—	27,295	28,295
Used Values ($)								
Base/SR ↑	4700	5900	6800	7900	8900	10,100	14,500	18,000
Base/SR ↓	3700	4600	5400	6500	7500	8500	12,900	17,000
2.0L Si ↑	6200	7400	8200	9300	10,300	11,500	—	—
2.0L Si ↓	5000	6100	6800	7500	8900	10,300	—	—
VTEC ↑	—	—	—	—	—	—	15,900	18,900
VTEC ↓	—	—	—	—	—	—	14,000	17,000
Reliability	③	④	⑤	⑤	⑤	⑤	⑤	⑤
Air conditioning	②	②	③	③	④	⑤	⑤	⑤
Body integrity	③	③	⑤	⑤	⑤	⑤	⑤	⑤
Braking system	①	①	①	③	③	④	④	④
Electrical system	②	②	②	③	③	④	④	④
Engines	③	④	⑤	⑤	⑤	⑤	⑤	⑤
Exhaust/Converter	②	②	③	⑤	⑤	⑤	⑤	⑤
Fuel system	④	④	④	④	④	⑤	⑤	⑤
Ignition system	④	④	④	④	④	⑤	⑤	⑤
Manual transmission	⑤	⑤	⑤	⑤	⑤	⑤	⑤	⑤
- automatic	③	③	③	④	⑤	⑤	⑤	⑤
Rust/Paint	②	②	④	⑤	⑤	⑤	⑤	⑤
Steering	②	②	③	④	⑤	⑤	④	④
Suspension	②	③	③	④	⑤	⑤	⑤	⑤
Dealer Service	④	④	④	④	④	④	⑤	⑤
Maintenance	⑤	⑤	⑤	⑤	⑤	⑤	⑤	⑤
Parts Availability	③	③	④	④	④	④	⑤	⑤
Repair Costs	⑤	⑤	⑤	⑤	⑤	⑤	⑤	⑤
Crash Safety	⑤	⑤	⑤	❷	❷	❷	⑤	⑤
Safety Features								
ABS	—	—	—	—	S	S	S	S
Airbag	—	—	—	—	—	D	D	D/P

HYUNDAI

Scoupe

Rating: Below Average buy (1991-94). An Excel cross-dressing as a sports car.

Price analysis: Average availability and fairly reasonably priced. Expect to pay about $300 annually for maintenance and repairs during the warranty period and $800 annually thereafter—more than enough reason to reject any Scoupe that doesn't have some of the original base warranty in effect. Other sports cars worth considering: Chrysler Laser/Talon 4X4 and Stealth • Ford Mustang or Probe • Honda Prelude or CRX • Mazda Miata, MX-3 or RX-7 • Nissan 240SX • Toyota Celica and MR2.

Technical Data

ENGINES	Litres/CID	HP	MPG	Model Years
OHC I-4 FI	1.5/90	81	25-31	1991-92
OHC I-4 FI	1.5/91	92	25-32	1993-95
OHC I-4T FI	1.5/91	115	23-29	1993-95

Strengths and weaknesses: This is essentially a cute coupe with an engine more suited to high gas mileage than hard driving. Except for its lighter weight, less luggage space and shorter overall length, the Scoupe's really an Excel clone, and there are better performing and more reliable sports coupes available. Plenty of interior room up front but the roof is too angular; if you are short and have to pull the seat up, your head almost touches the roof. Fuel efficient. Good heating and ventilation system.

This is far from a performance car, mainly due to the Excel's underpinnings and drivetrain. The 4-speed automatic transmission robs the base engine of much-needed horsepower making for poor acceleration on inclines and constant shifting between 2500 to 3500 rpm's when pushed. Suspension may be too firm for some. Plenty of body roll in turns; mediocre steering. Brakes are hard to modulate. Inadequate rear interior room.

Customer service has improved, if only because the dealers have more factory support. Body construction is sloppy, giving rise to wind/water leaks, rattles and breakage. Lots of engine and road noise intrudes into the interior. Owners also report frequent brake and wheel-bearing problems.

Confidential dealer service bulletins show the following problems on the 1993 models: harsh shifting with the automatic transmission when accelerating or coming to a stop, excessive disc brake noise, engine has difficulty reaching recommended operating temperature (MPI fault code #21), low fuel pressure; possible fuel leak at fuel gauge connection valve and wheel cover discoloration. DSBs for 1994 models address starting difficulties, transmission glitches, AC failures, noisy shock absorbers, and radio malfunctions.

Safety summary/recalls: A '91 Scoupe performed very well in the

404

NHTSA 57 km/h crash tests: both the driver and front passenger came out unscathed. Retested '93 and '94 models were judged to produce serious driver and passenger leg injuries. Airbags and ABS aren't available. *Recalls*: N/A.

Secret Warranties/Service Tips/DSBs

1991-Stalling when shifting into gear immediately after starting a cold engine may be corrected by installing a Cold Start Enrichment Kit (#39901-24Q00D).

1991-92-A harsh shift when coming to a stop or upon acceleration may be due to a misadjusted accelerator switch TCU.

1992-94-Hyundai has a field fix for manual transaxle gear clash/grind (DSB 9440-004).

1993-94-Hyundai has developed an improved spark plug (painted yellow on the tip) for better cold weather starting.

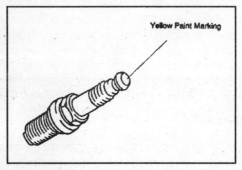

Yellow Paint Marking

1994-DSB 94-01-010-Hyundai will replace the AC discharge hose for free under a special service campaign.

• Rear shock noise may be silenced by installing upgraded shock absorbers.

• Model 840 radio noise can be corrected by installing a unit with an improved noise reduction filter.

Vehicle Profile

	1991	1992	1993	1994
Cost Price ($)				
Base	9645	10,125	10,995	11,595
LS	11,045	11,595	12,495	12,995
Used Values ($)				
Base ↑	5300	6700	7500	9400
Base ↓	4300	5400	6400	8000
LS ↑	5900	7400	8700	10,600
LS ↓	4700	6200	7500	9100

Reliability	③	③	③	③
Air conditioning	④	④	④	❷
Automatic transmission	③	③	③	③
Body integrity	❷	❷	③	③
Braking system	❷	❷	③	③
Electrical system	❷	❷	③	③
Engines	⑤	⑤	④	④
Exhaust/Converter	⑤	⑤	⑤	⑤
Fuel system	③	③	③	③
Ignition system	④	④	④	④
Rust/Paint	③	③	③	③
Steering	③	③	③	③
Suspension	⑤	⑤	④	④
Dealer Service	③	③	③	③
Maintenance	③	③	④	④
Parts Availability	④	④	④	④
Repair Costs	③	③	④	④
Crash Safety	⑤	⑤	❶	❶

MAZDA

MX-3, Precidia

Rating: Recommended buy (1992-94).

Price analysis: Below average availability and fairly expensive. According to the CAA, Mazda parts cost far more than average. Expect to pay about $300 annually for maintenance and repairs during the warranty period and $700 annually thereafter. Other sports cars worth considering: Chrysler Laser/Talon 4X4 • Ford Mustang or Probe • Honda Prelude or CRX • Nissan 200SX • Saturn SC • Toyota Celica or MR2.

Technical Data

ENGINES	Litres/CID	HP	MPG	Model Years
OHC I-4 FI	1.6/98	88	24-33	1992-93
DOHC I-4 FI	1.6/98	105	23-31	1994
DOHC V6 FI	1.8/113	130	20-26	1992-93

Strengths and weaknesses: The base 1.6L engine supplies plenty of power for most driving situations. When equipped with the optional 1.8L V6 powerplant (the smallest V6 on the market) and high-performance options, the Precidia transforms itself into a 130-

horsepower pocket rocket. In fact, the MX-3 GS sports coupe easily outperforms the 4-cylinder Honda del Sol, Toyota Paseo and Geo Storm for comfort and high-performance thrills. It does fall a bit short of the Saturn SC due to its limited low-end torque, and fuel economy is disappointing. Reverse gear sometimes hard to engage.

Brake and wheel-bearing problems are commonplace. Most of the MX-3's parts are used on other Mazda cars, so their overall reliability should be outstanding. Customer service has deteriorated a great deal and parts are sometimes hard to find.

Body assembly is average and rattles/squeaks are common. Owners have complained, of paint defects and sheet metal that is too thin above the door handles. Dents in the metal are caused where you would ordinarily place your thumb when closing the door. Some reports of wind and water leaks around the doors and windows. Moderate engine noise increases dramatically above 110 km/h.

Small door openings a hardship for tall occupants on entry and exit. Steering wheel rubs against thighs even when the seat is pushed as far back as it will go. Rear headroom and legroom limited. A high beltline and cowl add to a claustrophobic feeling. Trunk has a high liftover.

Safety summary/recalls: U.S. government 57 km/h frontal crash tests show both the driver and front passenger would escape serious injury. A retested '93 MX-3 showed the passenger would have received serious leg injuries. The car's tendency to understeer can be unnerving when taking corners at moderate speed. *Recalls*: N/A.

Secret Warranties/Service Tips/DSBs

1992-A front-end snapping noise during tight turns at walking speed is probably caused by excessive clearance between the wheel bearing and steering knuckle. Install modified wheel bearings.
• Idle fluctuation when applying an electrical load during idle or after deceleration from high rpm can be corrected by installing a new Electronic Control Unit.
• Poor AC performance may be due to insufficient airflow across the AC condenser.
• A noisy rear hatch can be silenced by changing the rear hatch glass, hinge or molding.
• Squeaking noise from the rear pillars is due to interference between the rear inner pillar and its reinforcement.
• A sulphur odor coming from the exhaust can be eliminated by installing an upgraded catalytic converter.
• Turn signals that cancel before the turn is completed need an upgraded combination switch.
1992-93-A cracking noise around the windshield can be corrected by inserting a felt pad between the area where the instrument panel contacts the frame.

1992-94-Freezing door and hatch lock cylinders are addressed in DSB 021/94.

• Clutch squealing can be silenced by installing an upgraded part with a thicker clutch cushioning plate.

1994-Timing belt noise can be silenced by replacing the tensioner pulley with an upgraded part.

All models/years-DSB 006/94 gives all of the possible causes and remedies for brake vibrations.

Vehicle Profile

	1992	1993	1994
Cost Price ($)			
Base	13,725	13,995	15,175
GS	16,725	17,065	19,010
Used Values ($)			
Base ↑	8800	10,300	11,800
Base ↓	7700	9000	10,400
GS ↑	10,900	12,400	13,900
GS ↓	9600	11,000	12,400
Reliability	④	⑤	⑤
Air conditioning	③	④	④
Automatic transmission	⑤	⑤	⑤
Body integrity	❷	③	④
Braking system	④	⑤	⑤
Electrical system	③	④	④
Engines	⑤	⑤	⑤
Exhaust/Converter	③	④	④
Fuel system	⑤	⑤	⑤
Ignition system	⑤	⑤	⑤
Rust/Paint	③	③	④
Steering	⑤	⑤	⑤
Suspension	④	⑤	⑤
Dealer Service	③	③	③
Maintenance	⑤	⑤	⑤
Parts Availability	③	③	③
Repair Costs	③	③	③
Crash Safety	⑤	❷	❷
Safety Features			
ABS	—	O	O
Airbag	—	—	D/P

Miata, MX-5

Rating: Recommended (1990-94).

Price analysis: Average availability and reasonably priced. Parts aren't easily found and cost more than average. Expect to pay about $300 annually for maintenance and repairs during the warranty period and $600 annually thereafter. Other sports cars worth considering: Chrysler Laser/Talon 4X4 and Stealth • Ford Mustang or Probe • Honda Prelude or CRX • Mazda MX-3 or RX-7 • Nissan 240SX • Toyota Celica and MR2.

Technical Data

ENGINES	Litres/CID	HP	MPG	Model Years
DOHC I-4 FI	1.6/98	116	23-31	1990-93
DOHC I-4 FI	1.8/112	128	22-26	1994-95

Strengths and weaknesses: The base 1.6L engine delivers adequate power and accelerates smoothly with a top speed of 115 mph. Acceleration from 0-to-60 mph is in the high eight-second range, which is on par with the 16-valve VW GTi but slower than the Honda CRX Si. The 5-speed manual transmission is easy shifting and has well-spaced gears. Lightness and 50/50 weight distribution make it an easy car to toss around corners but quite jittery on uneven roads. The double A-arm suspension front and rear helps to smooth out most of the bumps. Steering is crisp and predictable. Very effective vented front disc brakes. Rear solid disc brakes have a limiting valve if the rear end is a little light when stopping.

Incredible as it may seem, this little Mazda sportster has few factory-related defects or parts that wear out prematurely. Only electrical system failures and minor body and trim deficiencies are reported with any frequency.

Safety summary/recalls: Crash tests of a 1990 Miata concluded the front seat passenger would be well-protected, but the driver would have sustained severe leg injuries. A retested '93 model posted identical results. *Recalls*: **1990-93**-The optional hardtop's hoist accessory kit may have plastic buckles that break and allow the hardtop to suddenly fall, causing possible injury. **1991**-Faulty anti-lock brakes will be fixed by Mazda.

Secret Warranties/Service Tips/DSBs

1990-A hard-to-close trunk lid requires an upgraded rubber cushion (#B48156786).
• Poor AC performance is likely caused by the misalignment of the AC harness.
• A rattling noise coming from the exhaust manifold may require the replacement of the insulator bracket.
• Water may damage door speakers unless a speaker cover assembly (#B4Y5 7696X) is installed.
• A musty odor coming from the AC system can be cured by installing an upgraded resin-coated evaporator core (#NA0J 61II0A).
1990-91-Hard shifting into 2nd gear before the vehicle has warmed up can be corrected by installing an upgraded 2nd gear synchronizer ring and clutch hub sleeve (#JM1NA351-M-232720).
1990-95-Dirt and debris can clog up side sill drain holes allowing water to collect and corrosion to occur. The dealer will drill larger drain holes and repaint the area under the car's base warranty.
1992-94-If the window won't open fully, install a new cable fastener.
1994-Timing belt noise can be silenced by replacing the tensioner pulley with an upgraded part.
All models/years-DSB 006/94 gives all of the possible causes and remedies for brake vibration.

Vehicle Profile

	1990	1991	1992	1993	1994
Cost Price ($)					
Base	18,590	17,255	17,945	18,895	20,165
Used Values ($)					
Base ↑	10,300	11,400	12,900	13,900	15,600
Base ↓	8700	9700	10,900	11,800	13,400
Reliability	④	④	④	⑤	⑤
Air conditioning	④	④	④	⑤	⑤
Body integrity	❷	❷	❸	❸	❸
Braking system	④	④	④	④	④
Electrical system	❷	❷	❷	❸	❸
Engines	④	④	④	⑤	⑤
Exhaust/Converter	④	④	④	⑤	⑤
Fuel system	❸	④	④	⑤	⑤
Ignition system	❸	④	④	④	④
Manual transmission	⑤	⑤	⑤	⑤	⑤
- automatic	—	—	—	④	④
Rust/Paint	❸	④	⑤	⑤	⑤
Steering	⑤	⑤	⑤	⑤	⑤
Suspension	⑤	⑤	⑤	⑤	⑤

Dealer Service	❶	❶	❶	④	④
Maintenance	④	④	④	④	④
Parts Availability	④	④	④	④	④
Repair Costs	❷	③	③	⑤	⑤
Crash Safety	❷	❷	❷	❷	❷
Safety Features					
ABS	—	O	O	O	O
Airbag	D	D	D	D	D/P

RX-7

Rating: Recommended (1991-94); Above Average buy (1985-90).

Price analysis: Average availability and fairly expensive. Expect to pay about $300 annually for maintenance and repairs during the warranty period and $400 annually thereafter. Other sports cars worth considering: Chrysler Laser/Talon 4X4 and Stealth • Ford Mustang or Probe • Honda Prelude or CRX • Mazda Miata and MX-3 • Nissan 240SX • Toyota Celica and MR2.

Technical Data

ENGINES	Litres/CID	HP	MPG	Model Years
Wankel FI	1.3/80	160	15-18	1986-91
Wankel FI	1.3/80	200	14-17	1986-91
Wankel FI	1.3/81	255	13-17	1991-94

Strengths and weaknesses: The RX-7 is an impressive performer that goes from 0 to 100 km in eight seconds and covers the same distance in 6.2 seconds when equipped with a turbocharger. The ride can be painful on bad roads, though, due primarily to the car's stiff suspension. The GSL and Turbo models are very well equipped and luxuriously finished. Except for some oil-burning problems, apex seal failures and leaking engine O-rings, the RX-7 has served to dispel any doubts concerning the durability of rotary engines.

Nevertheless, careful maintenance is in order; contaminated oil or overheating will damage the engine. Clutches wear quickly if used hard. Disc brakes need frequent attention to the calipers and rotors. The MacPherson struts get soft more quickly than average. Be wary of leaky sun roofs. Radiators have a short lifespan. Rocker panels and body seams are prone to more serious rusting. The underbody on older cars should be inspected carefully for corrosion damage. Fuel economy has never been this car's strong suit.

RX-7s aren't as well made as Miatas, if one were to judge them both on the basis of consumer complaints relative to body hardware, brakes, fuel and exhaust system, electrical glitches, AC malfunctions and clutch failures. Fortunately, parts aren't difficult to find.

Safety summary/recalls: Crash tests of a 1985 RX-7 showed that the front passenger would sustain severe or fatal head injuries. In an '88 RX-7, the driver would have sustained serious leg injuries. Safety investigators believe that 1993 RX-7s could experience engine overheating and engine failure caused by a faulty turbocharger. Optional ABS first appeared on the '87 Turbo and GXL and became standard on all '93 versions. *Recalls*: **1979-83**-Idler arms may corrode, freeze or break after prolonged exposure to road salt. **1986-87**-Road salt may also cause excessive front brake disc pad liner corrosion. **1993-95**-Fuel hoses may crack and leak fuel.

Secret Warranties/Service Tips/DSBs

1979-91-Hard shifting into 2nd gear before the vehicle has warmed up can be corrected by installing an upgraded 2nd gear synchronizer ring and clutch hub sleeve (#JM1NA351-M-232720).
1986-87-Excessive suspension noise during acceleration or deceleration may be due to faulty subframe bolts.
1986-88-A hard-to-start cold engine can be fixed by changing to air gap spark plugs and disconnecting the sub-zero starting assist device.
• Misfire and hesitation over 6000 rpm can be corrected by installing an upgraded air flow meter.
• A rough idle may be caused by a short-circuit in the water temperature switch wiring.
• Erratic power window operation may require a new regulator guide assembly, motor bracket and sprocket.
1987-88-Turbo models with a rough idle or cold starting problems may need a new air control valve (#N332 13990).
1988-89-Front strut noise can be reduced by installing a modified mounting rubber on the front strut.
1993-94-To eliminate slipping clutch problems, Mazda will install, at no charge, an improved clutch disc.
All models/years-DSB 006/94 gives all of the possible causes and remedies for brake vibration.

Vehicle Profile

	1987	1988	1989	1990	1991	1992	1993	1994
Cost Price ($)								
RX-7	18,525	19,570	21,840	22,300	24,650	—	—	—
Convertible	—	34,520	40,690	41,670	38,950	—	—	—
Turbo	28,835	33,020	36,440	37,330	35,890	—	41,820	44,175

Used Values ($)

RX-7 ↑	4500	6000	7100	8800	9700	—	—	—
RX-7 ↓	3800	4400	5500	6800	7700	—	—	—
Convertible ↑	—	12,100	13,800	16,400	19,200	—	—	—
Convertible ↓	—	10,100	11,800	14,000	16,500	—	—	—
Turbo ↑	8200	9700	11,700	13,800	16,700	—	21,000	25,500
Turbo ↓	7000	8100	9700	11,800	14,200	—	18,000	22,000
Reliability	③	③	③	④	⑤	⑤	⑤	⑤
Air conditioning	③	④	④	④	④	⑤	⑤	⑤
Body integrity	③	③	③	③	⑤	⑤	⑤	⑤
Braking system	③	③	③	③	③	③	④	⑤
Electrical system	❷	❷	❷	⑤	⑤	⑤	⑤	⑤
Engines	⑤	⑤	⑤	⑤	⑤	⑤	⑤	⑤
Exhaust/Converter	③	③	③	③	⑤	⑤	⑤	⑤
Fuel system	❷	③	⑤	⑤	⑤	⑤	⑤	⑤
Ignition system	⑤	⑤	⑤	⑤	⑤	⑤	⑤	⑤
Manual transmission	③	③	③	③	④	④	④	④
- automatic	❷	❷	❷	③	④	④	④	④
Rust/Paint	③	③	⑤	⑤	⑤	⑤	⑤	⑤
Steering	⑤	⑤	⑤	⑤	⑤	⑤	⑤	⑤
Suspension	⑤	⑤	⑤	⑤	⑤	⑤	⑤	⑤
Dealer Service	③	③	③	③	③	③	③	③
Maintenance	③	③	③	③	③	③	③	③
Parts Availability	④	④	④	④	④	④	④	④
Repair Costs	❷	❷	❷	③	④	④	④	④
Crash Safety	❷	❷	❷	❷	❷	❷	❷	❷
Safety Features								
ABS	O	O	O	O	O	O	S	S
Airbag	—	—	—	D	D	D/P	D/P	D/P

NISSAN

200SX

Rating: Average buy (1988); Not Recommended (1983-87).

Price analysis: Hard to find but reasonably priced. Expect to pay about $300 annually for maintenance and repairs. Other sports cars worth considering: Chrysler Laser/Talon 4X4 and Stealth • Ford Mustang or Probe • Honda Prelude or CRX • Mazda MX-3, Miata, or RX-7 • Nissan 240SX • Toyota Celica and MR2.

Technical Data

ENGINES	Litres/CID	HP	MPG	Model Years
OHC I-4 FI	2.0/120	102	23-27	1985-88
OHC I-4T FI	1.8/110	120	22-25	1985-86
OHC V6 FI	3.0/181	160	19-23	1987-88

Strengths and weaknesses: Early 200SXs may look sporty, but their interiors are cramped and they provide only average power and handling. Later models are much sportier and have more passenger room. Prices are reasonable. Repair history is average. Parts are easy to obtain, and repairs are straightforward.

There is no solid reliability data available on the 1.8L turbocharged engine. The clutch has been the source of some complaints, along with occasional electrical malfunctions. Rapid brake wear and brake rotor damage are common problems and widespread surface rusting often leads to perforated body panels.

Safety summary/recalls: Crash tests of a 1984 200SX showed that the driver and front seat passenger would sustain serious injuries. A 1984 model showed the driver would have sustained severe or fatal head and leg injuries. The '87 version produced similar results. The underbody also rusts away very quickly on 1986-87 models. Careful inspection for corrosion damage is necessary. *Recalls*: **1982-84**-Nissan will repair faulty front seatbacks.

Secret Warranties/Service Tips/DSBs

1984-88-Improved brake pad material will cut brake noise and add to pad durability. Upgraded semi-metallic pads carry the Hitachi HP12 FE designation.
• Front brake shimmy and judder are covered in DSB TS89-105.
All models/years-DSB 006/94 gives all of the possible causes and remedies for brake vibration.

Vehicle Profile

	1983	1984	1985	1986	1987	1988
Cost Price ($)						
Base	9983	—	13,285	12,396	17,387	16,838
Used Values ($)						
Base ↑	1600	—	2900	3600	4400	5100
Base ↓	1200	—	2500	3000	4000	4500
Reliability	②	②	②	②	③	④
Crash Safety	❶	❶	❶	❶	❶	❶

414

240SX

Rating: Recommended (1992-93); Average buy (1989-91).

Price analysis: Average availability and fairly expensive. Only the convertible was carried over to the '94 model year. Expect to pay about $300 annually for maintenance and repairs during the warranty period and $500 annually thereafter. Other sports cars worth considering: Chrysler Laser/Talon 4X4 and Stealth • Ford Mustang or Probe • Honda Prelude or CRX • Mazda Miata, MX-3 or RX-7 • Nissan 200SX • Toyota Celica and MR2.

Technical Data

ENGINES	Litres/CID	HP	MPG	Model Years
OHC I-4 FI	2.4/146	140	21-25	1989-90
DOHC I-4 FI	2.4/146	155	22-27	1991-94

Strengths and weaknesses: This car doesn't have any major problems. The few problems reported concern electrical malfunctions, premature clutch wear, noisy brakes that wear out quickly, exhaust system rust-out, and fit and finish deficiencies.

Safety summary/recalls: Crash tests of a 1989 240SX concluded that the driver would sustain serious leg injuries. A 1991 model fared much better; both the driver and passenger were judged to have been well-protected. A retested '93 240SX showed the driver would sustain serious injury to one leg. ABS became optional on '91 SE and LE versions. *Recalls*: N/A.

Secret Warranties/Service Tips/DSBs

1989-Doors that won't lock from the outside are covered by a special service campaign that provides for a free door rod clip modification. • Another special service campaign covers the free replacement of the engine timing belt and tensioner. It's worth a fight for a partial refund. **1989-91**-Starting difficulties can often be traced to a connector not fully seated in the ECU. **1990**-Excessive squeaking from the front brakes can be fixed by increasing the front brake pad chamfer. **All models/years**-DSB 006/94 gives all of the possible causes and remedies for brake vibration.

Vehicle Profile

	1989	1990	1991	1992	1993
Cost Price ($)					
Base	17,989	18,890	17,890	22,090	22,890
Used Values ($)					
Base ↑	8000	9400	10,200	13,900	16,500
Base ↓	6600	8000	8700	12,300	14,500
Reliability	③	③	④	⑤	⑤
Air conditioning	③	③	④	④	④
Automatic trans.	③	③	⑤	⑤	⑤
Body integrity	③	③	③	④	④
Braking system	②	②	③	③	④
Electrical system	②	②	③	③	④
Engines	④	④	④	④	⑤
Exhaust/Converter	③	③	③	④	⑤
Fuel system	②	③	③	④	④
Ignition system	③	③	③	④	④
Rust/Paint	③	③	③	④	④
Steering	②	②	④	④	④
Suspension	④	④	④	④	⑤
Dealer Service	④	④	④	④	⑤
Maintenance	④	④	④	④	⑤
Parts Availability	④	④	④	④	⑤
Repair Costs	④	④	④	④	④
Crash Safety	②	②	⑤	⑤	②
Safety Features					
ABS	—	O	O	O	S
Airbag	—	—	—	—	D/P
Traction control	—	—	—	—	S

300ZX

Rating: Above Average buy (1992-94); Not Recommended (1985-91). Nissan's answer to the Corvette, this car has everything: high-performance capability, a heavy chassis, complicated electronics and minimal depreciation.

Price analysis: Average availability and unreasonably expensive. Expect to pay about $500 annually for maintenance and repairs during the warranty period and $800 annually thereafter, making it a good idea to shop around for a model that has some of Nissan's comprehensive warranty left. Insurance premiums are also likely to be very high on all years. Other sports cars worth considering: Chrysler Laser/Talon 4X4 and Stealth • Ford Mustang or Probe • Honda Prelude or CRX

• Mazda Miata, MX-3 or RX-7 • Nissan 240SX • Toyota Celica and MR2.

Technical Data

ENGINES	Litres/CID	HP	MPG	Model Years
OHC V6 FI	3.0/181	160-165	21-25	1988-89
OHC V6T FI	3.0/181	200-205	19-23	1988-89
DOHC V6 FI	3.0/181	222	21-25	1988-89
DOHC V6T FI	3.0/181	300	17-22	1990-93

Strengths and weaknesses: A high-performance car that also offers a high degree of luxury equipment. Turbocharged '90 and later models are much faster than previous versions. Traction is poor on slippery surfaces, however, and the rear suspension hits hard when going over speed bumps. Reliability is about average, but parts and servicing are way out of line. Just replacing the air cleaner and spark plugs is a task.

Lots more problems than you would find on the 240SX due to the complexity of all the 300ZX's bells and whistles. The best example of this is the electrical system—long a source of recurring, hard to diagnose shorts. The manual transmission has been failure prone, clutches don't last very long, front and rear brakes are noisy and wear out quickly, and the aluminum wheels are easily damaged by corrosion and road hazards. The exhaust system is practically biodegradable. The glitzy digital dash with three odometers and weird spongy/stiff variable shock absorbers are more gimmick than practical. Mediocre body assembly.

Safety summary/recalls: Crash tests of an '84 ZX concluded that the driver would sustain severe leg injuries, and the passenger would likely have severe or fatal head and leg injuries. A subsequent test of a '91 version showed both the driver and passenger would be unharmed. A retest of a '93 SX concluded that both the driver and passenger would sustain massive injuries to both legs. *Recalls*: **1979-87**-Nissan will install at no charge a shift interlock to prevent sudden acceleration.

Secret Warranties/Service Tips/DSBs

1984-87-Install a countermeasure mainshaft (#32241-V5280) to reduce transmission clunk.
1984-89-Front brake shimmy and vibration are covered in DSB TS89-105.
1990-Clunking when braking in Reverse can be eliminated by installing a retainer on each front brake pad.
1990-91-Starting difficulties can often be traced to a connector not fully seated in the Electronic Control Unit.

1991-An automatic transmission that shifts poorly or slips out of gear can be fixed by retorquing the band servo retainer bolts.

1992-An oil leak from the drive pinion oil seal can be fixed by installing an upgraded seal.

All models/years-Premature rear brake pad wear may be caused by poorly adjusted brakes or rusty rear rotors. Rear brake pad kit (#D4060-01P90) will help correct the problem. DSB 006/94 gives all of the possible causes and remedies for brake vibration.

Vehicle Profile

	1987	1988	1989	1990	1991	1992	1993	1994
Cost Price ($)								
Base	23,487	24,988	25,100	38,690	37,600	40,990	41,990	46,890
Used Values ($)								
Base ↑	5500	7000	8000	16,800	19,200	23,100	27,200	32,000
Base ↓	4200	5000	5900	14,300	16,700	20,100	24,200	30,000
Reliability	②	②	②	③	③	③	④	④
Air conditioning	③	④	④	④	④	⑤	⑤	⑤
Body integrity	③	③	③	③	③	④	④	④
Braking system	①	①	①	①	①	②	③	④
Electrical system	①	②	②	②	②	④	④	④
Engines	③	③	③	③	③	③	④	④
Exhaust/Converter	①	①	③	③	③	④	④	④
Fuel system	①	③	③	③	④	④	⑤	⑤
Ignition system	①	③	③	④	④	⑤	④	④
Manual transmission	①	③	④	④	④	④	⑤	⑤
- automatic	③	③	④	④	④	⑤	⑤	⑤
Rust/Paint	①	③	③	③	④	⑤	⑤	⑤
Steering	①	③	③	③	③	④	④	④
Suspension	①	③	③	③	③	④	④	④
Dealer Service	③	④	④	④	④	④	④	④
Maintenance	②	②	②	②	③	④	④	④
Parts Availability	③	③	③	③	③	④	④	④
Repair Costs	②	②	②	②	②	②	③	④
Crash Safety	①	①	①	②	⑤	⑤	①	①
Safety Features								
ABS	—	—	—	S	S	S	S	S
Airbag	—	—	—	—	D	D	D	D/P
Traction control	—	—	—	—	—	—	—	S

TOYOTA

Celica

Rating: Recommended (1991-94); Above Average buy (1986-90).

Price analysis: Excellent availability and fairly expensive. Parts cost less than average according to the Canadian Automobile Association. Expect to pay about $300 annually for maintenance and repairs during the warranty period and $400 annually thereafter. Other sports cars worth considering: Chrysler Laser/Talon 4X4 and Stealth • Ford Mustang or Probe • Honda Prelude or CRX • Mazda Miata, MX-3, or RX-7 • Nissan 240SX • Toyota MR2.

Technical Data

ENGINES	Litres/CID	HP	MPG	Model Years
OHC I-4 FI	2.0/122	97	23-27	1986
DOHC I-4 FI	2.0/122	115	24-28	1987-89
DOHC I-4 FI	2.0/122	135	21-25	1986-89
DOHC I-4T FI	2.0/122	190	20-23	1988-89
DOHC I-4 FI	1.6/97	103	23-29	1990-93
DOHC I-4T FI	2.0/122	200	19-23	1990-93
DOHC I-4 FI	2.2/132	135	21-26	1990-93
DOHC I-4 FI	1.8/108	110	26-30	1994-95
DOHC I-4 FI	2.2/132	135	23-27	1994-95

Strengths and weaknesses: The pre-1986 Celicas were not very sporty. Their excessive weight and soft suspension compromised handling and added a high fuel penalty. With the 1986 makeover, Celicas gained more power and much better handling, especially in the GT and GTS versions, but they are still more show than go with limited rear passenger room.

Redesigned '94 models are full of both show *and* go with more aerodynamic styling and an enhanced 1.8L that gives more pickup than the ST's 1.6L with better fuel economy. Among the upgraded models available, smart buyers should choose a used '94 ST for its more reasonable price, smooth performance, quiet running and high fuel economy.

All of these cars offer exceptional reliability and durability. Servicing and repair are straightforward and parts are easily found. The front-wheel-drive line performs very well and has not presented any problems to owners. Prices are high for Celicas in good condition, but some bargains are available with the base ST model. Pre-'91 models have the most complaints relative to brakes, electrical problems, AC malfunctions and premature exhaust wear-out. The '94 models may have a manual transmission that slips out of 2nd gear and hard starts caused by a faulty air flow meter #22250-74200. Other areas vulnerable to early rusting include rear wheel openings, suspension components, the area surrounding the gas filler cap, door bottoms, and trunk or hatchback lids.

Safety summary/recalls: Crash tests of a 1981, 1986 and 1991 two-door Celica all concluded that the driver and front seat passenger would be well-protected. A retested '93 model was judged to produce serious injury to the driver's two legs. ABS first became an option with the '88 All-Trac Turbo and then on later versions of the GT-S and GT. Even if you have 4X4 capability, it's imperative that snow tires be fitted to avoid dangerous control problems on snow and ice. *Recalls*: **1988-89 All-Trac Turbos**-The radiator and coolant will be replaced for free by Toyota. **1990**-Campaign L03 provides for the free replacement of the instrument panel light control switch.

Secret Warranties/Service Tips/DSBs

1985-86-Reduce excessive oil consumption by installing upgraded piston rings.
1985-88-Starter/ring gear clash can be corrected with an upgraded starter assembly (#28100-62011 or 62021).
1986-89-Reduce excessive engine ping and jerking by installing an upgraded TCCS Electronic Control Unit under the emissions warranty.
1986-91-Rattling headrests is a common problem addressed in DSB B091-010.
1989-91-Cruise controls that cancel their settings may need a modified filter circuit.
1990-Fujitsu players that eat CDs will be replaced free of charge.
All models/years-Older Toyotas with stalling problems should have the engine checked for excessive carbon buildup on the valves before any more extensive repairs are authorized. Faulty cruise control (reasonable durability is 5 years/80,000 km). Owner feedback and dealer service managers (who wish to remain anonymous) confirm the existence of Toyota's secret warranty that will pay for replacing front disc brake components that wear out before 2 years/40,000 km. The decade-old problem of brake pulsation/vibration is fully outlined and corrective measures detailed in DSB #BR94-002, issued February 7, 1994. To reduce front brake squeaks on ABS-equipped vehicles, ask the dealer to install new, upgraded rotors (#43517-32020).

Vehicle Profile

	1987	1988	1989	1990	1991	1992	1993	1994
Cost Price ($)								
Base	16,438	15,998	16,338	17,558	16,418	17,949	19,078	21,438
Used Values ($)								
Base ↑	3700	4800	5700	8200	9000	10,300	11,400	15,700
Base ↓	3000	3700	4300	6700	7500	8700	9800	13,600
Reliability	③	③	③	③	④	④	④	⑤
Air conditioning	②	②	③	③	⑤	⑤	⑤	⑤
Body integrity	③	②	②	②	②	③	③	⑤
Braking system	②	②	②	②	②	③	③	③
Electrical system	①	①	①	①	③	③	④	⑤
Engines	④	④	④	③	③	③	③	④
Exhaust/Converter	②	②	②	②	②	③	③	⑤
Fuel system	④	④	④	④	④	④	④	④
Ignition system	④	④	④	④	④	④	④	⑤
Manual transmission	③	③	④	④	④	④	④	⑤
- automatic	③	③	④	④	④	④	④	⑤
Rust/Paint	②	②	④	④	④	④	④	④
Steering	④	④	④	④	④	④	④	⑤
Suspension	④	④	④	④	④	④	④	⑤
Dealer Service	④	④	④	④	④	④	⑤	⑤
Maintenance	④	④	④	④	④	④	⑤	⑤
Parts Availability	④	④	④	④	④	④	⑤	⑤
Repair Costs	④	④	④	④	④	④	⑤	⑤
Crash Safety	⑤	⑤	⑤	⑤	⑤	⑤	①	①
Safety Features								
ABS	—	S	S	S	S	S	S	S
Airbag	—	—	—	O	O	O	O	O

MR2

Rating: Recommended (1992-94); Above Average buy (1987-1991).

Price analysis: Excellent availability and fairly expensive. Expect to pay about $200 annually for maintenance and repairs during the warranty period and $400 annually thereafter. Other sports cars worth considering: Chrysler Laser/Talon 4X4 and Stealth • Ford Mustang or Probe • Honda Prelude or CRX • Mazda Miata, MX-3, or RX-7 • Nissan 240SX • Toyota Celica.

Technical Data

ENGINES	Litres/CID	HP	MPG	Model Years
OHC I-4 FI	1.6/98	115	25-30	1988-90
OHC I-4 FI	1.6/98	145	23-28	1988-90
DOHC I-4 FI	2.2/132	135	23-27	1991-94
DOHC I-4T FI	2.0/122	200	21-25	1991-94

Strengths and weaknesses: The MR2 does everything a sports car should without fuss or surprises. Except for vague steering and some front-end instability, handling is practically flawless. The standard 16-valve 4-cylinder motor is smooth and adequate. The supercharged and turbocharged engines, though overpriced, produce more power than even a sporty car driver would want to use. On the downside, the engine's placement behind the driver's seat produces excessive noise and vibration that make long trips very uncomfortable.

A summary of the most common complaints on all MR2s would be, in order of frequency: brakes, electrical glitches and body hardware (fit and finish) deficiencies.

Safety summary/recalls: Crash tests of a 1985 MR2 concluded that the driver and front seat passenger would be well-protected. *Recalls*: N/A.

Secret Warranties/Service Tips/DSBs

1985-86-Premature brake wear and excessive front brake noise are common. New pads (#04491-17070) should eliminate these problems.
• A faulty remote trunk release requires a revised lock cylinder and bracket.
• Sunroof rattles can be reduced by installing upgraded components.
1985-88-Starter/ring gear clash can be corrected with an upgraded starter assembly (#28100-62011 or 62021).
1990-Fujitsu players that eat CDs will be replaced free of charge.
1991-To improve fuel door opening, Toyota has increased the spring force of the door hinge.
• The shape of the hood stay holder has been changed to increase its retention capability.
• Front brake squeal can be reduced by using new anti-squeal springs (#47743-32030).
• Sound system interference can be eliminated by changing the alternator.
All models/years-Toyota has a secret warranty that will pay for replacing front disc brake components that wear out before 2 years/40,000 km. The brake pulsation/vibration problem is fully outlined and corrective measures detailed in DSB #BR94-002, issued February 7, 1994.

422

Sometimes only the parts are covered, and the owner pays for labor.

Vehicle Profile

	1986	1987	1988	1989	1990	1991	1992	1993
Cost Price ($)								
Base	16,868	17,188	18,748	22,998	23,917	21,918	25,848	26,628
Used Values ($)								
Base ↑	4500	5300	6400	7800	9700	13,900	17,000	19,500
Base ↓	3900	4100	4900	6300	8200	12,300	15,500	18,000
Reliability	③	③	④	④	④	⑤	⑤	⑤
Air conditioning	②	②	④	④	⑤	⑤	⑤	⑤
Body integrity	②	②	③	③	③	⑤	⑤	⑤
Braking system	②	②	③	③	③	④	⑤	⑤
Electrical system	②	③	④	④	④	④	⑤	⑤
Engines	⑤	⑤	⑤	⑤	⑤	⑤	⑤	⑤
Exhaust/Converter	②	②	③	③	③	④	⑤	⑤
Fuel system	④	④	④	④	④	④	④	⑤
Ignition system	③	③	③	③	③	④	④	⑤
Manual transmission	③	③	③	③	③	⑤	⑤	⑤
- automatic	③	③	④	④	④	④	④	⑤
Rust/Paint	③	③	⑤	⑤	⑤	⑤	⑤	⑤
Steering	③	③	③	③	③	⑤	⑤	⑤
Suspension	③	③	③	③	③	③	③	⑤
Dealer Service	⑤	⑤	⑤	⑤	⑤	⑤	⑤	⑤
Maintenance	⑤	⑤	⑤	⑤	⑤	⑤	⑤	⑤
Parts Availability	③	③	③	③	③	⑤	⑤	⑤
Repair Costs	⑤	⑤	⑤	⑤	⑤	⑤	⑤	⑤
Crash Safety	⑤	⑤	⑤	⑤	⑤	⑤	⑤	⑤
Safety Features								
ABS	—	—	—	O	O	O	O	O
Airbag	—	—	—	—	—	—	D	D

Supra

Rating: Average buy (1990-94); Below Average buy (1986-89).

Price analysis: Average availability and very expensive. Supras are average sports cars that are way overpriced. Expect to pay about $500 annually for maintenance and repairs during the warranty period and $700 annually thereafter—a good reason to look for a Supra with some of the original warranty left. Other sports cars worth considering: Chrysler Laser/Talon 4X4 and Stealth • Ford Mustang or Probe • Honda Prelude or CRX • Mazda Miata, MX-3 or RX-7 • Nissan 240SX • Toyota Celica and MR2.

Technical Data

ENGINES	Litres/CID	HP	MPG	Model Years
DOHC I-6 FI	3.0/180	200	16-21	1986-92
DOHC I-6T FI	2.2/135	232	15-20	1987-92
DOHC I-6 FI	3.0/183	220	16-21	1993-94
DOHC I-6T FI	3.0/183	320	15-19	1993-94

Strengths and weaknesses: This is a nicely styled sports car that has caught the Corvette/Nissan 300ZX malady—cumulative add-ons that drive up the car's price and weight and drive down its performance and reliability. The 6-cylinder engines are smooth and powerful. Handling is sure and precise—slightly better than the Celica because of the independent rear suspension. The Supra has limited rear seating, fuel mileage is marginal around town and insurance premiums are likely to be much higher than average. Owners report major engine problems, frequent rear differential replacements, electrical short-circuits, AC malfunctions, and premature brake, suspension, and exhaust system wear. The engine is an oil-burner at times and cornering is often accompanied by a rear end growl. Body deficiencies are common. Seatbelt guides and the power antenna are failure prone.

Safety summary/recalls: No crash data is available. ABS became a standard feature on the '91 Turbo. *Recalls*: **1982-83**-Special Service Campaign #604 allows for the free replacement of front seat shoulder belts that fail to retract.

Secret Warranties/Service Tips/DSBs

1981-86-Valves must be adjusted annually or serious engine damage may occur.

1984-86-Defective catalytic converters are responsible for a rotten egg smell.

1985-88-Starter/ring gear clash can be corrected with an upgraded starter assembly (#28100-62011 or -62021).

1986-88-Excessive brake squeak and groaning can be reduced by installing revised brake pads (04491-14240).

1989-A defective center armrest pad will be replaced with an upgraded pad free of charge.

1989-90-Cold driveability and startability is improved with a modified TCCS Electronic Control Unit.

1990-Fujitsu players that eat CDs will be replaced free of charge.

1990-91-To improve brake pad durability, a new front brake pad material is now used (#04491-14280).

All models/years-Older Toyotas with stalling problems should have the engine checked for excessive carbon buildup on the valves before any more extensive repairs are authorized. Toyota has a secret warranty that will pay for replacing front disc brake components that wear out before 2 years/40,000 km. The brake pulsation/vibration problem is fully outlined and corrective measures detailed in DSB #BR94-002, issued February 7, 1994. Sometimes only the parts are covered, and the owner pays for labor.

Vehicle Profile

	1987	1988	1989	1990	1991	1992	1993	1994
Cost Price ($)								
Base	27,488	29,288	30,958	32,358	34,828	39,108	—	59,800
Used Values ($)								
Base ↑	7700	8900	10,700	14,400	17,300	20,000	—	35,000
Base ↓	6500	7100	8700	12,100	14,900	17,600	—	33,000
Reliability	2	2	2	3	3	3	—	3
Air conditioning	2	2	3	3	3	4	—	4
Body integrity	2	2	2	2	3	3	—	3
Braking system	2	2	2	2	2	2	—	3
Electrical system	2	2	2	2	2	3	—	3
Engines	3	3	3	3	4	4	—	4
Exhaust/Converter	2	2	2	2	3	3	—	3
Fuel system	2	2	2	2	4	4	—	4
Ignition system	4	4	4	4	4	4	—	4
Manual transmission	3	3	3	3	3	3	—	4
- automatic	3	3	3	3	3	3	—	4
Rust/Paint	2	2	2	3	4	4	—	4
Steering	3	3	3	3	3	3	—	4
Suspension	3	3	3	3	3	3	—	4
Maintenance	3	3	3	3	3	3	—	3
Parts Availability	4	4	4	4	4	4	—	4
Repair Costs	3	3	3	3	3	3	—	3
Crash Safety	—	—	—	—	—	—	—	—
Safety Features								
ABS	O	O	O	O	S	S	S	S
Airbag	—	—	—	D	D	D	D	D
Traction control	—	—	—	—	—	—	S	S

VOLKSWAGEN

Corrado

Rating: Above Average buy (1992-94); Not Recommended (1990-91).

Price analysis: Limited availability and fairly expensive. Outrageously high parts cost confirmed by the CAA. Owners complain that the alloy wheels are easily damaged and can cost over $450 to replace. Improved wheels cost over $900 each, but VW will cover the cost if you threaten court action. Expect to pay about $500 annually for maintenance and repairs during the warranty period and $900 annually thereafter— one big reason not to buy a used Corrado unless the comprehensive VW warranty is still in effect. Other sports cars worth considering: Chrysler Laser/Talon 4X4 and Stealth • Ford Mustang or Probe • Honda Prelude or CRX • Mazda Miata, MX-3 or RX-7 • Nissan 240SX • Toyota Celica and MR2.

Technical Data

ENGINES	Litres/CID	HP	MPG	Model Years
OHC I-4 FI	1.8/109	158	23-28	1990-92
OHC V6 FI	2.8/170	178	18-25	1992-93

Strengths and weaknesses: The Corrado is an attractive mid-size two-door coupe with a comfortable interior for the driver and front passenger. It gives good all-round performance with the accent on smooth acceleration, a firm but not harsh ride, and excellent handling with little body roll. The manual transmission's long shift throw is annoying and rear passenger room is quite limited.

Heating and defrosting system, brakes, electrical and fuel systems may be troublesome. Although the V6 engine runs quietly, there's lots of road/wind noise intrusion into the passenger compartment. Confidential dealer service bulletins show the 1993 models have excessive diagonal tire wear, excessive brake noise and faulty windshield wipers. DSBs issued in 1994 address AC expansion valve noise, an erratic idle, and abnormal rear tire wear due to the rear axle having too much positive toe.

Safety summary/recalls: There is no crash data available from government-run tests, but overall insurance injury claims are average for this type of vehicle. Rear visibility is seriously compromised by the high tail and spoiler. One Montreal owner of a '93 Corrado reports his car suddenly fishtailed out of control while rounding a curve at a moderate speed. *Recalls*: N/A.

Secret Warranties/Service Tips/DSBs

1990-91-Abnormal engine noise that occurs when the engine is warm can be corrected by installing an upgraded crankshaft (#026-105-101E).
• If the radiator fan stays on high speed, with the ignition off, discharging the battery, replace the radiator fan high-speed relay with part number #321-919-505A.
1991-93-AC expansion valve noises require the installation of an upgraded expansion valve.
1992-94-Poor 2.8L engine performance or a rough idle may be due to a misrouted EVAP vacuum hose or an improperly routed positive crankcase ventilation hose causing a vacuum leak.
1993-If the ABS warning light won't go out, a faulty start switch/lock is the likely culprit.
All models/years-Poor driveability (hard starts, surging, stalling low fuel economy) may be due to a deteriorated oxygen sensor (02S) wire shield or improper oxygen sensor wire shield ground.

Vehicle Profile

	1990	1991	1992	1993	1994
Cost Price ($)					
Base	26,350	24,930	27,600	29,175	29,050
Used Values ($)					
Base ↑	11,000	12,900	15,000	18,500	22,300
Base ↓	9500	11,500	14,000	17,000	21,000
Reliability	②	②	③	③	③
Air conditioning	③	③	④	④	④
Body integrity	③	③	③	④	④
Braking system	②	②	③	④	④
Electrical system	③	③	③	③	③
Engines	②	②	③	③	⑤
Exhaust/Converter	③	⑤	⑤	⑤	⑤
Fuel system	②	②	③	③	③
Ignition system	③	③	③	④	④
Manual transmission	⑤	⑤	⑤	⑤	⑤
- automatic	③	③	③	③	③
Rust/Paint	④	⑤	⑤	⑤	⑤
Steering	⑤	⑤	⑤	⑤	⑤
Suspension	③	③	③	④	④
Dealer Service	③	③	③	③	③
Maintenance	③	③	③	④	④
Parts Availability	③	③	③	③	③

Repair Costs	❷	❷	③	③	④
Crash Safety	—	—	—	—	—
Safety Features					
ABS	S	S	S	S	S
Airbag	—	—	—	—	D/P
Traction control	—	—	—	—	S

MINIVANS

1989 VW Vanagon: it's true; the van has gone for repairs—again.

Minivans and Multipurpose Vehicles

Minivans, vans, pickups and utility vehicles are often referred to as multipurpose vehicles (MPVs). There were 3,766,242 MPVs on Canada's roads as of July 1991, an increase of 25.1 percent over 1989, compared to car sales which had only had a 0.1 percent increase over the same period. MPV popularity is not surprising. They are versatile vehicles that can traverse rough terrain and carry cargo. Unfortunately, some MPVs lack government-mandated safety features like head restraints, rollover protection and side door beams, a safety feature found in small cars. Furthermore, the unforgiving handling of MPVs makes it easy to lose control of the vehicle and maximizes the probability of serious injury or death due to the lack of rollover protection.

Minivans

Chrysler launched the minivan concept with the Caravan/Voyager in 1984. Although poorly assembled, the tall, boxy vehicle was an instant success because it combined fuel efficiency, car-like maneuverability and increased cargo/passenger space in a smartly styled "garageable" van. On the other hand, Volkswagen's minivan—replaced by the EuroVan four years ago—had been on sale for over 20 years. Used mostly as a camper, it suffers from decades-old styling and has a reputation for being unreliable.

MPVs produced during the past few years have better crash test ratings, more safety features (airbags, etc.), more powerful engines and a greater variety of powertrains, better road handling, improved quality control, more competitive prices and greater parts availability. There's front-wheel drive, rear-wheel drive, four-wheel drive, all-wheel drive, front-engine, mid-engine, rear-engine, in-line 4, boxer-4 and V6 engine designs. Towing capacity varies between 1000 and 5000 pounds. Furthermore, many of the new minivans are more refined than Chrysler's original duo. They are more aerodynamic, highly styled and more car-like in their appearance and road performance.

If you must buy a minivan, remember that they fall into two categories: up-sized cars and down-sized trucks. The up-sized cars are "people movers." They are usually fwd, handle like a car and get great fuel economy. The post-'86 Chrysler Caravan/Voyager is the best example of this kind of minivan. GM's Astro/Safari and Ford Aerostar are down-sized trucks. Using rear-wheel drive, 6-cylinder engines and heavier mechanical components, these minivans handle cargo as well as passengers. Towing capacity varies between 3000 and 5000 pounds. On the negative side, fuel economy is no match for the fwd minivans, and highway handling on rear-drives is also more truck-like.

Minivan ownership costs are quite reasonable according to Runzheimer International, an American management consulting firm that has concluded it costs less to operate a minivan than it does many compact cars. Still, motorists who need a vehicle with large cargo and passenger carrying capacity should consider a cheaper GM Vandura or Chevy Van, even if it means sacrificing some fuel economy. You just can't beat the excellent forward vision and easy-to-customize interior these large vans provide.

Crash safety in collisions into a fixed barrier at 57 km/hr varies, with early Ford, GM and VW rear-drive minivans doing poorly. The 1990 front-drive Lumina APV and Trans Sport have done quite well. Chrysler's 1984-86 minivans failed the crash tests; the 1987-92 models did repectably well; the 1993-94s failed. The Highway Loss Data Institute's real-life claims statistics show that the Chrysler Caravan and Voyager, the Toyota Van and VW's Vanagon have consistently generated better (lower) than average claims. On the other hand, full-sized vans and 4X4s were singled out for having twice the fatality rate as their car counterparts, mostly because of rollover accidents.

The following used minivans are recommended:

Chrysler Caravan/Voyager (1994)
Ford Villager/Nissan Quest
Toyota Previa/4X4
Nissan Axxess

1993 Toyota Previa: Oh, what a feeling! To get rid of the old LE Van.

CHRYSLER

Caravan, Ram Van, Town and Country, Voyager

Rating: Recommended (1994); Average buy (1993); Not Recommended (1984-92). Chrysler minivans wouldn't be recommended at all if it weren't for the company's comprehensive seven-year warranty that covers most of these vehicles' serious body and powertrain defects.

Price analysis: Excellent availability and moderately priced. Expect to pay approximately $300 annually for maintenance and repairs during the first three years and about $600 each year thereafter. Buy an extended warranty if Chrysler's base warranty has expired—if none is available, stay away from these minivans. Owners speak of repeated visits to dealers to "repair" their repairs, and a "what, me worry?" attitude expressed by head office customer relations staff. If the dealer's service is lousy, you can have the vehicle repaired at an independent garage and force Chrysler to pay the cost. Now that the base warranty has been cut back, owners won't have the luxury of time to get proper warranty servicing through repeat repair bay visits. Other minivans that are likely to be as reliable: Ford and Nissan Villager/Quest • Nissan Axxess • Toyota Previa.

Technical Data

ENGINES	Litres/CID	HP	MPG	Model Years
OHC I-4 2 bbl.	2.2/135	101	17-21	1985-87
OHC I-4 2 bbl.	2.6/156	104	15-20	1985-87
OHC I-4 FI	2.5/153	102	17-22	1987-90
OHC I-4T FI	2.5/153	150	15-21	1989-90
OHC V6 FI	3.0/181	144	16-20	1987-94
OHV V6 FI	3.3/201	150-162	15-20	1990-95
OHC I-4 FI	2.5/153	100	18-22	1991-95
OHV V6 FI	3.8/232	162	14-19	1994-95

Strengths and weaknesses: These minivans are way underpowered with the 2.2L 4-cylinder motor, which has a history of head gasket failures, but it outshines the larger Mitsubishi 2.6L, guaranteed to self-destruct just as the warranty expires. The timing belt, piston rings and valves are particular weak points on the 2.6L powerplant. The two-piece camshaft oil seals are also prone to sudden leaks. The Chrysler-built 2.5L engine is fairly dependable and the 3.3L V6 is the most reliable of all. The Mitsubishi 3.0L V6 is much more reliable than its younger and smaller 2.6L version. Yet it lacks power on long climbs, has multiple fuel-injection and oil leak problems and produces a loud piston "slapping" noise during cold starts. Canada's climate presents additional problems for Chrysler minivan owners: one Red Deer, Alta. owner of an '89 Voyager says dealers in his area tell him his 3.0L engine seized because of "poor cold weather oil lubrication." If this is true, it spells trouble for many owners who are now nearing the end of Chrysler's original warranty coverage and have to drive in cold weather conditions. Another owner, this time from Hamilton, Ont., says her '92 Voyager's rear heater coolant tubes were badly corroded and had to be replaced after two years at a cost of $160.

Fuel injectors on all engines have been troublesome. Engine supports may be missing or not connected. Cruise control units often fail, accelerating or decelerating the vehicle without any warning.

The manual transmission performs well and has been relatively trouble free. Automatic transmissions haven't fared as well. The disastrous Ultradrive 4-speed automatic has been particularly troublesome on 1988-91 models; then it was renamed and continued to pile up complaints. For example, the Nepean, Ont. owner of a '94 Grand Caravan says the newer transmissions aren't much improved:

"...The car shudders at 65 km/h. The dealer says that the torque converter is locking up, but that it cannot be fixed. He says they are all like that and it is of no concern. I am still worried...!"

Take note: Chrysler, stung by critics, myself among others, that these transmissions were lemons, pledged that free corrections would be carried out on 1988-90 minivans.

Other automatic transmissions on the post-'90 versions have been known to leak, tend to shift noisily and "hunt" for the proper gear—the likely cause of some of the poor gas mileage claims.

One Toronto, Ont. owner of an SE equipped with a 3.3L engine calls the transmission malfunction a safety hazard: "I have experienced a transmission control module failure where the vehicle immediately dropped into second gear. . . . This could have been tragic if it had occurred on Highway 401 in heavy traffic. . . . These systems must be redesigned to be fault-tolerant or they may as well go back to mechanical devices which are much safer."

Other mechanical weaknesses include the premature wearing out of front suspension components, wheel bearings, front brake discs, brake master cylinder, water pump, the air-conditioning unit, engine-cooling system and manual transmission clutch.

The interior is well finished and provides quiet on most versions. However, overall fit and finish has gotten worse, not better, over the years—a worrisome trend (see *Service Tips*). Body hardware and interior trim are fragile and tend to break, warp or fall off (door handles are a good example). After about a year's use, the Caravan and its various spin-offs becomes a veritable rattle box with poorly anchored bench seats a major player.

1991-94 These minivans are significantly upgraded with a boost in horsepower, a restyled body, an improved, more comfortable interior, a more refined suspension, standard automatic transmission, all-wheel-drive, and optional ABS. On 1994 models, a 3.8L engine is standard with the Town and Country and optional with other models. Transmission choices include a 5-speed manual or 3-speed automatic, and a new, but failure prone, 4-speed Ultradrive automatic on the larger stretched versions.

These minivans have remained popular in spite of the poor reliability of early versions because Chrysler's comprehensive warranty paid for their shortcomings. I pulled the following DSB summary for a '93 Caravan/Voyager/Ram Van equipped with a V6 3.0L engine to give you an idea of the seriousness of Chrysler's quality problems and why these vehicles need extra warranty coverage if the original warranty has run out. Remember, many of these defects carry over to many other Chrysler models and model years. Bulletins are in alphabetical order; the date refers to the month and year the DSB was sent. If you want your own DSB summary or a copy of a bulletins mentioned below, fill out the order form found in the Appendix.

Oct-94 Underseat storage drawer cracks
Oct-94 Tire leads/drifts left
Oct-94 Smooth road vibration/shake/ wobble
Sep-94 Front door hem separates
Aug-94 Left B-pillar exhaust retention
Jul-94 AC evaporator whistle
Jul-94 Rough idle after cold start
Jun-94 Manual trans. squeak
May-94 AC evaporator odor
May-94 AC compressor locks up
Apr-94 Acceleration shudder

Apr-94 Revised sliding door ajar switch
Mar-94 Faulty front seat latch
Mar-94 Low heater performance
Feb-94 Smooth road vibration/shake
Feb-94 Harsh slow-speed shifting
Feb-94 Engine stalls on takeoff
Feb-94 Serpentine belt comes off
Feb-94 Fuel pump noise
Jan-94 Squeak in shock tower
Jan-94 Poor heater performance
Jan-94 Deceleration shudder

Dec-93 Trans. shift improvement
Dec-93 Slow fuel tank fill
Dec-93 AC noise
Dec-93 Carbon buildup on piston top
Dec-93 Improved shifting
Dec-93 Revised middle side glass latches
Nov-93 Front windows bind
Nov-93 Intake valve deposits
Oct-93 Relay failures
Oct-93 Key breaks off in lock cylinder
Sep-93 Trans. vent oil leak
Sep-93 Side vent glass misaligned
Sep-93 Right rear squeak
Sep-93 AC duct emit odor
Aug-93 AM radio reception
Aug-93 Improved rear wiper arm/blade
Jul-93 Poor radio reception
Jul-93 Quarter trim panel cracks
Jul-93 ABS open sensor circuit
Jun-93 Aluminum wheel cap retention
Jun-93 Repeated fuel pump failure
Jun-93 Headliner odor (fish)

Jun-93-Anti-chip paint repair
May-93 Door panel carpet warpage
May-93 Upgraded seatbelts/retraction
May-93 Trans. cooler line clamps faulty
May-93 Insufficient heat
Apr-93 Wind noise/"A" post
Apr-93 Faulty outside door handles
Apr-93 Interior trim panel rattle
Apr-93 Noisy left engine mount
Mar-93 Temperature control lever faulty
Mar-93 Intermittent speed control
Feb-93 Howling noise from rear
Feb-93 Front brake rotor wear/noise
Feb-93 Hard/no start in cold weather
Feb-93 Sliding door center hinge faulty
Feb-93 Squeak/exhaust manifold
Feb-93 Child seat rattle
Jan-93 Excessive oil burning, smoke
Jan-93 Snap noise/vent window latch
Jan-93 Whistling noise at idle/41TE and 42LE Trans.

Dec-92 Loss of AC cooling/flow
Dec-92 Repeated failure/cooling fan motor
Nov-92 Buzz in reverse-41TE trans.

Nov-92 Squeak when turning
Nov-92 Squeak/front suspension
Nov-92 Steering wheel vibration

Incidentally, I know the DSB relating to fishy-smelling headliners piqued your interest; actually, it's also a problem with 1993-94 Jeep Grand Cherokee and Grand Wagoneers. Here's the actual bulletin to rib friends or relatives who may own one of these aquatic oddities:

```
NO.: 23-12-93 Rev. B
GROUP: Body
DATE: Jun. 25, 1993
SUBJECT:
Odor From Headliner
NOTE:
THIS BULLETIN SUPERSEDES TECHNICAL SERVICE BULLETIN 23-12-93 REV. A WHICH SHOULD BE REMOVED FROM YOUR
FILES. ALL REVISIONS ARE HIGHLIGHTED WITH **ASTERISKS**
MODELS:
1993  (AS)  Caravan/Grand Caravan/Caravan CV
            Voyager/Grand Voyager/Town & Country
SYMPTOM/CONDITION:
An odor may be noticed inside some vehicles that is described to be similar to the odor of fish. This condition is most
noticeable during damp and warm weather conditions.
This odor is coming from the headliner and is due to a vendor manufacturing process. More specifically, the curing of the
fiberglass is not to process standards.
No health risks are associated with the odor.
DIAGNOSIS.
Verify the odor is present by smelling the interior of the vehicle. If an odor similar to fish is experienced, perform the repair
procedure.
```

Apart from their fishy smells, Chrysler's minivans ride and handle better than most truck-based minivans (although there is lots of room for improvement) and can carry up to seven passengers in comfort. Cargo hauling capability is less impressive, with a 3000-lb. maximum towing range.

Chrysler's 1991-94 minivans continue to offer a symphony of whistles, rattles, squeaks, moans and groans, including excessive engine noise caused by carbon buildup on the top of the piston, automatic transmission whines or whistles, AC noise caused by the absence of a clutch plate damper ring, and front coil spring noise caused by the springs coming into contact with the strut tower. Others noises: squeak from the right shock tower comes from the defective AC hose support bracket, instrument panel rattles, a high-pitched whistling caused by a defective idle air control motor, and left B-pillar creaking.

Safety summary/recalls: The NHTSA conducted crash tests on 1984, 1987, 1992, 1993 and 1994 minivans. The '84 model gave marginal injury protection to the driver dummy, but the passenger was technically killed. The 1987 Caravan showed the passenger would be well-protected but that the driver would be severely injured. A '92 Caravan and Voyager gave better results; both the driver and front seat passenger would have escaped serious injury. The '93 and '94 Caravan were judged to have produced serious driver and passenger leg injuries.

Rear seatbacks on 1984-1990 versions may collapse in a collision, throwing the passengers out of the car. U.S. Department of Transportation (NHTSA) probers are looking into accident reports to judge whether a recall should be initiated. U.S. government probers are also investigating the cause of the tailgate glass suddenly shattering for no apparent reason on 1992 models. Transport Canada has recorded one incident of the sudden failure of the right tie-rod end on a '91 Voyager and another incident of complete brake failure on a '94 Caravan. U.S. authorities are investigating 875 reports of ABS brake failures on 1990-93 models.

Driving these minivans is a bit tricky; when you ease up on the accelerator, the vehicle tends to wander. Front brakes have a tendency to lock up a bit soon on slippery ground and fade when wet. Most of the early minivans lack safety features found on ordinary cars such as head restraints, three-point rear seatbelts, rollover resistant roof panels and reinforced side doors. Try to get a more recent model with these safety features, especially because earlier versions have not done all that well in frontal crash tests. An innovative integrated child safety seat is an important optional safety feature found on recent models. ABS, optional with the base '91 Caravan, is standard on the Town and Country. *Recalls:* **1984-95**-All minivans are subject to a voluntary recall campaign that will fix a rear liftgate latch that may fail in a collision. **1985**-Dealers will install a protective cover over the brake proportioning valve. Fuel supply tube leaks on vehicles equipped with a 2.2L engine. **1986-7- and 8-passenger models**-First rear seats may detach in an accident. **1988**-Possible fuel tank leakage. **1988-89**-Notification #281T, applicable to vehicles with a trailer towing package, provides for a free oil cooler bypass valve to prevent transmission failure in cold weather. **1989-90**-Engine valve cover gasket may leak oil creating a fire hazard. Notification #466 provides for a free 3.3L engine valve spring. Safety recall #314T provides for the free installation of a reinforcing plate to the front seatbelt strap. **1990**-Incorrectly mounted proportioning valve may increase chance of skidding. Notification #281T free oil cooler bypass valve program extended to cars and 1990 minivans. **1991**-Faulty turn-signal flasher. **1991 ABS**-Hydraulic fluid leakage. **1992**-Safety recall #326T requires the replacement of all brake pedals which have been found to lack sufficient strength. Faulty steering column shaft coupling bolts. Improperly bent fuel tank flanges could cause a fire. **1993-94**-Possible separation of 15-inch steel wheels.

Secret Warranties/Service Tips/DSBs

1987-88-Rough-running 3.0L Mitsubishi engines may have blocked injectors or malfunctioning plugs, wires, distributor cap and EGR valve.

1987-89-Erratic 3.0L engine idle speed in cold weather may require the installation of a new AIS motor.

• Vehicles equipped with the 3.0L engine may experience loss of engine coolant from an external cylinder head gasket leak. Use the cylinder head gasket kit that includes an upgraded head gasket (#MD143540).

1987-90-An exhaust drone at 40 to 55 mph can be stopped by installing a new muffler support bracket, crossmember and heat shield.

1987-88-Vehicle sag, stumble or hesitation during initial startup and drive away likely requires the removal and cleaning of the throttle body bore and blade, disconnecting the EGR vacuum line, plugging the EGR vacuum port, and replacing the single module engine controller (SMEC).

• If the manual transmission fails to engage 2nd or 3rd gear, consider replacing the second and third thrust washer snap ring (#6033348).

1987-92-The heat and air-conditioning system may suddenly change to the defrost mode during a low vacuum condition, such as during trailer towing, hill climbing and acceleration. Install a revised vacuum check valve to correct this problem.

1987-93-3.0L engines that burn oil or produce a smokey exhaust at idle can be fixed by installing snap rings on the exhaust valve guides and replacing all of the valve guide stems or the cylinder head.

1988-A 3.0L engine surge with the speed control engaged may require a new SMEC.

1988-90-Intermittent rough running at idle signals a need for a new EGR. It's free under the emissions warranty.

1988-94-A sticking AC heater blend door can be corrected by spraying an anti-rust penetrant into the assembly.

1989-Leaking fuel injectors are a common problem.

1989-90-Cylinder head cover oil leaks with 2.2L and 2.5L engines are caused by poor sealing. The original cylinder head cover must be replaced with one that uses silicone sealant (RTV) instead of a gasket (DSB 09-17-89).

• Defective valve stem seals are the likely cause of high oil consumption with 2.2L and 2.5L engines (DSB HL-49-89C).

• Low-speed stalling with 3.0L and 3.3L engines may require the replacement of the SMEC.

• Squeaking from the exhaust flex joint requires the replacement of the exhaust manifold to exhaust pipe sealing ring.

• A high-pitched whine may signal the need to replace the wiring overlay harness and ballast resistor to silence the in-tank electric fuel pump.

• A-604 automatic transmission clutch slippage is a common problem addressed in DSB 21-09-9.

• A surge/buck at 35 to 55 mph with an automatic transmission can be corrected by installing driveability kit #4419447.

1990-A rough idle after cold engine start-up (3.0L only) requires the installation of a revised SBEC.

1990-91-3.3L engine oil leaks are likely caused by premature wear of the thrust bearing.

• Vehicles equipped with 2.2L and 2.5L engines that exhibit a rubbing or scraping noise at the front of the engine may need a new timing belt cover.

• Vehicles equipped with an A-604 automatic transmission may exhibit lit back up lights when the transmission is in Overdrive. Continued driving may cause clutch failure. Correct by replacing the PRNDL switch.

• A clicking/snapping noise emanating from the left side of the engine compartment while accelerating or decelerating, or a clunking noise from the front or right side of the engine compartment while shifting, may be caused by a faulty engine mount. Replace it with an upgraded mount.

1990-92-Erratic idle speeds occurring after deceleration from a steady cruising speed can be corrected by replacing the idle air control motor with a revised motor.

1990-94-Harsh automatic shifts can be tamed by installing the following revised parts: kickdown, accumulator, reverse servo cushion springs and the accumulator piston.

• Cold startup piston knocking noise can be eliminated by replacing the piston and connecting rod assembly.

1991-Loss of fuel pressure causing fuel pump noise, erratic transmission shifting, engine power loss or engine die out may be due to a defective fuel pump.

• An erratic idle with 2.2L and 2.5L engines can be cured by using an improved SMEC/SBEC engine controller.

• Faulty power door locks may need a new fuse, have a short-circuit or require a new door latch with power door lock assembly.

• An inaccurate fuel gauge may signal the need to replace the level unit assembly (#4713737).

1991-92-If the engine knocks when at full operating temperature and during light to medium acceleration, it may mean the single board engine controller (SBEC-Powertrain Control Module) needs replacing.

• Engines with a rough idle and stalling following a cold start also may require a new SBEC.

• A noise or rattle coming from the rear of the vehicle is likely caused by the right rear park brake cable vibrating in the cable hanger. Install urethane tubing onto the cable and replace the hanger with a revised part.

• Moisture may accumulate inside the fog lamp assembly. Change the fog lamp lens seal and drill two vent holes to correct the problem.

• If the interior dome light fails to illuminate, it's likely the problem is caused by corrosion at the M2 splice.

• The airbag warning lamp may continuously illuminate when the vehicle's ignition is in the ON position. This malfunction may be due to corrosion caused by water in the airbag six-way connector.

1991-93-Engines that stall following a cold start may need an upgraded Park/Neutral/Start switch.

1991-94-The serpentine belt may come off the pulley after driving through snow. Install an upgraded shield, screw and retainers.

• Noisy fuel pumps need to be replaced by an upgraded pump, wiring harness, fuel tank isolators and fuel tank straps.

• Noise when shifting into Reverse or when turning is addressed in DSB 09-14-94. Chrysler will make all repairs relative to this problem under warranty.

• A squeak in the right shock tower area is likely due to a faulty right shock tower AC hose support bracket.

1991-95-Poor AC performance while the AC blower continues to operate is likely due to the evaporator freezing because the powertrain control module (PCM) isn't properly disengaging the AC clutch via the relay.

• DSB 24-05-94 looks at all the causes and remedies for poor heater performance.

• If the vehicle tends to drift left cross-switch the tire and wheel assemblies, readjust the alignment or reposition the front crossmember.

1992-The brake pedal may not return to its fully released position causing the brake lights to remain illuminated. Install a pedal return kit (#4723625).

• Front door forward hem separation (the door seems to sag) can be corrected by welding the inner door panel to the outer door panel along the front door forward hem.

• Long crank times, a rough idle and hesitation may be corrected by replacing the intake manifold assembly.

• A vehicle that is hard to start may have a corroded ECT/sensor connector.

• An oil leak in the oil filter area may be corrected by installing a special oil filter bracket gasket (#MD198554).

• If the heater and ventilation system changes to the defrost mode during acceleration, trailer towing or hill climbing, the installation of a revised vacuum check valve should cure the problem.

• Intermittent failure of the power door locks, chimes, wipers, gauges and other electrical devices can be corrected by the replacement of defective relays with revised relays (#4713737).

1992-93-Some 41TE transaxles may produce a buzzing noise when shifted into Reverse. This problem can be corrected by replacing the valve body assembly or valve body separator plate.

• A deceleration shudder can be eliminated by replacing the powertrain control module with an upgraded version.

• Rough idling after a cold start with 2.2L and 2.5L engines can be corrected by installing an upgraded powertrain control module (PCM).

1992-94-AC duct odors are addresses in DSB 24-21-93.

• Poor heater performance may be the result of a misadjusted clip on the blend air door cable.

1993-A fuel pump check valve failure can cause startup die-out, reduced power, or erratic shifting.

1993-94-Acceleration shudder may be caused by automatic transmission front pump leakage.

• Improved automatic shifting can be had by installing an upgraded transmission control module.

• AC evaporator whistling requires the installation of upgraded AC expansion valves and gaskets.

• An AC moaning may be silenced by installing an AC clutch plate with a damper ring.

1994-Harsh, erratic or delayed transmission shifts can be corrected by replacing the throttle position sensor (TPS) with a revised part.

• A creaking left B-pillar can be silenced by repositioning the metal portion of the left B-pillar baffle.

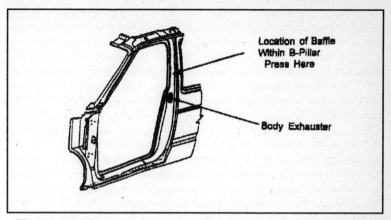

• Floor pan ticking can be stopped by applying Mopar spray gasket sealant between the floor pan and front mounting brackets.

• Coil spring noise is likely caused by the coil spring rubbing against the strut tower.

• Front seatback squeaks can be stopped by lubricating the seatback pivot bolt.

• A rattling heard from the lower left area of the instrument panel may be caused by a cracked fuse block mounting tab.

• Vent window latches that pop open or rattle should be readjusted or changed.

1994-95-Intake valve deposits are frequently the cause of poor driveability complaints.

• Intermittent no-cranks can be corrected by modifying the battery to starter cable terminal insulator at the starter connection.

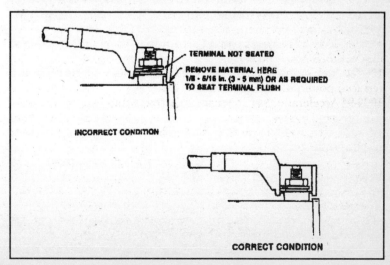

All models/years-Mitsubishi 2.6L engine balancer chains frequently wear out prematurely and can cause serious engine damage (up to $1500). The company has paid 100% towards the correction of this defect up to 5 years/80,000 km, but lately its handling of these engine complaints has been Scrooge-like. The problem can be prevented by adjusting the balancer chain every 24,000 km ($50 labor, no parts), changing the oil every three months or 5,000 km and using SAE 5W-30 motor oil rated for both gas and diesel.

MacPherson struts have been replaced free of charge by Chrysler dealers up to 75,000 km, but you may have a fight on your hands since no written documentation of this secret warranty has been found.

A rotten egg odor coming from the exhaust may be the result of a malfunctioning catalytic converter and there is *plenty* of written documentation to give you all the ammunition you need to stop Chrysler from weaseling out of its obligation to replace the catalytic converter for free under its emissions warranty.

Front brakes tend to wear out quickly on front-drive minivans. If pressed, owners say Chrysler will pay half the cost of brake repairs up to two years/40,000 km. Faulty steering assemblies are also often fixed free of charge up to 3 years/60,000 km (Ford and GM cover steering repairs two additional years).

Chrysler will pay 100% toward the correction of paint defects during the first 3 years/60,000 km and 50% up to the fifth year of ownership. Water leaks into the vehicle interior (a generic Chrysler affliction) will be plugged without charge up to the fifth year of ownership after the company tries to convince you it's either normal, or is part of routine maintenance. It's not—in both cases.

Vehicle Profile

	1987	1988	1989	1990	1991	1992	1993	1994
Cost Price ($)								
Ram	11,830	11,830	13,144	14,195	14,710	15,125	15,925	16,800
4X4	—	—	—	—	17,725	18,890	—	—
Caravan	13,008	13,664	14,528	15,530	15,200	15,810	15,935	16,860
4X4	—	—	—	—	19,515	20,750	20,900	—
Grand Caravan	14,739	15,794	16,676	20,555	18,170	19,105	19,685	20,425
4X4	—	—	—	—	20,050	21,300	21,860	23,680
Town & Country	—	—	—	33,065	30,230	31,470	32,490	34,874
Used Values ($)								
Ram ↑	3600	4500	5500	6400	7700	9400	11,000	12,700
Ram ↓	2800	3400	4000	5500	6600	8200	9500	11,200
4X4 ↑	—	—	—	—	8600	10,500	—	—
4X4 ↓	—	—	—	—	7300	8800	—	—
Caravan ↑	5400	6600	7600	8900	10,200	12,000	13,700	16,100
Caravan ↓	4500	5400	6500	7700	8800	10,500	12,100	14,500
4X4 ↑	—	—	—	—	11,000	12,500	15,000	—

4X4 ↓	—	—	—	—	10,000	11,000	14,000	—
Grand Caravan ↑	7000	6300	8400	9700	11,200	12,500	14,500	17,100
Grand Caravan ↓	5500	6300	7400	8600	9700	11,100	12,900	15,500
4X4 ↑	—	—	—	—	11,500	13,900	17,800	21,000
4X4 ↓	—	—	—	—	10,100	12,700	15,800	19,000
Town & Country ↑	—	—	—	17,000	19,000	21,000	23,000	26,500
Town & Country ↓	—	—	—	15,000	16,300	18,700	22,000	24,000
Reliability	①	①	①	①	②	②	③	④
Air conditioning	①	①	②	③	③	④	④	④
Body integrity	①	①	①	①	①	①	①	②
Braking system	①	①	①	①	①	②	③	②
Electrical system	①	①	①	①	②	②	③	③
Engines	①	①	①	②	②	③	③	④
Exhaust/Converter	②	②	②	③	③	③	④	⑤
Fuel system	①	①	①	①	③	③	③	③
Ignition system	②	③	③	③	③	④	⑤	⑤
Automatic trans.	②	②	②	②	②	③	③	③
Rust/Paint	①	①	①	①	①	①	①	②
Steering	①	①	①	①	③	③	④	④
Suspension	②	②	②	③	③	③	③	④
Dealer Service	③	③	③	③	③	③	③	④
Maintenance	③	③	③	③	③	④	④	⑤
Parts Availability	⑤	⑤	⑤	⑤	⑤	⑤	⑤	⑤
Repair Costs	①	①	①	③	③	⑤	⑤	⑤
Crash Safety	②	②	②	②	②	⑤	①	①
Safety Features								
ABS	—	—	—	—	O	O	O	O
Airbag	—	—	—	O	O	D	D	D/P

FORD

Aerostar

Rating: Above-Average buy (1993-94); Average buy (1992); Not Recommended (1986-91).

Price analysis: Excellent availability and reasonably priced. Buy an extended warranty if Ford's base warranty has expired, particularly if the vehicle is entering its fourth year, a point at which quality-control problems seem to proliferate. Expect to pay approximately $300 annually for maintenance and repairs during the first three years and about $800 each year thereafter. Ford has been coy about the Aerostar's future, but *Automotive News* confirms that the minivan will stay on the market, relatively unchanged, well into 1999. Other minivans that are likely to be more reliable and cheaper to service: Chrysler minivans

442

(only if the Chrysler warranty is still in effect) • Mercury and Nissan Villager/Quest • Nissan Axxess • Toyota Previa.

Technical Data

ENGINES	Litres/CID	HP	MPG	Model Years
OHC I-4 FI	2.3/140	88	21-25	1986-87
OHV V6 2 bbl.	2.8/171	115	17-22	1986
OHV V6 FI	3.0/182	145	16-22	1986-95
OHV V6 FI	4.0/244	155	15-21	1990-95

Strengths and weaknesses: 1986-91 models are at the bottom of the evolutionary scale as far as quality control is concerned. However, the last three model years have shown lots of improvement to the extent they would rival Chrysler if it weren't for Ford's limited warranty. Repair costs are reasonable, however, mainly because the Aerostar's myriad mechanical and body defects are covered by Ford warranty extensions (see *Secret Warranties*, below). The Aerostar's modern, swoopy shape belies its limited performance capabilities: the 3.0L and 4.0L engines are unreliable through the '92 model year and the 3.0L is a sluggish performer. Older 2.3L and 2.8L engines can barely pull their own weight. The 4-speed automatic transmission often has a hard time deciding which gear to choose, and the power steering transmits almost no road feel to the driver. The ride is bouncy, handling is sloppy and braking performance is poor. Reliability problems on all models make the Aerostar a risky buy, especially if the previous owner has been less than fastidious in maintenance and repairs.

Early models have compiled a miserable repair record. As soon as you plug one leak another leak springs up somewhere else; valve cover and rear main oil seal leaks are frequent, and leaks from the front axle vent tube often requires that the front axle assembly be replaced. Fuel injectors are either faulty or plugged. Other problems include expensive automatic transmission failures, electronic and electrical-system glitches, and premature wear-out of the air conditioner, power steering, suspension and brakes. An Amherstburg, Ont. owner wrote me that she spent $1000 on brake repairs for her '89 Limited over a two-year period. Another owner from Toronto had to replace the automatic transmission three times on his '86 Aerostar at a cost of $1322.50. Ford agreed to pay 50 percent if the dealer kicked in 25 percent. The dealer refused any compensation and was subsequently forced to pay the entire amount in a recent small claims court judgment. Says the owner, "I did some research on this matter to prepare my case, and it appears that this particular problem seems to be common to the Ford Aerostar, 1986-87."

A grinding/growling coming from the rear signals that the in-tank electric fuel pump is defective. Many mechanics find the electronic engine controls difficult to diagnose if problems arise. Routine repairs are very awkward because most components are buried under the windshield and dashboard. Windshield wipers are badly designed for Canadian winters. They freeze at the bottom of the windshield and wear out the wiper motor. Body hardware and integrity have earned low marks, as well.

Confidential dealer service bulletins show that 1993 models may have poorly performing AC systems with a slipping clutch at high ambient temperatures, noisy power-steering units and fuel pumps, inoperative door locks, a misaligned PRNDL shift lever indicator, and a rotten egg smell coming from the exhaust system.

DSBs applicable to '94 models address rough idle, hesitation, excessive fuel consumption and poor heater output that is likely caused by a thermostat sticking in an open position or opening before it should. Other problems include noise in radio speakers caused by faulty fuel pumps, and a defective electric rear window defroster.

Safety summary/recalls: NHTSA crash test results on an '87 Aerostar were disappointing: both the driver and passenger dummies sustained crash forces high enough to kill. An airbag-equipped '92 Aerostar passed the same test with flying colors: neither occupant would have been seriously injured. Model years '93 and '94 were tested and it was concluded that both of the driver's legs would be seriously injured. Basic Aerostars do not have front seat head restraints, unless equipped with the optional captain's chairs, and even then the restraints sit far too low for the average person. Reports of lower control arm suspension failures and subsequent accident injuries on '87 models are being investigated by NHTSA officials. Owners complain that the brake master cylinder and daytime running lights module may suddenly fail and that 1990 Aerostars' brakes lock up in wet weather. The hefty B-pillar (where the edge of the door meets the body behind the front seat) obstructs peripheral vision. The Ralph Nader-affiliated Center for Auto Safety in Washington, D.C., has opened an investigation of 1986-88 Ford Aerostars for safety-related defects, including rear brake lockup, side doors that fall off, electrical seat fires and fuel filler neck leaks. *Recalls*: **1986**-Rear suspension separating from the axle could cause steering loss. Recall #90S04 provides for a free fuel tank replacement. Lumbar seat wiring could short creating a fire hazard. **1986-87**-Possible fuel line leaks. Captain's chair may cut into seatbelt webbing. **1986-88**-Trailer towing package taillight wires may short circuit, creating a fire hazard. **1987-88**-Liftgate may suddenly fall. **1987-89**-The rear liftgate may fail due to defective ball studs attaching the lift cylinders to the body. **1989-90**-Ford will also replace, free of charge, faulty Quad Bucket seat assemblies. **1990**-Ford will replace, free of charge, faulty brake master cylinders. **1990-91**-Models with the A4LD automatic transmission may slip out of Park and roll as if in Neutral.

Secret Warranties/Service Tips/DSBs

1985-90-Noisy coil springs can be silenced by installing a sleeve over the rear upper coil spring.

1985-92-A buzz or rattle from the exhaust system may be caused by a loose heat shield catalyst.

1986-87-Ford will eliminate a rotten egg smell by installing a new catalytic converter (#E792-5F250-B).

• A 3.0L engine that stumbles or stalls at low speed may require a new EEC IV processor.

• Notification #88S55 provides for free repairs to improve the sliding door's poor durability.

• Leaking sliding windows require a body side window seal (#E792-11247A10-A).

• Owners are eligible for free replacement of prematurely worn seatbelts.

1986-88-Under Ford's M69 program, owners are eligible for free 3.0L V6 engine repairs up to 6 years/100,000 km. Try to get a partial refund.

• Hesitation or stall at idle with a 2.3L engine can be corrected by installing a new intake manifold gasket (E59Z-9439-A).

• Groaning front brakes: Ford will install new brake assemblies at the owner's expense.

1986-89-Sticking or squealing rear brakes may be fixed by installing upgraded brake linings (#E9TZ-2200-A and B) that are less sensitive to humidity.

• Hard starting/stalling may be caused by a defective fuel pump or sender assembly.

1986-91-3.0L engine knocking at idle may require the installation of a new, thicker thrust plate to reduce camshaft end play.

• Hard cold starts, hesitation and stalling may be caused by sludge in the throttle body and/or idle bypass valve. Install an idle air by-pass service kit (#F2DZ-9F939-A).

• Poor radio reception, including whining and buzzing, may be caused by electrical noise emanating from a faulty fuel pump. Install an electronic noise RFI filter on the fuel pump inside the fuel tank.

1986-92-A buzz or rattle from the exhaust system may be caused by a loose heat shield catalyst. Install worm clamps to secure the heat shield attachments.

• AC compressor noise, which sounds like a compressor failure, may be the result of a loose engine drive belt.

• Rear brakes that grab or squeal after the vehicle sits for a long period of time can be corrected by installing new brake shoe and lining assemblies that use material that is less sensitive to humidity.

1986-94-A speaker whine or buzz caused by the fuel pump can be stopped by installing an electronic noise RFI filter.

• Door glass binding can be remedied by replacing the worn channel glass run and removing the lower attachment clip from the door frame moulding.

1987-88-Crankshaft pulley separation is a common problem with 3.0L equipped Aerostars (DSB ON-M69).

1987-91-Improper operation of the heater or air conditioning system may be caused by sticking floor-panel air door lever or a distorted floor-panel air door.

1987-92-Brakes that stick or bind may have corroded brake caliper slide pins. Install corrosion resistant pins (#E8TZ-2C150-B).

1988-Delayed Reverse engagement can be corrected by installing a new separator plate.

1989-92-If popping or clunking and floorboard vibration occur when braking, they're likely caused by the front brake caliper suddenly springing away from the caliper abutment and returning. Adjusting the front brake pads and knuckle clearance will correct this problem.

1990-Delayed upshift or no upshift can be corrected by installing a new #4 thrust washer.

• Excessive steering noise can be reduced by installing an upgraded power-steering cooler.

• AC compressor shaft seal leaks can be best fixed by installing a new seal (#E9SZ-19D665-A).

1990-92-A 4.0L engine oil leak may occur around the rocker gasket because of variations in the gasket quality. Install two new rocker cover gaskets (Carrier type), along with conical spring screws.

• Automatic transmission fluid leakage may be caused by a faulty or loose transfer case rear output seal.

1990-93-Noise heard from the power-steering pump may be caused by air in the system. Purge the system.

1993-94-A squeak or chirp coming from the blower motor can be stopped by installing an upgraded blower motor with improved brush-to-commutator friction.

All models/years-Apply the 5 year/80,000 km emissions warranty to cure rotten egg smells caused by a defective catalytic converter. Ford's "goodwill" warranty extensions apply to fuel pumps and computer modules that govern engine, fuel injection and transmission functions. If Ford balks at refunding your money for a faulty computer module or fuel pump, apply the 5 year/80,000 km emissions warranty in small claims court.

Ford will pay 100% toward the correction of paint defects during the first 5 years/80,000 km and 50% up to the seventh year of ownership in keeping with the policy it first adopted to cover pickups, vans and 4X4s. Ford says its "Owner Dialogue" program was shut down earlier this year. I say the paint problems haven't ended and Ford needs to reopen its warranty extension program or get swamped by small claims lawsuits. Incidentally, the Owner Dialogue program also applied to almost all of Ford's model line over the past decade, and there are dozens of DSBs confirming this fact. Water leaks into the vehicle interior will be corrected without charge up to the fifth year of ownership. All of these programs include second owners.

Vehicle Profile

	1987	1988	1989	1990	1991	1992	1993	1994
Cost Price ($)								
Cargo	11,999	13,334	14,380	15,219	14,273	16,095	16,899	17,195
4X4	—	—	—	18,141	17,071	18,895	19,840	19,995
XL	13,068	13,865	14,912	15,390	14,396	16,395	17,215	18,095
4X4	—	—	—	18,448	17,395	19,095	20,050	20,495
Extended	—	—	15,659	16,299	15,195	17,395	18,265	19,295
4X4	—	—	—	19,052	18,495	20,195	21,205	21,595
Used Values ($)								
Cargo ↑	3700	4800	5700	6700	8100	9700	11,500	13,200
Cargo ↓	2900	3900	4700	5500	6800	8400	10,000	11,700
4X4 ↑	—	—	—	8000	9500	12,800	13,000	14,700
4X4 ↓	—	—	—	6800	8200	11,500	12,000	13,400
XL ↑	4800	5700	6500	8400	9400	12,800	14,700	16,900
XL ↓	3900	4600	5400	7200	8600	11,300	13,100	15,200
4X4 ↑	—	—	—	10,300	11,600	13,900	16,000	18,500
4X4 ↓	—	—	—	8900	10,200	12,700	15,000	17,000
Extended ↑	—	—	6900	8800	10,200	13,000	15,500	17,900
Extended ↓	—	—	5600	6600	8900	11,500	13,900	16,200
4X4 ↑	—	—	—	9500	11,800	14,500	17,200	19,800
4X4 ↓	—	—	—	8500	10,400	12,500	15,700	17,300
Reliability	1	1	1	2	2	3	4	4
Air conditioning	1	1	2	2	3	3	3	4
Body integrity	2	2	2	2	2	2	3	4
Braking system	1	1	1	1	1	1	3	4
Electrical system	1	1	1	1	1	1	3	4
Engines	1	1	1	3	3	3	3	4
Exhaust/Converter	1	1	1	2	3	3	4	4
Fuel system	1	1	3	3	4	4	4	4
Ignition system	3	3	4	4	4	5	5	5
Manual transmission	3	3	3	3	3	3	3	3
- automatic	1	1	3	3	3	3	4	4
Rust/Paint	2	2	2	2	3	3	4	4
Steering	2	2	2	3	3	3	4	4
Suspension	2	2	2	3	3	3	4	4
Dealer Service	3	3	3	3	3	3	3	3
Maintenance	3	3	3	3	3	3	3	3
Parts Availability	5	5	5	5	5	5	5	5
Repair Costs	1	1	1	2	2	3	4	4
Crash Safety	1	1	1	1	1	5	1	1
Safety Features								
ABS	—	—	—	S	S	S	S	S
Airbag	—	—	—	—	—	D	D	D

Villager, (Nissan) Quest

Rating: Recommended buy (1994); Above Average buy (1993).

Price analysis: Limited availability and prices are fairly high. According to the Canadian Automobile Association (CAA), parts are less expensive than most other minivans in this class. Expect to pay approximately $300 annually for maintenance and repairs during the first three years and about $600 each year thereafter. Other minivans worth considering: Chrysler minivans (only if the Chrysler warranty is still in effect) • Nissan Axxess • Toyota Previa.

Technical Data

ENGINES	Litres/CID	HP	MPG	Model Years
OHC V6 FI	3.0/181	151	18-23	1993-95

Strengths and weaknesses: The Villager/Quest's strongest features are its impressive highway performance and easy, no-surprise car-like handling. Additional assets are a 4-speed automatic transmission that is particularly smooth and quiet, and mechanical components that have been tested for years on the Maxima and other Ford vehicles. The ride on smooth and uneven highways is comfortable, overall highway stability is above reproach, and braking performance is quite good aided by standard ABS on the Villager that improves directional control by eliminating wheel lockup.

These fuel-thirsty minivans are heavier than the Aerostar by about 700 pounds, and the 3.0L engine has only 16 additional horses to carry the extra weight. GM's 2.8L engines produce more torque than what the Villager and Quest can deliver. Precise steering makes the Villager feel more responsive at highway speeds and during emergency maneuvers than it really is.

Interior space is impressive; the Villager is nearly a foot longer and two inches wider and higher than Chrysler's short-wheelbase minivans. There's better seating for three adults in the rear than with the Caravan, middle seatbacks fold flat, and the rear seats have tracks that allow them to slide forward all the way to the front or folded flat and converted to a serving area for tailgate parties. Body fit and finish are below par and there's lot of wind noise that enters the interior.

As far as proven reliability is concerned, these minivans are far more reliable than the Ford Aerostar and GM minivans. This isn't surprising since most of the important mechanical components have been used by Nissan on other models for some time.

Safety summary/recalls: Crash tests of a '93 and '94 Quest showed that the driver and passenger would likely sustain serious leg trauma. On

1993 Villagers, U.S. authorities are looking into fires due to materials being sucked into the engine's air intake. Safety investigators are looking into reports of electric door lock and power window failures, trapping occupants inside. *Recalls*: **1993**-Leaking fuel filler hoses will be replaced for free. Defective automatic seatbelt anchor bolts.

Secret Warranties/Service Tips/DSBs

1993-Noisy coil springs can be silenced by installing a sleeve over the rear upper coil spring.

• Harsh automatic transmission upshifts caused by metal contamination in the solenoid assembly can be fixed by replacing the solenoid assembly and transaxle pan gasket.

• An inoperative air conditioning blower motor can be fixed by installing a new blower motor resistor.

• An air conditioner blower that rattles, rumbles and emits an unusual odor may have foreign material that has entered the fresh air cowl and interfered with blower operation.

• A squeaking or rattling center bucket seat can be fixed by replacing the grommets and modifying the front latch mounting holes so that the front latches can be adjusted to provide better support.

• Rear bench seat squeaks or rattles may be caused by excessive clearance of the rear bench seat slide rails; normally due to improperly adjusted slide rails. Correct by adjusting the rear bench rollers.

• Stalling whenever the vehicle is shifted from P to D to R may mean the torque converter is stuck in the "lockup" mode. Install an upgraded valve body assembly (#F3XY-7A100-D) and transaxle oil pan gasket to fix the problem.

• Ford says the clearcoat layer of the basecoat/clearcoat paint may "microcheck" (crack and erode), turn white, flake or peel off horizontal surfaces.

• A ticking or clicking coming from the suspension strut area signals the need for an upgraded front strut spacer (#F3XY-3A120-A).

• Fogging or frosting of the side windows may be caused by a misconnected C261 electrical connector.

• If the keyless entry system becomes inoperative, install an upgraded keyless entry module (F4XY-14B001-A).

• If the front lapbelt retractors retract too quickly, nicking the door panel, install redesigned retractors that have a reduced spring force.

• If the liftgate light/door ajar light flickers, or the vehicle won't start, the rear liftgate latch may need to be changed.

• A whine or buzz coming from the radio speakers may signal the need to install an electronic noise RFI filter (F1PZ-18B925-A) on the fuel pump inside the fuel tank.

• A rear suspension clunk or thump when passing over bumps is likely caused by improperly calibrated rear shock absorbers.

• Install an upgraded speed control module (F3XY-9FS12-B) if the vehicle loses 3 to 5 mph on hills or grades with the present module.

• A steering wheel that squeaks when turned signals the need to lubricate the steering shaft bearing seal.

• A clicking or ticking noise when accelerating can be corrected by installing a new EGR tube with a redesigned fitting.

• A shudder or vibration that occurs during the 1-2 shift can be corrected by replacing the automatic transaxle valve body with an upgraded valve body and transaxle oil pan gasket.

1993-94-A squeak or chirp coming from the blower motor can be stopped by installing an upgraded blower motor with improved brush-to-commutator friction.

• Sliding door noise may need a new service spring in the upper hinge and the dovetail readjusted.

• A speaker whine or buzz caused by the fuel pump can be stopped by installing an electronic noise RFI filter.

• Body squeaks and rattles are thoroughly discussed in DSB 04-86-94.

| | | | VILLAGER SQUEAK AND RATTLE IDENTIFICATION CHART | | |
LOCATION	TYPE OF NOISE	TYPICALLY HEARD WHILE	POTENTIAL SOURCE	RECOMMENDED SERVICE PROCEDURE
SUSPENSION Front	Tick/Click	Normal Driving	Front Strut	Install Spacer Per TSB 93-21-11
Rear	Clunk/Thump	Driving Over Bumps	Rear Shocks	Replace shocks Per TSB 93-21-12
CHASSIS Front	Whining	Normal Driving	Front Wheel Bearing Bad	Replace Wheel Bearing
Front	Vibration	Hard Braking	ABS System Activating	Compare With Another Vehicle
DRIVETRAIN Transaxle	Shudder	1-2 Upshift at Over 1/2 Throttle	Valve Body Issue	Replace Valve Body Per TSB 93-25-13
BODY Front Doors	Rattle	Normal Driving/Closing Door	Loose Front Door Guard Beam	Secure Broken Welds Per TSB 94-4-9
Steering Column	Squeak	Turning The Steering Wheel	Intermed. Shaft Bearing Seal Or Steering Rack Seal	Lube Intermed. Shaft Seal Or Replace Steering Rack Per TSB 94-5-10
2nd Row Seat	Squeak/Rattle	While Driving With Center Seat Unoccupied	Grommets/Latch Do Not Provide Enough Support	Modify Latch Mount & Replace Bushings Per TSB 93-15-15
3rd Row Seat	Squeak/Rattle	While Driving With Rear Seat Unoccupied	Insufficient Clearance At Bench Slide Rails	Adjust Seat Rollers Per TSB 93-12-15

1993-95-The rear wiper motor may quit or stop intermittently because water has gotten into the motor printed circuit board.

All models/years-A rotten egg odor coming from the exhaust is probably caused by a malfunctioning catalytic converter that's covered by Ford's original warranty and the 5 year/80,000 km emissions warranty.

Vehicle Profile

	1993	1994
Cost Price ($)		
Villager GS	19,695	21,195
Villager LS	24,195	26,195
Quest XE	22,290	23,490
Quest GXE	26,590	—
Used Values ($)		
Villager GS ↑	14,600	17,100
Villager GS ↓	13,300	15,400
Villager LS ↑	16,000	19,100
Villager LS ↓	14,800	17,200
Quest XE ↑	16,000	18,500
Quest XE ↓	15,000	17,000
Quest GXE ↑	16,900	—
Quest GXE ↓	15,900	—
Reliability	④	⑤
Air conditioning	④	⑤
Automatic transmission	⑤	⑤
Body integrity	❷	❸
Braking system	④	⑤
Electrical system	③	④
Engines	⑤	⑤
Exhaust/Converter	⑤	⑤
Fuel system	⑤	⑤
Ignition system	⑤	⑤
Rust/Paint	④	⑤
Steering	④	⑤
Suspension	③	③
Dealer Service	⑤	⑤
Maintenance	⑤	⑤
Parts Availability	⑤	⑤
Repair Costs	⑤	⑤
Crash Safety	❶	❶
Safety Features		
ABS	S	S
Airbag	—	D

GENERAL MOTORS

Astro, Safari

Rating: Average buy (1992-94); Not Recommended (1985-91).

Price analysis: Excellent availability and severely depreciated prices on early models. Buy an extended warranty if GM's base warranty has expired, particularly if the vehicle is entering its fourth year when quality-control problems seem to multiply. Expect to pay approximately $400 annually for maintenance and repairs during the first three years and about $700 each year thereafter. Other minivans that are likely to be more reliable and cheaper to service: Chrysler minivans (only if the Chrysler warranty is still in effect) • Mercury and Nissan Villager/ Quest • Nissan Axxess • Toyota Previa.

Technical Data

ENGINES	Litres/CID	HP	MPG	Model Years
OHV I-4 FI	2.5/151	92-96	19-23	1985-88
OHV V6 4 bbl.	4.3/262	147	14-19	1985
OHV V6 FI	4.3/262	165	15-20	1986-94
OHV V6 FI	4.3/262	170-200	15-20	1991-95

Strengths and weaknesses: These models are the second-worst (VW is first) small van buy you can make. Introduced during the 1985 model year, they suffer from failure-prone automatic transmissions, a poor braking system, fragile steering components, and a weak and noisy 4-cylinder engine. The V6 provides ample power but also produces lots of noise, consumes excessive amounts of fuel, and tends to have leaking head gaskets and failure-prone oxygen sensors. Even though the 5-speed manual transmission shifts fairly easily, handling isn't particularly agile on these minivans, and the power steering doesn't provide the driver with enough road feel. Unloaded, the Astro provides very poor traction, the ride is not comfortable on poor road surfaces, and interior noise is rampant. Many drivers find the driving position awkward and the heating/defrosting system inadequate.

Reliability is much worse than average. The 4-speed automatic transmissions are poorly engineered and suffer from frequent failures. Excessive rear-end clunking and clanging occurs whenever the transmission shifts or downshifts when going around corners. One worker at GM's Oshawa plant, a 1993 Safari owner, wrote former GM Canada President George Peapples: "Do you as CEO really know what's going on or does middle management filter out the bad news?

GM's policy on warranty service is atrocious, your service representative was rude and your parts are substandard.... Your bulletin 93-4A-101 'Discouraging dealers from attempting to repair driveline clunk' is weaseling out on your responsibilities to the customer."

Other owners report that the front suspension, steering components, computer modules and the catalytic converter can wear out in as little as 60,000 km. There have also been lots of complaints about electrical, exhaust, cooling and fuel system bugs, as well as axle seals wearing out every 12 to 18 months. Body hardware is fragile and premature paint peeling/discoloration and surface rust are fairly common. Fortunately, finding parts and service is not a problem, and replacement parts are reasonably priced. Many engine components are hidden under the dashboard, making repair or maintenance awkward.

Safety summary/recalls: A 1985 and 1989 Astro did very poorly in crash tests: both the driver and front seat passenger were judged to have sustained fatal injuries. A subsequent NHTSA crash test of a '92 Astro confirmed the earlier results. A retested '93 did even more poorly: the driver and passenger would have had severe head and leg trauma. The 1994 model's score was similar, except that only the driver sustained severe head trauma. Furthermore, both the Astro and Safari have amassed a higher than average number of accident injury claims, according to insurance industry figures. 1987-88 Astros and Safaris have a design defect in the braking system that can cause the wheels to suddenly lock up under heavy braking, throwing the vehicle into a spin. Seatbelts may fail to retract on 1989 versions. The cargo vans may offer head restraints for the front seats. *Recalls*: **1985**-The steering gear may crack or break free, causing sudden steering loss. **1985-91**-Seatback may recline suddenly. **1989**-GM will install and relocate a new AC line under a recall campaign. **1990**-GM will repair for free the fuel return line fitting crimp.

Secret Warranties/Service Tips/DSBs

1983-89-Front brake noise (clicking, popping and squealing) can be traced to insufficiently clinched outboard brake pad tabs.
1985-87-Hard starting or stalling may be caused by a fuel pump dislodged in the gas tank or a loose fuel tank reservoir.
1985-86-Rough idling, surging or loss of power can often be traced to an overheated TPS module. Change the module and heat shield and the problem should disappear (DSB 86-122-6D).
1985-87-A defective 2.5L engine cylinder head leading to coolant loss is a common problem.
• Front brake squeal can be reduced or eliminated by installing noise insulated brake pads (called SAS II) with an insulator permanently attached to the metal portion of the brake pads.
1985-89-Poor radio reception may be linked to an antenna short-

circuit.

1985-90-Fuel starvation on Astros with TBI may be caused by deterioration of the in-tank fuel pump coupler.

• Some vehicles may experience a rear door noise or an inoperative rear door handle. These problems can be corrected by installing an upgraded door lock.

1985-91-Hydramatic 4L60/700R4 automatic transmission may have no upshift or appear to be stuck in 1st gear. The probable cause is a worn governor gear. It would be wise to also replace the retaining ring.

1985-92-If the cruise control operates intermittently, check for pinched wires exiting from the multi-functional lever.

1985-93-Vehicles equipped with a Hydramatic 4L60 transmission that buzzes when the vehicle is in Reverse or idle may need a new oil pressure regulator valve.

• A power-steering hiss can be silenced by replacing the power-steering valve assembly.

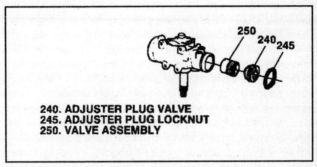

240. ADJUSTER PLUG VALVE
245. ADJUSTER PLUG LOCKNUT
250. VALVE ASSEMBLY

1986-4.3L engines may emit a rotten egg odor from the exhaust. If this occurs, change the PROM.

• A constant stalling problem when a warm 2.5L engine is restarted may signal the need for a new PROM module (#16085998).

1987-Hard starting or a pinging noise coming from cars equipped with a 2.5L engine: use a new upgraded PROM, fuel sender, pulsator and fuel pump (DSB 88-6-334).

1987-88-If the engine idles too fast prior to engaging the transmission, chances are the PROM software is defective and must be recalibrated (DSB 88-190-6B).

• No upshift or erratic shifting may mean a new governor driven gear is needed.

1988-A rotten egg odor coming from the 4.3L engine can be eliminated by relocating the oxygen sensor and installing a new PROM.

• Excessive oil consumption may be caused by one or more damaged intake valve stems (TSB 88-6-81).

1988-92-Hydramatic 4L60/700R4 automatic transmission may click or whine in 3rd or 4th gear. There may also be a rattling noise coming from the rear of the transmission. Correct by installing five new fiber plates in the low and reverse clutch. The new plates have a different groove configuration preventing 3rd and 4th gear vibration.

1989-91-THM 700-R4 automatic transmissions may exhibit a No Reverse or Delayed Reverse condition in cold weather. This problem can be corrected by replacing the piston outer seal with a long lip design. If a long lip design is already being used and there is no improvement, change the reverse input clutch housing.

• A binding sliding door requires the replacement of the center track rolling bracket, the center track assembly and lower track striker/ bumper assembly.

1990-A booming vibration can be reduced by installing an upgraded PROM (#16148810).

1991-Poor starting may be caused by the spring in early starter drives compressing too easily. Install an upgraded starter motor drive assembly (#10473700).

1992-94-The PCV hose may freeze, causing oil starvation to the engine and lead to engine failure. Owners who reside in Alaska are eligible for free higher flow calibrated PCVs under the emissions warranty. All other cold weather operators are supposed to be told of the problem and get free servicing on a case-by-case basis.

All models/years-Defective catalytic converters that cause a rotten egg smell in the interior will be replaced free of charge under the vehicle's 5 year/80,000 km emissions warranty. Spark knock with 2.5L engines can be fixed with the free installation of a new PROM module (#12269198) according to GM Bulletin 804-5812. Frequent stalling may require a new MAP sensor on 1990 vehicles (DSB 90-142-8A). GM has a serious rust/ paint peeling problem with all its domestic-made vehicles. Original owners will get 100% compensation for paint peeling/surface rusting up to six years (confirmed by GM in an internal memo to dealers reprinted in the Bonneville section of this *Guide*).

Vehicle Profile

	1987	1988	1989	1990	1991	1992	1993	1994
Cost Price ($)								
Cargo	10,917	13,400	15,057	16,747	15,650	16,798	17,638	18,198
CS	13,150	15,075	16,575	18,650	17,598	18,500	19,528	19,998
Used Values ($)								
Cargo ↑	3800	4900	5900	7000	8500	9800	11,200	13,000
Cargo ↓	2900	3900	4800	6000	7400	8500	9800	11,500
CS ↑	4500	6500	8000	9100	10,700	12,500	14,100	16,200
CS ↓	3600	5500	6700	7900	9200	10,800	12,500	15,500
Reliability	❶	❶	❶	❷	❷	③	③	③
Air conditioning	❷	❷	❷	③	③	③	④	④
Body integrity	❶	❶	❶	❶	❶	❶	❶	❶
Electrical system	❶	❶	❶	❶	❶	❶	❶	③
Engines	❶	❶	❶	③	④	④	④	⑤
Exhaust/Converter	❷	❷	③	③	③	④	④	④

Fuel system	③	④	④	④	④	④	④	④
Ignition system	③	④	④	④	④	④	④	④
Manual transmission	③	③	③	—	—	—	—	—
- automatic	③	③	③	③	③	③	③	④
Rust/Paint	❶	❶	❶	❶	❶	❶	❶	❶
Steering	❷	❷	③	③	③	③	④	④
Suspension	❷	❷	❷	❷	③	③	④	④
Dealer Service	③	③	③	③	③	③	③	③
Maintenance	❷	❷	③	③	③	③	③	③
Parts Availability	⑤	⑤	⑤	⑤	⑤	⑤	⑤	⑤
Repair Costs	❷	③	③	③	③	③	④	④
Crash Safety	❶	❶	❶	❶	❶	❶	❶	❶
Safety Features								
ABS	—	—	S	S	S	S	S	S
Airbag	—	—	—	—	—	—	—	D

Lumina APV, Trans Sport

Rating: Below Average buy (1993-94); Not Recommended (1990-92).

Price analysis: Excellent availability but prices remain relatively high on the used car market. Buy an extended warranty if GM's base warranty has expired. Expect to pay approximately $400 annually for maintenance and repairs during the first three years and about $800 each year thereafter. Parts are easily obtained at reasonable prices. Other minivans that are likely to be more reliable and cheaper to service: Chrysler minivans (only if the Chrysler warranty is still in effect) • Mercury and Nissan Villager/ Quest • Nissan Axxess • Toyota Previa.

Technical Data

ENGINES	Litres/CID	HP	MPG	Model Years
OHV V6 FI	3.1/191	120	17-22	1990-95
OHV V6 FI	3.8/231	170	16-21	1992-95

Strengths and weaknesses: GM's plastic-bodied, front-drive minivan looks more like a swoopy station wagon than the traditional minivan, as exemplified by the popular, boxy Chrysler Caravan. These vehicles use the Chevrolet Lumina (W-body) platform and, therefore, have more car-like handling than GM's Astro/Safari. Seating is limited to five adults (two up front and three on a removable bench seat) on the standard models, but this can be increased to seven if optional modular seats are ordered. Seats can be folded down flat, creating additional storage space.

Don't trust the towing limit specifications found in GM's owners manual. Carmakers publish tow ratings that are on the optimistic side and sometimes they even lie, as the following owner of a 1990 Lumina APV found out: "This spring, I decided to call the GM consumer information hotline to verify the towing capacity of our van for use in 1994. This is when I was told that it could pull a maximum of 1,000 pounds and that this was stated clearly in their 1990 owner's manual. Funny thing, that our 1990 owner's manual states 2,000 pounds with two passengers...." Two lessons learned from this reader's experience: make any sales promise an integral part of your contract (see "Misrepresentation" in Part 2) and reduce the promised tow rating by 20 percent.

The chassis and mechanical components come from GM's failure-prone W-bodies (Lumina, Regal, Cutlass Supreme and Grand Prix) and this explains why these minivans have so many of the same factory-related defects as their smaller cousins, notably, electronic module (PROM) and starter failures, short-circuits, automatic transmission breakdowns, abysmal fit and finish, sliding door malfunctions and faulty rear seat latches. Other problem areas include a 4-speed automatic transmission that isn't as durable as the less fuel-efficient 3-speed automatic, a poorly mounted sliding door, the side door glass that pops open, squeaks, rattles and clunks in the instrument panel cluster area and suspension, and a wind buffeting noise around the front doors.

The large dent-and rust-resistant plastic panels are robot-bonded to the frame with unique new adhesives, and they absorb engine and road noise very well. This combination of high-tech plastics, space-frame design and adhesive bonding has never been used before in any mass-produced vehicle which leads some body shops to complain that the innovative panels are in short supply and that damaged panels cannot be recycled, driving up the cost of repairs and causing insurance adjusters to simply write off repairable vehicles.

Be careful not to drop your keys between the windshield and the dash because you'll need a long stick to get them back.

Safety summary/recalls: Crash tests by the NHTSA of a 1990 Lumina APV and Trans Sport show both the driver and front seat passenger would escape serious injury. A tested '93 Trans Sport concluded that the driver's left leg would be seriously injured. A retested '94 Trans Sport did poorly; it was estimated that both of the driver's legs would be seriously injures and the passenger would sustain severe head trauma *and* massive leg injuries. NHTSA investigators are looking into reports of fuel line fires believed to be caused by a poor fuel line connection on 1990-92 models. Wheels that may crack and fracture on 1990-91 APVs are also under investigation. Some front door-mounted seatbelts cross uncomfortably at the neck. There's a nasty blind spot on the driver's side requiring a small stick-on convex mirror to correct. *Recalls*: **1990**-Defective modular rear seat latches replaced at no charge under recall #90C04. **1990-91 Trans Sport**-The upper glove box doors may not stay closed in an accident. **1993-94**-GM has recalled these minivans to fix a defect that could prevent the rear seat belt from retracting. The recall only concerns vehicles with power sliding doors.

Secret Warranties/Service Tips/DSBs

1990-Excessive brake squealing can be silenced by installing new brake linings (#12510008).
• A sliding side door that is difficult to unlatch may need a special clip (#10186100) to correct the problem.
• An upgraded switch (#10170226) will correct malfunctioning interior lights.
• Poor FM radio reception can be improved by installing a new RFI unit (#25027405).
• A sliding side door glass that pops open can be fixed by installing a new door bumper.
• Squeaks in the instrument panel cluster area require additional foam padding.
• A wind buffeting noise around the front doors can be reduced by changing the side mirrors.
1990-91-Hydramatic 4L60/700R4 automatic transmission may have no upshift or appear to be stuck in 1st gear. The probable cause is a worn governor gear. It would be wise to also replace the retaining ring.
1990-92-Vehicles with a 3T40 automatic transmission may slip in Low or Reverse gear. Correct by replacing the Low/Reverse clutch components, including the Low/Reverse release spring, clutch spring retainer and piston snap ring.
• A shudder or vibration at low speeds with vehicles equipped with a 3.1L engine may be caused by a faulty PROM electronic module.
• A power-steering shudder can be corrected by replacing the power-steering return hose/pipe assembly with a revised assembly and internal tuning cable (#26030907).
1990-94-An engine ticking at idle can be traced to rattling piston pins that must be replaced with upgraded parts.
1991 with 3.1L engine-Engine hesitation or stalling may require a new service calibration PROM that revises tip-in fueling. If the problem is reduced power, it may signal the need to replace the electronic spark control (ESC).
1991-92-A delayed shift between Drive and Reverse is likely caused by a rolled or cut input clutch piston outer seal.
1992-Power-steering shudder can be reduced by installing an upgraded power-steering outlet hose /pipe assembly (#260337593).
1992-94-Loss of Drive or erratic shifts may be caused by an intermittent short-circuit to ground on the A or B shift solenoid or an electrical short-circuit in the transaxle.
• A front-end clunking noise when driving over rough roads may

require the repositioning of the diagonal radiator support braces.

• A front end engine knock troubleshooting chart is found in DSB 306001.

1992-93-No Reverse or slipping in Reverse can be corrected by installing an upgraded lo/rev clutch return spring and spiral retaining ring.

1993-94-Owners who complain of automatic transmission low-speed miss, hesitation, chuggle or skip may find relief with an improved MEMCAL module that GM developed to remedy the problem.

1994-Front door glass window scraping/chattering can be eliminated by relocating the front lower guide attachment.

• Lazy front seat belt retractors will be replaced free of charge.

• A liftgate that fails to lock may have a loose or missing lock cylinder lock out pin.

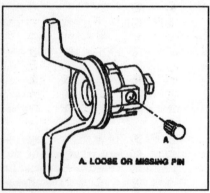

A. LOOSE OR MISSING PIN

• Manual sliding side doors that stick shut require a lock replacement.

All models/years-Defective catalytic converters that cause a rotten egg smell in the interior will be replaced free of charge under the 5 year/ 80,000 km emissions warranty. General Motors will repair defective steering assemblies free of charge up to 5 years/80,000 km and pay half the cost up to 100,000 km. Used vehicles and repairs carried out by independent garages are covered by this special program. GM has had a serious rust/paint peeling problem with all its domestic-made vehicles. Original owners will get 100% compensation for paint peeling/surface rusting up to six years (confirmed by GM in a letter to dealers reprinted in the Bonneville section of this *Guide*).

Vehicle Profile

	1990	1991	1992	1993	1994
Cost Price ($)					
Cargo	—	15,750	16,698	17,398	17,998
Passenger	18,898	17,198	18,098	18,798	19,598
Trans Sport/SE	20,450	18,498	18,950	19,698	20,298
GT	—	—	24,198	—	—

Used Values ($)

Cargo ↑	—	8100	9500	10,900	12,600
Cargo ↓	—	6500	8500	9600	11,200
Passenger ↑	9000	10,500	12,000	13,600	15,600
Passenger ↓	8000	9300	10,500	12,300	14,400
Trans Sport/SE ↑	9500	10,800	12,600	14,900	17,500
Trans Sport/SE ↓	8400	9700	11,200	13,500	16,000
GT ↑	—	—	15,700	—	—
GT ↓	—	—	13,900	—	—
Reliability	①	②	②	③	③
Air conditioning	③	③	③	④	④
Body integrity	①	①	①	②	②
Braking system	①	②	②	②	④
Electrical system	①	①	①	②	③
Engines	③	④	④	④	④
Exhaust/Converter	③	④	④	④	④
Fuel system	④	④	④	④	⑤
Ignition system	④	④	④	④	⑤
Automatic trans.	②	②	③	③	③
Rust/Paint	④	④	④	④	⑤
Steering	④	④	④	④	⑤
Suspension	④	④	④	④	⑤
Dealer Service	③	③	③	③	③
Maintenance	③	③	③	③	③
Parts Availability	⑤	⑤	⑤	⑤	⑤
Repair Costs	②	②	③	③	③
Crash Safety	⑤	⑤	⑤	①	①
Safety Features					
ABS	—	—	S	S	S
Airbag	—	—	—	—	D
Traction control	—	—	—	—	O

MAZDA

MPV

Rating: Average buy (1992-94); Below Average buy (1990-91).

Price analysis: The MPV is relatively easy to find, but it's way overpriced. New car dealers refuse to discount these popular minivans, so owners tend to boost their trade-in price in order to get back some of their initial investment. An extended warranty is recommended in view of the numerous expensive repair jobs reported by owners. Expect to pay approximately $600 annually for maintenance and repairs during the first three years and about $800 each year thereafter. Other minivans that are likely to be more reliable and cheaper to service: Chrysler minivans (only if the Chrysler warranty is still in effect) • Mercury and Nissan Villager/Quest • Nissan Axxess • Toyota Previa.

Technical Data

ENGINES	Litres/CID	HP	MPG	Model Years
OHC I-4 FI	2.6/159	121	17-23	1989-94
OHC V6 FI	3.0/180	150-155	16-22	1989-94

Strengths and weaknesses: Handling and overall highway performance, put the MPV in the top third of the minivan pack, but the poor reliability of early models that are no longer under warranty, unacceptable braking problems, mediocre servicing and high parts cost make it a below-average performer when it comes to overall operating costs. *Lemon-Aid* reader surveys show the quality of dealer servicing has declined dramatically during the past couple of years and parts are harder to find.

The base 2.6L 16-valve (121 hp) 4-cylinder engine is a dog, especially when hooked up to the automatic 4-speed transmission that robs it of what little power it has. The 3.0L 6-cylinder engine delivers more power and accelerates smoothly though there is a "dead" spot at around 60 km/h where pickup declines dramatically. Some cases of chronic engine knocking in cold weather with the 3.0L have been fixed by installing tighter-fitting, teflon-coated pistons. Valve lifter problems are also common with this engine. Winter driving is compromised by the MPV's light rear end and mediocre traction and low ground clearance means off-road excursions shouldn't be too adventurous.

The 5-speed manual transmission is easy shifting and has well-spaced gears, but it's relatively rare. The automatic performs fairly well but sometimes hesitates before going into gear at about 20 km/h and again at 60 km/h. Steering is crisp and predictable. Rear-drive setup makes for easy load carrying and trailer towing.

Owners report that the electronic computer module (ECU), automatic transmission drive-shaft, upper shock mounts, front 4X4 drive axles and lash adjusters, AC core and radiator fail within the first three years, cold temperatures tend to "fry" the automatic window motor, and the paint is easily chipped. Premature brake caliper and rotor wear is another frequent problem.

Safety summary/recalls: Crash tests of a 1991 MPV concluded that the driver would have been seriously or fatally injured but the front passenger would have been well-protected. Brake performance has been a chronic problem on 1990-91 MPVs. Owners report the front brake calipers suddenly grab and then release, losing their power, and rear brakes occasionally lock up in emergency situations. Some models (the '90 version, for example) have rear seatbelts that are too slack and lack head restraints. Lots of buffeting about by strong winds. *Recalls*: 1989-Rear brake shoes may fail. **1990-91**-Rear brakes may be too aggressive on braking at low speeds and cause the rear wheels to lock up with possible loss of vehicle control. The shoe linings on the rear brakes can change over time and increase friction, causing the rear-wheel ABS to activate prematurely.

Secret Warranties/Service Tips/DSBs

1988-91-Hard shifting after cold-weather starts can be corrected by installing upgraded synchronizer rings and clutch hub assemblies.
1989-Engine stalling in zero degree weather requires the replacement of the ECU under the emissions warranty (#JE151888IR).
1989-90-A transmission whine while the vehicle is idling in drive is likely caused by the torque converter contacting the weld at the torque converter sleeve. This problem can be fixed by installing an upgraded torque converter (#BV1119100A).
1989-91-Cold engine piston slapping requires replacement pistons to fix the problem.
1990-92-If parking on an incline makes your MPV impossible to start, the problem lies with the increased amount of play in the transmission linkage. When this occurs, the Park/Neutral circuit in the inhibitor switch fails to close, and the shift/lock mechanism won't disengage. Correct by installing an upgraded inhibitor switch and manual plate.
All models/years-DSB 006-94 looks into all the causes and remedies for excessive brake vibration.

Vehicle Profile

	1989	1990	1991	1992	1993	1994
Cost Price ($)						
5-pass. 4X2	16,590	18,440	16,900	18,495	19,345	20,615
5-pass. 4X4	—	23,890	21,850	23,595	—	—
7-pass. LX 4X2	17,740	19,290	17,000	18,895	23,745	24,975
7-pass. LX 4X4	—	27,240	24,950	26,095	26,345	28,375
Used Values ($)						
5-pass. 4X2 ↑	7500	9000	10,700	12,700	14,800	17,100
5-pass. 4X2 ↓	6700	8200	9500	11,400	13,500	15,600
5-pass. 4X4 ↑	—	10,000	12,000	15,900	—	—
5-pass. 4X4 ↓	—	9100	10,800	14,000	—	—
7-pass. LX 4X2 ↑	8100	9600	11,000	12,500	14,900	17,500
7-pass. LX 4X2 ↓	7200	8700	9800	11,300	13,900	16,000
7-pass. LX 4X4 ↑	—	11,200	13,000	16,900	18,500	21,500
7-pass. LX 4X4 ↓	—	9900	11,500	15,000	16,500	19,900
Reliability	②	②	②	③	③	④

Air conditioning	②	②	②	③	④	④
Body integrity	②	③	③	③	④	④
Braking system	①	①	①	②	②	③
Electrical system	①	①	①	②	③	③
Engines	②	②	②	②	③	④
Exhaust/Converter	②	③	③	④	④	⑤
Fuel system	③	③	③	④	④	⑤
Ignition system	④	④	④	④	④	⑤
Automatic trans.	②	②	②	③	③	④
Rust/Paint	③	③	③	③	③	④
Steering	②	②	③	③	④	⑤
Suspension	②	②	②	②	③	④
Dealer Service	③	③	③	③	③	③
Maintenance	②	②	②	③	④	⑤
Parts Availability	①	①	①	①	①	①
Repair Costs	②	②	②	③	④	④
Crash Safety	—	—	②	②	②	②
Safety Features						
ABS	—	—	—	S	S	S
Airbag	—	—	—	—	—	D/P

NISSAN

Multi

Rating: These compact vans were Average buys that are now Not Recommended due to their age, poor parts availability and inadequate crash protection.

Price analysis: Not many Multis were imported into Canada, and none was sold in the United States as the Multi. This makes it a two-year oddity with a surprisingly low value on the used car market. No cheaper commercial version is available. Other minivans that are likely to be more reliable but not as cheap: Chrysler minivans (only if the original warranty hasn't expired) • Mercury Villager • Nissan Axxess/Quest • Toyota Previa.

Vehicle Profile

	1987	1988
Cost Price ($)		
XE 4X2	14,987	15,588
GXE 4X2	16,987	—

Used Values ($)

XE 4X2 ↑	3400	4300
XE 4X2 ↓	2700	3500
GXE 4X2 ↑	4100	—
GXE 4X2 ↓	3300	—
Reliability	❶	❷
Crash Safety	❷	❷

Axxess

Rating: Recommended (1993-94); Average buy (1991-92); Not Recommended (1990).

Price analysis: Limited availability due to small number imported into Canada. Many of these small minivans found duty as taxis, so make sure you're not buying one with the mileage turned back. Fairly rapid depreciation makes these vehicles reasonably priced. The Euro model's extras are not essential and are overpriced. Expect to pay approximately $300 annually for maintenance and repairs during the first three years and about $400 each year thereafter. Other minivans that are likely to be more reliable: Chrysler minivans (only if the original warranty hasn't expired) • Mercury Villager • Nissan Quest • Toyota Previa.

Technical Data

ENGINES	Litres/CID	HP	MPG	Model Years
OHC I-4 FI	2.4/146	138	20-26	1990-94

Strengths and weaknesses: Some reports of electrical problems, premature wear of the front disc brakes, manual transmission malfunctions and paint defects.

Some owners have reported the resonator (located just behind the muffler) fails around the three-year mark and costs about $250 to replace. Mechanical parts aren't hard to find, and servicing is simple.

Safety summary/recalls: Government crash tests of the 1990 Axxess show poor protection for the driver and passenger. Airbags and ABS are not available. *Recalls*: **1987-90**-Nissan will install, at no charge, a new cooling fan and radiator to prevent an engine fire from occurring.

Secret Warranties/Service Tips/DSBs

1990-Improper automatic transmission shift timing may require the rerouting of the transmission breather hose.
• A noisy rear suspension can be fixed by installing revised rear shock absorbers and coil springs.
All models/years-DSB BR94-002 looks into the most and causes and cures for excessive steering wheel vibration.

Vehicle Profile

	1990	1991	1992	1993	1994
Cost Price ($)					
XE	17,490	16,090	16,290	17,190	17,490
XE 4X4	20,900	19,190	19,990	—	—
XE 4X4 Euro	23,490	21,490	—	—	—
SE	—	—	—	19,677	18,990
SE 4X4	—	—	—	22,673	21,890
Used Values ($)					
XE ↑	7500	9000	10,700	12,500	14,000
XE ↓	6500	7800	9400	11,500	12,700
XE 4X4 ↑	9000	11,000	12,700	—	—
XE 4X4 ↓	8000	9800	11,500	—	—
XE 4X4 Euro ↑	9800	11,900	—	—	—
XE 4X4 Euro ↓	8900	10,500	—	—	—
SE ↑	—	—	—	13,500	15,200
SE ↓	—	—	—	12,500	13,900
SE 4X4 ↑	—	—	—	14,900	16,800
SE 4X4 ↓	—	—	—	13,700	15,900
Reliability	❶	③	③	④	⑤
Air conditioning	③	④	⑤	⑤	⑤
Body integrity	❶	❷	❷	③	③
Braking system	❷	❷	❷	③	③
Electrical system	❷	❷	③	④	④
Engines	③	③	③	⑤	⑤
Exhaust/Converter	③	③	③	④	⑤
Fuel system	❷	❷	❷	③	④
Ignition system	❷	③	③	④	④
Manual transmission	③	③	③	⑤	⑤
- automatic	③	③	③	③	④
Rust/Paint	❶	❷	③	③	④
Steering	③	③	③	④	④
Suspension	❷	③	③	⑤	⑤
Dealer Service	③	③	③	③	③
Maintenance	④	④	④	⑤	⑤
Parts Availability	⑤	⑤	⑤	⑤	⑤

Repair Costs	⑤	⑤	⑤	⑤	⑤
Crash Safety	❶	❶	❶	❶	❶
Safety Features					
ABS	—	—	—	O	O
Airbag	—	—	—	D/P	D/P
Traction control	—	—	—	O	O

TOYOTA

LE, Previa

Rating: Recommended (1991-94); Not Recommended (1984-90).

Price analysis: Fair availability but extravagantly priced. Dealers sell these minivans for the full sticker price, which owners try to recoup by selling used versions for much more than their worth. Early LEs are less popular than the Previa, and their resale value has taken a beating.

Buy an extended warranty if Toyota's base warranty has expired. Expect to pay approximately $250 annually for maintenance and repairs during the first three years and about $400 each year thereafter. Other minivans worth considering: Chrysler minivans (only if the original warranty hasn't expired) • Mercury Villager • Nissan Axxess and Quest.

Technical Data

ENGINES	Litres/CID	HP	MPG	Model Years
OHC I-4 FI	2.2/135	101	23-27	1988-90
DOHC I-4 FI	2.4/149	138	20-25	1991-94
DOHC I-4 FI	2.4/149	161	18-23	1994-95

Strengths and weaknesses: Previa yes, LE no. That pretty well sums up Toyota's minivan qualities.

The LE uses a conventional mechanical layout borrowed from the Toyota truck line. This means the vehicle, with its short wheelbase, has an unusually high center of gravity and a tendency to tip precariously in tight turns. Add to this the tendency of the brakes to lock up upon hard application and you have a recipe for disaster with these early minivans. The engine's placement under the front seats takes first prize for poor design and makes routine maintenance an all-day affair. Furthermore, the only way to go from the front to the rear of the vehicle is to get out and get back in. The LE is also extremely vulnerable to side winds flinging it about, and the short wheelbase accentuates the discomfort experienced when going over bumpy roads.

LE reliability isn't very good with owners reporting lots of premature fuel pump and air-conditioning failures, faulty engine oil pressure sensors and cruise-control mechanisms, excessive front brake pad and disc wear, poorly engineered and rust-prone steering components, and high service charges caused by poor design and expensive parts. For example, the fuel pump costs about $300 and is located inside the fuel tank. It takes two hours to replace.

The Previa is almost another vehicle in that its performance and reliability are so much improved over its predecessor. In fact, from a safety and quality control standpoint, the '93 Previa seems to be the *cuvée* of choice. It's not perfect, however, and owners have had some problems with premature front brake wear, electrical glitches, AC malfunctions, and fit and finish blemishes. 4X4 models with automatic transmissions steal lots of power from the 4-cylinder powerplant.

Safety summary/recalls: The NHTSA's crash test results on an '86 Van showed both the driver and passenger would sustain severe or fatal injuries. A subsequent test of an '89 LE also gave disappointing scores: the driver sustained crash forces high enough to be seriously injured or killed. The passenger would have had only minor injuries. A '93 airbag-equipped Previa showed that both the driver and passenger would have been well-protected. Unfortunately, a retested '94 showed the driver and passenger would sustain serious leg injuries. Some wind buffeting. *Recalls:* **1991**-Dealers will replace faulty electrical components in Fujitsu Ten radios to eliminate a fire hazard.

Secret Warranties/Service Tips/DSBs

LE Van
1985-86-Chronic stalling or hard starting may be caused by a defective ignition-control module.
1986-88-Special Service Campaign #K01 provides for the free replacement of the steering bevel gear.
• Engine piston slap can be reduced by installing an upgraded distributor assembly (#19040-73010).
• Poor idle or hard starting may require the installation of a regulator and valve kit, or a water temperature sensor.
1988-92-In its memo to dealers No. 89-11, issued 2/21/89, Toyota says it will pay for the replacement of the oxygen sensor up to 80,000 miles on all its trucks and vans.
Previa
1990-If the sliding door makes a scraping noise as it travels, it signals the need to replace the center rail with an improved part (#68303-28020).
1991-A short-circuit could occur in the radio leading to a fire. Toyota will replace the radio free of charge.

1990-92-The seat cushion cover tail section may separate from the seat frame. Correct by installing new clips that attach the seat cover to the seat frame.

1991-Under a special service program, Toyota will replace at no charge the radiator, fan and fan shroud with improved parts.

• Under Special Service Program LO5, Toyota will replace at no charge the cylinder head core plugs and gaskets with improved components.

1992-93-Panasonic CD players that skip or won't play were upgraded as of 6/93.

All models/years-Owners feedback confirms that front brake pads and discs will be replaced free of charge if they are prematurely worn before 2 years/40, 000 km. Improved disc brake pad kits are described in DSB BR94-004. Another generic Toyota problem: brake pulsation/vibration is fully addressed in DSB BR94-002 "Cause and Repair of Vibration and Pulsation."

Vehicle Profile

	1987	1988	1989	1990	1991	1992	1993	1994
Cost Price ($)								
LE	15,368	16,838	18,498	—	—	—	—	—
4X4	21,178	20,178	21,608	—	—	—	—	—
Commercial	11,889	13,078	14,618	—	—	—	—	—
Commercial 4X4	15,578	16,888	—	—	—	—	—	—
Previa	—	—	—	—	18,918	20,778	21,448	24,748
4X4	—	—	—	—	22,438	27,278	26,538	29,178
Used Values ($)								
LE ↑	4500	5700	7000	—	—	⌐	—	—
LE ↓	3500	4700	5800	—	—	—	—	—
4X4 ↑	5400	6500	7900	—	—	—	—	—
4X4 ↓	4400	5500	6700	—	—	—	—	—
Commercial ↑	3600	4500	5500	—	—	—	—	—
Commercial ↓	2800	3500	4500	—	—	—	—	—
Commercial 4X4 ↑	4400	5300	—	—	—	—	—	—
Commercial 4X4 ↓	3400	4000	—	—	—	—	—	—
Previa ↑	—	—	—	—	13,500	15,700	18,400	20,500
Previa ↓	—	—	—	—	12,100	14,300	16,400	18,800
4X4 ↑	—	—	—	—	15,500	17,500	21,000	23,300
4X4 ↓	—	—	—	—	14,500	16,500	19,500	21,800
Reliability	③	③	③	—	④	⑤	⑤	⑤
Air conditioning	❷	❷	③	—	③	④	⑤	⑤
Body integrity	③	③	③	—	④	⑤	⑤	⑤
Braking system	❶	❶	❶	—	③	③	④	⑤
Electrical system	③	③	③	—	❶	❶	❷	④
Engines	③	③	③	—	④	⑤	⑤	⑤
Exhaust/Converter	③	③	③	—	④	⑤	⑤	⑤

Fuel system	③	③	③	—	④	⑤	⑤	⑤
Ignition system	③	③	③	—	④	⑤	⑤	⑤
Automatic trans.	④	③	③	—	④	⑤	⑤	⑤
Rust/Paint	③	④	④	—	④	⑤	⑤	⑤
Steering	③	④	④	—	③	④	④	④
Suspension	③	③	③	—	③	④	④	④
Dealer Service	③	③	③	—	③	③	③	③
Maintenance	❶	❶	❶	—	④	⑤	⑤	⑤
Parts Availability	❶	❶	❶	—	③	③	③	③
Repair Costs	③	③	③	—	③	③	③	③
Crash Safety	❶	❶	❷	—	❷	❷	⑤	❶
Safety Features								
ABS	—	—	—	—	—	O	O	O
Airbag	—	—	—	—	—	D	D	D/P

VOLKSWAGEN

Camper, EuroVan, Vanagon

Rating: Not Recommended (1985-94). Although the reliability of the 1993 and 1994 models is average, this may simply reflect the strength of VW's warranty or that it's too early for VW's generic deficiencies to appear.

Price analysis: Relatively rare vehicles, these minivans are not very popular, although the Camper version has attracted a cult following. Prices are generally higher for Campers due to their popularity and extensive standard equipment. An extended warranty is essential. Expect to pay approximately $400 annually for maintenance and repairs during the first three years and about $600 each year thereafter. Other minivans that are likely to be more reliable: Chrysler minivans (only if the original warranty hasn't expired) • Mercury Villager • Nissan Axxess and Quest • Toyota Previa.

Technical Data

ENGINES	Litres/CID	HP	MPG	Model Years
OHC I-5 FI	2.5/150	109	16-20	1992-95
OHC I-5D FI	2.4/145	77	22-26	1993-94

Strengths and weaknesses: VW minivans are ugly, grossly underpowered and predictably unpredictable. They handle poorly and are easily flung about in crosswinds. They provide poor traction (except in the

4X4 mode) on slippery roads and take a long time to get up to cruising speed. Heating and air conditioning are inadequate. Although these are the most spacious minivans on the market today, they are also the most expensive to own. Repairs are costly and difficult to come by, and there are few independent parts suppliers for other than routine maintenance items. Excessive tire, wind, road and engine noise.

Reliability is the pits for all years. Both air-cooled and water-cooled engines are unreliable. The water-cooled version in particular has a tendency to form air pockets in the water jacket, resulting in engine overheating and poor heater performance. Other major problem areas are the air-conditioning and fuel systems, brakes, driveline, manual and automatic transmissions and the suspension.

The '92 EuroVan has a more powerful engine than its predecessor, but it is still overwhelmed by the vehicle's excess weight. It is unbelievably slow to accelerate. Towing is not recommended for any VW minivan.

Safety summary/recalls: A 1988 Vanagon did very poorly in crash tests; the driver would have sustained fatal injuries, and the front passenger would have been severely injured. A crash tested 1993 and 1994 EuroVan showed the driver would have sustained severe or fatal injuries. The passenger would not have been injured. One Winnipeg, Man. owner of a '90 Camper reports that the fuel injectors may pump fuel onto the engine manifold. Airbags and ABS are not available. *Recalls*: **1986-87**-Stalling and rough running likely caused by defective fuel tank/filter. **1993 VW EuroVan**-Dealers will install a new locking bolt to secure the collapsible steering column.

Secret Warranties/Service Tips/DSBs

1983-Coolant leaking or noise coming from the rear water pump can be fixed by installing a revised Gurney (#537990) water pump.
1983-90-Rough running and poor idle may be caused by an air intake boot clamp leak. Install a new clamp (#191129647).
1984-91-Defective overhead air-conditioning consoles are under investigation by U.S. safety authorities.
1993-If the ABS warning light won't go out, a faulty start switch/lock is the likely culprit.
All models/years-Install a new ATF strainer cover and gasket if the automatic transmission slips on turns or after stops.

Vehicle Profile

	1987	1988	1989	1990	1991	1992	1993	1994
Cost Price ($)								
EuroVan	—	—	—	—	—	21,275	21,610	27,545
EuroVan Camper	—	—	—	—	—	29,250	29,865	35,850
Transporter	17,160	18,020	18,870	18,200	16,990	18,275	—	21,695
Commercial	16,530	17,355	18,135	—	—	—	—	—
Vanagon	21,565	22,435	22,590	22,955	—	—	—	—
Vanagon 4X4	25,020	—	—	—	—	—	—	—
Vanagon Camper	26,230	27,910	29,070	27,740	25,895	—	—	—
Camper 4X4	30,810	32,660	—	25,890	30,200	—	—	—
Used Values ($)								
EuroVan ↑	—	—	—	—	—	14,600	17,200	19,000
EuroVan ↓	—	—	—	—	—	12,900	15,400	17,000
EuroVan Camper ↑	—	—	—	—	—	17,600	20,100	23,000
EuroVan Camper ↓	—	—	—	—	—	16,000	19,000	21,000
Transporter ↑	3100	4400	6100	7400	9300	11,500	—	14,500
Transporter ↓	2400	3000	5000	6300	8100	10,200	—	13,500
Commercial ↑	3800	5000	6300	—	—	—	—	—
Commercial ↓	2900	4000	5300	—	—	—	—	—
Vanagon ↑	5200	6500	7800	10,200	—	—	—	—
Vanagon ↓	4500	5300	6600	8900	—	—	—	—
Vanagon 4X4 ↑	7000	—	—	—	—	—	—	—
Vanagon 4X4 ↓	6000	—	—	—	—	—	—	—
Camper ↑	10,500	12,000	13,800	15,600	17,000	—	—	—
Camper ↓	9000	11,000	12,300	14,000	16,000	—	—	—
Camper 4X4 ↑	12,500	14,000	—	17,500	20,500	—	—	—
Camper 4X4 ↓	11,500	13,000	—	16,500	19,000	—	—	—
Reliability	②	②	②	②	②	②	③	③
Air conditioning	②	②	②	②	③	③	③	④
Body integrity	③	③	③	③	③	③	③	③
Braking system	②	②	③	③	③	③	④	④
Electrical system	③	③	③	③	③	③	③	③
Engines	②	②	②	②	②	②	④	④
Exhaust/Converter	②	③	③	③	③	③	③	⑤
Fuel system	②	②	②	②	②	②	②	③
Ignition system	③	③	③	③	③	③	④	④
Manual transmission	②	③	③	③	③	④	④	⑤
- automatic	③	③	③	②	③	④	④	⑤
Rust/Paint	③	③	③	③	③	④	④	⑤
Steering	③	③	③	③	④	④	④	④
Suspension	③	③	③	③	③	④	④	④
Dealer Service	②	②	②	②	②	②	②	②
Maintenance	②	②	②	②	②	②	②	②
Parts Availability	②	②	②	②	②	②	②	②
Repair Costs	②	②	②	②	②	②	③	⑤
Crash Safety	①	①	①	①	①	①	②	②

Appendix I

Lemon-Proofing Before You Buy

Now that you've chosen a vehicle that's priced right and seems to meet your needs, take 20 minutes to assess its interior, exterior and highway performance by following the checklist below.

Safety Check

1. Is outward visibility good in all directions? (You can't see the nose of the Lumina APV, so you'll have to park by ear.)
2. Are there large blind spots impeding vision (i.e., side pillars)?
3. Are the mirrors large enough for good side and rear views?
4. Does the rear-view mirror have a glare-reducing setting?
5. Is there a rear window washer and wiper?
6. Are all instrument displays clearly seen and controls easily reached?
7. Is the hand brake easy to reach and use?
8. Are the head restraints adjustable or non-adjustable? (The latter are better if you're forgetful about setting them.)
9. Are the head restraints designed to permit rear visibility? (Some are annoyingly obtrusive.)

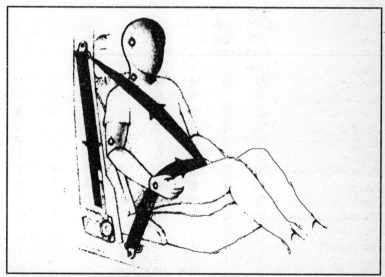

Three-point rear shoulder belts reduce spinal cord injury.

10. Are there rear three-point shoulder belts similar to the front seats? Two-point belts are not as good. (Some older minivans don't have

three-point belts anywhere.)
11. Is the seatbelt latch plate easy to find and reach?
12. Does the seatbelt fit comfortably across the chest without rubbing against the face or falling off the shoulder? (A serious problem with the Chrysler Aries and Reliant.)
13. Do you feel too much pressure against you from the shoulder belt?
14. Does the seatbelt release easily and retract smoothly?
15. Are there child seat anchorage locations?
16. Are there automatic door locks controlled by the driver or child-proof rear door locks?
17. Do the rear windows roll only halfway down?

Exterior Check

Rust is a four-letter word that means trouble. Don't buy any used vehicle with extensive corrosion in the trunk, wheel wells, door bottoms or rocker panels. Body work in these areas is usually only a temporary solution.

Cosmetic rusting (trunk lid, exhaust system, front hood) is acceptable and can even help push the price way down as long as the chassis and other major structural members are not affected. Bumps, bubbles or ripples under the paint may be due to repairs resulting from an accident, or premature corrosion. Don't dismiss this as a mere cosmetic problem; the entire vehicle will have to be stripped down, reprimed and repainted.

Use a flashlight to check for exhaust system and suspension component rust-out. Make sure the catalytic converter is present. In the past, many drivers removed this pollution control device in the mistaken belief that it would improve fuel economy (this was only true in the first several years converters were used). Police can now fine you for not having the converter and force you to buy one ($300 to $400) before certifying your vehicle.

Accident repairs should not rule out any vehicle, but they do require a further inspection by an independent body shop to see if the frame is aligned and the vehicle is tracking correctly. Frameless, unit body cars and minivans need extensive and expensive work to straighten them out. In British Columbia, all accidents involving more than $2000 in repairs must be reported to subsequent buyers.

What to Look For
1. If the vehicle has been repainted recently, check the quality of the job by inspecting the engine and trunk compartments and the inside door panels. Do it on a clear day so you'll find any waves in the paint.
2. Inspect the paint for tiny bubbles. They may identify a poor priming job or premature rust.
3. Have the bumpers been damaged or recently repaired? Check the

bumper support struts for corrosion damage.

4. See if the hood, trunk lid and side doors on minivans open and close without difficulty. Make sure they look properly aligned.
5. Test the shock absorbers by pushing hard on a corner of the vehicle. If it bounces around like a ship at sea, the shocks need replacing.
6. Look at the muffler and exhaust pipe to detect premature rust or displacement from a low-impact collision; this could channel deadly carbon monoxide into the passenger area.
7. Make sure the trunk has a spare tire, a jack and tools necessary for changing a flat. Can you get at the spare easily? Also look for premature rusting in the side wheel wells and for water in the trunk.
8. Knock gently on the front fenders, door bottoms, rear wheel wells and rear doors, places where rust usually occurs first. Even if these areas have been repaired with plastic, lead, metal plates or fiberglass, once rusting starts it is difficult to stop. Use a small magnet to check which body panels have been repaired with non-metallic body fillers.
9. Look at how the vehicle sits. If one side or end is higher than the other, it could mean the suspension is defective.
10. Ask the seller to turn on the headlights (low and high beam), turn signals, parking lights, emergency blinking lights, and blow the horn. From the rear, check that the brake lights, back-up lights, turn indicators, tail lights and licence plate light all work.

Tires

Don't be concerned if the tires are worn; retreads are inexpensive and easy to find. Look at tire wear for clues that the vehicle is out of alignment, needs suspension repairs or has serious chassis problems. An alignment and new shocks and springs are part of routine maintenance and are relatively inexpensive in the aftermarket. However, if it's a 4X4 or the MacPherson struts have to be replaced, you're looking at a $1000 repair bill.

Interior Check

The number of kilometers on the odometer is not as important as how well the car was driven and maintained. Still, high-mileage vehicles depreciate rapidly because most people consider them risky buys. Calculate 20,000 kilometers per year as average and take off about $200 for each additional 10,000 km above this average. Be suspicious of the odometer reading. Confirm it by checking the vehicle's maintenance records.

Often, the interior will give you an idea as to how the vehicle was used and maintained. For example, sagging rear seats and a front passenger seat in pristine condition indicate the car is probably an ex-taxi. Delivery vans will have the paint on the driver's door sill rubbed down to the metal, while the passenger door sill will look like new.

What to Look For

1. Excessive wear of the seats, dash, accelerator and brake pedal, armrests and roof lining.
2. Check the dash and roof lining for radio or cellular phone mounting holes (police, taxi, delivery van). Is the radio tuned to local stations?
3. Turn the steering wheel: listen for unusual noises and watch for excessive play (more than an inch).
5. Test the emergency brake with the vehicle parked on a hill.
6. Inspect the seatbelts. Is the webbing in good condition? Do the belts retract easily.
7. Make sure door latches and locks are in good working order. If rear doors have no handles or locks, or if they have just been replaced, the car may have been a police cruiser.
8. Can the seats be moved into all the positions intended by the manufacturer. Look under them to make sure the runners are functioning as they should.
9. Can head supports be adjusted easily?
10. Peel back the rugs and check the metal floor for signs of rust or dampness.

Road Test

1. Start the vehicle and listen for unusual noises. Shift automatic into park; manuals into neutral with the hand brake engaged. Open the hood to check for fluid leaks. This test should be done with the engine running and be repeated 10 minutes after the engine has been shut down following the completion of the test drive.
2. With the motor running, check out all dashboard controls; windshield wipers, heater and defroster, radio.
3. If the engine stalls or races at idle, a simple adjustment may fix the trouble. Loud clanks or low oil pressure could mean potentially expensive repairs.
4. Check all ventilation systems. Do the rear side windows roll down? Are there excessive air leaks around door handles?
5. While in Neutral, push down on the accelerator abruptly. Black exhaust smoke may only require a minor engine adjustment; blue smoke may signal major engine repairs.
6. Shift an automatic into Drive with the motor still idling. The vehicle should creep forward slowly without stalling or speeding. Listen for unusual noises when the transmission is engaged. Manual transmissions should engage as soon as the clutch is released. Slipping or stalling could require a new clutch. Make absolutely sure that 4-wheel drive can be engaged while driving without

unusual noises or hesitation.

7. Shift an automatic transmission into Drive. While the motor is idling, apply the emergency brake. If the motor is not racing and the brake is in good condition, the car should stop.
8. Accelerate to 50 km/h while slowly moving through all gears. Listen for transmission noises. Step lightly on the brakes; the response should be immediate and equal for all wheels.
9. In a deserted parking lot, test the vehicle's steering and suspension by driving in figure eights at low speeds.
10. Make sure the highway is clear of traffic and pedestrians. Drive at 30 km/h and take both hands off the steering wheel to see whether the vehicle veers from one side to the other. If it does, the alignment or suspension could be defective, or the car could have been in an accident.
11. Test the suspension by driving over some rough terrain.
12. Stop at the foot of a small hill and see if the car or minivan can climb it without difficulty.
13. On an expressway, it should take no longer than 20 seconds for most cars and minivans to accelerate from a standing start to 100 km/h.
14. Drive through a tunnel with the windows open. Try to detect any unusual motor, exhaust or suspension sounds.
15. After the test drive, verify the performance of the automatic transmission by shifting from drive to Neutral to Reverse. Listen for clunking sounds during transmission engagement.

Undoubtedly, many of these tests will turn up some defects, which may be major or minor (even new cars have an average of a half dozen major and minor defects). Ask an independent mechanic for an estimate and try to convince the seller to pay part of the repair bill if you buy the vehicle.

It's important to eliminate as many duds as possible through your own 20-minute check, because you'll later invest two hours and about $100 for a thorough mechanical inspection of your choice. Garages approved by the Automobile Protection Association or members of the Canadian Automobile Association usually do a good job. CAA inspections run from $100 to $150 for non-members. Oil company affiliated diagnostic clinics are recommended only if they don't do repairs.

Appendix II

Survey and Bulletin Search

Rate Your Vehicle
Much of the information found in this book has been garnered from motorists' responses to surveys conducted by the author. Your answers to the survey on the next page will help us to force automakers and dealers to improve their product and conduct. Include any photographs, diagrams, contracts or work orders that expose a defect or dishonest practice. Survey comments will help me zero in on bulletins that may be helpful to you if you also order a bulletin summary.

If you know of others who would like to participate in this survey or who wish to have a dealer service bulletin summary for their vehicle's ills, feel free to photocopy these two pages and pass them around. I can't answer every inquiry, but don't be surprised if I call or write you with my comments.

Cut Repair Costs • Fight Fraud and Incompetence with . . .

LEMON-AID'S SERVICE BULLETIN SUMMARY

Order by mail:
"Lemon-Aid DSB," 2805 E. Oakland Park Blvd., Suite 211, Ft. Lauderdale, FL 33306. Make your check or money order payable to "Lemon-Aid DSB".

Nothing gives you a stronger argument with a service manager or mechanic than pulling out a confidential dealer service bulletin that says a failure is factory related or is covered by an extended warranty.

For a $10 (Cdn.) search fee (this includes computer time and mailing costs), you will receive an exhaustive summary of all DSBs (published in the U.S) that concern **your** 1980-95 vehicle. **With each bulletin summary order, we will give you your vehicle's present wholesale and retail value**

For $5 for each bulletin thereafter, you can then order bulletins that address your concerns (DSBs show diagnostic shortcuts, labor time, lists of upgraded parts, probable defects, recall campaigns or secret warranties.

Order by FAX (954) 563-2448, 24 hours a day, 7 days a week. If you urgently need a bulletin summary, (warranty dispute, inflated repair bill, or repairs that never fix the problem,) FAX us the Survey/DSB Summary Request on the next page. We will mail or FAX the information to you (FAX costs an additional $3 for a total fee of $13). Set your FAX to receive. The FAX will be sent in the evening.

LEMON-AID SURVEY/DSB SUMMARY REQUEST

❏ I don't need a DSB summary; my survey comments are below.
❏ Please mail me a DSB summary for my car ($10 fee enclosed) and an estimate of its worth.
❏ Please FAX me the above information ($13).
FAX #_____ VISA # _____
Signature: _____

Name: _____
Address:_____
Province: _____ Postal code: _____

MY VEHICLE'S PROFILE

Make: _____ Model:_____ Year: _____
Engine (litres): _____ Mileage: _____

GENERAL COMMENTS
(Include a photo, diagram or bill.)

Safety: _____

Reliability:_____
_____
_____

Performance: _____
_____
_____

JOY OF OWNERSHIP
(Recommended ⑤, Above Average ④, Average ③,
Below average ❷, Not recommended ❶)

Overall Reliability

Air conditioning	Ignition system
Automatic transmission	Rust resistance
Body integrity	Steering
Braking system	Suspension
Electrical system	**Dealer service**
Engine	**Maintenance**
Exhaust/converter	**Parts availability**
Fuel system	**Repair costs**